A Cross Section of Educational Research

Journal Articles for Discussion and Evaluation

Third Edition

Lawrence S. Lyne

Editor

Pyrczak Publishing

P.O. Box 250430 ♦ Glendale, CA 91225

"Pyrczak Publishing" is an imprint of Fred Pyrczak, Publisher, A California Corporation.

This edition was prepared in collaboration with Randall R. Bruce.

Although the editor and publisher have made every effort to ensure the accuracy and completeness of information contained in this book, we assume no responsibility for errors, inaccuracies, omissions, or any inconsistency herein. Any slights of people, places, or organizations are unintentional.

Project Director: Monica Lopez.

Scanning and editing services by Karen M. Disner.

Editorial assistance provided by Cheryl Alcorn, Brenda Koplin, Erica Simmons, and Sharon Young.

Printed in the United States of America by Malloy, Inc.

ISBN 1-884585-65-5

Contents

continued →

Program Evaluation

Qualitative Research

Combined Qualitative/Quantitative Research

continued →

Meta-Analysis

Review of Empirical Research

Appendices

Introduction to the Third Edition

This book is designed for students who are learning how to evaluate published educational research. The 37 research articles in this collection provide the stimulus material for such a course.

Selection of the Articles

Several criteria were used in the selection of the articles. The first criterion was that the articles needed to be comprehensible to students taking their first research methods course. Thus, to be selected, an article needed to illustrate straightforward designs and the use of only basic statistics.

Second, because most education majors become teachers, the articles needed to deal with topics of interest to classroom teachers. To apply this criterion, students taking an educational research methods course were given the titles and abstracts (i.e., summaries) of a large number of articles to rate for interest. Only those that received moderate to high average ratings survived the screening of the initial pool of potential articles.

Third, the articles as a whole needed to illustrate a wide variety of approaches to research. You will notice in the table of contents that the articles represent 13 types of research such as Qualitative Research, Quantitative Research, Content Analysis, Survey Research, Correlational Research, True Experimental Research, and so on.

Finally, the articles as a whole needed to be drawn from a large number of different journals. Because each journal has its own genre as well as criteria for the selection of submissions for publication, students can learn about the wide variations in educational research only by reading articles from a number of different journals. Application of this criterion resulted in 37 articles drawn from 21 different journals.

How to Use this Book

In the field tests, articles were assigned for homework at each class meeting. Students were required to read the articles and answer the questions at the end of each one. At the next class meeting, the articles were discussed with the instructor leading the discussion. Other arrangements are, of course, possible. For example, each student might be responsible for leading the discussion of one of the articles after all members of the class have read the article.

About the Questions at the End of Each Article

There are three types of questions at the end of each article. First, there are *Factual Questions*. The answers for these are explicitly stated in the articles. In addition to writing down the answers, students should record the line numbers where they found the answers. The line numbers will facilitate discussions if there are disagreements as to what constitutes a correct answer to a question.

Second, there are *Questions for Discussion*. Because these are designed to stimulate classroom discussions, most of these questions ask for students' opinions on various decisions made by the researchers in conducting and writing up their research. In the field tests, these questions led to lively classroom discussions. Because professional researchers often debate such issues with each other, students should not be surprised by such debates in their own classrooms.

Third, students are asked to make *Quality Ratings* for each article. This is done by applying 11 fundamental criteria for evaluating research, using rating scale items that are repeated at the end of each article. These criteria may be supplemented by the more extensive list presented in Appendix A or with lists of criteria that are found in some research methods textbooks.

Reading the Statistics in this Book

Students who have taken a statistics class as a prerequisite to their research methods class should feel quite comfortable with the overwhelming majority of statistics found in this collection because articles that contained large numbers of obscure or highly advanced statistics were excluded from this book.

Students who are learning about statistics for the first time in the course in which they are using this book may need some additional help from their instructors. Keep in mind that it is not realistic to expect instructors of a research methods class to also teach a full-fledged course in statistical methods. Thus, there may be times when an instructor asks students to concentrate on the researcher's *interpretation* of statistics without extensive discussions of the theory underlying specific statistics.

The Classification of the Articles

Educational research methods textbooks vary somewhat in how various types of research are classified. While some labels such as "true experiment," "qualitative research," and "survey" are common to almost all textbooks, others may be more idiosyncratic. In addition, some categories of research overlap each other. For instance, when analyzing the results of a survey, a researcher may compute correlation coefficients, making it unclear whether it should be classified as survey research or as correlational research. An interesting classroom discussion topic is whether a given article can be classified as representing more than one type of research.

About the Third Edition

Many of the articles from the Second Edition were retained in this edition. New to this edition are articles 1, 2, 3, 4, 5, 9, 12, 14, 17, 18, 21, 23, 24, 26, 27, 28, 30, 31, 32, 36, and 37. In addition, Appendix B provides information that should be helpful in the evaluation of qualitative research.

Acknowledgments

I am grateful to Mildred L. Patten, who is the author of a similar collection titled *Educational and Psychological Research: A Cross Section of Journal Articles for Analysis and Evaluation*. Her collection emphasizes broad issues of interest to psychologists and educators, while this book emphasizes topics of interest to classroom teachers. Nevertheless, some structural elements of her book were employed in this one, such as the inclusion of three types of questions at the end of each article. She also provided me with advice on the criteria for selecting articles and numerous technical matters while I was preparing this book.

I also am indebted to the publishers who hold the copyrights to the articles in this book. Without their cooperation, it would not be possible to amass a collection such as you find here.

Lawrence S. Lyne

Article 1

Teachers' Knowledge of Facts and Myths About Suicide

MICHAEL G. MacDONALD
Oakland University

SUMMARY. Suicidal behavior is a serious public health concern that has prompted the development of prevention strategies, which include increasing community members' knowledge about suicide. Given that teachers are in a key position to recognize and respond to suicidal behavior, this study examined teachers' knowledge about suicide to identify how they need to be educated relative to its prevention. Eighty-two Canadian schoolteachers from middle and high schools were administered a revised version of the 32-item Facts on Suicide Quiz to examine their knowledge of suicide. Analysis indicated that general information about suicide was limited, while knowledge of clinically relevant information about suicide (e.g., "Suicide rarely happens without warning") was relatively high.

From *Psychological Reports*, 95, 651–656. Copyright © 2004 by Psychological Reports. Reprinted with permission.

Suicide and nonfatal suicidal behavior are a significant public health concern both in North America (Sakinovsky, 1998; Minino, Arias, Kochanek, Murphy, & Smith, 2002) and throughout the world (Diekstra, 5 1989).[1] Of particular relevance for teachers and schools is that data indicate suicide is a leading cause of death among 15- to 24-yr.-olds. One component in comprehensive programs for suicide prevention involves the education and training of community members or 10 "gatekeepers" who may have contact with suicidal youth. In this regard, it has been recognized that teachers are positioned to be instrumental in preventing suicide (Cole & Siegel, 1987; Ryerson, 1990; Range, 1993).

15 Although teachers generally endorse the idea that both schools and educators should be involved in suicide prevention (Allen, 1987; Laporte, 1990; Te, 2001), research also suggests that teachers perceive themselves to be underprepared to recognize and respond to 20 suicidal students (Schepp & Biocca, 1991; Nieschowski, 1996; Barron Jones, 1998; King, Price, Telljohann, & Wahl, 1999; Tran, 2002). Specifically, studies of secondary schoolteachers report they have low knowledge for signs of suicide risk (Leane & Shute, 25 1998; Scouller & Smith, 2002; Tran, 2002), while also believing various "myths" about suicide such as associating unrelated factors to increased risk (Gust, 1999; Te, 2001). The present study investigated Canadian teachers' knowledge of suicide to provide direction for 30 educational programming that would prepare teachers to work in suicide prevention.

Method

Eighty-two Canadian teachers (43 women, 39 men) from Ontario were administered a version of the Facts on Suicide Quiz (McIntosh, Hubbard, & Santos, 1985) 35 adapted for this study with permission of the test authors to assess teachers' knowledge about suicide. The sample included 12 elementary and 70 secondary schoolteachers who were either enrolled in continuing education courses at an urban university or worked in 40 one semirural county.

The 32-item scale has 16 true and 16 false items pertaining to suicide facts and myths. Items presenting demographic information address perceived associations of suicide with factors such as age, sex, climate 45 conditions, and race. "Suicide is most common among lower socioeconomic groups" is an example of a demographic item. Clinically relevant items include statements such as "The suicidal person wants to die and is fully intent on dying." These items are themati- 50 cally similar to the myths implied in anecdotal literature (e.g., Schneidman & Mandelkorn, 1970). Items that referred to the USA were changed to Canada for this Canadian sample.

Following the procedure employed by McIntosh, et 55 al. (1985), participants were instructed to read and respond to each statement by circling True, False, or Undecided and then return to evaluate the undecided items. Ten demographic items on participants such as age, sex, grade taught, and their educational and per- 60 sonal experiences with suicide followed the items about knowledge. Descriptive statistics were computed for items, and *t* tests evaluated whether participants' knowledge scores differed as a function of demographic or experiential variables, for example, to assess 65 whether these teachers' knowledge was influenced by personal experience with suicidal individuals.

---

[1] World Health Organization (2002). Suicide statistics, international suicide statistics. [On-line] Available: http://www.befrienders.org/info/statistics.htm.

Table 1
Participants' Responses on Selected Facts on Suicide Quiz Items (N = 82)

Item (correct answer)*	Response (% correct)
31. If you ask someone directly "Do you feel like killing yourself?" it will likely lead them to make a suicide attempt. (False)	99
18. Suicide rates are increasing among the young. (True)	96
3. Nothing can be done to stop a person from making the attempt once they have made up their mind to kill themselves. (False)	89
12. Most people who attempt suicide fail to kill themselves. (True)	84
25. Suicide is most common among lower socioeconomic groups. (False)	84
26. The suicidal person wants to die and is fully intent on dying. (False)	84
24. If seen by a psychiatrist, everyone who commits suicide would be diagnosed as depressed. (False)	80
32. Suicide rarely happens without warning. (True)	76
15. Native Canadians (aboriginal peoples) have the highest suicide rate of any racial group in Canada. (True)	74
1. There is a strong correlation between alcoholism and suicide. (True)	72
22. Suicide usually happens during the day. (True)	30
8. Suicide by shooting oneself is less common than using drugs in Canada. (False)	27
21. Winter is the season of the highest number of suicides. (False)	26
11. Suicide rates are higher among the young than the old. (False)	24
10. Oppressive weather (e.g., rain, etc.) has been found to be very related to suicidal behavior. (False)	13

* Reproduced from Facts on Suicide Quiz (McIntosh, Hubbard, & Santos, 1985) with permission of Drs. J. L. McIntosh and R. W. Hubbard.

Results

Only six of the teachers reported they had received training in suicide prevention or crisis intervention. Twenty-two respondents also indicated that they had a variety of direct and indirect experiences with individuals who have attempted or completed suicide. One respondent indicated that she had made a suicide attempt that could be described as having a low probability of death, and 21 participants indicated that they had contemplated suicide. The majority of respondents reported knowing people who had either attempted suicide (n = 48) or completed suicide (n = 51). In contrast to previous research (Durocher, Leenaars, & Balance, 1989), scores for respondents who reported knowing a close friend who had completed suicide (n = 5, M = 23 items correct) were significantly higher than those of respondents who did not know such a person (n = 31, M = 17.9 items correct; t_{35} = 8.94, p = .01). All other overall scores were not significantly different across demographic and experiential variables.

The mean correct score for suicide information was only slightly greater than chance, 20.1 or 63% correct of the 32 items. This clearly represents low overall knowledge about suicide and is consistent with findings using the same measure with college students (McIntosh, et al., 1985) and other measures of general knowledge with middle-aged adults (Stillion, McDowell, & May, 1989) and Australian secondary school-teachers (Leane & Shute, 1998). It should be noted that only cautious and speculative comparisons can be made when contrasting these and other findings from studies in which tests, methods, and samples were different.

Knowledge of clinically relevant items (that is, items most often believed to be myths that are particularly important for suicide prevention) was relatively high (76% correct) and comparable to other research with Canadian and U.S. adults (McIntosh, et al., 1985; Leenaars, Balance, Pellarin, Aversano, Magli, & Wenckstern, 1988; Durocher, et al., 1989; Domino, 1990; McIntosh & Hubbard, 2003). As presented in Table 1, correctly answered items by the majority of the respondents included (a) if you asked someone directly about suicide that it would not likely lead them to make a suicide attempt, (b) suicide rates have increased among the young, (c) something can be done to stop a person from making an attempt once they have made up their mind to kill themselves, (d) most people who attempt suicide do not kill themselves, (e) suicide is not more common among lower socioeconomic groups, (f) the suicidal person is ambivalent about living and dying, (g) not all people who commit suicide would be diagnosed as depressed, (h) suicide rarely happens without warning, (i) aboriginal peoples have the highest suicide rate in Canada, and (j) there is a strong correlation between alcoholism and suicide.

In contrast, Table 1 also presents responses indicating that the majority endorsed several misconceptions that indicated suicidal behavior is related to oppressive weather, suicide rates are higher among the young than the old, and suicide by shooting oneself is less common than using drugs in Canada. The majority also incorrectly rejected items that indicated that suicide usually happens during the day, black groups have a lower suicide rate than white groups, suicidal persons often seek medical help, and men kill themselves at least twice as often as do women.

Discussion

The present study investigated Canadian teachers' general (declarative) knowledge about suicide. Analysis indicated that while knowledge for primarily demographic items was low, average scores for clinical items which described common misconceptions about suicide were relatively high. These teachers' information about suicide which has particular relevance for prevention was consistent with prior research (Leenaars, et al., 1988; Durocher, et al., 1989). One may infer tentatively that important information is often understood. Researchers should evaluate teachers' knowledge about suicide with larger and more diverse samples and also should employ inventories which evaluate concerns specific to adolescents and young adults (e.g., Scouller & Smith, 2002; McIntosh & Hubbard, 2003). Also, further study of what teachers know about suicide intervention (procedural) should be undertaken, especially within the context of their attitudes, subjective norms, and perceived behavioral control (see Ajzen, 2002).

Interventions aimed at preparing teachers to recognize and respond to suicidal behavior should move beyond simply raising awareness and increasing general knowledge (White, 2002). Development of caregivers' competencies for suicide intervention should include education about attitudes, knowledge, and skills (Tierney, 1994; MacDonald, 1999). Given that suicide is complex, a multidimensional response is required (Leenaars, 1996). The development of effective intervention should be part of a comprehensive public health response with broad-based community involvement (Silverman & Feiner, 1995; White, 1998).

References

Ajzen, I. (2002). Perceived behavioral control, self-efficacy, locus of control, and the theory of planned behavior. *Journal of Applied Social Psychology, 32,* 665–683.

Allen, D. R. (1987). A comparative study of the attitudes toward and knowledge of suicide between secondary teachers who have and those who have not attended a school suicide awareness program. Unpublished doctoral dissertation, University of Pittsburgh.

Barron Jones, J. D. (1998). A qualitative analysis of preservice and inservice teachers' preparedness to help children cope with stress, manage crisis, avoid suicide, and foster resilience. Unpublished doctoral dissertation, Indiana University of Pennsylvania.

Cole, E., & Siegel, J. A. (1987). Alleviating hopelessness: Suicide prevention in the schools. *Public Health Reviews, 15,* 241–255.

Diekstra, R. F. W. (1989). Suicide and attempted suicide: An international perspective. *Acta Psychiatrica Scandinavica, 80,* 1–24.

Domino, G. (1990). Popular misconceptions about suicide: How popular are they? *Omega: Journal of Death and Dying, 21,* 167–175.

Durocher, G. J., Leenaars, A. A., & Balance, W. D. G. (1989). Knowledge about suicide as a function of experience. *Perceptual and Motor Skills, 68,* 26.

Gust, K. L. (1999). An exploratory study of suicidal behaviors and school personnel's knowledge and perceptions of suicide at state-supported, residential high schools for academically gifted students. Unpublished doctoral dissertation, Ball State University, Indiana.

King, K. A., Price, J. H., Telljohann, S. K., & Wahl, J. (1999). High school health teachers' perceived self-efficacy in identifying students at risk for suicide. *Journal of School Health, 69,* 202–207.

Laporte, L. C. (1990). An assessment of teachers' awareness of the indicators of suicide among adolescents. Unpublished master's thesis, University of Manitoba (Canada).

Leane, W., & Shute, R. (1998). Youth suicide: The knowledge and attitudes of Australian teachers and clergy. *Suicide and Life-threatening Behavior, 28,* 165–173.

Leenaars, A. A. (1996). Suicide: A multidimensional malaise. *Suicide and Life-threatening Behavior, 26,* 221–236.

Leenaars, A. A., Balance, W. D. G., Pellarin, S., Aversano, G., Magli, A., & Wenckstern, S. (1988). Facts and myths of suicide in Canada. *Death Studies, 12,* 195–206.

MacDonald, M. G. (1999). Suicide intervention training evaluation: A study of immediate and long-term training effects. Unpublished doctoral dissertation, University of Calgary (Canada).

McIntosh, J. L., & Hubbard, R. W. (2003). The expanded and revised Facts on Suicide Quiz. Paper presented at the annual conference of the American Association of Suicidology, Santa Fe, NM.

McIntosh, J. L., Hubbard, R. W., & Santos, J. F. (1985). Suicide facts and myths: A study of prevalence. *Death Studies, 9,* 267–281.

Minino, A. M., Arias, E., Kochanek, K. D., Murphy, S. L., & Smith, B. L. (2002). Deaths: Final data for 2000. In *National Vital Statistics Reports.* Hyattsville, MD: National Center for Health Statistics. *50*(15). [DHHS Publication No. (PHS) 2002-1120]

Niesluchowski, L. M. (1996). Levels of knowledge about preadolescent suicide among middle school teachers. Unpublished master's thesis, California State University, Long Beach.

Range, L. M. (1993). Suicide prevention: Guidelines for schools. *Educational Psychology Review, 5,* 135–154.

Ryerson, D. (1990). Suicide awareness education in schools: The development of a core program and subsequent modifications for special populations or institutions. *Death Studies, 14,* 371–390.

Sakinovsky, I. (1998). The epidemiology of suicide in Canada. In A. A. Leenaars, S. Wenckstern, I. Sakinovsky, R. J. Dyck, M. J. Kral, & R. C. Bland (Eds.), *Suicide in Canada.* Toronto, ON: University of Toronto Press. Pp. 37–66.

Schepp, K. G., & Biocca, L. (1991). Adolescent suicide: Views of adolescents, parents, and school personnel. *Archives of Psychiatric Nursing, 5,* 57–63.

Schneidman, E. S., & Mandelkorn, P. (1970). How to prevent suicide. In E. Schneidman, N. Farberow, & R. E. Litman (Eds.), *The psychology of suicide.* New York: Science House. Pp. 125–143.

Scouller, K. M., & Smith, D. I. (2002). Prevention of youth suicide: How well informed are the potential gatekeepers of adolescents in distress? *Suicide and Life-threatening Behavior, 32,* 67–79.

Silverman, M. M., & Feiner, R. D. (1995). Suicide prevention programs: Issues of design, implementation, feasibility, and developmental appropriateness. *Suicide and Life-threatening Behavior, 25,* 92–104.

Stillion, J. M., McDowell, E. E., & May, J. H. (1989). *Suicide across the lifespan: Premature exits.* Washington, DC: Hemisphere.

Te, L. H. (2001). An assessment of teachers' knowledge of adolescent suicide. Unpublished master's thesis, California State University, Long Beach.

Tierney, R. J. (1994). Suicide intervention training evaluation: A preliminary report. *Crisis, 15,* 69–76.

Tran, A. (2002). High school teachers' level of knowledge about teenage suicide. Unpublished master's thesis, California State University, Long Beach.

White, J. (1998). Comprehensive youth suicide prevention: A model for understanding. In A. A. Leenaars, S. Wenckstern, I. Sakinovsky, R. J. Dyck, M. J. Kral, & R. C. Bland (Eds.), *Suicide in Canada.* Toronto, ON: University of Toronto Press. Pp. 37–66.

White, J. (2002). Suicide awareness is not enough. *SIEC Current Awareness Bulletin, 5,* 1–2.

Address correspondence to: Dr. Michael G. MacDonald, Teacher Development and Educational Studies Department, Oakland University, Rochester, MI 48309. E-mail: mmacdona@oakland.edu

Exercise for Article 1

Factual Questions

1. According to the literature review, do teachers generally endorse the idea that both schools and educators should be involved in suicide prevention?

2. Were there more elementary *or* more secondary schoolteachers in the sample?

3. In addition to circling "True" *or* "False," what other choice could the teachers circle?

4. In this study, scores for respondents who reported knowing a close friend who had completed suicide were significantly higher than scores for respondents who did not know such a person. Is this particular finding consistent with the results in the literature?

5. What was the mean correct score for suicide information? What is the correct corresponding percentage?

6. What percentage marked "True" to the statement "Suicide rarely happens without warning"?

Questions for Discussion

7. In your opinion, is it likely that the teachers in this study are representative of Canadian teachers in general? Explain.

8. The scale had 16 true and 16 false items. In your opinion, would it have been better to have all 32 items be false? Explain.

9. In lines 58–59, the researcher states that among other things, demographic information on age, sex, and grade taught was collected. Would it have been desirable for the researcher to report on these variables (e.g., percentage who were men)? (Also, see lines 83–85.) Explain.

10. About half the items and the percentages correct are shown in Table 1. In your opinion, would it have been desirable to show all 32 items? Why? Why not?

11. In lines 143–152, the researcher makes some suggestions for future research. Do you think that these suggestions are important? Why? Why not?

12. Do any of the results of this study surprise you? Explain.

Quality Ratings

Directions: Indicate your level of agreement with each of the following statements by circling a number from 5 for strongly agree (SA) to 1 for strongly disagree (SD). If you believe an item is not applicable to this research article, leave it blank. Be prepared to explain your ratings.

A. The introduction establishes the importance of the study.

SA 5 4 3 2 1 SD

B. The literature review establishes the context for the study.

SA 5 4 3 2 1 SD

C. The research purpose, question, or hypothesis is clearly stated.

SA 5 4 3 2 1 SD

D. . The method of sampling is sound.

SA 5 4 3 2 1 SD

E. Relevant demographics (for example, age, gender, and ethnicity) are described.

SA 5 4 3 2 1 SD

F. Measurement procedures are adequate.

SA 5 4 3 2 1 SD

G. All procedures have been described in sufficient detail to permit a replication of the study.

SA 5 4 3 2 1 SD

H. The participants have been adequately protected from potential harm.

SA 5 4 3 2 1 SD

I. The results are clearly described.

SA 5 4 3 2 1 SD

J. The discussion/conclusion is appropriate.

SA 5 4 3 2 1 SD

K. Despite any flaws, the report is worthy of publication.

SA 5 4 3 2 1 SD

Article 2

Adolescent Smoking Cessation Services of School-Based Health Centers

JAMES H. PRICE
University of Toledo

JOSEPH A. DAKE
Wayne State University

FAITH YINGLING
University of Toledo

SUSAN K. TELLJOHANN
University of Toledo

ABSTRACT. A national sample of 390 junior and senior high school-based centers were mailed an 18-item survey to assess their institutional stages of change regarding smoking cessation education, referral, and prescription nicotine replacement therapy (NRT) services and their perceived barriers and benefits regarding the provision of these services. Nearly half were in the maintenance stage for cessation education programs, one-third were in the maintenance stage for referral services, and 12% were in the maintenance stage for NRT. The most frequently cited perceived benefits included an increased awareness of short- and long-term effects of smoking (education programs and referral services) and increasing student access to cessation methods (NRT). The greatest barriers cited were a lack of financial resources (education programs), problems with student transportation (referral services), and staff not having the authority to provide prescription services (NRT). School-based centers can do more to help stop adolescents from using tobacco.

From *Health Education & Behavior, 30*, 196–208. Copyright © 2003 by SOPHE. Reprinted with permission.

Approximately 1 million youths take up smoking annually. According to the latest results from the *Monitoring the Future Study*, 15%, 24%, and 31% of the 8th-, 10th-, and 12th-graders, respectively, reported
5 smoking at least once in the prior 30 days. The comparable proportions of adolescent daily smokers were 7%, 14%, and 21%.[1] In fact, the majority (90%) of adult smokers in the United States began smoking during adolescence.[2,3] Approximately 36% of those youths
10 who try cigarettes progress to daily use, most within 2 years after first trying a cigarette.[4] Furthermore, three-fourths of youths who smoke daily as high school seniors will still be daily smokers 8 years later.[5] Once a male adolescent begins smoking, he will continue to
15 smoke for an average of 16 years.[6]

If current youth smoking levels continue, approximately 5 million youth who are now younger than 18 years of age will eventually die from smoking-attributable diseases.[7] These smoking-attributable dis-
20 eases may result in $200 billion in future health care costs.[7] Because smoking prevention activities do not prevent all adolescents from becoming regular smokers, it is essential that adolescent smokers become a major point of intervention for reducing the toll ciga-
25 rette smoking addiction will make in this population.

A recent review of the behavioral treatment of smoking among adolescents found an average end-of-treatment abstinence rate of 21% and 3 to 6 months follow-up abstinence rates averaging 13%.[8] Further-
30 more, adolescents who smoke but do not smoke daily are almost seven times more likely to quit than daily smokers.[9,10] This may indicate that adolescents who are addicted to nicotine may have more difficulty quitting. Thus, nicotine replacement therapy (NRT) may be use-
35 ful for some adolescent smokers who attempt to quit. Initial research has found that nicotine patch therapy is safe and well tolerated in adolescents with an adverse side-effect profile similar to adult users.[11] Evidence from the largest adolescent smoking cessation trial to
40 date indicates that in-school smoking cessation clinics with minimal recruitment efforts can entice one-third of the schools' smokers into such clinics and that about half of the clinic enrollees will complete the entire program.[12] Thus, a potential point of attack for smoking
45 cessation efforts for adolescents could be through school-based health centers (SBHCs).

SBHCs were developed to meet the physical, mental, and social health needs of adolescents that were not being met by the traditional health care enterprise.[13]
50 SBHCs are perceived as a way of meeting adolescents' primary health care needs through the integration of services that promote and preserve health.[14] A variety of studies have been published studying the services used by adolescents in SBHCs. These studies often
55 explore service use for mental health and substance abuse services, including alcohol use, but they do not mention services regarding tobacco cessation.[15-17] The few studies that have examined the relationship between SBHCs and smoking have only investigated the
60 existence of a SBHC in the school on smoking frequency with no evidence of effect; they did not investigate intervention methods by the SBHCs.[18-20] This may

65 indicate that SBHCs are not directly addressing tobacco cessation in youths, that the techniques that they
may be using are ineffective, or that adequate evaluation designs are not being used.

Parents find tobacco use counseling to be one of the
top four counseling services they would like to see
offered in SBHCs.[21] Furthermore, at least one study has
70 found that 74% of occasional adolescent smokers and
65% of daily smokers wanted to quit.[22] However, the
percentage of adolescents who make an attempt to quit
in the previous 6 months decreases as their age increases.[23] Thus, research is needed on whether SBHC
75 personnel are involved in smoking cessation activities,
if the services are available in junior high and high
schools, and if they are, what activities they are conducting to help reduce the number of adolescent smokers. More specifically, the purposes of this study were
80 to find answers to the following questions: To what
extent do SBHC personnel provide smoking cessation
education programs? To what extent do SBHC personnel refer students who smoke to outside agencies? To
what extent do SBHC personnel provide prescription
85 NRT for adolescent smokers? What are the perceived
benefits SBHC personnel cite for offering smoking
cessation education programs, referring adolescents
who smoke, and prescribing NRT? What do SBHC
personnel cite as the perceived barriers to offering
90 smoking cessation education programs, referring adolescents who smoke, and prescribing NRT?

Method

Participants

Personnel at SBHCs at junior high and high schools
across the United States were surveyed regarding education, referral, and prescription NRT services relative
95 to cigarette smoking cessation. Names and addresses of
nurses at SBHCs across the United States were obtained from a list purchased from a market data company (Market Data Retrieval). The entire list of 390
different SBHCs was used (27 junior high and 363
100 senior high schools).

Instrument

The 18-item survey instrument was developed
based on a comprehensive review of the adolescent
smoking literature to establish face validity of the questionnaire. The questionnaire was sent to five national
105 authorities in the area of adolescent smoking to establish content validity. The feedback obtained from the
authorities was used to refine the wording of some of
the items on the instrument. The response format required the participants to select from a list of possible
110 responses, with the last option being "other."

Prochaska's stages of change model[24-26] provided
the theoretical basis of the instrument and was used to
assess SBHCs activity regarding cigarette smoking
cessation education, referral, and prescription services.
115 The stages of change model is a technique for assessing
the readiness of individuals to change a behavior and

has been found to be useful in outlining behavior
change interventions.[24] The six stages of change include precontemplation (not thought about changing),
120 contemplation (thinking about changing), preparation
(taking steps to change a behavior in the near future),
action (recently made a behavioral change), maintenance (have maintained the behavior change over an
extended period of time), and relapse (used to but no
125 longer engage in the behavior). The stages of change
model has been found to be applicable to a variety of
health-related personal behaviors.[25,26] This study, however, used the stages of change model on an institutional level rather than a personal one. Research indi-
130 cates that the stages of change model also works well
with assessing stages of organizational change.[27]

Personnel at SBHCs were also asked about the
benefits and barriers of providing cigarette smoking
cessation educational, referral, and prescription NRT
135 services to their students. These two components of the
health belief model have also been shown to be useful
with assessing institutions.[27,28]

Procedure

Data were collected in the spring of 2001. The initial mailing to the SBHCs consisted of a brief cover
140 letter and a copy of the questionnaire. Several techniques were used to increase the response rate, including a $1 incentive; a postage-paid, self-addressed, re-
turn envelope; a hand-signed cover letter ensuring confidentiality; and colored paper.[29] The surveys were
145 coded to track returns and facilitate follow-up mailings.
Approximately 2 weeks after the initial mailing, a second mailing was sent to nonresponding SBHCs that
included a second cover letter, another copy of the survey, and another postage-paid return envelope. Ap-
150 proximately 2 weeks after the second mailing, a colored postcard reminder was sent to nonrespondents.

Data Analysis

SPSS 10.0[30] was used for data entry and analysis.
Characteristics of SBHC by stages of change were analyzed using Kruskal-Wallis and post hoc Wilcoxon-
155 Mann-Whitney U tests with a p value set at .05. Chi-
square tests were used to analyze the perceived benefits
and barriers to offering each of the smoking cessation
services by whether personnel at the SBHC offered
such services. Due to the number of chi-square tests
160 run, p values were set at .01 to reduce potential Type I
errors.

Results

Demographic Characteristics

Of the 390 potential responses, there were 25 no
longer in existence and 2 nondeliverables. Professionals from 250 SBHCs responded, resulting in a 69%
165 response rate. The centers that responded were primarily from the West ($n = 77$), South ($n = 72$), and Northeast ($n = 67$) (Table 1). They were most likely to be
urban (55.2%), located in a school or on school

Table 1
Demographic Characteristics of Responding School-Based Health Centers (SBHCs)

Item	Number	Percentage
Geographic location		
Midwest	28	11.2
Northeast	67	26.8
South	72	28.8
West	77	30.8
Setting in which school is located		
Urban	138	55.2
Rural	76	30.4
Suburban	33	13.2
Location that best describes SBHC		
Located in the school or on school grounds	242	96.8
Located near the school but off school grounds	1	0.4
Other	6	2.4
Primary sponsoring agency of SBHC		
Health department	65	26.0
Hospital/medical center	58	23.2
School system	38	15.2
Community health center	30	12.0
Nonprofit health organization	17	6.8
Medical and/or nursing school	15	6.0
Other	23	9.2
Primary funding source of SBHC		
State/local funding including state/local grants	85	34.0
Private foundation and other grants	32	12.8
School districts	31	12.4
Maternal and child health block grant	24	9.6
Medicaid	23	9.2
Community health center	11	4.4
Tobacco monies	7	2.8
Federal funding	5	2.0
Other	33	13.2

	Mean	Standard deviation
Number of years SBHC has been in existence (range: 1–30 years)	8.87	6.18
Number of professional full-time-equivalent (FTE) staff members in the SBHC (range: 1–14 FTE)	2.68	1.83

Note. N = 250.

grounds (96.8%), and sponsored by a health department or hospital medical center (49.2%). The primary funding source for the plurality of respondents was state and local funding (34%). The average number of professional full-time-equivalent staff members was 2.68 (*SD* = 1.83).

Stages of Change for Smoking Cessation Services

175   SBHC personnel were assessed regarding their center's provision of three smoking cessation services: educational programs, referral services, and provision of prescriptions for NRT. A plurality of center personnel reported that their centers were in the maintenance 180 stage (provided the service for 1 year or longer) for educational programs (47.2%) and referral services (33.2%). However, the majority of respondents claimed their centers had not seriously thought about offering prescription services for NRT (70.0%) (Table 2). It is 185 noteworthy that 8% of the SBHCs previously offered educational programs for smoking cessation but no longer do. Unfortunately, space limitation on the questionnaire precluded further explanation as to why this was so.

190   A series of three Kruskal-Wallis tests (nonparametric ANOVAs) by geographic location (Midwest, Northeast, South, and West) and stages of change for education programs, referral services, and provision of prescriptions for NRT were calculated. Significant 195 Kruskal-Wallis tests were found for geographic location by education programs on smoking cessation (χ^2 = 17.386, df = 3, p = .001), the offering of referral services (χ^2 = 18.824, df = 3, p < .001), and providing prescription services for NRT (χ^2 = 23.959, df = 3, p < 200 .001).

Post hoc Wilcoxon-Mann-Whitney U tests found that midwestern versus western SBHCs (z = –2.211, p = .027), northeastern versus southern SBHCs (z =

Table 2
Stages of Change for Offering Specific Services for Smoking Cessation

Item (stage)	Education programs		Referral services[a]		Prescription services for NRT	
	n	%	*n*	%	*n*	%
Have not thought seriously about offering (precontemplation)	34	13.6	69	27.6	175	70.0
Are thinking about providing (contemplation)	31	12.4	20	8.0	21	8.4
Have made plans to provide and are currently taking steps to implement (preparation)	27	10.8	15	6.0	2	0.8
Have been providing for less than a year (action)	19	7.6	10	4.0	4	1.6
Have provided for 1 year or longer (maintenance)	118	47.2	83	33.2	29	11.6
Provided in the past but no longer do so (relapse)	20	8.0	5	2.0	6	2.4

Note. $N = 250$. NRT = nicotine replacement therapy.
[a]A total of 17.6% responded that they do not have referral services because they offer programs themselves.

-3.008, $p = .003$), and southern versus western SBHCs
205 ($z = -3.669$, $p < .001$) were significantly different in
their stages of change regarding the provision of smoking cessation education programs. The SBHCs located
in the West were twice as likely to have provided cessation education programs for more than 1 year com-
210 pared to SBHCs located in the Midwest (58.4% vs. 28.6%, respectively). In comparing the Northeast versus the South, SBHCs in the Northeast were more than
twice as likely (62.7% vs. 28.4%, respectively) to be in
the maintenance stage and less than half as likely
215 (9.0% vs. 23.0%, respectively) to be in the precontemplation stage (have not seriously thought about providing a smoking cessation education program). Finally,
western SBHCs were twice as likely as southern
SBHCs (58.4% vs. 28.4%, respectively) to have pro-
220 vided cessation education for more than 1 year and
nearly one-third as likely (7.8% vs. 23.0%, respectively) to have not seriously thought about providing
this service.

Post hoc Wilcoxon-Mann-Whitney *U* tests were
225 also used to compare geographic region of SBHC and
stages of change regarding referral services for smoking cessation and provision of prescriptions for NRT.
Northeastern versus southern SBHCs ($z = -2.590$, $p =$
.010) and southern versus western SBHCs ($z = -4.419$,
230 $p < .001$) were significantly different in the stages of
change in regard to offering referral services for tobacco cessation. The results of the Wilcoxon-Mann-
Whitney *U* tests for NRT prescription services indicated that midwestern versus western SBHCs ($z =$
235 -2.682, $p = .007$) and southern versus western SBHCs
($z = -4.109$, $p < .001$) were significantly different in
their stages of change.

The personnel at SBHCs located in the South were
more likely than those in the Northeast (40.5% vs.
240 28.8%) to report that their centers have never seriously
thought about offering referral services for smoking
cessation. Personnel at SBHCs in the South were also
more than twice as likely as those in the West (40.5%

vs. 15.8%, respectively) to report that their center was
245 in the precontemplation stage regarding referral services. In regards to offering prescription services for
NRT, SBHCs in the Midwest and the South were similar to SBHCs in the West. The western SBHCs were
twice as likely as those in the South or the Midwest
250 (20.8% vs. 8.3% and 10.7%, respectively) to have offered prescription services for NRT. Similar geographic differences were found with southern and
midwestern SBHCs more likely to be in the precontemplation stage (not seriously thought about offering
255 prescription services for NRT) than those SBHCs located in the West (82.1% and 84.7% vs. 52.8%, respectively).

Finally, in relation to offering the three forms of
smoking cessation services, a series of three Wilcoxon-
260 Mann-Whitney *U* tests were conducted to compare the
location of the school (rural vs. urban) by the stages of
change for each of the three services (cessation education, referral for smoking cessation, and NRT), and
none of the tests were significant ($p > .05$).

Perceived Benefits of Smoking Cessation Services

265   Respondents at the SBHCs were asked to check
their perceived benefits from a list of seven potential
benefits of offering smoking cessation education programs and the category "other." The majority of center
respondents agreed with all seven benefits (Table 3).
270 Almost four out of five or more reported the following
benefits of education programs: creates awareness of
the short- and long-term effects of smoking (89.6%),
helps adolescents recognize smoking triggers (84.4%),
creates an opportunity to discuss smoking (84.4%), and
275 provides adolescents with coping strategies (78.8%).

A series of Pearson chi-squares were calculated for
whether (maintenance stage) or not (precontemplation,
contemplation, or preparation) smoking cessation education programs were offered by the seven potential
280 benefits, and one benefit was found to be significant at
$p < .01$. Those that offered education programs were
more likely to perceive that such programs created an

Table 3
Perceived Benefits to Providing Specific Services for Smoking Cessation

Item	Education programs		Referral services		Prescription services for NRT	
	n	*%*	*n*	*%*	*n*	*%*
Increases students' awareness of short- and long-term effects of smoking	224	89.6	178	71.2	NA	
Assists students in recognizing smoking triggers (e.g., peer pressure, stress)	211	84.4	169	67.6	NA	
Creates an opportunity to discuss the issue of smoking with students	211	84.4	NA		NA	
Provides students with coping strategies	197	78.8	178	71.2	NA	
Increases students' motivation to quit smoking	177	70.8	166	66.4	NA	
Increases students' likelihood of quitting smoking	155	62.0	160	64.0	132	52.8
Decreases students' cigarette consumption	141	56.4	138	55.2	NA	
Creates opportunity to link students with individualized attention	NA		182	72.8	NA	
Increases students' access to prescription services	NA		127	50.8	NA	
Increases students' access to cessation methods	NA		NA		147	58.8
Provides students with appropriate cessation methods	NA		NA		129	51.6
There are no other providers who prescribe NRT to minors in the community	NA		NA		53	21.2
Other	28	11.2	19	7.6	38	15.2
There are no benefits	0	0.0	3	1.2	12	4.8

Note. $N = 250$. NRT = nicotine replacement therapy; NA = not applicable for this service. Respondents could check all that apply.

opportunity to discuss the issue of smoking with students compared to those that did not offer the services (93.2% vs. 77.2%, respectively).

Respondents were asked to check all that apply from a list of eight potential benefits for referring students who smoked cigarettes to smoking cessation services. The majority of all center respondents agreed with all eight benefits, even though their support for these benefits was not as strong as it was for education programs. The three benefits of referrals most strongly supported were an opportunity to link students with individualized attention (72.8%), provides students with coping strategies (71.2%), and creates awareness of short- and long-term effects of smoking (71.2%) (Table 3).

A series of Pearson chi-squares were calculated for whether referral programs existed and the eight potential benefits of such programs and three were found to be significant at $p < .01$. The SBHC personnel who did not currently refer students were less likely than SBHC personnel who did refer students to believe it would increase the likelihood of quitting smoking (61.5% vs. 77.1%, respectively), that it increased students' access to prescription services (39.4% vs. 63.9%, respectively), and that it would create an opportunity to link students with individualized attention (66.3% vs. 84.3%, respectively).

From a list of four potential benefits for prescribing NRT and the category "other," respondents were to select all with which they agreed. Three of the four

potential benefits were agreed to by the majority of respondents, but the level of support for the perceived benefits was lowest for this service when compared to education programs and referral services (Table 3).

A series of Pearson chi-square tests by whether the SBHCs offered NRT by the four potential benefits found two significant differences at $p < .01$. SBHCs that did not offer NRT were less likely than SBHCs that did offer NRT to believe that it provides students with appropriate cessation methods (45.6% vs. 93.1%, respectively) and that offering NRT prescription services increases students' access to cessation methods (55.1% vs. 89.7%, respectively).

Perceived Barriers to Services for Smoking Cessation

Center respondents were asked to select all of the barriers that apply to offering an educational program from a list of 10 potential barriers. There were 3 main barriers to offering smoking cessation education programs: not having the financial resources (31.6%), students would not use this service (22.0%), and staff not having the necessary experience to offer such programs (19.2%) (Table 4).

A series of chi-square tests by whether the SBHC offered education programs by the 10 potential barriers found 1 significantly different barrier at $p < .01$. SBHCs that did not offer smoking cessation education programs were more likely than SBHCs that did offer such programs to cite that their funding source did not

Table 4
Perceived Barriers to Providing Specific Services for Smoking Cessation

Item (stage)	Education programs		Referral services		Prescription services for NRT	
	n	%	*n*	%	*n*	%
There are no barriers to providing this service	84	33.6	79	31.6	45	18.0
Do not have the financial resources	79	31.6	28	11.2	NA	
Students would not use this service	55	22.0	82	32.8	50	20.0
Our staff does not have the necessary experience to provide this	48	19.2	NA		68	27.2
Our funding source does not allow us to provide this	13	5.2	16	6.4	53	21.2
Not enough students smoking in our school to warrant this	12	4.8	4	1.6	6	2.4
School administration is not supportive of this	9	3.6	NA		NA	
This is not one of our responsibilities	8	3.2	8	3.2	30	12.0
Parents of students would object to this	7	2.8	19	7.6	60	24.0
This would encourage smoking among students	3	1.2	2	0.8	7	2.8
Sponsoring agency does not allow us to provide this	3	1.2	8	3.2	36	14.4
Transportation to referral services would be difficult for students	NA		107	42.8	NA	
Cost to students for referral services would be too great	NA		50	20.0	NA	
No providers of cessation programs in our community	NA		40	16.0	NA	
Our staff does not have the authority to provide prescription services for NRT	NA		NA		73	29.2
Students would abuse the NRT	NA		NA		67	26.8
Other	78	31.2	32	12.8	55	22.0

Note. N = 250. NRT = nicotine replacement therapy; NA = not applicable for this service. Respondents could check all that apply.

340 allow them to provide this service (7.7% vs. 0%, respectively).

A series of Pearson chi-square tests of perceived barriers to referring students by whether the SBHCs referred students who smoke to outside sources found 345 two significant differences at *p* < .01. Respondents of SBHCs that did not refer students were more likely than SBHCs that did refer students to claim there were no providers of smoking cessation programs in the community (24.3% vs. 7.4%, respectively) and were 350 more likely to claim that their funding source did not allow them to refer students (11.7% vs. 1.2%, respectively).

A series of Pearson chi-square tests of perceived barriers to providing NRT by whether the SBHCs pro- 355 vided NRT found five significant differences at *p* < .01. Respondents for SBHCs that did not provide NRT were more likely than SBHCs that did provide NRT to believe that students would not use NRT services (22.3% vs. 11.1%, respectively), students would abuse 360 NRT (31.5% vs. 0%, respectively), parents would object to offering NRT (28.4% vs. 3.7%, respectively), their staff did not have sufficient experience to provide NRT (32.0% vs. 3.7%, respectively), and their staff did not have the authority to provide prescription service 365 for NRT (35.0% vs. 3.7%, respectively).

Discussion

School-based programs that have addressed tobacco use have traditionally provided an emphasis on prevention of tobacco use. However, the Centers for Disease Control and Prevention's *Guidelines for School Health* 370 *Programs to Prevent Tobacco Use and Addiction*[31] has as one of its recommendations the need for schools to support efforts to help adolescents quit using tobacco products. The guidelines go on to state, "Schools should identify available resources in the community 375 and provide referral and follow-up services to students. If cessation programs for youth are not available, such programs might be jointly sponsored by the school" (p. 13). Thus, this study examined smoking cessation services for adolescents that are offered by SBHCs.

380 The results of this study indicated that SBHCs in the South were the least likely of the geographic regions to offer smoking cessation education programs or to offer referral services for smoking cessation. This may indicate less support in more traditional tobacco- 385 growing regions of the country for schools to become involved in smoking cessation activities. It may also indicate that more limited resources are provided to SBHCs in the South, a region known to have limited financial resources.

390 An assessment of specific services for smoking cessation in SBHCs found that these centers tend to follow

a more traditional education mission in that they were more likely to have provided education programs (47.2%) than referral (33.2%) or prescription services for NRT (11.6%). In fact, 7 out of 10 SBHCs had never seriously thought about offering prescription services for NRT. There may be a number of explanations for the high level of precontemplation for NRT by SBHC personnel. First, because much of the staff at SBHCs are nurses, they may have no one on staff with prescriptive authority. In fact, almost one-third of the SBHC personnel cited this as a barrier. Second, because there have not been randomized, placebo-controlled trials to establish the efficacy of NRT in adolescents, some SBHCs may have questioned the efficacy and safety of such adjuncts to adolescent smoking cessation. Yet, initial research supports the safety of nicotine-patch therapy in adolescents.[12,32] A potential third reason why SBHC personnel may have not thought about prescription NRT services may be that they did not perceive prescription NRT as any more effective than over-the-counter NRT (e.g., gums and patches). Finally, the respondents may not have thought about prescribing NRT because of concerns about the financial costs to students. In fact, two studies found that financial costs associated with adolescent smoking cessation programs had a negative impact on the use of the services or were perceived as inhibiting attempts to quit smoking.[33,34]

Further research is needed in several areas associated with adolescent smoking cessation. First, research is needed to identify the nature of the smoking cessation education programs and referral services offered by SBHCs. Second, how best to structure a smoking cessation program for adolescent smokers has yet to be determined. Third, research is needed regarding parents' support for various components of adolescent smoking cessation programs. In the current study, one-fourth of the respondents perceived that parents would not be supportive of prescription services for NRT. Fourth, further research is needed to assess the level of nicotine abuse adolescents may be involved in when using NRT. Initial research does not imply that this is a significant problem.[12,32]

The limitations of this study that could result in potential bias of the results should be examined. First, a nonresponse bias may exist because the response rate was 69%, possibly limiting the external validity of the results. It is probable that the nonrespondents were less likely to have smoking cessation programs than those that did respond. Thus, the results may overestimate the percentage of SBHCs that offer such services. Second, the survey was a closed-format instrument, which did not attempt to obtain other important aspects of smoking cessation services from respondents other than that addressed in each item. To the extent that the category "other" was selected by respondents, this may indicate a threat to the internal validity of the study. Third, the monothematic nature of the survey may have

caused some respondents to answer some of the items in a unique manner. If this had resulted in some socially desirable responses, then this would be a threat to the internal validity of the study. Fourth, all data were self-report, a limitation of most survey research. Thus, to the extent that responses were not truthful, this would have limited the internal validity of the findings. Fifth, when the survey was initiated, *Making the Grade* had identified a national total of 616 middle and high school SBHCs in 1998–1999.[35] Our original sample of 390 SBHCs represented only 63% of this total population. Thus, to the extent that the SBHCs not included in our sample differed on some important characteristic related to tobacco services, this might have been a threat to the external validity of our results. Finally, because the authors did not wish to limit the definition of "smoking cessation education programs," no definition of the programs was provided to the respondents. This may have caused different respondents to answer these items in different ways. To the extent that this might have occurred, it would also be a threat to the internal validity of the study. However, in spite of the aforementioned potential limitations, this study has several important strengths. It is the first national survey of the smoking cessation activities of SBHCs. The constructs explored in this study are of importance to health education. Thus, these results provide a foundation on which to further assess school-based smoking cessation programs.

Implications for Practice

To further the implementation of tobacco cessation programs in schools, professional health education organizations (e.g., American Association for Health Education, American School Health Association) need to formulate position statements in support of these programs. More states need to use their tobacco lawsuit funds to financially support comprehensive school-based smoking cessation programs. One-third of the respondents in this study claimed they did not have sufficient financial resources to offer smoking cessation education programs. One in five respondents claimed they did not have the necessary experience to offer smoking cessation education programs. Professional health education organizations need to do more to educate their members regarding adolescent smoking cessation services. More specifically, this education should focus on recruitment strategies and effective cessation program components.

Many adolescents who currently smoke are not motivated to quit. In fact, many teen smokers are in the precontemplation stage (have not thought about quitting).[36] There are several strategies that can be used to gain access to students who are in need of cessation services:

- Schools could offer required attendance at a smoking cessation program as an alternative to suspension for being caught smoking.

11

- School personnel could make personal contact with students who smoke, inviting them to attend the program.[36]

510
- Peer leaders could recruit smokers to attend the program.

- Schools could use a social marketing campaign targeted to both students and parents to recruit students to the cessation program. The student portion

515 of the campaign should be tailored based on the values of students within the specific school.[36] The parent portion of the campaign should use a school newsletter to inform parents about the details and importance of the cessation program as well as the parents' role in assisting their child's cessation ef-

520 forts (e.g., role modeling).

Once students are enrolled in the smoking cessation program, there are a variety of intervention techniques that should be used. The limited literature available on smoking cessation suggests that programs for adoles-

525 cents include the following:

- peer-led programs;
- offering incentives;
- correct use of NRT;
- education about normal quit patterns (e.g.,

530 stages of change, recidivism);
- information about the early onset of health problems associated with smoking;
- confidentiality of participants;
- specific attainable goals;

535 - contracts with rewards;
- social support;
- avoidance, stress management, and refusal skills;
- opportunity to practice skills that will help them remain nonusers; and

540 - newsletters to parents about parent cessation and role modeling.[8,31,36]

If school districts cannot afford or do not have trained personnel to conduct cessation programs, school personnel should create partnerships with com-

545 munity agencies that may already offer cessation programs (e.g., local hospitals, American Lung Association, American Cancer Society). In addition, school districts should be encouraged to evaluate the effectiveness of their cessation programs so that information

550 can be added to the limited literature on effective adolescent smoking cessation programs.

References

1. Johnston LD, O'Malley PM, Bachman JG: *Monitoring the Future National Survey Results on Drug Use, 1975–1999. Volume 1: Secondary School Students*. Bethesda, MD: National Institute on Drug Abuse, 2000. (NIH Pub. No. 00-4802.)

2. U.S. Department of Health and Human Services: *Preventing Tobacco Use Among Young People: A Report of the Surgeon General*. Washington, DC: Government Printing Office, 1994.

3. Gilpin E, Lee L, Evans N, Pierce J: Smoking initiation rates in adults and minors: U.S. 1944–1988. *Am J Epidemiol* 140:535–543, 1994.

4. U.S. Department of Health and Human Services: Incidence of initiation of cigarette smoking. *MMWR* 47:837–840, 1998.

5. Johnston LD, O'Malley PM, Bachman JG: *National Survey Results on Drug Use From the Monitoring the Future Study, 1975–1998. Volume 1: Secondary School Students*. Rockville, MD: National Institute on Drug Abuse, 1999.

6. Pierce J, Choi W, Gilpin E, Farkas A, Merritt R: Validation of susceptibility as a predictor of which adolescents take up smoking in the United States. *Health Psychol* 15:355–361, 1996.

7. Centers for Disease Control and Prevention: Projected smoking-related deaths among youth—United States. *MMWR* 45:971–974, 1996.

8. Sussman S, Lichtman K, Ritt A, Pallonen UE: Effects of thirty-four adolescent tobacco use cessation and prevention trials on regular users of tobacco products. *Subst Use Misuse* 34:1469–1503, 1999.

9. Ershler J, Leventhal H, Fleming R, Glynn K: The quitting experience for smokers in sixth through twelfth grades. *Addict Behav* 14:365–378, 1989.

10. Sargent JD, Mott LA, Stevens M: Predictors of smoking cessation in adolescents. *Arch Pediatr Adolesc Med* 152:388–393, 1998.

11. Sussman S, Dent CW, Lichtman KL: Outcomes of a teen smoking cessation program. *Addict Behav* 26:425–438, 2001.

12. Smith TA, House RF, Croghan IT, Gauvin TR, Coligan RC, Offord KP, Gorney-Dahl LC, Hurt RD: Nicotine patch therapy in adolescent smokers. *Pediatrics* 98:659–667, 1996.

13. Brindis CD, Sanghui RV: School-based health clinics: Remaining viable in a changing health care delivery system. *Ann Rev Public Health* 18:567–587, 1997.

14. Maternal and Child Health Bureau: *Primary Care for Children and Adolescents: Definition and Attributes*. Rockville, MD: U.S. Department of Health and Human Services, Health Resources and Services Administration, 1994.

15. Keyl PM, Hurtado MP, Barber MM, Borton J: School-based health centers: Students' access, knowledge, and use of services. *Arch Pedriatr Adolesc Med* 150:175–180, 1996.

16. Anglin TM, Naylor KE, Kaplan DW: Comprehensive school-based health care: High school students' use of medical, mental health, and substance abuse services. *Pediatrics* 97:318–330, 1996.

17. Pastore DR, Juszczah L, Fisher MM, Friedman SB: School-based health center utilization: A survey of users and non-users. *Arch Pediatr Adolesc Med* 152:763–767, 1998.

18. Kisker EE, Brown RS: Do school-based health centers improve adolescents' access to health care, health status, and risk-taking behavior? *J Adolesc Health* 18:335–343, 1996.

19. Kirby D, Waszac C, Ziegler J: *An Assessment of Six School-Based Clinics: Services, Impact and Potential*. Washington, DC: Center for Population Options, 1990.

20. Weathersby AM, Lobo ML, Williamson D: Parent and student preferences for services in a school-based clinic. *J Sch Health* 65:14–17, 1995.

21. Lowe JM, Knapp ML, Meyer MA, Gall GB, Hampton JG, Dillman J, Roover ML: School-based health centers as a locus for community health improvement. *Quality Management in Health Care* 9(4):24–32, 2001.

22. Stone SL, Kristeller JL: Attributes of adolescents toward smoking cessation. *Am J Prev Med* 14:405–407, 1992.

23. Moss AJ, Allen KF, Giovino GA, Mills SL: *Recent Trends in Adolescent Smoking, Smoking Uptake Correlates, and Expectations About the Future*. Washington, DC: Vital and Health Statistics, U.S. Department of Health and Human Services, Public Health Service, Centers for Disease Control [Advance Data 221], 1992.

24. Prochaska JO, Diclemente CC, Norcross JC: In search of how people change: Applications to addictive behaviors. *Am Psychol* 47:1102–1114, 1992.

25. Prochaska JO, Velicer WF, Rossi JS, Goldstein MG, Marcus BH, Rakowski W, et al: Stages of change and decisional balance for twelve problem behaviors. *Health Psychol* 13:39–46, 1994.

26. Prochaska JO: Strong and weak principles for progressing from precontemplation to action based on twelve problem behaviors. *Health Psychol* 13:47–51, 1994.

27. Price JH, Oden, L: Reducing firearm injuries: The role of local public health departments. *Pub Health Rep* 114:533–539, 1999.

28. McCarthy S, Telljohann S, Price J, Coventry B: *Emergency Contraceptive Pills: Education, Referral, and Prescription Services in School-Based Health Clinics*. Paper presented at the American School Health Association, Albuquerque, NM, November 2001.

29. King KA, Pealer LN, Bernard AL: Increasing response rates to mail questionnaires: A review of inducement strategies. *Amer J Health Educ* 32:4–15, 2001.

30. SPSS: *SPSS 10.0 for Windows*. Chicago: SPSS Inc., 1999.

31. Centers for Disease Control and Prevention: Guidelines for school health programs to prevent tobacco use and addiction. *MMWR* 43(RR-2):1–18, 1994.

32. Hurt RD, Croghan GA, Beede SD, Wolter TD, Croghan IT, Patten CA: Nicotine patch therapy in 101 adolescent smokers. *Arch Pediatr Adolesc Med* 154:31–37, 2000.

33. Gillespie A, Stanton W, Lowe, JB, Hunter B: Feasibility of school-based smoking cessation programs. *J Sch Health* 65:432–437, 1995.

34. Hines D: Young smokers' attitudes about methods for quitting smoking: Barriers and benefits to using assisted methods. *Addict Behav* 21:531–535, 1996.
35. Lear JG, Eichner N, Koppelman J: The growth of school-based health centers and the role of state policies: Results from a national survey. *Arch Pediatr Adolesc Med* 153: 1177–1180, 1999.
36. Balch GI: Exploring perceptions of smoking cessation among high school smokers: Input and feedback from focus groups. *Prev Med* 27:A55–A63, 1998.

About the authors: James H. Price, Ph.D., MPH, and Faith Yingling, MS, Ed, Department of Public Health, University of Toledo. Joseph A. Dake, Ph.D., MPH, College of Education, Division of HPER, Wayne State University. Susan K. Telljohann, HSD, CHES, Department of Public Health, University of Toledo.

Address correspondence to: Dr. James H. Price, Department of Public Health, University of Toledo, Toledo, OH 43606. E-mail: jprice@utnet.utoledo.edu

Exercise for Article 2

Factual Questions

1. The acronym "SBHCs" stands for what words?

2. The acronym "NRT" stands for what words?

3. How did the researchers obtain the names and addresses of nurses at SBHCs?

4. The entire list of 390 SBHCs included how many senior high schools?

5. After how many weeks was a second mailing sent to nonrespondents?

6. What percentage of the responding SBHCs had state/local funding?

Questions for Discussion

7. Have the researchers convinced you that the questionnaire is valid? (See lines 101–108.)

8. The researchers used a $1 incentive to increase the response rate. What is your opinion on using such an incentive? (See lines 140–142.)

9. In your opinion, is a response rate of 69% acceptable for a survey of this type? (See lines 163–165 and lines 436–442.)

10. In your opinion, how important are the results relating to regional/geographic differences? (See lines 201–264.)

11. In lines 420–434, the researchers list four suggested areas for future research. Do you believe that all four are important? Explain.

12. In lines 453–456, the researchers note the limitation of using self-reports. In your opinion, are respondents to this type of survey likely to not be truthful in their responses? Explain.

Quality Ratings

Directions: Indicate your level of agreement with each of the following statements by circling a number from 5 for strongly agree (SA) to 1 for strongly disagree (SD). If you believe an item is not applicable to this research article, leave it blank. Be prepared to explain your ratings.

A. The introduction establishes the importance of the study.

SA   5   4   3   2   1   SD

B. The literature review establishes the context for the study.

SA   5   4   3   2   1   SD

C. The research purpose, question, or hypothesis is clearly stated.

SA   5   4   3   2   1   SD

D. The method of sampling is sound.

SA   5   4   3   2   1   SD

E. Relevant demographics (for example, age, gender, and ethnicity) are described.

SA   5   4   3   2   1   SD

F. Measurement procedures are adequate.

SA   5   4   3   2   1   SD

G. All procedures have been described in sufficient detail to permit a replication of the study.

SA   5   4   3   2   1   SD

H. The participants have been adequately protected from potential harm.

SA   5   4   3   2   1   SD

I. The results are clearly described.

SA   5   4   3   2   1   SD

J. The discussion/conclusion is appropriate.

SA   5   4   3   2   1   SD

K. Despite any flaws, the report is worthy of publication.

SA   5   4   3   2   1   SD

Article 3

Elementary Teachers' Beliefs and Knowledge About Grade Retention: How Do We Know What They Know?

STACIE M. WITMER
Carlisle Area School District

LYNN M. HOFFMAN
Bucknell University

KATHARYN E. NOTTIS
Bucknell University

ABSTRACT. Elementary teachers' beliefs, knowledge, and practice relating to retention were explored using an adapted version of the Teacher Retention Beliefs Questionnaire (Tomchin & Impara, 1992). A researcher-developed knowledge section was added to the original questionnaire to measure teachers' propositional knowledge of retention. Thirty-five K–4 teachers from a rural school district in the northeastern United States completed the questionnaire. Teachers from all grade levels believed retention was an acceptable practice. Students' academic performance was the most influential factor in retention decisions. Significant differences between K–2 and 3–4 teachers were found on several belief statements. Teachers' knowledge about the effects and outcomes of retention, measured by factual questions, was low regardless of grade taught. The majority correctly answered knowledge questions based upon hypothetical students. No significant correlation was found between teachers' knowledge and retention practice. Issues related to the measurement of teacher knowledge and implications of the findings are discussed.

From *Education, 125*, 173–193. Copyright © 2004 by Project Innovation, Inc. Reprinted with permission.

Introduction

Years of research have shown that retention provides limited academic advantages to students (McCoy & Reynolds, 1999; Meisels & Liaw, 1993; Reynolds, 1992; Shepard & Smith, 1989), and yet the practice

5 continues. According to the National Association of School Psychologists (NASP) (2003), approximately 15% of all American students are retained each year with 30–50% being held back before the ninth grade. Retention rates have increased over the last 20 years

10 (NASP, 2003) as pressure to end social promotion has increased and satisfactory performance on newly introduced end-of-year standards-based assessments has become a new expectation for promotion to the next grade.

15 When decisions are made to retain students in grade, the primary goal is to remediate academic difficulties (Nason, 1991). However, grade retention is not an effective educational strategy for long-term academic improvement (McCoy & Reynolds, 1999; Meis-

20 els & Liaw, 1993; Owings & Magliaro, 1998; Shepard & Smith, 1989). Any small positive effects that have been seen with the retained students usually have not been sustained beyond a few years (Roderick, 1995). In addition, retention has been associated with a variety of

25 negative effects, including greater academic failure (Meisels & Liaw, 1993; Reynolds, 1992), higher dropout rates (Roderick, 1995), and lower self-concept (Nason, 1991). Repeating a grade has been found to be the third most stressful imagined event in a child's life,

30 surpassed only by going blind and losing a parent (Shepard & Smith, 1990).

Teachers usually make the recommendation to promote or retain their students, with the final decision mitigated by varying input or pressure from parents

35 and administrators (Kelly, 1999). Since teachers have this responsibility, it is important to identify and understand their beliefs and knowledge about retention.

Teachers' Beliefs About Retention

Pajares (1992) has suggested that beliefs are the best indicators of the decisions individuals make

40 throughout their lives. Beliefs are different from knowledge (Enters, 1994; Shepard & Smith, 1989; Tomchin & Impara, 1992) and often described interchangeably as attitudes, judgments, values, opinions, perceptions, ideology, and internal mental processes

45 (Eisenhart, Shrum, Harding, & Cuthbert, 1988; Pajares, 1992). Beliefs are relatively static whereas knowledge changes as more and different knowledge is acquired (Nespor, 1987).

Teachers' beliefs appear to underlie their judgments

50 about students (Fang, 1996; Tomchin & Impara, 1992), although many times these beliefs are interwoven with knowledge, making it difficult to separate the two (Shepard & Smith, 1989). Many researchers (e.g., Shepard & Smith, 1989; Stipek & Byler, 1997) have

55 identified teachers' beliefs about retention as a way to explain their practice of retention. However, few studies have documented how teachers create their own belief systems throughout their teaching careers (Kagan, 1992).

60   It is known that teachers rarely alter their beliefs based on research studies they have read and are more likely to do so as a result of personal experiences or advice from colleagues (Kagan, 1992). Knowledge of research findings has been referred to as propositional

65   knowledge (Smith, 1989) while knowledge from personal experiences has been labeled practical knowledge (Fenstermacher, 1994). Practical knowledge, "[I]s bounded by time, place, or situation. To claim to know something practically is to claim to know something

70   about an action, event, or situation in a particular instance" (Fenstermacher, 1994, p. 28). This delineation is supported further by Calderhead's (1996) efforts to differentiate among different sorts of teacher knowledge. It may be that straightforward questions about

75   research results require teachers' theoretical knowledge, while situational questions activate their personal practice or case knowledge. Consistent with the previous findings, research has also shown that teachers have tended to rely on practical knowledge more often

80   than formal knowledge when making retention decisions (Shepard & Smith, 1989).

Researchers have examined teachers' beliefs about grade retention using both questionnaires and vignettes with hypothetical situations (Manley, 1988; Tomchin

85   & Impara, 1992). Manley (1988) used a researcher-developed questionnaire generated from two earlier studies (Faerber & Van Dusseldorp, 1984; Frazier, 1978), augmenting it with three vignettes describing a child with a school-related problem. Tomchin and Im-

90   para (1992) developed the Teacher Retention Beliefs Questionnaire (TRBQ) to assess teachers' explicit views of retention. Items were originally developed from students' permanent records, written policies, teacher interviews, and previous literature (Tomchin &

95   Impara, 1992). The Retention Decision Simulation instrument was also developed by Tomchin and Impara (1992) to assess teachers' implicit beliefs about retention. It consists of 40 vignettes about hypothetical students and was constructed using ten retention decision

100   factors. Studies using these and other assessments have indicated that academic achievement is the most influential factor teachers consider when deciding to promote or retain a student (Enters, 1994; Kirby, 1996; Manley, 1988; Pouliot, 1999; Tomchin & Impara,

105   1992).

Previous research (e.g., Tomchin & Impara, 1992) has found that teachers' beliefs may vary by grade taught. For example, Tomchin and Impara (1992) found that teachers in the earlier grades (K–3) had

110   different beliefs than those in later grades (4–7). Teachers surveyed in the earlier grades agreed that students must master the basic skills before moving on to the next grade, reflecting an adherence to the prescribed curriculum and its standards for performance.

115   Upper grade teachers' beliefs about retention were not as consistent, with some teachers indicating approval of retention as a way to improve student outcomes,

maintain standards, or demonstrate that lack of effort results in retention.

120   How does an awareness of research findings or propositional knowledge influence teachers' retention decisions? Few studies have researched this question. Enters (1994) attempted to do so by adding a knowledge section to Tomchin and Impara's (1992) TRBQ.

125   However, this additional "knowledge" section inferred teachers' knowledge was from workshops attended or books read, and asked them how personally important this knowledge was rather than assessing actual knowledge of research findings. There still appears to

130   be a need to assess teachers' knowledge about retention and its source (personal experience or research findings).

Purpose of the Study

Retention is an ineffective practice for helping academically slow or immature learners, yet many

135   teachers continue to recommend that students be retained (McCoy & Reynolds, 1999; Shepard & Smith, 1989). These continuing recommendations appear to be based on teachers' short-term personal experiences with retained students (Shepard & Smith, 1989).

140   These experiences lead teachers to believe retention is beneficial despite research to the contrary (Pouliot, 1999; Tomchin & Impara, 1992). However, these beliefs have been found to vary according to the grades a teacher has taught (Tomchin & Impara, 1992).

145   Enters (1994) attempted to measure teachers' knowledge as well as beliefs about retention by adding questions to the TRBQ (Tomchin & Impara, 1992). These added knowledge questions assessed the source of their knowledge and its importance. An assessment

150   is still needed to determine teachers' actual knowledge of retention research.

Therefore, the purpose of this pilot study was to develop a knowledge assessment to measure teachers' propositional knowledge about retention (knowledge of

155   research findings) that could be easily added to a pre-existing instrument, in this case, an adapted version of the TRBQ (Tomchin & Impara, 1992). It was hoped that by including both beliefs and knowledge about grade retention in the same instrument a more complete

160   picture of why teachers continue to recommend retention would emerge. In addition to the development of a knowledge test, the following questions were examined:

1.   What are elementary teachers' beliefs about
165   grade retention and do they differ by grade taught?
2.   What factors influence teachers' decisions to retain students?
3.   How much propositional knowledge do elemen-
170   tary teachers have about grade retention?
4.   Do elementary teachers have higher levels of practical or propositional knowledge about grade retention?

5. What is the relationship between teachers' propositional knowledge about retention and their practice of retaining students?

Method

Participants

Forty-one questionnaires were distributed, one per teacher, to those teaching kindergarten to fourth grade in the same rural school district in the northeastern part of the United States. The district consisted of four elementary schools with three enrolling approximately 100 students each and one reporting 696 students. All four schools were supervised by one principal housed at the largest school. The school district from which the sample was drawn had a history of retaining students. Records from 1996–2000, provided by district administrators, showed that 55 students had been retained in the four elementary schools.

Completed questionnaires were received from 35 teachers (85% response rate). There were 27 female and 8 male teachers. All respondents were Anglo American. Questionnaires were then grouped into two categories (K–2 and 3–4). There were 21 teachers in the K–2 group and 14 teachers in the 3–4 group.

Materials

A researcher-developed knowledge section was added to an adapted version of Tomchin and Impara's (1992) Teacher Retention Beliefs Questionnaire, prompting the original name of the questionnaire to be changed to the Teacher Retention Beliefs and Knowledge Questionnaire (TRBKQ). The new knowledge section then became the third part of the four-part questionnaire. Overall retention rates were also collected from the elementary school principal as well as information about the current district's retention policy.

Part I of TRBKQ measured teachers' beliefs about grade retention using a four-choice Likert-scale format ranging from agree to disagree (1 = Agree, 2 = Tend to Agree, 3 = Tend to Disagree, and 4 = Disagree) and two open-ended questions. One item related to teachers of older students was altered from the TRBQ (Tomchin & Impara, 1992) to better reflect the sampled school district's policy. "Students who do not make passing grades in two of the three major subject areas should be retained" (Tomchin & Impara, 1992, p. 203) was changed to read, "Students retained once in elementary school (grades K–4) should not be retained again in elementary school."

Part II of the questionnaire assessed the differential importance of factors influencing teachers' decision-making processes when deciding whether to retain a student. Subjects were requested to distribute 100 points across 11 factors. Seven of the listed factors had previously been found to be the most common in terms of influencing teachers' decisions: (a) academic performance, (b) social/emotional maturity, (c) age in relation to others, (d) home environment, (e) effort being put forth, (f) child's self-esteem, and (g) ability (Tom-

chin & Impara, 1992). However, in the current study, four factors were added after area school personnel enrolled in a graduate course at a small, private university in the same geographical area were asked to list factors that they considered when deciding to retain a student. These added factors were: parental input, presence of a learning disability, student transience, and attendance. Two factors found on the original questionnaire (Tomchin & Impara, 1992), size in relation to others and gender, were removed because none of the area school personnel mentioned them.

The researchers developed a 16-item knowledge retention assessment for Part III of the questionnaire. It consisted of thirteen multiple-choice and three open-ended questions. Five of the multiple-choice questions (#26, #28, #30, #33, #36) were patterned after the vignettes previously used in the literature (e.g., Tomchin & Impara), asking subjects to respond to hypothetical students and situations using their knowledge of the retention literature. These questions were designed to measure teachers' practical knowledge. The other eight multiple-choice questions asked participants to respond to information about retention presented in a factual format. These questions were designed to measure teachers' propositional knowledge. Five of the propositional knowledge questions (#35, #32, #37, #29, #31) were matched with the practical knowledge questions, each assessing the same information. Content validity for this part of the questionnaire was obtained by asking five university professors in the education department of a small private university to review questions in both formats. Their feedback was incorporated into the final version, found in Appendix A of this article. The open-ended questions asked respondents to indicate some predictors of retention, alternatives to retention, and to identify their primary source of knowledge about retention.

Part IV collected demographic information about the teachers as well as information about their practice of retention. Teachers' practice of retention was assessed by asking teachers to indicate the number of students retained in the previous school year, the number of students recommended for retention but promoted in the previous school year, and the largest number of students retained in one school year. These three questions were additions to the original Teacher Retention Beliefs Questionnaire (Tomchin & Impara, 1992).

Finally, three multiple-choice questions added by Enters (1994) to the original TRBQ were also used. These questions assessed how teachers obtained their knowledge about retention by asking them to indicate the last time they read a journal article or other literature that discussed retention or attended a workshop or conference relating to retention, and to reflect on the amount of knowledge they had about retention.

Table 1
Descriptive Statistics for Beliefs of Those Teaching Grades K–2 and 3–4

	Belief	Grade taught	% who agreed	% who disagreed	Median[1] score	n
1.	Retention is an effective means of preventing students from facing daily failure in the next higher grade.	K–2 3–4	19.0 28.5	9.5 0.0	2.0 2.0	21 14
2.	Retention is necessary for maintaining grade level standards.**	K–2 3–4	0.0 14.2	33.3 0.0	3.0 2.0	20 14
3.	Retaining a child in grades K–2 harms a child's self-concept.	K–2 3–4	14.2 0.0	42.8 28.5	3.0 3.0	21 14
4.	Retention prevents classrooms from having wide ranges in student achievement.	K–2 3–4	4.7 0.0	52.3 35.7	4.0 3.0	21 14
5.	Students who do not apply themselves should be retained.**	K–2 3–4	0.0 0.0	57.1 14.2	4.0 3.0	21 14
6.	Knowing that retention is a possibility does motivate students to work harder.	K–2 3–4	4.7 0.0	28.5 14.2	3.0 3.0	21 14
7.	Retaining a child in grades 3–4 harms a child's self-concept.	K–2 3–4	23.8 0.0	4.7 0.0	2.0 2.5	21 14
8.	Retention is an effective means of providing support in school for the child who does not get support at home.	K–2 3–4	9.5 7.1	33.3 35.7	3.0 3.0	21 14
9.	Students retained once in elementary school (K–4) should not be retained again in elementary school.**	K–2 3–4	57.1 28.5	0.0 0.0	1.0 2.0	21 14
10.	Students who make passing grades but are working below grade level should be retained.	K–2 3–4	4.7 0.0	52.3 35.7	4.0 3.0	19 14
11.	Retention in grades K–2 is an effective means of giving the immature child a chance to catch up.	K–2 3–4	28.5 21.4	4.7 7.1	2.0 2.0	21 14
12.	Retention in grades 3–4 is an effective means of giving the immature child a chance to catch up.	K–2 3–4	0.0 7.1	19.0 14.2	3.0 2.0	21 14
13.	Students receiving services from a learning support teacher should not be retained.	K–2 3–4	42.8 21.4	9.5 7.1	2.0 3.0	21 14
14.	If students are to be retained, they should be retained no later than 4th grade.	K–2 3–4	23.8 14.2	4.0 14.2	2.0 3.0	21 14
15.	In grades K–2, overage children (more than a year older than their classmates) cause more behavior problems than other children.**	K–2 3–4	4.7 0.0	66.6 21.4	4.0 3.0	21 14
16.	In grades 3–4, overage children (more than a year older than their classmates) cause more behavior problems than other children.	K–2 3–4	9.5 0.0	33.3 28.5	3.0 3.0	20 14
17.	Retention in grades K–2 permanently labels a child.	K–2 3–4	0.0 0.0	61.9 35.7	4.0 3.0	21 14
18.	Retention in grades 3–4 permanently labels a child.	K–2 3–4	4.7 0.0	42.8 28.5	3.0 3.0	20 14
19.	Children who have passing grades but excessive absences should be retained.	K–2 3–4	0.0 0.0	57.1 57.1	4.0 4.0	21 14
20.	Children should never be retained.	K–2 3–4	0.0 0.0	71.4 78.5	4.0 4.0	21 14

**Significant differences in responses given by the two groups of teachers.
[1]Scores ranged from 1–4, with 1 = agree, 2 = tend to agree, 3 = tend to disagree, 4 = disagree.

Design and Procedure

A within-subjects posttest design with no control groups was used for the current study. All subjects received all parts of the TRBKQ. Descriptive statistics were used to answer questions related to overall beliefs and knowledge of the respondents. Responses of teachers in different grade levels on Part I of the TRBKQ were compared for two of the four response categories:

285

290

17

Agree and Disagree. Due to the small, nonrandom sample, group comparisons and descriptions of the relationship between knowledge and the practice of retention were made using nonparametric tests.

295 *Pre-Study Preparation.* Prior to the study, the TRBQ (Tomchin & Impara, 1992) was adapted for use. The 10 factors considered for retention decisions in Part II were adapted based on responses from 10 local teachers enrolled in a university graduate education
300 course. In addition, a section assessing teachers' propositional knowledge of retention developed by the researchers was added. Content validity was obtained and revisions were made based on the reviewers' comments.

305 *Data Collection.* The researchers and the elementary principal supervising all four buildings developed a memo encouraging teachers' participation. This memo was distributed prior to data collection and was also attached to the TRBKQ. Teachers anonymously
310 and individually completed the questionnaire (TRBKQ) and returned it in an envelope to a specially marked box in the mailroom of the largest elementary school in the district. These were collected and the data obtained were analyzed.

Results

315 Thirty-seven percent of the 35 teachers who returned the questionnaire had been teaching between one to ten years, 17% of the teachers had been teaching between 11 to 20 years, and 37% had been teaching 21 to 29 years. Only 8% of the teachers had been teaching
320 for over 30 years. Sixty percent of the teachers reported that their highest level of education was a master's degree.

Teachers' Beliefs About Retention

Part I of the Teachers Retention Beliefs and Knowledge Questionnaire was used to discern elemen-
325 tary teachers' beliefs about grade retention and whether they differed as a function of grade level category (K–2, 3–4). It was hypothesized that teachers would agree that retention is an effective practice, and this was supported. It was found that 77% of the respondents be-
330 lieved retention was an effective practice for preventing failure in later grades and 94% of them disagreed with the statement, "Children should never be retained" (Item #20).

It was also hypothesized that there would be sig-
335 nificant differences between the beliefs of the two groups of teachers (K–2 and 3–4), and some differences were found. Descriptive statistics for each item, along with variations in the responses provided by participants teaching grades K–2 and 3–4, can be seen in
340 Table 1.

The Mann-Whitney test revealed there were significant differences on responses to four of the 20 questions. There was a significant difference between the two groups of teachers on whether retention is neces-
345 sary to maintain grade level standards (Item #2). More

teachers in grades K–2 disagreed with this statement than teachers in grades 3–4 ($U = 44.50$, $p < .01$). A significant difference was also found between the two groups of teachers on whether pupils who do not apply
350 themselves in their studies should be retained (Item #5). More K–2 teachers than 3–4 teachers disagreed with that statement ($U = 78.0$, $p < .05$). Also, significantly more K–2 than 3–4 teachers disagreed with the statement, "In grades K–2…overage children cause
355 more behavioral problems than other children" (Item #15), ($U = 83.0$, $p < .05$).

Finally, responses to Item #9, which stated, "Students retained once in elementary school (K–4) should not be retained again in elementary school," tended to
360 be in agreement with the school district's retention policy that students can only be retained once in elementary school. Although the median response was 2.0, which equaled "tend to agree," significantly more K–2 than 3–4 teachers agreed that students should only
365 be retained once in elementary school, ($U = 88.0$, $p < .05$).

Open-ended responses revealed that some teachers relied more heavily on support services and their own interventions to prevent retention than they had in the
370 past. One teacher noted that she had seen retention be both successful and unsuccessful while another indicated that she hesitated to recommend retention because of potential conflict with parents who disagreed with her recommendation.

Factors Considered in the Retention Decision

375 Responses to the second part of the Teachers Retention Beliefs and Knowledge Questionnaire indicated factors that influenced participants' decisions to retain. Respondents distributed 100 points across 11 factors to indicate the relative weight of each factor in their deci-
380 sions. It was hypothesized that academic performance would be the most influential factor and this was confirmed. On average, academic performance was considered twice as important as the second most important factor. Table 2 shows the mean number of points
385 assigned to each factor by K–2 and 3–4 grade teachers.

After academic performance, three other factors clustered together as second most important. Effort being put forth, ability, and social/emotional maturity had approximately the same mean score. None of the
390 teachers added other factors in the blank space provided. There were some differences found between the K–2 and 3–4 teachers although the child's self-esteem was the only factor where a significant difference was found. Kindergarten through second-grade teachers
395 gave significantly more weight to a child's self-esteem than third- and fourth-grade teachers ($U = 88.0$, $p < .05$).

Teachers' Knowledge of Retention

Part III of the Teacher Retention Beliefs and Knowledge Questionnaire was used to determine the
400 teachers' knowledge about grade retention and to dis-

18

Table 2
Factors that Influence Retention Decisions: A Comparison of Mean Number of Points Assigned by K–2 (n = 21) and 3–4 (n = 14) Teachers

Factor	Grades taught	Mean # of points[1]	SD
Parental input	K–2	9.5	7.4
	3–4	10.0	7.1
Learning disability	K–2	6.8	5.8
	3–4	10.9	6.9
Academic performance	K–2	21.4	10.4
	3–4	26.8	12.5
Social/emotional maturity	K–2	11.7	6.0
	3–4	11.0	7.4
Transient student	K–2	4.0	4.6
	3–4	2.7	3.4
Age in relation to others	K–2	6.0	3.4
	3–4	4.0	3.4
Number of absences	K–2	3.6	3.6
	3–4	2.1	3.1
Home environment	K–2	4.8	3.7
	3–4	4.2	5.5
Effort being put forth	K–2	11.0	9.2
	3–4	13.0	14.2
Child's self-esteem**	K–2	9.8	7.5
	3–4	5.1	4.0
Ability	K–2	12.6	8.2
	3–4	11.0	7.3

**Significant difference, ($p < .05$)
[1]Points ranged from 0–100.

tinguish whether this knowledge was practical or propositional. It was hypothesized that teachers would have limited propositional knowledge about the effects of grade retention and this was supported. When scores were examined by grade groups, mean scores were comparable; both groups had a mean score of approximately 30%.

It was also suspected that teachers would more often correctly respond to questions about hypothetical situations where practical knowledge was assessed rather than factual questions where propositional knowledge was assessed, and this was supported. A Wilcoxon test revealed that teachers had significantly higher scores for hypothetical than factually based ($T = -3.70, p < .001$).

Sources of Knowledge

Thirty-two of the respondents indicated the source of their knowledge about retention. Forty-four percent of this group reported that personal experiences with retained students contributed the most to their knowledge while 22% attributed their knowledge base to talking to colleagues. Only three teachers (9%) reported that their knowledge about retention came from reading journal articles and/or attending workshops on retention.

When asked to indicate when they last read a journal article or other literature that discussed grade reten-

tion, 76% of the total sample of teachers reported a year or more. Eighty-seven percent of the teachers also reported that they attended a workshop, conference, or meeting on retention more than a year ago. Six percent ($n = 2$) of respondents noted that they had never attended a workshop, conference, or meeting on retention.

When asked to rate their knowledge of the current research about retention and its effects on students, 23% of the teachers reported that they had extremely limited knowledge, 56% of the teachers explained that they had somewhat limited knowledge about retention, and 21% of the teachers said they had moderate but not extensive knowledge about retention. No one indicated that his/her knowledge about retention was extensive.

Relationship Between Teachers' Knowledge and Practice of Retention

The last research question examined the relationship between teachers' knowledge about retention as measured in Part III of the Teacher Retention Beliefs and Knowledge Questionnaire and their practice of retaining students. Teachers' practice of retention was operationally defined as the number of students recommended for retention last school year and the largest number of students recommended for retention in one school year. It was hypothesized that there would be a negative relationship between teachers' knowledge level and the number of students they retained. Spearman rank correlations revealed that there was no significant relationship between teachers' knowledge scores and their practice of retention.

When asked to give an estimate of the total number of students recommended for retention in each of the grade levels taught during their careers, the greatest number of retained students was listed at the kindergarten level. Seven teachers (20%) had taught kindergarten at some time during their teaching careers and had retained a total of 53 students. The second largest number of students was retained in first grade. Twenty-eight percent ($n = 10$) had taught first grade at some time during their teaching career, and these teachers retained a total of 43 students. When asked "What is the largest number of students you have retained in one school year?" the overall mean was one student/school year ($M = 1.13$, $SD = .99$), although almost a third reported that they had never retained any students. However, four of these teachers reported that this was their first year teaching.

Discussion

Several studies have examined teachers' beliefs about and their practice of retention (Keaton, 1997; Shepard & Smith, 1989; Stipek & Byler, 1997; Tomchin & Impara, 1992) but few have looked at teachers' knowledge of retention and its relationship to their practice. Enters (1994) added a knowledge section to the Teacher Retention Beliefs Questionnaire (Tomchin & Impara, 1992) but questions inferred knowledge of retention from the number of articles read and workshops attended. The current study, through the development and administration of the Teacher Retention Beliefs and Knowledge Questionnaire, attempted to assess teachers' knowledge of retention research as well as their beliefs about retention to determine whether there was a relationship between their knowledge and practice of retention.

Consistent with other research findings (e.g., Byrnes & Yamamoto, 1986; Enters, 1994; Tomchin & Impara, 1992), K–4 teachers in this study believed that retention was an effective practice that could help certain students be more successful in the classroom. Also consistent with the results reported by Tomchin and Impara (1992), teachers' beliefs about retention differed according to whether they taught younger or older elementary students.

Significant differences were found between teachers' beliefs in grades K–2 and 3–4 on four different belief statements. First, teachers in grades K–2 tended to disagree more strongly than teachers of grades 3–4 that retention was useful in maintaining grade level standards. It is possible that teachers of older students were more mindful of the high-stakes state assessments that many students first encounter in the primary grades. Second, consistent with previous findings (Enters, 1994; Tomchin & Impara, 1992), K–2 teachers

tended to disagree more strongly than their 3–4 counterparts that students who did not demonstrate effort and apply themselves to their studies would be candidates for retention. Perhaps teachers of younger students equated their lack of success with an inability to master basic skills while teachers of older students expected to see the development of "habits of mind," including observable effort, as a condition for promotion (Marzano, Pickering, & McTighe, 1993). Third, K–2 teachers disagreed more than grade 3–4 teachers that overage, retained students presented more behavioral problems than other students.

The majority of the participants agreed that students should not be retained more than once in their K–4 years. This overall agreement aligns with the school district's policy on multiple retentions and supports the findings of previous researchers (e.g., Smith & Shepard, 1988; Tomchin & Impara, 1992) who found that teachers in the same school tended to share similar beliefs. Smith and Shepard (1988) noted, "The beliefs held by individuals are related to beliefs held by others in the same environment; beliefs appear to be interwoven within school structure and social climate" (p. 330). While the teachers in this study represented four school buildings, they were all influenced by this small district's beliefs and policies about retention and were overseen by the same administrator. However, although there tended to be overall agreement, significantly more K–2 than 3–4 teachers agreed with the statement, perhaps reflecting the widely held belief that retention is better for students in earlier grades than it is for students in later grades.

Teachers considered a number of factors when deciding to retain or promote a student, although some factors were more influential than others. Consistent with previous research (e.g., Nason, 1991; Reynolds, 1992), respondents identified students' academic performance as the most influential factor, a finding that is not surprising considering the major reason given for retaining students is to improve their academic achievement. Additional factors such as students' ability, effort, and social and emotional maturity were also identified by participants as playing important roles in their decision-making. Teachers teaching grades K–2 weighted ability as the second most important factor, whereas teachers teaching grades 3–4 identified effort as their second most influential factor. Marzano, Pickering, and McTighe (1993) described the "habits of mind," or attitudes and perceptions that students must cultivate if they are to become successful independent learners. Perhaps teachers of older students expected that these productive mental habits, such as perseverance in the face of difficulty and active engagement in the learning process, should be more firmly entrenched and observable in older students.

A significant difference was found between the two groups of teachers on the importance of a child's self-esteem in relation to retention. Teachers in the K–2 group placed more weight on a child's self-esteem than teachers in the 3–4 group. This is in contrast to the results of Enters' (1994) research, in which teachers in the upper grades listed students' self-esteem as a more important factor to consider. However, Enters' (1994) older grade level group extended to grade 7; perhaps middle school teachers are more aware of self-esteem issues among students at that transitional level. It is also possible that, after careful consideration, the teachers in the current study concluded that retention would not result in damage to the self-esteem of the particular students they had retained. Jimerson (1999) has noted that teachers sometimes feel that retention gives students a "gift" of an additional year in grade to improve reading and other academic skills, thereby increasing students' efficacy and self-esteem.

Of the four additional factors listed on the second part of the Teacher Retention Beliefs and Knowledge Questionnaire, two appeared to influence teachers' decision-making: parental input and the presence of a learning disability. Additional research with other groups of teachers will be needed to confirm the importance of parental input and a student's identification as a special needs student as possible factors in teachers' retention decisions.

Sakowicz (1996) noted that, "[Of] all the major issues in education, grade retention represents one of the clearest examples of noncommunication between research and practice" (p. 16). Responses to the knowledge questions support this observation. Teachers had minimal knowledge about the effects of retention; the average knowledge score was 30%. Despite their low level of propositional knowledge, teachers did respond more accurately to hypothetical questions about student retention, a finding that is not surprising given previous research (e.g., Schon, 1983) that has suggested that when a problem is situated, professionals tend to form intuitions based upon their own successes and failures that guide their practice. Shepard and Smith's (1989) conclusion that a discrepancy exists between teachers' personal and propositional knowledge about retention also appears to be supported here.

Overall, teachers described their knowledge of retention research as limited. The majority attributed their knowledge to personal experiences with retained students. Talking to colleagues was the second most frequently cited source of knowledge. This supports previous research (e.g., Kagan, 1992) that has suggested that teachers alter their personal beliefs based primarily on their own experiences or through the shared experiences of their colleagues rather than through the acquisition of knowledge derived from current research. Kennedy (1997) has suggested that teachers' lack of familiarity with research and research's minimal influence on their practice may be the result of one or more of the following: the research itself may not be sufficiently persuasive, the research is not relevant to teachers' practice, ideas from research

have not been accessible to teachers, or the education system itself is unable to change. Teachers' responses indicated that they might not have had access to recent research on retention. They generally reported reading a journal article on retention or attending a workshop where retention was discussed one or more years ago.

It was hypothesized that a negative relationship would be found between teachers' knowledge levels, as measured by the Teacher Retention Beliefs and Knowledge Questionnaire, and the number of students they had retained. However, no significant correlation was found. This could be due to the small, nonrandom sample in this study, as well as the generally low knowledge levels of all participants. Low knowledge levels could be related to the type of questions used to measure that knowledge. Although content validity was obtained, reliability of the knowledge section of the instrument was not determined. Future research should determine reliability of the instrument as well as use larger, random samples from multiple school districts. Follow-up interviews with participants targeting their knowledge-base acquisition and their decision-making process would also provide a more in-depth understanding of their practice, as well as insights into their interpretation of the knowledge questions.

Ultimately, educators need to address how to improve students' academic skills and reduce failure. Teachers need to learn about and implement promising practices that prevent retention in their own school and in their own classrooms. In order for this to happen, meaningful strategies need to be designed to provide teachers with more accurate knowledge about retention either at the preservice or practice level. Tanner and Combs (1993) have suggested that teachers continue to perceive retention as a successful intervention either because they are unaware of retention research and promising alternatives to retention, or because they know the literature and discard its implications in favor of their personal beliefs. Connecting teachers effectively with retention research might be the first step in changing this ineffective practice.

References

Byrnes, D., & Yamamoto, K. (1986). Views on grade repetition. *Journal of Research and Development in Education, 20*, 14–20.

Calderhead, J. (1996). Teachers: Beliefs and knowledge. In D. C. Berliner & R. C. Calfee (Eds.), *Handbook of educational psychology.* New York: Simon & Schuster Macmillan, pp. 709–725.

Eisenhart, M. A., Shrum, J. L., Harding, J. R., & Cuthbert, A. M. (1988). Teacher beliefs: Definitions, findings, and directions. *Educational Policy, 2*, 51–70.

Enters, T. (1994). *Grade retention: A survey of elementary school teachers' beliefs.* Unpublished master's thesis, University of Wisconsin–Whitewater.

Faerber, K., & Van Dusseldorp, R. (1984). *Attitudes toward elementary school student retention.* (ERIC Documents Reproduction Services No. ED 250 109).

Fang, Z. (1996). A review of research on teacher beliefs and practices. *Educational Research, 38*, 47–63.

Fenstermacher, G. D. (1994). The knower and the known: The nature of knowledge in research on teaching. In L. Darling-Hammond (Ed.), *Review of Research in Education: Vol. 20* (pp. 3–56). Washington, DC: American Educational Research Association.

Frazier, C. (1978). *Teacher attitudes toward retention.* Unpublished master's thesis, Tennessee Technological University, Cookeville.

Jimerson, S. R. (1999). On the failure of failure: Examining the association between early grade retention and education and employment outcomes during late adolescence. *Journal of School Psychology, 37*, 243–272.

Kagan, D. M. (1992). Implications of research on teacher beliefs. *Educational Psychologist, 27*, 65–90.

Keaton, D. M. (1997). *Teacher beliefs about grade level retention in high and low retaining elementary schools.* Unpublished doctoral dissertation, University of North Carolina.

Kelly, K. (1999). Retention vs. social promotion: Schools search for alternatives. *Harvard Education Letter, 15*, 1–3.

Kennedy, M. M. (1997). The connection between research and practice. *Educational Researcher. 26*, 4–12.

Kirby, N. K. (1996). *A study analyzing practitioners' practices and beliefs about grade retention.* Unpublished doctoral dissertation, Ohio University.

Manley, J. (1988). *Study of primary teachers' attitudes toward grade retention.* Unpublished doctoral dissertation, University of Kansas.

Marzano, R., Pickering, D., & McTighe, J. (1993). *Assessing student outcomes.* ASCD: Alexandria, VA.

McCoy, A. R., & Reynolds, A. J. (1999). Grade retention and school performance: An extended investigation. *Journal of School Psychology, 37*, 273–298.

Meisels, S. J., & Liaw, F. R. (1993). Failure in grade: Do retained students catch up? *Journal of Educational Research, 87*, 69–77.

Nason, B. R. (1991). Retaining children, is it the right decision? *Childhood Education, 67*, 300–304.

National Association of School Psychologists (NASP) (2003). Position Statement: Student Grade Retention and Social Promotion. Silver Spring, MD: Author.

Nespor, J. (1987). The role of beliefs in the practice of teaching. *Journal of Curriculum Studies, 19*, 317–328.

Owings, W. A., & Magliaro, S. (1998). Grade retention: A history of failure. *Educational Leadership, 56*, 86–88.

Pajares, M. F. (1992). Teachers' beliefs and educational research: Cleaning up a messy construct. *Review of Educational Research, 62*, 307–332.

Pouliot, L. (1999, April). *A double method approach for a double need: To describe teachers' beliefs about grade retention and to explain the persistence of these beliefs.* Paper presented at the Annual Meeting of the American Educational Research Association, Montreal, Quebec, Canada. (ERIC Document Reproduction Service No. ED 429 946).

Reynolds, A. J. (1992). Grade retention and school adjustment: An explanatory analysis. *Education Evaluation and Policy Analysis, 14*, 101–121.

Roderick, M. (1995). Grade retention and school dropout: Policy debate and research questions. *Research Bulletin of Phi Delta Kappa Center for Evaluation, Development, and Research, 15*, 1–5.

Sakowicz, A. B. (1996). *The effect of retention, in grade one, on the slow reader.* Unpublished master's thesis, Kean College, New Jersey.

Schon, D. (1983). *The reflective practitioner: How professionals think in action.* New York: Basic Books.

Shepard, L.A., & Smith, M. L. (1989). Academic and emotional effects of kindergarten retention in one school district. In L.A. Shepard & M. L. Smith (Eds.), *Flunking grades: Research and policies on retention* (pp. 79–107). Philadelphia: Falmer.

Shepard, L. A., & Smith, M. L. (1990). Synthesis of research on grade retention. *Educational Leadership, 47*, 84–88.

Smith, M. L. (1989). Teachers' beliefs about retention. In L. A. Shepard & M. L. Smith (Eds.), *Flunking grades: Research and policies on retention* (pp. 132–150). Philadelphia: Falmer.

Smith, M. L., & Shepard, L. A. (1988). Kindergarten readiness and retention: A qualitative study of teachers' beliefs and practices. *American Educational Research Journal, 25*, 307–311.

Stipek, D. J., & Byler, P. (1997). Early childhood education teachers: Do they practice what they preach? *Early Childhood Research Quarterly, 12*, 305–325.

Tanner, C. K., & Combs, F. E. (1993). Student retention policy: The gap between research and practice. *Journal of Research in Childhood Education, 8*, 69–77.

Tomchin, E. M., & Impara, J. C. (1992). Unraveling teachers' beliefs about grade retention. *American Educational Research Journal, 29*, 199–223.

Appendix A
Part III
Retention Knowledge Assessment

24. What is the current educational position on retention and social promotion?
    a. Schools should keep both social promotion and grade retention.
    b. Schools should end both social promotion and grade retention.*
    c. Schools should end social promotion and keep grade retention.
    d. Schools should keep social promotion and end grade retention.

25. Whether a student is promoted or retained, what does the majority of the current research say about the long-term effects on students' academic achievement?
    a. Retention does not effectively increase academic achievement among low-achieving students.*
    b. Social promotion does not effectively increase academic achievement among low-achieving students.
    c. Neither social promotion nor retention effectively increase academic achievement.
    d. Both social promotion and retention effectively increase academic achievement.

26. According to the current research, how will Steven, a first-grader, most likely feel when he hears that he is going to be retained?
    a. He will be indifferent toward the decision.
    b. He will feel relieved because now he can "catch up" on his basic skills.
    c. He will feel like he is being punished.*
    d. He will feel happy because he will be the leader in the class.

27. In general, what does the current research say about an extra year in kindergarten, pre-kindergarten programs, and/or transitional first programs?
    a. Students do not experience any benefits from these extra-year programs.*
    b. Students become more mature as a result of these extra-year programs.
    c. Students experience a benefit in academic achievement in these extra-year programs.
    d. Students experience higher self-esteem from these extra-year programs.

28. According to current research, which student is most likely to drop out of school?
    a. John who was held back one time in elementary school.
    b. Brian who has been held back once in elementary school and once in middle school.*
    c. Matt who has been performing below average every school year, but has never been retained.
    d. David who was recommended for retention but was promoted to the next grade level.

29. In general, what does the majority of the current research say about grade retention and academic gains?
    a. Academic gains are not noticed until three or four years after the retention.
    b. Any academic gains made during the repeated year increase over time.
    c. Retained students make more academic gains than those who are promoted.

d. Any academic gains made during the repeated year fade over time.*

30. According to current research, which student is most likely to be retained?
    a. Brad, a White male, who is young for his grade and whose family is in the low socioeconomic status (SES) group.
    b. Jerome, an African American male, who is young for his grade, family is in the low SES group.*
    c. Maria, a Hispanic female, whose primary language is not English, family is in the high SES group.
    d. Lisa, a White female, the smallest and youngest in her class, family is in the high SES group.

31. What does the current research suggest when comparing the behavior of students who have been retained or socially promoted with students who have NOT been retained or promoted?
    a. Grade retention is not associated with children's behavior problems.
    b. Grade retention is associated with decreased rates of behavior problems.
    c. Grade retention is associated with increased rates of behavior problems. *
    d. Social promotion is associated with increased rates of behavior problems.

32. In general, what does the majority of the current research say about retention and school drop-out rate?
    a. Students who are retained are more likely to drop out of school.*
    b. There is no correlation between being retained and dropping out of school.
    c. Students who are retained are less likely to drop out of school.
    d. Students are likely to drop out of school only if they have been retained more than once.

33. Tricia, Jen, Michelle, and Julie are all struggling academically. According to current research, which student would you expect to perform better academically three or four years from now?
    a. Jen who was retained at the end of the year.
    b. Michelle who was recommended for retention but was promoted to the next grade.*
    c. Tricia who was retained due to parent request.
    d. Julie who was retained due to social immaturity.

34. In general, what does the majority of research say about peer relatedness and grade retention in the elementary grades?
    a. Students will more often pick the retained student for help with academics, but not as a play partner.*
    b. Students will more often pick the retained student as a play partner, but not for help with academics.

c. Retained students are not treated differently by their peers in elementary school.
    d. Promoted students experience rejection by their peers more often than retained students do.

35. In general, what does the majority of the current research say about retention and students' self-concepts?
    a. Children in kindergarten and first grade are unaffected because of their age.
    b. Retention produces more positive effects than negative effects on students' self-concepts.
    c. Retention has no effect on students' self-concepts.
    d. Retention produces more negative effects than positive effects on students' self-concepts. *

36. According to current research, which student will most likely be causing the most behavior problems in the elementary grades?
    a. Scott who is age appropriate for his grade and was never retained.
    b. Paul who is young for his grade due to his summer birthday.
    c. Jessica who is age appropriate for her grade, but was promoted to the next grade level.
    d. Kristin who is old for her grade due to being retained.*

37. In general, what does the literature say are some of the predictors of early grade retention among students?

38. What alternatives are there to retention?

39. Please check the one that most contributes to how you have obtained your knowledge about grade retention and social promotion.
    __ reading journal articles and attending workshops
    __ personal experiences with retained students
    __ talking to colleagues
    __ recent university coursework
    __ other (please explain)

*Keyed answer.

About the authors: Stacie M. Witmer is a school psychologist in the Carlisle Area School District in Carlisle, PA. Her research interests include academic and behavioral issues of school-age children. Lynn M. Hoffman is an assistant professor of education at Bucknell University in Lewisburg, PA. Her research interests are in high school culture and adolescent rites of passage and their manifestation in yearbooks. Her teaching interests are in school administration and in the preparation of novice teachers. Katharyn E. Nottis is an associate professor of education at Bucknell University in Lewisburg, PA. An educational psychologist, she is primarily interested in conceptual learning in science and gender issues. Most recently, she has investigated the generation of science analogies by pre-service teachers and studied the effect of learner and instructional variables on the learning of point and plane group symmetry in chemistry. Her teaching interests are in educational psychology and in the preparation of novice teachers.

Address correspondence to: Lynn M. Hoffman, Education Department, Bucknell University, Moore Avenue, Lewisburg, PA 17837.

Exercise for Article 3

Factual Questions

1. According to Smith (1989), how is "propositional knowledge" defined?

2. To whom were the questionnaires distributed?

3. In Part I of the questionnaire, what does a response of "3" indicate?

4. How was the content validity of Part III of the questionnaire determined?

5. What percentage of the teachers teaching in grades K–2 agreed with the statement, "Retention is necessary for maintaining grade level standards"?

6. What percentage of the responding teachers reported that their knowledge about retention came from reading journal articles and/or attending workshops on retention?

Questions for Discussion

7. The researchers cite a study indicating that teachers rarely alter their beliefs based on research studies they have read. Speculate on the reasons for this. Have you personally altered your beliefs based on a research study? Explain. (See lines 60–63.)

8. Teachers anonymously completed the questionnaire. In your opinion, is anonymity important for a study on this topic? Explain. (See lines 309–310.)

9. The teachers in the four schools returned their completed questionnaires to a mailbox in the largest of the elementary schools in the district. If you had conducted this study, is this how you would have had the teachers return them? Explain. (See lines 309–313.)

10. The researchers hypothesized that there would be a negative relationship between teachers' knowledge level and the number of students they retained. If you had been planning this study, would you have made this hypothesis? Explain. (See lines 450–452.)

11. The researchers suggest that follow-up interviews would be desirable in future studies on this topic. Do you agree? Explain. (See lines 644–648.)

12. If you were conducting a study on the same topic, what changes in the research methodology, if any, would you make?

13. What is your opinion of the knowledge questions in Appendix A of this article? (The appendix appears just below the references in this article.) To what extent does the inclusion of the actual questions help you comprehend the results of this study? Explain.

Quality Ratings

Directions: Indicate your level of agreement with each of the following statements by circling a number from 5 for strongly agree (SA) to 1 for strongly disagree (SD). If you believe an item is not applicable to this research article, leave it blank. Be prepared to explain your ratings.

A. The introduction establishes the importance of the study.

SA   5   4   3   2   1   SD

B. The literature review establishes the context for the study.

SA   5   4   3   2   1   SD

C. The research purpose, question, or hypothesis is clearly stated.

SA   5   4   3   2   1   SD

D. The method of sampling is sound.

SA   5   4   3   2   1   SD

E. Relevant demographics (for example, age, gender, and ethnicity) are described.

SA   5   4   3   2   1   SD

F. Measurement procedures are adequate.

SA   5   4   3   2   1   SD

G. All procedures have been described in sufficient detail to permit a replication of the study.

SA   5   4   3   2   1   SD

H. The participants have been adequately protected from potential harm.

SA   5   4   3   2   1   SD

I. The results are clearly described.

SA   5   4   3   2   1   SD

J. The discussion/conclusion is appropriate.

SA   5   4   3   2   1   SD

K. Despite any flaws, the report is worthy of publication.

SA   5   4   3   2   1   SD

Article 4

Bullying and Victimization: Prevalence and Relationship to Gender, Grade Level, Ethnicity, Self-Esteem, and Depression

DOROTHY SEALS
Delta State University

JERRY YOUNG
Delta State University

ABSTRACT. This study investigated the prevalence of bullying and victimization among students in grades seven and eight. It also explored the relationship of bullying and victimization to gender, grade level, ethnicity, self-esteem, and depression. Three survey instruments were used to obtain data from a convenience sample of 454 public school students. Twenty-four percent reported bullying involvement. Chi-square tests indicated significantly more male than female bullying involvement, seventh-graders reported more involvement than did eighth-graders, and there were no statistically significant differences in involvement based on ethnicity. Both bullies and victims manifested higher levels of depression than did students who were neither bullies nor victims. There were no significant differences between groups in terms of self-esteem.

From *Adolescence*, 38, 735–747. Copyright © 2003 by Libra Publishers, Inc. Reprinted with permission.

The destructive consequences of bullying behavior in U.S. schools have sparked public concern for students' safety (Spivak & Prothrow-Stith, 2001). School shootings have increased awareness that bullying may
5   serve as a precursor to these violent eruptions. Further, bullying and victimization have been associated with negative consequences in adulthood (Olweus, 1991; Perry, Kusel, & Perry, 1988; Tritt & Duncan, 1997).

Research on school bullying has found higher
10   prevalence rates in the United States than in other countries (Duncan, 1999; Hoover, Oliver, & Hazler, 1992). Information on the prevalence of bullying could be useful to school boards, administrators, counselors, and teachers as they plan ways to deal with this in-
15   creasingly common problem. Not only would it be helpful to know the extent of the problem, but knowing who is involved, where it occurs, the types of bullying, and its effects on both bullies and victims of bullying would be valuable. For example, males have been
20   found to be more involved in physical bullying, while females use more covert forms (Olweus, 1991). Borg (1998) reported that the prevalence of bullying only appears to decline as students mature; it actually

changes from aggressive forms to more passive, verbal
25   forms.

Ethnicity as a possible factor in bullying has not been widely studied, though Kaufman, Chen, Choy, Chandler, Chapman, Rand, and Ringel (1998), reporting the results of a national survey, indicated that eth-
30   nicity was not as significant as gender and grade level. The effects of bullying behaviors on bullies and victims in the areas of self-esteem and depression have been studied, but results have been mixed. Duncan (1999), Rigby and Slee (1991), and Tritt and Duncan
35   (1997) noted that victims of bullying manifested lower levels of self-esteem than did bullies, but O'Moore and Hillery (1989), in their study of Irish school children, found that bullies had lower levels of self-esteem. In their study of Australian school children, Rigby and
40   Slee (1991) found that bullies had high levels of self-esteem but were more depressed than those who were neither bullies nor victims of bullying.

The present study attempted to answer three questions: (1) How prevalent is self-reported bullying and
45   victimization as perceived by students? (2) What is the relationship of bullying and victimization to the variables of gender, grade level, and ethnicity? (3) What is the relationship of bullying and victimization to measures of self-esteem and depression? Students in grades
50   seven and eight were chosen for this study because adolescence has been characterized as a period of transitional stress resulting in impulsive behaviors and rapid fluctuations in emotions, and exposure to repeated insults and rejection by peers can generate
55   deadly results, such as suicide or homicide (Olweus, 1991). Participants were drawn from seven public schools in Mississippi, in an area of the state that has a high concentration of African American students. This provided a sample that differed ethnically from those
60   used in most prior studies of school bullying in the U.S., which have been composed primarily of Caucasian students (Duncan, 1999; Hoover, Oliver, & Hazler, 1992).

Method

This descriptive study used a sample obtained from a total population of 1,126 students enrolled in seventh and eighth grades in five school districts in the northern delta region. Approval was obtained from the Institutional Research Board of Delta State University and the superintendents of each school district. Parental consent forms were distributed, and 454 signed forms were returned (40%). The ages of the students ranged from 12 to 17 years. The participants were primarily African American (79%) and Caucasian (18%). Fifty-nine percent were female and 41% were male. Forty-eight percent were in schools classified as urban and 52% were in rural/suburban schools.

Instruments

Three instruments were used to collect data: the Peer Relations Questionnaire (PRQ; Rigby & Slee, 1995), the Rosenberg Self-Esteem Scale (RSE; Rosenberg, 1965), and the Children's Depression Inventory (CDI; Kovacs, 1983). The PRQ is a twenty-item survey that consists of three scales: Bully, Victim, and Prosocial. These scales describe bullying and present an example, followed by general questions about bullying. Items regarding victimization address frequency and duration of bullying, types of bullying experienced, and feelings about being bullied. Content validity was established by Rigby and Slee (1995). Duncan (1999) determined that the PRQ is valid and reliable for surveying students in seventh and eighth grades.

The RSE is a ten-item measure of global self-esteem. Five items are positively worded and five are negatively worded. Examples include: "I do not have much to be proud of," "I am proud of myself," and "I take a positive attitude toward myself."

The CDI has a third-grade reading level and is suitable for use with those between the ages of 7 and 17 years. Total scores range from 0 to 54, with higher scores indicating greater depression. Kovacs (1992) recommended using scores of 17 or above to indicate depression in a heterogeneous population. Comparison of CDI items with symptom criteria for depression in the American Psychiatric Association's *Diagnostic and Statistical Manual of Mental Disorders* indicated high content validity (Hodges & Seigal, 1985). Kovacs (1983) reported high test–retest reliability in studies of pediatric patients with diabetes and public school children.

Procedure

School superintendents at the selected school districts were given a written overview of the proposed research, along with copies of the instruments and parental consent forms to be used. With approval of the superintendents and school board (when necessary), school principals were contacted to set up dates, times, procedures, and places for the surveys. Procedures for maintaining confidentiality and anonymity were discussed. On the specified dates, designated teachers or counselors collected signed parental consent forms. No attempt was made to ascertain the reason for either not returning the form or declining permission to participate.

Testing sessions lasted fifty minutes and were conducted by one of the researchers, who read the instructions to participating students at the beginning of each session. A consistent format was used at each site. Each student was given a number-coded packet containing the instruments. Students were cautioned not to identify themselves on any of the documents. Data for each school were later provided to the respective superintendent, as requested.

Data Analysis

Coded data were analyzed using descriptive statistics. Frequencies, percentages, and cross-tabulation were used to analyze responses to individual items on the PRQ and to categorize participants according to their level of involvement in bullying: bully, victim, bully/victim, and nonbully/nonvictim. Bullies indicated engagement in individual or group bullying (or both) one or more times per week; victims indicated being bullied by an individual or group one or more times per week. Bullies/victims met both the bully and victim criteria (bully others one or more times per week and victimized one or more times per week). Those who did not indicate they had bullied or had been victimized were designated as nonbullies/nonvictims. Cross-tabulation and the chi-square statistic were used to determine relationships.

The relationship of gender, grade level, and ethnicity to classification (bully vs. victim) was addressed by a series of 2×2 cross-tabulations using male vs. female, grade seven vs. grade eight, and African American vs. Caucasian. Significant interactions at the $p < .05$ level were identified. Since the category of bully/victim included only six students, this group was not included in the analysis.

The relationship of bullying and victimization to measures of self-esteem and depression, specifically bullying involvement (bully, victim, and nonbully/nonvictim) and scores on the RSE and CDI, was analyzed. One-way ANOVAs were used, with statistical significance set at $p < .05$.

Results

Responses to the PRQ were analyzed to determine the frequency and location of bullying, as well as the types of bullying experienced, and to group students according to their level of involvement in bullying (bully, victim, nonbully/nonvictim). One hundred nine students (24%) reported bullying involvement (bullying or victimization). The perception of frequency of bullying based on grade level was determined: 45.4% of the seventh graders and 41.8% of the eighth graders perceived bullying to occur "often" at school. However, the difference was not significant, $\chi^2(2, N = 454)$ = 1.77, $p = .41$.

In order to assess the types of behaviors involved in bullying, students were asked to rate five bullying behaviors on a three-point scale ("never," "sometimes," or "often"). Nine percent of the students reported often being teased in an unpleasant way, 13.5% reported often being called hurtful names, 6.6% reported often being threatened with harm, and 10.8% reported often being hit or kicked (see Table 1). Using the same three-point scale, the students were asked where the bullying occurred: 18.9% stated that the bullying often occurred in class, 30.2% reported that it often occurred at lunch or recess, 8.8% reported that the bullying often occurred on the way to school, and 20.7% reported that it often happened on the way home from school (see Table 2).

The demographic variables of gender, grade, and ethnicity were compared among three categories of students (see Table 3). Results showed that males comprised 66.7% of the bullies, 43.6% of the victims, and 37.3% of the nonbullies/nonvictims. Significantly more males than females were involved in bullying, $\chi^2(2, N = 454) = 15.17$, $p = .01$. Further, seventh-graders comprised 58.3% of the bullies, 49.1% of the victims, and 40.2% of the nonbullies/nonvictims. Significantly more seventh-graders than eighth-graders were involved in bullying, $\chi^2(2, N = 454) = 6.57$, $p = .04$. No significant differences were found between the African American and Caucasian students, $\chi^2(2, N = 439) = 0.31$, $p = .86$. In addition, when type of school (urban or rural/suburban) was examined, no significant differences were found, $\chi^2(2, N = 454) = 1.25$, $p = 54$.

Table 1
Type and Frequency of Bullying During the Past School Year

Bullying behavior	n	%
Physical		
Never	306	67.7
Sometimes	97	21.5
Often	49	10.8
Threats of harm		
Never	349	77.2
Sometimes	73	16.2
Often	30	6.6
Name calling		
Never	225	49.8
Sometimes	166	36.7
Often	61	13.5
Mean teasing		
Never	255	56.3
Sometimes	157	34.7
Often	41	9.0
Exclusion		
Never	307	67.9
Sometimes	112	24.8
Often	33	7.3

Table 2
Location and Frequency of Bullying

Location of bullying	n	%
In class		
Never	94	20.7
Sometimes	274	60.4
Often	86	18.9
At lunch or recess		
Never	92	20.3
Sometimes	225	49.5
Often	137	30.2
On the way to school		
Never	294	64.8
Sometimes	120	26.4
Often	40	8.8
On the way home		
Never	164	36.1
Sometimes	196	43.2
Often	94	20.7

Table 3
Demographic Variables and Involvement in Bullying

Variable	Bully		Victim		Nonbully/ nonvictim	
	n	%	n	%	n	%
Gender						
Male	32	66.7	24	43.6	131	37.3
Female	16	33.3	31	56.4	220	62.7
Grade level						
7th	28	58.3	27	49.1	141	40.2
8th	20	41.7	28	50.9	210	59.8
Ethnicity						
Caucasian	7	15.2	10	18.5	63	18.6
African American	39	84.8	44	81.5	276	81.4
School type						
Urban	25	52.1	25	45.5	153	43.6
Rural/suburban	23	47.9	30	54.5	198	56.4

A subgroup analysis of the 48 identified bullies in the sample was conducted to examine involvement in individual or group bullying. Thirty (62.5%) exhibited bullying behavior only in group situations, while 18 (37.5%) exhibited bullying as an individual or in conjunction with others. Of those who bullied only in a group, 56.7% were males; of those who bullied as an individual or in conjunction with others, 83.3% were males. This difference did not attain statistical significance, $\chi^2(1, N = 48) = 3.60$, $p = .06$.

Next, a subgroup analysis based on reports by 55 victims was performed to determine the gender of those who bully. When the bully was male, 66.7% of the victims were male as well; when the bully was female, only 12.2% of the victims were male; and when the bullying was by either a male or female, or a combination of males and females, 34.6% of the victims were male. The chi-square value was significant $\chi^2(2, N = 55) = 8.54$, $p = .01$. The gender of the bully and the gender of the victim were independent. Male victims reported more bullying by individual males, groups of males, or a combination of males and females.

An analysis of the gender of the bully and grade levels showed that when a male bully was involved,

47.6% of the victims were eighth-graders; when a female bully was involved, 87.5% of the victims were eighth-graders; and when male and female bullies acted together, 42.3% of the victims were eighth graders. The chi-square value was not significant, $\chi^2(2, N = 55) = 5.15$, $p = .08$. Seventh- and eighth-grade victims did not differ in respect to reported bullying by individual male or female bullies or by mixed-gender groups of bullies.

In addition, the gender of the bully and the ethnicity of the victim were examined. The chi-square value was not significant. African American and Caucasian victims did not differ according to whether they were bullied by male or female bullies, either alone or in groups.

Table 4 displays frequency of bullying behavior (reported as occurring "often") by gender. The percentages for male students were as follows: physical (49.0%), threats of harm (65.0%), name calling (44.3%), mean teasing (53.7%), and exclusion (42.4%). However, the chi-square test was not significant, $\chi^2(4, N = 216) = 1.64$, $p = .80$. Male and female victims did not differ significantly in their reports of bullying behaviors experienced.

Table 4
Bullying Behavior Reported As Occurring "Often" by Gender

Bullying behavior	Male		Female	
	n	%	*n*	%
Physical	25	49.0	26	51.0
Threats of harm	26	65.0	14	35.0
Name calling	27	44.3	34	55.7
Mean teasing	22	53.7	19	46.3
Exclusion	14	42.4	19	57.6

Table 5 presents frequency of bullying behavior (reported as occurring "often") by grade level. The percentages for eighth-grade students were as follows: physical (54.2%), threats of harm (46.7%), name calling (52.5%), mean teasing (48.8%), and exclusion (63.6%). However, the chi-square test was not significant, $\chi^2(4, N = 216) = 2.55$, $p = .64$. Seventh- and eighth-graders did not differ significantly in their reports of bullying behaviors experienced.

Table 5
Bullying Behavior Reported As Occurring "Often" by Grade Level

Bullying behavior	7th grade		8th grade	
	n	%	*n*	%
Physical	22	45.8	26	54.2
Threats of harm	16	53.3	14	46.7
Name calling	29	47.5	32	52.5
Mean teasing	21	51.2	20	48.8
Exclusion	12	36.4	21	63.6

Table 6 displays frequency of bullying behavior (reported as occurring "often") by ethnicity. The percentages for African American students were as fol-

lows: physical (77.6%), threats of harm (76.7%), name calling (76.7%), mean teasing (80.5%), and exclusion (84.4%). However, the chi-square test was not significant, $\chi^2(4, N = 216) = .0.96$, $p = .92$. African American and Caucasian students did not differ significantly in their reports of bullying behaviors experienced.

Table 6
Bullying Behavior Reported As Occurring "Often" by Ethnicity

Bullying behavior	Caucasian		African American	
	n	%	*n*	%
Physical	11	22.5	38	77.6
Threats of harm	7	23.3	23	76.7
Name calling	14	23.3	46	76.7
Mean teasing	8	19.5	33	80.5
Exclusion	5	15.6	27	84.4

The three groups (bullies, victims, and nonbullies/nonvictims) were compared in terms of self-esteem. Bullies ($M = 31.9$, $SD = 4.8$) scored higher than victims ($M = 30.7$, $SD = 4.9$), as did nonbullies/nonvictims ($M = 31.4$, $SD = 5.0$), but these differences were minimal. A one-way analysis of variance was not significant, $F(2, 451) = .70$, $p < .50$.

The three groups were compared in regard to depression. Their scores were as follows: bullies ($M = 14.3$, $SD = 7.9$), victims ($M = 15.6$, $SD = 8.3$), and nonbullies/nonvictims ($M = 9.1$, $SD = 6.4$). A one-way analysis of variance was significant, $F(2, 451) = 29.66$, $p < .01$. Scheffé post hoc tests revealed that the mean scores for bullies and victims were not significantly different; however, both bullies and victims had significantly higher depression scores than did nonbullies/nonvictims.

Discussion

The students in this study perceived a high frequency of bullying. Of the 454 students surveyed, 45% of the seventh-graders and 42% of the eighth-graders reported that bullying occurred "often" in the delta schools participating in this project. In addition, 24% (109 students) reported direct involvement in bullying: 10% bullied others one or more times per week, 13% were victimized at the same rate, and 1% both were bullied and bullied others on a weekly basis. These results indicate a lower rate of bullying than the 29% reported by Nansel et al. (2001) and Duncan (1999), but this may be due to the criteria used to designate bullies and victims. The present findings are consistent with other research that shows that rural schools are not immune to this form of aggression. This is a cause for concern in that a recent study of rural fourth- through sixth-graders indicated that bullying and victimization were correlated with being aggressive and holding attitudes that promote violence as a primary method of conflict resolution (Stockdale, Handaduambo, Duys, Larson, & Sarvela, 2002).

Gender, grade level, and ethnicity were also exam-
310 ined. Males were significantly more involved in bullying than were females, with twice as many males identified as bullies. In regard to grade level, results indicated that seventh-graders were more involved in bullying than were eighth-graders.
315 Additionally, both male and female bullies who
bullied alone tended to target victims of the same gender. However, more females than males were involved
in mixed-gender group bullying. Results also indicated
that physical bullying did not decline in eighth grade,
320 with more females in this grade reporting being hit,
kicked, or shoved than those in seventh grade. Verbal
name calling represented the most prevalent form of
bullying experienced, followed by physical aggression.
There were no significant grade-level differences in the
325 prevalence of the various types of bullying. Further,
there were no significant differences between African
American and Caucasian students.

In terms of self-esteem, bullies, victims, and non-
bullies/nonvictims were not significantly different from
330 one another. However, bullies had the highest level of
self-esteem, followed by nonbullies/nonvictims and
then victims. The six bullies/victims had the lowest
self-esteem. These findings are consistent with those
presented by Rigby (1996), who found that bullies
335 were generally more popular in school and had high
levels of self-esteem, while victims viewed themselves
as less popular and had the lowest self-esteem. Although the lack of adequate sample size prohibited
inclusion of the bullies/victims in the analysis, this
340 group requires further attention because of the higher
degree of pathological behavior reported by several
researchers (Kumpulainen, Rasanen, & Henttonen,
1998; Olweus, 1991; Slee & Rigby, 1993).

This study's findings in regard to depression are in
345 accord with those reported by Slee (1995) and others
(Duncan, 1999; Tritt & Duncan, 1997), who found that
victims were more depressed than bullies and students
not involved in bullying, but that bullies also showed a
degree of depression. In the present study, both bullies
350 and victims were more depressed than students who
were neither bullies nor victims. This has implications
for educators in that depression is often associated with
self-destructive behaviors and diminished social interaction, as well as with decreased academic perform-
355 ance. An analysis of CDI items revealed that 5% of the
students in this sample had thoughts of self-harm.
While this is a small percentage, the association of impulsive behaviors with thoughts of self-harm is a cause
for concern (Kumpulainen et al., 1998). In addition,
360 depression has often been associated with risk-taking
behaviors in adolescence, such as smoking and substance abuse (Nansel et al., 2001).

Conclusions

Recent acts of school violence have shown that bullying can no longer be viewed as merely a part of

365 growing up. We now recognize that exposure to this
form of behavior can also have detrimental long-term
effects. In addition, the use of force can prevent students from learning more adaptive methods of resolving interpersonal conflicts.
370 More needs to be known about the frequency and
magnitude of this problem among students, as well as
its relationship to depression and self-esteem. Further
investigation into the relationship of bullying to self-
destructive thoughts and behaviors and acts of revenge
375 is needed. Since this study did not show a decline in
physical aggression in the eighth grade, studies of high
school students should be conducted. A large, cross-
sectional study of students in all grades would indicate
the possible evolution of bullying and its relationship
380 to behavioral problems and academic performance.

References

Borg, M. G. (1998). The emotional reactions of school bullies and their victims. *Educational Psychology, 18*, 433–435.

Duncan, R. (1999). Maltreatment by parents and peers: The relationship between child abuse, bully victimization, and psychological distress. *Child
Maltreatment, 19*, 45–56.

Hodges, K, & Seigal, L. J. (1985). Depression in children and adolescents. In
E. Beckham & W. Berber (Eds.), *Depression: Treatment, assessment, and
research.* Homewood, IL: Dow-Jones-Irwin.

Hoover, J. H., Oliver, R. L., & Hazler, R. J. (1992). Bullying: Perceptions of
adolescent victims in midwestern USA. *School Psychology International,
13*, 5–16.

Kaufman, P., Chen, X., Choy, S. P., Chandler, K. A., Chapman, C. D., Rand,
M. R., & Ringel, C. (1998). *Indicators of school crime and safety.* Washington, DC: U.S. Department of Education and Justice.

Kovacs, M. (1983). The Children's Depression Inventory. *Psychopharmacol
ogy Bulletin, 21*, 995–998.

Kovacs, M. (1992). *Children's Depression Inventory manual.* New York:
Multi-Health Systems.

Kumpulainen, K., Rasanen, E., & Henttonen, I. (1998). Bullying and psychiatric symptoms among elementary school-aged children. *Child Abuse and Neglect, 22*, 705–717.

Nansel, T. R., Overpeck, M., Pilla, R. S., Ruan, W. J., Simons-Morton, B., &
Scheidt, P. (2001). Bullying behaviors among U.S. youth: Prevalence and
association with psychosocial adjustment. *Journal of the American Medical
Association, 285*, 2094–2100.

Olweus, D. (1991). Bully/victim problems among school children: Basic
effects of a school-based intervention program. In D. Pepler & K. Rubin
(Eds.), *The development and treatment of childhood aggression* (pp. 411–
448). New Jersey: Erlbaum.

O'Moore, A. M., & Hillery, B. (1989). Bullying in Dublin schools. *Irish Journal of Psychology, 10*, 426–441.

Perry, D. G., Kusel, S. J., & Perry, L. C. (1988). Victims of peer aggression.
Developmental Psychology, 24, 807–814.

Rigby, K. (1996). *Bullying in school: What to do about it.* Melbourne: Acer.

Rigby, K., & Slee, P. T. (1991). Bullying among Australian school children:
Reported behavior and attitudes to victims. *Journal of Social Psychology,
11*, 615–627.

Rigby, K., & Slee, P. T. (1995). *Manual for the Peer Relations Questionnaire
(PRQ).* Underdale, South Australia: University of South Australia.

Rosenberg, M. (1965). *Society and the adolescent self-image.* Princeton, NJ:
Princeton University Press.

Salmon, G., James, A., & Smith, D. M. (1998). Bullying in schools: Self-
reported anxiety, depression and self-esteem in secondary school children.
British Medical Journal, 31, 924–925.

Slee, P. T. (1995). Peer victimization and its relationship to depression among
Australian primary school children. *Personality and Individual Differences,
18*, 57–62.

Slee, P. T., & Rigby, K. (1993). The relationship of Eysenck's personality
factors and self-esteem to bully–victim behavior in Australian schoolboys.
Journal of Personality and Individual Differences, 14, 371–373.

Spivak, H., & Prothrow-Stith, D. (2001). The need to address bullying: An
important component of violence prevention. *Journal of the American Medical Association, 286*, 16–17.

Stockdale, M., Handaduambo, S., Duys, D., Larson, K., & Sarvela, P. (2002).
Rural elementary students', parents', and teachers' perceptions of bullying.
American Journal of Health Behavior, 26, 266–277.

Tritt, C., & Duncan, R. D. (1997). The relationship between childhood bullying and young adult self-esteem and loneliness. *Journal of Humanistic Education and Development, 67*, 35–44.

About the authors: Jerry L. Young, Division of Curriculum, Instruction, Leadership, and Research, Delta State University. Dorothy L. Seals, School of Nursing, Delta State University.

Address correspondence to: Dorothy L. Seals, School of Nursing, Delta State University, Cleveland, Mississippi 38733. E-mail may be sent to: lseals@deltastate.edu

Exercise for Article 4

Factual Questions

1. Do the researchers provide any information to indicate that the Peer Relations Questionnaire is valid and reliable?

2. For which one of the three instruments used in this study is the "test–retest reliability" mentioned?

3. How long did each testing session last?

4. Was the difference between the perception of the frequency of bullying at the two grade levels statistically significant? What was the probability associated with this comparison?

5. At what location was bullying most "often" reported as happening? What is the corresponding percentage?

6. The researchers report that significantly more males than females were involved in bullying. At what probability level was this significant?

Questions for Discussion

7. Five school districts from one region were used in this study. Would you be interested in seeing other studies on this topic conducted in other regions of the U.S.? Explain. (See lines 64–67.)

8. The sample in this study is larger than the samples in most other studies in this book. In your opinion, is this an important strength of this study? Explain. (See lines 69–71.)

9. In your opinion, does the fact that only 40% of the parents returned consent forms potentially affect the validity of the results of this study? Explain. (See lines 69–71.)

10. The researchers do not discuss the validity and reliability of the RSE. In your opinion, is this an important omission? Explain. (See lines 92–96.)

11. This research article contains more statistical tables (i.e., Tables 1 through 6) than most other articles in this book. Is the presentation of results in tables a strength of this article? Explain.

12. The researchers relied on self-reports of bullying and victimization. In your opinion, might some students deliberately not report their experiences on this issue even though the questionnaire was administered anonymously? If yes, does this pose a serious threat to the validity of the results of this study? Explain.

Quality Ratings

Directions: Indicate your level of agreement with each of the following statements by circling a number from 5 for strongly agree (SA) to 1 for strongly disagree (SD). If you believe an item is not applicable to this research article, leave it blank. Be prepared to explain your ratings.

A. The introduction establishes the importance of the study.

SA   5   4   3   2   1   SD

B. The literature review establishes the context for the study.

SA   5   4   3   2   1   SD

C. The research purpose, question, or hypothesis is clearly stated.

SA   5   4   3   2   1   SD

D. The method of sampling is sound.

SA   5   4   3   2   1   SD

E. Relevant demographics (for example, age, gender, and ethnicity) are described.

SA   5   4   3   2   1   SD

F. Measurement procedures are adequate.

SA   5   4   3   2   1   SD

G. All procedures have been described in sufficient detail to permit a replication of the study.

SA   5   4   3   2   1   SD

H. The participants have been adequately protected from potential harm.

SA   5   4   3   2   1   SD

I. The results are clearly described.

SA   5   4   3   2   1   SD

J. The discussion/conclusion is appropriate.

SA   5   4   3   2   1   SD

K. Despite any flaws, the report is worthy of publication.

SA   5   4   3   2   1   SD

Article 5

The "Nuts and Dolts" of Teacher Images in Children's Picture Storybooks: A Content Analysis

SARAH JO SANDEFUR
University of Tennessee, Chattanooga

LEANN MOORE
Texas A & M University, Commerce

ABSTRACT. Children's picture storybooks are rife with contradictory representations of teachers and school. Some of those images are fairly accurate. Some of those images are quite disparate from reality. These representations become subsumed into the collective consciousness of a society and shape expectations and behaviors of both students and teachers. Teachers cannot effectuate positive change in their profession unless and until they are aware of the internal and external influences that define and shape the educational institution. This ethnographic content analysis examines 62 titles and 96 images of teachers to probe the power of stereotypes/clichés. The authors found the following: The teacher in children's picture storybooks is overwhelmingly portrayed as a white, non-Hispanic woman. The teacher in picture storybooks who is sensitive, competent, and able to manage a classroom effectively is a minority. The negative images outnumbered the positive images. The teacher in children's picture storybooks is static, unchanging, and flat. The teacher is polarized and does not inspire in his or her students the pursuit of critical inquiry.

From *Education*, *125*, 41–55. Copyright © 2004 by Project Innovation, Inc. Reprinted with permission.

A recent children's book shares the story of a teacher. Miss Malarkey, home with the flu, narrates her concern about how her elementary students will behave with and be treated by the potential substitutes available to the school. Among the substitutes represented are Mrs. Boba, a 20-something woman who is too busy painting her toenails to attend to Miss Malarkey's students. Mr. Doberman is a drill sergeant of a man who snarls at the children: "So ya think it's time for recess, HUH?" Mr. Lemonjello, drawn as a small, bald, nervous man, is taunted by the students with the class iguana and is subsequently covered in paint at art time (*Miss Malarkey Won't Be In Today*, Finchler, 1998).

In this text, which is representative of many that have been published with teachers as central characters, teachers are portrayed as insensitive, misguided, victimizing, or incompetent. We perceive these invalidating images as worthy of detailed analysis, based on a hypothesis that a propensity of images painting teachers in an unflattering light may have broader consequences on cultural perceptions of teachers and schooling. Our ethnographic content analysis herein examines 96 images of teachers as they are found in 62 picture storybooks from 1965 to present. It is our perspective that these images in part shape and define the idea of "Teacher" in the collective consciousness of a society.

Those of us in teacher education realize our students come to us with previously constructed images of the profession. What is the origin of those images? When and how are these images formed and elaborated upon? It appears that the popular culture has done much to form or modify those images. Weber and Mitchell (1995) suggest that these multiple, often ambiguous, images are "...integral to the form and substance of our self-identities as teachers" (p. 32). They suggest that "...by studying images and probing their influence, teachers could play a more conscious and effective role in shaping their own and society's perceptions of teachers and their work" (p. 32). We have supported this "probing of images" by analyzing children's picture storybooks, examining their meanings and metaphors where they intersect with teachers and schooling. It is our intention that by sharing what we have learned about the medium's responses to the profession, we will better serve teachers in playing that "conscious role" in defining their work.

We submit that children's picture storybooks are not benign. Although the illustrations of teachers are often cartoon-like and at first glance fairly innocent, when taken as a whole they have power not just in teaching children and their parents about the culture of schooling, but in shaping it, as well. This is of concern particularly when the majority of the images of teachers are negative, mixed, or neutral as we have found in our research and will report herein. Gavriel Salomon, well known for his research in symbolic representations and their impact on children's learning and thinking, has this to say about the power of media:

Media's symbolic forms of representation are clearly not neutral or indifferent packages that have no effect on the represented information. Being part and parcel of the information itself, they influence the meanings one arrives at, the mental capacities that are called for, *and the ways* one comes to view the world. Perhaps more important, the culture that creates the media and develops their symbolic forms of representation also *opens the door for those forms to act on the minds of the young* in both more and less desirable ways. [italics added] (1997, p. 13).

We see Salomon's work here as foundational to our own in this way: If those images children and parents see of "teacher" are generally negative, then they will create a "world view" of "teacher" based upon stereotype. The many negative images of teachers in children's picture storybooks may be the message to readers that teachers are, at best, kind but uninspiring, and at worst, roadblocks to be torn down in order that children may move forward successfully.

Why Study Images of Teachers from Popular Culture?

As we were preparing to teach a graduate class titled "Portrayal of Teachers in Children's Literature and in Film," we began gathering a text set of picture storybooks that focused on teachers, teaching, and the school environment. We quickly became aware of the propensity of negative images of teachers, from witch to dragon, drill sergeant to milquetoast, incompetent fool to insensitive clod. We realized early in the graduate course that many teachers had not had the opportunity to critically examine images of their own profession in the popular media. They were unaware of the negative portrayals in existing texts, particularly in children's literature. Teachers may not have considered that the negative images of the teacher "may give the public further justification for a lack of support of education" (Crume, 1989, p. 36).

Children's literature is rife with contradictory representations of teachers and school. Some of those images are fairly accurate and some of those images are quite disparate from reality (Farber, Provenso, & Holm, 1994; Joseph & Burnaford, 1994; Knowles, Cole, & Presswood, 1994; Weber & Mitchell, 1995). These representations become subsumed into the collective consciousness of a society and shape expectations and behaviors of both students and teachers. They become a part of the images that children construct when they are invited to "draw a teacher" or "play school," and indeed the images that teachers draw of themselves. Consider, for example, the three-year-old boy with no prior schooling experience, who, in playing school, puts the dolls in straight rows, selects a domineering personality for a female teacher, and assigns homework (Weber & Mitchell, 1995).

This exploration into teacher images is a critical one at multiple levels of teacher education. Preservice teachers need to analyze via media images their personal motivations and expectations of the teaching profession and enter into teaching with clear understandings of how the broad culture perceives their work. In-service teachers need to heighten their awareness of how children, parents, and community members perceive them. These perceptions may be in part media-induced and not based on the complex reality of a particular teacher. If information is indeed power, then perhaps those of us in the profession can better understand that popular images contribute to the public's frequent suspicion of our efficacy, and this heightened awareness can support us in addressing the negative images head on.

Research Perspectives

How do we as teachers, prospective teachers, and teacher educators come to so fully subscribe to the images we have both experienced and imagined? Have those images formed long before adulthood, perhaps even before the child enters school? Weber and Mitchell (1994) contend, "Even before children begin school, they have already been exposed to a myriad of images of teachers, classrooms and schools which have made strong and lasting impressions on them" (p. 2). Some of those images and attitudes form from direct experience with teachers. Barone, Meyerson, and Mallette (1995) explain, "When adults respond to the question of which person had the greatest impact on their lives, other than their immediate family, teachers are frequently mentioned" (p. 257). Those early images are not necessarily positive, often convey traditional teaching styles, and are marked with commonalities across the United States (Joseph & Burnaford, 1994; Weber & Mitchell, 1995).

In addition to the years of "on-the-job" experience with teaching and teachers that one acquires as a student sitting and observing "on the other side of the desk," a person has also acquired images and stereotypes of teaching and teachers from the person's experiences with literature and media. Lortie calls this "the apprenticeship-of-observation" (1975, p. 67). These forms of print media (literature) and visual media are part of "popular culture," which is inclusive of film, television, magazines, newspapers, music, video, books, cartoons, etc. In the past decade the literature on popular culture has grown dramatically as an increasing number of educators, social scientists, and other critical thinkers have begun to study the field (Daspit & Weaver, 1999; Giroux, 1994; Giroux, 1988; Giroux & Simon, 1989; McLaren, 1994; Trifonas, 2000; Weber & Mitchell, 1995). Weber and Mitchell (1994) explain, "So pervasive are teachers in popular culture that if you simply ask, as we have, schoolchildren and adults to name teachers they remember, not from school but from popular culture, a cast of fictionalized characters emerges that takes on larger-than-life proportions" (p. 14). These authors challenge us to examine how it is that children—even young children—would hold such strong images and that there be such similarity among the images they hold.

Studies of children's literature have previously examined issues of stereotyping (race, gender, ethnicity, age) as well as moral and ethical issues within stories (Dougherty & Engel, 1987; Hurley & Chadwick, 1998; Lamme, 1996). Recently, Barone, Meyerson, and Mallette (1995) examined the images of teachers in children's literature. They found a startling paradox: "On one hand, teachers are valued as contributing members of society; on the other hand, teachers are frequently portrayed in the media and literature as inept and not very bright" (p. 257).

Barone et al. (1995) found two types of teachers portrayed: traditional, non-child centered and nontraditional, more child-centered. The more prevalent type, the traditional teacher, was not usually liked nor respected by the students in the stories. The nontraditional teacher was seldom portrayed, but when the portrayal was presented, the teacher was shown to be valued and well liked. They contend that the reality of teaching is far too complex to fall into two such simple categories; that the act of teaching is complex. They point out that "…the authors of children's books often negate this complexity of teaching and learning, and classify teachers as those who care about students and those who are rigid or less sensitive to students' needs" (p. 260). Their study led to several disturbing conclusions: (a) the ubiquitous portrayal of traditional teachers as mean and strict make schools and schooling appear to be a dreadful experience, (b) the portrayal of teachers is frequently one in which the teacher is shown as having less intelligence than the students have, and (c) teachers are portrayed as having little or no confidence in their students and their abilities. Weber and Mitchell (1995) assert that "the stereotypes that are prevalent in the popular culture and experience of childhood play a formative role in the evolution of a teacher's identity and are part of the enculturation of teachers into their profession" (p. 27). Joseph and Burnaford (1994) address the numerous examples of caricatures or stereotypes as being somewhat different, but "…all are negative and all reduce the teacher to an object of scorn, disrespect, and sometimes fear" (p. 15).

What Research Framework Guided Our Study?

To answer our questions concerning the elements of the children's texts, we required a methodological framework from which we could examine the "character" of the texts. We found that framework in accessing research theories from anthropology and literary criticism which suggested an appropriate approach to content analysis.

Submitting that all research directly or indirectly involves participant observation, David Altheide (1987) finds an ethnographic approach applicable to content analyses, in that the writings or electronic texts are ultimately products of social interaction. Ethnographic content analysis (ECA) requires a reflexive and highly interactive relationship between researcher and data with the objective of interpreting and verifying the communication of meaning. The meaning in the text message is assumed to be reflected in the multiple elements of form, content, context, and other nuances. The movement between researcher and data throughout the process of concept development, sampling, data collection, data analysis, and interpretation is systematic but not rigid, initially structured but receptive to emerging categories and concepts.

As we proceeded through the multiple readings of the picture storybooks, we attempted to foreground three main concepts: (a) to attempt to discover "meaning" is an attempt to include the multiple elements that make up the whole: appearance, language, subject taught, gender issues, racial/ethnic diversity, and other nuances as they became apparent; (b) the multiple readings of the selected sample of children's literature to understand and to interpret the structures of the texts are not to conform the texts to our analytic notions but to inform them; and (c) in the intimacy of our relationship with the data we are acting on them and changing them, just as the data are changing us and the way we perceive past and present texts. As we encountered new texts, we attempted to consistently return to previous texts and to be receptive to new or revised interpretations that were revealed.

What Was Our Research Methodology?

We used Follett Library Resources' database to find titles addressing "teachers" and "schools." This resulted in a list of 62 titles and 96 teacher images published from 1965 to present (Appendix A at the end of this article). No chapter books or *Magic Schoolbus* series books were reviewed, as they did not qualify under the definition of "picture storybook" (Huck et al., 1997, p. 198). We specifically did not attend to publication dates or "in print/out of print" status, as many of these texts appear on school and public library shelves decades after they have gone out of print. Our approach provided us with the majority of children's picture storybooks available in the United States for purchase or available through public libraries.

To better guide our examinations about the images of teachers, ensure that we reviewed the titles consistently, and in order to record the details of the texts we reviewed, we noted details of each teacher representation in aspects of Appearance, Language, Subject, Approach, and Effectiveness. The specific details we were seeking under each category for each teacher represented in the sample literature are further described below:

Appearance: observable race, gender, approximate age, name, clothing, hairstyle, weight (thin, average, plump)

Language: representative utterances by the teacher represented in the book or as reported by the narrator of the book

285 *Subject*: the school subject(s) that the teacher was represented as teaching: reading/language arts, math, geography, history, etc.

Approach: any indicators of a teaching philosophy, including whether children were seated in rows, were working together in learning centers, were re-
290 citing memorized material, whether the teacher was shown lecturing, etc.

Effectiveness: indicators included narrator's point of view, images or language about children's learn- ing from that teacher; images or language about
295 children's emotional response to the teacher, etc.

We also attempted to note the absence of data as well as the presence of data. For example, we noted the occurrences of a teacher remaining nameless through the book, of a teacher not being represented as teaching
300 any curriculum, or of a teacher failing to inspire any critical thinking in her students.

We entered data in the foregoing categories about each teacher representation onto forms, which we then reviewed in order to group the individually represented
305 teachers into four more specific categories: positive representations, negative representations, mixed re- view, and neutral. A teacher fitting into the category of "positive teacher" was represented as being sensitive to children's emotional needs, supportive of meaningful
310 learning, compassionate, warm, approachable, able to exercise classroom management skills without resort- ing to punitive measures or yelling, and was respectful and protective of children. A teacher would be classi- fied as a "negative teacher" if he or she were repre-
315 sented as dictatorial, using harsh language, unable to manage classroom behavior, distant or removed, inat- tentive, unable to create a learning environment, allow- ing teasing or taunting among students, or unempa- thetic to students' diverse backgrounds. A teacher was
320 categorized as "mixed review" if they possessed char- acteristics that were both positive and negative: for example, if a teacher were otherwise represented as caring and effective in the classroom, but did nothing to halt the teasing of a child. The fourth category for
325 consideration was that of "neutral," in which a teacher was represented in the illustration of a text, but had neither a positive nor a negative effect on the children.

A doctoral student focusing on reading in the ele- mentary school and who is well versed in children's
330 literature served as an inter-rater for this part of the analysis. After having conferred on the characteristics of each category, she read each text independently of the researchers and categorized each teacher as "posi- tive," "negative," "mixed review," and "neutral." We
335 achieved 100% agreement in the category of "positive representations of teachers" and 93% agreement re- garding the "negative" images. We had 75% agreement on the "neutral" images and 100% agreement on the category of "mixed" images (two images). Upon fur-
340 ther discussion of our qualifications for "neutral," we

were able to agree on all 14 images as having neither a positive nor negative impact on the children as repre- sented in the text.

What Were the Findings?

Our findings regarding the preponderance of the
345 images are detailed in the following paragraphs.

The teacher in children's picture storybooks is overwhelmingly portrayed as a white, non-Hispanic woman. There were only eight representations of Afri- can American teachers, and only three of them were
350 the protagonists of the books: *The Best Teacher in the World* (Chardiet & Maccarone, 1990); *Show and Tell* (Munsch, 1991); and *Will I Have a Friend?* (Cohen, 1967). Two Asians, no Native Americans, and no other persons of color are shown in the 96 teacher images,
355 making the total number of culturally diverse images represented at only 11% of the total.

The teacher in picture storybooks who is sensitive, competent, and able to manage a classroom effectively is a minority. The teacher who met the standards we
360 described for a "positive teacher," which include an ability to construct meaningful learning environments, compassion, respect, and management skills for a group of children, exists in only 42% of the teacher images in our sample. This means only 40 images out
365 of a total 96 images were demonstrative of teacher effi- cacy. Some examples of the "positive teacher" are found in Mr. Slingerland in *Lilly's Purple Plastic Purse* (Henkes, 1996), Mr. Falker in *Thank You, Mr. Falker* (Polacco, 1998), and Arizona Hughes in *My*
370 *Great-aunt Arizona* (Houston, 1992).

The negative images outnumbered the positive im- ages. Teachers who were dictatorial, used harsh lan- guage with children, were distant or removed, or al- lowed teasing among students comprised 42% of the
375 total number of 96 teacher representations. Examples of the "negative teacher" are found in the nameless teacher in *John Patrick Norman McHennessy—The Boy Who Was Always Late* (Burningham, 1987), Miss Tyler in *Today Was a Terrible Day* (Giff, 1980), and
380 Miss Landers in *The Art Lesson* (de Paola, 1989). There were only two teachers in the sample who re- ceived a "mixed review," which was by definition a generally positive teacher with some negative strate- gies, approaches, or statements (Mrs. Chud in *Chrysan-*
385 *themum* [Henkes, 1991] and Mrs. Page in *Miss Alaineus: A Vocabulary Disaster* [Frasier, 2000]). Fourteen teacher images, or 15% of the total number, were represented as "neutral," meaning that the teacher in the text had neither a positive nor a negative impact
390 on the students. The nameless teachers in *Oliver Button Is a Sissy* (de Paola, 1979) and *Amazing Grace* (Hoff- man, 1991) are representative of "neutral" teacher im- ages.

The teacher in children's picture storybooks is
395 *static, unchanging, and flat.* An unexpected finding in this content analysis was that teachers in picture story-

books are never shown as learners themselves, never portrayed as moving from less effective to more effective. Like the nameless teacher in Miriam Cohen's *Welcome to First Grade!* series, if she is a paragon of kindness and patience, she will remain so unfailingly from the beginning of the text to its conclusion. If he is an incompetent novice, like Mr. Lemonjello in *Miss Malarkey Won't Be In Today* (Finchler, 1998), he will not be shown reflecting, learning, and reinventing himself into an informed and effective educator by book's end. Perhaps the evolution from mediocrity to effectiveness holds little in the way of entertainment value, but it could hold great value in the demonstration that teachers are complex human beings with a significant capacity for growth. The potential to paint realistic portraits of teachers is present, but we see little evidence of the medium's desire to construct such an image.

The teacher in children's picture books is polarized. Other researchers have also noted our concerns that we as teachers represented in picture storybooks are "healers or wounders...sensitive or callous, imaginative or repressive" (Joseph & Burnaford, 1994, p. 12). Only 15% of the teachers presented in our sample are neutral images, neither positively nor negatively impacting the children in the fictional classroom, and only two images out of the 96 examined qualified as a "mixed review" of mostly positive characteristics with some negative aspects of educational practice. Therefore, approximately 84% of the teachers represented in our sample are either very good or horrid. The teacher paragon in picture books "generally is a woman who never demonstrates the features of commonplace motherhood—impatience, frustration, or possibly interests in the world other than children themselves—demonstrates to children that the teacher is a wonderfully benign creature" (Joseph & Burnaford, 1994, p. 11). Ms. Darcy in *The Best Teacher in the Whole World* (Chardiet & Maccarone, 1990), and Mrs. Beejorgenhoosen in *Rachel Parker, Kindergarten Show-off* (Martin, 1992) fit neatly into the mold of "paragon." They are not represented exhibiting any less-than-perfect, but realistic, characteristics of exhaustion, short-temperedness, or lapses in good judgment.

Several texts offer "over the top" representations of bad teachers. The often-reviewed *Black Lagoon* series depicts the teachers in children's imaginations as fire-breathing dragons or huge, green gorillas. The well-known *Miss Nelson* series (Allard) has created substitute teacher Viola Swamp in the likeness of a witch, complete with incredible bulk, large features, warts, and a perpetual bad hair day. The teachers in *The Big Box* (Morrison, 1999), put a child who "just can't handle her freedom" in a big, brown box. Other books offer slightly more subtle, but still alarming, representations of negative teaching practice. Consider Miss Tyler, the heavy-lidded, unsmiling teacher in *Today Was a Terrible Day* (Giff, 1980), who humiliates Ronald

five times in the course of the story; or Mrs. Bell, who in *Double Trouble in Walla-Walla* (Clements, 1997) takes a child to the principal for her unique language style. Even worse is the nameless teacher who repeatedly (and falsely) accuses a student of lying and threatens to strike him with a stick *(John Patrick Norman McHennessey—The Boy Who Was Always Late*, Burningham, 1987). In less drastic representations, but still of concern to those of us who believe that literature informs expectations about reality, teachers are represented as failing to protect children from their peers' taunts. Teachers are shown doing nothing to stop the teasing of children in *Chrysanthemum* (Henkes, 1991), *The Brand New Kid* (Couric, 2000), *Today Was a Terrible Day* (Giff, 1980), and *Miss Alaineus: A Vocabulary Disaster* (Frasier, 2000). If children are learning about teachers and school from the children's books read to them, we propose that there is cause for concern about the unrealistic expectations children could develop from such polarized and unrealistic images.

The teacher in children's picture books does not inspire in his or her students the pursuit of critical inquiry. The overwhelming majority of texts that represent teachers in a positive light—and these number in our sample only 42% of the total number of school-related children's literature—show them as kind caregivers who dry tears (Miss Hart in *Ruby the Copycat*, Rathmann, 1991), resolve jealousy between children (Mrs. Beejorgenhoosen in *Rachel Parker, Kindergarten Show-off*, Martin, 1992), restore self-esteem (Mrs. Twinkle in *Chrysanthemum*, Henkes, 1991), teach right from wrong (Ms. Darcy in *The Best Teacher in the Whole World*, Chardiet & Maccarone, 1990). However, few teachers are represented as having a substantial impact on a child's learning. Joseph and Burnaford (1994) found that teachers are not seen "leading students toward intellectual pursuits—toward analyzing and challenging existing conditions of community and society.... The 'successful' teacher [in children's literature]...does not awaken students' intelligence. Such teachers value order; order is what they strive for, what they are paid for" (p. 16).

Our analysis confirms their findings. Examples are common in which teachers actually provide roadblocks to children's success. Tommy in *The Art Lesson* (de Paola, 1989) must wage battle to use his own crayons, use more than just one sheet of paper, and to create art based on his own vision and not the tired model of the art teacher. Miss Kincaid in *The Brand New Kid* (Couric, 2000) actually establishes the opportunity for children to tease the new boy who is an immigrant: "We have a new student...His name is a different one, Lazlo S. Gasky." Young Lazlo's mother must help him find his way into the culture of the school and community. In *David Goes to School* (Shannon, 1999), young David is met with negatively framed demands from his nameless and faceless teacher: "No, David!" "You're tardy!" "Keep your hands to yourself!" "Shhhhh!" and "You're staying after school!"

Only six books in our sample represent teachers as intellectually inspiring. Mr. Isobe in *Crow Boy* (Yashima, 1967) is represented as child-centered and appreciative of Chibi's knowledge of agriculture and botany, who values his drawings and stays after school to talk with young Chibi. He is represented as the catalyst for the crow imitations at the school talent show, which gain Chibi recognition and a newfound respect among his peers. In *Lilly's Purple Plastic Purse* (Henkes, 1996), Mr. Slingerland is such an effective teacher that he inspires Lilly to want to be a teacher (when she isn't wanting to be "a dancer or a surgeon or an ambulance driver or a diva…"). Mr. Cohen in *Creativity* (Steptoe, 1997) uses the arrival of a new immigrant in his class to teach about the history of immigration in this country and to deliver a message about tolerance and shared histories. Mrs. Hughes in *My Great-aunt Arizona* (Houston, 1992) teaches generations of children about "words and numbers and the faraway places they would visit someday." The nameless teacher in *When Will I Read?* (Cohen, 1977) helps young Jim come to the realization that he is a reader, and Mr. Falker in *Thank You, Mr. Falker* (Polacco, 1998) helps fifth-grader Trisha learn to read in three months and cries over her achievement when she reads her first book independently. Although these are excellent examples of how teachers can be represented as dedicated supporters of learning, only six texts out of the 62 in our sample construct images of teacher as an educated professional.

Discussion

Other researchers have found bias, prejudice, and stereotypical presentations of characters in children's books, and our study specifically about images of teachers does not dispute those findings (Barone, Meyerson, & Mallette, 1995; Hurley & Chadwick, 1998; Hurst, 1981). From our extensive 62-book sample of picture storybooks widely available to children, parents, and teachers, we have found a parade of teachers who discourage creativity, ignore teasing, and even threaten to hit children with sticks. We have also found teachers in children's literature who, in great devotion to the human good and the educative process, save children: from boredom, from illiteracy, and from the devastating effects of social isolation. Our deep concern is that the books in which the teacher is demonstrated as intelligent and inspiring (six in our 62-book sample) are dwarfed by the number of books in which the image of Teacher is one of daft incompetence, unreasonable anger, or rigid conformity.

We do not find images of teachers as transformative intellectuals, as educators, who "go beyond concern with forms of empowerment that promote individual achievement and traditional forms of academic success" (Giroux, 1989, p. 138). Instead, we find representations of teachers whose negatively metaphoric/derogatory surnames indicate the level of respect for the profession: Mr. Quackerbottom, Mrs. Nutty, Ima Berpur, Miss Bonkers, and Miss Malarkey.

Referring back to the graduate class we taught on representations of teachers in popular culture, we perceived a naïveté in these teachers as to the power of the media, to the power of stereotypes to shape the teaching profession, and the power that teachers have to combat the negative images. An overwhelming majority of our graduate students valued the traditional teacher who maintained order, was nurturing and caring, and whose focus was on the emotional well-being of the child. They failed to notice that it was an extremely rare image in picture storybooks that showed a teacher as an intellectually inspiring force.

Teachers cannot effectuate positive change in their profession unless and until they are aware of the internal and external influences that define and shape the educational institution. We want to encourage reflection and conversation about schooling and teaching, careful evaluation of extant images in popular culture in order to develop meaningful dialogue about the accuracy of those images, and to encourage teachers to examine their own memories of teachers and how they form current perceptions.

Implications for Future Research

Our explorations into the representations of teachers in picture storybooks have led to other and further questions regarding images that cultures create of its education professionals.

There is much information to be gleaned from a careful study of the portrayals of school administrators in picture storybooks. How are teachers and administrators represented in basal literature? How often do basal publishers select literature or write their own literature that has school as a setting and what is the ratio of positive representations to negative ones? Do children's authors in other cultures and countries create similar negative images of educators with the same frequency and ire as they do in the U.S.? How are teachers and administrators portrayed in literature for older children, as in beginning- and intermediate-chapter books, young adult novels? How have the images of teachers and administrators evolved over time in our culture? Was there a time in our history that teachers were consistently portrayed in a positive light, and was there perhaps a national event or series of events which caused the images to take on more negative characteristics?

Conclusion

Before we began this study we came across a book titled *Through the Cracks* (Sollman, Emmons, & Paolini, 1994), which we decided not to include in our literature sample as we perceive this text to be more for teachers and teacher educators than children. The text now takes on new importance in light of our findings.

625 It chronicles change on one school campus through the eyes of an elementary-age student, Stella. Early in the story Stella and some of her peers begin to physically shrink and literally fall through the cracks of the classroom floor because of boredom—boredom with both the content and delivery of the school curriculum. The teachers initially are illustrated as lecturing to day-
630 dreaming children, running off dittos, and grading papers during class time; one image even shows a teacher sharply reprimanding a child for painting her pig blue instead of the pink anticipated in the teacher's lesson plan. The children have become lost in a kind of aca-
635 demic purgatory under the floorboards. Here they remain until substantial changes are made on their campus. The children at first watch, then come up through the floor to become involved in a curriculum that has become relevant, child-centered, and integrative of the
640 arts. Teachers are then represented as supporting children's learning through highly integrated explorations of Egypt, the American Revolution, geometry, life in a pond. Their images are shown guiding the children in recreating historical and social events; supporting stu-
645 dent inquiry; exploring painting, building, drawing, dancing, and playing music as a way of knowing; cooking; becoming involved in community clean-up projects; interviewing experts; conducting science experiments; and more.
650   Linda Lamme (1996) concludes that "...children's literature is a resource with ample moral and ethical activity, that, when shared sensitively with children, can enhance their moral development and accomplish the lofty goals to which educators in a democracy as-
655 pire" (p. 412). Our point in sharing the contents of *Through the Cracks* is this: The picture storybook format has the potential to share with readers the reality of an effective and creative teacher. As opposed to an object of ridicule or scathing humor, a teacher can be
660 represented as an intellectual who inspires children to stretch, grow, and explore previously unknown worlds and communicate that new knowledge through multiple communicative systems. The picture storybook has the potential to encourage a child to anticipate the
665 valuable discoveries that are possible in the school setting; it can also demonstrate to parents how school ought to be and how teachers support children in cognitive and psychosocial ways. Children's literature can also provide positive enculturation for preservice
670 teachers and validation for inservice teachers of the possibilities inherent in their social contributions. Positive representations of teachers have the potential to empower all the partners in the academic community: the children, their parents, teachers and administrators,
675 and the community at large.

References

Altheide, D. (1987). Ethnographic content analysis. *Qualitative Sociology, 10,* 65–76.

Barone, D., Meyerson, M., & and Mallette, M. (1995). Images of teachers in children's literature. *The New Advocate, 8,* 257–270.

Crume, M. (1989). Images of teachers in films and literature. *Education Week,* October 4, 3.

Daspit, T. & Weaver, J. (1999). *Popular culture and critical pedagogy: Reading, constructing, connecting.* New York: Garland.

Dougherty, W. & Engle, R. (1987). An 80s look for sex equality in Caldecott winners and honor books. *The Reading Teacher, 40,* 394–398.

Farber, P., Provenzo, E. & Holm, G. (1994). *Schooling in the light of popular culture.* Albany. New York: State University of New York Press.

Giroux, H. (1988). *Teachers as intellectuals: Toward a critical pedagogy of learning.* Granby, MA: Bergin and Garvey.

Giroux, H. (1989). Schooling as a form of cultural politics: Toward a pedagogy of and for difference. In Henry A. Giroux & Peter L. McLaren (Eds.), *Critical pedagogy, the state and cultural struggle,* (pp. 125–151). Albany, NY: SUNY Press.

Giroux, H. (1994). *Disturbing pleasures.* New York: Routledge.

Giroux, H. & Simon, R. (1989). *Popular culture, schooling and everyday life.* New York: Bergin & Garvey.

Huck, C., Hepler, S., Hickman, J., & Kiefer, B. (1997). *Children's literature in the elementary school* (6th ed.), Boston: McGraw.

Hurley, S., & Chadwick, C. (1998). The images of females, minorities, and the aged in Caldecott Award-winning picture books, 1958–1997. *Journal of Children's Literature, 24,* 58–66.

Hurst, J. B. (1981). Images in children's picture books. *Social Education, 45,* 138–143.

Joseph, P. B. & Burnaford, G. E. (1994). *Images of schoolteachers in Twentieth-Century America.* New York: St. Martin's Press.

Knowles, J. G., & Cole, A. L. (with Presswood, C. S.) (1994). *Through preservice teachers' eyes: Exploring field experiences through narrative and inquiry.* New York: Merrill.

Lamme, L. L. (1996). *Digging deeply: Morals and ethics in children's literature. Journal for a just and caring education, 2,* 411–419.

Leitch, V. B. (1988). *American literary criticism from the 30s to the 80s.* New York: Columbia UP.

Lepman, J. (Ed.) (1971). *How children see our world.* New York: Avon.

Lortie, D. C. (1975). *Schoolteacher: A sociological study.* Chicago: University of Chicago Press.

McLaren, P. (1994). *Life in schools: An introduction to critical pedagogy in the foundations of education.* White Plains, New York: Longman.

Salomon, G. (1997). Of mind and media: How culture's symbolic forms affect learning and thinking. *Phi Delta Kappan, 78,* 375–380.

Sollman, C., Emmons, B., & Paolini, J. (1994). *Through the cracks.* Worcester, MA: Davis Publications.

Trifonas, P. (2000). *Revolutionary pedagogies: Cultural politics, instituting education. and the discourse of theory.* New York: Routledge.

Weber, S. & Mitchell, C. (1995). *That's funny, you don't look like a teacher: Interrogating images and identity in popular culture.* Washington, DC: The Falmer Press.

Appendix A
Children's book references

Allard, H. (1985). *Miss Nelson has a field day.* Illustrated by James Marshall. New York: Scholastic.

Allard, H. (1982). *Miss Nelson is back.* Illustrated by James Marshall. Boston: Houghton Mifflin.

Allard, H. (1977). *Miss Nelson is missing.* Illustrated by James Marshall. Boston: Houghton Mifflin.

Burningham, J. (1987). *John Patrick Norman McHennessy—The boy who was always late.* New York: Crown.

Chardiet, B., & Maccarone, G. (1990). *The best teacher in the world.* Illustrated by G. Brian Karas. New York: Scholastic.

Clements, A. (1997). *Double-trouble in Walla-Walla.* Illustrated by Sal Murdocca. Brookfield, CT: Millbrook.

Cohen, M. (1977). *When will I read?* Illustrated by Lillian Hoban. New York: Bantam.

Cohen, M. (1967). *Will I have a friend?* Illustrated by Lillian Hoban. New York: Aladdin.

Couric, K. (2000). *The brand new kid.* Illustrated by Majorie Priceman. New York: Doubleday.

de Paola, T. (1989). *The art lesson.* New York: Putnam.

de Paola, T. (1979). *Oliver Button is a sissy.* San Diego, CA: HBJ.

Finchler, J. (1995). *Miss Malarkey doesn't live in Room 10.* Illustrated by Kevin O'Malley. New York: Scholastic.

Finchler, J. (1998). *Miss Malarkey won't be in today.* Illustrated by Kevin O'Malley. New York: Walker.

Frasier, D. (2000). *Miss Alaineus*: A vocabulary disaster. San Diego, CA: Harcourt.

Giff, P. R. (1980). *Today was a terrible day.* New York: Puffin.

Hallinan, P. K. (1989). *My teacher's my friend.* Nashville, TN: Ideals.

Henkes, K. (1991). *Chrysanthemum.* New York: Greenwillow.

Henkes, K. (1996). *Lilly's purple plastic purse.* New York: Greenwillow.

Hoffman, M. (1991). *Amazing Grace.* Illustrated by Caroline Binch. New York: Scholastic.

Houston, G. (1992). *My great-aunt Arizona.* Illustrated by Susan Condie Lamb. New York: Harper-Collins.

Martin, A. M. (1992). *Rachel Parker, kindergarten show-off.* Illustrated by Nancy Poydar. New York: Holiday House.

McGovern, A. (1993). *Drop everything, it's D.E.A.R. time!* Illustrated by Anna DiVito. New York: Scholastic.

Morrison, T. & Morrison, S. (1999). *The big box.* Illustrated by Giselle Potter. New York: Hyperion.

Munsch, R. (1991). *Show and tell.* Illustrated by Michael Martchenko. Toronto, Canada: Annick.

Munsch, R. (1985). *Thomas' snowsuit.* Illustrated by Michael Martchenko. Toronto, Canada: Annick.

Polacco, P. (1998). *Thank you, Mr. Falker.* New York: Philomel.

Rathmann, P. (1991). *Ruby the copycat.* New York: Scholastic.

Schwartz, A. (1988). *Annabelle Swift, kindergartner.* New York: Orchard.

Seuss, Dr. (1978). *Gerald McBoing Boing.* New York: Random House.

Shannon, D. (1999). *David goes to school.* New York: Scholastic.

Yashima, T. (1965). *Crow Boy.* New York: Scholastic.

About the authors: Sarah Jo Sandefur is UC Foundation assistant professor of literacy education, University of Tennessee, Chattanooga. Leann Moore is assistant dean, College of Education and Human Services, Texas A & M University, Commerce.

Address correspondence to: Dr. Sarah Jo Sandefur, UTC Teacher Preparation Academy, Dept. 4154, 203B Hunter Hall, 615 McCallie Avenue, Chattanooga, TN 37403.

Exercise for Article 5

Factual Questions

1. In the "Research Perspectives" section of this article, the researchers cite a "startling paradox." What is the paradox?

2. Which database did the researchers use to find the titles analyzed in this study?

3. The researchers noted details in five areas, including "Subject." To what does "Subject" refer?

4. What percentage of the 96 teacher images were culturally diverse images?

5. What was an "unexpected finding" of this study?

6. How many of the books represent teachers as intellectually inspiring?

Questions for Discussion

7. In your opinion, does the first paragraph provide convincing information? Explain. (See lines 1–13.)

8. The researchers attempted to note "the absence of data." In your opinion, is this important? Explain. (See lines 296–301.)

9. The researchers examined inter-rater agreement. Is this important? Why? Why not?

10. In the researchers' discussion of "Implications for Future Research," the researchers list a number of possible research questions. If you had to pick one to conduct a study on, which one would you pick? Explain the reason for your choice. (See lines 594–616.)

11. Overall, does this study convince you that images of teachers in children's picture storybooks influence the public's perceptions of the teaching profession? Explain.

12. Overall, what is your impression of content analysis as a method for obtaining important information on the education profession? How has this study influenced your answer?

Quality Ratings

Directions: Indicate your level of agreement with each of the following statements by circling a number from 5 for strongly agree (SA) to 1 for strongly disagree (SD). If you believe an item is not applicable to this research article, leave it blank. Be prepared to explain your ratings.

A.   The introduction establishes the importance of the study.

   SA   5   4   3   2   1   SD

B.   The literature review establishes the context for the study.

   SA   5   4   3   2   1   SD

C.   The research purpose, question, or hypothesis is clearly stated.

   SA   5   4   3   2   1   SD

D.   The method of sampling is sound.

   SA   5   4   3   2   1   SD

E.   Relevant demographics (for example, age, gender, and ethnicity) are described.

   SA   5   4   3   2   1   SD

F.   Measurement procedures are adequate.

   SA   5   4   3   2   1   SD

G.   All procedures have been described in sufficient detail to permit a replication of the study.

   SA   5   4   3   2   1   SD

H.   The participants have been adequately protected from potential harm.

   SA   5   4   3   2   1   SD

I.   The results are clearly described.

   SA   5   4   3   2   1   SD

J.   The discussion/conclusion is appropriate.

   SA   5   4   3   2   1   SD

K.   Despite any flaws, the report is worthy of publication.

   SA   5   4   3   2   1   SD

Article 6

A Comparison of How Textbooks Teach Mathematical Problem Solving in Japan and the United States

RICHARD E. MAYER
University of California, Santa Barbara

VALERIE SIMS
University of California, Santa Barbara

HIDETSUGU TAJIKA
Aichi University of Education, Japan

ABSTRACT. This brief report compared the lesson on addition and subtraction of signed whole numbers in three seventh-grade Japanese mathematics textbooks with the corresponding lesson in four U.S. mathematics textbooks. The results indicated that Japanese books contained many more worked-out examples and relevant illustrations than did the U.S. books, whereas the U.S. books contained roughly as many exercises and many more irrelevant illustrations than did the Japanese books. The Japanese books devoted 81% of their space to explaining the solution procedure for worked-out examples compared to 36% in U.S. books; in contrast, the U.S. books devoted more space to unsolved exercises (45%) and interest-grabbing illustrations that are irrelevant to the lesson (19%) than did the Japanese books (19% and 0%, respectively). Finally, one of the U.S. books and all three Japanese books used meaningful instructional methods emphasizing (a) multiple representations of how to solve worked-out examples using words, symbols, and pictures and (b) inductive organization of material beginning with familiar situations and ending with formal statements of the solution rule. The results are consistent with classroom observations showing that Japanese mathematics instruction tends to emphasize the process of problem solving more effectively than does U.S. mathematics instruction (Stevenson & Stigler, 1992).

From *American Educational Research Journal*, 32, 443–460. Copyright © 1995 by the American Educational Research Association. Reprinted with permission.

National and international assessments of mathematics achievement have consistently revealed that students in the United States perform more poorly than their cohorts in other industrialized nations, particularly students from Asian nations such as Japan (Robitaille & Garden, 1989; Stevenson, Lee, Chen, Stigler, Hsu, & Kitamura, 1990; Stevenson & Stigler, 1992; Stigler, Lee, & Stevenson, 1990). The relatively poor performance of U.S. students occurs not only on tests of basic computational skills but also on tests of mathematical problem solving.

Converging evidence suggests that an explanation for cross-national differences can be found in the *exposure hypothesis*: cross-national differences in mathematics achievement are related to differences in the quantity and quality of mathematics instruction (Mayer, Tajika, & Stanley, 1991; McKnight et al., 1987; Stevenson & Stigler, 1992). Stevenson, Stigler, Lee, Kitamura, Kimura, and Kato (1986) point out that Japanese students spend approximately twice as many hours per week on mathematics as U.S. students spend. Perhaps even more important, Stevenson and Stigler (1992) provide evidence that Japanese schools tend to emphasize the process of problem solving whereas U.S. schools tend to emphasize the mastery of facts and procedures for computing the correct answer. For example, compared to U.S. elementary school mathematics teachers, Japanese teachers provide more verbal explanations, engage students in more reflective discussion, are more likely to use concrete manipulatives to represent abstract concepts, are more likely to include a real-world problem in a lesson, present more coherent lessons, ask questions that require longer answers, provide more critical feedback, and focus on fewer problems in more depth (Stevenson & Stigler, 1992).

The present study compared how mathematical problem solving is taught in mathematics textbooks used in Japan and in the United States. In particular, we examined the hypothesis that a typical Japanese textbook is more oriented toward teaching conceptual understanding and problem-solving skills whereas typical U.S. textbooks are more oriented toward teaching isolated facts and rote computation. This study extends earlier research comparing how mathematical problem solving is taught in Japanese and U.S. classrooms (Stevenson & Stigler, 1992) and contributes to an emerging research base on cross-national comparisons of textbooks (Chambliss & Calfee, 1989; Okamoto, 1989; Stevenson & Bartsch, 1991).

Cross-national comparisons of mathematics textbooks are important in light of evidence that U.S. textbooks constitute a sort of de facto national curriculum. For example, Armbruster and Ostertag (1993, p. 69) assert that "the powerful role of textbooks in the American curriculum is by now well established."

Garner (1992, p. 53) notes that "textbooks serve as critical vehicles for knowledge acquisition in school" and can "replace teacher talk as the primary source of information." Glynn, Andre, and Britton (1986, p. 245) propose that across many disciplines students experience "a heavy reliance on textual materials for a great deal of their knowledge." It follows that examining the content and teaching methods used in American and Japanese mathematics textbooks provides a partial account of how mathematics is taught in the two nations.

Method

Materials

The data source consisted of lessons on addition and subtraction of signed whole numbers taken from three Japanese textbooks (Fukumori et al., 1992, pp. 19–25; Kodaira, 1992, pp. 27–32; Fujita & Maehara, 1992, pp. 17–25) and four U.S. textbooks (Bolster, Crown, Hamada et al., 1988, pp. 354–359; Fennell, Reys, Reys, & Webb, 1988, pp. 428–431; Rucker, Dilley, Lowry, & Ockenga, 1988, pp. 332–335; Willoughby, Bereiter, Hilton, & Rubinstein, 1991, pp. 260–265) commonly used to teach seventh-grade mathematics. The number of pages for the lesson in the Japanese books ranged from 7 to 9 based on an average page size of 5.5×7.5 inches, and from 4 to 6 in the U.S. books based on a page size averaging 7×9.5 inches. The Japanese books were approved by the Japanese Ministry of Education and were highly similar to one another because they conformed to detailed governmental specifications; the U.S. books were from publishers' series that were approved for adoption by the California State Department of Education. The books were selected as typical based on consultations with teachers and school administrators in Japan and the United States. The lesson in all books described how to add and subtract positive and negative whole numbers, such as $3 + 8 = \_, -3 + 8 = \_, 3 + -8 = \_, -3 + -8 = \_, 3 - 8 = \_, -3 - 8 = \_, 3 - -8 = \_,$ and $-3 - -8 = \_.$ In each of the Japanese books, the material was contained in the lesson titled, "Addition and Subtraction," taken from the chapter titled, "Positive and Negative Numbers" (Fujita & Maehara, 1992; Fukumori et al., 1992; Kodaira, 1992). In the U.S. books, the material was contained in lessons titled, "Adding and Subtracting Signed Numbers" (Willoughby, Bereiter, Hilton, & Rubinstein, 1991); "Adding Integers" and "Subtracting Integers" (Fennell, Reys, Reys, & Webb, 1988; Rucker, Dilley, Lowry, & Ockenga, 1988); or "Adding Integers: Same Sign," "Adding Integers: Different Signs," and "Subtracting Integers" (Bolster, Crown, Hamada et al., 1988). We also included the exercises involving addition and subtraction of signed integers in the end-of-the-chapter test. We did not include sections on addition and subtraction of signed fractions, signed decimals, or three or more signed numbers because this material was not covered in all books. In short, the data source consisted of seven lessons on addition and sub-traction of signed integers, ranging from 4 to 9 pages in length.

Procedure

To conduct a quantitative analysis of the instructional methods used for teaching students how to solve signed arithmetic problems, two independent raters broke each lesson into four parts—exercises, irrelevant illustrations, relevant illustrations, and explanation—and resolved conflicts by consensus. First, the raters circled the exercise portions of each lesson using a colored marker. We defined an exercise as a symbol-based problem involving addition or subtraction of two signed integers for which no answer or explanation was provided, such as $-8 + 3 = \_$. In the Japanese books, the exercises were labeled as "Problem" or "Exercise"; contained the instructions, "Calculate the following"; and were numbered consecutively. In the U.S. books, the exercises were presented under labels such as "Exercise" or "Practice"; contained instructions such as, "Give each sum," "Give each difference," "Add," or "Subtract"; and were numbered consecutively. The raters counted the number of exercise problems involving addition or subtraction of two signed numbers in each lesson, including exercise problems given at the end of the chapter. We did not include exercises involving fractions, decimals, or more than two numbers. There were no unresolved disagreements between the raters.

Second, the raters circled the irrelevant illustrations in each lesson using a colored marker and circled the relevant illustrations using a different-colored marker. We defined an illustration as any line drawing, chart, picture, or photograph. Furthermore, we defined a relevant illustration as any line drawing or chart that represented the steps in the solution of a signed arithmetic problem and an irrelevant illustration as a picture or photograph that did not correspond to the steps in the solution of a signed arithmetic problem. To ensure consistency, the raters maintained a list of illustrations that were classified as relevant and a list of illustrations that were classified as irrelevant. Relevant illustrations included line drawings showing changes in the water level of a water storage tank, changes in position on a number line, or changes in mixtures of negative and positive ions in a beaker; irrelevant illustrations included a picture of a tape measure, a drawing of a ski village, a drawing of a mad scientist, a drawing of a submarine, a mural from an ancient Egyptian pyramid, a photo of a woman swinging a golf club, and a photo of hockey players skating on ice. A series of line drawings about the same problem presented together on a page was counted as one illustration. The raters counted the number of relevant and irrelevant illustrations in each lesson. There were no unresolved disagreements.

Third, the remaining portions of the lesson constituted the explanation and were circled with a colored marker designating explanation. Each rater counted the number of worked-out examples in the explanation portion of the lesson. A worked-out example was defined as a signed arithmetic problem in which the answer and verbal description of how it was generated were given. In most cases, the worked-out examples were presented under the heading, "Example." Each rater also counted the number of words in the explanation section of the lesson; words in headings and in relevant illustrations were included. A word was defined as any letter or letter group found in a dictionary. We did not include mathematical symbols such as numerals, +, −, or =. There were no unresolved disagreements between the raters.

One of the raters used a ruler to measure the space (in square inches) occupied by exercises, irrelevant illustrations, relevant illustrations, and explanation for each lesson. In measuring the areas, margin space was not included. Given the objective nature of these measurements, a second rater was not needed.

In sum, the quantitative data for each lesson included the number of exercises, the number of irrelevant illustrations, the number of relevant illustrations, the number of worked-out examples, the number of words, the area occupied by exercises, the area occupied by irrelevant illustrations, the area occupied by relevant illustrations, and the area occupied by explanation.

Results and Discussion

The instructional lesson is much longer in Japan than in the U.S., but the exercise set is about the same length in both nations. Research on instructional methods has emphasized the role of meaningful explanation rather than unguided hands-on symbol manipulating activities in promoting problem-solving competence (Mayer, 1987). The instructional part of the lesson—that is, the part of the lesson that did not contain to-be-solved exercises—was more than four times longer in the Japanese books than in the U.S. books: The mean number of words in the U.S. books was 208 compared to 925 in the Japanese books. However, the exercise part of the lesson, which emphasizes unguided symbol manipulation, was about the same in the two nations: The Japanese books contained an average of 63 exercises on addition and subtraction of signed numbers, whereas the U.S. books averaged 51 exercises. In both nations, additional worksheets and workbooks are available to supplement the textbook exercises. Overall, these data show a difference in the relative emphasis of Japanese and U.S. books: There were 14.7 words of instruction per exercise in the Japanese books compared to an average of 3.9 words of instruction per exercise in the U.S. books.

Worked-out examples and concrete analogies are more common in Japan than in the U.S. Research on multiple representations, case-based reasoning, and analogical reasoning has demonstrated the important role of worked-out examples and concrete analogies in helping students to improve their problem-solving skills (Mayer, 1987). Worked-out examples serve to model appropriate problem-solving processes, and concrete analogies provide a means for connecting procedures to familiar experience. On average, worked-out examples were three times more common in the Japanese textbooks than in the U.S. textbooks: U.S. books averaged approximately 4 worked-out examples compared to 15 in the Japanese lessons.

The Japanese books employed the same concrete analogy throughout the lesson on addition and subtraction of signed numbers. For example, one book presented a tank for storing water in which a rise in the water level is expressed by a positive number and a fall in the water level is expressed by a negative number. According to this analogy, addition of signed numbers occurs when the water level is changed twice—for example, a first change in the water level plus a second change in the water level produces a total change in the water level; subtraction of signed numbers occurs when one knows the total change and the second change but wants to find the first change. The analogy was represented in multiframe illustrations 9 times, indicating changes that corresponded to arithmetic operations. Another book used the analogy of walking east or west along a path, which was portrayed as arrows along a number line. The book contained 7 multiframe illustrations showing the process of taking two trips along the number line. For example, the problem $(+8) + (−3) =$ ___ was represented as two parts of a trip: an arrow from 0 to 8 (labeled as +8) and an arrow from 8 to 5 (labeled as −3). Below this figure, the solution was represented as an arrow from 0 to 5 (labeled as $+8 − 3$). A third book represented addition and subtraction of signed numbers as movement along a number line, including 6 sets of illustrations of number lines.

In contrast, the U.S. books used concrete analogies such as changes in temperature on a thermometer, keeping score in golf or hockey, matter and antimatter annihilation, and beakers containing positive and negative ions. However, in three out of four cases, the analogy used to represent addition was different from the analogy used to represent subtraction, and none of the analogies was represented in a multiframe illustration depicting changes that correspond to addition or subtraction. In the U.S. books, analogies used to describe addition of signed numbers were insufficient to describe subtraction of signed numbers. For example, in the matter/antimatter analogy, combining 5 bricks and 2 antibricks yielded 3 bricks (analogous to $5 + −2 = 3$). However, this analogy breaks down for situations in which a negative number is subtracted from another number (such as $5 − −2 = 7$), so the textbook used a different analogy, temperatures on a thermometer, to represent subtraction of signed numbers.

Relevant illustrations were more common in Japanese books than in U.S. books, but irrelevant illustra-

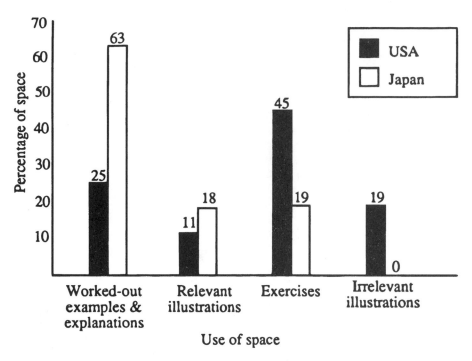

Figure 1. Proportion of page space devoted to explanations, relevant illustrations, exercises, and irrelevant illustrations in Japan and in the United States.

tions were more common in U.S. books than in Japanese books. Research on illustrations reveals that some kinds of illustrations have more instructional value than
285   others (Levin & Mayer, 1993; Mayer, 1993). Illustrations that simply decorate the page are instructionally irrelevant, whereas illustrations that explain the process of signed arithmetic are instructionally relevant. Other than the first page of the chapter, the Japanese books
290   contained more relevant and fewer irrelevant illustrations than U.S. books: The Japanese books contained an average of 0 irrelevant and 11 relevant illustrations compared to an average of 2 irrelevant and 4 relevant illustrations in the U.S. books. The irrelevant illustra-
295   tions in U.S. textbooks may be intended to make the material more interesting, but recent research on seductive details reveals that the addition of highly interesting and vivid material to a text often diminishes students' recall of the important information (Garner,
300   Brown, Sanders, & Menke, 1992; Wade, 1992).

In summary, the foregoing analyses indicate that the Japanese books contain far more worked-out examples and relevant illustrations than the U.S. books, whereas U.S. books contain roughly as many exercises
305   and more irrelevant illustrations than Japanese books. Another way to examine these kinds of differences is to compare the allocation of page space in Japanese and U.S. lessons, which is done in the next section.

Japanese books excel in devoting page space to ex-
310   *planation of problem-solving procedures, whereas U.S. books excel in devoting page space to unsolved exercises and interest-grabbing illustrations.* The allocation

of space in Japanese and U.S. textbooks represents the values of the cultures that produced them. An emphasis
315   on understanding the process of problem solving is reflected in the use of worked-out examples, which model the problem-solving process in words, symbols, and illustrations. Research on the teaching of problem-solving processes indicates that successful pro-
320   grams rely on the use of cognitive modeling techniques—such as detailed descriptions of worked-out examples (Mayer, 1992). On average, 81% of the page space in Japanese books was devoted to explanation of problem-solving procedures (63% emphasizing
325   worked-out examples and 18% for corresponding illustrations) compared to 36% in U.S. books (25% emphasizing worked-out examples and 11% for corresponding illustrations).

In contrast, an emphasis on the product of problem
330   solving is reflected in the presentation of lists of to-be-solved exercise problems. On average, 45% of the page space in U.S. books was devoted to presenting lists of exercise problems compared to 19% in Japanese books. Perhaps to compensate for what might be
335   considered the boring task of having to solve exercise problems without guidance, authors of U.S. books added interest-grabbing illustrations that were irrelevant to the problem-solving procedures. On average, U.S. books devoted 19% of their space to irrelevant
340   illustrations compared to 0% in Japanese books. Figure 1 summarizes these differences in the use of space in Japanese and U.S. textbooks.

2a. Excerpt from Japanese textbook that includes verbal, visual, and symbolic representations for each of three problem-solving steps.

We have a tank for storing water. If we put in or take out water, the water level in the tank goes up or down. If we express a change which raises the water level with a positive number, then we can express a change which lowers the water level with a negative number. If the water level rises 5 cm, the change in the water level is +5 cm. If the water level decreases 3 cm, the change in the water level is -3 cm...When the water level changes twice in succession we can express the change as:...

If the first change is:	-3 cm
and the second change is:	+8 cm
then the total change is:	(-3) + (+8)
and this is +5 cm.	(-3) + (+8) = +5

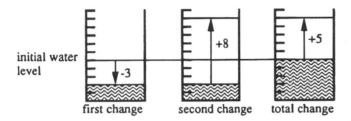

2b. Excerpt from Japanese textbook that includes verbal, visual, and symbolic representations for each of three problem-solving steps.

When you walk from A...you first walk 3 m to the east and then 5 m to the west. The two movements...will be expressed using positive and negative numbers. The first movement is +3 m, the second movement is -5 m, the result is -2 m... The calculation is expressed as follows: (+3) + (-5) = -2.

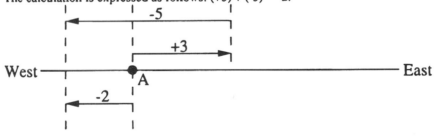

Figure 2. Representations used in Japanese textbooks to teach addition of numbers with different signs.

Note. 2a is adapted from Kodaira (1992); 2b is adapted from Fujita and Maehara (1992).

Meaningful instructional methods emphasizing the coordination of multiple representations were more common in Japanese books than in U.S. books. Research in mathematics education emphasizes the importance of helping students build connections among multiple representations of a problem and of helping students induce solution rules based on experience with familiar examples (Grouws, 1992; Hiebert, 1986). To analyze these aspects of meaningful instruction and to supplement the foregoing quantitative analyses, we analyzed the ways that the textbooks explained one type of signed arithmetic—namely, adding two numbers with different signs, such as $(+3) + (-8) = -5$ or $(-4) + (+3) = -1$. To assess the use of multiple representations in each lesson, we examined whether the lesson presented complete symbolic, verbal, and pictorial representations of a problem-solving procedure for addition of integers with different signs. In particular, we evaluated whether or not the lesson included symbolic, verbal, and visual representations for the first

3a. Excerpt from U.S. textbook that includes visual and symbolic representations for some of three problem-solving steps.

Example. -5 + +1 = ?

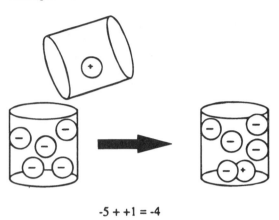

-5 + +1 = -4

3b. Excerpt from U.S. textbook that includes verbal, visual, and symbolic representations for each of three problem-solving steps.

Find 4 + (-7)

Starting at zero, move 4 units to the right.
From there, move 7 units to the left.

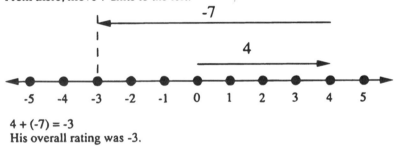

4 + (-7) = -3
His overall rating was -3.

Figure 3. Representations used in U.S. textbooks to teach addition of numbers with different signs.

Note. 3a is adapted from Rucker, Dilley, Lowry, and Ockenaga (1988); 3b is adapted from Bolster et al. (1988).

step (i.e., determining the value of the first number), the second step (i.e., adding the value of the second number), and the third step (i.e., using the resulting number as the final answer). To assess the use of an inductive method in each lesson, we determined whether or not the lesson progressed from familiar examples to a formal statement of the rule for addition of integers with different signs.

All three of the Japanese books systematically built connections among symbolic, verbal, and pictorial representations for each of three steps in solving the prob-

lem. In explaining how to add two numbers with different signs, one Japanese book (Kodaira, 1992) began by describing a water tank analogy in words. The book (p. 27) stated that "when the water level changes twice in succession, we can express the changes, starting with the first change as: (the first change) + (the second change)." In relating this analogy to addition of two numbers with different signs, the book (p. 28) described the situation in words: "If the first change is −3 cm and the second change is +8 cm, then the total change is (−3) + (+8), and this is +5

385 cm." Then the book presented the problem in symbolic form as "$(-3) + (+8) = +5$." Next to this was a pictorial representation of the problem consisting of three labeled frames, as shown in Figure 2a. Each step in the problem was represented, starting with negative 3, add-
390 ing positive 8, and ending with positive 5. At the end of a series of examples, the book presented a rule for addition of numbers with different signs (p. 30):

> In seeking the sum of two numbers with different signs, consider only their absolute values and subtract the
> 395 smaller absolute value from the larger. Then assign to the sum the sign of the number with the larger absolute value. If the absolute values are equal, then the sum is 0.

Thus, the lesson was organized inductively, beginning with a familiar analogy and ending with a formal
400 statement of the solution rule.

A second Japanese book (Fujita & Maehara, 1992) began its discussion of addition of different-signed integers by describing a walk along a road (p. 17):

> Imagine that you are walking along a road which runs
> 405 east and west in a straight line…. You first walk 3 meters to the east and then walk 5 meters to the west. Moving to the east will be used as the positive numbers and moving to the west will be used as the negative numbers.

Then, the book describes the computation in words and
410 symbols (p. 17): "Two movements and their results will be expressed as follows, when positive and negative numbers are used…. The first movement is +3 m, the second movement is −5 m, the result is −2 m." On the right, the book presented a number line with an
415 arrow from 0 to 3 corresponding to the first movement, from 3 to −2 corresponding to the second movement, and from 0 to −2 corresponding to the answer. This illustration is summarized in Figure 2b. Next, the example was expressed in symbolic form (p. 18):

> 420 When moving twice in succession, the results…are expressed as follows by adding two numbers: (the first movement) + (the second movement). When the results are expressed like this, the calculation for the example is as follows: (+3) + (−5). The answer is −2, and so the
> 425 computation is expressed as follows: (+3) + (−5) = −2.

Finally, after presenting several examples in verbal, visual, and symbolic forms, the section ended with a statement of the general principle (p. 20): "The sum of numbers with different signs: You can subtract the
430 smaller absolute value from the larger one and assign to the sum the sign of the number with the larger absolute value. When the absolute values are equal, the sum is 0." As in the other Japanese book, this lesson was organized inductively—beginning with a familiar
435 situation of walking east and west along a road and ending with a formal statement of the procedure for addition of numbers with different signs.

The third book (Fukumori et al., 1992, pp. 18–19) also used verbal, visual, and symbolic representations
440 to explain what to do "when you add a positive and negative number." The book connected symbols,

words, and pictures as follows: "$(-7) + 5$ means to get a number that is 5 larger than −7. A number 5 larger than −7 is the number −2, which is 2 smaller than 0, as
445 you can see on the number line below." Directly below was an illustration of a number line with an arrow from −7 to −2, and below that was the symbolic form of the problem, "$(-7) + 5 = -2$." After presenting several other examples of the same form in the same way, the
450 section ended with a statement of general principle: "Addition of a negative and positive number means subtraction of the negative number from the positive number… $3 + (-5) = 3 - 5 = -2$." Again, as in the other Japanese books, instruction moved from the familiar
455 statement of a problem in words and pictures to a formal statement of the solution procedure as a rule.

In contrast, only one of the four U.S. books contained symbolic, verbal, and pictorial representations of example problems involving addition of integers with
460 different signs. For example, one U.S. textbook (Willoughby, Bereiter, Hilton, & Rubinstein, 1991) began by presenting word problems about familiar analogies such as a thermometer: "The temperature is −4C. If it goes up 3C, what will it be?" For each word problem,
465 the book stated the problem in symbolic form but did not give an answer, such as "$-4 + 3 = ?$" Thus, the book presented only the first two steps in the problem—namely, starting at negative 4 and adding positive 3; it failed to describe the third step—namely, end-
470 ing at negative 1. The book also failed to connect the verbal and symbolic representation of the problem to a pictorial representation. In the next section of the chapter, titled "Adding and Subtracting Signed Numbers," the book (p. 263) listed rules such as: "To add 2 signed
475 numbers, if the signs are different, subtract the smaller absolute value from the larger and use the sign of the one with the larger absolute value." Then, the book provided exercises such as "$(-8) + (+7) = n$" along with instructions to use the above rule. This is a deductive
480 approach because it begins with stating a rule and then tells the learner to apply the rule to exercise problems.

In another U.S. textbook (Rucker, Dilley, Lowry, & Ockenga, 1988), the section on "Integers" began by representing positive and negative integers as beakers
485 containing positive and negative charges. Then, in the section on "Adding Integers," the book presented several examples. For each, there was a picture of one beaker containing positive or negative charges being poured into another beaker containing positive or nega-
490 tive charges and the resulting beaker; below the picture was a symbolic representation of the problem. For example, Figure 3a shows a beaker containing one positive charge being poured into a beaker containing 5 negative charges, and the result is a beaker containing
495 4 free negative charges. Directly under this picture was the equation, "$-5 + +1 = -4$." This lesson used symbols and pictures to present all three steps in the procedure—starting with negative 5, adding positive 1, and ending with negative 4—but failed to connect them to

words. There was no verbal description other than the general statement, "To understand how to add integers, you can think about putting charges together." The book then moved directly to exercises without ever presenting the solution rule.

Another book (Fennell, Reys, Reys, & Webb, 1988) used a creative analogy about annihilation of matter and antimatter to explain addition of signed integers (p. 428):

> In a galaxy totally different from our own, a scientist named Dr. Zarkov discovered antimatter. When he puts antimatter together with antimatter nothing happens. For example, if he puts 4 cups of antiwater together with 3 cups of antiwater, he gets 7 cups of antimatter. Strange as it may seem, however, when he puts equal amounts of matter and antimatter together, they both disappear. For example, if he puts 2 telephones and 2 antitelephones together, he is left with nothing. In his latest experiment, Dr. Zarkov added 2 antibricks to a box containing 5 bricks. There was a blinding flash of light. When the smoke cleared, he was left with 3 bricks.

There was no illustration for the bricks example, although there was an illustration depicting 2 light and 2 dark telephones being placed together, and then disappearing in a "poof." Later in the section, the bricks example was represented symbolically as, "2 antibricks + 5 bricks = 3 bricks," and as, "−2 + 5 = 3." In this case, the book described the three steps in the addition of signed integers within the context of an interesting situation and related them to a symbolic representation but failed to relate them to a pictorial representation. In addition, the book failed to state the solution rule in a formal way, but it asked the students to do so as an exercise (p. 429): "State rules for adding a positive integer and a negative integer."

Finally, the fourth U.S. book (Bolster et al., 1988) used a hockey analogy to explain addition of signed integers in a section titled "Adding Integers: Different Signs." The section (p. 356) started by describing a hockey-scoring procedure: "Angelo's hockey coach uses a plus/minus system to rate the performance of the players. If a player is on the ice when his team scores, he gets 1. If he is on the ice when the other team scores, he gets −1. For his first 10 games, Angelo's plus rating was 4, and his minus rating was −7. What was his overall rating?" Next the book stated the problem symbolically: "Find 4 + (−7)." Finally, the book used a captioned number line illustration as shown in Figure 3b to represent the three steps in solving the problem. The caption described the steps: "Starting at zero, move 4 units to the right. From there, move 7 units to the left. His overall rating was −3." Although very short, this lesson makes connections among symbolic, verbal, and visual representations of all three steps in the example problem. Unlike the Japanese book, which included many complete examples, however, this book presented only one complete example. Finally, the lesson ended with a statement of the solution rule (p. 357): "To add two integers with different signs, consider the distance each integer is from zero. Subtract the shorter distance from the longer distance. In your answer, use the sign of the number farther from zero." Like the Japanese book, this textbook used an inductive approach, moving from familiar examples to a formal statement of the rule.

In summary, the books differed in their use of multiple representations to explain how to add a negative and positive integer and in their inclusion of a statement of the solution rule. The Japanese books presented complete explanations of at least two examples of addition of a positive and negative integer; in these examples, all three steps in the procedure were presented symbolically, verbally, and pictorially, and the solution rule was clearly stated at the end of the explanation. In contrast, one U.S. textbook presented a complete explanation of one example and a statement of the rule, one presented an explanation that lacked a pictorial representation and a statement of the rule, one presented an explanation that lacked a verbal representation and a statement of the rule, and one presented an explanation that lacked a pictorial representation and lacked portions of the symbolic and verbal representations. Overall, all of the Japanese books presented multiple representations of example problems and presented material in inductive order, whereas most of the U.S. books did not employ these meaningful instructional methods.

The lesson was better integrated into the Japanese books than into the U.S. books, and the U.S. books were much longer than the Japanese books. Research on text structure has highlighted the importance of organizing topics in a simple and coherent structure (Britton, Woodward, & Binkley, 1993; Jonassen, Beissner, & Yacci, 1993). The Japanese books, averaging less than 200 pages in length, contained an average of 7 chapters with each one divided into two or three coherent sections, whereas the U.S. textbooks, averaging 475 pages in length, contained an average of 12 chapters with each including approximately a dozen loosely related topics. For example, each of the Japanese books contained an entire chapter, titled "Positive and Negative Numbers," devoted exclusively to signed numbers. The chapter consisted of three related sections involving an introduction to signed numbers, addition/subtraction of signed numbers, and multiplication/division of signed numbers. In contrast, lessons on addition and subtraction of signed numbers were presented as short fragments within more diverse chapters throughout most of the U.S. books. In three U.S. books, material on addition and subtraction of signed numbers was in the same chapter as solving equations and coordinate graphing of equations; in another, it was taught in a chapter that included units of measure, mixed numbers, and improper fractions. Overall, compared to the U.S. textbooks, the Japanese textbooks were more

615 compact, presented a clearer structure, and covered fewer topics in more depth.

Conclusion

If textbooks serve as a sort of national curriculum, then international comparisons of textbook lessons can provide a partial picture of not only what is taught but
620 also how it is taught across nations. Two competing methods for teaching students how to solve mathematics problems are drill and practice—in which page space is devoted to unexplained exercises involving symbol manipulation—and cognitive modeling—in
625 which page space is devoted to presenting and connecting multiple representations of step-by-step problem-solving processes through worked-out examples. The drill-and-practice approach follows from a view of learning as knowledge acquisition that emphasizes the
630 *product of problem solving*—that is, getting the right answer; in contrast, the cognitive modeling approach follows from a view of learning as knowledge construction, which emphasizes *the process of problem solving*—that is, how to get the right answer (Mayer,
635 1989).

In this study, we are concerned with how much space in Japanese and U.S. mathematics textbooks is devoted to unexplained exercises consisting of symbol manipulation and how much space is devoted to build-
640 ing and connecting multiple representations for problem solving through worked-out example problems. Building on the exposure hypothesis, which originally focused on the allocation of instructional time (Mayer, Tajika, & Stanley, 1991; Stevenson & Stigler, 1992),
645 the amount of space in mathematics textbooks that is devoted to meaningful explanation of problem-solving strategies may be an important determinant of students' mathematical problem-solving competence.

If textbook page space is viewed as a limited re-
650 source, then the allocation of that space reflects the priorities of the cultures that produced them. In Japan, the major use of page space is to explain mathematical procedures and concepts in words, symbols, and graphics, with an emphasis on worked-out examples and
655 concrete analogies. In U.S. books, where the use of page space for explanation is minimized relative to Japanese books, the major use of page space is to present unexplained exercises in symbolic form for the students to solve on their own. These lessons are sup-
660 plemented with attention-grabbing graphics that, unlike those in the Japanese books, are interesting but irrelevant. Japanese textbooks devote over 80% of their space, and U.S. books devote less than 40% of their space to instruction in the process of problem solving
665 (i.e., words, pictures, and symbols that explain how to add and subtract signed numbers), whereas U.S. books devote over 60% of their space, and Japanese books devote less than 20% of their space to hands-on exercises without guidance and interesting-but-irrelevant
670 illustrations. A further analysis of lessons provides converging evidence: All three of the Japanese books and only one of the four U.S. books presented worked-out examples that explained how to solve problems in words, symbols, and pictures.

675 In Japan, the textbooks provide worked-out examples that model successful problem-solving strategies for students; in the U.S., textbooks are more likely to provide lots of exercises for students to solve on their own without much guidance. In Japan, the textbooks
680 provide concrete analogies that help the student relate the concepts of addition and subtraction of signed numbers to a familiar situation; in the U.S., textbooks may give rules without much explanation. In Japan, the textbooks devote space to explaining mathematical
685 ideas in words, whereas U.S. textbooks devote relatively more space to manipulating symbols.

The picture that emerges from our study of mathematics textbooks is that cognitive modeling of problem-solving processes is emphasized more in Japan
690 than in the United States, whereas drill and practice on the product of problem solving is emphasized more in the United States than in Japan. Japanese textbooks seem to assume the learner is a cognitively active problem solver who seeks to understand the step-by-step
695 process for solving a class of problems. In contrast, U.S. textbooks seem to assume the learner is a behaviorally active knowledge acquisition machine who learns best from hands-on activity in solving problems with minimal guidance and who needs to be stimulated
700 by interesting decorative illustrations.

Our study is limited and should be interpreted as part of a converging set of research results. First, our data source involves only three Japanese and four U.S. books. Although we chose books that are widely used,
705 we did not exhaustively review other books and supplemental materials, such as workbooks. Second, we examined only one lesson—amounting to a few pages in each of the books in our sample. Although the material is a typical component of the mathematics curricu-
710 lum in both nations, we did not review other lessons. Furthermore, our subsequent analysis was even more restrictive, examining only addition of signed numbers with different signs. Finally, we focused on properties of the lessons that are related to problem-solving
715 instruction, rather than other aspects of the text such as its readability. Ultimately, the practical goal of this study is to provide suggestions for the improvement of textbooks aimed at mathematical problem solving. The following suggestions need to be subjected to research
720 study: (a) present a few basic topics in depth, organized into coherent lessons, rather than a huge collection of fragments; (b) embed the lesson within a familiar situational context so that verbal, visual, and symbolic representations are interconnected; (c) use worked-out
725 examples to emphasize the process of problem solving; (d) present a verbal statement of the solution rule after presenting familiar worked-out examples. Finally, it should be noted that additional research is needed to

730 determine not only how to design effective textbooks but also how to use them successfully in classrooms (Driscoll, Moallem, Dick, & Kirby, 1994).

References

Armbruster, B., & Ostertag, J. (1993). Questions in elementary science and social studies textbooks. In B. K. Britton, A. Woodward, & M. Binkley (Eds.), *Learning from textbooks: Theory and practice* (pp. 69–94). Hillsdale, NJ: Erlbaum.

Bolster, L. C., Crown, W., Hamada, R., Hansen, V., Lindquist, M. M., McNerney, C., et al. (1988). *Invitation to mathematics* (7th grade). Glenview, IL: Scott, Foresman & Co.

Britton, B. K., Woodward, A., & Binkley, M. (Eds.) (1993). *Learning from textbooks: Theory and practice.* Hillsdale, NJ: Erlbaum.

Chambliss, M. J., & Calfee, R C. (1989). Designing science textbooks to enhance student understanding. *Educational Psychologist, 24,* 307–322.

Driscoll, M. P., Moallem, M., Dick, W., & Kirby, E. (1994). How does the textbook contribute to learning in a middle school science class? *Contemporary Educational Psychology, 19,* 79–100.

Fennell, F., Reys, B. J., Reys, R. E., & Webb, A. W. (1988). *Mathematics unlimited* (7th grade). New York: Holt, Rinehart & Winston.

Fujita, H., & Maehara, S. (Eds.) (1992). *New math* (in Japanese). Tokyo: Shoseki.

Fukumori, N., Kikuchi, H., Miwa, T., Iijima, Y., Igarashi, K., Iwai, S., et al. (1992). *Math 1* (in Japanese). Osaka, Japan: Keirinkan.

Garner, R. (1992). Learning from school texts. *Educational Psychologist, 27,* 53–63.

Garner, R., Brown, R., Sanders, S., & Menke, D. J. (1992). "Seductive details" and learning from text. In K. A. Renninger, S. Hidi, & A. Krapp (Eds.), *The role of interest in learning and development* (pp. 239–254). Hillsdale, NJ: Erlbaum.

Glynn, S. M., Andre, T., & Britton, B. K. (1986). The design of instructional text. *Educational Psychologist, 21,* 245–251.

Grouws, D. A. (Ed.) (1992). *Handbook of research on mathematics teaching and learning.* New York: Macmillan.

Hiebert, J. (Ed.) (1986). *Conceptual antiprocedural knowledge: The case of mathematics.* Hillsdale, NJ: Erlbaum.

Jonassen, D. H., Beissner, K., & Yacci, M. (1993). *Structural knowledge.* Hillsdale, NJ: Erlbaum.

Kodaira, K. (Ed.) (1992). *Japanese grade 7 mathematics* (H. Nagata, Trans.). Chicago: University of Chicago. (Original work published 1984)

Levin, J. R., & Mayer, R. E. (1993). Understanding illustrations in text. In B. Britton, A. Woodward, & M. Binkley (Eds.), *Learning from textbooks: Theory and practice* (pp. 95–113). Hillsdale, NJ: Erlbaum.

Mayer, R. E. (1987). *Educational psychology: A cognitive approach.* New York: Harper Collins.

Mayer, R. E. (1989). Cognition and instruction in mathematics. *Journal of Educational Psychology, 81,* 452–456.

Mayer, R. E. (1992). *Thinking, problem solving, cognition* (2nd ed.). New York: Freeman.

Mayer, R. E. (1993). Illustrations that instruct. In R. Glaser (Ed.), *Advances in instructional psychology* (Vol. 4, pp. 253–284). Hillsdale, NJ: Erlbaum.

Mayer, R. E., Tajika, H., & Stanley, C. (1991). Mathematical problem solving in Japan and the United States: A controlled comparison. *Journal of Educational Psychology, 83,* 69–72.

McKnight, C. C., Crosswhite, F. J., Dossey, J. A., Kifer, E., Swafford, J. O., Trayers, K. J., & Cooney, T. J. (1987). *The underachieving curriculum: Assessing U.S. school mathematics from an international perspective.* Champaign, IL: Stipes.

Okamoto, Y. (1989, April). *An analysis of addition and subtraction word problems in textbooks: An across national comparison.* Paper presented at the Annual Meeting of the American Educational Research Association, San Francisco.

Robitaille, D. F., & Garden, R. A. (1989). *The IEA study of mathematics II: Contexts and outcomes of school mathematics.* Oxford, England: Pergamon.

Rucker, W. E., Dilley, C. A., Lowry, D. W., & Ockenga, E. G. (1988). *Heath mathematics* (7th grade). Lexington, MA: D. C. Heath.

Stevenson, H. W., & Bartsch, K. (1991). An analysis of Japanese and American textbooks in mathematics. In R. Leetsma & H. Walberg (Eds.), *Japanese educational productivity.* Ann Arbor: Center for Japanese Studies.

Stevenson, H. W., Lee, S-Y., Chen, C., Stigler, J. W., Hsu, C-C., & Kitamura, S. (1990). Contexts of achievement: A study of American, Chinese, and Japanese children. *Monographs of the Society for Research in Child Development, 55* (1–2, Serial No. 221).

Stevenson, H. W., & Stigler, J. W. (1992). *The learning gap.* New York: Summit.

Stevenson, H. W., Stigler, J. W., Lee, S-Y., Kitamura, S., Kimura, S., & Kato, T. (1986). Achievement in mathematics. In H. Stevenson, H. Azuma, & K. Hakuta (Eds.), *Child development and education in Japan* (pp. 201–216). New York: Freeman.

Stigler, J. W., Lee, S-Y., & Stevenson, H. W. (1990). *Mathematical knowledge of Japanese, Chinese, and American elementary school children.* Reston, VA: National Council of Teachers of Mathematics.

Wade, S. E. (1992). How interest affects learning from text. In K. A. Renninger, S. Hidi, & A. Krapp (Eds.), *The role of interest in learning and development* (pp. 254–277). Hillsdale, NJ: Erlbaum.

Willoughby, S. S., Bereiter, C., Hilton, P., & Rubinstein, J. H. (1991). *Real math* (7th grade). La Salle, IL: Open Court.

Note: This project was supported by a grant from the Pacific Rim Research Program. Hidetsugu Tajika translated two of the Japanese textbook lessons into English.

About the authors: Richard E. Mayer is a professor of psychology and education, Department of Psychology, University of California, Santa Barbara, CA 93106. His specializations are educational and cognitive psychology. Valerie Sims is a Ph.D. candidate, Department of Psychology, University of California, Santa Barbara, CA 93106. Her specializations are cognitive and developmental psychology. Hidetsugu Tajika is an associate professor, Department of Psychology, Aichi University of Education, Kariya, Aichi 448 Japan. His specializations are memory and cognitive processes.

Exercise for Article 6

Factual Questions

1. The researchers explicitly state their research hypothesis for this study in which line(s)?

2. The lessons examined in this study ranged from a low of how many pages to a high of how many pages?

3. On the average, what percentage of the page space in Japanese textbooks is devoted to explanations of problem-solving procedures? What is the corresponding percentage for U.S. textbooks?

4. Which country's textbooks cover fewer topics?

5. According to the authors, which country's textbooks assume that students are "behaviorally active knowledge acquisition machines"?

6. The researchers note the need for research on how to use textbooks effectively in which lines?

Questions for Discussion

7. In lines 47–49, the researchers state that this study "contributes to an emerging research base on cross-national comparisons of textbooks" and cite three references for this statement. Would it have been appropriate for them to discuss this research base in more detail? Explain.

8. In lines 63–66, the researchers state that examining the content and teaching methods in textbooks "provides a partial account of how mathematics is taught...." Although it is partial, is it important?

What else might be examined to get a fuller account? Explain.

9. The researchers examined only one type of lesson in only five textbooks. Is this an important limitation? Is the study of value despite this limitation? Explain.

10. The researchers state that the selected textbooks were "typical." How did they determine this? How would you determine it? (See lines 86–89.)

11. The researchers used two "independent raters." Why did they bother to use two raters? What does "independent" mean? (See line 114–138.)

12. Beginning in line 114, the researchers describe their *quantitative* analysis. Beginning in line 188, they describe their *qualitative* analysis as a supplement to the quantitative one. In your opinion, which analysis yielded more important information about the differences between the two sets of textbooks? Explain.

13. Have these researchers demonstrated that differences between the two nations' textbooks are the *cause* of the differences in the mathematics achievement of the students in the two nations? Explain.

14. This study is an example of content analysis (also known as documentary analysis) in which the contents of documents are analyzed. Are there advantages and disadvantages to using content analysis as a research method for collecting information on problems in education? Explain.

Quality Ratings

Directions: Indicate your level of agreement with each of the following statements by circling a number from 5 for strongly agree (SA) to 1 for strongly disagree (SD). If you believe an item is not applicable to this research article, leave it blank. Be prepared to explain your ratings.

A. The introduction establishes the importance of the study.

   SA   5   4   3   2   1   SD

B. The literature review establishes the context for the study.

   SA   5   4   3   2   1   SD

C. The research purpose, question, or hypothesis is clearly stated.

   SA   5   4   3   2   1   SD

D. The method of sampling is sound.

   SA   5   4   3   2   1   SD

E. Relevant demographics (for example, age, gender, and ethnicity) are described.

   SA   5   4   3   2   1   SD

F. Measurement procedures are adequate.

   SA   5   4   3   2   1   SD

G. All procedures have been described in sufficient detail to permit a replication of the study.

   SA   5   4   3   2   1   SD

H. The participants have been adequately protected from potential harm.

   SA   5   4   3   2   1   SD

I. The results are clearly described.

   SA   5   4   3   2   1   SD

J. The discussion/conclusion is appropriate.

   SA   5   4   3   2   1   SD

K. Despite any flaws, the report is worthy of publication.

   SA   5   4   3   2   1   SD

Article 7

Symptoms of Anxiety Disorders and Teacher-Reported School Functioning of Normal Children

PETER MURIS
Maastricht University, The Netherlands

COR MEESTERS
Maastricht University, The Netherlands

SUMMARY. Correlations between scores on the Spence Children's Anxiety Scale, a questionnaire for measuring symptoms of anxiety disorders and a report of school functioning by teachers, were computed for 317 primary school children and 13 teachers in The Netherlands. Analysis showed a small but significant negative correlation between scores for total anxiety and school functioning ($r = -.20$, $p < .001$). The finding is consistent with the notion that high symptoms indicating anxiety disorders in children are accompanied by less optimal functioning in school.

From *Psychological Reports*, *91*, 588–590. Copyright © 2002 by Psychological Reports. Reprinted with permission.

Anxiety disorders are among the most common types of psychopathology in children (Bernstein, Borchardt, & Perwien, 1996). It is also well known that subclinical manifestations of these disorders are highly prevalent among youths of all ages (e.g., Bell-Dolan, Last, & Strauss, 1990). Despite this high prevalence rate, only a small proportion of children with anxiety disorders seeks treatment (Spence, 2001). This is probably because anxiety is a so-called internalizing problem, which causes relatively little burden to others in the children's environment. Although it is generally assumed that anxiety disorders can potentially interfere significantly with children's functioning in a wide range of domains, relatively few studies have actually addressed this issue (but see Strauss, Frame, & Forehand, 1987). The present investigation examined the relation between magnitude of children's symptoms indicating anxiety disorders and school functioning as perceived by their teachers.

Primary school children (154 boys and 163 girls, aged 10 to 12 years) completed a shortened version of the Children's Anxiety Scale (Spence, 1998), a 20-item 4-point rating scale with anchors of 0 = never and 3 = always for measuring symptoms of social phobia, panic disorder, separation anxiety disorder, and generalized anxiety disorder. Examples of items are "I feel afraid that I will make a fool of myself in front of people," "All of a sudden I feel really scared for no reason at all," "I feel scared if I have to sleep on my own," and "I worry that something bad will happen." Subscale scores and a total anxiety score can be computed by summing across relevant items. In addition, children's teachers ($n = 13$) completed the Pyramid Test (Smits, 1983), a sociometric ranking procedure on which the teacher ranks all children in class on four 9-point "normal distribution"-based scales representing the following aspects of school functioning: learning attitude, relation with teacher, relation with peers, and self-esteem.

All assessment scales were reliable, with Cronbach's alphas between .74 (separation anxiety disorder) and .88 (total score) for the Spence Children's Anxiety Scale, and .77 for the total score of school functioning. Various correlations between scores on the Spence scale and school functioning (see Table 1) were significant. For example, the correlation between the Total Anxiety and General School Functioning scores was $-.20$ ($p < .001$). Furthermore, anxiety scores appeared particularly associated with two specific domains of school functioning, *viz.*, Relation with Peers and Self-Esteem. Finally, the most substantial connection emerged between Social Phobia symptoms and children's Relation with Peers ($r = -.29$, $p < .001$). In all cases, correlations were negative, indicating that higher symptoms of anxiety disorder were accompanied by lower school functioning.

Although this study was cross-sectional in nature so one cannot draw causal conclusions, the data indicate that teachers perceive some impairment in the school functioning of children with more intense symptoms related to anxiety disorders. At the same time, it should be acknowledged that correlations between such anxiety symptoms and school functioning were rather low. None accounted for more than 9% of the common variance. This seems to indicate that children's problems with anxiety in most cases remain largely hidden. If one is willing to implement early intervention programs for childhood anxiety disorders in the schools (see Dadds, Spence, Holland, Barrett, & Laurens,

Table 1
Correlations (Corrected for Sex) Between Scores on Spence Children's Anxiety Scale and School Functioning As Ranked by Teachers

			Teacher-reported school functioning				
Spence Children's Anxiety Scale	M	SD	General functioning	Learning attitude	Relation with teacher	Relation with peers	Self-esteem
Total anxiety	10.4	7.5	−.20**	−.10	−.06	−.27**	−.18*
Social phobia	3.3	2.7	−.26**	−.16*	−.10	−.29**	−.24**
Panic disorder	2.2	2.3	−.09	−.02	−.03	−.15*	−.07
Separation anxiety disorder	1.5	2.0	−.14*	−.07	−.02	−.19**	−.14*
Generalized anxiety disorder	3.3	2.7	−.11*	−.05	−.02	−.17*	−.08

* $p < .05$, ** $p < .05/25$ (i.e., Bonferroni correction).

70 1997), screening by means of self-report anxiety measures seems potentially useful.

References

Bell-Dolan, D. J., Last, C. G., & Strauss, C. C. (1990). Symptoms of anxiety disorders in normal children. *Journal of the American Academy of Child and Adolescent Psychiatry, 29*, 759–765.

Bernstein, G. A., Borchardt, C. M., & Perwien, A. R. (1996). Anxiety disorders in children and adolescents: A review of the past 10 years. *Journal of the American Academy of Child and Adolescent Psychiatry, 35*, 1110–1119.

Dadds, M. R., Spence, S. H., Holland, D. E., Barrett, P. M., & Laurens, K. R. (1997). Prevention and early intervention for anxiety disorders: A controlled trial. *Journal of Consulting and Clinical Psychology, 65*, 627–635.

Smits, J. A. E. (1983). *Piramide Techniek (PT), een methode voor het beoordelen van leerlingen door leidsters en leerkrachten.* Nijmegen: Berkhout.

Spence, S. H. (1998). A measure of anxiety symptoms among children. *Behaviour Research and Therapy, 36*, 545–566.

Spence, S. H. (2001). Prevention strategies. In M. W. Vasey & M. R. Dadds (Eds.), *The developmental psychopathology of anxiety.* New York: Oxford University Press., pp. 325–351.

Strauss, C. C., Frame, C. L., & Forehand, R. (1987). Psychosocial impairment associated with anxiety in children. *Journal of Clinical Child Psychology, 16*, 235–239.

Address correspondence to: Dr. Peter Muris, Department of Medical, Clinical, and Experimental Psychology, Maastricht University, P.O. Box 616, 6200 MD Maastricht, The Netherlands. E-mail: p.muris@dep.unimaas.nl

Exercise for Article 7

Factual Questions

1. The researchers speculate that anxiety is a so-called internalizing problem that causes what?

2. What was the age range of the students in this study?

3. Who performs the ranking on the Pyramid Test?

4. Was the relationship between Total Anxiety and General School Functioning direct (i.e., positive) *or* inverse (i.e., negative)?

5. The strongest relationship was found between which two variables?

6. What was the value of the correlation coefficient for the relationship between Social Phobia and Learning Attitude?

Questions for Discussion

7. In the second paragraph, the researchers present sample items from the Children's Anxiety Scale. To what extent do the sample items help you understand what the scale measures?

8. In the third paragraph, the researchers report that all Cronbach's alphas were between .74 and .88. If you have studied measurement, what does this mean?

9. Are you surprised that all the coefficients in this report are negative? Explain.

10. If you were conducting a study on the same topic, what changes, if any, would you make in the research methodology?

Quality Ratings

Directions: Indicate your level of agreement with each of the following statements by circling a number from 5 for strongly agree (SA) to 1 for strongly disagree (SD). If you believe an item is not applicable to this research article, leave it blank. Be prepared to explain your ratings.

A. The introduction establishes the importance of the study.

SA 5 4 3 2 1 SD

B. The literature review establishes the context for the study.

SA 5 4 3 2 1 SD

C. The research purpose, question, or hypothesis is clearly stated.

SA 5 4 3 2 1 SD

D. The method of sampling is sound.

SA   5   4   3   2   1   SD

E. Relevant demographics (for example, age, gender, and ethnicity) are described.

SA   5   4   3   2   1   SD

F. Measurement procedures are adequate.

SA   5   4   3   2   1   SD

G. All procedures have been described in sufficient detail to permit a replication of the study.

SA   5   4   3   2   1   SD

H. The participants have been adequately protected from potential harm.

SA   5   4   3   2   1   SD

I. The results are clearly described.

SA   5   4   3   2   1   SD

J. The discussion/conclusion is appropriate.

SA   5   4   3   2   1   SD

K. Despite any flaws, the report is worthy of publication.

SA   5   4   3   2   1   SD

Article 8

The Significance of Language and Cultural Education on Secondary Achievement: A Survey of Chinese-American and Korean-American Students

STEVEN K. LEE
California State University, Dominguez Hills

ABSTRACT. This study attempted to answer the question: What is the significance of language and cultural orientation on academic achievement? This study examined the relationship between the students' level of interest in maintaining their heritage language and culture and their achievement in school. The subjects for this study were 105 U.S.-born, Chinese-American and Korean-American students attending public high schools in Southern California. The study found that those who valued the acculturation process (adapting to the mainstream culture while preserving their language and culture) had superior academic achievement levels to those who were most interested in the assimilation process and who adopted the values and lifestyles of the dominant culture. In light of the implementation of the "English Only" policy in California's public schools, this study has important implications in public education—that curriculum and instruction should focus on helping language and cultural minority students to develop and maintain their heritage while exposing them to new ideas.

From *Bilingual Research Journal*, *26*, 213–224. Copyright © 2002 by National Association for Bilingual Education. Reprinted with permission.

There is a prevalent stereotype in the American society that Asian-American students are high achievers; hence, the term "model minority" is often used in reference to Asian-Americans. Such use emerged during
5 the 1960s in the midst of the civil rights movement (Osajima, 1988; Sue & Kitano, 1973). It was coined as a hegemonic device, attempting to divert attention away from the racial and ethnic tension of the period and laud the economic success of Asian-Americans
10 outside of the movement. Thus, the term was not really used to recognize the important contribution of Asian-Americans to American society. On the contrary, the model minority stereotype was propagated by the media to subdue growing demands from the African-
15 American and other minority groups for equal rights. The media often cited Asian-Americans as an example of a model group that achieved educational and social

prosperity in the absence of government assistance or intervention in schools and in employment, and who
20 were able to seek educational and employment opportunities—thereby delegitimizing the issue of racial inequality and suppressing public outcry for rectification and improvements in educational and social systems of the United States.
25 According to many scholars (e.g., Caplan, Choy, & Whitmore, 1991; Hsu, 1971; Kitano, 1969; Mordkowitz & Ginsberg, 1987; Sung, 1987) Asian-Americans are more successful in school because their culture emphasizes the value of education. In addition, the
30 family-oriented nature of Asian cultures, in which academic success is equated with upholding the family honor, is seen as facilitating conditions for educational success. Suzuki (1980), one of the first to examine educational achievement from a historical cultural per-
35 spective, posited that academic success of Asian-Americans was a reaction to social stratification that existed in the United States: Exclusion of Asian-Americans from social participation forced parents to push for education for their children to overcome the
40 social and political barriers. More recent studies (e.g., Hirschman & Wong, 1986; Mark & Chih, 1982; Sue & Okazaki, 1990) seem to support Suzuki's theory that perception of education as a key to social mobility is a contributing factor in academic achievement of Asian-
45 Americans. Stacey Lee (1996) found that among the different Asian-American student groups, the group that held the highest regard for education as the most essential for social mobility had superior academic achievement than those groups who did not see school
50 as the key to upward mobility in the society. Whereas the former group felt obligated to do their best in school, the latter group placed little interest in education.

In explaining the difference in academic achieve-
55 ment among minority groups, Ogbu (1989) distinguished between voluntary and involuntary minorities. According to this theory, voluntary immigrants do bet-

ter in school because they accept the host culture. This theory also posits that voluntary immigrants believe
60 that their future is determined by their ability to overcome social and economic hurdles through academic success. Studies by Mark and Chih (1982) and Lee (1996) seem to support this theory: They found that parents of Asian-American students often reminded
65 their children to excel in school to overcome racial prejudice and discrimination. In other words, Asian-Americans perceived education as the most important form of empowerment for social mobility. Considering that a relatively high percentage (5.3%) of Asian-
70 Americans enter colleges and universities, Asian-American parents seem to have a great influence on their children's educational interests. Involuntary immigrants are thought to reject the dominant culture because they perceive the mainstream culture to be a
75 threat to their own identity. Thus, according to this theory, involuntary immigrants may regard school success as giving up their culture at the expense of assimilating to the dominant culture with which school is associated.
80   Although it is true that Asian-Americans are generally more successful in education than other minority groups—measured in terms of SAT scores and the percentage of Asian-Americans who have completed or are currently enrolled in higher education—there is
85 growing evidence to suggest that not all Asian-American students are doing well in school. Rumbaut and Ima (1988) found that among the Southeast Asian students, the Khmer and the Lao had a grade point average (GPA) below that of the majority (white) stu-
90 dents, whereas the GPA of the Vietnamese and Chinese-Vietnamese students was well above the average of the majority students. More recent studies (e.g., Trueba, Cheng, & Ima, 1993) seem to point in the direction that there is a need to clarify conceptual find-
95 ings by examining intra-group differences within the Asian-American population. That is, academic achievement of Asian-Americans can no longer be predicted based simply on the notion that all Asian-Americans share a common culture. The implicit mes-
100 sage is that the socio- and psycho-cultural dynamics of Asian-American students are as complex as any other ethnic group's. As such, studies related to educational achievement of Asian-American students must go beyond the rudimentary task of developing a conceptual
105 framework based on collective descriptions.
    In explaining inter-group differences in academic achievement, Ogbu (1989) classifies all Asian-Americans as belonging to one group. That is, according to Ogbu's framework, fifth-generation Asian-
110 Americans are no different from recent immigrants—both belong to the voluntary immigrant group. Although this framework provides an interesting and dichotomous view of the relationship between culture and academic achievement, it fails to consider intra-
115 group and individual differences. That is, why are

some groups within the Asian-American population, presumably who came to the United States voluntarily to seek improved livelihood, doing better than others? And why do some Asian-American students excel
120 while others barely make it through high school?
    Caudill and De Vox (1956) were among the first to examine educational achievement of Asian-Americans from a cultural perspective. Based on their research on Japanese-Americans, they reported that Japanese-
125 Americans are more successful because their cultural characteristics are those highly regarded by the mainstream society. Kitano (1969) and Caplan, Choy, and Whitmore (1991) concluded that Asian-Americans are more successful in the schools because of compatibility
130 of their culture with middle-class American culture. Although these postulations provide interesting perspectives, they seem to reinforce the "model minority" stereotype by assuming that all Asian-Americans share similar cultural backgrounds. For example, what does
135 Hmong culture have in common with Korean or Japanese culture? Or, do middle-class Americans really hold high regard for Cambodian culture? Studies based on the stereotypical treatment of Asian-Americans as a homogeneous group ignore the importance of adaptive
140 strategies and other psychological and social variables that may influence the learning experiences of Asian-American students.
    Gibson (1988) observed that among Punjabi students, there was a positive correlation between their
145 arrival in the United States and school success: The longer the students have been in the United States, the better their performance. Gibson's studies clearly suggest that appropriate behavior cannot be the most important determinant factor of academic achievement.
150 That is, assimilation is more likely for those students who have been exposed longer to the dominant culture than for those who have recently arrived in the United States, so that there may be more cultural similarities between mainstream students and those students who
155 have been in the United States longer than with the newcomers. Considering this, theories based on behavior and cultural compatibility do not adequately explain the educational achievement of Asian-American students. For example, if we were to accept the notion that
160 Asian-American students do better in school than other minority students because there is "cultural match" with the mainstream culture, it predicates not only that Asian-American students share the same culture, but also that there is no heuristic process within the Asian
165 and Asian-American culture.
    The purpose of this study was to examine the significance of language and cultural identity on academic achievement of Chinese-American and Korean-American students in secondary schools. This
170 study was motivated by the emergence of studies that indicate that there is variation in academic achievement among Asian-American students. This study attempted to answer the question: Is there a correlation between

175 the students' level of interest in and awareness of cultural heritage and the level of academic achievement? This study investigated the possibility that educational achievement may be related to the students' involvement, interest, and awareness of their ancestral culture.

Method

Subjects

Subjects for this study were 105 male and female
180 students of Chinese ($n = 57$) and Korean ($n = 48$) heritage enrolled in two high schools in an upper-middle-class community of Orange County, California. All the subjects, between the ages of 15 and 17, were enrolled in regular classes. Both schools offered courses in Chi-
185 nese and Korean as foreign language classes. The two groups represented the largest minority group (approximately 20%) in the community. All subjects were born in the United States.

Instrument

The questionnaire, consisting of 10 closed-ended
190 questions, was pretested on 23 high school students for clarification and appropriateness of the questions contained in the survey. The randomly selected students each received a questionnaire to be completed prior to beginning their class. Questions surveyed the subjects'
195 background, interest, awareness, and views on cultural identity. They included:

1. Have you attended a Chinese or Korean language/culture school for more than one year while you were in middle or high school?
200 2. Do you know much about the history/culture of China or Korea?
3. Have you studied Chinese or Korean for more than one year at your high school?
4. Do you regularly attend (at least once a month)
205 Chinese- or Korean-related cultural events/activities, including religious functions?
5. Do you speak Chinese or Korean in the home and/or with relatives/friends?
6. Are you interested in learning more about your
210 cultural heritage?
7. Do you feel it is important for you to maintain your cultural identity?
8. Do you feel your culture/heritage contributes to the American culture/heritage?
215 9. Do you feel there should be diverse cultures represented in the United States?
10. Do you feel people should have a greater interest in their own ethnic culture/heritage than in the mainstream culture?

220 In addition to the questionnaire, Asian-American students were observed and interviewed during lunchtime for a total of approximately 20 hours.

Procedures

A research assistant distributed and collected the
265 questionnaires. The research assistant also provided

225 instructions prior to administering the questionnaire. The investigator personally observed and interviewed the students. Interviews were recorded on a cassette tape with the subjects' permission.

Results

Responding "yes" to the questions on the survey
230 indicated orientation toward acculturation, an additive process of adapting to the mainstream culture while preserving the heritage culture. Conversely, responding "no" on the survey suggested orientation toward assimilation, toward adopting the values, behaviors, be-
235 liefs, and lifestyles of the dominant culture. The subjects' GPAs in relation to the number of affirmative responses were used to establish a correlation.

Although there was a wide range, 0 to 10, the majority of the subjects (about two-thirds) responded af-
240 firmatively to six to nine questions. The grade point average (GPA) ranged from 2.98 to 3.81 with a mean of 3.54. With the exception of two subjects who responded affirmatively to three questions, and who had a GPA of 2.98, there was a pattern in the relationship
245 between the number of affirmative responses and the subjects' GPA; the subjects' GPA increased as the number of affirmative responses increased. Using the Pearson product-moment correlation coefficient (r) to find the strength of the relationship at the critical value
250 of .05, 96 degrees of freedom (df), the correlation (r) was .94. Thus, the statistical analysis indicated that there was a strong correlation between the students' GPAs and the extent to which the subjects showed an interest in their cultural heritage. The level of signifi-
255 cance for a two-tailed test at this level for a sample size of 105 is .201. Hence, the results revealed that students who had a greater awareness for and interest in developing biculturalism had superior grade point averages than their counterparts who had less interest in their
260 heritage. The correlation was very significant, statistically.

Table 1
GPA in Relation to Number of Affirmative Responses

Subjects ($n = 105$)	No. of "Yes" Responses	GPA ($M = 3.54$)
2	0	3.17
2	3	2.98
6	4	3.19
10	5	3.25
17	6	3.27
23	7	3.58
19	8	3.76
17	9	3.78
9	10	3.81

It is interesting to note that only 38% indicated that they knew much about the history/culture of China or Korea. This is in sharp contrast to the 86% who responded that they were interested in learning more about their cultural heritage. This strongly suggests that

Asian-American students were not receiving an adequate amount of exposure to Asian history and culture in and outside the home. Also, while 81% of the subjects indicated that they have attended a Chinese or Korean language/culture school for at least a year, only 25% responded that they have studied Chinese or Korean at a high school. Thus, it seems most Chinese-American and Korean-American students are receiving educational language and cultural lessons at community-based private schools rather than at the public high schools. Considering the fact that both schools offered instructions in Chinese and Korean, the disparity between the two seems to suggest that the public schools may not be offering the kinds of instruction and experience students expect from the language classes.

Also worth noting is the great disparity between the percentage of subjects who indicated the importance of maintaining cultural identity (90%) and the percentage who thought their heritage contributed to American culture (41%). It seems the majority of the subjects perceived cultural heritage to be more important for personal identification than for actual contribution to United States culture. When subjects were asked this question during interviews, many thought that most Americans of different racial, ethnic, and/or cultural backgrounds did not recognize Chinese or Korean culture as part of U.S. culture. Therefore, it appears that for many, cultural contribution is based on their perception of the level of acceptance by other Americans. This was supported by 93% of the respondents, who indicated that cultural diversity should exist in the United States (see Table 2).

Table 2
Percentage of Affirmative Responses

Question	Percentage
1. Attended Chinese or Korean community school	81%
2. Knowledge about Chinese or Korean history/culture	38%
3. Studied Chinese or Korean at high school	25%
4. Attended Chinese- or Korean-related cultural activity	90%
5. Speak Chinese or Korean at home/with relatives/friends	78%
6. Interested in learning more about cultural heritage	86%
7. Important to maintain cultural identity	90%
8. Cultural heritage contributes to American culture	41%
9. Cultural diversity should exist in the United States	93%
10. Greater interest for own culture than mainstream culture	60%

Discussion

As one of the fastest growing minority groups in the United States, Asian-Americans are expected to account for 10% of the total population of the United States by 2040 (González, 1990). In California, Asian-American students already outnumber African-American students. Yet the model minority stereotype seems to have desensitized the need for inclusion of Asian-Americans on discussions of race and education; Asian-Americans are often treated as outsiders needing no special consideration. The results of this study seem to suggest that there are indeed intra-group and individual differences in academic achievement within the Chinese-American and Korean-American student populations. The study found that there was a strong correlation between the students' cultural interest/identity and their academic achievement.

Suzuki (1980) stated that Asian-American students receive favorable evaluations from their teachers due to compatibility between the Asian culture and the teachers' expectations. That is, certain Asian cultural characteristics, such as obedience, conformity, and respect for authority, were viewed favorably by teachers. In fact, Suzuki claimed that teachers may assign good grades to Asian-American students based on behavior rather than on academic performance. Both Goldstein (1985) and Lee (1996) reported that teachers' evaluation of Asian-American students was often based on observable characteristics and not on actual academic achievement. According to E. Lee and M. Lee (1980), acculturation vis-à-vis assimilation plays an important factor in academic achievement of Asian-American students because it allows them to exhibit those behaviors favored by teachers. Although these studies are helpful in understanding how behavior can influence teachers' assessment of students, they seem to discredit the achievement of Asian-American students by generating yet another overly simplified proposition—that behavior is what sets Asian-American students apart from other students. These findings do not substantiate (a) why some Asian-Americans fail while other Asian-Americans are successful, (b) why Asian-Americans generally score higher than other minority students on standardized tests in which observable behavior has no influence on the outcome, and (c) why grades based on behavior are Asian-American specific.

The results of this study have revealed that there are indeed intra-group differences among U.S.-born Chinese-American and Korean-American students. Those students who had had greater experience and interest in developing bilingualism and biculturalism enjoyed higher academic achievement than those who were less interested in their cultural heritage. Thus, this study not only invalidated the deeply rooted stereotype that Asian-Americans belong to a group that adheres to common cultural values and practices, but also that personal interest in bilingualism and biculturalism is related to academic achievement. The results revealed a positive correlation between the students' language and cultural identity and their academic achievement.

This study was an attempt to examine educational achievement of Chinese-Americans and Korean-

360 Americans from an intra-cultural perspective. That is, rather than attempting to devise an overly simplified concept based on collective treatment of Asian-Americans as a group, this study examined the issue of educational attainment from a psychocultural perspec-

365 tive of Chinese-Americans and Korean-Americans as individuals. This study has found that among Chinese-American and Korean-American students, the cultural interests and experiences of Asian-American students vary, and that these differences may influence their

370 academic performance. Thus, the implication from this study is that the educational community must recognize the significant contribution of education programs that promote heritage, language, and culture for language- and cultural-minority students.

375 There is no doubt that inclusion of Asian and Asian-American experiences, as well as the recognition of the importance of their presence in schools, will empower Asian-American students to participate in the learning process. It is hypothesized that those students

380 who had greater interest in their language and cultural identity had superior academic achievement than their counterparts because they had greater motivation for a diversified learning experience and interest. That is, these students had superior cognitive, meta-cognitive,

385 and socioaffective strategies to help them do better in school. Hence, rather than emulating their peers to conform to the norm of the dominant culture (cultural compensatory strategy), these students were interested in empowering themselves by developing awareness

390 and pride in their heritage while undergoing personal experiences in the mainstream culture (cultural enrichment strategy). Thus, in this dichotomy, students who utilize the cultural enrichment strategy draw upon the positive qualities of at least two cultures from

395 which to adapt to the learning needs of the classroom. On the contrary, students applying the cultural compensatory strategy are at a disadvantaged position because their primary interest is to assimilate to the mainstream culture at the expense of losing their heritage.

400 Thus, cultural compensatory strategy tends to devalue one's ancestral culture while placing a high priority on adopting the mainstream culture.

As diversity within the Asian-American community increases, so is the likelihood that students will come to

405 school with varying interests in their cultural heritage. In 1992, approximately 41% of Asian-Americans were foreign born (Wong, 1992). By the year 2000, this percentage is projected to increase to about 50%. The increasing presence of Asian-American students in our

410 schools will inevitably demand that institutions of learning prepare themselves to be able to provide facilitative instruction in which bilingualism and biculturalism are encouraged and promoted for all students, including Asian-American students. This study has

415 shown that the issue of language and culture in academic achievement is more than a collective interpretation of similarities and differences between two cul-

tures: It is about accepting and supporting the students' language and culture while allowing them the opportu-

420 nity to experience diversity in thinking and practice. To this end, bilingual education programs in which the students' first language and culture are valued, respected, and encouraged—while students are exposed to a new language and culture—are invaluable to stu-

425 dents' eventual success in school.

References

Caplan, N., Choy, M. H., & Whitmore, J. K. (1991). *Children of the boat people: A study of educational success.* Ann Arbor, MI: University of Michigan Press.

Caudill, W., & De Vox, G. (1956). Achievement, culture and personality: The case of the Japanese Americans. *American Anthropologist, 58,* 1102–1127.

Gibson, M. (1988). *Accommodation without assimilation: Sikh immigrants in an American high school.* Ithaca, NY: Cornell University Press.

Goldstein, B. (1985). *Schooling for cultural transitions: Hmong girls and boys in American high schools.* Unpublished doctoral dissertation, University of Wisconsin, Madison.

González, R. (1990). When minority becomes majority: The challenging face of English classrooms. *English Journal, 79*(1), 16–23.

Hirschman, C., & Wong, M. G. (1986). The extraordinary educational attainment of Asian Americans: A search for historical evidence and explanations. *Social Forces, 65*(1), 1–27.

Hsu, F. L. K. (1971). *The challenge of the American dream: The Chinese in the United States.* Belmont, CA: Wadsworth.

Kitano, H. H. L. (1969). *Japanese Americans: The evolution of a subculture.* Englewood Cliffs, NJ: Prentice-Hall.

Lee, E., & Lee, M. (1980). *A study of classroom behaviors of Chinese American children and immigrant Chinese children in contrast to those of Black American children and White American children in an urban head start program.* Unpublished doctoral dissertation, University of San Francisco.

Lee, S. J. (1996). *Unraveling the model minority stereotype.* New York, NY: Teachers College Press.

Mark, D. M. L., & Chih, G. (1982). *A place called America.* Dubuque, IA: Kendall Hunt.

Mordkowitz, E. R., & Ginsberg, H. P. (1987). Early academic socialization of successful Asian-American college students. *Quarterly Newsletter of the Laboratory of Comparative Human Cognition, 9,* 85–91.

Ogbu, J. U. (1989). The individual in collective adaptation: A framework for focusing on academic underperformance and dropping out among involuntary minorities. In L. Weis, E. Farrar, & H. G. Petrie (Eds.), *Dropouts from school: Issues, dilemmas, and solutions* (pp. 181–204). Albany: State University of New York Press.

Osajima, K. (1988). Asian Americans as the model minority: An analysis of the popular press image in the 1960s and 1980s. In G. Y. Okihiro, S. Hune, A. A. Hansen, & J. M. Liu (Eds.), *Reflections on shattered windows: Promises and prospects for Asian American studies* (pp. 165–174). Pullman: Washington State University Press.

Rumbaut, R. G., & Ima, K. (1988). *The adaptation of Southwest Asian refugee youth: A comparative study.* Washington, DC: U.S. Office of Refugee Settlement.

Sue, S., & Kitano, H. H. L. (1973). Stereotypes as a measure of success. *Journal of Social Issues, 29*(2), 83–98.

Sue, S., & Okazaki, S. (1990). Asian-American educational achievements: A phenomenon in search of an explanation. *American Psychologist, 45*(8), 913–920.

Sung, B. L. (1987). *The adjustment experience of Chinese immigrant children in New York City.* New York: Center for Migration Studies.

Suzuki, R. H. (1980). Education and the socialization of Asian Americans: A revisionist analysis of the "model minority" thesis. In R. Endo, S. Sue, & N. N. Wagner (Eds.), *Asian-Americans: Social and psychological perspectives, Vol. 2* (pp. 155–175). Ben Lomond, CA: Science and Behavior Books.

Trueba, H. T., & Ima, K. (1993). *Myth or reality: Adaptive strategies of Asian Americans in California.* Washington, DC: The Farmer Press.

Wong, G. (1992). *California State University Asian Language BCLAD Consortium proposal.* Long Beach, CA: California State University Asian Language BCLAD Consortium.

Exercise for Article 8

Factual Questions

1. According to the literature review, Ogbu classifies Asian-Americans as belonging to how many groups?

2. How many of the subjects in this study were of Korean ancestry?

3. Responding "yes" to the questions on the survey indicated orientation toward
   A. acculturation.   B. assimilation.

4. In this report, what is the symbol for correlation?

5. What is the value of the correlation coefficient for the relationship between GPA and affirmative responses to the survey?

6. What was the GPA of the nine subjects who responded "yes" to all 10 survey questions?

7. Among all subjects, what percentage responded in the affirmative to studying Chinese or Korean at high school?

Questions for Discussion

8. The researcher states: "In addition to the questionnaire, Asian-American students were observed and interviewed during lunchtime for a total of approximately 20 hours." In your opinion, is this an important part of the study? Explain. (See lines 220–222.)

9. The researcher states that the correlation coefficient in this study was very statistically significant. However, he does not indicate the probability level at which it was significant. In your opinion, is this an important omission? Explain. (See lines 247–254.)

10. Would you characterize the correlation coefficient reported in this study as being "strong"? Explain. (See lines 247–261.)

11. In your opinion, does the correlation coefficient of .94 lend support to the possibility that acculturation *causes* higher achievement as indicated by students' GPAs? Does it indicate *proof of causation*? Explain.

12. In your opinion, to what extent do you think the results of this study support this implication stated by the researcher: "…the educational community must recognize the significant contribution of education programs that promote heritage, language, and culture for language- and cultural-minority students"? (See lines 371–374.)

Quality Ratings

Directions: Indicate your level of agreement with each of the following statements by circling a number from 5 for strongly agree (SA) to 1 for strongly disagree (SD). If you believe an item is not applicable to this research article, leave it blank. Be prepared to explain your ratings.

A. The introduction establishes the importance of the study.

   SA   5   4   3   2   1   SD

B. The literature review establishes the context for the study.

   SA   5   4   3   2   1   SD

C. The research purpose, question, or hypothesis is clearly stated.

   SA   5   4   3   2   1   SD

D. The method of sampling is sound.

   SA   5   4   3   2   1   SD

E. Relevant demographics (for example, age, gender, and ethnicity) are described.

   SA   5   4   3   2   1   SD

F. Measurement procedures are adequate.

   SA   5   4   3   2   1   SD

G. All procedures have been described in sufficient detail to permit a replication of the study.

   SA   5   4   3   2   1   SD

H. The participants have been adequately protected from potential harm.

   SA   5   4   3   2   1   SD

I. The results are clearly described.

   SA   5   4   3   2   1   SD

J. The discussion/conclusion is appropriate.

   SA   5   4   3   2   1   SD

K. Despite any flaws, the report is worthy of publication.

   SA   5   4   3   2   1   SD

Article 9

Test–Retest Reliability of the Self-Assessed Physical Activity Checklist

TRENT D. BROWN
RMIT University

BERNIE V. HOLLAND
RMIT University

SUMMARY. To estimate the test–retest reliability of a modified version of the Self-assessed Physical Activity Checklist, two administrations separated by five days were conducted for 52 boys and 51 girls in grade 6 in Australia. Intraclass correlation coefficients were calculated to assess the reliability. Similar test–retest reliabilities were found between boys and girls for light, moderate, and total physical activity, with the largest difference for vigorous physical activity (.44 vs. .12). The results suggest that the checklist is a more appropriate measure of boys' physical and sedentary activity, as boys reported higher reliability coefficients on all categories except for light physical activity and TV/video watching.

From *Perceptual and Motor Skills*, 99, 1099–1102. Copyright © 2004 by Perceptual and Motor Skills. Reprinted with permission.

Many physical activity questionnaires for children have been developed. Of those readily available, recall periods vary from one day to one year. Among these, one of the most commonly used physical activity surveys is the Self-assessed Physical Activity Checklist (5, 11). This checklist is a 24-hr. recall scale which measures type, frequency, and intensity of physical and sedentary activity, is inexpensive, easy to administer, and has been validated (9). Furthermore, the scale uses a segmented day for recall, so children recall physical activity before school, during school and after school, as this method is more accurate than reporting activity for the whole day (2). Despite the wide use of children's self-report surveys, little attention has been paid to their test–retest reliabilities and in particular of the checklist (10).

The accuracy of self-report has been questioned, especially as recall periods lengthen, primarily because children are limited in their accurate recall of physical activity (1). To overcome this limitation of memory, the use of the previous day has been suggested (4). In a recent review of such scales (8), only five of the 17 self-report scales examined used 24-hr. or previous-day recall and test–retest periods varied from 3 hr. to 4 wk. Cale (4) reported a test–retest reliability coefficient over 4 wk. of .62 using a one-day recall administered for two weekdays and two weekend days by a sample of 12 children. In another study (12), for the test–retest

reliability of the Previous Day Physical Activity Recall, after 1 hr. the correlation was .98. In each study coefficients were available for the overall sample, not for boys and girls separately.

Only a small number of studies could be located with sex-specific values of validation and reliability of self-report scales by children and adolescents (3, 6) so the present purpose was to estimate the test–retest r of the Self-assessed Physical Activity Checklist protocol. Also, aims were to provide sex-specific reliability coefficients for light, moderate, vigorous, and total physical activity and to examine the stability of two common sedentary activities: television viewing and computer/video game use.

Method

A total of 103 volunteers (52 boys and 51 girls) from five different grade 6 classes in physical education from primary schools within the city of Melbourne were recruited. The M ± SD for subjects' ages were 11.7 ± .05 yr. for all 103; 11.8 ± 0.5 yr. for boys and 11.7 ± 0.5 yr. for girls. The RMIT University Human Research and Ethics Committee and Victorian Department of Education and Training approved the study. Prior to participation, written approved consent was obtained from participants' parents or guardians.

A modified version of the Self-assessed Physical Activity Checklist was used to assess light, moderate, vigorous, and total physical activity and the time engaged in sedentary activities of television viewing and computer use. The checklist was modified to include activities more common to the Australian lifestyle and context: cricket, Australian rules football and netball replaced activities of ice hockey and American football. This provided a checklist of 24 physical activities to choose from, with three blank sections titled "other activities" so each participant could add an activity not on the checklist. Also, television viewing and computer use were also listed and reported in hours and minutes engaged in each activity. The original checklist is a modified version of the Yesterday Activity Checklist (7) and is reliable and valid. Subjects completed the modified checklist twice with a minimum of five days between administrations in the presence of the first author, who read the instructions. Participants were

Table 1
Means and Standard Deviations for Test and Retest and Intraclass Coefficients for Physical and Sedentary Activity

Measure	Boys (*n* = 52)					Girls (*n* = 51)				
	Test		Retest			Test		Retest		
	M	*SD*	*M*	*SD*	*r*	*M*	*SD*	*M*	*SD*	*r*
Physical activity (min./day)										
Light	78.4	58.7	57.4	44.6	.43	46.7	44.3	40.6	38.9	.47
Moderate	37.6	41.7	17.7	25.3	.36	20.7	28.4	25.3	25.0	.27
Vigorous	31.2	27.9	31.3	32.6	.44	50.7	52.2	30.6	43.8	.12
Total	147.1	71.1	106.4	47.0	.20	118.2	73.3	96.5	59.4	.19
Sedentary activity (min./day)										
TV/Video	105.5	88.7	73.1	60.8	.20	76.7	62.2	66.8	64.7	.38
Computer use	63.6	83.3	30.2	52.2	.40	30.3	46.9	24.2	46.9	.35
Total	169.1	125.0	103.3	82.6	.36	107.0	89.5	90.9	79.7	.34

reminded to recall physical or sedentary activity that lasted longer than 5 min.

75   Time in minutes spent performing each physical and sedentary activity were summed to provide a measure of total minutes in light, moderate, and vigorous physical activity. Activities have previously been classified as light, moderate, vigorous, and sedentary (5). Another category, total physical activity, was cre-

80   ated by summing time in light, moderate, and vigorous activities. Minutes spent watching TV/video and playing video/computer games were summed for total sedentary activity. After an exploratory analysis, because data were skewed, a square root-transformation was

85   used. The intraclass correlation coefficients were calculated based on a two-way mixed-effect analysis of variance.

Results and Discussion

Table 1 shows the means, standard deviations, and test–retest reliabilities for light, moderate, vigorous,

90   and total physical activity, TV/video watching, playing computer/video games, and total sedentary activity. Mean times spent in physical and sedentary activities were greater for boys than for girls in all categories at both test times except for vigorous activity during the

95   test and moderate activity during the retest. These results for physical activity are consistent with prior reports (5).

As shown in Table 1, the reliability coefficients for all categories varied from .12 to .47. Values were

100   somewhat higher for boys than for girls, as in other studies of sex differences at test–retest of physical activity (6). Test–retest reliabilities were lower than previously reported for a number of reasons. Perhaps children cannot accurately recall their physical activity.

105   For example, girls may report their physical activity behavior more accurately than boys (3); however, our results contradict this. Perhaps the difference then reflects types of activities participants remember. Second, improved reliability may be gained through the

110   use of a 7-day as opposed to a 5-day test–retest format. As children's physical activity behavior is highly variable from day to day, recall error may be reduced by

using the same day during the retest as on the first day (8).

115   As no previous study has examined the test–retest scores of this checklist, the moderate reliabilities of light physical activity for both boys and girls and vigorous physical activity for boys are useful.

References

1.   Baranowski, T. (1988). Validity and reliability of self-report measures of physical activity: An information-processing perspective. *Research Quarterly for Exercise and Sport, 59*, 314–327.
2.   Baranowski, T., Dworkin, R. J., Cieslik, C. J., Hooks, P., Clearman, D. R., Ray, L., Dunn, J. K., & Nader, P. R. (1984). Reliability and validity of self-report of aerobic activity: Family health project. *Research Quarterly, 55*, 309–317.
3.   Booth, M. L., Okely, A. D., Chey, T., & Bauman, A. (2002). The reliability and validity of the adolescent physical activity recall questionnaire. *Medicine and Science in Sports and Exercise, 34*, 1986–1995.
4.   Cale, L. (1994). Self-report measures of children's physical activity: Recommendations for future development and a new alternative measure. *Health Education Journal, 53*, 439–453.
5.   Myers, L., Strikmiller, P. K., Webber, L. S., & Berenson, G. S. (1996). Physical and sedentary activity in school children grades 5–8: The Bogalusa Heart Study. *Medicine and Science in Sports and Exercise, 28*, 852–859.
6.   Sallis, J. F., Buono, M. J., Roby, J. J., Micale, F. G., & Nelson, J. A. (1993). Seven-day recall and other physical activity self-reports in children and adolescents. *Medicine and Science in Sports and Exercise, 25*, 99–108.
7.   Sallis, J. F., Condon, S. A., Goggin, K. J., Roby, J. J., Kolody, B., & Alcaraz, J. E. (1993). The development of self-administered physical activity surveys for 4th grade students. *Research Quarterly for Exercise and Sport, 64*, 25–31.
8.   Sallis, J. F. & Saelens, B. E. (2000). Assessment of physical activity by self-report: Status, limitations, and future directions. *Research Quarterly for Exercise and Sport, 71*, 1–14.
9.   Sallis, J. F., Strikmiller, P. K., Harsha, D. W., Feldman, H. A., Ehlinger, S., Stone, E. J., Williston, J., & Woods, S. (1996). Validation of interviewer- and self-administered physical activity checklists for fifth grade students. *Medicine and Science in Sports and Exercise, 28*, 840–851.
10.   Sirard, J. R., & Pate, R. R. (2001). Physical activity assessment in children and adolescents. *Sports Medicine, 31*, 439–454.
11.   Treuth, M. S., Sherwood, N. E., Butte, N. F., McClanahan, B., Obarzanek, E., Zhou, A., Ayers, C., Adolph, A. L., Jordan, J., Jacobs, D. R., Jr., & Rochon, J. (2003). Validity and reliability of activity measures in African-American girls for GEMS. *Medicine and Science in Sports and Exercise, 35*, 532–539.
12.   Weston, A. T, Petosa, R., & Pate, R. R. (1997). Validation of an instrument for measurement of physical activity in youth. *Medicine and Science in Sports and Exercise, 29*, 138–143.

Address correspondence to: Dr. Trent D. Brown, Monash University, Faculty of Education, Northways Road, Churchill, Victoria, Australia 3842. E-mail: trent.brown@education.monash.edu.au

Exercise for Article 9

Factual Questions

1. Of the 103 students in this study, how many were girls?

2. What was the mean age for the boys in this study?

3. What was the mean number of minutes girls reported vigorous activity on the test? What was the mean number of minutes they reported vigorous activity on the retest?

4. What was the value of the test–retest correlation coefficient for vigorous activity reported by girls?

5. For girls, which physical activity was measured the most reliably? What is the value of the test–retest reliability coefficient (r) of this activity?

6. From test to retest, was the average number of minutes boys reported engaging in vigorous physical activities similar?

Questions for Discussion

7. The scale in this study asks children to recall activities separately during which three segments of a 24-hour day? In your opinion, is this important to know? (See lines 9–13.)

8. The researchers state that they used "volunteers." Is this important to know? Explain. (See line 43.)

9. The checklist was modified to include activities more common to the Australian lifestyle. In your opinion, does this restrict the generalizability of the results to Americans? Explain. (See lines 57–61.)

10. The purpose of the checklist is to measure physical activity. Yet, items were included on sedentary activities. In your opinion, does the inclusion of items on sedentary activities provide important information? Explain.

11. The researchers state that the data were "skewed." What is your understanding of the meaning of this term? (See lines 83–84.)

12. Based on your knowledge of correlation coefficients and their application in assessing reliability, does the checklist appear to be adequately reliable? Explain.

13. The researchers speculate that the reliabilities might have been higher if a 7-day instead of a 5-day retest had been used (i.e., test twice on the same day of the week; for instance, test on one Friday and retest on the next Friday). Do you agree? Why? Why not? (See lines 108–110.)

Quality Ratings

Directions: Indicate your level of agreement with each of the following statements by circling a number from 5 for strongly agree (SA) to 1 for strongly disagree (SD). If you believe an item is not applicable to this research article, leave it blank. Be prepared to explain your ratings.

A. The introduction establishes the importance of the study.

    SA   5   4   3   2   1   SD

B. The literature review establishes the context for the study.

    SA   5   4   3   2   1   SD

C. The research purpose, question, or hypothesis is clearly stated.

    SA   5   4   3   2   1   SD

D. The method of sampling is sound.

    SA   5   4   3   2   1   SD

E. Relevant demographics (for example, age, gender, and ethnicity) are described.

    SA   5   4   3   2   1   SD

F. Measurement procedures are adequate.

    SA   5   4   3   2   1   SD

G. All procedures have been described in sufficient detail to permit a replication of the study.

    SA   5   4   3   2   1   SD

H. The participants have been adequately protected from potential harm.

    SA   5   4   3   2   1   SD

I. The results are clearly described.

    SA   5   4   3   2   1   SD

J. The discussion/conclusion is appropriate.

    SA   5   4   3   2   1   SD

K. Despite any flaws, the report is worthy of publication.

    SA   5   4   3   2   1   SD

Article 10

The Effects of Computer-Assisted Instruction on First-Grade Students' Vocabulary Development

CHARLOTTE BOLING
The University of West Florida

SARAH H. MARTIN
Eastern Kentucky University

MICHAEL A. MARTIN
Eastern Kentucky University

ABSTRACT. The purpose of the present study was to determine the effect of computer-assisted instruction on first-grade students' vocabulary development. Students participating in this study were randomly divided into experimental and control groups. The students in both groups were involved in DEAR (Drop Everything And Read) as part of their instruction in a balanced literacy program. During their normal DEAR time, the control group used a book and tape to explore stories. The experimental group explored stories using computerized storyboards. The results of the study show a significant difference for both groups on pre- and posttests. However, the mean difference demonstrates a much larger gain for students in the experimental group.

From *Reading Improvement*, *39*, 79–88. Copyright © 2002 by Project Innovation, Inc. Reprinted with permission.

What can teachers do to ensure that the children they teach will develop into successful readers? This is a question that has puzzled the educational community for years. Most educators have their individual opinion
5 as to how the reading process occurs. Morrow and Tracey (1997) state that some educators believe in a behaviorist approach, where reading is taught in a skills-based environment through a prescribed curriculum. Others believe in a more constructivist approach,
10 where a relationship between the context and child must be developed where students build knowledge and gain skills through immersion in a literature-rich environment (Czubaj, 1997; Daniels & Zemelman, 1999). Whatever one believes, these approaches to
15 reading instruction—behaviorist or constructivist— continue to be the subject of debates in our classrooms and communities.

The core beliefs that teachers possess have a great impact on students learning to read. Teachers' personal
20 beliefs concerning the processes involved in learning to read greatly influence their instructional choices. A teacher's beliefs are based on his or her personal knowledge, experiences with instructional techniques, and the way students respond to the instructional
25 strategies in classroom situations (Dillon, 2000; How-

ard, McGee, Purcell, & Schwartz, 2000; Kinzer and Leu, 1999). Therefore, while teachers maintain their core beliefs about how children best learn to read, they are continuously striving to find the technique(s) that
30 will have the greatest impact on their students.

Since the early 1920s, educators have used a multi-sensory approach to teaching reading by combining reading, writing, and speaking in a natural context and not through deliberate teaching (Chall, 1992). This has
35 been particularly useful in the teaching of vocabulary. It stands to reason then that the most active vocabulary growth occurs in the early years of life. A child learns to connect an object with the sight, sound, smell, taste, and feel associated with the object. This experience is
40 followed by certain sounds made to represent the object. Thus, communication begins and the concept associated with the object develops into vocabulary. For example, a child understands the physical properties of an apple. He knows how the object looks, tastes, feels,
45 smells, and sounds. A loving parent then builds vocabulary in a natural context by adding the word associated to this object—apple. Then, this label is connected to the experience. "You are eating an apple."

As the vocabulary increases, children realize words
50 are used in many contexts. Children must then reach beyond the actual word and activate their schema of the context in which the word is used to understand the meaning. For example, the word "mouse" can have different meanings, such as a small rodent or a com-
55 puter device. A child needs to experience words being used in different contexts to understand the complexity of our language. The more children experience vocabulary in context, the sooner they will begin to realize that it is the concept of the word in question in the
60 given context that provides meaning.

As a child progresses through the various aspects of literacy development (listening, speaking, reading, and writing), his/her communication skills become more interdependent upon vocabulary development. Vocabu-
65 lary development involves understanding the "labeling" that goes with the "concept" that makes the word meaningful. It is acquired through direct experience,

multiple exposure, context, association, and comprehension. As students become comfortable with new vocabulary words, they are more likely to use the words when communicating.

Elements of our "Technological Age" often influence the instructional decisions that teachers make in the classroom. One such decision is the role that computers will play in the reading development of the children one teaches. Computer-based teaching and learning have produced positive effects in the classroom. Students seem to be motivated by learning through this medium (Forcier, 1999). Therefore, it is essential that today's teachers change as our society changes (Hoffman & Pearson, 2000). Children who enter today's primary classrooms have been processing multisensory concepts for most of their young lives. Home computers, interactive games, television, the Internet, and software companies capitalize on this multisensory concept.

Software companies have developed many programs for beginning reading that appeal to the senses and interests of the young child who is learning to read. This multimedia concept stimulates the learner with sight, sound, and action while integrating skills necessary for language development. Instructional technology offers virtual multisensory perception that should provide meaningful instruction.

Teacher-centered instruction is one approach to the use of instructional technology in the classroom (Forcier, 1999). The teacher-centered approach is similar to the direct-instruction approach in that the teacher is directing the children through the learning in order to achieve the goals of the lesson. One category of the teacher-centered approach is computer-assisted instruction. When using computer-assisted instruction, the teacher organizes the learning situation. He/she selects the targeted learning goal, situates the learning environment, and then allows exploratory time as students engage in learning. The teacher then monitors the learning activities and modifies the instructional level as needed to meet the various needs of the children involved.

Classroom teachers have the unique opportunity to infuse a variety of technological components with multisensory learning while situating the learning situation. One area where this is especially true is in the teaching of reading to young children. The research study being reported employed a teacher-centered, computer-assisted instructional technique that situated progressive reading material in an attempt to answer the following question:

Will a computerized multisensory approach to the teaching of reading increase first graders' vocabulary development?

Review of Literature

Many software programs offer "read alongs" and "edutainment" that assist students as they learn letter sounds, vocabulary concepts, comprehension, and to enjoy literature. Interactive multimedia allows the printed word to take on sight, sound, and action, which visually and mentally stimulates the individual.

One such program is DaisyQuest I and II (Mitchell, Chad & Stacy, 1984–2000). An in-depth study investigated the phonological awareness in preschool children utilizing this software (Brinkman & Torgesen, 1994). Each child in the treatment group interacted with a computerized story concerning "Daisy the friendly dragon." A computer, monitor, mouse, and standard headphone were provided to allow the child, as he/she listened to the story, to discover clues revealing where the dragon was hiding. The clues were revealed by correctly answering at least four correct answers in a row. The skills assessed were rhyming words, beginning sounds, ending sounds, middle sounds, and whether a word contained a given number of sounds. This study revealed that children in the treatment group responded at a higher and faster rate of reading readiness than children in the control group. Not only did the children in the treatment group gain knowledge to aid in their ability to read, these pre-schoolers had fun!

In another study, two literacy teachers (one a Reading Recovery teacher, the other a Title I reading teacher) wrote simple, predictable texts using the multimedia software HyperStudio (Wagner, 1978). These teachers created "talking books" for their students, with a focus on high-frequency words with graphics and animation to offer sight, sound, and movement. Students enjoyed experiencing the stories as the computer "read" the story to them as the cursor (pointing finger) touched each word. This process came full circle by the end of the school year, as these students were writing and reading their own stories. Students were then encouraged to use invented spelling, graphics, and sounds while they created their own stories using the Kid Pix Software program (Hickman, 1984–2000). "The computer serves as a motivational tool in their journey to literacy" (Eisenwine & Hunt, 2000, p. 456).

There are many reasons why computer-assisted reading instruction has been effective. The computer provides immediate responses and practice for the child learning a skill. Struggling readers interface with the computer and practice a skill without embarrassing situations in the classroom. Interaction with a multisensory format provides motivation and a positive attitude toward reading and learning (Case & Truscott, 1999; Forcier, 1999).

A word of caution accompanies much of the literature, warning educators to focus on the targeted instructional goals and not be "enchanted" by the entertainment that makes software packages so appealing (Case & Truscott, 1999; Sherry, 1996). While this multisensory approach is highly motivating for young readers, the instructional purpose is to enable them to become better readers. Educators should choose the types of software and technological resources carefully in order to maximize learning without being entangled in the "bells and whistles."

The benefits of using instructional technology include "an intrinsic need to learn technology…motivation increases engagement time…students move beyond knowledge and comprehension and into application and analysis…and students develop computer literacy by applying various computer skills as part of the learning process" (Dockstader, 1999, p. 73). As Ray and Wepner (2000) suggest, the question as to whether or not technology is the valuable educational resource we think it is may be a moot point because it is such an integral part of our lives. However, the question concerning the most productive methods of using technology in the classroom still needs to be addressed. Therefore, the purpose of this study was to investigate the effects of computer-assisted instruction on first-grade students' vocabulary development. Specifically, this study investigated the impact of the WiggleWorks program (CAST & Scholastic, 1994–1996) on first-grade students' vocabulary development.

Method

Sample

A first-grade classroom at a mid-Atlantic elementary school was selected for this research project. The subjects were 21 first-grade students. There were 10 boys and 11 girls involved in this study. The ethnic background of this class was as follows: 13 Caucasian students, six African American students, one Hispanic student, and one Pakistani student. Students were from a lower socioeconomic status and had limited exposure to educational experiences outside the school. The subjects were assigned to either the control or experimental group by using a table of random numbers and applying those numbers to the students. Ten students were assigned to the control group and 11 to the experimental group.

Computer-Assisted Program

The WiggleWorks (1994–1996) software program was used in this study. Co-developed by CAST and Scholastic, Inc., this program offers a literacy curriculum based on a combination of speech, sounds, graphics, text, and customizable access features. The software program features 72 trade books, audiocassettes, and a variety of computer-based activities. Students use the trade books and audiocassettes to read independently with or without the support of the audiocassette. Using the software program, students may listen to a story, read along with a story, or read a story silently. As they read, students are encouraged to review the suggested vocabulary words by selecting My Words. Students may listen to a pronunciation of the word by clicking on it or hear the word contextually in the story. Students may add new words to their vocabulary list by clicking on the selected word and the plus sign or remove words by clicking on the subtraction sign. Students may read and reread the story as they wish. Students may also create word families or practice spelling using a magnetic alphabet.

After listening to or reading a story, students have the option of composing their own stories. WiggleWorks provides a story starter, close-structured text, or free writing to help young students write their story. After composing a story, students may illustrate personal stories using basic drawing tools, stamps of the story characters, and/or story event backgrounds. Students may share their stories with others by recording their stories or printing the story and creating a book. These functions are available in a Read Aloud, Read, Write, My Book, and Magnet Board menu available to the individual user.

WiggleWorks is a managed instructional system. The management functions allow the teacher the opportunity to customize the computer-assisted instruction for each child. For instance, in Read Aloud, the settings can be adjusted so that the story is read to the student using a word-by-word, line-by-line, or whole-page approach. The management system also keeps a running log of individual and class activities. The Portfolio Management feature provides a reading record for each child (tracks the stories read, date and time individual stories were read, etc.), including reading and writing samples. The WiggleWorks software program provides a multimedia approach to literacy while supporting traditional methods with the accompanying trade books and audiocassettes.

Variables

The research project tested the independent variable of computer-assisted instruction on reading vocabulary development. Eleven students received the treatment monitored by one of the researchers. The dependent variable was a pre- and post-vocabulary test. The test was an independent word list administered by the researcher to the experimental and control groups at the beginning and end of each session.

Measurement

The instrument used to determine the effect of computer-assisted instruction on vocabulary was a pre- and posttest designed by one of the researchers. Six high-frequency vocabulary words from each of the seven stories were selected by the researcher and placed on an independent list. The independent list of words served as the pre- and post-vocabulary test for each. All results were compared to determine the effect the treatment had on these subjects.

Procedure

As a part of the regular curriculum, all students received reading vocabulary instruction. The teacher utilized the reading instructional curriculum adopted by the county, which consisted of reading textbooks, related materials, and charts provided by the publishing company. Students participated in daily reading instruction. Each student in the class was randomly assigned into two groups: a control group and an experimental group. In an attempt to limit extraneous learning, both groups continued to receive regular reading instruction by the researcher/teacher. The regular reading curriculum had a 20-min time block, where students participated in a DEAR (Drop Everything And Read) program. The researchers used this block of time to implement this research project.

Seven predetermined stories were used for this research project. The stories were available on book and tape as well as on interactive, computerized storyboards. The control group experienced the story in a variety of ways. First, they listened to the assigned story as the teacher/researcher read the story to them. Next, students listened to the story on tape and read along with an accompanying book. Last, students were provided with an assortment of literature: library books, classroom literature, or the students' personal books to read at their leisure after the predetermined book and tape assignment had been completed. During that 20-min time span, the 10 students in the experimental group visited the media computer lab and explored the same story using the computerized storyboard. A computer, monitor, mouse, and headphone were provided for each subject. During the first session, the teacher/researcher explained the working mechanics of the computer laboratory and answered any questions from the students. Then, the lessons began as students listened to enjoy the story. Next, the students revisited and identified words unknown to them by clicking on the word. The computerized storyboards served as a remediator. These subjects saw the printed word highlighted and heard it as the word was produced in sound. Students were required to listen to the story once while reading along.

After completing those requirements, students could listen to and/or read any story previously read or any story at a lower level. Students were introduced to a new WiggleWorks story every other day. During this project, students experimented with seven different stories that became progressively more challenging. The ability levels of the stories ranged from kindergarten to second grade. The project continued for 6 weeks.

Results

The results were analyzed using a paired-samples *t* test. An alpha level of .05 was set incorporating a two-tailed significance level. The analyses showed significant positive changes for both groups. The mean scores confirm that students using computerized storyboards demonstrate significant gains in their ability to recall a greater amount of new vocabulary words (see Table 1). The pre- and posttest were analyzed using a paired-samples *t* test. The results demonstrate a statistically significant difference ($p < .002$) in the experimental (computer) group. A significant difference ($p < .01$) was also found (see Table 2) in the control group (Book/Tape).

Table 1
Means and Standard Deviations

Group	Pretest		Posttest	
	M	*SD*	*M*	*SD*
Computer	3.7	4.37	16.9	13.17
Book/Tape	1.8	2.68	5.45	6.07

The mean scores of the pre- and post-vocabulary tests indicate a significant gain in the experimental (computer storyboard) group (MeanPre = 3.7; MeanPost = 16.9). A further analysis involving the reading ability of the individual students demonstrated that students with higher reading ability scored higher in the experimental and control groups than average-ability or low-ability students. Those students who were performing successfully in their reading scored significantly higher than those students who were performing at a lower level.

Table 2
Paired-Samples t Test

Group	*df*	*t*	*p*
Computer	9	4.18	0.002
Book/Tape	10	3.17	0.010

Discussion

The stories selected for this project were progressively more challenging so as to meet the needs of as many young readers as possible. Students with greater reading ability scored higher on the pretests and showed greater improvement on the posttests. These students seemed to possess a greater command of reading and technological skills required in maneuvering the storyboards.

Students with less reading ability did not gain as much from the experience. While they seemed to enjoy the stories, they were greatly challenged by the pre- and posttest. These students would have been more successful with stories developmentally appropriate for their reading ability. Overall, the ability level of the students in the classroom seemed to mirror their performance in the computer-based reading instruction. Strong readers worked somewhat independently, average-ability students were at an instructional level with reading and technology skills, while students with less reading ability needed assistance with reading and technology. Students in the experimental group (computer storyboards) were greatly motivated by the use of computers. They enjoyed the interactive, multisensory aspect of learning. This was evidenced by the students' request to spend more time listening to stories on the computers. Multisensory teaching seemed to make their learning fun.

Implications and Significance

This research project was designed to investigate the effects of computer-assisted instruction on first-

385 grade students' vocabulary development. With the integration of sights, colors, sounds, actions, plus the printed word, vocabulary lessons took on a new meaning. Students recognized the word on sight, remembered the word through association and phonemes, and

390 quite a few could use the word as a part of their spoken and written vocabulary. Students were able to recognize the words in isolation and in text.

Overall, implications of this research project are that a 20-min DEAR time using computerized story-

395 boards directly results in improved vocabulary development among first-grade students. Learning new vocabulary words took place at a faster pace with greater accuracy than with the direct teaching format. "Technology brings to your classroom the capability of con-

400 necting dynamic, interactive vocabulary learning with reading, writing, spelling, and content learning" (Fox & Mitchell, 2000, p. 66).

Computerized classroom instruction does not imply inflated test scores or a magic potion for teaching. It is

405 a motivating medium that enhances good teaching. The infusion of technology and literacy is a lifelong learning gift we create for our students.

Recommendations

Computer-assisted instruction has a positive influence on students' motivation, interest, and learning.

410 This research project validates the effect that computer-assisted instruction has on first graders' vocabulary development during a crucial time when they are learning to read. To improve upon this study, a concentrated effort should be made to determine the developmental

415 reading level of each student. Students could then receive more individualized instruction at their appropriate reading level. Additionally, teachers/researchers need to move students from dependent direct instruction to more independent learning. A natural follow-up

420 to this study could be to see if this move to more independent learning is facilitated by differing uses of technology in the classroom.

References

Brinkman, D., & Torgeson, J. (1994). Computer administered instruction in phonological awareness: Evaluation of the DaisyQuest program. *The Journal of Research and Development in Education, 27*(2), 126–137.

Case, C., & Truscott, D. M. (1999). The lure of bells and whistles: Choosing the best software to support reading instruction. *Reading and Writing Quarterly, 15*(4), p. 361.

Chall, J. (1992). The new reading debates: Evidence from science, art, and ideology. *Teachers College Record, 94*(2), 315.

Czubaj, C. (1997). Whole language literature reading instruction. *Education, 117*(4), 538.

Daniels, H., & Zemelman, S. (1999). Whole language works: Sixty years of research. *Educational Research, 57*(2), 32.

Dillon, D. R. (2000). Identifying beliefs and knowledge, uncovering tensions, and solving problems. *Kids' insight: Reconsidering how to meet the literacy needs of all students* (pp. 72–79). Newark, DE: International Reading Association.

Dockstader, J. (1999). Teachers of the 21st century know the what, why, and how of technology integration. *T.H.E. Journal, 26*(6), 73–74.

Eisenwine, M. J., & Hunt, D. A. (2000). Using a computer in literacy groups with emergent readers. *The Reading Teacher, 53*(6), 456.

Forcier, R. C. (1999). Computer applications in education. *The computer as an educational tool* (pp. 60–93). Upper Saddle, NJ: Prentice-Hall, Inc.

Fox, B. J., & Mitchell, M. J. (2000). Using technology to support word recognition, spelling, and vocabulary acquisition. In R. Thurlow, W. J. Valmont,

& S. B. Wepner (Eds.). *Linking Literacy and Technology.* Newark, DL: International Reading Association, Inc.

Hickman, C. (1984–2000). Kid Pix. Deluxe Version. [Unpublished computer software]. Available: http://www.pixelpoppin.com/kidpix/index.html

Hoffman, J., & Pearson, P. D. (2000). Reading teacher education in the next millennium: What your grandmother's teacher didn't know that your granddaughter's teacher should. *Reading Research Quarterly, 35*(1), 28–44.

Howard, B. C., McGee, S., Purcell, S., & Schwartz, N. (2000). The experience of constructivism: Transforming teacher epistemology. *Journal of Research on Computing in Education, 32*(4), 455–465.

Kinzer, C. K., & Leu, D. J. (1999). *Effective Literacy Instruction.* Upper Saddle River, NJ: Prentice-Hall, Inc.

Mitchell, C., & S. (1984–2000). DaisyQuest. [Unpublished computer software]. Available: http://www.greatwave.com/html/daisys.html

Morrow, L. M., & Tracey, D. H. (1997). Strategies used for phonics instruction in early childhood classrooms. *The Reading Teacher, 50*(8), 644.

Ray, L. C., & Wepner, S. B. (2000). Using technology for reading development. In R. Thurlow, W. J. Valmont, & S. B. Wepner (Eds.). *Linking Literacy and Technology.* Newark, DL: International Reading Association, Inc.

Sherry, L. (1996). Issues in distance learning. *International Journal of Educational Telecommunications, 1*(4), 337–365.

Wagner, R. (1978). HyperStudio. [Unpublished computer software]. Available: http://www.hyperstudio.com/

WiggleWorks [Computer Software]. (1994–1996). New York: CAST and Scholastic, Inc.

Exercise for Article 10

Factual Questions

1. What is the research question explored by this study?

2. What "caution" is mentioned in the Review of Literature?

3. How many students participated in this study?

4. Who designed the instrument used in this study?

5. What is the value of the posttest mean for the book/tape group?

6. Were the gains by the experimental group statistically significant? If yes, at what probability level?

Questions for Discussion

7. The first five paragraphs provide a general background for the study. The use of computers is introduced in the sixth paragraph. In your opinion, how important are the first five paragraphs in establishing a context for the study?

8. The researchers state that the students were assigned at random to one of the two groups. How important is this? Would it be better to use a different method for assigning students? Explain. (See lines 211–216.)

9. In your opinion, is the Procedure described in sufficient detail? Explain. (See lines 282–331.)

10. Has this study convinced you of the superiority of computer-assisted instruction for improving vocabulary development? Explain.

11. If you were conducting a study on the same topic, what changes in the research methodology, if any, would you make?

Quality Ratings

Directions: Indicate your level of agreement with each of the following statements by circling a number from 5 for strongly agree (SA) to 1 for strongly disagree (SD). If you believe an item is not applicable to this research article, leave it blank. Be prepared to explain your ratings.

A. The introduction establishes the importance of the study.

  SA   5   4   3   2   1   SD

B. The literature review establishes the context for the study.

  SA   5   4   3   2   1   SD

C. The research purpose, question, or hypothesis is clearly stated.

  SA   5   4   3   2   1   SD

D. The method of sampling is sound.

  SA   5   4   3   2   1   SD

E. Relevant demographics (for example, age, gender, and ethnicity) are described.

  SA   5   4   3   2   1   SD

F. Measurement procedures are adequate.

  SA   5   4   3   2   1   SD

G. All procedures have been described in sufficient detail to permit a replication of the study.

  SA   5   4   3   2   1   SD

H. The participants have been adequately protected from potential harm.

  SA   5   4   3   2   1   SD

I. The results are clearly described.

  SA   5   4   3   2   1   SD

J. The discussion/conclusion is appropriate.

  SA   5   4   3   2   1   SD

K. Despite any flaws, the report is worthy of publication.

  SA   5   4   3   2   1   SD

Article 11

The Effect of a Computer Simulation Activity versus a Hands-on Activity on Product Creativity in Technology Education

KURT Y. MICHAEL
Central Shenandoah Valley Regional Governor's School, Virginia

Computer use in the classroom has become a popular method of instruction for many technology educators. This may be due to the fact that software programs have advanced beyond the early days of drill and
5 practice instruction. With the introduction of the graphical user interface, increased processing speed, and affordability, computer use in education has finally come of age. Software designers are now able to design multidimensional educational programs that include
10 high-quality graphics, stereo sound, and real time interaction (Bilan, 1992). One area of noticeable improvement is computer simulations.

Computer simulations are software programs that either replicate or mimic real world phenomena. If im-
15 plemented correctly, computer simulations can help students learn about technological events and processes that may otherwise be unattainable due to cost, feasibility, or safety. Studies have shown that computer simulators can:

20 1. Be equally as effective as real life, hands-on laboratory experiences in teaching students scientific concepts (Choi & Gennaro, 1987).
2. Enhance the learning achievement levels of students (Betz, 1996).
25 3. Enhance the problem-solving skills of students (Gokhale, 1996).
4. Foster peer interaction (Bilan, 1992).

The educational benefits of computer simulations for learning are promising. Some researchers even sus-
30 pect that computer simulations may enhance creativity (e.g., Betz, 1996; Gokhale, 1996; Harkow, 1996); however, after an extensive review of literature, no empirical research has been found to support this claim. For this reason, the following study was conducted to com-
35 pare the effect of a computer simulation activity versus a traditional hands-on activity on students' product creativity.

Background

Product Creativity in Technology Education

Historically, technology educators have chosen the creation of products or projects as a means to teach
40 technological concepts (Knoll, 1997). Olson (1973), in describing the important role projects play in the industrial arts/technology classroom, remarked, "The project represents human creative achievement with materials and ideas and results in an experience of self-
45 fulfillment" (p. 21). Lewis (1999) reiterated this belief by stating, "Technology is in essence a manifestation of human creativity. Thus, an important way in which students can come to understand it would be by engaging in acts of technological creation" (p. 46). The result
50 of technological creation is the creative product.

The creative product embodies the very essence of technology. The American Association for the Advancement of Science (Johnson, 1989) stated, "Technology is best described as a process, but is most com-
55 monly known by its products and their effects on society" (p. 1). A product can be described as a physical object, article, patent, theoretical system, an equation, or new technique (Brogden & Sprecher, 1964). A creative product is one that possesses some degree of un-
60 usualness (originality) and usefulness (Moss, 1966). When given the opportunity for self-expression, a student's project becomes nothing less than a creative product.

The creative product can be viewed as a physical
65 representation of a person's "true" creative ability encapsulating both the creative person and process (Besemer & O'Quin, 1993). By examining the literature related to the creative person and process, technology educators may gain a deeper understanding of the crea-
70 tive product itself.

The Creative Person

Inventors such as Edison and Ford have been recognized as being highly creative. Why some people reach a level of creative genius while others do not is still unknown. However, Maslow (1962), after studying
75 several of his subjects, determined that all people are

creative, not in the sense of creating great works, but rather, creative in a universal sense that attributes a portion of creative talent to every person. In trying to understand and predict a person's creative ability, two factors have often been considered: intelligence and personality.

Intelligence

A frequently asked question among educators is "What is the relationship between creativity and intelligence?" Research has shown that there is no direct correlation between creativity and intelligence quotient (I.Q.) (Edmunds, 1990; Hayes, 1990; Moss, 1966; Torrance, 1963). Edmunds (1990) conducted a study to determine whether there was a relationship between creativity and I.Q. Two hundred and eighty-one randomly selected students, grades eight to eleven, from three different schools in New Brunswick, Canada, participated. The instruments used to collect data were the *Torrance Test of Creative Thinking* and the *Otis-Lennon School Ability Test*, used to test intellectual ability. Based on a Pearson product moment analysis, results showed that I.Q. scores did not significantly correlate with creativity scores. The findings were consistent with the literature dealing with creativity and intelligence.

On a practical level, findings similar to the one above may explain why I.Q. measures have proven to be unsuccessful in predicting creative performance. Hayes (1990) pointed out that creative performance may be better predicted by isolating and investigating personality traits.

Personality Traits

Researchers have shown that there are certain personality traits associated with creative people (e.g., DeVore, Horton, & Lawson, 1989; Hayes, 1990; Runco, Nemiro, & Walberg, 1998; Stein, 1974). Runco, Nemiro, and Walberg (1998) identified and conducted a survey investigating personality traits associated with the creative person. The survey was mailed to 400 individuals who had submitted papers and/or published articles related to creativity. The researchers asked participants to rate, in order of importance, various traits that they believed affected creative achievement. The survey contained 16 creative achievement clusters consisting of 141 items. One hundred and forty-three surveys were returned reflecting a response of 35.8%. Results demonstrated that intrinsic motivation, problem finding, and questioning skills were considered the most important traits in predicting and identifying creative achievement. Though personality traits play an important part in understanding creative ability, an equally important area of creativity theory lies in the identification of the creative process itself.

The Creative Process

Creativity is a process (Hayes, 1990; Stein, 1974; Taylor, 1959; Torrance, 1963) that has been represented using various models. Wallas (1926) offered one of the earliest explanations of the creative process. His model consisted of four stages that are briefly described below:

1. Preparation: This is the first stage in which an individual identifies then investigates a problem from many different angles.
2. Incubation: At this stage the individual stops all conscious work related to the problem.
3. Illumination: This stage is characterized by a sudden or immediate solution to the problem.
4. Verification: This is the last stage at which time the solution is tested.

Wallas' model has served as a foundation upon which other models have been built. Some researchers have added the communication stage to the creative process (e.g., Stein, 1974; Taylor, 1959; Torrance, 1966). The communication stage is the final stage of the creative process. At this stage, the new idea confined to one's mind is transformed into a verbal or nonverbal product. The product is then shared within a social context in order that others may react to and possibly accept or reject it. A more comprehensive description of the creative process is captured within a definition offered by Torrance (1966):

> Creativity is a process of becoming sensitive to problems, deficiencies, gaps in knowledge, missing elements, disharmonies, and so on; identifying the difficult; searching for solutions, making guesses or formulating hypotheses about the deficiencies, testing and re-testing these hypotheses and possibly modifying and re-testing them, and finally communicating the results (p. 8).

Torrance's definition resembles what some have referred to as problem solving. For example, technology educators Savage and Sterry (1990), generalizing from the work of several scholars, identified six steps to the problem-solving process:

- Defining the problem: Analyzing, gathering information, and establishing limitations that will isolate and identify the need or opportunity.
- Developing alternative solutions: Using principles, ideation, and brainstorming to develop alternate ways to meet the opportunity or solve the problem.
- Selecting a solution: Selecting the most plausible solution by identifying, modifying, and/or combining ideas from the group of possible solutions.
- Implementing and evaluating the solution: Modeling, operating, and assessing the effectiveness of the selected solution.
- Redesigning the solution: Incorporating improvements into the design of the solution that address needs identified during the evaluation phase.

185   • Interpreting the solution: Synthesizing and communicating the characteristics and operating parameters of the solution (p. 15).

By closely comparing Torrance's (1966) definition of creativity with that of Savage and Sterry's (1990)
190   problem-solving process, one can easily see similarities between the descriptions. Guilford (1976), a leading expert in the study of creativity, made a similar comparison between steps of the creative process offered by Wallas (1926) with those of the problem-solving
195   process proposed by the noted educational philosopher, John Dewey. In doing so, Guilford simply concluded that "Problem solving is creative; there is no other kind" (p. 98).

Hinton (1968) combined the creative process and
200   problem-solving process into what is now known as creative problem solving. He believed that creativity would be better understood if placed within a problem-solving structure. Creative problem solving is a subset of problem solving based on the assumption that not all
205   problems require a creative solution. He surmised that when a problem is solved with a learned response, no creativity has been expressed. However, when a simple problem is solved with an insightful response, a small measure of creativity has been expressed; when a com-
210   plex problem is solved with a novel solution, genuine creativity has occurred.

Genuine creativity is the result of the creative process that manifests itself into a creative product. Understanding the creative process as well as the creative
215   person may play an important role in realizing the true nature of the creative product. Though researchers have not reached a consensus as to what attributes make up the creative product (Besemer & Treffingger, 1981; Joram, Woodruff, Bryson, & Lindsay, 1992; Stein,
220   1974), identifying and evaluating the creative product has been a concern of some researchers. Notable is the work of Moss (1966) and Duenk (1966).

Evaluating the Creative Product in Industrial Arts/ Technology Education

Moss (1966) and Duenk (1966) have arguably conducted the most extensive research establishing criteria
225   for evaluating creative products within industrial arts/technology education. Moss (1966), in examining the criterion problem, concluded that unusualness (originality) and usefulness were the defining characteristics of the creative product produced by industrial
230   arts students. A description of his model is presented below:

1. Unusualness: To be creative, a product must possess some degree of unusualness [or originality]. The quality of unusualness may, theoretically, be
235   measured in terms of probability of occurrence; the less the probability of its occurrence, the more unusual the product (Moss, 1966, p. 7).

2. Usefulness: While some degree of unusualness is a necessary requirement for creative products, it is
240   not a sufficient condition. To be creative, an industrial arts student's product must also satisfy the minimal principle requirements of the problem situation; to some degree it must "work" or be potentially "workable." Completely ineffective, ir-
245   relevant solutions to teacher-imposed or student-initiated problems are not creative (Moss, 1966, p. 7).

3. Combining Unusualness and Usefulness: When a product possesses some degree of both unusual-
250   ness and usefulness, it is creative. But because these two criterion qualities are considered variables, the degree of creativity among products will also vary. The extent of each product's departure from the typical and its value as a problem solu-
255   tion will, in combination, determine the degree of creativity of each product. Giving the two qualities equal weight, as the unusualness and/or usefulness of a product increases so does its rated creativity; similarly, as the product approaches the conven-
260   tional and/or uselessness its rated creativity decreases (Moss, 1966, p. 8).

In establishing the construct validity of his theoretical model, Moss (1966) submitted his work for review to 57 industrial arts educators, two measurement spe-
265   cialists, and six educational psychologists. Results of the review found the proposed model was compatible with existing theory and practice of both creativity and industrial arts. No one disagreed with the major premise of using unusualness and usefulness as defining
270   characteristics for evaluating the creative products of industrial arts students.

To date, little additional research has been conducted to establish criteria for evaluating the creative products of industrial arts and/or technology education
275   students. If technology is best known by its creative products, then technology educators are obligated to identify characteristics that make a product more or less creative. Furthermore, educators must find ways to objectively measure these attributes and then teach
280   students in a manner that enhances the creativity of their products. A possible approach to enhancing product creativity is by incorporating computer simulation technology into the classroom. However, no research has been done in this area to measure the true effect of
285   computer simulation on product creativity. For that reason, other studies addressing computer use in general and product creativity will be explored.

Studies Related to Computers and the Creative Product

A study conducted by Joram, Woodruff, Bryson, and Lindsay (1992) found that average students pro-
290   duced their most creative work using word processors as compared to students using pencil and paper. The researchers hypothesized that word processing would hinder product creativity due to constant evaluation and

editing of their work. To test the hypothesis, average and above-average eighth-grade writers were randomly assigned to one of two groups. The first group was asked to compose using word processors while the second group was asked to compose using pencil and paper. After collecting the compositions, both the word-processed and handwritten texts were typed so that they would be in the same format for the evaluators. Based on the results, the researchers concluded that word processing enhances the creative abilities of average writers. The researchers attributed this to the prospect that word processing may allow the average writer to generate a number of ideas, knowing that only a few of them will be usable and the rest can be easily erased. However, the researchers also found that word processing had a negative effect on the creativity of above-average writers. These mixed results suggest that the use of word processing may not be appropriate for all students relative to creativity.

Similar to word processing, computer graphics programs may also help students improve the creativeness of their products. In a study conducted by Howe (1992), two advanced undergraduate classes in graphics design were assigned to one of two treatments. The first treatment group was instructed to use a computer graphic program to complete a design project whereas the other group was asked to use conventional graphic design equipment to design their product. Upon completion of the assignment, both groups' projects were collected and photocopied so that they would be in the same format before being evaluated. Based on the results, the researcher concluded that students using computer graphics technology surpassed the conventional method in product creativity. The researchers attributed this to the prospect that computer graphics programs may enable graphic designers to generate an abundance of ideas, then capture the most creative ones and incorporate them into their designs. However, due to a lack of random assignment, results of the study should be generalized with caution.

Like word processing and computer graphics, simulation technology is a type of computer application that allows users to freely manipulate and edit virtual objects. Thus, it was surmised that computer simulation may enhance creativity. This notion led to the development of the study reported herein.

Purpose of the Study

This study compared the effect of a computer simulation activity versus a traditional hands-on activity on students' product creativity. A creative product was defined as one that possesses some measure of both unusualness (originality) and usefulness. The following hypothesis and sub-hypotheses were examined.

Major Research Hypothesis

There is no difference in product *creativity* between the computer simulation and traditional hands-on groups.

Research Sub-Hypotheses

1. There is no difference in product *originality* between the computer simulation and traditional hands-on groups.
2. There is no difference in product *usefulness* between the computer simulation and traditional hands-on groups.

Method

Subjects

The subjects selected for this study were seventh-grade technology education students from three different middle schools located in Northern Virginia, a middle-to-upper-income suburb outside of Washington, D.C. The school system's middle school technology education programs provide learning situations that allow the students to explore technology through problem-solving activities. The three participating schools were chosen because of the teachers' willingness to participate in the study.

Materials

Kits of *Classic Lego Bricks*™ were used with the hands-on group. The demonstration version of *Gryphon Bricks*™ (Gryphon Software Corporation, 1996) was used with the simulation group. This software allows students to assemble and disassemble computer-generated Lego-type bricks in a virtual environment on the screen of the computer. Subjects in the computer simulation group were each assigned to a Macintosh computer on which the *Gryphon Bricks* software was installed. Each subject in the hands-on treatment group was given a container of Lego bricks identical to those available virtually in the Gryphon software.

Test Instrument

Products were evaluated based on a theoretical model proposed by Moss (1966). Moss used the combination of *unusualness* (or originality) and *usefulness* as criteria for determining product creativity. However, Moss' actual instrument was not used in this study due to low inter-rater reliability. Instead, a portion of the *Creative Product Semantic Scale* or *CPSS* (Besemer & O'Quin, 1989) was used to determine product creativity. Sub-scales "Original" and "Useful" from the *CPSS* were chosen to be consistent with Moss' theoretical model.

The *CPSS* has proven to be a reliable instrument in evaluating a variety of creative products based on objective, analytical measures of creativity (Besemer & O'Quin, 1986, 1987, 1989, 1993). This was accomplished by the use of a bipolar, semantic differential scale. In general, semantic differential scales are good for measuring mental concepts or images (Alreck, 1995). Because creativity is a mental concept, the semantic differential naturally lends itself to measuring the creative product. Furthermore, the *CPSS* is flexible enough to allow researchers to pick various subscales based on the theoretical construct being investigated,

400 like the use of the "Original" and "Useful" subscales in this study. In support of this, Besemer and O'Quin (1986) stated, "… the subscale structure of the total scale lends itself to administration of relevant portions of the instrument rather than the whole" (p. 125).

405 The *CPSS* was used in a study conducted by Howe (1992). His reliability analysis, based on Cronbach's alpha coefficient, yielded good to high reliability across all subscales of the *CPSS*. Important to this study were the high reliability results for subscales
410 "Original" (.93) and "Useful" (.92). These high reliability coefficients are consistent with earlier studies conducted by Besemer and O'Quin (1986, 1987, 1989).

The Pilot Study

A pilot study was conducted in which a seventh-grade technology education class from a Southwest
415 Virginia middle school was selected. The pilot study consisted of 16 subjects who were randomly assigned to either a hands-on treatment group or a simulation treatment group. As a result of the pilot study, the time allocated for the students to assemble their creative
420 products was reduced from 30 minutes to 25 minutes because most of them had finished within the shorter time. Precedence for limiting the time needed to complete a creative task was found in Torrance's (1966) work in which 30 minutes was the time limit for a vari-
425 ety of approaches to measuring creativity.

Procedure

One class from each of the three participating schools was selected for the study. Fifty-eight subjects participated, 21 females and 37 males, with an average age of 12.4 years. Subjects were given identification
430 numbers, then randomly assigned to either the hands-on or the computer simulation treatment group. The random assignment helped ensure the equivalence of groups and controlled for extraneous variables such as students' prior experience with open-ended problem-
435 solving activities, use of Lego blocks and/or computer simulation programs, and other extraneous variables that may have confounded the results. The independent variable in this study was the instructional activity and the dependent variable was the subjects' creative prod-
440 uct scores as determined by the combination of the "Original" and "Useful" subscales from the *CPSS* (Besemer & O'Quin, 1989).

Subjects in both the hands-on and the simulation groups were asked to construct a "creature" that they
445 believed would be found on a Lego planet. The "creature" scenario was chosen because it was an open-ended problem and possessed the greatest potential for imaginative student expression. The only difference in treatment between the two groups was that the hands-
450 on group used real Lego bricks in constructing their products whereas the simulation treatment group used a computer simulator. Treatments were administered simultaneously and overall treatment time was the same for both groups. The hands-on treatment group

455 met in its regular classroom whereas the simulation treatment group met in a computer lab. The classroom teacher at each school proctored the hands-on treatment group and the researcher proctored the simulation treatment group.

460 The subjects in the hands-on treatment group were given five minutes to sort their bricks by color while subjects in the simulation treatment group watched a five-minute instructional video explaining how to use the simulation software. By having the students sort
465 their bricks for five minutes, the overall treatment time was the same for both groups, thus eliminating a variable that may otherwise influence the results. Then, the subjects in both groups were given the following scenario:

470 Pretend you are a toy designer working for the Lego Company. Your job is to create a "creature" using Lego bricks that will be used in a toy set called Lego Planet. What types of creatures might be found on a Lego planet? Use your creativity and make a creature that is
475 *original* in appearance yet *useful* to the toy manufacturer.

One more thing: The creature you construct must be able to fit within a five-inch cubed box. That means you must stay within the limits of your green base plate and make your creature no higher than 13 bricks.

480 You will have 25 minutes to complete this activity. If you finish early, spend more time thinking about how you can make your creature more creative. You must remain in your seat the whole time. If there are no questions, you may begin.

485 When the time was up, the subjects were asked to stop working. The hands-on treatment group's products were labeled, collected, and then reproduced in the computer simulation software by the researcher. This was done so that the raters could not distinguish from
490 which treatment group the products were created. Finally, the images of the products from both groups were printed using a color printer.

Product Evaluation

To evaluate the students' solutions, two raters were recruited: a middle school art teacher and a middle
495 school science teacher. The teachers were chosen because of their willingness to participate in the study and had a combined total of 36 years of teaching experience. To help establish inter-rater reliability, a rater training session was conducted during the pilot study.
500 The same teacher-raters used in the pilot study were used in the final study. The training session provided the teacher-raters with instructions on how to use the rating instrument and allowed them to practice rating sample products. During the session, disagreements on
505 product ratings were discussed and rules were developed by the raters to increase consistency. The pilot study confirmed that there was good inter-rater reliability across all the scales and thus the experimental procedures proceeded as designed. No significant differ-

ence in creativity, originality, or usefulness was found between the two treatment groups during the pilot study.

For the actual study, the teacher–raters were each given the printed images of the products from each of the 58 subjects and were instructed to independently rate them using the "Original" and "Useful" subscales of the *CPSS* (Besemer & O'Quin, 1989). Three weeks were allowed for the rating process.

Findings

Once the ratings from the two raters had been obtained, an inter-rater reliability analysis, based on Cronbach's alpha coefficient, was conducted. Analysis yielded moderate to good inter-rater reliability (.74 to .88) across all the scales. The stated hypotheses were then tested using one-way analysis of variance (ANOVA).

- No difference in product *Creativity* scores was found between the computer simulation group ($M = 41.7$, $SD = 7.67$) and the hands-on group ($M = 42.0$, $SD = 5.58$). Therefore, the null hypothesis was not rejected, $F(5,52) = 0.54$, $p = 0.75$.

- No difference in product *Originality* scores was found between the computer simulation group ($M = 20.59$, $SD = 4.44$) and the hands-on group ($M = 21.10$, $SD = 3.10$). Thus, the null hypothesis was not rejected, $F(5,52) = 1.07$, $p = 0.39$.

- No difference in product *Usefulness* scores was found between the computer simulation group ($M = 21.15$, $SD = 4.17$) and the traditional hands-on group ($M = 20.90$, $SD = 3.20$). Once again, the researcher failed to reject the null hypothesis, $F(5,52) = 0.49$, $p = 0.78$.

Conclusion

Though there are only a few empirical studies to support their claims, some researchers believe that computers in general may improve student product creativity by allowing students to generate an abundance of ideas, capture the most creative ones, and incorporate them into their product (Howe, 1992; Joram, Woodruff, Bryson, & Lindsay, 1992). Similarly, some researchers speculate that the use of computer simulations may enhance product creativity as well (Betz, 1996; Gokhale, 1996; Harkow, 1996). However, based on the results of this study, the use of computer simulation to enhance product creativity was not supported. The creativity, usefulness, or originality of the resulting products appears to be the same whether students use a computer simulation of Lego blocks or whether they manipulated the actual blocks.

Because the simulation activity in this study was nearly identical to the hands-on task, one might conclude that product creativity may be more reliant upon the individual's creative cognitive ability rather than the tools or means by which the product was created.

This would stand to reason based on Besemer and O'Quin's (1993) belief that the creative product is unique in that it combines both the creative person and process into a tangible object representing the "true" measure of a person's creative ability. With this in mind, when studying a computer simulation's effect on student product creativity, researchers may want to focus more attention on the creative person's traits and the cognitive process used to create the product rather than focusing on the tool or means by which the product was created. This approach to understanding student product creativity may lend itself more to qualitative rather than quantitative research.

If quantitative research is to continue in this area of study, researchers may wish to consider using a different theoretical model and instrument for measuring the creative product. For example, if replicating this experiment, rather than using only the two subscales of the *Creative Product Semantic Scale* (Bessemer & O'Quin, 1989), the complete instrument might be used, yielding additional dimensions of creativity. Additional research regarding the various types of simulation programs is needed, along with the different effects they might have on student creativity in designing products. The use of computer simulations in technology education programs appears to be increasing with little research to support their effectiveness or viable use.

References

Alreck, T. L., & Settle, B. R. (1995). *The survey research handbook* (2nd Ed.). Chicago: Irwin Inc.

Besemer, S. P., & O'Quin, K. (1993). Assessing creative products: Progress and potentials. In S. G. Isaksen (Ed.), *Nurturing and developing creativity: The emergence of a discipline* (pp. 331–349). Norwood, New Jersey: Ablex Publishing Corp.

Besemer, S. P. & O'Quin, K. (1989). The development, reliability, and validity of the revised creative product semantic scale. *Creativity Research Journal, 2*, 268–279.

Besemer, S. P., & O'Quin, K. (1987). Creative product analysis. Testing a model by developing a judging instrument. In S. G. Isaksen, *Frontiers of creativity research: Beyond the basics.* (pp. 341–357). Buffalo, NY: Bearly Ltd.

Besemer, S. P., & O'Quin, K. (1986). Analysis of creative products: Refinement and test of a judging instrument. *Journal of Creative Behavior, 20*(2), 115–126.

Besemer, S. P., & Treffinger, D. (1981). Analysis of creative products: Review and synthesis. *Journal of Creative Behavior, 15*, 158–178.

Betz, J. A. (1996). Computer games: Increase learning in an interactive multi-disciplinary environment. *Journal of Technology Systems, 24*(2), 195–205.

Bilan, B. (1992). *Computer simulations: An integrated tool.* Paper presented at the SAGE/6th Canadian Symposium, The University of Calgary.

Brogden, H., & Sprecher, T. (1964). Criteria of creativity. In C. W. Taylor. *Creativity, progress and potential.* New York: McGraw Hill.

Choi, B., & Gennaro, E. (1987). The effectiveness of using computer simulated experiments on junior high students' understanding of the volume displacement concept. *Journal of Research in Science Teaching, 24*(6), 539–552.

DeVore, P., Horton, A., & Lawson, A. (1989). *Creativity, design, and technology.* Worcester, Massachusetts: Davis Publications, Inc.

Duenk, L. G. (1966). *A study of the concurrent validity of the Minnesota Test of Creative Thinking, Abbr. Form VII, for eighth-grade industrial arts students.* Minneapolis: Minnesota University. (Report No. BR-5-0113).

Edmunds, A. L. (1990). Relationships among adolescent creativity, cognitive development, intelligence, and age. *Canadian Journal of Special Education, 6*(1), 61–71.

Gokhale, A. A. (1996). Effectiveness of computer simulation for enhancing higher order thinking. *Journal of Industrial Teacher Education, 33*(4), 36–46.

Gryphon Software Corporation (1996). *Gryphon Bricks Demo* (Version 1.0) [Computer Software]. Glendale, CA: Knowledge Adventure. [On-line] Available: http://www.kidsdomain.com/down/mac/bricksdemo.html

Guilford, J. (1976). Intellectual factors in productive thinking. In R. Mooney & T. Rayik (Eds.), *Explorations in creativity*. New York: Harper & Row.

Harkow, R. M. (1996). *Increasing creative thinking skills in second and third grade gifted students using imagery, computers, and creative problem solving*. Unpublished master's thesis, NOVA Southeastern University.

Hayes, J. R. (1990). *Cognitive processes in creativity*. (Paper No. 18). University of California, Berkeley.

Hinton, B. L. (1968, Spring). A model for the study of creative problem solving. *Journal of Creative Behavior*, 2(2), 133–142.

Howe, R. (1992). Uncovering the creative dimensions of computer-graphic design products. *Creativity Research Journal*, 5(3), 233–243.

Johnson, J. R. (1989). *Project 2061: Technology* (Association for the Advancement of Science Publication 89-06S). Washington, DC: American Association for the Advancement of Science.

Joram, E., Woodruff, E., Bryson, M., & Lindsay, P. (1992). The effects of revising with a word processor on writing composition. *Research in the Teaching of English*, 26(2), 167–192.

Knoll, M. (1997). The project method: Its vocational education origin and international development. *Journal of Industrial Teacher Education*, 34(3), 59–80.

Lewis, T. (1999). Research in technology education: Some areas of need. *Journal of Technology Education*, 10(2), 41–56.

Maslow, A. (1962). *Toward a psychology of being*. Princeton, NJ: Van Nostrand.

Moss, J. (1966). *Measuring creative abilities in junior high school industrial arts*. Washington, DC: American Council on Industrial Arts Teacher Education.

Olson, D. W. (1973). *Tecnol-o-gee*. Raleigh: North Carolina University School of Education, Office of Publications.

Runco, R. A., Nemiro, J., & Walberg, H. J. (1998). Personal explicit theories of creativity. *Journal of Creative Behavior*, 32(1), 1–17.

Savage, E., & Sterry, L. (1990). *A conceptual framework for technology education*. Reston, VA: International Technology Education Association.

Stein, M. (1974). *Stimulating creativity: Vol. 1. Individual procedures*. New York: Academic Press.

Taylor, I. A. (1959). The nature of the creative process. In P. Smith (Ed.), *Creativity: An examination of the creative process* (pp. 51–82). New York: Hastings House Publishers.

Torrance, E. P. (1966). *Torrance test on creative thinking: Norms-technical manual* (Research Edition). Lexington, MA: Personal Press.

Torrance, E. P. (1963). Creativity. In F. W. Hubbard (Ed.), *What research says to the teacher* (Number 28). Washington, DC: Department of Classroom Teachers American Educational Research Association of the National Education Association.

Wallas, G. (1926). *The art of thought*. New York: Harcourt, Brace and Company.

About the author: Kurt Y. Michael is a technology education teacher at Central Shenandoah Valley Regional Governor's School, Fishersville, Virginia. E-mail: michael@csvrgs.k12.va.us

Exercise for Article 11

Factual Questions

1. According to Moss (1966), a creative product is one that possesses what two things?

2. What two factors does the researcher mention as being often considered when trying to understand and predict creative ability?

3. The researcher cites a study in which the effects of word processors on creativity were evaluated. Were the results of this study conclusive? Explain.

4. The subjects were drawn from how many different middle schools?

5. *CPSS* stands for what words?

6. What does the researcher identify as "the independent variable in this study"?

7. ANOVA stands for what words?

8. What was the mean *Originality* score of the hands-on group?

Questions for Discussion

9. The researcher cites a reference published in 1926. Do you think this helps provide a historical context for this study? Do you think that providing a historical context is important? Explain. (See lines 130–144.)

10. The literature review is longer than those in the other research articles in this book. Do you think it is about the right length given the nature of this study? Explain.

11. The major research hypothesis and the research sub-hypotheses predict "no difference." Is this what you would have predicted in hypotheses if you had conducted the study? Explain. (See lines 344–354.)

12. In your opinion, are the materials used in this study described in sufficient detail? Explain. (See lines 365–376.)

13. To what extent does the fact that the researcher conducted a pilot study increase your overall evaluation of the study? (See lines 413–425.)

14. The researcher assigned students at random to the two groups. Do you agree with him that this was a desirable way to assign the students? Explain. (See lines 429–437.)

15. The researcher describes the inter-rater reliability as good. Do you agree? Explain. (See lines 506–509.)

16. Despite the findings of no differences between the groups, do you think that additional quantitative research should be conducted on this topic? Explain. (Consider the researcher's discussion of this issue in lines 519–542 before answering this question.)

Quality Ratings

Directions: Indicate your level of agreement with each of the following statements by circling a number from 5 for strongly agree (SA) to 1 for strongly disagree (SD). If you believe an item is not applicable to this research article, leave it blank. Be prepared to explain your ratings.

A. The introduction establishes the importance of the study.

      SA   5   4   3   2   1   SD

B. The literature review establishes the context for the study.

      SA   5   4   3   2   1   SD

C. The research purpose, question, or hypothesis is clearly stated.

      SA   5   4   3   2   1   SD

D. The method of sampling is sound.

      SA   5   4   3   2   1   SD

E. Relevant demographics (for example, age, gender, and ethnicity) are described.

      SA   5   4   3   2   1   SD

F. Measurement procedures are adequate.

      SA   5   4   3   2   1   SD

G. All procedures have been described in sufficient detail to permit a replication of the study.

      SA   5   4   3   2   1   SD

H. The participants have been adequately protected from potential harm.

      SA   5   4   3   2   1   SD

I. The results are clearly described.

      SA   5   4   3   2   1   SD

J. The discussion/conclusion is appropriate.

      SA   5   4   3   2   1   SD

K. Despite any flaws, the report is worthy of publication.

      SA   5   4   3   2   1   SD

Article 12

Efficacy of a Mail Survey Appeal
for a Dissertation

JOHN F. GASKI

University of Notre Dame

SUMMARY. Of all the determinants of mail survey response investigated, a dissertation as the purpose is one type of appeal not used in a covering letter. Two parallel field experiments involving populations of wholesale organizations (N = 743 and 509) are reported in which such an appeal was tested. Lack of statistically significant findings indicates use of this appeal did not enhance response rate or quality.

From *Perceptual and Motor Skills*, *99*, 1295–1298. Copyright © 2004 by Perceptual and Motor Skills. Reprinted with permission.

Scientific examination of tactics influencing response to mail surveys has a substantial history. Researchers who use mail questionnaires have a pragmatic interest in more complete and timely survey returns. An important segment of this body of research focuses on the covering letter's appeal. Subject variables have included sponsorship (Houston & Nevin, 1977; Jones & Lang, 1980; Goyder, 1982), benefit of compliance (Robertson & Bellenger, 1978; Hubbard & Little, 1988), imposition of a deadline (Henley, 1976; Nevin & Ford, 1976; Vocino, 1977; Roberts, McCrory, & Forthofer, 1978), and ingratiating text content (Hendrick, Borden, Giesen, Murray, & Seyfried, 1972). Houston and Nevin (1977) manipulated thematic appeal via the text of the covering letter.

One previously untested feature may have practical significance for conducting survey research for a doctoral dissertation: Should that purpose even be mentioned in a covering letter? Would such disclosure help, hurt, or make no difference whatsoever? Since the literature yielded no answer, a field experiment was designed to test the efficacy of a dissertation-purpose-based appeal. The operative hypothesis (H_a) was that a dissertation-related appeal would enhance response rate or quality. Possible reasons would be sympathy for a student's project, were the purpose understood by respondents; or if respondents did not understand what a dissertation was, the word may connote importance or leave an elevated impression. Support is found in the common tendency for university survey sponsorship to elicit higher response rates (Albaum, 1987). Perhaps a similar effect would occur for other academic-related appeals.

The alternative hypothesis (H_b) was that a dissertation appeal could detract from response if perception of a student or academic—rather than professional or commercial—purpose reduced the sense of seriousness attached; or the word "dissertation" would possibly be confusing or distracting and, whether understood or not, could be psychologically off-putting. The null hypothesis (H_o) was that the appeal would have no effect at all.

Method

Procedure

The experiment was conducted along with data collection for a mail survey study of a manufacturer, Gillette, and its distributors. (That is, a field experiment was overlaid upon a survey.) A randomly selected group of questionnaire recipients was exposed to this covering letter appeal:

> I am conducting a study of relations between suppliers and dealers of various products and have the permission of Mr. ___ of Gillette–Paper Mate to survey Paper Mate dealers for this purpose. (The study is being done in conjunction with a doctoral dissertation.)

A control group received the same text excluding the parenthetic sentence. The manipulation was then repeated for a pair of groups from a different population, as described below.

Subjects

The entire population of 509 U.S. "mass market" dealers of the Gillette Company's Paper Mate division was surveyed. These wholesalers serve drug, department, variety, and discount retail stores, as well as supermarkets. A randomly selected half of the population (254 dealers per systematic randomization) received the experimental covering letter, the remainder the other version. Designated addressee for each recipient firm was the owner, president, or general manager.

The experiment was repeated with Paper Mate's office products distribution system. This population (N = 743) included wholesalers who serve stationery, office supply, and school supply stores.

Table 1
Group Characteristics and t Tests: Indices of Effectiveness of Covering Letter Appeal

Group	Rate (%)	Response time*	Incompleteness[†]
Mass Market Dealers (N = 509)			
Experimental Group	18.1	17.9	3.5 (4.5%)
Control Group	18.0	15.5	3.3 (4.2%)
p	ns	*p* < .10 (*t* = 1.67)	ns
statistical power @ .05	.05	.67	.13
effect size	.03	.19	.05
Office Products Dealers (N = 743)			
Experimental Group	18.1	19.8	4.8 (6.1%)
Control Group	16.8	17.5	3.9 (4.9%)
p	ns	ns	*p* < .10 (*t* = 1.64)
statistical power @ .05	.14	.88	.49
effect size	.08	.21	.12

*Mean number of elapsed days between questionnaire mailing and return postmark.
[†]Mean item nonresponse out of 79 questionnaire items.

Nonresponse Bias Test Procedure

To verify the representativeness of the sample, two standard tests of nonresponse bias were done for each population. First, adapting the Armstrong and Overton approach (1977), response time-lag was correlated with all (15) variables measured in the substantive study, mostly multi-item scales comprising 79 total questionnaire items.[1] The rationale was that, if late respondents differ from early ones, then *non*respondents are also likely to differ from early or all respondents. For each distributor population, only one significant correlation was found, about what would occur by chance, indicating similarity between early and late respondents.

The second test was a comparison of the geographic profile of respondents and population. Chi-square indicated a nonsignificant difference between population and respondents within each category.

Results

Multivariate analysis of variance was applied to the data, with response time and item nonresponse as the dependent variables. Comparisons were nonsignificant for each population. In Table 1 are responses for each measure and individual *t* ratios between the groups. A third dependent variable of this analysis was response rate, tested at the aggregate level by *t* test for proportions.

There appears to be no significant difference for response rate associated with use of the dissertation appeal or for response time. Consistent across both populations, a higher elapsed mean time for the experimental group was noted, although significant statistically per one-tail test for one population only. Unambiguously, in neither population was there evidentiary support in terms of item nonresponse for use of the dissertation appeal. The nonsignificance of results was influenced by a few outliers inflating the variance for response time and item nonresponse. Yet statistical power is high for three of the six comparisons.

Contrary to the primary hypothesis, a dissertation reference in a covering letter for a mail survey did not enhance response rate or quality, according to three common measures for two populations. Interpretation of failure to reject a null hypothesis cannot be done definitely, as is well known.

References

Albaum, G. (1987). Do source and anonymity affect mail survey results? *Journal of the Academy of Marketing Science, 15,* 74–81.

Armstrong, J. S., & Overton, T. S. (1977). Estimating nonresponse bias in mail surveys. *Journal of Marketing Research, 14,* 396–402.

Goyder, J. C. (1982). Further evidence on factors affecting response rates to mailed questionnaires. *American Sociological Review, 47,* 550–553.

Hendrick, C., Borden, R., Giesen, M., Murray, E. J., & Seyfried, B. A. (1972). Effectiveness of ingratiation tactics in a cover letter on mail questionnaire response. *Psychonomic Science, 26,* 349–351.

Henley, J. R., Jr. (1976). Response rate to mail questionnaires with a return deadline. *Public Opinion Quarterly, 40,* 374–375.

Houston, M. J. & Nevin, J. R. (1977). The effects of source and appeal on mail survey response patterns. *Journal of Marketing Research, 14,* 374–378.

Hubbard, R., & Little, E. L. (1988). Promised contributions to charity and mail survey responses: Replication with extension. *Public Opinion Quarterly, 52,* 223–230.

Jones, W. H., & Lang, J. R. (1980). Sample composition bias and response bias in a mail survey: A comparison of inducement methods. *Journal of Marketing Research, 17,* 69–76.

Nevin, J. R., & Ford, N. M. (1976). Effects of a deadline and a veiled threat on mail survey responses. *Journal of Applied Psychology, 61,* 116–118.

Roberts, R. E., McCrory, O. F., & Forthofer, R. N. (1978). Further evidence on using a deadline to stimulate responses to a mail survey. *Public Opinion Quarterly, 42,* 407–410.

Robertson, D. H., & Bellenger, D. N. (1978). A new method of increasing mail survey responses: Contributions to charity. *Journal of Marketing Research, 15,* 632–633.

Vocino, T. (1977). Three variables in stimulating responses to mailed questionnaires. *Journal of Marketing, 41,* 76–77.

Address correspondence to: John F. Gaski, Department of Marketing, Mendoza College of Business, University of Notre Dame, Notre Dame, IN 46556-5646. E-mail: gaski.1@nd.edu

[1] Focal variables included sociological phenomena such as social power, conflict, dependence, and system performance in an interorganizational business setting. (Actual scales are available from the author.)

Exercise for Article 12

Factual Questions

1. What is the "alternative hypothesis" for this study?

2. What is the "null hypothesis" for this study?

3. Did the control group receive exactly the same covering letter? Explain.

4. What were the three dependent variables?

5. In Table 1, how is "Response Time" defined?

6. For the Office Products Dealers, did the experimental *or* the control group have a higher response rate?

Questions for Discussion

7. Is it important to know that the researcher selected individuals for the experimental and control groups at random? Explain. (See lines 62–65.)

8. In your opinion, is this study primarily a nonexperimental survey *or* an experiment? Explain.

9. The researcher speculates that "if late respondents differ from early ones, then *non*respondents are also likely to differ from early or all respondents." Do you agree? Explain. (See lines 77–79.)

10. In Table 1, this symbol appears twice: "$p < .10$." Do you know what this means? Explain.

11. The researcher indicates that the null hypothesis was *not* rejected. To the best of your knowledge, does this mean that the differences were statistically significant *or* that they were insignificant?

Quality Ratings

Directions: Indicate your level of agreement with each of the following statements by circling a number from 5 for strongly agree (SA) to 1 for strongly disagree (SD). If you believe an item is not applicable to this research article, leave it blank. Be prepared to explain your ratings.

A. The introduction establishes the importance of the study.

SA   5   4   3   2   1   SD

B. The literature review establishes the context for the study.

SA   5   4   3   2   1   SD

C. The research purpose, question, or hypothesis is clearly stated.

SA   5   4   3   2   1   SD

D. The method of sampling is sound.

SA   5   4   3   2   1   SD

E. Relevant demographics (for example, age, gender, and ethnicity) are described.

SA   5   4   3   2   1   SD

F. Measurement procedures are adequate.

SA   5   4   3   2   1   SD

G. All procedures have been described in sufficient detail to permit a replication of the study.

SA   5   4   3   2   1   SD

H. The participants have been adequately protected from potential harm.

SA   5   4   3   2   1   SD

I. The results are clearly described.

SA   5   4   3   2   1   SD

J. The discussion/conclusion is appropriate.

SA   5   4   3   2   1   SD

K. Despite any flaws, the report is worthy of publication.

SA   5   4   3   2   1   SD

Article 13

Using Virtual Reality to Teach Disability Awareness

JAYNE PIVIK
University of Ottawa

IAN MacFARLANE
Nortel Networks

JOAN McCOMAS
University of Ottawa

MARC LaFLAMME
University of Ottawa

ABSTRACT. A desktop virtual reality (VR) program was designed and evaluated to teach children about the accessibility and attitudinal barriers encountered by their peers with mobility impairments. Within this software, children sitting in a virtual wheelchair experience obstacles such as stairs, narrow doors, objects too high to reach, and attitudinal barriers such as inappropriate comments. Using a collaborative research methodology, 15 youth with mobility impairments assisted in developing and beta-testing the software. The effectiveness of the program was then evaluated with 60 children in grades 4–6 using a controlled pretest/posttest design. The results indicated that the program was effective for increasing children's knowledge of accessibility barriers. Attitudes, grade level, familiarity with individuals with a disability, and gender were also investigated.

From *Journal of Educational Computing Research*, 26, 203–218. Copyright © 2002 by Baywood Publishing Company, Inc. Reprinted with permission.

Inclusive education of children with disabilities in public education institutions is now common in developed countries. In Canada, this means that 373,824 children with special needs between the ages of 5–14 years attend regular classes [1]. Inclusive education is considered by most as a positive experience for both children with and without disabilities and an important social policy toward ensuring full participation and accessibility for individuals with disabilities [2]. Theoretically, inclusive education allows children with disabilities the opportunity for "free and appropriate public education" as determined by the Education of the Handicapped Act (EHA) in the United States in 1975.

However, in reality, children with disabilities often have to contend with structural, physical, and attitudinal barriers for the 30 hours per week they spend at school. Examples of structural barriers include steep ramps, uncut sidewalk curbs, heavy doors, and one-inch thresholds [3, 4]. Stairs, narrow bathrooms, revolving doors, and turnstiles also have been reported as impediments that limit access and inclusion for individuals who use wheelchairs [5]. In addition to structural barriers, children with disabilities have to manage the physical limitations inherent to their disability. For example, a child with spina bifida may have to contend with poor upper extremity function (limiting fine motor skills such as writing), poor hand–eye coordination, potential neurological deficits, and difficulties with organizational skills [6].

Perhaps the most difficult type of barrier encountered by children with disabilities is negative attitudes expressed by their peers [7]. Attitudinal barriers experienced in educational integration, such as rejection and stereotyping [8, 9] or covert and overt bullying [10], can further isolate children with a disability and impact on their feelings of social acceptance and self-esteem. Social isolation has been linked to difficulty with future peer relations [4] and lower academic and cognitive development [11].

In order to increase social awareness, understanding, and acceptance toward children with disabilities by their nondisabled peers, disability awareness programs have been developed. Current methods of disability awareness programs for school children include: 1) simulating a disability (e.g., sitting in a wheelchair or wearing a blindfold), 2) providing information about disabilities, 3) live and video presentations/testimonials by individuals with disabilities, 4) pairing disabled and nondisabled children together in a buddy system, 5) group discussions about disability, and 6) a combination of the above methods [7]. Along with disability awareness, Roberts and Smith [12] recommend providing children without a disability with knowledge and practical skills that assist with social interactions with their disabled peers. Logic dictates that one of the most effective ways to impart knowledge about the realities for children with disabilities is to try to simulate the experience of the disability. In other words, to provide an opportunity where the child without a disability literally experiences different situations, viewpoints, perceptions, and interactions from the perspective of a child with a disability.

Simulation has been the cornerstone of virtual reality (VR), and in fact, the first uses of VR involved the

65 simulation of military experiences as noted by Kozak, Hancock, Arthur, and Chrysler [13]. VR is defined as a three-dimensional, participatory, computer-based simulation that occurs in real time and is often multisensory [14]. In other words, VR responds to the user's actions,
70 has real-time 3-D graphics, and provides a sense of immersion. There are many advantages to using VR for simulation. For example, VR provides a safe environment for practicing a skill, such as learning to cross street intersections [15–17]. Simulations using VR may
75 also be less costly than real-world simulations [18] and provide the user the opportunity for repetitive practice [19, 20]. Experiences that are not available in the real world can be simulated in a virtual environment, such as moving through a cellular structure or visiting his-
80 torical sites that are presently nonexistent or too far away to be accessible. Past experience has shown us that children using VR find it very interesting and stimulating, thus motivating the training experience [21]. Finally, desktop VR can provide a simulation that
85 can be made widely accessible through dissemination via the Internet.

The purpose of this project was to develop and evaluate a desktop VR program designed to teach children about the accessibility and attitudinal barriers
90 faced by children with mobility impairments. Desktop VR utilizes a personal computer, where the virtual environment is displayed on a conventional computer monitor and movement within the environment is effected through either a mouse, keyboard, or joystick.
95 Although less immersive than systems that use head-mounted display units, desktop VR systems have the advantages of being less expensive, more portable, and easier to use. The developed program, titled *Barriers: The Awareness Challenge*, used desktop VR to simu-
100 late the experiences of a child in a wheelchair in an environment familiar to most children—an elementary school. The specific objectives of this project were to examine the effectiveness of using a disability simulation with virtual reality to: 1) increase children's
105 knowledge of accessibility and attitudinal barriers that impact individuals with disabilities and 2) promote more positive attitudes toward children with disabilities.

Method

There were four phases to The Barriers Project. The
110 first was to utilize a collaborative research methodology, where youth with mobility impairments (our Disability Awareness Consultants) identified the barriers that would comprise the content of the software. The second phase was to develop the software, which in-
115 volved organizing the barriers into a script or storyboard, building the virtual environment, and then beta-testing it with our consultants. The third phase of the project involved evaluating the software to examine the impact of the program on youth without disabilities.
120 The final phase involved disseminating information about the program and providing free access to the software via the Internet.

Collaborative Software Development

In order to ensure that the software reflected the current status of accessibility and inclusion within an
125 elementary school setting, a collaborative research methodology was used. Fifteen Disability Awareness Consultants assisted in the content development and testing of the software. The consultants (aged 9–16 years) attended eight different schools on a full-time
130 basis and had either cerebral palsy ($n = 11$) or spina bifida ($n = 5$). Their mobility impairments ranged from difficulty walking (on uneven surfaces and/or for long periods of time) to constant use of an electric wheelchair for independent mobility. The barriers to full in-
135 clusion in their schools and the proposed solutions to these barriers were identified by these consultants during three focus group meetings. The final list of barriers and proposed solutions was then prioritized by the focus group participants, where each person was given
140 seven stickers and was asked to place one or more of the stickers on the barrier(s) they felt were necessary to include in the software. The barriers with the greatest number of stickers became the basis for the script or storyboard of the software program. Using this script, a
145 virtual elementary school was developed, which includes the exterior of a school, an outside playground, hallways, a classroom, a library, and two washrooms (one inaccessible). The children using the program were told that they were to travel in a "virtual wheel-
150 chair" and seek out all of the "building" and "bad attitude" barriers in the school. There are 24 barriers in the program, which include building barriers such as narrow hallways, crowded classrooms, a ramp that is too steep, a locker hook that is too high, and inaccessible
155 bathroom fixtures. The attitudinal barriers include comments from virtual students such as "Hey, look at the kid in the wheelchair!" or "Ha! Ha! You can't play here!"

The program presents a gaming style interface with
160 a first-person point of view during navigation through the world. The user moves within the virtual school using the cursor keys and can activate events such as opening doors or using the elevator by pressing the left button of the mouse. Two message areas are used: a
165 task message area and an information message area. The task messages instruct the child to complete specific tasks such as performing an action or going to a specific location. The information message center gives feedback to the child when barriers are identified. A
170 "wheelchair damage" display is used to encourage children to be careful as they navigate through the world and is activated when they bump into walls, objects, or people. As each barrier is correctly identified, the score is updated. A number of icons (such as a coat,
175 key, and book) are also displayed. The icons are added and removed as the student completes specific tasks. At

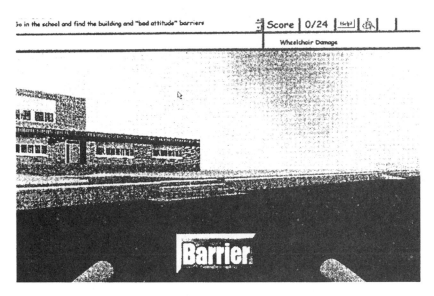

Figure 1. When first entering the world, the user is placed in the parking lot facing the school.

the end of the program, a results section is displayed listing all the barriers and each one is labeled as to whether it was found or not during the program.

180   The program was developed in VRML 2.0 (Virtual Reality Modeling Language) using CosmoWorlds. The CosmoPlayer 2.1 plug-in (for Netscape Navigator and Microsoft Internet Explorer) was used as the 3D viewer. The virtual school that was developed used the scripting capabilities of VRML to control interactions with the virtual objects and people in the school. Fields, events, proximity nodes, and collision sensors are used extensively throughout the virtual world. Each barrier, whether it is structural or attitudinal, is activated by a proximity node. A number of fields are used to record the state of the world in relation to the location of the wheelchair and the interactions that have taken place. The child identifies a structural barrier by moving close to the barrier and clicking on the "Barrier" button that floats just in front of the virtual wheelchair. For example, when first entering the world, the user is placed in the parking lot facing the school (Figure 1).

A proximity node surrounds the front steps that lead up to the school. A number of fields indicate where the wheelchair is and which barriers have been found. For the front steps, the "atSidewalkSteps" field is initially "false" and the "SidewalkStepsIDed" field (which records whether the steps have been identified as a barrier or not) is set to "false." If the "Barrier" button is clicked when the wheelchair is not at any of the barriers, an audio clip that indicates an incorrect choice is played. When the child navigates closer to the steps, the virtual wheelchair collides with the proximity node that surrounds the steps. This collision triggers an event that sets the "atSidewalkSteps" field to "true." Now, if the "Barrier" button is clicked, a number of

events occur: 1) the number of correct barriers found is incremented, 2) an appropriate message is displayed in the information message area (in this case, it informs the child that wheelchairs cannot go up stairs), 3) the "SidewalkStepsIDed" field is set to "true," which is used in the results section to indicate which barriers were found and which were not found, 4) the proximity sensor is permanently disabled, and 5) an HTML page that corresponds to the current running total of the number of barriers found is loaded in the score frame. If the child navigates out of the proximity node without identifying the barrier, the value of the "atSidewalk-Steps" field is toggled back to "false."

Attitudinal barriers are identified by clicking on the "Barrier" button after hearing an audio "bad attitude" comment. The script works in a manner similar to the structural barriers, except that an audio node is triggered when a collision with the corresponding proximity node occurs. For example, when the child enters the classroom, a collision with a proximity node that is located just inside the door is triggered. This event triggers a sound node to play an audio clip "It's the kid in the wheelchair" (said in a nasty, sarcastic tone indicating "a bad attitude"). While the wheelchair remains in the proximity node, the child can identify the attitudinal barrier (Figure 2). However, if the child moves farther into the classroom, they will leave the proximity node and will be unable to identify the barrier unless they move back in (which will re-trigger the playing of the audio clip).

There are three distinct areas of the virtual world: outside the school, inside the school, and the results section. The transition between the areas is accomplished by using a touch sensor to trigger an event that uses a switch node to change to the next "level." The touch sensor for the transition from the outside to the

Figure 2. While the wheelchair remains in the proximity node, the child can identify the attitudinal barrier.

inside is the automatic door opener, and the one that triggers the loading of the results is on the computer in the library. Once you have left an area, you cannot go back. The switch node is used so that the entire program can be implemented in a single VRML file that interacts with the HTML frames in which the world is loaded. The single file was necessary so that the running score for the entire world could be maintained without the need for applications, CGIs, or servlets running on a server. This permits schools and other users with slow Internet connections to download the entire set of files once and then run them locally on their machine whenever they want. Six of the Disability Awareness Consultants returned to the Rehabilitation Sciences Virtual Reality Lab at the University of Ottawa to beta-test the program for content validity and general usability. Modifications to the software were made based on their feedback.

Evaluation of the Software

Study Design

In order to evaluate the effectiveness of The Barriers software, a controlled pretest/posttest design was used. Using random assignment, half of the sample was given the VR intervention and the other half received an alternate desktop VR program—similar in length and based in a school setting, but without disability awareness information—in order to control for computer practice effects. The control program titled "Wheels," developed by R. J. Cooper & Associates, is an excellent desktop VR program designed to teach children how to use electric wheelchairs. Hence, the viewpoint of the control program is also from the first-person perspective at wheelchair height. As well, the control program also simulates wheelchair usage such as orienting oneself properly to enter doorways. The main difference between the two virtual environments is the presence of barriers (physical and attitudinal) in the intervention program. The hypotheses were that children receiving the Barriers Program would at posttest have: 1) a greater knowledge of barriers than the control group and 2) more positive attitudes toward peers with a disability compared to the control group.

Participants

Sixty youth (aged 9–11 years) participated in the study. All were from a local urban school and attended grade 4 ($n = 20$), grade 5 ($n = 19$), or grade 6 ($n = 21$). There were 24 males and 36 females in the sample. Half the sample ($n = 30$) received the Barriers intervention and the other half received the control program. Both programs took one-half hour to complete. Each child was tested individually and completed the program one time.

Measures

Two questionnaires were administered to the entire sample one week before and one week after the VR intervention. The Knowledge Questionnaire consisted of simply asking all the children to write out as many "building" and "people" barriers they could think of that might impact on children who use wheelchairs or crutches at school. Barriers were defined as "things that stop a person from doing what everybody else can do or cause people to be treated differently because of a disability." The building barrier example that was given was "smooth elevator buttons for people who are blind," and the people barrier example given was "someone who has a 'bad attitude' toward those who are different." Although this questionnaire was not a standardized measure, it was a simple, effective method for determining the youth's current knowledge of accessibility and attitudes within a school setting. For each accurate statement, the youth received one point.

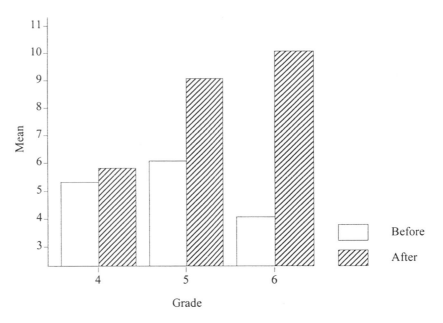

Figure 3. Pre- and postknowledge of barriers by grade for intervention group.

The attitude measure used was the Children's Social Distance from Handicapped Persons Scale, a scale developed specifically for school settings, which has
320   shown to be a quick, reliable measure of affective attitudes toward peers with a disability ($r = .78$) [22]. Concern over the word "handicapped" was allayed through conversations with experts in attitude measurement who indicated that the word "handicapped" is better
325   understood by children than the word "disabled" (Hazzard; Rosenbaum, personal communications, 1999). An example item of this measure is, " It would be okay if a handicapped kid sat next to me in class," to which the child could respond with "yes," "maybe
330   yes," "maybe no," or "no." Scores on this scale range from 0–30, with higher scores indicating more positive affective attitudes. The children also were asked to indicate whether they knew someone who was handicapped, to indicate what that handicap was, whether
335   the person was a friend, an acquaintance or a family member, and finally, how much they liked this person.

Results

Knowledge

The self-report Knowledge Scale was used to ascertain knowledge of both building or structural barriers and people or attitude barriers for both groups using
340   ANOVAs (group membership × time). Overall knowledge of barriers was examined by adding both the structural and attitude barriers together. Table 1 describes the building and attitudinal barriers for both groups before and after the intervention.
345   These results indicate that prior to the VR intervention, both the control group and the intervention group reported similar levels of knowledge within their

school setting; however, following the intervention, the youth in the Barriers group reported a significantly
350   greater number of barriers than the control group, $F(1,57) = 5.35$, $p < .05$. When broken down by type (building or attitude barriers), there was a significant difference in post-reported barriers between the two groups for the building barriers, $F(1,56) = 11.27$, $p =$
355   .001, with the Barriers group reporting more barriers.

Table 1
Mean (SD) Knowledge Scores Before and After VR Intervention

	Time	
Group	Before	After
Barriers		
Building	2.9 (1.9)	6.4 (3.9)
Attitude	2.2 (1.8)	3.2 (2.6)
Total	5.2 (3.3)	9.6 (6.0)
Control		
Building	2.5 (1.7)	3.4 (2.6)
Attitude	2.5 (1.4)	2.9 (2.1)
Total	5.0 (2.7)	6.4 (4.2)

There were no differences between groups for knowledge of attitudinal barriers, which was not unexpected because only 4 of the 24 barriers in the program were "bad attitude" barriers. Gender was also not a
360   significant factor for knowledge of barriers. There was a significant difference for children receiving the Barriers intervention by grade level on the total barriers reported following the VR intervention, $F(2,57) = 3.26$, $p < .05$, with grades 5 and 6 showing the greatest learn-
365   ing curve (see Figure 3).

Attitude and Previous Experience

No differences were found between the two groups or within groups for affective attitude measured with the Children's Social Distance from Handicapped Persons Scale [22]. However, there was a significant difference between males and females on the post-attitude scale, $F(1,57) = 4.68$, $p < .05$, with males reporting higher affective attitudes than females. Previous experience of knowing someone with a disability has been shown to impact on attitude scores. In this study, neither knowledge nor attitude scores showed differences for children who knew: 1) someone with a disability, 2) the type of disability of that person, 3) whether that person was a friend, an acquaintance, or a family member, or 4) how much they liked that person. Interestingly, 54 of the 60 children reported they knew someone with a disability.

Discussion

Based on the results of this study, *Barriers: The Awareness Challenge* software was effective for increasing the knowledge of barriers within a familiar setting for children in grades 4, 5, and 6. Building barriers were remembered most often, with grades 5 and 6 showing the greatest change. It is unclear whether the older children remembered more of the program at the posttest or whether their greater change in scores reflected previous findings that older children are more knowledgeable about disabilities [22] and are more accepting of their peers with a disability [23]. Regardless, sensitizing individuals to the difficulties associated with accessibility in public buildings remains an important component to disability awareness promotion. Rowley-Kelly provides an excellent checklist of potential accessibility barriers that school administrators can use to evaluate their structural resources for all different types of disabilities [24]. Examples include the need for wider aisles for access by people who use wheelchairs, tactile markings for individuals with visual impairments, flashing lights for fire alarms for individuals who are hearing impaired, and pictorial signage for those who have difficulty reading.

Although it has been 25 years since the precedent-setting Education of Handicapped Act, our children's schools are still riddled with accessibility barriers that serve to further isolate them from full participation and inclusion. More resources need to be allocated to improve accessibility in schools and attention paid to making adjustments to existing provisions [25, 26]. Another recommendation for school resource allocation that arose from the focus groups with our Disability Awareness Consultants was the necessity for ensuring that teachers and support staff have disability awareness training. This suggestion has been reinforced in the literature and specifically recommends that teachers be provided with training, sufficient materials, and on-site assistance [27, 28].

The lack of differences in attitude scores between the control and experimental groups was in all likelihood a function of the very high attitude scores of all the students participating in the study. On both the pretest and posttest scores, both groups had attitude scores

just under 90%; thus, either the measure was not sensitive enough and/or a ceiling effect occurred. Other factors that have been shown to impact the effectiveness of disability awareness programs include gender, where females report more positive attitudes, and familiarity, where knowing someone with a disability positively influences knowledge of and attitudes toward persons with disabilities [29]. In our study, gender did not differentiate the two groups on knowledge of barriers or attitude before the VR intervention; however, males did report a significantly higher posttest attitude score. This result is inconsistent with the literature [30, 31]. One possible explanation is that males were more familiar with the interactive gaming aspect of the VR program, as indicated by their higher game scores during the program ($M = 16.5$, $SD = 4.56$) vs. females ($M = 14.39$, $SD = 3.57$). This gaming familiarity may have allowed the males to focus on the educational material being presented vs. maneuverability and orientation.

Regarding familiarity with disability issues, the high attitude scores were most likely influenced by the great number of children in the study who knew someone with a disability [29]; in this case, 90% of the total sample. As such, knowledge and attitude scores showed no differences for children who knew someone with a disability, the type of disability of that person, whether that person was a friend, acquaintance or family member, or how much they liked them. However, in evaluating the effectiveness of the software, even though most of the study sample knew someone with a disability, and, as a group had very positive attitudes, they were still able to learn about accessibility barriers. This is important because increased knowledge about disabilities is believed to be necessary for creating a lasting influence on positive attitudes [32].

The authors realize that no simulation program will ever be able to truly describe the experiences and perceptions associated with having a disability. The concern expressed by French is that simulation programs trivialize the cumulative social and psychological effects of a disability and that they do not address the environmental and social barriers associated with a disability [33]. On the other hand, a lack of knowledge and understanding about issues related to a disability has been shown to lead to discrimination and isolation in schools [8, 24]. The Barriers Project was designed with these concerns and issues in mind. The collaboration of youth with disabilities in the design of the program provided assurances of content validity as well as support for the concept of using VR to impart knowledge to their peers. As well, the focus of the program is not based on simulating a sense of the physical limitations associated with a disability, but rather on the environmental and social barriers encountered by persons with a disability. Utilizing the social–political model of disability, the Barriers Project revolved around the impact of the environment (both physical and social) on the experiences of a person using a wheelchair [2].

Every effort was made to accurately design a program that simulates maneuverability in a wheelchair in order to highlight structural barriers such as narrow aisles, doorways, washroom stalls, and crowded classrooms. Although this provided a sense of frustration for the children tested on the program, it served to provide a sense of environmental constraints as well as to highlight the capabilities of their peers who use a wheelchair.

The program also attempted to provide facilitated learning by using a problem-solving approach. In designing an environment that required active exploration for solutions, we anticipated that the children would remember more barriers—a recommendation suggested by previous researchers [34–36]. However, during the beta-testing phase, when the entire VR school was open to exploration, we found that the children missed many areas important to the learning objective. It appeared that in providing a totally unstructured environment, the children focused on exploration vs. barrier identification. Thus, the program was modified to be semi-structured (i.e., where the children were directed to different areas, such as the library, where they could search and identify the barriers specific to that location). Overall, this was found to be an effective strategy based on the results and the anecdotal comments reported by the students testing the program. The anecdotal comments included that: 1) it gave them a better understanding of the accessibility barriers that are all around them that they had not previously noticed, 2) "bad attitudes" are just as difficult as, if not more difficult than, building barriers, 3) the VR program was good at simulating maneuverability in a wheelchair and could be extremely frustrating at times, 4) they had a new appreciation of the capabilities of people who use wheelchairs, and 5) the program was very motivating and they were interested in trying it again.

Limitations and Recommendations

The most obvious limitation of this study is the lack of effect of attitudinal change. This was probably due to positive attitudes of the students toward peers with a disability before the intervention as well as the relatively few attitudinal barriers in the program. The school that agreed to be in the study is one of eight schools out of 128 that is identified as "accessible" by the school board. From a structural point of view, however, the school had all the accessibility barriers that were identified in the program. As part of the "accessible distinction," it is likely that there is a greater incidence of children with disabilities in this school (however, there were no children who used wheelchairs or crutches in the three classes tested), and, thus, greater disability awareness. For future studies, we would recommend controlling for place effects by testing the program in settings with and without previous awareness and sensitivity training.

Another likely influence that impacted on attitudinal scores was the small percentage of attitudinal barriers presented in the program (four of twenty-four). Poor attitudes were depicted as nasty or sarcastic comments by virtual students. The use of these students or avatars in the program use up a considerable amount of memory, which in turn slows down the program. For ease of use, we decided to include as few avatars as possible. However, as both the hardware and software capabilities improve in the future, more avatars can be used to depict attitudinal barriers. The content of the attitudinal barriers also posed difficulties. Many of the statements that our Disability Awareness Consultants proposed (such as the word "crip") were not included for fear of promoting or teaching negative attitudes. For that reason, this program could serve as a jump start for discussing negative attitudes toward people who are different.

VR was chosen as a teaching medium for a number of reasons: 1) it provided first-person simulation effects, 2) allowed us to control the environment (e.g., define and place barriers where we chose), 3) is accessible to many individuals if distributed over the Internet, and 4) has shown to be an enjoyable experience for children. However, because this is the first VR program that provides disability awareness, we would recommend future studies compare it to traditional forms of disability awareness training such as real-world wheelchair simulation, presentations, testimonials, and videos.

As well, because this project is the first of its kind to use VR to promote disability awareness, in this case, for mobility impairments, it would be interesting to develop and test the effectiveness of VR for simulating other types of disabilities. It also would be interesting to give the user the opportunity to make modifications that would erase barriers within the virtual environment. For example, the user could widen aisles or lower drinking fountains in order to make them more accessible.

Even in a school whose students had very positive attitudes about peers with disabilities, they were still able to learn about structural barriers in their environment that negatively impact the lives of individuals with disabilities. Hence, *Barriers: The Awareness Challenge* was considered successful in teaching about the environmental conditions faced by individuals with mobility limitations and, thus, was made available free of charge via the Internet at http:/www.health. uottawa.ca/vrlab. We hope that along with children utilizing the program, teachers, staff, and parents also try the software. Along with raising awareness about structural and attitudinal barriers, we hope this program will serve to initiate further discussions about disabilities, highlight how environmental constraints and attitudes impact society's views toward their members with a disability, and provide a forum that emphasizes the capabilities of individuals who have disabilities.

References

1. Statistics Canada, *1991 Canadian Census*, Statistics Canada, Ottawa, Ontario, 1992.
2. M. Law and W. Dunn, Perspectives on Understanding and Changing the Environments of Children with Disabilities, *Physical & Occupational Therapy in Pediatrics*, *13*:3, pp. 10–17, 1993.
3. M. Law, Changing Disabling Environments through Participatory Research, *Canadian Journal of Rehabilitation*, *7*:1, pp. 22–23, 1993.
4. S. R. Asher and A. R. Taylor, Social Outcomes of Mainstreaming: Sociometric Assessment and Beyond, in *Social Development of Exceptional Children*, P. Strain (ed.), Aspen Systems, Rockville, Maryland, pp. 1–18, 1982.
5. S. B. Baker and M. A. Rogosky-Grassi, Access to the School, in *Teaching the Student with Spina Bifida*, L. Fern, F. Rowley-Kelly, and D. H. Reigel (eds.), Paul H. Brooks Publishing, Baltimore, pp. 31–70, 1993.
6. M. Rogosky-Grassi, Working with Perceptual-Motor Skills, in *Teaching the Student with Spina Bifida*, L. Fern, F. Rowley-Kelly, and D. H. Reigel (eds.), Paul H. Brooks Publishing, Baltimore, pp. 193–209, 1993.
7. J. Donaldson, Changing Attitudes toward Handicapped Persons: A Review and Analyses of Research, *Exceptional Children*, *46*:7, pp. 504–513, 1980.
8. J. Gottlieb, Attitudes toward Retarded Children: Effects of Labeling and Academic Performance, *American Journal of Mental Deficiency*, *78*, pp. 15–19, 1980.
9. J. Gottlieb, L. Cohen, and L. Goldstein, Social Contact and Personal Adjustment as Variables Relating to Attitudes toward EMR Children, *Training School Bulletin*, *71*, pp. 9–16, 1974.
10. A. Llewellyn, The Abuse of Children with Physical Disabilities in Mainstream Schooling, *Developmental Medicine and Child Neurology*, *37*, pp. 740–743, 1995.
11. H. Gardner, Relations with Other Selves, in *Developmental Psychology* (2nd Edition), M. H. Bornstein and M. Lamb (eds.), Lawrence Erlbaum Associates, Hillsdale, New Jersey, pp. 72–98, 1982.
12. C. Roberts and P. Smith, Attitudes and Behavior of Children toward Peers with Disabilities, *International Journal of Disability, Development and Education*, *46*:1, pp. 35–50, 1999.
13. J. J. Kozak, P. A. Hancock, E. J. Arthur, and S. T. Chrysler, Transfer of Training from Virtual Reality, *Ergonomics*, *36*, pp. 777–784, 1993.
14. K. Pimentel and K. Teixeiera, *Virtual Reality: Through the New Looking Glass*, McGraw-Hill, Toronto, 1995.
15. D. P. Inman and K. Loge, Teaching Motorized Wheelchair Operation in Virtual Reality, in *Proceedings of the 1995 CSUN Virtual Reality Conference*, California State University, Northridge, 1995.
16. D. Strickland, L. M. Marcus, G. B. Mesibov, and K. Hogan, Brief Report: Two Case Studies Using Virtual Reality as a Learning Tool for Autistic Children, *Journal of Autism and Developmental Disorders*, *26*:6, pp. 651–659, 1996.
17. F. D. Rusch, R. E. Cimera, D. L. Shelden, U. Thakkar, D. A. Chapman, Y. H. Khan, D. D. Moore, and J. S. LeBoy, Crossing Streets: A K–12 Virtual Reality Application for Understanding Knowledge Acquisition, in *Proceedings of the IEEE Virtual Reality Annual International Symposium*, IEEE Press, New York, 1997.
18. J. W. Regian, W. L. Shebilske, and J. M. Monk, Virtual Reality: An Instructional Medium for Visual-Spatial Tasks, *Journal of Communication*, *42*, pp. 136–149, 1992.
19. P. N. Wilson, N. Foreman, and D. Stanton, Virtual Reality, Disability and Rehabilitation, *Disability and Rehabilitation*, *19*:6, pp. 213–220, 1997.
20. B. R. Lowery and F. G. Knirk, Micro-Computer Video Games and Spatial Visualization Acquisition, *Journal of Educational Technology Systems*, *11*, pp. 155–166, 1982.
21. J. McComas, J. Pivik, and M. Laflamme, Children's Transfer of Spatial Learning from Virtual Reality to Real Environments, *CyberPsychology & Behavior*, *1*:2, pp. 115–122, 1998.
22. A. Hazzard, Children's Experience with Knowledge of and Attitude toward Disabled Persons, *Journal of Special Education*, *17*:2, pp. 131–139, 1983.
23. G. Royal and M. Roberts, Students' Perceptions of and Attitudes toward Disabilities: A Comparison of Twenty Conditions, *Journal of Clinical Child Psychology*, *16*:2, pp. 122–132, 1987.
24. F. Rowley-Kelly, Social Acceptance and Disability Awareness, in *Teaching the Student with Spina Bifida*, L. Fern, F. Rowley-Kelly, and D. H. Reigel (eds.), Paul H. Brooks Publishing, Baltimore, pp. 245–250, 1993.
25. S. B. Baker and M. A. Rogosky-Grassi, Access to the School, in *Teaching the Student with Spina Bifida*, L. Fern, F. Rowley-Kelly, and D. H. Reigel (eds.), Paul H. Brooks Publishing, Baltimore, pp. 31–70, 1993.
26. G. Clunies-Ross and K. O'Meara, Changing the Attitudes of Students toward Peers with Disabilities, *Australian Psychologist*, *24*:2, pp. 273–284, 1989.
27. A. Hazzard and B. Baker, Enhancing Children's Attitudes toward Disabled Peers Using a Multi-Media Intervention, *Journal of Applied Developmental Psychology*, *3*, pp. 247–262, 1982.
28. W. Henderson, Recommendations of Program Presenters about the Design and Implementation of Disability Awareness Programs for Elementary Students, doctoral dissertation, University of Massachusetts, 1987, *Dissertation Abstracts International*, *48*:09, p. 153, 1988.
29. P. L. Rosenbaum, R. W. Armstrong, and S. M. King, Determinants of Children's Attitudes toward Disability: A Review of Evidence, *Children's Health Care*, *17*:1, pp. 32–39, 1988.
30. Y. Leyser, C. Cumblad, and D. Strickman, Direct Intervention to Modify Attitudes toward the Handicapped by Community Volunteers: The Learning about Handicaps Programme, *Educational Review*, *38*:3, pp. 229–236, 1986.
31. A. Tripp, R. French, and C. Sherrill, Contact Theory and Attitudes of Children in Physical Education and Programs toward Peers with Disabilities, *Adapted Physical Activity Quarterly*, *12*, pp. 323–332, 1995.
32. M. Karniski, The Effect of Increased Knowledge of Body Systems and Functions on Attitudes toward the Disabled, *Rehabilitation Counseling Bulletin*, *22*, pp. 16–20, 1978.
33. S. French, Simulation Exercises in Disability Awareness Training: A Critique, in *Beyond Disability: Towards an Enabling Society*, G. Hales (ed.), The Open University, Bristol, Pennsylvania, pp. 114–123, 1996.
34. K. Diamond, Factors in Preschool Children's Social Problem-Solving Strategies for Peers With and Without Disabilities, *Early Childhood Research Quarterly*, *9*:2, pp. 195–205, 1994.
35. J. Kilburn, Changing Attitudes, *Teaching Exceptional Children*, *16*, pp. 124–127, 1984.
36. S. Thurston, R. Wideman, M. Wideman, and P. Willet, Promoting Positive Attitudes on the Disabled, *History and Social Science Teacher*, *21*, pp. 39–43, 1985.

Acknowledgments: This project was funded by Human Resources Development Canada and Nortel Networks. The authors would like to thank our Disability Awareness Consultants, The Ottawa Children's Treatment Centre, The Canadian Paraplegic Association, Jason Odin, and Corpus Christi School for their assistance in this project.

Address correspondence to: Dr. Jayne Pivik, School of Rehabilitation Sciences, University of Ottawa, 451 Smyth Road, Ottawa, Ontario, Canada K1H 8M5

Exercise for Article 13

Factual Questions

1. How is VR defined in this article?

2. What was the age range of the Disability Awareness Consultants?

3. What type of assignment was used to place students into the two programs?

4. How many students received the Barriers intervention treatment?

5. What was the mean post-reported (i.e., after intervention) building barriers score for the Barriers group? What was the corresponding mean for the control group?

6. Was the difference between the two means in your answer to Question 5 statistically significant? If yes, at what probability level?

7. Was there a difference between the Barriers group and the Wheels group on the Children's Social Distance from Handicapped Persons Scale?

Questions for Discussion

8. In lines 30–32, the researchers indicate that negative attitudes expressed by their peers may be the most difficult type of barrier encountered by children with disabilities. Would you recommend this program to educators who are looking for a tool to help reduce negative attitudes? Explain.

9. The control group also received a VR program (i.e., "Wheels"). Do you think it would be worthwhile to conduct another study in which the control group did not receive a program? Explain. (See lines 274–281.)

10. In your opinion, is the control program ("Wheels") described in sufficient detail? Explain.

11. When scores are very high (near the top of a scale) at the beginning of an experiment, there is little room for improvement. Thus, it is not possible to obtain large increases. This problem is called the "ceiling effect," which the researchers refer to in lines 423–426. Were you previously aware of this type of problem in conducting research? How important do you think it was in this study?

12. If you were conducting a study on the same topic, what changes in the research methodology, if any, would you make?

Quality Ratings

Directions: Indicate your level of agreement with each of the following statements by circling a number from 5 for strongly agree (SA) to 1 for strongly disagree (SD). If you believe an item is not applicable to this research article, leave it blank. Be prepared to explain your ratings.

A. The introduction establishes the importance of the study.

SA   5   4   3   2   1   SD

B. The literature review establishes the context for the study.

SA   5   4   3   2   1   SD

C. The research purpose, question, or hypothesis is clearly stated.

SA   5   4   3   2   1   SD

D. The method of sampling is sound.

SA   5   4   3   2   1   SD

E. Relevant demographics (for example, age, gender, and ethnicity) are described.

SA   5   4   3   2   1   SD

F. Measurement procedures are adequate.

SA   5   4   3   2   1   SD

G. All procedures have been described in sufficient detail to permit a replication of the study.

SA   5   4   3   2   1   SD

H. The participants have been adequately protected from potential harm.

SA   5   4   3   2   1   SD

I. The results are clearly described.

SA   5   4   3   2   1   SD

J. The discussion/conclusion is appropriate.

SA   5   4   3   2   1   SD

K. Despite any flaws, the report is worthy of publication.

SA   5   4   3   2   1   SD

Article 14

Project Trust: Breaking Down Barriers Between Middle School Children

MARY ELLEN BATIUK
Wilmington College

JAMES A. BOLAND
Wilmington College

NORMA WILCOX
Wright State University

ABSTRACT. This paper analyzes the success of a camp retreat weekend called Project Trust involving middle school students and teachers. The goal of the camp is to break down barriers between cliques identified as active in the school. The camp focuses on building team relationships across clique membership and incorporates elements of peace education and conflict resolution. A treatment group (campers) and comparison group (noncampers) were administered an adaptation of the Bogardus Social Distance Test and the Piers-Harris Children's Self-Concept Scale before and after the camp. Attendance was found to lower social distance scores for nine of the ten groups/cliques. Campers also had higher self-concept scores after the retreat.

From *Adolescence*, *39*, 531–538. Copyright © 2004 by Libra Publishers, Inc. Reprinted with permission.

The *Final Report and Findings of the Safe School Initiative* indicates that from 1993 to 1997, the "odds that a child in grades 9–12 would be threatened or injured with a weapon in school were 8 percent, or 1 in 13 or 14; the odds of getting into a physical fight at school were 15 percent, or 1 in 7" (Vossekuil, Fein, Reddy, Borum, & Modzeleski, 2002, p. 12). Such widespread experiences of school violence have led to what McLaren, Leonardo, and Allen (2000) call a "bunker mentality" on many school campuses. As Tompkins (2000) points out, "increased levels of security suggest to students and teachers that they learn and teach in a violent environment where students cannot be trusted and are under suspicion" (p. 65). This is doubly unfortunate, not only because positive school climates promote learning, but that they have been found to be strong predictors of the absence of school violence (Welsh, 2000).

Further, one of the ten key findings of the analysis of the Safe School Initiative is that "many attackers felt bullied, persecuted or injured by others prior to the attack" (Vossekuil et al., 2002, p. 18). In a word, attackers felt excluded. Kramer (2000) has established that patterns of individual exclusion in school settings contribute to violence among students because exclusion separates them from the informal social control networks provided by parents, schools, and communities. This lack of informal social control has been linked to diminishing social and cultural capital (Hagen, 1985) and ultimately delinquency (Cullen, 1994, Currie, 1998; Sampson & Laub, 1993). Exclusion also preempts the kind of dialogue that can resolve conflicts (Aronowitz, 2003).

As a result, many educators have called for curricular changes incorporating programs in peace education (Caulfield, 2000; Harris, 1996; Pepinsky, 2000) and conflict resolution (Bretherton, 1996; Children's Defense Fund, 1998). For example, 10 years ago, Wilmington College collaborated with a local middle school to provide programming aimed at eliminating patterns of mistrust and exclusion fostered by student cliques. The collaboration was a natural one since Wilmington College offers extensive teacher education programs and maintains a strong tradition of conflict resolution and peacemaking tied to its Quaker heritage.

The training emphasized a mutual and reflexive process of problem solving and conflict resolution in which involved parties actively frame the understanding of both the problem and its solution. Teachers and students at the middle school overwhelmingly pointed to the ongoing problem of conflicts arising from student cliques. As a response, teachers and students designed activities that would help break down barriers among the cliques. From this collaboration emerged Project Trust—a weekend camp retreat in which student opinion/clique leaders engaged in discussions, role-playing, and noncompetitive risk-taking tasks.

The present paper focuses on a program for middle school children that incorporates principles of peace education and conflict resolution techniques to address the pervasive sources of these conflicts within networks of student cliques. It was hypothesized that by engaging student leaders in activities focused on cooperation and breaking down barriers, these same students would become more receptive to interacting with members of other cliques. It was also hypothesized that participation in the retreat weekend would lead to increased self-esteem in the participants.

Method

Project Trust

In the fall of 1990, middle school teachers and stu-

70 dents were asked to brainstorm about the kinds of cliques that were active in the school. A list of 24 groups, active within the school, emerged from these initial brainstorming sessions. Discussions with both students and teachers allowed project managers to hone

75 the list to eight, and these groups became the focal point for Project Trust. The groups included: (1) preps—smart and well dressed, well to do or at least giving the perception that they are, doing what they are told to do; (2) alternatives—baggy clothes, various

80 colors of hair, might be skaters, long hair; (3) jocks—athletes or individuals whose lives are dominated by sports interests, wearing NBA and NFL jerseys; (4) hoods/gangsters/thugs—rule-breakers, tough, like to fight, might be in a gang, wearing black; (5) dorks—

85 geeks, socially awkward, nonathletic; (6) cheerleaders—attractive and active girls; (7) hicks/hillbillies—rural kids, possibly live in trailer parks, like country music; and (8) dirties—poor kids, dirty and cannot help it, poor hygiene.

90 The names of the cliques came directly from the students and teachers. Ethnic groups were not mentioned by the students but were added by the project managers after discussions with the teachers (i.e., whites and African Americans).

Treatment and Comparison Groups

95 Project Trust camp retreats include student opinion/clique leaders who are identified by teachers and invited to spend the weekend at a local camp that regularly provides team-building exercises to local civic groups and businesses. Middle school teachers receive

100 training from Wilmington College project managers in group process and team building. Both teachers and Wilmington College professors lead the retreats. Once at the camp, students and teachers are placed into Family Groups of 8–10 members designed to cut across

105 clique memberships. Students are encouraged to take ownership of the weekend agenda by developing contracts with retreat leaders. Contracting processes involve eliciting from students what they hope to "get" from the weekend (everything from food to fun activi-

110 ties) and what they are willing to "give" to get those things. During the course of the weekend (Friday evening through Sunday afternoon), student family groups take part in discussions, cooperative tasks, and team building and survival exercises.

115 One team-building activity, titled Toxic Waste, involves blindfolded team members "dumping" a cupful of sludge into another cup inside of a 4 × 4 square. Unsighted family team members cannot cross into the square, have access only to 4 bungee cords, the cup of

120 sludge and a rubber band, and are given directions by their sighted team members. Another activity, called Plane Crash, involves the completion of various tasks by team members who have received several handicaps (broken bones, loss of sight) and limited supplies

125 (food, water, blankets). Also included in the retreat are an extended outdoor trust walk and a structured discussion about the harmful effects of put-downs and techniques for resolving conflicts around them. Students and teachers discuss the case study of a young girl who

130 committed suicide, leaving a note explaining the exclusion she felt because of being called a "fat hog" by her classmates.

Family groups are brought together regularly to assess how the retreat is progressing. Plenty of snacks,

135 pizza, and pop are provided to foster an environment of fun and relaxation during the time that students and teachers spend together.

In addition to this treatment group, fellow students who did not attend the camp were selected on the basis

140 of availability and assessed using the same instrument, for the purposes of comparison. Treatment group students were identified by teachers on the basis of being "opinion leaders."

Assessments

145 Assessment of Project Trust weekends relies primarily on an adaptation of the Bogardus (1933) Social Distance Scale to measure the social distances between the students and identified groups before and after the camp experience. The scale was chosen because of its ease of scoring and high reliability (Miller, 1991;

150 Owen et al., 1981). In addition, the scale has also been successfully and widely adapted for use with school-age children (Cover, 2001; Lee, Sapp, & Ray, 1996; Mielenz, 1979; Payne, 1976; Williams, 1992). On this modified scale, students were asked to rate all ten

155 groups on a scale of 0–7, with 7 representing the greatest degree of social distance: 0–be best friends with; 1–invite over to my house; 3–choose to eat lunch with; 4–say "hi" to only; 5–as a member of my homeroom only; 6–as a member of my school only; 7–exclude

160 them from my school. Both treatment and comparison groups completed this scale immediately before the retreat weekend and within one month after the camp.

In addition, treatment and nontreatment groups completed the Piers-Harris Children's Self-Concept

165 Scale (Piers, 1984). This self-report scale measures self-concept using 80 yes/no questions and is intended for use with youths aged 8–18. The scale was administered to the treatment group before and after the camp experience, and to the comparison group before the

170 camp experience.

Results

Camps have been held from 1998 through 2002 in both the fall and spring. An independent-samples t test (equal variances not assumed) comparing the pretest mean scores of the treatment group ($n = 298$) and com-

175 parison group ($n = 215$) found significant differences between only two groups: preps ($t = 5.058$, $df = 405$, $p < .01$) and jocks ($t = 2.654$, $df = 378$, $p < .01$). In both cases, the means of the treatment group social distance scores were lower than for the comparison group: preps

180 ($M = 2.28$, $SD = 2.06$, for campers, vs. $M = 3.34$, $SD =$

2.24, for noncampers), jocks ($M = 2.07$, $SD = 2.14$, for campers, vs. $M = 2.66$, $SD = 2.43$, for noncampers). Thus, treatment and comparison students were roughly equivalent in their perceptions of social distance from their classmates with the exception of the preps and the jocks. In these two instances, the campers reported statistically significant lower social distance scores when compared to noncampers.

A paired-samples t test was calculated for both the treatment group ($n = 216$) and comparison group ($n = 80$). Table 1 reports the results for the treatment group. For all eight cliques, attendance at the camp significantly reduced perceptions of social distance. In addition, perceptions of social distance were significantly reduced for African Americans but not whites. Mean scores for whites were already low (pretest $M = .54$, $SD = 1.00$) and did fall (posttest $M = .47$, $SD = .86$), though not to a statistically significant degree. The greatest change for campers was in their perceptions of dirties, moving an average of 1.55 points on the 7-point scale (pretest $M = 5.55$, $SD = 1.40$; posttest $M = 4.00$, $SD = 1.71$); dorks, moving an average of 1.37 points (pretest $M = 4.60$, $SD = 2.10$; posttest $M = 3.23$, $SD = 1.65$); and hicks, moving an average of 1.23 points (pretest $M = 4.38$, $SD = 2.07$; posttest $M = 3.15$, $SD = 1.96$).

Table 1

Paired-Samples Two-Tailed t Test for the Treatment Group (n = 216)

Campers	t	df	p
Preps	6.816	212	.000
Alternatives	5.254	196	.000
Jocks	6.532	207	.000
Hoods	6.709	205	.000
Dorks	10.810	206	.000
Cheerleaders	3.282	213	.001
Hicks	8.608	203	.000
Dirties	11.751	204	.000
African Americans	2.500	208	.013
Whites	1.141	206	.255

Table 2 reports the results for the comparison group (noncampers). The only statistically significant shift was for preps (pretest $M = 3.18$, $SD = 2.23$; posttest $M = 2.74$, $SD = 2.37$). In all other instances, there were no statistically significant changes. However, there were two instances, for dorks and African Americans, in which social distance scores actually regressed.

On the Piers-Harris Children's Self-Concept Scale, self-concept scores also shifted for the treatment (camper) group. The mean score on the pretest was 61.37 ($SD = 12.6$) and the mean on the posttest was 66.13 ($SD = 11.32$). The difference was statistically significant ($p < .01$).

Conclusions

The results suggest that educational programs for middle school children that incorporate peace education and conflict resolution hold potential for reducing divisive student cliques built around difference, mistrust, and exclusion, that often result in the violence found in schools today. While this is only one study in a rural area of a mid-Atlantic state with a unique subculture, it does offer hope of greater validity and reliability with its longitudinal character. Obviously, the study needs to be replicated in a variety of cultural and institutional contexts and across different age groups. However, there is much to be gained by such replication in a society struggling to understand the attitudes of the "other."

Table 2

Paired-Samples Two-Tailed t Test for the Comparison Group (n = 80)

Noncampers	t	df	p
Preps	2.035	72	.046
Alternatives	0.967	63	.337
Jocks	0.150	65	.881
Hoods	0.567	61	.573
Dorks	−0.068	68	.946
Cheerleaders	0.935	72	.353
Hicks	2.264	72	.353
Dirties	1.589	67	.117
African Americans	−0.271	74	.787
Whites	0.090	206	.928

References

Aronowitz, S. (2003). Essay on violence. In *Smoke and mirrors: The hidden context of violence in schools and society* (pp. 211–227). New York: Rowman and Littlefield.

Bogardus, E. S. (1933). A social distance scale. *Sociology and Social Research, 17*, 265–271.

Bretherton, D. (1996). Nonviolent conflict resolution in children. *Peabody Journal of Education, 71*, 111–127.

Caulfield, S. L. (2000). Creating peaceable schools. *ANNALS: The American Academy of Political and Social Science, 567*, 170–185.

Children's Defense Fund. (1998). *Keeping children safe in schools: A resource for states.* Available: http://www.childrensdefense.org.

Cover, J. D. (1995). The effects of social contact on prejudice. *The Journal of Social Psychology, 135*, 403–405.

Cullen, F. T. (1994). Social support as an organizing concept for criminology: Presidential address to the Academy of Criminal Justice Sciences. *Justice Quarterly, 11*, 527–559.

Currie, E. (1998). *Crime and punishment in America.* New York: Metropolitan Books.

Hagen, J. (1985). *Modern criminology: Crime, criminal behavior and its control.* New York: McGraw-Hill.

Harris, I. M. (1996). Peace education in an urban school district in the United States. *Peabody Journal of Education, 71*, 63–83.

Kramer, R. (2000). Poverty, inequality, and youth violence. *ANNALS: The American Academy of Political and Social Science, 567*, 123–139.

Lee, M. Y., Sapp, S. G., & Ray, M. C. (1996). The Reverse Social Distance Scale. *The Journal of Social Psychology, 136*, 17–24.

McLaren, P., Leonardo, Z., & Allen, R. L. (2000). Rated "cv" for cool violence. In S. U. Spina (Ed.), *Smoke and mirrors: The hidden context of violence in schools and society* (pp. 67–92). New York: Rowman and Littlefield.

Mielenz, C. C. (1979). Non-prejudiced Caucasian parents and attitudes of their children toward Negroes. *The Journal of Negro Education, 1979*, 12–21.

Miller, D. (1991). *Handbook of research design and social measurement.* Newbury Park, CA: Sage Publications.

Owen, C. A., Eisner, H. C., & McFaul, T. R. (1981). A half century of social distance research: National replication of the Bogardus studies. *Sociology and Social Research, 66*, 80–98.

Payne, W. J. (1976). Social class and social differentiation: A case for multidimensionality of social distance. *Sociology and Social Research, 61*, 54–67.

Pepinsky, H. (2000). Educating for peace. *ANNALS: The American Academy of Political and Social Science, 567,* 157–169.

Piers, E. V. (1984). *Piers-Harris Children's Self-Concept Scale revised manual 1984.* Los Angeles: Western Psychological Services.

Sampson, R. J., & Laub, J. H. (1993). *Crime in the making: Pathways and turning points through life.* Cambridge, MA: Harvard University Press.

Tompkins, D. E. (2000). School violence: Gangs and a culture of fear. *ANNALS: The American Academy of Political and Social Science, 567,* 54–71.

Vossekuil, B., Fein, R A., Reddy, M., Borum, R., & Modzeleski, W. (2002). *The final report and findings of the Safe School Initiative: Implications for the prevention of school attacks in the United States.* Washington, DC: U.S. Secret Service and U.S. Department of Education.

Welsh, W. N. (2000). The effects of school climate on school disorder. *ANNALS: The American Academy of Political and Social Science, 567,* 88–107.

Williams, C. (1992). The relationship between the affective and cognitive dimensions of prejudice. *College Student Journal, 26,* 50–54.

About the authors: Mary Ellen Batiuk, Department of Social and Political Studies, Wilmington College. James A. Boland, Department of Education, Wilmington College. Norma Wilcox, Department of Sociology, Wright State University.

Address correspondence to: Mary Ellen Batiuk, Department of Social and Political Studies, Wilmington College, Wilmington, OH 45177. E-mail: mebatiuk@wilmington.edu

Exercise for Article 14

Factual Questions

1. What resulted from the brainstorming sessions?

2. On the Social Distance Scale, what does a rating of "3" represent?

3. On the Social Distance Scale, does a high rating (e.g., "7") represent the greatest degree of social distance *or* does it represent the least degree of social distance?

4. In terms of social distance, the greatest change for campers from pretest to posttest was in their perceptions of what group?

5. In Table 1, all differences are statistically significant except for one group. Which group?

6. Was the treatment group's pretest to posttest difference on self-concept statistically significant? If yes, at what probability level?

Questions for Discussion

7. Keeping in mind that this is a research report and not an instructional guide, is the description of the treatment in lines 95–137 described in sufficient detail so that you have a clear picture of it? Explain.

8. For the comparison group, fellow students who did not attend the camp were selected on the basis of availability. How much stronger would this experiment have been if students had been randomly assigned to the treatment and comparison groups? Explain. (See lines 138–143.)

9. In your opinion, is the Piers-Harris Children's Self-Concept Scale described in sufficient detail? Explain. (See lines 163–170.)

10. The researchers state that "the study needs to be replicated in a variety of cultural and institutional contexts and across different age groups." In your opinion, are the results of this study sufficiently promising to warrant such replications? Explain.

11. What changes, if any, would you suggest making in the research methodology used in this study?

Quality Ratings

Directions: Indicate your level of agreement with each of the following statements by circling a number from 5 for strongly agree (SA) to 1 for strongly disagree (SD). If you believe an item is not applicable to this research article, leave it blank. Be prepared to explain your ratings.

A. The introduction establishes the importance of the study.

SA   5   4   3   2   1   SD

B. The literature review establishes the context for the study.

SA   5   4   3   2   1   SD

C. The research purpose, question, or hypothesis is clearly stated.

SA   5   4   3   2   1   SD

D. The method of sampling is sound.

SA   5   4   3   2   1   SD

E. Relevant demographics (for example, age, gender, and ethnicity) are described.

SA   5   4   3   2   1   SD

F. Measurement procedures are adequate.

SA   5   4   3   2   1   SD

G. All procedures have been described in sufficient detail to permit a replication of the study.

SA   5   4   3   2   1   SD

H. The participants have been adequately protected from potential harm.

SA   5   4   3   2   1   SD

I. The results are clearly described.

SA   5   4   3   2   1   SD

J. The discussion/conclusion is appropriate.

SA   5   4   3   2   1   SD

K. Despite any flaws, the report is worthy of publica-
    tion.

SA   5   4   3   2   1   SD

Article 15

Using a Psychoeducational Approach to Increase the Self-Esteem of Adolescents at High Risk for Dropping Out

DON WELLS
Louisiana Tech University

JEROME TOBACYK
Louisiana Tech University

MARK MILLER
Louisiana Tech University

ROBERT CLANTON
Louisiana Tech University

ABSTRACT. The effectiveness of an ecologically oriented approach in changing the self-concepts of 80 high-risk adolescents was investigated. Participants were administered a self-esteem scale before and after an eight-week psychoeducational program designed for dropout prevention. Results indicated significant reductions in dropout rates and increased self-esteem among participants.

From *Adolescence*, 37, 431–434. Copyright © 2002 by Libra Publishers, Inc. Reprinted with permission.

Over 10% of white adolescents, 15% of African American adolescents, and 35% of Hispanic adolescents drop out of school (U.S. Department of Commerce, 1995). In addition, Kelly (1963) contends that many young adolescents continue to attend school even though they have mentally dropped out.

There are numerous reasons why adolescents drop out of school, including lack of interest in school, low grades, misconduct, low reading and math abilities, financial problems, personality problems, parental influence, family background, and other socioeconomic factors (Browne & Rife, 1991; Buhrmester, 1990; Horowitz, 1992; Kupersmidt & Coie, 1990; Sarigiani et al., 1990; Zarb, 1984). Finally deciding to drop out, however, appears to be a decision made over time. Many adolescents, by the time they do drop out, have lost all confidence in their ability to succeed in school (Nunn & Parish, 1992) and have developed feelings of inferiority (Cairns, Cairns, & Neckerman, 1989). This study addresses the issue of feelings of inferiority and low self-esteem in adolescents. Specifically, it describes the changes in self-esteem of high-risk students who participated in an eight-week residential program designed to reduce dropout rates.

Method

An eight-week summer program was designed and implemented to prevent high-risk adolescents from dropping out of school. Identified by their high school counselors as being at high risk for dropping out, participants were provided a total immersion curriculum that included academic and vocational instruction, as well as personal counseling services. They were housed on a Southern university campus for the entire eight weeks, including weekends. Five days a week, participants received four hours of academic instruction by master's level schoolteachers and four hours of vocational instruction. Each evening they received 1–4 hours of individual and/or group counseling by counseling psychology graduate students.

Participants

The participants were 80 economically disadvantaged adolescents who were at high risk for dropping out. They ranged from 14 to 16 years of age. There were 32 females and 48 males.

Instrument

The Coopersmith Self-Esteem Inventory–School Form (Coopersmith, 1986) was administered to measure the participants' self-esteem. This 58-item measure consists of five subscales: General Self, Social Self–Peers, Home–Parents, School–Academic, and Total Self. A pretest was administered to participants upon entry into the program, and a posttest administration was completed eight weeks later, just prior to leaving the program.

Results

Table 1 provides the results of the two administrations of the Coopersmith Self-Esteem Inventory–School Form for participants in the program. Significant differences were found between pretest and posttest self-esteem total scores (i.e., Total Self) ($t = 3.24$, $p < .003$), as well as between Home–Parents subscale scores ($t = 4.22$, $p < .001$).

A follow-up study of participants' school retention rates was conducted over the two years directly after participation in the dropout prevention program. The first year after intervention yielded a dropout rate of

Table 1
Self-Esteem Scores for 80 At-Risk Adolescents

	Pretest		Posttest			
	M	*SD*	*M*	*SD*	*t*	*p*
General Self	32.2	7.8	31.8	8.0	−1.52	ns
Social Self–Peers	10.7	3.7	10.5	4.1	−0.83	ns
Home–Parents	9.5	4.3	11.2	4.1	4.22	< .001
School–Academic	8.9	3.5	9.1	3.8	1.98	ns
Total Self	61.3	14.9	62.6	15.3	3.24	< .003

Maximum possible scores: General Self, 52; Social Self–Peers, 16; Home–Parents, 16; School–Academic, 16; and Total Self, 100.

zero. Following the second year, the dropout rate of participants was 6%. For a control group of similar
65 individuals not receiving intervention, the dropout rate was 21.2% for the same time period.

Discussion

The psychoeducational theory providing the foundation of the program involved removing adolescents from their current home environments. Therapists and
70 educators were then afforded the opportunity of presenting an alternative to their current course, that is, potentially dropping out of school. In addition to increasing academic abilities and providing prevocational training, the program offered participants the opportu-
75 nity to consult with counselors on a daily basis, all of which most likely contributed to the success of the program in reducing dropout rates.

Underlying these changes, however, were apparent changes in self-esteem. Curiously, the subscale on
80 which scores most significantly changed during the program was Home–Parents, the area from which they were intentionally removed for the eight-week program. During that time, these adolescents apparently experienced perceptional changes they related to their
85 homes and families.

Significant changes in self-concept cannot fully account for the dramatic reduction in the dropout rates of participants. Given, however, that increasing the self-esteem of these high-risk dropouts was a central focus
90 of the therapeutic milieu, further investigations may reveal the specific relationships between increases in self-esteem and reductions in dropout rates.

References

Browne, C. S., & Rife, J. C. (1991). Social, personality, and gender differences in at-risk and not-at-risk sixth-grade students. *Journal of Early Adolescence*, *11*, 482–495.

Buhrmester, D. (1990). Intimacy of friendships, interpersonal competence, and adjustment during preadolescence and adolescence. *Child Development*, *61*, 1101–1111.

Cairns, R. B., Cairns, B. D., & Neckerman, H. J. (1989). Early school dropout: Configuration and determinants. *Child Development*, *60*, 1436–1452.

Coopersmith, S. (1986). *Self-Esteem Inventory*. Palo Alto, CA: Consulting Psychologist Press.

Horowitz, T. R. (1992). Dropout—Mertonian or reproduction scheme? *Adolescence*, *27*, 451–459.

Kelly, E. C. (1963). The dropout—Our greatest challenge. *Educational Leadership, 20*, 294–296.

Kupersmidt, J. B., & Coie, J. D. (1990). Preadolescent peer status, aggression, and school adjustment as predictors of externalizing problems in adolescence. *Child Development*, *61*, 1350–1362.

Nunn, G. D., & Parish, T. S. (1992). The psychosocial characteristics of at-risk high school students. *Adolescence*, *27*, 435–440.

Sarigiani, P. A., Wilson, J. L., Peterson, A. C., & Viocay, J. R. (1990). Self-image and educational plans of adolescents from two contrasting communities. *Journal of Early Adolescence, 10*, 37–45.

U.S. Department of Commerce, Bureau of the Census. (1995). *Statistical abstract of the United States, 1995*. Washington, DC: U.S. Government Printing Office.

Zarb, J. M. (1984). A comparison of remedial failure and successful secondary school students across self-perception and past and present school performance variables. *Adolescence, 19*, 335–348.

Address correspondence to: Don Wells, Department of Psychology and Behavioral Sciences, Louisiana Tech University, P.O. Box 10048, Ruston, LA 71272.

Exercise for Article 15

Factual Questions

1. In the literature review, the researchers state that "There are numerous reasons why adolescents drop out of school," followed by a list of reasons. How many references are cited for this portion of the literature review?

2. Where were students "housed" during the program?

3. Who conducted the counseling in the evenings?

4. The difference between the pretest and posttest means on the Home–Parents subscale scores was statistically significant. At what probability level was it significant?

5. What was the pretest mean on the Home–Parents subscale?

6. On the Home–Parents subscale, the posttest mean is how many points higher than the pretest mean?

7. What was the dropout rate for the control group?

Questions for Discussion

8. The researchers mention that "many young adolescents continue to attend school even though they have mentally dropped out." In your opinion, is this an important point to make in the introduction to this particular study? If so, would you find it useful to have more information on this issue? (See lines 5–6.)

9. The program is described in lines 25–38. In your opinion, is it described in sufficient detail? Explain. The researchers state that the participants were "economically disadvantaged." Is this important to know? Explain.

10. Speculate on the meaning of the abbreviation "ns" in Table 1.

11. The researchers mention the dropout rate for a control group in lines 64–66. They state that the control group consisted of "similar individuals." Would it be helpful to know how the researchers determined their similarity? Explain.

12. The researchers use the term "curiously" in discussing one of the differences. Do you agree that it is curious? (See lines 79–83.)

13. If you were conducting a study on the same topic, what changes, if any, would you make in the research methodology?

Quality Ratings

Directions: Indicate your level of agreement with each of the following statements by circling a number from 5 for strongly agree (SA) to 1 for strongly disagree (SD). If you believe an item is not applicable to this research article, leave it blank. Be prepared to explain your ratings.

A. The introduction establishes the importance of the study.

SA   5   4   3   2   1   SD

B. The literature review establishes the context for the study.

SA   5   4   3   2   1   SD

C. The research purpose, question, or hypothesis is clearly stated.

SA   5   4   3   2   1   SD

D. The method of sampling is sound.

SA   5   4   3   2   1   SD

E. Relevant demographics (for example, age, gender, and ethnicity) are described.

SA   5   4   3   2   1   SD

F. Measurement procedures are adequate.

SA   5   4   3   2   1   SD

G. All procedures have been described in sufficient detail to permit a replication of the study.

SA   5   4   3   2   1   SD

H. The participants have been adequately protected from potential harm.

SA   5   4   3   2   1   SD

I. The results are clearly described.

SA   5   4   3   2   1   SD

J. The discussion/conclusion is appropriate.

SA   5   4   3   2   1   SD

K. Despite any flaws, the report is worthy of publication.

SA   5   4   3   2   1   SD

Article 16

Academic Achievement and Between-Class Transition Time for Self-Contained and Departmental Upper-Elementary Classes

CAROLE J. McGRATH
Lincoln County Schools

JAMES O. RUST
Middle Tennessee State University

ABSTRACT. This study investigated the relationship between elementary school classroom organizational structure (i.e., self-contained versus departmental formats) and standardized achievement scores, transition time between classes, and instruction time. Participants included 103 fifth-grade and 94 sixth-grade students from one school district. Based on previous findings, students from self-contained classes were predicted to achieve significantly more than comparable students from departmentalized classes, take significantly less time to change classes, and spend more time in instruction. Results indicated that the self-contained group gained significantly more on Total Battery, Language, and Science subtests compared to the departmentalized group. Departmentalized classes took significantly longer to transition from subject to subject than did the self-contained classes. No differences were evident for instructional time. Findings were consistent for fifth and sixth grades. The results are limited because of using only one school district.

From *Journal of Instructional Psychology*, *29*, 40–43. Copyright © 2002 by *Journal of Instructional Psychology*. Reprinted with permission.

Educators have debated elementary school organizational structure since the beginning of the twentieth century (Gibb & Matala, 1962; Lamme, 1976). One aspect of organizational structure involves the number
5   of subject areas covered by each teacher. In the self-contained approach, the teacher acts as a generalist and carries responsibility for the curriculum all day. The other extreme is the departmentalized approach. Here, students change teachers for instruction in different
10 subjects. Thus, teachers cover fewer subject areas (Roger & Palardy, 1987; Mac Iver & Epstein, 1992). Advocates for a self-contained organizational pattern argue that it promotes instruction that is children-centered rather than subject-centered. Self-contained
15 classrooms allow the teacher and students the opportunity to become well acquainted. Moreover, self-contained teachers know their students' strengths, weaknesses, and personality traits, enabling better accommodation of the students' individual learning styles
20 (Squires, Huitt, & Segars, 1983). Additionally, self-contained classes allow for greater flexibility in scheduling. Elkind (1988) argues that the time students spend gathering books and papers and moving to other departmental classes cuts into valuable instruction
25 time.

On the other hand, some educators have found that departmentalized organizational approaches offer distinct advantages for the student (e.g., Culyer, 1984). Anderson (1962) presented a strong case for specialization when he reported that only 4 of 260 teachers con-
30 sidered themselves well prepared in all subject areas. Walker (1990) noted greater emphasis on curriculum matters in departmentalized elementary schools.

This paper is similar to one by Garner and Rust
35 (1992), which found that fifth-grade students in self-contained rooms scored significantly higher on group achievement tests compared to their departmentalized peers. The present study added measures of transition time and actual instruction time.

Method

Participants

40 The participants included 197 students (103 fifth graders and 94 sixth graders) from two kindergarten–sixth-grade schools in rural Tennessee. There were 109 students from School A. Of these students, 58 fifth graders (30 boys and 28 girls) and 51 sixth graders (23
45 boys and 28 girls) attended departmentalized classes. School B's participants included 88 students. Of these students, 45 fifth graders (20 boys and 25 girls) and 43 sixth graders (21 boys and 22 girls) attended self-contained classrooms. All of the participants attended
50 self-contained classrooms in the fourth grade. School A used departmentalized fifth- and sixth-grade classes. School B maintained self-contained classes through grade 6. The social class compositions of Schools A and B were similar, with 27% of the students at each
55 school getting free or reduced-fee lunch.

Apparatus

The scale scores and normal curve equivalents of the norm-referenced component of the Tennessee Comprehensive Assessment Program (TCAP) were

dependent variables. The primary aim of the instrument
is to provide a measure of achievement of basic skills
in reading, spelling, language, mathematics, study
skills, science, and social studies. The Tennessee Department
of Education considers the scale scores obtained
on the TCAP useful for measuring growth of
students or groups of students from year to year (Tennessee
Comprehensive Assessment Program, 1993).
Scores range from 0 to 999. Parents, students, and
teachers can monitor annual progress up the scale in
each subject from 0 toward 999. McWherter and Smith
(1993) refer to year-to-year scale score comparisons as
value-added assessment. The TCAP also supplies traditional
normal curve equivalents (NCEs), which have
many of the characteristics of percentile ranks, but
have the additional advantage of being based on an
equal-interval scale. NCEs have a mean of 50 and a
standard deviation of 10 (Bock & Wolfe, 1996).

Transition time was recorded by direct observation.
Each group was observed for two full days, not consecutively,
and not the same day of the week. Actual
time was recorded and rounded to the nearest minute
from the closing of one subject until the beginning of
the next. Instruction time was recorded during the same
days. Subject matter was noted. The first author made
these observations.

Results

Normal curve equivalents (NCEs) and scale scores
from the TCAP Total Battery and subtests (reading,
language, mathematics, science, and social studies)
were analyzed in six separate 2 (Grades: 5, 6) × 2 (Organizational
Structure: Self-contained and Departmental)
× 2 (Male, Female) analyses of variance. The mean
gains were calculated by subtracting the difference
between TCAP pretest scale scores from posttest scale
scores (see Table 1). School A implemented a departmentalized
organizational structure, and School B implemented
a self-contained structure.

Table 1
Mean Value-Added Scores

Test	Departmentalized		Self-contained	
	5th	*6th*	*5th*	*6th*
Total battery	7.62	19.60	16.24	27.88
Reading	16.24	14.51	18.04	21.49
Language	2.15	12.87	20.00	18.94
Mathematics	4.98	30.90	9.49	44.47
Science	−5.60	8.16	13.28	28.22
Social studies	23.82	5.53	21.62	19.93

Significant effects were found for gain scores using
the TCAP scale scores. Self-contained students gained
significantly more than departmentalized students in
total battery, language, and science in fifth and sixth
grades (see Table 1). No differences were found in
reading, mathematics, or social studies. Inspection of
Table 1 reveals wide differences in gain scores. One of
the fifth-grade classes lost points in science. All of the

other groups improved compared to the previous year's
scores. The gain scores found here are more variable
and more modest than those presented in a longitudinal
study of the TCAP (Bock & Wolfe, 1996).

In the NCE analyses, there were no significant main
effects or interactions for organizational structure.
Transition time was significantly more efficient in the
self-contained classes compared to the departmentalized
school (average transition time was 3.27 minutes
for the self-contained groups compared to 4.55 minutes
for the departmental groups). However, there was no
significant difference in actual instruction time. Departmentalized
classes averaged 48 minutes of instruction
time per hour while self-contained classes were
engaged in instruction an average of 46 minutes. That
difference was not significant. Anecdotal observations
revealed that teachers in self-contained classes offered
instruction in academically oriented areas that were not
included in the study. Computer lab, creative writing,
and journal writing are some examples.

Discussion

Implications for practice resulting from this study
include some support for self-contained instruction for
fifth- and sixth-grade children. As hypothesized, significantly
higher gains were found in three academic
areas. These findings support those of Garner and Rust
(1992).

There were two additional measures in the present
study: transition time and instruction time. Transition
time findings agree with those of Culyer (1984) and
Elkind (1988) that students spend more time transitioning
from class to class in schools that follow a departmental
structure compared to those organized in self-contained
groups.

One would logically assume, as Culyer (1984) did,
that the self-contained structure would increase time-on-task
because of the reduced time required to organize
materials and change classrooms. Elkind (1988)
posited also that the extra time spent changing classes
would cut into valuable instruction time. However, the
present study did not find that to be the case. The present
study found no meaningful differences between
departmental and self-contained situations for instruction
time. Despite the longer transition time, the departmental
teachers allotted a similar amount of instructional
time in the five major subject areas compared
to self-contained teachers. The reason for the
nonsignificant difference of instruction time appeared
to be that the self-contained teachers included time for
computer lab, creative writing, and art. The study included
some support for self-contained instruction for
these children. As hypothesized, significantly higher
gains were found in language, science, and total battery.
However, no differences were evident in reading,
mathematics, and social studies.

The study was limited by the small number of
classes used in one small southern town. Observation

160   lasted only two days for determining transition and instruction time. Future studies will need to expand this database to allow for generalization.

References

Anderson, R. C. (1962). The case for teacher specialization in the elementary school. *Elementary School Journal, 62,* 253–260.

Bock, R. D., & Wolfe, R. (1996). Audit and review of the Tennessee value-added assessment system (TVAAS): Preliminary report (Technical Report, pp. 1–35). Tennessee Office of Education Accountability, Comptroller of the Treasury, Nashville, TN.

Culyer, R. C. (1984). The case for self-contained classroom. *Clearing House, 57,* 417–419.

Elkind, D. (1988). Rotation at an early age. *Principal, 36,* 11–13.

Garner, S. S., & Rust, J. O. (1992). Comparison of fifth-grade achievement in departmentalized and self-contained rural schools. *Tennessee Educational Leadership, 19,* 32–37.

Gibb, E. G., & Matala, D. C. (1962). Studies on the use of special teachers of science and mathematics in grades 5 and 6. *School Science and Mathematics, 62,* 565–585.

Lamme, L. L. (1976). Self-contained to departmentalized: How reading habits changed. *Elementary School Journal, 76,* 208–218.

Mac Iver, D. J., & Epstein, J. L. (1992). Middle grades education. In M. Alkin (Ed.) *Encyclopedia of educational research* (6th ed., pp. 834–844). New York: MacMillan/American Educational Research Association.

McWherter, N., & Smith, C. E. (1993). *21st Century Schools Value Added Assessment.* Nashville: Tennessee Department of Education.

Roger, J. S., & Palardy, J. M. (1987). A survey of organizational patterns and grouping strategies used in elementary schools in the southeast. *Education, 108,* 113–118.

Squires, D. A., Huitt, W. G., & Segars, J. K. (1983). *Effective schools and classrooms: A research-based prospective.* (ASCD No. 611–83298). Alexandria, VA: Association for Supervision and Curriculum Development.

Tennessee Comprehensive Assessment Program: Guide to test interpretation. (1993). Monterey, CA: CTB, Macmillan/McGraw-Hill.

Walker, D. (1990). *Fundamentals of Curriculum.* San Diego, CA: Harcourt Brace Jovanovich.

Address correspondence to: James O. Rust, Box 533, MTSU Station, Murfreesboro, TN 37132. E-mail: jorust@mtsu.edu

Exercise for Article 16

Factual Questions

1. In the literature review, the results by Anderson (1962) were cited to support which type of organizational approach?

    A. Departmentalized organizational approach.
    B. Self-contained organizational approach.

2. How many of the participants in School A were girls? How many of the participants in School B were girls?

3. TCAP is an acronym for the name of what test?

4. What term do McWherter and Smith (1993) use to refer to year-to-year scale score comparisons?

5. The departmentalized sixth graders gained how many points on Language?

6. Which group lost points in Science?

7. Was the difference between the two averages for transition time significant?

Questions for Discussion

8. Is it important to know that the social class compositions of the two schools were similar? Explain. (See lines 53–55.)

9. Apparently, individual students were *not* assigned at random to attend one of the two schools (i.e., random assignment was not used). In your opinion, if it were possible to assign the students at random, would the study be improved? Why? Why not?

10. Observations of transition time were done on two different days of the week. Speculate on why the researchers used two days instead of one (e.g., both on Mondays).

11. Instruction time was determined by observations made by one of the researchers. In your opinion, would it be an important improvement to use more than one observer? Explain.

12. In your opinion, are the anecdotal observations described in lines 119–123 important? Explain.

13. The researchers indicate that their results include "some support" for self-contained instruction. In your opinion, how strong is this support? Explain. (See lines 124–126.)

14. The researchers state that "The study was limited by the small number of classes used in one small southern town." Do you think that this is an important limitation? Explain. (See lines 158–159.)

Quality Ratings

Directions: Indicate your level of agreement with each of the following statements by circling a number from 5 for strongly agree (SA) to 1 for strongly disagree (SD). If you believe an item is not applicable to this research article, leave it blank. Be prepared to explain your ratings.

A. The introduction establishes the importance of the study.

    SA   5   4   3   2   1   SD

B. The literature review establishes the context for the study.

    SA   5   4   3   2   1   SD

C. The research purpose, question, or hypothesis is clearly stated.

    SA   5   4   3   2   1   SD

D. The method of sampling is sound.

    SA   5   4   3   2   1   SD

E. Relevant demographics (for example, age, gender, and ethnicity) are described.

    SA   5   4   3   2   1   SD

F. Measurement procedures are adequate.

    SA   5   4   3   2   1   SD

G. All procedures have been described in sufficient detail to permit a replication of the study.

    SA   5   4   3   2   1   SD

H. The participants have been adequately protected from potential harm.

    SA   5   4   3   2   1   SD

I. The results are clearly described.

    SA   5   4   3   2   1   SD

J. The discussion/conclusion is appropriate.

    SA   5   4   3   2   1   SD

K. Despite any flaws, the report is worthy of publication.

    SA   5   4   3   2   1   SD

Article 17

Effects of Parent Education on Knowledge and Attitudes

MARY BETH MANN
Southwest Missouri State University

PEGGY T. PEARL
Southwest Missouri State University

PAMELA D. BEHLE
Jackson County Family Court

ABSTRACT. This study evaluated 42 pregnant and parenting adolescents (aged 13 to 20 years) and adults (who began parenting as adolescents) enrolled in parenting classes. The Parent As a Teacher Inventory and the Adult-Adolescent Parenting Inventory were used to measure change in knowledge and attitudes following participation in the classes. The findings indicated significant improvement as a result of parent education.

From *Adolescence, 39,* 355–360. Copyright © 2004 by Libra Publishers, Inc. Reprinted with permission.

Every year, nearly half a million adolescent girls in the U.S. give birth (U.S. Census Bureau, 2002). About 95% keep and raise their children, which has serious implications since adolescent parenthood and child

5 maltreatment are linked (Coren, Barlow, & Stewart-Brown, 2003; Dukewich, Borkowski, & Whitman, 1999). Lack of both emotional maturity and parenting skills are contributing factors in this maltreatment. While teen parents express empathy and concern for

10 their children, they often lack necessary life experiences and knowledge of child development (Weinman, Schreiber, & Robinson, 1992). Compared with older parents, teen mothers are less knowledgeable about normal developmental milestones for infants and chil-

15 dren; display fewer and poorer-quality vocalizations; are less aware of, and responsive to, their child's needs; are less inclined to engage in spontaneous play, and the give-and-take during play is of lower quality; are less likely to spend time looking at their babies; are more

20 ambivalent about being a mother; and are more inclined to use physical punishment (Dukewich, Borkowski, & Whitman, 1999; Miller & Moore, 1990).

There are other problems associated with adolescent parenthood. For example, children born to adoles-

25 cents often have low birth weights (Alan Guttmacher Institute, 1999; Children's Defense Fund, 1997; Mann & Hunt, 1989; Ventura, Curtin, & Mathews, 2000). Further, the majority (approximately three-fourths) are born out of wedlock (Alan Guttmacher Institute, 1999;

30 Children's Defense Fund, 1998). In fact, for adolescents in the U.S., the rate of out-of-wedlock birth is higher than for any other industrialized nation (Alan Guttmacher Institute, 1999; Clewell, Brooks-Gunn, &

Benasich, 1989; Coley & Chase-Lansdale, 1998;
35 Coren, Barlow, & Stewart-Brown, 2003).

Adolescents often have inappropriate expectations of their children and favor spanking as their primary means of discipline (Bolton, 1980, as cited in Miller & Moore, 1990; Coren, Barlow, & Stewart-Brown, 2003;

40 O'Callaghan, Borkowski, Whitman, Maxwell, & Keogh, 1999). Lack of parenting skills is another factor that puts their children at risk for abuse and neglect (Danoff, Kemper, & Sherry, 1994; Dukewich, Borkowski, & Whitman, 1999). As noted by Bavolek

45 (1989), parent education is often cited as an appropriate means of teaching noninjurious discipline techniques to adolescent parents.

Research has documented the effectiveness of parent education programs for adolescent mothers. Since

50 the 1960s, family life programs have yielded positive results in terms of increasing both knowledge of child development and parent-child interaction skills among low-income families, as well as changing parental attitudes (Clewell, Brooks-Gunn, & Benasich, 1989;

55 Coren, Barlow, & Stewart-Brown, 2003; Weinman, Schreiber, & Robinson, 1992). Such programs have also been found to increase the likelihood that teen parents will return to school and obtain significantly more education. In comparison, teen mothers who have

60 not attended parenting classes have been found to demonstrate more dependency, greater isolation, less interest in activities, more stress raising their children, and more unrealistic expectations of their children (Clewell et al., 1989; Coren et al., 2003).

65 The Parenting Life Skills Center (PLSC), serving at-risk adolescents and families in a medium-sized Midwestern community, offers one such program. Life skills are taught in a caring, nurturing, and accessible environment designed to improve self-worth and qual-

70 ity of life. In addition to attending parent education classes, participants meet weekly as a support group, are given incentives for participation in the program, and share a weekly family-style meal. The parent education curriculum follows a consistent format over a

75 nine-month period.

The purpose of the present study was to evaluate the PLSC program by measuring change in knowledge

and attitudes as a result of participation in parenting classes. In particular, the following areas were assessed: creativity (parental acceptance of the child's creativity and willingness to encourage its development), frustration (parental frustration as a result of inconsistency between parental expectations and the child's developmental abilities), control (scope of child control required by parent), play (parental understanding of play and its influence on child development), teaching-learning (parental views about the ability to foster intellectual development), parental expectations for the child, parental empathy for the child's needs, parental value of physical punishment, and parent-child role reversal.

Method

Participants

The 42 participants were pregnant or parenting adolescents (aged 13 to 20 years) and adults (who began parenting as adolescents). They attended parenting classes, were from economically disadvantaged households, and possessed weak academic skills. The majority were from child-abusive and substance-abusing families, in which their mothers began parenting at a young age.

Measures

The Parent As a Teacher Inventory (PAAT; Strom, 1984) and the Adult-Adolescent Parenting Inventory (AAPI; Bavolek, 1985) were used to measure change in participants' knowledge and attitudes. Both instruments are norm-referenced, reliable, and valid for population under investigation in the present study (Bavolek, 1989; Strom, Johnson, Strom, & Strom, 1992).

The 50-item PAAT contains statements that describe parents' desires and expectations for their child, ways they interact with their child, and the actions taken in response to certain child behaviors. PAAT items are grouped into five subscales (creativity, frustration, control, play, and teaching-learning) that parallel key domains of child development.

The 32-item AAPI was selected to assess participants' attitudes. It consists of four subscales: parental expectations for the child, parental empathy for the child's needs, parental value of physical punishment, and parent-child role reversal. The inventory was carefully developed and normed, using separate samples of abusive adults and abused adolescents (Fox, Baisch, Goldberg, & Hochmuth, 1987).

The curriculum of the parenting classes (i.e., child growth and development, role of play, child discipline and guidance) closely parallels the concepts measured by the PAAT and the AAPI. In addition, a demographic questionnaire was developed to gather information about participants, their family of origin (including physical maltreatment and substance abuse), and their children.

Procedure

The instruments were administered within the first three weeks of participation in the parenting classes, and again four months later or when participants left the Parenting Life Skills Center. Informed consent was obtained. Participants were told that (a) there were no right or wrong answers; (b) it would take about 25 minutes to complete the inventories and questionnaire; (c) their answers were confidential and would be pooled with those of about 30–50 other respondents; and (d) the materials would be identified by number only. Participants received a voucher for groceries upon completion of the instruments.

Results

Comparison of pretest and posttest scores using paired-samples t tests indicated statistically significant improvement in six of nine areas ($p < .05$). Participants showed significant gains on four out of five subscales of the PAAT (creativity, control, play, and teaching-learning), and the fifth subscale (frustration) approached significance. Participants also showed significant gains on two of the four subscales of the AAPI (parental expectations for the child and parental value of physical punishment).

Discussion

The six subscales that were statistically significant are related to the content of the curriculum—units were taught on child growth and development, appropriate discipline techniques, and the value of play. These findings support the idea that knowledge about parenting can be imparted, and that the PLSC program is an appropriate means of delivery.

The remaining three subscales—frustration, parental empathy for child's needs, and parent-child role reversal—are related more closely to attitudes and feelings, which are more psychological in nature. Psychological changes may be harder to achieve or take longer to occur. Perhaps conducting the study over a longer period of time would have revealed significant changes in attitudes, specifically frustration, empathy, and role reversal.

Overall, the gains in knowledge were modest (it should be noted that some participants attended classes sporadically). Because this was a short-term study, large gains were not expected. However, anecdotal reports from program educators indicated that participants with good attendance records increased their positive behaviors, such as staying in or returning to school, maintaining sobriety, utilizing community resources, and delaying subsequent pregnancies.

It should also be noted that systematic collection of data from this population was a challenge. Some participants had no permanent home, making it difficult to contact them in order to collect data after they left the program. Some had difficulty reading the inventories and questionnaire and were reluctant to ask for help. Further, self-report measures were used, and social

185 desirability bias may have been a factor in their responses.

Nevertheless, the findings of this study suggest that knowledge about child growth and development can be increased through parent education. It is hoped that
190 such gains will result in better parenting behaviors and fewer instances of child abuse and neglect.

References

Alan Guttmacher Institute (1999). *Teen sex and pregnancy.* Retrieved October 13, 2003, from http://www.agi-usa.org/pubs/fbs_teen_sex.html

Bavolek, S. J. (1985). *Handbook for the Adult-Adolescent Parenting Inventory.* Schaumburg, IL: Family Development Associates.

Bavolek, S. J. (1989). Assessing and treating high-risk parenting attitudes. *Early Child Development and Care, 42,* 99–112.

Children's Defense Fund. (1997). *The state of America's children yearbook 1997.* Washington, DC: Author.

Children's Defense Fund. (1998). *The state of America's children yearbook 1998.* Washington, DC: Author.

Clewell, B. C., Brooks-Gunn, J., & Benasich, A. A. (1989). Evaluating child related outcomes of teenage parenting programs. *Family Relations, 8,* 201–209.

Coley, R. L., & Chase-Lansdale, P. L. (1998). Adolescent pregnancy and parenthood: Recent evidence and future directions. *American Psychologist, 53,* 152–166.

Coren, E., Barlow, J., & Stewart-Brown, S. (2003). The effectiveness of individual and group-based parenting programmes in improving outcomes for teenage mothers and their children: A systematic review [Electronic version]. *Journal of Adolescence, 26,* 79–103.

Danoff, N. L., Kemper, K. J., & Sherry, B. (1994). Risk factors for dropping out of a parenting education program. *Child Abuse & Neglect, 18,* 599–606.

Dukewich, T. L., Borkowski, J. G., & Whitman, T. L. (1999). Longitudinal analysis of maternal abuse potential and developmental delays in children of adolescent mothers. *Child Abuse & Neglect, 23,* 405–420.

Fox, K. A., Baisch, M. J., Goldberg, B. D., & Hochmuth, M. C. (1987). Parenting attitudes of pregnant adolescents. *Psychological Reports, 61,* 403–406.

Mann, M. B., & Hunt, S. N. (1989, March). *Impact of a parenthood education course on adolescents' knowledge.* Paper presented at the annual meeting of the American Educational Research Association, San Francisco.

Miller, B. C., & Moore, K. A. (1990). Adolescent sexual behavior, pregnancy, and parenting: Research through the 1980s. *Journal of Marriage and the Family, 52,* 1025–1044.

O'Callaghan, M. F., Borkowski, J. G., Whitman, T. L., Maxwell, S. E., & Keogh, D. (1999). A model of adolescent parenting: The role of cognitive readiness to parent. *Journal of Research on Adolescence, 9,* 203–226.

Strom, R (1984). *The Parent As a Teacher Inventory.* Chicago: Scholastic Testing Service.

Strom, R, Johnson, A., Strom, S., & Strom, P. (1992). Parental differences in expectations of gifted children. *Journal of Comparative Family Studies, 23,* 69–77.

U.S. Census Bureau. (2002). *Statistical abstracts of the United States: 2002.* Retrieved October 13, 2003, from http://www.census.gov/prod/2003pubs/02statab/vitstat.pdf

Ventura, S. J., Curtin, S. C., & Mathews, T. J. (2000). Variations in teenage birth rates, 1991–98: National and state trends. *National Vital Statistics Reports, 48,* 1–16.

Weinman, M. L., Schreiber, N. B., & Robinson, M. (1992). Adolescent mothers: Were there any gains in a parent education program? *Family Community Health, 15,* 1–10.

Acknowledgments: The authors thank the students and colleagues involved in collecting, transcribing, and coding the data, and the participants at the Parenting Life Skills Center.

About the authors: Mary Beth Mann, Child Development Center, Southwest Missouri State University. Peggy T. Pearl, Early Childhood and Family Development, Southwest Missouri State University. Pamela D. Behle, Jackson County Family Court, Kansas City, Missouri.

Address correspondence to: Mary Beth Mann, Child Development Center, Southwest Missouri State University, 901 South National Avenue, Springfield, Missouri 65804. E-mail: mem032f@smsu.edu

Exercise for Article 17

Factual Questions

1. What is the stated purpose of this study?

2. What was the sample size?

3. Is there any indication that the PAAT is valid?

4. What probability level was used to determine statistical significance?

5. Participants showed significant gains on how many of the AAPI subscales?

6. What type of reports indicated that participants with good attendance records increased their positive behaviors?

7. Did all the participants find it easy to read the inventories and questionnaire?

Questions for Discussion

8. Do you believe that the program offered by the PLSC is described in sufficient detail? Explain. (See lines 65–75.)

9. In your opinion, would it be important to know more about the demographics of the participants? (See lines 92–99 and 126–130.)

10. The researchers mention that "informed consent" was obtained. Is this important? Explain. (See lines 134–135.)

11. The researchers report that there were significant differences on four out of five of the PAAT subscales. Would you be interested in seeing the mean (i.e., average) scores on these subscales? Explain. (See lines 145–152.)

12. Do you think that the inclusion of a control group in this experiment would have improved its validity? Explain.

13. The researchers mention the possibility of "social desirability bias" on the self-report measures that they used. Do you think this might have impacted the validity of this study? See lines 184–186.

Quality Ratings

Directions: Indicate your level of agreement with each of the following statements by circling a number from 5 for strongly agree (SA) to 1 for strongly disagree (SD). If you believe an item is not applicable to this research article, leave it blank. Be prepared to explain your ratings.

A.   The introduction establishes the importance of the study.

        SA   5   4   3   2   1   SD

B.   The literature review establishes the context for the study.

        SA   5   4   3   2   1   SD

C.   The research purpose, question, or hypothesis is clearly stated.

        SA   5   4   3   2   1   SD

D.   The method of sampling is sound.

        SA   5   4   3   2   1   SD

E.   Relevant demographics (for example, age, gender, and ethnicity) are described.

        SA   5   4   3   2   1   SD

F.   Measurement procedures are adequate.

        SA   5   4   3   2   1   SD

G.   All procedures have been described in sufficient detail to permit a replication of the study.

        SA   5   4   3   2   1   SD

H.   The participants have been adequately protected from potential harm.

        SA   5   4   3   2   1   SD

I.   The results are clearly described.

        SA   5   4   3   2   1   SD

J.   The discussion/conclusion is appropriate.

        SA   5   4   3   2   1   SD

K.   Despite any flaws, the report is worthy of publication.

        SA   5   4   3   2   1   SD

Article 18

Improving Textbook Reading in a Middle School Science Classroom

RICH RADCLIFFE
Southwest Texas State University

DAVID CAVERLY
Southwest Texas State University

CYNTHIA PETERSON
Southwest Texas State University

MATT EMMONS
Prairie Lea Independent School District

ABSTRACT. Ineffective approaches for teaching with print may prevent textbook reading from being a useful learning resource in middle school. University faculty mentored a middle school science teacher as he implemented a textbook study-reading approach, PLAN (Caverly, Mandeville, & Nicholson, 1995), in 2 classes (*n* = 33). PLAN orchestrates 4 strategies through student-created mapping. After 3 months of strategy use, students gained in a self-report of strategic reading and in comprehension as reflected by maps. Post-assessment interviews revealed that the teacher had changed his instructional routine, moving through stages of strategy awareness, understanding, and adaptation. The teacher changed his expectation that students would complete textbook reading and that it increased student learning. The students changed their expectation that they could read and learn from the textbook.

From *Reading Improvement*, 41, 145–156. Copyright © 2004 by Project Innovation. Reprinted with permission.

Although educators have long debated the role of the textbook for learning, in middle school the science textbook appears to be an important learning resource. According to the National Assessment of Educational Progress (2000), 80% of eighth-grade science teachers reported using the textbook regularly. It may play a stronger instructional role in the classroom when student prior knowledge or the teacher's relative familiarity with the topic is low (Driscoll, Moallem, Dick, & Kirby, 1994).

Weaknesses in textbook content and ineffective approaches for teaching with print may prevent textbook reading from being effective. The American Association for the Advancement of Science (2002) reported that science textbooks do a poor job of following standards-based principles for concept learning, a reason science teachers might avoid assigning textbook reading. In a case study of a middle school science classroom (Driscoll et al., 1994), the teacher presented textbook reading as the learning option for "book people," a style claimed by few students, according to the study results. In this classroom, other sources of learning, such as hands-on activities, seemed more valued. The textbook was used for definitional-level learning while hands-on activities were used for problem solving. The students' low average score (59%) on a unit test of facts and vocabulary suggested that using the textbook as a dictionary was not effective.

To address some of these issues, Haury (2000) recommended that science teachers help students adopt a purposive stance and a questioning attitude for textbook reading. This stance and attitude can be operationalized in the classroom as strategies for content area reading.

The Effectiveness of Reading Strategy Instruction

A substantial body of research documents the effectiveness of strategic reading instruction for middle school students on their comprehension of text (Trabasso & Bouchard, 2002). Explicit strategies prompt students to engage their prior knowledge and to monitor their comprehension. Despite evidence of the effectiveness of these strategies, a number of studies (reviewed by Pressley, 2002) report that few teachers use them in their instruction. To change their instructional routines, teachers likely need added support.

Teachers looking to follow Haury's (2000) recommendation for the science classroom will find little research to recommend the most popular strategy specific to study–reading with textbooks, SQ3R, as it has not shown advantages over traditional studying or students' existing approaches (Graham, 1982). A newer strategy for comprehending and studying textbooks called PLAN has been demonstrated to be effective with middle school students (Caverly, Mandeville, & Nicholson, 1995). It orchestrates a repertoire of strategies that have been validated with upper elementary and middle school students: relating the text to prior knowledge, questioning, summarizing (Pressley, Johnson, Symons, McGoldrick, & Kurikta, 1989), and using imagery and setting a purpose for reading (Brown, 2002). Specifically, PLAN begins with an assessment of the reading task demand, such as taking a chapter test or writing a paper. With the task for reading in mind, students *predict* (P) the content of the text and construct a tentative map; *locate* (L) on the map what is known by placing checkmarks and what is not known by placing question marks; *add* (A) notes during the reading of the textbook to confirm checkmarks and to address the question marks; and *note* (N) a reformulated understanding by revising the map, writing a summary, or performing any other task that might be aligned with the purposes for reading. In utilizing mapping, PLAN improves upon other strategic approaches to textbook reading. The value of student construction of concept maps has been well documented for the science classroom (Al-Kunified & Wandersee, 1990).

The purpose of this research was to examine the effects of introducing the PLAN study–reading strategy into two middle school science classrooms taught by one of the authors of this study [Caverly], a middle school science teacher subsequently referred to as the teacher. First, we asked how this middle school science teacher would change his instruction over a school year as he was mentored in teaching with the PLAN strategy. Second, we asked whether his students were able to learn using PLAN. Finally, we wanted to know how students perceived their use of the strategy.

Methods

The study followed a single-group pretest-posttest design that included multiple post assessments. This multiple posttest approach was used to strengthen the single-group design and because we expected a time delay between implementing the strategic reading strategies and generating benefits.

Participants

Participants were the science teacher from a small, rural middle school and the 15 seventh-grade and 18 eighth-grade students in his two science classes. The teacher held a master's degree in biology and had more than three years of teaching experience. As the only science teacher for the school, he taught the same students for both fall and spring semesters. Students' scores on the district's recently administered STAR test of reading ability (Advantage Learning Systems, 1998) indicated mixed-ability classes. Four students who scored third grade or below on the STAR test were eliminated from the data analyses, as they lacked basic decoding skills. The 29 students included in the analyses were categorized in roughly equal groups by gender and ethnicity (Anglo and Hispanic, though a few students were African American).

Data Sources

Three instruments were administered before and after four weeks of PLAN instruction by the teacher: (a) reading comprehension tests, (b) reading strategy checklists, (c) student-created concept maps. After nine months of strategy implementation, semi-structured interviews of the teacher and students were conducted and transcribed.

Textbook chapter reading comprehension tests. The teacher followed his regular instructional routine for creating chapter tests by selecting six questions from the textbook publisher's test bank. The test for one chapter served as the pretest and a test for a different chapter was the posttest. Each test balanced multiple choice, true-false, and matching questions. The purpose of the tests was to assess students' comprehension of the textbook chapters.

Concept maps. The students created concept maps based upon the science chapters that they were reading. These pretest and posttest assessments provided a second measure of reading comprehension and revealed information about the students' reading processes. The rubric to score these maps (see Appendix at the end of this article) was adapted from one developed by Stoddart, Abrams, Gaspar, and Canaday (2000).

Reading strategy checklist. We adapted a checklist developed by a colleague who had used it for many semesters with developmental college readers. Ten true-false questions asked students about which strategies they used for reading a textbook chapter and for monitoring comprehension (see Appendix at the end of this article).

Field notes. A notebook documented the conversations with the teacher and observations held throughout the nine months of the study.

Teacher and student interviews. The teacher and four of the students were interviewed nine months after the teacher introduced the PLAN strategy into the classroom. Using parallel sets of 12 open-ended questions, one of us (who had not worked with the teacher during the nine months) conducted an hour-long interview with the teacher while another of us conducted shorter, individual interviews with the students. The teacher selected these students because their performance fell in the middle of the range of student performance in the classes. These students were very willing to be interviewed. Questions to the teacher focused on his expectations of students and his instructional routines. Questions to the students focused on their expectations of the textbook and their perceptions of learning from it. The transcriptions of the taped interviews were analyzed using a constant comparative method for identifying themes.

Procedures

The study proceeded in three phases: (a) a preparation phase during which the teacher gained strategy awareness; (b) an implementation phase during which the teacher gained contextual strategy knowledge; and (c) an adaptation phase during which the teacher gained strategy control.

Preparation. The teacher had completed a summer graduate course taught by one of us [Peterson] that focused on integrating reading strategies into content-area teaching. The course included the modeling of specific comprehension strategies for content learning and practice by class members in small groups. PLAN for study–reading was modeled during one class session and practiced by students using a chapter from the course textbook. After expressing interest in trying out the PLAN strategy in his classroom, the teacher was invited to participate in this study.

Implementation. During three months of the fall semester, the teacher met weekly, a total of over 15 hours, with two of us [Caverly and Radcliffe] subsequently referred to as the mentors. During the meetings, the mentors and the teacher held in-depth discussions of the processes of strategic textbook reading and the challenges of implementing it in a middle school classroom. Concurrently, the teacher taught the PLAN strategy in his seventh- and eighth-grade science classes through the following major steps: (a) PLAN was introduced as a new way for students "to read hard material in the science textbook," (b) the teacher illustrated how to create concept maps on the board, (c) the students created concept maps in groups and then individually, and (d) the students individually completed the four steps in the PLAN strategy based on content in their science textbook. The instruction followed Pearson and Gallagher's (1983) steps of explicit instruction by modeling the strategy for students, providing scaffolding during guided practice, and structuring time for independent strategy use for students to internalize the processes.

Adaptation. In the spring semester, the teacher did not meet with the mentors, but remained in email contact. At this point, the teacher focused on integrating PLAN into his instructional routine and on promoting in students the idea of adapting it to be an individual "plan" for strategic textbook reading.

Findings

Changes in the Teacher's Perception of the Textbook

The field notes recorded the teacher's perceptions of textbook readings. Before his participation in the study, the teacher doubted the effectiveness of textbooks for science learning. His own experience had not been positive: "When I was in school the word textbook was like a four-letter word" and he did not know how to teach well with it: "I hadn't realized that I had no experience with someone teaching me how to read and understand a science textbook." Compounding these doubts about the relative importance of the textbook was his preparation for teaching science: "Doing experiments is what science is all about." This preparation was supported by his teaching experience: "Before I taught here, I taught at a project-based learning school and textbooks were completely forbidden."

Changes in the Teacher's Instruction

Three findings emerged from analysis of the transcript of the interview conducted at the end of the study. In comparing his teaching of a unit the previous spring with the teaching of the same unit with the PLAN strategy, these changes were evident at the adaptation phase.

1. The teacher had integrated the PLAN strategy into his instructional routine. "I will begin [the unit] with the PLAN strategy... Near halfway in the first period [I'll say] 'Your assignment is to read the first section. I want you to do the P, the L, and at least get started on the A.' We kind of got in the routine." In class, he leads a discussion of what students already know. Students then have about 20 minutes to get started. They take their books home to complete their PLAN maps and return with them the next day for a grade.

2. He modified the strategy in three ways. First, he used PLAN as a way for students to build background knowledge from the textbook: "The textbook now has become a background knowledge thing." The background knowledge increased student preparation for unit activities: "They come to class ready to discuss and learn things." His second modification was to allow students to choose a mapping format: "Some of the seventh-graders like *Inspiration* (2003), a mapping program with the concept maps on the computer. So some of them have moved on to that while others like doing it by hand." His third modification was that in the "N" step he assigned students to answer the comprehension questions at the end of the section. "Part of the thing I did with the note thing was to ask yourself, did you get out of the reading what the author wanted you to get? And the way to do that is to look at your concept map and look at the question and [ask] do you have the information the author is trying to get you to get."

3. His expectations of his students had changed. "The things that I teach are the same and I use the same materials but my expectations are different."

Effectiveness of Strategy for Student Learning

Comprehension tests. Students' scores on comprehension tests and reading strategy checklists were analyzed using a paired *t* test statistic (two-tailed). Differences in the students' scores on the 10-point reading comprehension pretest *(M = 4.9)* and posttest *(M = 3.9)* were not statistically significant, $t(22) = 1.427$, $p = .167$. Although the slight drop in scores was not statistically significant and too small to be practically significant, this result was unexpected and inconsistent with other findings in this study. The small number of test questions and possible differences in student prior knowledge of the chapter topics may have confounded the results.

Concept maps. Beginning with the first PLAN map, students were able to accurately represent the major headings and subheadings of the chapter. Content accuracy remained stable from the first to the final PLAN maps, with an average of 98% of the propositions recorded correctly. What did increase was the percentage of propositions that reflected paraphrasing of content and higher order thinking (a growth of 9% to 14%). There was also a decline in the percentage of propositions that were simply copied from the text (a decline from 91% to 86%).

Reading checklists. Comparison of the students' performance on the 10-item reading strategy checklist revealed a statistically significant difference, $t(22) = -2.102$, $p = .047$, between the pretest *(M = 5.5)* and posttest *(M = 6.4)* scores. This small gain in reading strategy scores was supported by the teacher's and students' responses in interviews that investigated the expanded use of reading strategies.

Teacher interview. Analysis of interview transcripts revealed four findings from the teacher's perspective on the effectiveness of PLAN.

1. He saw improvement in his students' learning. "They were coming in with more understanding of the material." He saw that "mean grades of the class increased" because students were better prepared for the labs. At the same time he came to believe that the publisher-provided chapter tests were inadequate measures of student learning: "By talking to them on what they learned, I know they have learned more than what they can write on a test."

2. His students moved from needing group support with strategic reading to being independent in their strategy use and able to do the reading as homework. "First, I was teaching group concepts but by February they could do them individually."

3. He believed the benefits to students in using PLAN developed over time: "I use 12 weeks [in the fall] teaching it. [After winter break] we do a refresher PLAN strategy. That is actually where I really started seeing the benefits of it, after we came back and reviewed it again. They had some time to absorb it and think about it and to see."

4. At the end of the Adaptation phase, he observed that students were more willing to complete the textbook reading. In discussing his teaching of the same unit during the previous academic year he stated: "I assigned it but it wasn't getting done." In discussing his teaching this spring he said: "We stand outside the classrooms in between classes and students will run up to you and ask you if they need their textbooks today. [It's] the way they ask [the] question, "Do we have to have our textbooks today?" versus "Do we need our textbooks today?" I think that portrays the kind of attitude shift away from it is your enemy...[when they get an assignment] instead it's I can do that, I understand that, I can answer those questions."

Student interviews. Analysis of interview transcripts revealed three findings from the students' perspectives on the effectiveness of PLAN.

1. The students saw PLAN as part of the classroom routine. They said the teacher prompted them to use the PLAN strategy when they took their science books home to read, and when they created concept maps. All students reported that they took their books home to read twice a week. Some days they were assigned to read a whole chapter at home, other times to read a chapter that was started in class using PLAN. One student said: "We have our PLAN thing [to do]; [we] do the webs." In some cases the concept maps were completed in class, other times the students prepared them while reading at home. A student explained one of the steps: "I start out looking at the main titles in the chapter, and then I break it off into subtitles, and then I will read each paragraph to put information [into the concept map]."

2. The students emphatically reported an increase in their reading since implementing the PLAN strategy: "I have read a lot more this year." Consistently, the interviewed students explained that they had become better readers. "I think I am a lot better, better reader." They elaborated, sharing that they understood more of what they read and that they were using elements of the PLAN strategy. One student explained: "I can understand it a lot better because doing concept maps helped me." In response to an inquiry about changes in reading, another student shared that she used to be scared to read textbooks and did not have any confidence, but now "I like to read." She reported that in addition to reading more in her science book than a year ago, she now reads more in social studies and other subjects.

3. Consistent with the teacher's description, the four interviewed students reported that they were doing well in science; two students explained that their grades had improved during the academic year. Strategic reading appeared to be contributing to their success. Three students explained that they liked to read and that it was helpful: "I like reading the chapters, I like understanding where I got it," "It helps me learn," and "I feel like I get a lot from reading my textbook."

Discussion

This study reveals how a middle school science teacher implemented strategic reading instruction through a collection of strategies for study–reading called PLAN. It reports the subsequent gains in his students' willingness and ability to learn from textbook reading. Consistent with the case study of Driscoll et al. (1994), this teacher was reluctant to rely on textbooks for learning and did not expect his students to be successful in reading a science textbook. More than adding a teaching strategy to his repertoire, he had to overcome his negative perceptions and experiences related to using textbooks to teach science. The

395 short chapter tests, only six questions from the publisher test bank, may have reflected his low expectation that students would read the text or that the test would be a valuable assessment.

400 Consistent with the research of Caverly, Mandeville, and Nicholson (1995), the middle school students in the current study benefited from their use of PLAN as documented by the concept maps. Their posttest scores on the reading strategy checklist indicated that they also engaged in additional reading
405 strategies, such as summarizing what they had read. The students interviewed reported that reading their science textbook helped them to learn science.

A major finding in this study was that adopting this strategic reading strategy in a middle school science
410 classroom involved substantial time and effort by the teacher to modify his instructional routine. He had to develop skills in strategic reading instruction and gain confidence that students would learn from *his* delivery of it. Over a nine-month period, he progressed through
415 three stages as he implemented PLAN: (a) awareness of the strategy, (b) a deeper knowledge and understanding of both why and how to teach it, and (c) control of it to meet his students' needs for learning science content. Scaffolds in this process included a
420 summer graduate course in reading strategies and 15 meetings with two mentors during the fall school term. Consistent with Pressley (2002), this teacher developed in his ability to teach students effective study–reading strategies from simply being aware of the need
425 to teach them, to understanding how to teach them, to the control of teaching them as demonstrated by both his choice to continue to teach them and his willingness to adapt them to fit his needs.

A second major finding in this study was that the
430 benefits of learning the strategies for textbook reading took time to develop. After four weeks of strategy instruction and implementation, the students did not gain on the textbook chapter test, but did improve in their ability to represent the details and to translate the
435 content into their own words through concept maps. They also reported that they were reading more strategically. The teacher believed the students needed more than four weeks to internalize the processes. During the following semester (with the same students in
440 class), he observed that they understood more than what was on the chapter test, as they were better prepared for lab work and better able to use science vocabulary. At the end of the nine months, he saw increases in his students' science grades, which he at-
445 tributed to their better performance in the lab work.

The students reported that they read more often than in the previous school year and they found reading more enjoyable. PLAN engages students in taking responsibility for reading skills by requiring concrete
450 evidence of their reading in the form of a map. In contrast, SQ3R prompts in-the-head operations that may be difficult for the student and teacher to monitor. The

teacher reported that students shifted from initially relying on his instruction about PLAN to relying on
455 small-group support, and finally to independent use of the strategy. This sequence follows Pearson and Gallagher's (1983) steps of explicit instruction.

Finally, this study documents the process of strategy control by the teacher. In the spring semester, after
460 mentoring had ended, the teacher revised the "Note" step in PLAN. (Recall, the Note step is map revision or content reformulation.) Instead, the teacher assigned students to read and answer the comprehension questions at the end of the chapter. Yet, the teacher
465 presented this traditional assignment in a way that prompted students' metacognition: He asked them to compare their maps to what the textbook author saw as most important, as expressed in the chapter questions. A second modification was his focus on using the
470 strategy for building background knowledge in preparation for lab work. This modification shows that the teacher redefined his purpose for having students read the textbook based upon his observations of what they were learning by using the strategy.

Conclusions

475 Textbook reading in this middle school science classroom changed from being an assignment that students were not expected to complete to one that students completed and from which they learned science content. The teacher's expectations of students moved
480 from doubt to confidence that they would read the textbook. Over a period of nine months, the teacher's classroom routine changed to include strategic reading instruction for the use of textbooks through a study–reading strategy called PLAN. Students changed their
485 learning strategies by completing concept maps at home on textbook chapters. The teacher moved through three stages: (a) strategy awareness, (b) understanding, and (c) control, while the students progressed from observing the teacher model PLAN to using it in
490 small groups, to individual classroom practice and homework.

After four weeks of strategy implementation, an evaluation of the students' concept maps indicated an increase in the use of higher order thinking. They
495 gained in their self-reported use of reading strategies. The teacher observed deeper improvement after several months of implementation. At the end of the year, students reported that they were reading their textbooks more often and were understanding more of
500 what they read. Consistent with prior studies, such as Trabasso and Bouchard (2002), we concluded that strategic reading instruction helped students learn from their textbooks.

In this study the teacher modified the strategy to
505 suit his instructional needs. We believe that this adaptation phase is important, specifically that strategic reading instruction must be integrated into the teacher's instructional routine. For example, using

510 PLAN as a vehicle for students to develop general knowledge and concepts served to link textbook reading and the hands-on activities that are often preferred in teaching science.

515 Although these findings support and extend prior research about PLAN (Caverly et al., 1995), they are limited by several factors. First, some of the findings are based on the teacher's and students' perceptions of the implementation. The four-week time span between pre- and posttests likely was not enough time to show the full benefit of the strategy adoption and adaptation.

520 The study is also limited because the approach was to compare the same students' performance over time; the use of a quasi-experimental research design is recommended for future investigation.

Implementation took considerable time and effort, 525 a year's commitment, and a combination of graduate course work and mentor support. Therefore, teacher-educators need to evaluate whether reading workshops or a single reading strategy course are sufficient to enable participants to implement complex new strate-530 gic reading routines, such as the PLAN strategy.

References

Al-Kunified, A., & Wandersee, J .H. (1990). One hundred references related to concept mapping. *Journal of Research in Science Teaching. 27*(10), 1069–1075.

American Association for the Advancement of Science (2002). *AAAS Project 2061: Middle grades science textbooks: A benchmarks-based evaluation.* Retrieved May 19, 2003, from http://www.project2061.org/tools/textbook/mgsci/mgbooks.htm

Caverly, D., Mandeville, T., & Nicholson, S. (1995). PLAN: A study reading strategy for informational text, *Journal of Adolescent and Adult Literacy. 39*(3). 190–199.

Driscoll, M. P., Moallem, M., Dick, W., & Kirby, E. (1994). How does the textbook contribute to learning in a middle school science class? *Contemporary Educational Psychology, 19,* 79–100.

Graham, S. (1982). Comparing the SQ3R method with other study techniques for reading improvement. *Reading Improvement, 19*(1), 45–47.

Haury, D. L. (2000). *High school biology textbooks do not meet national standards.* (ERIC Document Reproduction Service No. ED 463949)

Inspiration Software, Inc. (2003). Inspiration 7.0. Retrieved Jul 24, 2003, from http://www.inspiration.com

Pearson, P. D., & Gallagher, M. (1983). The instruction of reading comprehension. *Contemporary Educational Psychology. 8,* 317–244.

Pressley, M., Johnson, C. J., Symons, S., McGoldrick, J. A., & Kurikta, J. A. (1989). Strategies that improve children's memory and comprehension of text. *Elementary School Journal, 90,* 3–32.

Pressley, M. (2002). Comprehension strategies instruction: A turn-of-the-century report. In C. C. Block & M. Pressley (Eds.). *Comprehension instruction: Research-based best practices* (pp. 11–27). NY: Guilford Press.

Stoddart, T., Abrams, R., Gaspar, E., & Canaday, D. (2000). Concept maps as assessment in science inquiry learning — A report of methodology. *International Journal of Science Education, 22,* 1221–1246.

Trabasso, T., & Bouchard, E. (2002). Teaching readers how to comprehend text strategically. In C. C. Block & M. Pressley (Eds.) Comprehension instruction: *Research-based best practices* (pp. 176–200). NY: Guilford Press.

U.S. Department of Education. Office of Educational Research and Improvement. National Center for Education Statistics. (2001) *The Nation's Report Card: Science Highlights 2000,* NCES 2002–452, by National Center for Education Statistics. Washington, DC.

Address correspondence to: Rich Radcliffe, Department of Curriculum and Instruction, 214 Commons Hall, Southwest Texas State University, San Marcos, TX 78666.

Appendix

Concept Map Rubric

Proposition #	Accuracy							Depth		Complexity	
	Accurate	Partially accurate	Common knowledge	Inaccurate	Affective	Question	Don't know	Basic description	Higher order description	Simple elaboration	Complex elaboration
1.											
2.											
3.											

Each map was scored by categorizing map nodes and links into proposition units, formed by two nodes (bubbles on the concept map) connected by a link. Each proposition was numbered starting with first-level links from the superordinate node, then second-level, and so on. If partially illegible, the text was rewritten. If completely illegible, the proposition was classified as "Don't Know."

Each proposition was scored using the following categories (adapted from Stoddart et al., 2000).

I. Content Accuracy
1. *Accurate*: Correct statement confirmed by text and expert
   • for example, – "acceleration equals net force divided by mass"
2. *Partially accurate*: Correct statement but only partially correct
   • for example, – "Newton's law states a net force changes the velocity of an object"
3. *Common knowledge*: Common or popular knowledge not stated in the text
   • for example, – "Newton's Apple" (TV show)

4. *Inaccurate*: Misconception or confusion
   • for example, – "the lower the mass the greater the inertia"
   or, inappropriately linked
   • for example, – linked to superordinate when should be linked to coordinate concept
5. *Affective*: Statements that express emotions, feelings, or personal thoughts
   • for example, – "boring!"
6. *Question*: Proposition in form of question that cannot be judged
   • for example, – "mass vs. acceleration?"
   (Also, don't classify in the Depth of Explanation or Complexity categories)
7. *Don't know*: Cannot be scored because the meaning of the proposition is unclear or scorer has insufficient knowledge
   • for example, – "Newton developed"
   Cannot be scored because unintelligible due to handwriting or spelling
   • for example, – "dsjalf dasfa werter"
   (Also, do not classify in the Depth of Explanation or Complexity categories)

II. Depth of Explanation
   1. *Basic description*: Statements copied directly from the text
      • for example, – "a force that resists motion between two surfaces that are in contact"
   2. *Higher-order description*: Explanations that paraphrase the text or add function or purpose, such as "how" or "why"
      • for example, – "the rougher the surfaces the greater the friction"

III. Complexity
   1. *Simple elaboration*: The proposition is a single subject-object clause
      • for example, – "Newton's Laws of Motion" are "First Law," "Second Law," "Third Law"
   2. *Compound elaboration*: contains one or more dependent clauses as explanations
      • for example, – "An object will not change its motion unless a force is acted upon it"

Reading Strategy Checklist

_____   _____
code   **date**

Directions: Carefully read the following statements and honestly respond to them using the scale below. Circle either A or B.

A. = Yes, I did this in preparation for this quiz.

B. = No, I did not do this in preparation for this quiz.

A. B.	1.	I made predictions about what the author would say next or what would happen next.
A. B.	2.	I connected ideas from my own experience to what I read.
A. B.	3.	I figured out new words by the ones around them.
A. B.	4.	I created a map of the ideas from the reading.
A. B.	5.	I created examples from my own experience to help my understanding.
A. B.	6.	I memorized key terms.
A. B.	7.	I reviewed the passage after reading to make sure I understood.
A. B.	8.	I skipped parts I didn't understand.
A. B.	9.	I tried to put the important ideas in my own words.
A. B.	10.	I identified the purpose the author had for writing.

Exercise for Article 18

Factual Questions

1. Who used PLAN in this study?

2. On what basis were four students eliminated from the data analyses?

3. How many students were included in the analyses?

4. Was the difference between the pretest and posttest scores on the reading comprehension test statistically significant?

5. What was the mean score on the reading checklist at the pretest? What was it at the posttest?

6. What is the name of the statistical test used to test the significance of the difference between pretest and posttest means on the reading checklist?

Questions for Discussion

7. In your opinion, are the steps in PLAN described in sufficient detail? Keep in mind that this is a research article. (See lines 60–75.)

8. Are the results of this experiment sufficiently promising that you would recommend conducting additional research on PLAN?

9. In your opinion, was interviewing four students sufficient in light of the purposes of this study? (See lines 144–161.)

10. In your opinion, is a 10-point reading comprehension test adequate for a study of this type? (See lines 263–275.)

11. To determine effectiveness in terms of student learning, the researchers used a variety of measures. Is this an important strength of this experiment? Explain. (See lines 263–382.)

12. Is the absence of a control group an important weakness of this study? Explain.

Quality Ratings

Directions: Indicate your level of agreement with each of the following statements by circling a number from 5 for strongly agree (SA) to 1 for strongly disagree (SD). If you believe an item is not applicable to this research article, leave it blank. Be prepared to explain your ratings.

A. The introduction establishes the importance of the study.

SA   5   4   3   2   1   SD

B. The literature review establishes the context for the study.

SA   5   4   3   2   1   SD

C. The research purpose, question, or hypothesis is clearly stated.

SA   5   4   3   2   1   SD

D. The method of sampling is sound.

SA   5   4   3   2   1   SD

E. Relevant demographics (for example, age, gender, and ethnicity) are described.

SA   5   4   3   2   1   SD

F. Measurement procedures are adequate.

SA   5   4   3   2   1   SD

G. All procedures have been described in sufficient detail to permit a replication of the study.

SA   5   4   3   2   1   SD

H. The participants have been adequately protected from potential harm.

SA   5   4   3   2   1   SD

I. The results are clearly described.

SA   5   4   3   2   1   SD

J. The discussion/conclusion is appropriate.

SA   5   4   3   2   1   SD

K. Despite any flaws, the report is worthy of publication.

SA   5   4   3   2   1   SD

Article 19

The Use of Accelerated Reader
with Emergent Readers

MEGHAN J. CUDDEBACK
Albion Central School District

MARIA A. CEPRANO
Buffalo State College

From *Reading Improvement*, 39, 89–96. Copyright © 2002 by
Project Innovation, Inc. Reprinted with permission.

Introduction

Accelerated Reader (AR) is a computer-based reading and management program that is designed for students in grades K–12. AR is developed and distributed by Advantage Learning Systems, a Wisconsin-based
5 company. The goal of AR is to provide measurable reading practice time for each student participant. It purports to supplement any class-based reading curriculum by providing the teacher and each student in the class immediate feedback on how well reading ma-
10 terial has been comprehended.

AR data measure three aspects of students' reading practice: quantity, quality, and challenge. Quantity is defined as the number of books read and the number of points earned. Quality is indicated by how well the
15 students score on AR tests. Level of challenge refers to the relationship between the difficulty of books read and the students' tested reading ability ("Idaho State-wide Implementation of Reading Renaissance," 1999).

Description and Rationale for AR

According to AR providers (Advantage Learning
20 Systems, Inc., 1999) teachers in non-AR classrooms often are unable to measure comprehension of material students read independently without carrying on a one-on-one discussion with the student or evaluating journal entries or worksheets pertaining to books com-
25 pleted by the reader. The AR computer system provides more than 27,000 different books, both fiction and nonfiction, at different reading levels or zones. Students having access to the system first choose a book in their reading zone and read the story. After
30 reading the story at least once, the students take a computerized multiple-choice test, which usually contains 5, 10, or 20 questions. The test measures the students' knowledge and comprehension of the story. After the students complete the test, they are given immediate
35 feedback regarding their score and questions that were answered incorrectly. The students then earn a number of points based on difficulty level and how many questions were answered correctly. The points accumulate to make the students eligible for a number of prizes
40 (Carter, 1996). AR's management system allows teachers to create reports to track students' progress, number of books read, number of questions answered correctly, and number of points earned (Briggs & Clark, 1997).
45 According to AR providers, teachers can be fairly sure that students have read and basically comprehended the story with AR test products. AR provides continuous assessment and accountability for literature-based reading (Paul, Vanderzee, Rue, & Swanson,
50 1996).

Background

One of the occasional criticisms directed at the AR system, including its related assessments, has been that use of it fosters "lower-level" comprehension of what is read. Lower-level comprehension, sometimes re-
55 ferred to as "literal comprehension," generally is accepted as referring to the understanding of information explicitly stated in the text. As opposed to lower-level comprehension, higher-level comprehension requires understanding as well as a use of background knowl-
60 edge to make critical judgments about the text (Leu & Kinzer, 1995). Both lower- and higher-level comprehension are subsumed under a general definition of comprehension—the awareness of that which is being read and the ability to initiate strategies that help when
65 something is not being understood (Bossert & Schwantes, 1995–1996).

Another criticism directed at the AR system centers over its use of an extrinsic reward system to encourage wide reading. While it is agreed that AR helps schools
70 earn higher standardized test scores, some literacy specialists are concerned that these higher scores may come at a great price. Briggs and Clark (1997) maintain that AR devalues reading by rewarding students with extrinsic motivators, such as points and prizes for
75 their reading. Supported by a fair amount of research arising from behavioral conditioning ideology, Briggs and Clark hold that a tangible reward system inhibits the students' development of an intrinsic appreciation and/or love of reading. Students, particularly those who
80 would be struggling readers, are apt to be conditioned to read only when they can garner extrinsic rewards.

As pertains to the above-noted criticisms, providers of the AR system maintain that they are unjustified. AR developers hold that literal comprehension is important. When educators promote higher-level over lower-level comprehension, students begin to see lower-level thinking as unimportant. Higher-order skills often reflect students' backgrounds rather than their achievement so that comprehension gleaned from text is biased for experience. AR tests are less subject to bias and, therefore, all students who read the book and understand it at a basic level receive the same score (Institute for Academic Excellence, April 1999).

Disputing claims on the inadvisability of providing extrinsic rewards, the Institute (November, 1997) points to an experimental study completed in 1994 by Cameron and Pierce indicating that extrinsic motivators, when properly administered, actually enhance intrinsic motivation by positively affecting attitude, behavior, and interest.

A fair amount of research provides insights on how AR affects children in selected age groups. A five-year longitudinal study by Peak and DeWalt (1993) concluded that AR students scored higher on reading measures and had better reading attitudes than their non-AR peers. Briggs and Clark (1997) showed that AR students reported reading more hours per week and checking out more library books per grading period than the non-AR students, and Vollands, Topping, and Evans (1996) showed that sixth graders who used AR and Reading Renaissance (techniques on how to use AR) acquired higher scores in reading comprehension and showed greater improvements in reading attitudes. A doctoral thesis by McKnight (1992) revealed that AR effectively motivates students and helps them acquire better reading habits (cited in Advantage Learning Systems, Inc., 1999), while a study reported by Briggs and Clark (1997) concluded that the more students use AR effectively, the better chance they will have of passing the Texas Assessment of Academic Skills (TAAS). Finally, a study by Topping and Paul (1999) showed that the more students practice reading, the better they become. Topping and Paul concurred that the easier reading becomes for students, the greater chance they will have of spending more time reading. As students increase their reading time, they may then acquire a love for reading. A review of the literature investigating the effects of AR on emergent readers yielded little, if any, insights about its effectiveness.

Purpose

The purpose of this study was to determine if AR is beneficial to the reading development of young emergent readers' comprehension. More specifically, will AR improve young struggling readers' comprehension skills and attitudes so that they can more easily become true independent readers?

Method

Subjects who received AR treatment were 12 of 36 students from a rural high-need school who, after completing first grade, did not meet the district DRP benchmark (a score of at least 12) for promotion. The students receiving AR had been randomly assigned to one of three different summer school classrooms. Their instructor is the first author of this article.

Summer school encompassing the AR program ran over a 4-week period. The children attended school 4 days per week for 4 hours a day. The 12 children examined for effects received AR treatment for periods of approximately 30 to 40 minutes a day every day, with the exception of the last day of each week, when they were expected to write about their favorite AR book using a story grammar guide provided by the teacher. Specifically, the guide asked students to write about or dictate for the teacher or aide (Crawley & Merritt, 2000) the following elements pertaining to the AR book that was their favorite of the week: Title, Characters, Problem, Solution.

During the first 2 weeks of AR time, the children were required to read books within their reading zone (for this study, these were levels 1.0–1.9) and take at least one AR test every day. During the second 2 weeks, the level of books provided was increased, with students having a choice of books that ranged up through 2.9. A motivational bulletin board located in the classroom encouraged students to read and accumulate points. Prizes were awarded to students each week based on the number of points they had accumulated. When the students were not working with AR, they received direct instruction in phonics, sight words, use of context clues (mini-book making), and math.

Whether engaged in AR testing or writing, students were allowed access to the books with which they were working so that they could locate the responses to questions presented. For some students, scaffolding was provided to help them with vocabulary difficulties they encountered while reading a particular book or taking a test.

Finally, to help determine the specific benefits of AR on attitudes, children were administered a short survey at the end of their 4-week program. In a series of three multiple-choice items, the survey asked: What did you like best?,…second best, and…least about learning how to read this summer:…taking AR test?, …playing vowel games?,…making mini-books?,…or writing?

The answers were then tabulated for the final results.

Report of Findings: Literal Comprehension

Displayed [on the next page] is a chart of the 12 students' AR comprehension scores (% received out of 100%) for each of the 4 weeks. The middle and end columns provide a comparison between achievements for the first 2 weeks when book levels available were levels 1.0–1.9 and weeks 3 and 4 when choice was

Comprehension Scores

Students*	Week 1	Week 2	Weeks 1 & 2	Week 3	Week 4	Weeks 3 & 4
Madison	70	86.7	Increase +16.7	60	86.7	Increase +20.7
Cody	86.7	88.6	Increase +2.6	68	83.3	Increase +15.3
Jacob	88	100	Increase +12.0	80	90	Increase +10.0
Calvin	66.7	76	Increase +9.3	46.7	66.7	Increase +20.0
Melissa	44	72	Increase +28.0	80	60	**Decrease –20.0**
Shaquille	80	90	Increase +10.0	80	64	**Decrease –16.0**
Dillan G.	86.7	86.7	Same	93.3	90	**Decrease –3.3**
Dillan S.	100	100	Same	93.3	68	**Decrease –25.3**
Caitlyn	83.3	80	**Decrease –3.3**	73.3	84	Increase +10.7
Ryan	85.7	62.9	**Decrease –22.8**	47.5	68	Increase +20.5
Richard	86	80	**Decrease –6.0**	75	70	**Decrease –5.0**
Samantha	85	84	**Decrease –1.0**	93.3	86.7	**Decrease –6.6**

*Names of subjects have been changed for confidentiality purposes.

provided from books ranging in between levels 1.0–2.9.

Using a 5-point gain or loss from week 1 to week 2, it can be noted that all but two children maintained or improved their literal understandings of stories read, with only one of the children performing below the 70% level of performance often used to determine adequate silent reading performance on many publicized informal reading inventories (IRIs) (e.g., Ekwall/Shanker Reading Inventory, 1993).

When students were given a choice of materials with the option of choosing books that might well be above their reading zones, five students showed a decrease in their literal comprehension performances, though three of these students performed at adequate levels of silent reading comprehension performance, according to publicized IRIs.

Overall, the class mean increased from 81% to 83.9% from week 1 to week 2 and from 74.2% to 76.4% from week 3 to 4. While the conclusions drawn from this facet of the study are limited due to the time over which children's comprehension at different levels was evaluated, most students seem to benefit from their experiences with AR.

With regard to influence of extrinsic motivators utilized in conjunction with this aspect of the study, the instructor felt that they were not harmful. When AR was not in use, students appeared to have just as much enthusiasm as they did when AR was in use. AR was seen as giving some students a "jump start" into reading books for the first time.

Report of Findings: Higher-Level Comprehension

To determine if AR affected higher-level comprehension, students answered four questions pertaining to story grammar elements of their favorite book each week. They were given 45 minutes to answer these questions on paper. The following chart shows how many students correctly answered each of the four aspects of story grammar week by week.

	Week 1	Week 2	Week 3	Week 4
Title	12	12	11	11
Characters	11	12	11	11
Problem	7	9	10	10
Solution	2	4	8	7
n	12	12	11	11

n = number of students

In order to receive a correct answer, the student must have correctly identified the particular aspect of story grammar. A correct answer is as follows: (1) Title: The correct title must be written, (2) Characters: The main characters must be written, (3) Problem: At least one problem must be identified from the story, and (4) Solution: The correct solution to the problem stated must be expressed.

As the chart shows, identification of title and characters (literal comprehension) of the stories they had read posed no difficulty for most of the students. With regard to identifying the problem and solution within each story (higher-level comprehension), this skill, being relatively weak in comparison to identifying title and character during the initial week of the study, was improved for several of the students by the final week of the study.

Case Studies

The written drafts comparing each of two children's understandings of story grammar components for the first week as compared to the final week are displayed below so that qualitative improvements in performance might be observed. Both samples reflect great strides in ability to express understanding. It should be noted here that improvements shown below reflect efforts of the instructor to promote students' story grammar understanding as well as written/oral expression apart from the directives and materials provided by AR.

Madison:

First Week:

All Tutus should be pink. (Title)

Emily and little g (Characters)

Final Week:

More Spaghetti I Say. (Title)

Freddy and Minnis (Characters)

265 Minnis won't play with Freddy because she is eating spaghetti. (Problems)

She got sick. From eating spaghetti.

Now Freddy is going to play (?) with spaghetti, too. (Solution)

270 Madison began the program by being able to write only the title and half the characters. As can be seen by the above example, after 4 weeks she improved tremendously and wrote to all four aspects of the story quite well, though details could have been more clear

275 with regard to the solution.

Calvin:

First Week:

(Note: Calvin simply copied the model provided by the teacher in a demonstration lesson. When asked to write

280 his own answers to the questions, Calvin merely copied the last sentence in the book.)

Final Week:

The title is up up and away (Title)

The characters is a boy and girl (Characters)

285 They get in a rocket

They get in the car

They go back home

As can be noted, Calvin went from copying and not showing any comprehension at all to writing the cor-

290 rect title, characters, and sequence of events (with some exclusions). The book he wrote about is a simple book that has no apparent problem and solution, yet his sequencing and organization of the story were accurate.

Children's Perceptions of Instructional Materials

The survey that was administered to the children

295 during the final week of the program provides some merit for the activities. When students were asked what part of summer school helped them most to become better readers, the majority of students chose AR. Interestingly enough, the vowel games, although played

300 widely and enjoyed by the students, received only one vote. Most of the students indicated that AR gave them more practice reading and therefore made them better readers. Furthermore, 100% of the students put AR as one of their top two choices when asked to indicate

305 their favorite summer school activity.

Conclusion

The findings led the authors to conclude that AR did contribute to students' reading comprehension improvement when utilized in conjunction with other materials and teaching procedures. AR by itself is very

310 motivating and, as with many programs, can be made even more effective when coupled with instructional directives that promote comprehension improvement—both literal and higher level. AR does accomplish its goal of giving students more reading practice time and

315 also goes beyond the goal by increasing comprehension knowledge.

It is our feeling that AR can be beneficial if teachers are trained on how to use the program correctly and also how to supplement the program to increase higher-

320 level thinking skills.

Limitations and Recommendations

One limitation of this study was the shortness of its duration. Only 4 weeks of data were collected. A longer period of observation may have revealed results that would be considered more reliable.

325 A second limitation of this study arises from the fact that it was conducted with at-risk readers. Thus, the benefits of AR cannot be generalized to a normal population.

It is recommended that consideration be given to

330 completing the study with a heterogeneous group of first graders approximately halfway through the regular school year. It is also recommended that the element of choice of books from a wider range of reading levels be studied, with more careful attention to experimental

335 controls.

References

Advantage Learning Systems, Inc. (1999, October). *Research summary* (Issue No. LO331). Wisconsin Rapids, WI.

Bossert, T., & Schwantes, F. (1995–1996). Children's comprehension monitoring: Training children to use rereading to aid comprehension. *Reading Research and Instruction, 35*(2), 109–121.

Briggs, K., & Clark, C. (1997). *Reading programs for students in the lower elementary grades: What does the research say?* (Clearinghouse No. CS013213). Austin, Texas: Texas Center for Educational Research. (ERIC Document Reproduction Service No. ED 420 046)

Cameron, J., & Pierce, W. D. (1994). Reinforcement, reward, and intrinsic motivation: A meta-analysis. *Review of Educational Research, 64*(3), 363–423.

Carter, B. (1996). Hold the applause! *School Library Journal, 42*(10), 22–26.

Crawley, S., & Merritt, K. (2000). *Remediating reading difficulties* (Rev. ed.). Boston, MA: McGraw Hill.

Eisenberger, R., & Cameron, J. (1996). Detrimental effects of reward: Reality or myth? *Journal of the American Psychological Association, 51*(11), 1153–1166.

Ekwall, E. E., & Shanker, J. L. (1994). *Ekwall/Shanker Reading Inventory* (Third Edition 1993). Allyn and Bacon.

Fowler, D. (1998). Balanced reading instruction in practice. *Educational Leadership, 55*(6), 11–12.

Idaho Statewide Implementation of Reading Renaissance. (1999). Madison, WI: Institute for Academic Excellence.

Institute for Academic Excellence. (1997, November). *Toward a balanced approach to reading motivation: Resolving the intrinsic–extrinsic rewards debate.* Madison, WI. (ERIC Document Reproduction Service No. ED 421 687)

Institute for Academic Excellence. (1999, April). *The design of reading practice and literacy skills assessments* (Issue No. LO334). Madison, WI.

Institute for Academic Excellence. (1999, October). *ZPD guidelines: Helping students achieve optimum reading growth.* Madison, WI.

Leu, D., & Kinzer, C. (1995). *Effective reading instruction.* (Rev. ed.). Englewood Cliffs, NJ: Prentice-Hall.

Paul, T. (1996). *Patterns of reading practice.* Madison, WI: Institute for Academic Excellence.

Paul, T., Vanderzee, D., Rue, T., & Swanson, S. (1996). *Impact of the accelerated reader.* Atlanta, GA: Institute for Academic Excellence. (ERIC Document Reproduction Service No. ED 421 684)

Paul, T. (1998). *How accelerated reader quizzes are designed* (Clearinghouse No. CS 013256). Madison, WI: Institute for Academic Excellence. (ERIC Document Reproduction Service No. ED 421 690)

Peak, J., & DeWalt, M. (1993, February). Effects of the computerized accelerated reader program on reading achievement. Paper presented at the annual meeting of the Eastern Educational Research Association, Clearwater Beach, FL.

Sterl, A. A. (1996). Controversial issues relating to word perception. *The Reading Teacher, 50*(1), 10–13.

Topping, K., & Paul, T. (1999). Computer-assisted assessment of practice at reading: A large-scale survey using accelerated reader data. *Reading and Writing Quarterly, 15*(3), 213–231.

Vollands, S., Topping, K., & Evans, H. (1996, October). *Experimental evaluation of computer-assisted self-assessment of reading comprehension: Effects on reading achievement and attitude.* Paper presented at the National Reading Research Center Conference "Literacy and Technology for the 21st century," Atlanta, GA.

Exercise for Article 19

Factual Questions

1. In the AR system, how is quantity defined?

2. According to the researchers, one of the occasional criticisms of the AR system and its related assessments is that it fosters what?

3. How many subjects participated in this study?

4. How often were prizes awarded to students?

5. What was administered to determine the specific benefits of AR on attitudes?

6. From week 1 to week 2, Jacob's percentage points increased from 88 to what value?

Questions for Discussion

7. The researchers note the controversy on the use of extrinsic motivation, which is used in the AR system. What is your opinion on this controversy? Did the literature cited by the researchers on this topic influence your opinion? Explain. (See lines 67–100.)

8. Does the chart showing increases and decreases for individual children help you understand the results? Would you be just as informed if the researchers provided only means and standard deviations for each week? Explain.

9. Do the findings convince you that AR had a positive effect on higher-level comprehension? Explain.

10. In your opinion, how important are the case studies that are reported in lines 247–293 for understanding the effects of AR?

11. Do you agree with the researchers regarding generalizing the results? (See lines 325–328.)

12. To what extent would including a control group improve this study? (See lines 329–332.)

Quality Ratings

Directions: Indicate your level of agreement with each of the following statements by circling a number from 5 for strongly agree (SA) to 1 for strongly disagree (SD). If you believe an item is not applicable to this research article, leave it blank. Be prepared to explain your ratings.

A. The introduction establishes the importance of the study.

    SA   5   4   3   2   1   SD

B. The literature review establishes the context for the study.

    SA   5   4   3   2   1   SD

C. The research purpose, question, or hypothesis is clearly stated.

    SA   5   4   3   2   1   SD

D. The method of sampling is sound.

    SA   5   4   3   2   1   SD

E. Relevant demographics (for example, age, gender, and ethnicity) are described.

    SA   5   4   3   2   1   SD

F. Measurement procedures are adequate.

    SA   5   4   3   2   1   SD

G. All procedures have been described in sufficient detail to permit a replication of the study.

    SA   5   4   3   2   1   SD

H. The participants have been adequately protected from potential harm.

    SA   5   4   3   2   1   SD

I. The results are clearly described.

    SA   5   4   3   2   1   SD

J. The discussion/conclusion is appropriate.

    SA   5   4   3   2   1   SD

K. Despite any flaws, the report is worthy of publication.

    SA   5   4   3   2   1   SD

Article 20

Effects of Holding Students Accountable for Social Behaviors During Volleyball Games in Elementary Physical Education

CRAIG A. PATRICK
Pepper Ridge Elementary School

PHILLIP WARD
University of Nebraska—Lincoln

DARRELL W. CROUCH
Carlock Elementary School

ABSTRACT. This study investigated the effects of a semiformal accountability intervention (a modified version of the good behavior game) on the occurrence of appropriate and inappropriate social behaviors, and appropriate skill attempts during a 20-lesson volleyball unit. Participants were 67 students in grades 4, 5, and 6. Following the collection of baseline data, students received intervention consisting of (a) differential awarding and removing of points for appropriate and inappropriate behavior, (b) public posting of team points, (c) the establishment of daily criteria, (d) a special activity for teams that met the criteria, and (e) an end-of-unit activity for teams that consistently met the criteria. A multiple baseline design across students showed that the intervention was effective in reducing inappropriate social behaviors and increasing appropriate social behaviors, but did not affect the number of correct volleyball skills performed. Results are discussed relative to task systems and social skills.

From *Journal of Teaching in Physical Education*, *17*, 143–156. Copyright © 1998 by Human Kinetics Publishers, Inc. Reprinted with permission.

The promotion of socially responsible behavior in the form of moral character, conformity to social rules and norms, cooperation, and positive styles of social interaction has been a traditional and valued educational objective for American...public schools in almost every educational policy statement since 1848, being promoted with the same frequency as the development of academic skills. (Wentzel, 1991, p. 2)

Despite the implied equity between academic and social objectives in Wentzel's statement, there is a substantive difference between the number of studies that investigate academic outcomes and those that investi-
5 gate social outcomes. Nonetheless, social skills are commonly investigated in several literatures, including classroom management, social competence, and fair play. In each literature, a shared objective for social skills is that students learn and apply the rules of a par-
10 ticular context. Because the contexts often differ, the type of social skill required varies (e.g., the skills needed to work together to complete a group assign-

ment in a classroom are different from those needed to respond to point losses during volleyball games). Fur-
15 thermore, the theoretical perspective through which social skills are viewed by a particular literature also influences the type and function of social skill observed (e.g., management versus fair play).

In the classroom management literature, the pur-
20 pose of social skills is viewed primarily, but not exclusively, as contributing to classroom order by developing skills necessary to participate successfully in classroom events (Colvin & Sugai, 1988; Doyle & Carter, 1984; Soar & Soar, 1979). In physical education, sev-
25 eral researchers have addressed the theme of what it takes to be a "member in good standing" in a class, often concurrent with their primary focus, and often from the perspective of preventative management (Hastie & Pickwell, 1996; Johnston, 1995; Oslin, 1996;
30 O'Sullivan & Dyson, 1994). While the problem of inadequate social skills is acknowledged in physical education (e.g., Hellison, 1995; Sharpe, Brown, & Crider, 1995), there has been little effort to empirically examine efforts to remedy it.

35 In the social competence literature, the purpose of social skill development is to learn the rules not just of the classroom and the school, but to acquire skills that generalize beyond the classroom to other settings (e.g., home, after school, present and future work settings). It
40 includes studies of moral citizenship and values education (Kohler & Fowler, 1985; Ostroky & Kaiser, 1995; Wentzel, 1991). In physical education, social competence studies have investigated self-responsibility for delinquency-prone youth (DeBusk & Hellison, 1989),
45 moral development (Gibbons, Ebback, & Weiss, 1995; Romance, Weiss, & Brockover, 1986; Weiss & Bredemeier, 1986), and values education (Chen, 1996; Ennis, 1992; Wandzilak, Carroll, & Ansorge, 1988).

Though similar to investigations of social compe-
50 tence, the fair play literature is specific to physical education. Within the past decade, a small number of researchers have investigated social skills in the context of game play (Giebink & McKenzie, 1985; Grant, 1992; Sharpe et al. 1995). Of particular interest are the

55 studies conducted by Giebink and McKenzie (1985) and Sharpe et al. (1995). Giebink and McKenzie (1985), using a multitreatment reversal design (A–B–C–D–A), intervened on three behaviors during softball lessons: (a) compliment your teammates, (b) play fair,
60 and (c) accept the consequences. The behaviors were assessed across baseline (A) and three experimental conditions: teacher instructions and praise for fair play behaviors (B), modeling of fair play behaviors (C), and a point system for fair play behaviors (D). All three
65 interventions increased fair play behaviors and decreased inappropriate behaviors when compared to baseline. The behaviors developed in softball, however, did not generalize to a new setting: recreational basketball games. Giebink and McKenzie (1985) then inter-
70 vened in the recreation setting using a multitreatment reversal design (A–B–A–C) to compare baseline (A) with the teacher instructions and praise for fair play behaviors (B) and the point system (C). In the recreational basketball setting, inappropriate social behaviors
75 decreased in both experimental conditions compared to baseline levels; however, fair play behaviors did not improve in any condition.

Sharpe et al. (1995) used an intervention designed to teach conflict resolutions and leadership skills in
80 physical education and reported that these behaviors generalized to regular classroom settings. The Sharpe et al. (1995) study is particularly significant because of evidence of generalization of social skills to classroom settings, and because it provides an empirical valida-
85 tion of a social skills curriculum. At least three other social skills curricula have been developed to address the context-specific needs of children in sports: *Fair Play for Kids* (1990), *Sport Education* (Siedentop, 1994), and *Teaching Responsibility Through Physical*
90 *Activity* (Hellison, 1995).

One conclusion from the above review is that unless planned for and taught by the teacher, appropriate social skills often remain underdeveloped. If one accepts that improving social skills ought to be part of
95 the functional curriculum, then teaching social skills becomes one of the tasks of teaching. Given this conclusion, the task system paradigm provides a useful framework to empirically investigate the improvement of social skills in education and physical education in
100 particular. Though originally derived from the classroom management literature, the task system framework has great utility as a tool for investigating dimensions of classroom life. The major task systems in physical education are instructional, managerial, and
105 social (Siedentop, 1991; Tousignant & Siedentop, 1983). Within a task system, tasks are defined and maintained by the effectiveness of the accountability used by the teacher. When there is no accountability, or when it is ineffective, task accomplishment may be
110 incomplete, or the task may be modified by the student in such a manner as to change the intended outcome (Doyle, 1983). Holding students accountable for the

accomplishment of social tasks is a key instructional procedure to ensure that such skills taught by the
115 teacher are acquired by students.

This study was occasioned by a concern of the first author (an elementary school physical education teacher), who noted that during game play in volleyball (including applied tasks with modified rules), students
120 in his classes were seldom encouraging and supportive of each other and that at times some students behaved inappropriately. He wanted to find a proactive strategy designed not only to reduce the occurrences of inappropriate behaviors, but to increase the occurrence of
125 encouraging and supportive behavior. After some discussion, we decided to modify an intervention called the "good behavior game" (Barrish, Saunders, & Wolf, 1969) to meet the teacher's goals. The good behavior game is a group contingency that typically operates as
130 follows: A class is divided into at least two groups, and when any member of the group misbehaves, a point is marked against that group. At the end of a period of time, the group with the fewest points wins. Winning typically allowed the group members to engage in
135 some special activity. In short, the group is held accountable for its members' inappropriate behavior. In our discussions, we decided to modify the good behavior game to hold students accountable for both appropriate and inappropriate behaviors by adding points for
140 appropriate behaviors and removing them for inappropriate behaviors. Furthermore, we decided that rather than have teams compete against each other, we would instead have them compete against a daily criterion. Thus, any and all teams that met the criterion would
145 "win."

In classroom studies of social competence, an implied outcome of social skill improvement has often been improved academic performance (Wentzel, Weinberger, Ford, & Feldman, 1990). One possible
150 explanation for improved achievement in the classroom is that with fewer inappropriate social skills less disruption and distraction occurs, which improves the opportunity to learn. In the present study, in addition to assessing the effects of the intervention on social skills,
155 we were also interested in determining whether or not the number of successful forearm passes and overhead passes were affected as a result of the social skills intervention.

Three experimental questions guided our investiga-
160 tion during volleyball game play:

1. What is the effect of the modified good behavior game on the number of occurrences of inappropriate social behaviors?
2. What is the effect of the modified good behavior
165 game on the number of occurrences of appropriate social behaviors?
3. What is the effect of the modified good behavior game on the number of successful forearm passes and overhead passes?

Method

Participants and Setting

170 Participants in the study were the students enrolled in three intact physical education classes and their physical education teacher at a suburban elementary school: a fourth-grade class consisting of 21 students (12 boys, 9 girls), a fifth-grade class consisting of 25

175 students (11 boys, 14 girls), and a sixth-grade class consisting of 21 students (11 boys, 10 girls). Parental consent for participation was obtained for all students. In addition, each student volunteered to participate in the study. The teacher was in his tenth year of teaching.

180 Physical education classes were held daily for 20 minutes in grade 4, and daily for 30 minutes in grades 5 and 6. The lessons were conducted in half of the school gymnasium, in an area approximately the size of one basketball court (90 × 50 ft). During each of the 20

185 lessons in the volleyball unit, 10 minutes were allocated for game play with modified rules. Students in each class were grouped into four teams of 5–6 students. The students remained in these teams for the duration of the study. Teams typically played against

190 each other on a rotated schedule.

Data Collection Procedures

Three classes of behavior were measured: (a) the number of appropriate social behaviors per class, (b) the number of inappropriate social behaviors per class, and (c) the number of correct forearm passes and sets

195 per class. Appropriate and inappropriate social behaviors were further subdivided into three categories: physical acts, verbal statements, and gestures committed by students. The following list presents the behaviors, definitions, and examples of each category:

Appropriate Social Behaviors

200 • *Physical*: Physical contact between students that is supportive in nature or that is a response to good play (e.g., high five, pat on the back, handshake).
• *Verbal*: Statements made by students that are supportive in nature or that are a response to good

205 play (e.g., "good job," "good try," and "way to go").
• *Gestures*: Gestures made by students that are supportive in nature or that are a response to good play (e.g., thumbs up, clapping hands following a

210 good performance).

Inappropriate Social Behaviors

• *Physical*: Physical contact between students that is combative in nature (e.g., pushing, fighting), acts of vandalism (e.g., pulling net; slamming, kicking, or throwing the ball), acts of anger (e.g., leaving

215 the game; nonparticipation).
• *Verbal*: Statements made by students that are discouraging or offensive in nature (e.g., "shut up," ridiculing others, arguing and/or shouting, laughing at others' mistakes).

220 • *Gestures*: Gestures made by students that are discouraging or offensive in nature (e.g., making faces in jest, clapping hands following a poor performance).
• *False acts*: Appropriate behaviors emitted in the

225 absence of any play for the purpose of achieving points.

Volleyball Skills

• *Forearm pass*: With hands together, player contacts ball off the forearms, and lands inbounds.
• *Overhead pass*: With two hands, player contacts

230 ball with fingers, and lands inbounds.

In coding an instance of an appropriate behavior, we made a judgment regarding an observed contingent relationship between the appropriate behavior and the events that preceded it. In addition, a separate subcate-

235 gory labeled "false acts" was included to record instances where students used an appropriate behavior that was not contingent upon some success or effort by team members but occurred in the presence of the teacher merely to earn a point. For example, during a

240 break in the game and as the teacher passes by, one student turns to another and says "well done."

Data were collected via videotape for a 5-minute block of the 10-minute game for all 20 lessons of the unit. "Interactions during game play" was selected as

245 the unit of analysis because the teacher had observed the most inappropriate acts during this phase of the lesson. Two games occurred concurrently. Data collection was limited to 5 minutes of each game due to equipment limitations and also to standardize the ob-

250 servation interval. Data collected for appropriate and inappropriate social behaviors were limited to the sensitivity of the camera's microphone and the lens of the camera. Because of the need to capture the verbal comments of the students, the camera was placed to the

255 side and at an angle to the court. As such, it was quite obtrusive. The school, however, was a regular site for student teachers who were supervised and videotaped by university personnel. The practice of videotaping was therefore a common event in the school and in

260 these classes in particular. Students were informed that the camera would be used to help the teacher make judgments about their performance during the volleyball unit.

The forearm pass and overhead pass skills were se-

265 lected because they represented the content of the instruction that preceded games for each class and were the most frequently used skills in the game. The physical education teacher for the class determined the criteria for correct performance of the volleyball skills.

Independent Variable

270 The independent variable consisted of five components. Each will be discussed in turn.

Differential Awarding and Removing of Points. During the 10 minutes of game play, the teacher moved between the two games and awarded points to teams

275 when members demonstrated appropriate behaviors. Points were removed from the team score if the teacher observed instances of inappropriate behavior. A "false act" also resulted in a lost point.

Public Posting of Team Points. During scheduled
280 breaks in the game, students recorded the points that were awarded for appropriate behavior and/or lost due to inappropriate behavior on a wall poster under their team name.

The Establishment of Daily Point Criteria. At the
285 beginning of each class, the teacher established a criterion for each group to meet or exceed during the daily game. On the first day of the intervention, the teacher established a criterion that was 10 times that of the teams' baseline. With the exception of the first day of
290 the intervention, teams were required to meet or exceed the previous day's performance, or a criterion established by the teacher in the case of an occasion where there were an exceptional number of points accrued on the previous day.

295 *Daily Special Activity.* Teams that met the daily criterion played an additional 3 minutes of game play each lesson. Teams that did not meet the criterion were not awarded the special game time. Any and all teams that met the criterion were awarded the special game
300 time.

Special End-of-Unit Activity. A special end-of-unit lunchtime game was provided for the two (or more, if they were equal) teams in each class that met the daily criterion most often. Thus, though a team may have
305 exceeded the criterion each day, in order to participate in this lunchtime game, the criterion had to be consistently met over the duration of the unit of instruction.

Experimental Design and Procedure

A multiple baseline design across classes (Cooper, Heron, & Heward, 1987) was used to assess the effi-
310 cacy of the modified good behavior game in holding students accountable for the targeted social behaviors. In single-subject designs, judgments about internal validity are made on the basis of visual analysis of changes in the data as a consequence of changing ex-
315 perimental conditions (which includes the removal or introduction of a baseline). The multiple baseline design uses a time-lagged strategy to assess internal validity when changes in the data path (level and trend) plotted on the first tier occur at the point of interven-
320 tion, without changes occurring in the underlying tiers. This effect, when reproduced in Tier 2, and in particular in Tier 3, increases confidence that changes in the dependent variable are in fact due to the presence of the independent variable (see Cooper et al., 1987, for a
325 more detailed explanation).

Baseline. During baseline, students played the game of volleyball.

Intervention. On Day 1 of the intervention, the teacher took 10–15 minutes to (a) explain the rules of
330 the good behavior game, (b) have the students put the

poster on the wall with their team names marked on it, (c) allow a short rehearsal where the teacher awarded points for good behavior, and (d) establish the daily criterion. Later during that lesson and for the remainder
335 of the unit, points were awarded or removed contingent upon the targeted behaviors during game play. Due to the time-lagged strategy of the multiple baseline design, grade 5 received the intervention first, followed by grade 4 and then grade 6. We made the decision to
340 intervene in this order based on the stability and trend of the data paths of each class.

Interobserver Agreement

Judgments of correct and incorrect performance of volleyball skills made by the teacher were compared to those of a second trained observer (another physical
345 education teacher in the school) to determine the percentage of interobserver agreement. The second observer was not directly involved with the study's implementation and had been trained using direct observation and video recordings to a criterion of three ses-
350 sions at 80% or higher prior to the start of the study. Both observers coded the dependent variables from the videotape independent of each other. Interobserver agreement (IOA) was assessed on 50% of the sessions distributed across baseline and intervention phases
355 (typically, every other day). The IOA percentages were calculated using a trial-by-trial method, by dividing the number of agreements by the number of agreements plus disagreements and multiplying by 100. Mean IOA percentages for social behaviors were: grade 5, 85%
360 (range = 73–93%); grade 4, 85% (range = 74–97%), and grade 6, 87% (range = 70–98%).

Interobserver agreement was also conducted on 25% of the sessions (two baseline and three intervention sessions for each class) for the correct perform-
365 ance of the forearm pass and overhead pass. The means for correct volleyball skills were calculated similarly for social behaviors (i.e., trial-by-trial) and were: grade 5, 93% (range = 91–95%); grade 4, 89% (range = 81–96%); and grade 6, 92% (range = 90–95%).

370 While the IOA means for social behaviors in each grade lie in the mid-80s, the range of the IOAs for each grade indicate there was at least one occasion per class (in Grade 4 there were two occasions) where IOA agreement scores were in the 70s. In contrast, the IOA
375 means for the forearm pass and overhead pass were quite high with a small range. The difference in variability in the ranges and level of agreement between the IOAs for social behaviors and volleyball skills may be an artifact of the difficulty of coding the less obvi-
380 ous social behaviors versus the more overt volleyball skills. This problem of lower reliability for social skills has been reported elsewhere (Dugan et al., 1995).

Procedural Integrity

During both baseline and intervention, in order to standardize instruction, the teacher was instructed to
385 (a) only stop a game to deal with managerial problems

Table 1
Means and Ranges for Appropriate and Inappropriate Social Behaviors

	Appropriate behaviors				Inappropriate behaviors			
	Baseline		Intervention		Baseline		Intervention	
	M	Range	*M*	Range	*M*	Range	*M*	Range
Grade 5	12	8–16	102	35–184	25	21–30	3	1–6
Grade 4	10	2–16	121	53–196	23	15–43	2	0–4
Grade 6	12	6–20	135	100–153	25	8–41	1	0–2

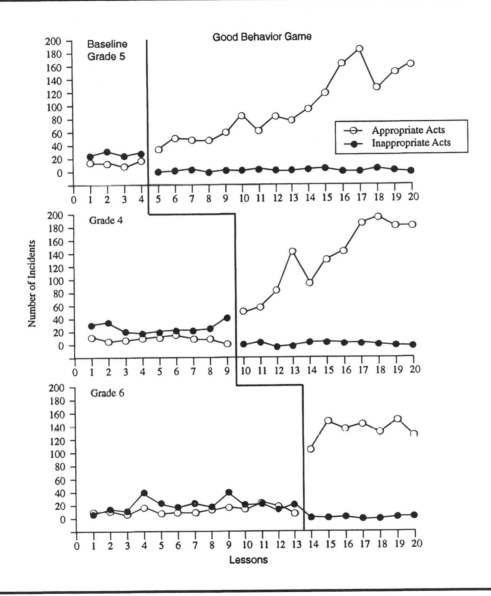

Figure 1. Number of appropriate and inappropriate behaviors per class.

(e.g., arguments over the score fights) or to allow the points accrued during the intervention to be posted on the wall chart, (b) restrict his feedback, and (c) maintain his monitoring (movement around the court perimeter) of games.

390 rimeter) of games.

Results

Four primary dependent measures (inappropriate and appropriate social behaviors, and correct and incorrect skill trials) were totaled for each day and plotted. In addition, the mean and range for each variable during baseline and intervention were calculated. Also of interest, and totaled for each day, were two secondary

395

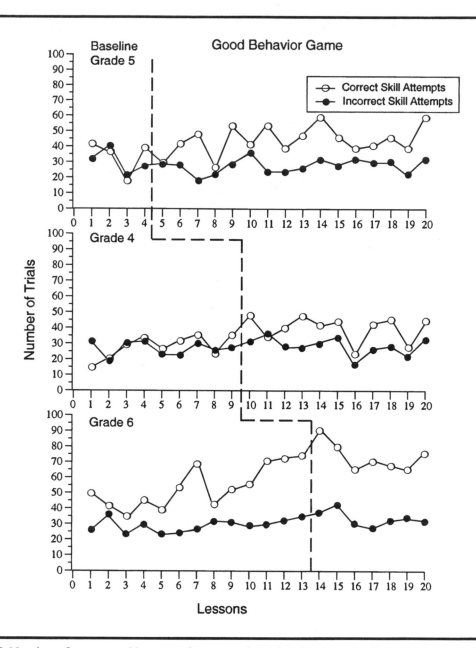

Figure 2. Number of correct and incorrect forearm and overhead passes per class.

variables: the number of false acts and the days where teams reached their criterion level of points.

The first question addressed in this study was 400 "What is the effect of the modified good behavior game on the number of occurrences of inappropriate social behaviors?" As shown in Table 1, mean baseline measures were 25, 23, and 25 for grades 5, 4, and 6, respectively. During intervention, the means dropped 405 to 3, 2, and 1. Visual inspection of the graphed data in Figure 1 indicates that the change in level was immediate and was maintained throughout the intervention for each class.

The second question addressed in this study was 410 "What is the effect of the modified good behavior

game on the number of occurrences of appropriate social behaviors?" Mean baseline measures for appropriate behaviors were 12, 10, and 12 for grades 5, 4, and 6 415 (see Table 1). When the intervention was implemented, the means rose to 102, 121, and 135, respectively. Visual inspection of the graphed data in Figure 1 indicates that the change in level was immediate and increased throughout the study for grades 5 and 4, and was relatively stable after Day 1 of the intervention for grade 6.

420 There were few false acts observed. No false acts were observed in grade 5. In grade 4, on Day 16, four false acts were committed by the same student. In grade 6, on Day 11, two acts (by different students) occurred, and on Day 16, one false act was observed.

425 Data were collected on the number of days a team in any class did not meet its established criterion. For grades 5 and 6, there were no instances when teams in either class failed to meet the criterion. In grade 4, there were two occasions (two separate teams) when
430 the criterion was not met.

The final question addressed in this study was "What is the effect of the modified good behavior games on the number of successful forearm and overhead passes?" Figure 2 displays the number of correct
435 and incorrect forearm passes and overhead passes performed by members of each class. The vertical dotted line indicates when the good behavior game intervention occurred for each class. Changes in the level or trend of the data at and following that point in time
440 would indicate that the intervention targeted on the social behaviors influenced the volleyball skill performances as well. Visual inspection of the graphed data in Figure 2 indicates that there were no concurrent changes for any of the classes at the time of the social
445 skills intervention. Data paths for correct and incorrect volleyball skill performances maintained their trends.

Discussion

The results of this study show that the modified version of the good behavior game was effective in reducing inappropriate social behaviors and increasing
450 appropriate social behaviors, but did not affect the quality of students' skill attempts. During the baseline in each class, more inappropriate social behaviors occurred than appropriate social behaviors. This finding was also obtained by Giebink and McKenzie (1985) in
455 both the softball and basketball settings they investigated. The finding is also consistent with the conclusions from the classroom management, social competence, and fair play research that suggest that appropriate social skills often remain underdeveloped unless
460 planned for and taught by the teacher.

The good behavior game represents one strategy that can be used by teachers to teach social skills in physical education. Focusing on the group rather than on specific individuals in the good behavior game al-
465 lows those individuals who have fewer social skills to be in the presence of peers who can model correct behaviors and who are present at the time of an inappropriate behavior to discourage it. One possible negative outcome of such contingencies is that an individual
470 within the group may be unfairly punished by members for the inappropriate behavior if it prevents the group from achieving the daily criterion. In this study, there were only two occasions in the entire study where teams did not meet their established criterion and there-
475 fore did not play in the daily special event. Furthermore, no instances were observed where one member of a group was unfairly treated by other group members. One explanation for this may lie in how the criteria were established. Each teams' criterion was based
480 on the previous day's score of that team (i.e., meet or

exceed the previous day's performance) and was not a mean of the class or an arbitrary judgment made by the teacher.

Although students were not interviewed to assess
485 their enjoyment and sense of the intervention, the teacher reported that during the intervention, the students seemed to relax and there was less pressure to do well. He suggested that this was because it was less likely that a student would be ridiculed if a bad play
490 was made during the intervention, and because playing the game under the good behavior game conditions was fun.

The finding that volleyball skills remained unaffected by the intervention is interesting. Social compe-
495 tence studies suggest that social competence and achievement in classrooms may be causally related (Wentzel, 1991). If so, then improved volleyball skill performance during the intervention would have occurred concurrent with the introduction of the interven-
500 tion. It did not, which suggests either (a) that the social and psychomotor response classes are unrelated (i.e., there is no causal link, as Wentzel suggests), or (b) that the baseline conditions in this study for social skills were not sufficiently "inappropriate" to influence the
505 performance of volleyball skills. One explanation for this might be that the inappropriate behaviors deemed undesirable by the teacher and researchers did not functionally affect student achievement. Another explanation is that the intervention did not produce condi-
510 tions that were positive enough to influence skill achievement. This seems quite unlikely given the level of appropriate social skills demonstrated. It is more likely that the positive environment did not influence the skill performance. Similar findings have been re-
515 ported in classroom studies (Soar & Soar, 1979). Soar and Soar (1979), in their studies of classroom climates, found little difference in achievement gains in classrooms where the climate was either neutral or positive, but they found negative correlations in classrooms
520 where the climate was negative.

The previous discussion notwithstanding, the development of social skills does not require the rationale of improved student learning. As Wentzel (1991) noted, the development of social skills and social com-
525 petence as educational objectives was a component of "every educational policy statement since 1848" (p. 2). There are three challenges for researchers in the area of social skills training. First, strategies designed to improve social skill competence need to be empirically
530 assessed. Second, such assessment should demonstrate that changes resulting from social skills training and interventions can be maintained in the setting. Third, researchers need to assess the generalization of social skills to new settings. In the present study, while the
535 efficacy of a strategy designed to improve social skills was assessed, maintenance and generalization were not. In physical education, few studies have assessed the effects of maintenance and generalization of social

skills. Giebink and McKenzie (1985) found that social skills training did not generalize from a softball setting to a basketball setting. Sharpe et al. (1995), however, did report generalization of conflict resolution skills from the gymnasium to classroom settings. These mixed findings, relative to the generalization of social skills in physical education, reflect a larger problem of generalizing social skills from one setting to another. In a review of social skills in preschool settings, the most extensively and rigorously studied setting for social skills, Chandler, Lubeck, and Fowler (1992) noted that "generalization and maintenance have been particularly difficult to obtain in applied research with peer interactions and young children" (p. 416). Future studies in physical education should try to assess the maintenance and generalization of social skills and, in particular, the generalization of social skills to classrooms and playgrounds, as well as to different units of instruction.

Framing social competence as skill development allows social skills to be viewed in the same manner as cognitive and psychomotor skills. In this study, doing so allowed social skill to be examined within the tasks systems or ecological paradigm (Doyle 1979, 1986). In this paradigm, a task, a social skill in the present case, can be treated as a dependent variable, and some form of accountability (e.g., teacher monitoring, public posting, peer mediation) can be used as an independent variable to assess and improve task accomplishment. The task systems framework has allowed researchers in physical education to investigate different dimensions of teaching and learning. For example, researchers have (a) examined the specific systems in operation in physical education (e.g., Silverman, Kulinna, & Crull, 1995; Tousignant & Siedentop, 1983); (b) examined the congruence between tasks stated by the teacher and the actual tasks performed by students (e.g., Jones, 1992; Lund, 1992); and (c) examined the ecology of the social system that operates in different physical education contexts, such as camp, dance, and sports settings (e.g., Hastie & Pickwell, 1996; Hastie & Saunders, 1990); and (d) most recently, used task accomplishment as a dependent variable and accountability as an independent variable to improve student achievement (Crouch, Ward, & Patrick, 1997; Ward, Smith, & Sharpe, 1997).

The present study's use of the good behavior game to increase socially appropriate behavior and reduce socially inappropriate behaviors extends the research on tasks and accountability in at least two ways. First, it assesses the efficacy of the good behavior game as a type of semiformal accountability. Second, the study represents an initial step toward expanding the empirical base of the task systems paradigm (specifically, tasks and accountability) into domains other than the psychomotor—in this case, the affective domain. In addition, the study represents one of a small number of studies that empirically validate strategies designed to improve social skill competence in physical education.

We hope that additional research efforts along these lines will lead to other strategies that will focus on the affective domain in physical education.

References

Barrish, H. H., Saunders, M., & Wolf, M. M. (1969). Good behavior game: Effects of individual contingencies for group consequences on disruptive behavior in a classroom. *Journal of Applied Behavior Analysis, 2,* 119–124.

Chandler, L. K., Lubeck, R. C., & Fowler, S. A. (1992). Generalization and maintenance of preschool children's social skills: A critical review and analysis. *Journal of Applied Behavior Analysis, 25,* 415–428.

Chen, A. (1996). Validation of personal meaning in secondary physical education. *Research Quarterly for Exercise and Sport, 67* (Suppl.), A76.

Colvin, G., & Sugai, G. (1988). Proactive strategies for managing social behavior problems: An instructional approach. *Education and Treatment of Children, 11,* 341–348.

Cooper, J. O., Heron, T. E., & Heward, W. L. (1987). *Applied behavior analysis.* Columbus, OH: Merrill.

Crouch, D. W., Ward, P., & Patrick, C. A. (1997). The effects of peer-mediated accountability on task accomplishment during volleyball drills in elementary physical education. *Journal of Teaching in Physical Education, 17,* 26–39.

DeBusk, M., & Hellison, D. (1989). Implementing a physical education self-responsibility model for delinquency-prone youth. *Journal of Teaching in Physical Education, 8,* 104–112.

Doyle, W. (1979). Classroom tasks and student abilities. In P. L. Peterson & H. J. Walberg (Eds.), *Research on teaching: Concepts, findings, and implications* (pp. 183–205). Berkeley, CA: McCutchan.

Doyle, W. (1983). Academic work. *Review of Educational Research, 53,* 159–199.

Doyle, W. (1986). Classroom organization and management. In M. C. Wittrock (Ed.), *Handbook of research on teaching* (3rd ed., pp. 392–431). New York: Macmillan.

Doyle, W., & Carter, K. (1984). Academic tasks in classrooms. *Curriculum Inquiry, 14,* 129–149.

Dugan, E., Kamps, D., Leonard, B., Watkins, N., Rheinberger, A., & Stackaus, J. (1995). Effects of cooperative learning groups during social studies for students with autism and fourth-grade peers. *Journal of Applied Behavior Analysis, 28,* 175–188.

Ennis, C. D. (1992). The influence of value orientations in curriculum decision making. *Quest, 44,* 317–329.

Fair Play for Kids. (1990). Ottawa, ON, Canada: Commission for Fair Play.

Gibbons, S. L., Ebback, V., & Weiss, M. R. (1995). Fair Play for Kids: Effects on the moral development of children in physical education. *Research Quarterly for Exercise and Sport, 66,* 247–255.

Giebink, M. P., & McKenzie, T. L. (1985). Teaching sportsmanship in physical education and recreation: An analysis of interventions and generalization effects. *Journal of Teaching in Physical Education, 4,* 167–177.

Grant, B. C. (1992). Integrating sport into the physical education curriculum in New Zealand secondary schools. *Quest, 44,* 304–316.

Hastie, P. A., & Pickwell, A. (1996). Take your partners: A description of a student social system in a secondary school dance class. *Journal of Teaching in Physical Education, 15,* 171–187.

Hastie, P. A., & Saunders, J. E. (1990). A study of monitoring in secondary school physical education classes. *Journal of Classroom Interaction, 25,* 47–54.

Hellison, D. (1995) *Teaching responsibility through physical activity.* Champaign, IL: Human Kinetics.

Johnston, B. D. (1995). Withitness: Real or fictional? *The Physical Educator, 52,* 22–28.

Jones, D. L. (1992). Analysis of task structures in elementary physical education classes. *Journal of Teaching in Physical Education, 11,* 411–425.

Kohler, F. W., & Fowler, S. A. (1985). Training prosocial behaviors to young children: An analysis of reciprocity with untrained peers. *Journal of Applied Behavior Analysis, 18,* 187–200.

Lund, J. (1992). Assessment and accountability in secondary physical education. *Quest, 44,* 352–360.

Oslin, J. L. (1996). Routines as organizing features in middle school education. *Journal of Teaching in Physical Education, 15,* 319–337.

Ostroky, M. M., & Kaiser, A. P (1995). The effects of a peer-mediated intervention on the social communicative interactions between children with and without special needs. *Journal of Behavioral Education, 5,* 151–171.

O'Sullivan, M., & Dyson, B. (1994). Rules, routines, and expectations of 11 high school physical education teachers. *Journal of Teaching in Physical Education, 13,* 361–374.

Romance, T. J., Weiss, M. R., & Brockover, J. (1986). A program to promote moral development through elementary school physical education. *Journal of Teaching in Physical Education, 5,* 126–136.

Sharpe, T., Brown, M., & Crider, K. (1995). The effects of a sportsmanship curriculum intervention on generalized positive social behavior of urban elementary school students. *Journal of Applied Behavior Analysis, 28,* 401–416.

Siedentop, D. (1991). *Developing teaching skills in physical education* (3rd ed.). Palo Alto, CA: Mayfield.

Siedentop, D. (1994). *Sport education.* Champaign, IL: Human Kinetics.

Silverman, S., Kulinna, P. H., & Crull, G. (1995). Skill-related task structures, explicitness, and accountability: Relationships with student achievement. *Research Quarterly for Exercise and Sport, 66,* 32–40.

Soar, R., & Soar, R. (1979). Emotional climate and management. In P. L. Peterson & H. J. Walberg (Eds.), *Research on teaching: Concepts, findings, and implications* (pp. 97–118). Berkeley, CA: McCutchan.

Tousignant, M., & Siedentop, D. (1983). A qualitative analysis of task structures in required secondary physical education classes. *Journal of Teaching in Physical Education, 1,* 47–57.

Wandzilak, T., Carroll, T., & Ansorge, C. J. (1988). Values development through physical activity. *Journal of Teaching in Physical Education, 8,* 13–23.

Ward, P., Smith, S., & Sharpe, T. (1997). The effects of accountability on task accomplishment in collegiate football. *Journal of Teaching in Physical Education, 17,* 40–51.

Weiss, M. R., & Bredemeier, B. J. (1986). Moral development. In V. Seefeldt (Ed.), *Physical activity and well-being* (pp. 373–390). Reston, VA: American Alliance for Health, Physical Education, Recreation, and Dance.

Wentzel, K. R. (1991). Social competence at school: Relation between social responsibility and academic achievement. *Review of Educational Research, 61,* 1–24.

Wentzel, K. R., Weinberger, D. A., Ford, M. E., & Feldman, S. S. (1990). Academic achievement in preadolescence: The role of motivational, affective, and self-regulatory processes. *Journal of Applied Developmental Psychology, 11,* 179–193.

About the authors: Craig Patrick is with the Pepper Ridge Elementary School, Bloomington, IL 61701. Phillip Ward is with the Department of Health and Human Performance, 247 Mabel Lee Hall, University of Nebraska-Lincoln, Lincoln, NE 68588-0229. Darrell Crouch is with the Carlock Elementary School in Carlock, IL 61725.

Acknowledgments: Special thanks to Mary O'Sullivan and Bill Murphy for their comments on the manuscript.

Exercise for Article 20

Factual Questions

1. Which body of literature is specific to physical education?

2. Did all the parents grant consent for their children to participate in this evaluation?

3. How are "false acts" defined?

4. What did the students do during the *baseline*?

5. IOA stands for what words?

6. What was the mean number of inappropriate behaviors observed among the fifth graders during the baseline?

7. According to the researchers, what is the first of the "three challenges for researchers" working in the area of social skills training?

Questions for Discussion

8. In your opinion, are the definitions of appropriate and inappropriate social behaviors adequate? (See lines 200–226.) Given these definitions, do you think you could reliably observe for the same behaviors? Explain.

9. Do you think the use and placement of the camera might have influenced students' behavior? Do you think that the results of this study will generalize to other settings where a camera may not be present (i.e., will students in settings without cameras be likely to behave the same)?

10. All students in this study received the independent variable. Thus, this study does not have a traditional "control group." However, students in different grade levels were given the treatment at different points in time (see Figures 1 and 2). In your opinion, would it be desirable to have a traditional control group under these circumstances? Explain.

11. The researchers studied the interobserver agreement (i.e., reliability). In your opinion, is it adequate? Explain. (See lines 342–382.)

12. The differences among the means in Table 1 were not tested for statistical significance. Despite this fact, do you think the differences are sufficiently large to be considered important? Would you characterize the differences as being "dramatic"? Explain.

13. Were you surprised that the independent variable seemingly had no effect on the volleyball skills (i.e., forearm passes and overhead passes)? Explain.

14. The researchers note that they did not interview the students to assess their enjoyment. Do you think it would be a good idea to do so in a future study? Explain.

15. Do you think there is sufficient evidence here to justify tryouts of the independent variable in elementary physical education classes in your community? Why? Why not?

Quality Ratings

Directions: Indicate your level of agreement with each of the following statements by circling a number from 5 for strongly agree (SA) to 1 for strongly disagree (SD). If you believe an item is not applicable to this research article, leave it blank. Be prepared to explain your ratings.

A.   The introduction establishes the importance of the study.

    SA   5   4   3   2   1   SD

B.   The literature review establishes the context for the study.

    SA   5   4   3   2   1   SD

C.   The research purpose, question, or hypothesis is clearly stated.

    SA   5   4   3   2   1   SD

D.   The method of sampling is sound.

    SA   5   4   3   2   1   SD

E.   Relevant demographics (for example, age, gender, and ethnicity) are described.

    SA   5   4   3   2   1   SD

F.   Measurement procedures are adequate.

    SA   5   4   3   2   1   SD

G.   All procedures have been described in sufficient detail to permit a replication of the study.

    SA   5   4   3   2   1   SD

H.   The participants have been adequately protected from potential harm.

    SA   5   4   3   2   1   SD

I.   The results are clearly described.

    SA   5   4   3   2   1   SD

J.   The discussion/conclusion is appropriate.

    SA   5   4   3   2   1   SD

K.   Despite any flaws, the report is worthy of publication.

    SA   5   4   3   2   1   SD

Article 21

Supporting High School Students to Engage in Recreational Activities with Peers

CAROLYN HUGHES
Vanderbilt University

STEPHANIE E. FOWLER
Vanderbilt University

SUSAN R. COPELAND
Vanderbilt University

MARTIN AGRAN
University of Northern Iowa

MICHAEL L. WEHMEYER
University of Kansas

PENNY P. CHURCH-PUPKE
Vanderbilt University

ABSTRACT. The authors investigated the effects of an intervention package to support five high school students with extensive support–needs to initiate and engage in recreational activities with general-education peers in their physical education classes. The intervention components were (a) assessing participants' recreational activity goals, (b) teaching self-prompting using a picture book, (c) programming common stimuli, and (d) asking participants to assess daily performance and evaluate daily goal achievement. The intervention was associated with increases in participants' initiation of and engagement in recreational activities with general-education peers as well as increases in ratings of quality of interaction. In addition, participants typically assessed with accuracy their performance of recreational activities and whether they had achieved their recreational goals. Findings are discussed with respect to future research and practice.

From *Behavior Modification*, 28, 3–27. Copyright © 2004 by Sage Publications, Inc. Reprinted with permission.

A primary intent of the Individuals with Disabilities Education Act (IDEA) Amendments of 1997 (PL 105–17) is that students with disabilities access the range of opportunities typically available to their general-
5 education peers. The amendments support the argument that success in adulthood requires more than academic or employment skills (Schleien & Ray, 1997). For example, participation in socially inclusive recreational activities, such as physical education classes,
10 school clubs, or sports teams, may provide students opportunities to learn appropriate social behaviors, develop social relationships, enjoy lifetime leisure pursuits, or experience enhanced community membership (Wilson, Arnold, & Rowland, 1997). Educational pro-
15 gramming that promotes engagement in recreational activities may relate to increased participation in the community (Bullock & Mahon, 1992).

Some students, however, may not have the requisite skills or support needed to initiate or engage in recrea-
20 tional activities, even when access to these activities is available (Hunt & Goetz, 1997; O'Reilly, Lancioni, & Kierans, 2000). For example, Nietupski et al. (1986) reported that three high school students with extensive support–needs required considerable prompting before
25 picking a recreational activity from an array of activity choices and sustaining engagement with the activity. Activities performed were solitary versus interactive, however, and occurred in a self-contained special-education classroom rather than in a setting with gen-
30 eral-education peers.

Few investigators have addressed skills and support needed to initiate and sustain engagement in recreational activities with general-education high school peers (e.g., Gaylord-Ross, Haring, Breen, & Pitts-
35 Conway, 1984; Rynder et al., 1993). Four strategies in combination may be effective in supporting recreational-activity engagement: (a) assessing students' recreational goals, (b) teaching self-prompting using a picture book, (c) programming common stimuli, and
40 (d) promoting self-assessment and goal evaluation.

First, assessing students' recreational–activity goals may help determine if they wish to participate in activities with their general-education peers. For example, Hughes, Killian, and Fischer (1996) queried high
45 school students with disabilities about their social goals prior to and after teaching them a strategy to increase social interaction with general-education peers. Participating students indicated that (a) prior to the intervention they wished they could interact more frequently
50 with their general-education peers and (b) after intervention they believed they had progressed toward their goals.

Second, students may use self-prompting to improve their performance (Wehmeyer, Palmer, Agran,
55 Mithaug, & Martin, 2000). For example, Hughes et al. (2000) involved general-education students as peer trainers for five high school students with extensive support needs. Peer trainers taught participants to use a communication book to prompt themselves to initiate
60 conversations with their general-education peers. All participants used the self-prompting strategy to engage in social interactions with both familiar and unfamiliar general-education peers across general-education settings.

65 Third, incorporating into training physical and social stimuli that typically are found in the everyday environment may promote generalization of skills (i.e., programming common stimuli, Stokes & Baer, 1977). For example, McMahon, Wacker, Sasso, Berg, and 70 Newton (1996) introduced into a training setting peers and board games that were present in the classroom setting. Participants in game-playing training generalized game skills learned and increased interaction with their general-education peers in the classroom setting.

75 Fourth, asking students to assess their performance may prompt them to evaluate goal achievement. For example, Agran, Blanchard, and Wehmeyer (2000) asked high school students with disabilities to evaluate their performance of transition-related skills (e.g., mak- 80 ing transportation arrangements) in relation to a goal. Participants improved their performance of targeted skills when they assessed their goals. However, we found no published research in which high school students with disabilities were asked to evaluate their en- 85 gagement in recreational activities with general-education peers.

The purpose of this study was to combine promising strategies into an intervention to support students with extensive support–needs to initiate and engage in 90 recreational activities with general-education peers in their physical-education classes. To determine if participants would benefit from participation, we assessed their recreational-activity goals prior to intervention and at the beginning of each training session (Hughes 95 et al., 2000). To promote generalization of skills, participants were taught to prompt their initiation of engagement in recreational activities across a variety of general-education peers using a picture-book strategy (Hunt, Alwell, Goetz, & Sailor, 1990). To increase the 100 saliency of recreational activities available in the physical-education class to participants, we introduced materials and verbal cues associated with these activities into training and generalization sessions (McMahon et al., 1996). To prompt participants to evaluate if 105 they had achieved their recreational-activity goals, we asked them to assess their engagement in recreational activities (Agran et al., 2000). The effects of training were evaluated with respect to participants' initiation of and engagement in recreational activities with gen- 110 eral-education peers. We also asked participants, after intervention, if they perceived that they had met their recreational-activity goals.

Method

Setting

The study was conducted in a gymnasium of a large urban high school during two ninth-grade physical- 115 education classes. The student population of the school was 1,079, of which 77% were African American, 20% were Caucasian, and 3% were other ethnicities. Fifty-four percent of the students received free or reduced lunches. Between 35 to 50 general- and special- 120 education students and two teachers typically were present during each physical-education class. At the beginning of each class, students were expected to enter the gym, sit in assigned positions on the floor, and wait for roll call. After roll call, the teachers verbally 125 instructed the students, "It's time to go do something." This statement was designed to prompt students to select an available sport or recreational activity in which to participate. Typically, the teachers provided two to four activities (e.g., volleyball, basketball, or badmin- 130 ton) per class period from which students could choose. Students also talked or looked at magazines or pictures with each other while waiting for an activity to become available or while in between engaging in activities.

Participants

Five high school students chosen from a pool of 26 135 students enrolled in classes for students with extensive support–needs participated in this study. Selection was based on (a) enrollment in a physical-education class, (b) 8 weeks of prebaseline observation of participants in their physical-education classes, which indicated that 140 they rarely engaged in recreational activities with their general-education peers, and (c) an individualized education program (IEP) goal to increase engagement in peer interaction and/or recreational activities. Two participants were enrolled in the school's first-period 145 physical-education class and three were enrolled in the second-period class. In addition to attending physical-education classes, all participants ate lunch with their general-education peers. Two of the participants were enrolled in an additional general-education class (cos- 150 metology), and all students participated in employment training in the community one class period per day.

Jesse was a 15-year-old African American young man diagnosed with mental retardation and a speech and articulation impairment. He characteristically 155 spoke softly in two- to three-word phrases. Prebaseline observation indicated that Jesse typically interacted with only other special-education students during physical education or sat on the gym floor by himself. He participated in large group activities in the 160 class (e.g., walking laps) when directed by the teacher but did not speak or otherwise interact with others while doing so. While in the gym, Jesse was observed never to initiate interactions and rarely to make eye contact with others when spoken to.

165 Marshea was a 14-year-old African American young woman identified with mental retardation and a speech and language impairment. She spoke in short sentences, which were difficult to understand, and rarely smiled or expressed other emotion. Observation 170 in Marshea's physical-education class indicated that she rarely interacted with her general-education peers and only in response to their occasional initiations. Characteristically, she sat throughout the class period with one or two other special-education students in a 175 corner of the gym and watched as other students par-

Table 1
Participant Characteristics

Participant	Diagnosis and IQ assessment	Adaptive behavior assessment[a]	Speech and language assessment	Medical and behavioral history
Jesse, 15, African American male	Mental retardation, speech impairment; 46[b]	Composite: 58	Articulation impairment: 83.5[c]	Premature birth; mother had toxemia during pregnancy; shortened right leg; low birth weight; history of repeated ear infections; delayed language development
Marshea, 14, African American female	Mental retardation, speech/language impairment; 40[b]	Composite: 77	Articulation impairment: expressive: 50; receptive: 50[d]	None reported
Marlice, 16, African American female	Mental retardation; 42[e]	Composite: 33	MA 2–5: auditory comprehension: 54; verbal ability: 49; LA: 53[f]	History of hospitalization as infant for poor weight gain; history of heart murmur, vision, and dental problems
Aaliyah, 18, African American female	Mental retardation; 52[g]	Composite: 52	None reported	Born with some atypical physical features, including asymmetry of head, eyes, ears, and hands; ptosis of right eyelid; history of arthritis
Tanisha, 18, African American female	Mental retardation, language impairment; 40[b]	Composite: 41	LA: 3 years, 7.5 months[h]	First talked at 2.5 years; history of developmental delays

Note. WISC = Wechsler Intelligence Scale for Children; MA = mental age; LA = language age.
a. Vineland Adaptive Behavior Scale.
b. WISC-Revised.
c. Arizona Articulation Proficiency Scale.
d. Clinical Evaluation of Language Fundamentals Revised.
e. Stanford-Binet, Form L-M.
f. Expressive Word Picture Vocabulary Test.
g. WISC-3.
h. Preschool Language Scale.

ticipated in class activities. She participated in recreational activities (e.g., badminton) with a special-education peer only when her teacher or the peer suggested it.

Marlice was a 16-year-old African American young woman with mental retardation. She communicated with others using short sentences. Although she was observed to smile and laugh frequently and occasionally greet familiar special-education or general-education peers, she did not engage in conversations or sustained interactions with these peers. Observation indicated that unless instructed by her teacher, she did not participate in physical-education activities. Instead, she occasionally interacted with other special-education students enrolled in the class and watched from the edge of the gym as peers in the class participated in their class activities.

Aaliyah was an 18-year-old African American young woman with mental retardation who communicated using short sentences. Aaliyah rarely smiled or appeared animated and often appeared angry. Her teachers characterized her as "moody." During physical education class, Aaliyah was observed to sit on the floor by the wall of the gym with one to two special-education students, to whom she was often observed giving verbal orders (e.g., "Come here" or "Give me that"). When directed by the teacher to participate in a class activity, she did so with only other special-education students. Aaliyah reported that she did not

like the class because it was "too boring" and because there was nothing to do.

Tanisha was an 18-year-old African American young woman identified with mental retardation and a language impairment. Tanisha typically spoke quietly in one- to two-word phrases that were difficult to understand. She often appeared sullen or angry and occasionally would yell when approached by adults or other students. Similar to the other participants, Tanisha was observed never to engage in class activities unless instructed to do so by the teacher. Instead, she sat by herself or with a small group of special-education students in the corner of the gym. She did not initiate interaction with her general-education peers but did respond briefly verbally or with facial expression to their infrequent initiations. (Additional participant characteristics are found in Table 1.)

Participants' recreational activity goals. Participants' recreational-activity goals were assessed once prior to training and reassessed at the beginning of each training session to determine if engaging in recreational activities with a peer was a desired activity. First, the trainer met individually with participants and verbally asked three yes or no questions, asking clarifying questions as needed. The trainer immediately recorded all responses, including gestures or facial expressions. Next, following affirmative responses from all participants, the trainer suggested that participants could achieve their goals by performing three steps: (a) choosing a recreational activity, (b) asking a peer to

131

235 participate in the activity, and (c) initiating performing the activity with the peer. All participants responded affirmatively when asked if they would like to perform these three steps to meet their goals. After each gener-

240 alization session during the training and maintenance conditions, participants were asked to assess their performance of the three steps and to evaluate if they had met their performance goals. At the conclusion of the study, participants were verbally asked five postinter-

245 vention questions to determine if they perceived they had met their recreational-activity goals and if their picture books were helpful.

Recreational-Activity Partners

Twenty-one general-education students in the participants' physical-education classes volunteered to serve as recreational-activity partners during training

250 sessions (three for Marlice, four for Aaliyah, six for Marshea and Tanisha, and eight for Jesse, respectively) and 70 volunteers to serve during generalization sessions (number of volunteers ranged from 21 to 25 per participant). Recreational-activity partners were rotated

255 randomly across participants. All partners were recruited by the authors by asking for volunteers to participate in recreational activities with special-education classmates. The only criteria for participation were consent to volunteer and availability. Seventy-three

260 percent of all partners were young women, 79% were African American, and 21% were Caucasian.

Picture Books

Participants were taught to use picture books to prompt themselves to initiate a recreational activity with an activity partner. The picture book was a 12 cm

265 by 17 cm photograph album containing two color photographs. The first photograph showed a young man grasping an object and was designed to prompt participants to choose a recreational activity. The second photograph showed several young people interacting with

270 each other and was intended to prompt participants to ask an activity partner to participate in the chosen recreational activity.

Participants were taught to (a) pick up the picture book in response to the verbal instruction, "It's time to

275 go do something," which was used daily by the physical-education teachers to direct all students in their classes to choose an activity in which to participate; (b) turn to the first photograph in the book; (c) look at and point to the photograph; (d) perform the action repre-

280 sented by the photograph (i.e., choose an activity); (e) turn the page; (f) look at and point to the second photograph; (g) perform the action depicted in the photograph (i.e., ask an activity partner to participate in the activity); (h) put the picture book down; and (i) initiate

285 performing the activity with the partner (e.g., begin playing badminton).

Outcome Measures

Outcome measures assessed during training and

generalization sessions were (a) % of intervals in which participants engaged in a recreational activity

290 with their partners, (b) quality of interaction, (c) % of self-prompting steps performed, (d) % of recreational-activity initiation steps performed, (e) accuracy with which participants assessed their performance of recreational-activity initiation steps, and (f) accuracy with

295 which participants evaluated their recreational-activity goal achievement. Engaging in a recreational activity was defined as participants and activity partners performing verbal or nonverbal behaviors directed to each other or related to the recreational activity (Kasari,

300 Sigman, Mundy, & Yirmiya, 1990; Kennedy & Itkonen, 1994). Quality of interaction was rated using a Likert-type scale ranging from 1 (low) to 5 (high) based on frequency, duration, content, and reciprocity of exchanges between participants and partners and

305 their overall affect (e.g., facial expression, body posture, or attentiveness) during the interaction (Fryxell & Kennedy, 1995; Koegel & Egel, 1979).

Self-prompting was defined as participants performing the six picture-book steps designed to prompt

310 initiation of engagement in a recreational activity: (a) pick up picture book (Step 1); (b) turn to first photograph in book (Step 2); (c) look at and point to first photograph (Step 3); (d) turn page in book (Step 4); (e) look at and point to second photograph (Step 5); and (f)

315 put book down (Step 6). Recreational activity initiation was defined as participants performing the three steps required to initiate engagement in a recreational activity, which were designed to be prompted by performance of the picture-book steps. Specifically, (a) follow-

320 ing performance of picture-book Step 3 (look at and point to first photograph in book), participants were taught to choose a recreational activity; (b) after performing Step 5 (look at and point to second photograph in book), participants were taught to ask a partner to

325 participate in the activity; and (c) after performing Step 6 (put picture book down), they were taught to initiate performing the activity with the partner. Choose an activity was defined as participants picking up materials with which to engage in a recreational activity (e.g.,

330 a badminton racquet or a deck of cards). Ask a partner was defined as participants performing verbal or nonverbal behaviors directed toward their activity partners to elicit their participation in an activity (e.g., saying, "Want to play?" or holding a magazine toward a part-

335 ner with an expectant look on his or her face). Initiate performance of activity was defined as participants performing motor behavior required to begin engagement in activity (e.g., holding a badminton racquet and walking toward an area of the gym with the badminton

340 net or putting checkers in place on a checkerboard).

Accuracy of self-assessment of performance referred to the degree of agreement between participants' and observers' reports of number of recreational-activity initiation steps performed by participants per

345 session. Accuracy of self-evaluation of goal achieve-

ment was defined as the degree of agreement between participants' and observers' reports that participants had achieved their recreational-activity goal, as determined by the number of recreational-activity initiation steps performed per session.

Experimental Design and Conditions

A multiple-baseline-across-participants design (Kazdin, 1982) was used to examine the effects of the intervention on participants' initiation of and engagement in recreational activities with activity partners. There were three experimental conditions—(a) baseline, (b) training, and (c) maintenance—during which generalization data were collected daily. Participants received self-prompted picture-book training daily during the training condition only, prior to generalization sessions.

Baseline. During each baseline session, a physical-education teacher provided a variety of recreational activities in which students could choose to participate—such as playing basketball or walking laps around the gym—by displaying the requisite materials or equipment (e.g., a volleyball and a net). The teacher also delivered the verbal instruction to the class, "It's time to go do something." During each session, participants were observed for 5 min while they were within proximity (i.e., 1.5 min) of a general-education classmate who had volunteered to engage in an activity with the participants (i.e., recreational-activity partner). Recreational-activity partners were told to stay within proximity of participants and to respond to but not initiate an initial interaction with participants. No additional instructional feedback was provided.

Training. Following baseline, we introduced self-prompted picture-book training in the gym with Jesse, with training for the other participants following sequentially. Training sessions averaged 13 min (average length ranged from 5 to 21 min) and followed a training script (available on request). During training sessions, materials associated with three recreational activities available in the gym were placed near participants (e.g., a badminton racquet, a volleyball, and a video game). Activity choices were based on students' preferences, teachers' daily lesson plans, and observation of typical activities engaged in by general-education students in the physical-education classes. Activity choices included volleyball, badminton, basketball, board games, card games, paper-and-pencil games, drawing with markers, video games, and looking at magazines or school yearbooks. Choices available were rotated daily across participants.

Each training session consisted of five steps. First, the trainer (the second author) reassessed participants' activity goals by asking if they would like to engage in more recreational activities with friends in their class and if they wished to learn to perform three steps that would help them achieve their goals. Next, an observer stated the verbal instruction used by the physical-education teachers to direct students to begin participation in class activities (i.e., "It's time to go do something"). Next, the trainer used the picture book to model the six self-prompting steps and the three corresponding recreational-activity initiation steps (see Outcome Measures) to engage in a recreational activity with a general-education volunteer (i.e., recreational-activity partner). As during baseline, activity partners were instructed to respond to but not initiate interaction. The trainer then provided direct instruction as participants self-prompted using their picture books to perform the three recreational-activity initiation steps with the activity partner. Repeated opportunities to practice and corrective feedback were provided if participants failed to perform a self-prompting or recreational-activity initiation step. Finally, at the end of a session, the trainer reminded participants to use their picture books during physical-education classes when they heard the verbal prompt, "It's time to go do something." Fidelity of treatment assessed across 43% of participants' training sessions indicated that the trainer correctly followed 100% of the training steps across sessions.

Maintenance. Maintenance was assessed after self-prompting training was withdrawn for each of the participants on Sessions 12, 19, 22, 27, and 36 for Jesse, Marshea, Marlice, Aaliyah, and Tanisha, respectively. Three criteria were used to terminate training: (a) 100% independent performance of all six self-prompting steps and all three recreational-activity initiation steps for three consecutive training sessions, (b) 90% intervals engaging in a recreational activity with a partner during three consecutive generalization sessions, and (c) 100% independent performance of all self-prompting and recreational-activity initiation steps during three consecutive generalization sessions. The total number of training sessions was 8, 8, 3, 4, and 7 sessions for Jesse, Marshea, Marlice, Aaliyah, and Tanisha, respectively (data available on request).

During maintenance, baseline conditions were in effect with the following exceptions. (a) In addition to the recreational-activity choices provided by the physical-education teachers, three choices of activities were placed near participants and their activity partners, as during training. (b) Prior to each session, an observer repeated the verbal instruction used by the physical-education teachers to prompt students to select a recreational activity in which to engage (i.e., "It's time to go do something"). The observer then moved out of the eye gaze of the participant and partner. When the 5-min observation was completed, the observer left the area, allowing the participants and partners to continue to engage in the chosen recreational activity.

Self-assessment of performance and self-evaluation of goal achievement. During the training and maintenance conditions following each generalization session, the trainer met individually with each participant. First, she verbally asked participants three forced-choice

460 questions related to their performance of the three recreational-activity initiation steps: Did you (a) choose an
activity, (b) ask a partner to participate in the activity,
and (c) initiate performing the activity with the partner.
She recorded their responses as yes or no on a sheet of
465 paper on which the three questions were typed. Next,
the trainer showed the written responses to participants
and asked them to count aloud the number of yeses
recorded. She then recorded this number on the sheet.
Next, she asked participants to look at this number and
470 determine if they had met their recreational-activity
goal (i.e., performed all three recreational-activity initiation steps), which had been assessed prior to training
(see Participants' Recreational Activity Goals) and
reassessed during each training session (see Training).
475 She recorded their responses as yes or no.

Observation and Recording Procedures

Participants and their recreational-activity partners
were observed once daily for one 5-min session at randomly chosen times during their 50-min physical-
education classes across all generalization sessions. If
480 participants did not initiate engagement in a recreational activity with their partners during 3 consecutive
minutes, however, a session was discontinued. Participants and partners were also observed during training
that occurred daily during the self-prompting training
485 condition, before the generalization sessions.

We used a 10-s observe, 5-s record partial-interval
recording system to assess % of intervals engaging in
recreational activities, which was scored as occurred or
did not occur per interval. We used a checklist to assess
490 (a) % of self-prompting steps performed, (b) % of
recreational-activity initiation steps performed, (c) accuracy with which participants assessed their performance of recreational-activity initiation steps, and (d)
accuracy with which participants evaluated their
495 recreational-activity goal achievement. Quality of interaction was measured using a Likert-type scale (see
Outcome Measures) at the end of each observation
session.

Observers and Observer Training

Three graduate students in special education served
500 as observers. Prior to data collection, the observers
read and discussed definitions and descriptions of outcome measures and observation procedures. The observers then practiced the observation and recording
procedures in the participants' physical-education
505 classes by observing students as they engaged in recreational activities. Observers were required to reach a
criterion of 80% interobserver agreement for all outcome measures for two consecutive practice sessions
before collecting data.

Interobserver Agreement

510 Interobserver agreement was assessed during a
minimum of 29% of generalization sessions per participant per condition ($M = 38\%$ across participants and

conditions) and during a minimum of 25% of training
sessions per participant ($M = 38\%$ across participants).
515 The point-by-point agreement method (Kazdin, 1982)
was used to assess % of agreement for all measures.
Overall interobserver-agreement means and ranges
across generalization conditions were as follows: for %
of intervals engaging in recreational activity, $M = 98\%$
520 and range = 80% to 100%; for quality of interaction,
$M = 97\%$ and range = 60% to 100%; for % of self-
prompting steps performed, $M = 100\%$; for % of
recreational-activity initiation steps performed, $M =
100\%$; for accuracy of self-assessment of performance,
525 $M = 100\%$; and for accuracy of self-evaluation of goal
achievement, $M = 100\%$. Overall interobserver-
agreement means and ranges during training were as
follows: for % of self-prompting steps performed, $M =
97\%$ and range 94% to 100%; and for % of recrea-
530 tional-activity initiation steps performed, $M = 98\%$ and
range = 90% to 100%.

Social Validation Measures

In addition to assessing participants' recreational-
activity goals, we also queried recreational-activity
partners regarding their interactions with participants.
535 Following each generalization session during the training and maintenance conditions, we asked recreational-
activity partners to complete a written questionnaire in
which they rated their perceptions of their interactions
with participants while engaging in recreational activi-
540 ties.

Results

*Percentage of Intervals Engaging in Recreational
Activities*

Percentage of intervals in which participants engaged in recreational activities with partners during
generalization sessions is shown in Figure 1 and Figure
2 (upper panels). During baseline, only one participant
545 (Tanisha) engaged in recreational activities with a
general-education peer (41% of intervals during Session 1). After training was introduced, all participants
immediately increased their percentage of intervals of
recreational-activity engagement. Mean percentage of
550 engagement across participants during the training
condition was $M = 91\%$ and range = 83% to 99%. After self-prompting training was withdrawn, percentage
of intervals of engagement in recreational activities
remained high across all participants. Mean percent-
555 ages of intervals of engagement during the maintenance condition were $M = 95\%, 96\%, 97\%, 94\%,$ and
98% for Jesse, Marshea, Marlice, Aaliyah, and Tanisha, respectively.

Quality of Interaction

Ratings of quality of interaction between partici-
560 pants and their partners while engaging in recreational
activities are shown in Figure 1 and Figure 2 (upper
panels, right ordinates). Quality of the one interaction

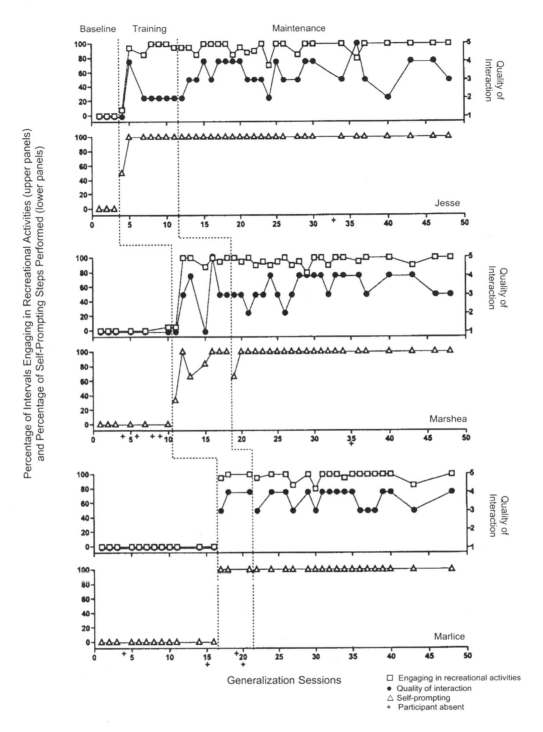

Figure 1. Percentage of intervals engaging in recreational activities (upper panels, left ordinates), rating of quality of interactions (upper panels, right ordinates), and percentage of self-prompting steps performed (lower panels) for Jesse, Marshea, and Marlice.

that occurred during baseline (Tanisha in Session 1) was rated as low ($M = 1.06$). Mean rating across participants during the training condition was $M = 2.86$ and range = 2.14 to 3.67. Mean ratings for Jesse, Marshea, Marlice, Aaliyah, and Tanisha during the maintenance condition were $M = 3.36, 3.36, 3.61, 3.32,$ and 4.0, respectively.

% of Self-Prompting Steps Performed

The lower panels of Figure 1 and Figure 2 show % of the six self-prompting steps designed to prompt initiation of engagement in a recreational activity, which were performed by participants during generalization sessions. During baseline, no participants self-prompted initiation of engagement in recreational ac-

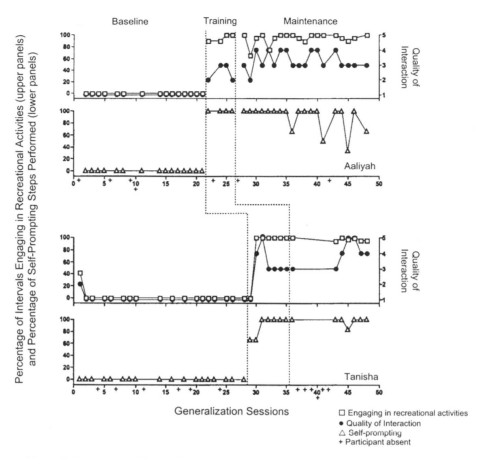

Figure 2. Percentage of intervals engaging in recreational activities (upper panels, left ordinates), rating of quality of interactions (upper panels, right ordinates), and percentage of self-prompting steps performed (lower panels) for Aaliyah and Tanisha.

tivities. Throughout training and maintenance sessions, Marlice performed 100% of self-prompting steps. Mean % of self-prompting steps performed across sessions for the remaining participants was $M = 94\%$ and range = 83% to 100% during the training condition and $M = 97\%$ and range = 90% to 100% during maintenance.

% of Recreational-Activity Initiation Steps Performed

During baseline, no participant performed any of the three recreational-activity initiation steps. During the training condition, all participants performed the first two steps (choose activity and ask partner) across 100% of sessions except for Tanisha, who performed these steps across 71% of sessions. Marlice and Aaliyah performed Step 3 (initiate activity) across 100% of sessions during the training condition and Jesse, Marshea, and Tanisha did so across 86% of sessions. During maintenance, all participants performed all three steps across 100% of sessions with one exception: Aaliyah performed Step 1 and Step 2 across 95% of sessions.

Accuracy of Self-Assessment of Performance

During baseline, participants did not have an oppor-

tunity to self-assess their performance. During training and maintenance conditions, participants accurately assessed whether they had performed each of the three steps across 100% of sessions with three exceptions: Marshea accurately assessed whether she initiated an activity during 86% of maintenance sessions, Aaliyah accurately assessed whether she chose an activity and asked a partner during 95% of maintenance sessions, and Tanisha accurately assessed whether she chose an activity and asked a partner across 86% of training sessions.

Accuracy of Self-Evaluation of Goal Achievement

Following self-assessment of performance of the three recreational-activity initiation steps, participants were asked to determine whether they had achieved their recreational-activity goal during each preceding generalization session. Participants accurately evaluated whether they had met their goal, as determined by comparison with observers' records, with $M = 94\%$ and range = 86% to 100% for sessions during the training condition and $M = 99\%$ and range = 95% to 100% for sessions during the maintenance condition (data available upon request).

Participants' Recreational-Activity Goals

Prior to intervention, all participants indicated that they would like to participate in more activities with their classmates during their physical-education classes. They also indicated that they would like to learn new ways to make friends in class. During postintervention interviews, all participants indicated that they had engaged in more activities with their classmates (e.g., basketball, volleyball, or checkers), that they enjoyed these interactions, and that they had made new friends in class. Four of the five participants indicated that the picture book was helpful.

Social Validation

Following generalization sessions during training and maintenance conditions, recreational-activity partners rated the appropriateness and enjoyableness of their interactions with participants by completing a 5-item questionnaire using a 5-point Likert-type scale with poles marked 1 (*never*) and 5 (*always*). Overall average means across items and participants were $M = 4.20$ and range = 3.0 to 5.0 during training and $M = 4.18$ and range = 3.4 to 4.7 during maintenance. Individual items indicated that partners enjoyed their interactions, that they believed participants interacted appropriately, and that they had similar interactions with their general-education friends. For example, comments included, "I had fun. I would at any time like to do this again" and "Marshea is a great friend."

Discussion

An intervention package was found to be effective at supporting high school students with extensive support–needs in increasing their initiations of and engagement in recreational activities with their general-education peers during physical-education classes. Virtually no engagement in recreational activities with peers was observed across participants during baseline despite that (a) peers were in proximity, (b) verbal cues were given by teachers to engage in recreational activities, and (c) recreational materials were available to participants. Introduction of the support package was associated with increases in participants' initiation of and engagement in recreational activities with peers, in addition to increases in ratings of quality of interaction. Findings extend the literature on strategies to increase recreational engagement with peers as follows.

First, the self-prompting strategy, which was designed to initiate recreational activity engagement, was rapidly acquired across participants (i.e., 3 to 8 training sessions; $M = 13$ min per session). Rapidity of acquisition may have related to the simplicity of the self-prompting strategy. The self-prompting picture book contained only two photographs, which participants used to perform only six self-prompting steps (i.e., pick up book, turn to first photograph, look at and point to first photograph, turn page, look at and point to second photograph, and put book down). Further, recreational-activity initiation prompted by picture-book use required participants to perform only three steps (i.e., choose activity, ask partner, and initiate activity). In comparison, high school students with extensive support–needs in Copeland and Hughes's (2000) study were required to use as many as 19 pictures to prompt their performance of 19 corresponding cleaning tasks. Despite as many as 26 training sessions, trainer prompts for both picture-prompt use and task performance were required throughout the study for participants to initiate and complete assigned tasks. When teaching students with extensive support–needs to prompt themselves to perform expected behavior, it may be critical to limit the number and complexity of self-prompting steps that students are expected to perform.

Second, we introduced into training and generalization sessions multiple stimuli that were present in participants' everyday physical-education class environments (i.e., recreational materials, a verbal cue to engage in recreational activities, or multiple classmates as recreational partners). During training, participants were provided repeated practice in choosing from a range of recreational materials found in their everyday classroom and in asking a variety of their general-education classmates to participate in a recreational activity. Participants did so in response to the same verbal cue used by their physical-education teachers to prompt recreational-activity engagement for the entire class. Repeated practice in initiating recreational-activity engagement using the same stimuli available in participants' daily classes may have increased the saliency of (a) expected behavior in physical-education class (i.e., engaging in recreational activities with peers) and (b) accessibility of recreational opportunities available in the gym (e.g., playing badminton with a peer) during generalization sessions. Although these stimuli were available every day during physical-education classes, they did not serve as discriminative stimuli for participants to initiate and engage in recreational activities until the intervention package was introduced. Researchers report that students with extensive support–needs often do not engage in expected classroom behavior in general-education classes unless direct assistance is provided to prompt and support them to do so (e.g., Mu, Ellin, Siegel, & Allinder, 2000; Schnorr, 1997). Programming common stimuli may be one means of teaching students what behaviors are expected in a general-education class environment and supporting them in performing these behaviors.

Third, we taught participants simply to initiate rather than actually engage in recreational activity-interaction with peers. Participants were taught to only (a) choose an activity, (b) ask a peer to engage in the activity with them, and (c) initiate the activity with the peer. We did not attempt to teach participants or partners how to engage in the activity, such as how to look at and discuss a magazine with a peer, how to hit a volleyball, or how to place game pieces on a board

game. Further, we did not teach participants or partners how to interact socially when engaging in an activity such as how to ask a peer if she would like to turn the page in a magazine or how to engage in casual conver-
735 sation with a peer while playing a game. Nonetheless, simply initiating a recreational activity by participants resulted in nearly continuous engagement in the activity with peers across participants throughout generalization sessions, as well as increases in quality of inter-
740 actions (e.g., affect, frequency of communicative exchanges, or attentiveness) while engaging in activities. Observational data gathered during generalization sessions indicated that either (a) participants already had the skills needed to engage in a particular activity or
745 (b) recreational partners showed participants how to engage in an activity if needed. However, participants did not engage in recreational activities until they were taught to initiate recreational-activity engagement. Schnorr (1997) suggested that students with extensive
750 support–needs should be taught strategies to initiate activities with their peers in general-education environments as a means to promote social interaction and mutual engagement. Our findings indicate that, for some students with extensive support–needs, simply
755 learning to initiate an activity, rather than receiving possibly more extensive recreational- or social-skills training, may result in quality interactions with peers in general-education settings.

Fourth, the intervention included components de-
760 signed to support participants in establishing and assessing their recreational-activity goals. Specifically, we asked participants prior to intervention and on a daily basis prior to training sessions whether engaging in recreational activities was a personal goal and if they
765 wanted to perform three steps (i.e., choose an activity, ask a partner, and initiate activity) to achieve this goal. Participants consistently responded affirmatively to these queries. In addition, immediately following each generalization session, we asked participants to assess
770 their performance of recreational-activity initiation and whether they had achieved their goal of performing all three steps to initiate an activity with a peer. Participants assessed both their performance and goal achievement with considerable accuracy, although nei-
775 ther prompts nor corrective feedback were provided. Locke and Latham (1990), in reviewing goal evaluation studies, suggested that frequent feedback on progress toward goal achievement may enhance performance. However, feedback typically is provided by in-
780 terventionists—and typically on only an intermittent basis—rather than by frequently asking participants to assess their own performance or goal achievement (Locke & Latham). (See Grossi & Heward, 1998, for a notable exception.) Asking participants in our study to
785 self-assess performance and self-evaluate goal achievement may have increased the saliency of steps required to initiate recreational-activity engagement and achieve daily performance goals.

Several limitations of the study are noteworthy.
790 During generalization sessions throughout training and maintenance conditions, we (a) asked general-education classmates to serve as recreational partners, (b) put recreational materials in proximity of participants, and (c) provided the verbal cue, "It's time to go
795 do something," used by the physical-education teachers to prompt recreational-activity engagement. Although all of these stimuli (i.e., classmates, recreational materials, and verbal cue) were present every day in the gym during physical-education classes, participants did
800 not respond to them as prompts to engage in recreational activities. In addition, we handed participants their self-prompting picture books at the beginning of each session and asked them to self-assess performance and goal achievement after each session. Although our
805 presence must be considered a component of the intervention, we provided no verbal or physical prompts or corrective feedback for performance; rather, we set the occasion for performance to occur by providing discriminative stimuli. Further, we argue that our inter-
810 vention is a support package, some components of which (e.g., providing materials or verbal cue) may need to be permanently retained to support performance. Future interventionists should examine the extent to which classroom teachers, other practitioners, or
815 general-education peers could provide these supports alone—without research-staff assistance—following self-prompting picture-book training for participants.

References

Agran, M., Blanchard, C., & Wehmeyer, M. L. (2000). Promoting transition goals and self-determination through student self-directed learning: The self-determined model of instruction. *Education and Training in Mental Retardation and Developmental Disabilities, 35,* 351–364.

Bullock, C. C., & Mahon, M. J. (1992). Decision making in leisure: Empowerment for people with mental retardation. *Journal of Physical Education, Recreation, and Dance, 63,* 36–40.

Copeland, S. R., & Hughes, C. (2000). Acquisition of a picture prompt strategy to increase independent performance. *Education and Training in Mental Retardation and Developmental Disabilities, 35,* 294–305.

Fryxell, D., & Kennedy, C. H. (1995). Placement along the continuum of services and its impact on students' social relationships. *Journal of the Association for Persons with Severe Handicaps, 20,* 259–269.

Gaylord-Ross, R. J., Haring, T. G., Breen, C., & Pitts-Conway, V. (1984). The training and generalization of social interaction skills with autistic youth. *Journal of Applied Behavior Analysis, 17,* 229–247.

Grossi, T. A., & Heward, W. L. (1998). Using self-evaluation to improve the work productivity of trainees in a community-based restaurant training program. *Education and Training in Mental Retardation and Developmental Disabilities, 34,* 235–259.

Hughes, C., Killian, D. J., & Fischer, G. M. (1996). Validation and assessment of a conversational interaction intervention. *American Journal on Mental Retardation, 100,* 493–509.

Hughes, C., Rung, L. L., Wehmeyer, M. L., Agran, M., Copeland, S. R., & Hwang, B. (2000). Self-prompted communication book use to increase social interaction among high school students. *Journal of the Association for Persons with Severe Handicaps, 15,* 153–166.

Hunt, P., Alwell, M., Goetz, L., & Sailor, W. (1990). Generalized effects of conversation skill training. *Journal of the Association for Persons with Severe Handicaps, 15,* 250–260.

Hunt, P., & Goetz, L. (1997). Research on inclusive educational programs, practices, and outcomes for students with severe disabilities. *The Journal of Special Education, 31,* 3–29.

Individuals with Disabilities Education Act Amendments of 1997, PL 105–17, 20 U. S. C. § 1400 *et seq.*

Kasari, C., Sigman, M., Mundy, P., & Yirmiya, N. (1990). Affective sharing in the context of joint attention interactions of normal, autistic, and mentally retarded children. *Journal of Autism and Developmental Disorders, 20,* 87–100.

Kazdin, A. E. (1982). *Single case research design: Methods for clinical and applied settings.* New York: Oxford University Press.

Kennedy, C. H., & Itkonen, T. (1994). Some effects of regular class participation on the social contacts and social networks of high school students with severe disabilities. *Journal of the Association for Persons with Severe Handicaps, 19*, 1–10.

Koegel, R. L., & Egel, A. L. (1979). Motivating autistic children. *Journal of Abnormal Psychology, 88*, 418–426.

Locke, E. A., & Latham, G. P. (1990). *A theory of goal setting and task performance.* Englewood Cliffs, NJ: Prentice Hall.

McMahon, C. M., Wacker, D. P., Sasso, G. M., Berg, W. K., & Newton, S. M. (1996). Analysis of frequency and type of interactions in a peer-mediated social skills intervention: Instructional vs. social interactions. *Education and Training in Mental Retardation and Developmental Disabilities, 31*, 339–352.

Mu, K., Ellin, B., Siegel, E. B., & Allinder, R. M. (2000). Peer interactions and sociometric status of high school students with moderate or severe disabilities in general education classrooms. *Journal of the Association for Persons with Severe Handicaps, 25*, 142–152.

Nietupski, J., Hamre-Nietupski, S., Green, K., Varnum-Teeter, K., Twedt, B., LePera, D., Seebold, K., & Hanrahan, M. (1986). Self-initiated and sustained leisure activity participation by students with moderate/severe handicaps. *Education and Training of the Mentally Retarded, 21*, 259–264.

O'Reilly, M. F., Lancioni, G. E., & Kierans, I. (2000). Teaching leisure social skills to adults with moderate mental retardation: An analysis of acquisition, generalization, and maintenance. *Education and Training in Mental Retardation and Developmental Disabilities, 35*, 250–258.

Rynder, J. E., Schleien, S. J., Meyer, L. H., Vandercook, T. L., Mustonen, T., Colond, J. S., & Olson, K. (1993). Improving interaction outcomes for children with and without severe disabilities through cooperatively structured recreation activities: A research synthesis. *Journal of Special Education, 26*, 386–407.

Schleien, S. J., & Ray, M. T. (1997). Leisure education for a quality transition to adulthood. *Journal of Vocational Rehabilitation, 8*, 155–169.

Schnorr, R. (1997). From enrollment to memberships: "Belonging" in middle and high school classes. *Journal of the Association for Persons with Severe Handicaps, 21*, 1–15.

Stokes, T. F., & Baer, D. M. (1977). An implicit technology of generalization. *Journal of Applied Behavior Analysis, 10*, 349–367.

Wehmeyer, M. L., Palmer, S. B., Agran, M., Mithaug, D. E., & Martin, J. E. (2000). Promoting causal agency: The self-determined learning model of instruction. *Exceptional Children, 66*, 439–453.

Wilson, A., Arnold, M., & Rowland, S. T. (1997). Promoting recreation and leisure activities for individuals with disabilities: A collaborative effort. *Journal of Instructional Psychology, 24*, 76–79.

About the authors: Carolyn Hughes is an associate professor in the Department of Special Education at Vanderbilt University. She has published extensively in the area of self-management for persons with developmental disabilities and social interaction among high school students with disabilities and their general-education peers. Stephanie E. Fowler is a research assistant in the Department of Special Education at Vanderbilt University. She has conducted studies in the areas of goal setting and self-directed behavior in high school settings among students with developmental disabilities. Susan R. Copeland is a research associate in the Department of Special Education at Vanderbilt University. Her research interests include self-determination and goal setting. She has published her findings in the *American Journal on Mental Retardation* and related journals. Martin Agran is a professor in the Department of Special Education at the University of Northern Iowa. He has a lengthy publication history in the areas of self-directed learning and problem solving among high school students and adults with developmental disabilities in general-education and community settings. Michael L. Wehmeyer is an associate professor and the director of Self-Determination Projects at the Beach Center on Families and Disability at the University of Kansas. He is highly sought as a keynote speaker in the area of secondary transition and is a frequent contributor to journals in the field of developmental disabilities. Penny P. Church-Pupke is a research assistant in the Department of Special Education at Vanderbilt University. She has conducted literature reviews in the area of supports for persons with developmental disabilities and studies investigating social interaction in high school settings.

Address correspondence to: Dr. Carolyn Hughes, Peabody College of Vanderbilt University, Peabody #329, 230 Appleton Place, Nashville, TN 37203-5721.

Exercise for Article 21

Factual Questions

1. Participants' recreational-activity goals were assessed once prior to training. When were they reassessed?

2. When rating the quality of interaction, were nonverbal communications included? Explain.

3. Who served as observers?

4. After training, how many participants immediately increased their percentage of five-minute intervals of recreational-activity engagement?

5. Did the researchers attempt to teach participants how to engage in recreational activities with peers?

6. Did the researchers provide corrective feedback in order to influence participants' behavior?

Questions for Discussion

7. What is your understanding of the term "baseline" as used in this study? (See lines 361–376.)

8. Is the description of the training sufficiently specific to give you a clear indication of how the training was conducted? Explain. (See lines 377–424.)

9. Each participant and his or her partner was observed for five minutes during each 50-minute physical education class. In your opinion, is this amount of time (across a number of class sessions) sufficient for the purposes of this study? Explain. (See lines 476–479.)

10. Is it important to know that the observers were required to reach a criterion of 80% interobserver agreement for all outcome measures? (See lines 506–509.)

11. Does a comparison of "baseline data" with "training data" in Figures 1 and 2 convince you that the training caused improvements in participants' behavior? In your opinion, would the inclusion of a separate control group provide more convincing data? Explain.

12. In your opinion, how important are the social validation data? Would the study be just as convincing without them? Explain. (See lines 532–540 and 630–644.)

Quality Ratings

Directions: Indicate your level of agreement with each of the following statements by circling a number from 5 for strongly agree (SA) to 1 for strongly disagree (SD). If you believe an item is not applicable to this research article, leave it blank. Be prepared to explain your ratings.

A. The introduction establishes the importance of the study.

    SA 5 4 3 2 1 SD

B. The literature review establishes the context for the study.

    SA 5 4 3 2 1 SD

C. The research purpose, question, or hypothesis is clearly stated.

    SA 5 4 3 2 1 SD

D. The method of sampling is sound.

    SA 5 4 3 2 1 SD

E. Relevant demographics (for example, age, gender, and ethnicity) are described.

    SA 5 4 3 2 1 SD

F. Measurement procedures are adequate.

    SA 5 4 3 2 1 SD

G. All procedures have been described in sufficient detail to permit a replication of the study.

    SA 5 4 3 2 1 SD

H. The participants have been adequately protected from potential harm.

    SA 5 4 3 2 1 SD

I. The results are clearly described.

    SA 5 4 3 2 1 SD

J. The discussion/conclusion is appropriate.

    SA 5 4 3 2 1 SD

K. Despite any flaws, the report is worthy of publication.

    SA 5 4 3 2 1 SD

Article 22

Drug Use Patterns Among High School Athletes and Nonathletes

ADAM H. NAYLOR
Boston University

DOUG GARDNER
ThinkSport® Consulting Services

LEN ZAICHKOWSKY
Boston University

ABSTRACT. This study examined drug use patterns and perceptions of drug intervention programs among adolescent interscholastic athletes and nonathletes. In particular, it explored the issue of whether participation in high school athletics is related to a healthier lifestyle and decreased use of recreational drugs and ergogenic aids. One thousand five hundred fifteen Massachusetts high school students completed a 150-item survey that assessed illicit and nonillicit substance use. Chi square analyses revealed that athletes were significantly less likely to use cocaine and psychedelics, and were less likely to smoke cigarettes, compared with nonathletes. Conversely, nonathletes were less likely to use creatine than were athletes. There was no difference in the use of anabolic steroids and androstenedione between athletes and nonathletes. Descriptive analyses appear to indicate that drug interventions for athletes are falling short of their objectives. This study suggests that athletes have a healthier lifestyle and that the efficacy of intervention programs must be further examined.

From *Adolescence, 36,* 627–639. Copyright © 2001 by Libra Publishers, Inc. Reprinted with permission.

Drug use by athletes has made newspaper headlines, sport governing body rulebooks, and doctors' waiting rooms on a regular basis. Despite this, the relationship between drug use and participation in athletics

5   is not yet a clear one. On one hand, it has been suggested that participation in athletics leads to a healthier lifestyle and wiser decisions about substance use (Anderson, Albrecht, McKeag, Hough, & McGrew, 1991; Shephard, 2000; Shields, 1995). Conversely,

10   others have suggested that drug use is inherent in sports and its culture (Dyment, 1987; Wadler & Hainline, 1989). In between these two perspectives, one is left wondering if there is any difference in the substance use patterns of athletes and the general public (Adams,

15   1992; Anshel, 1998).

One way to begin clarifying this issue is to differentiate between recreational substances and ergogenic aids. Recreational substances are typically used for intrinsic motivates, such as to achieve altered affective

20   states. Examples of such drugs are alcohol, tobacco, marijuana, psychedelics, and cocaine. Ergogenic substances are used to augment performance in a given

domain. In sports, such drugs are typically used to assist athletes in performing with more speed and

25   strength, and to endure more pain than normal. Examples of ergogenic aids are creatine, androstenedione, anabolic steroids, major pain medication, barbiturates, and amphetamines. The categorization of specific substances is debatable in some cases (Adams, 1992). For

30   instance, although marijuana is traditionally viewed as a recreational substance, it recently has been banned by the International Olympic Committee for its performance-enhancing potential (i.e., lowering of physiological arousal) (H. Davis, personal communication, Octo-

35   ber 4, 1999). Similarly, amphetamines have been used for recreational purposes. Nevertheless, the attempt to label substances as either recreational or ergogenic assists in clarifying differences between athletes and nonathletes in their drug use patterns.

Recreational Drugs

40   It has been traditionally believed that participation in athletics leads to a healthier lifestyle and less use of recreational drugs. Increased physical activity not only creates a physically healthier person, but also may lead to changes in overall lifestyle, highlighted by "a pru-

45   dent diet and abstinence from cigarette smoking" (Shephard, 2000). Some research has supported the popular notion that substance use is negatively correlated with healthful activities. In the university setting, athletes have self-reported less alcohol and drug use

50   than their peers (Anderson et al., 1991), providing further evidence that the high-level physical and mental demands of sports are incompatible with recreational drug use. Shields (1995) indicated that high school athletic directors perceived that students who partici-

55   pated in athletics were less likely to smoke cigarettes, consume alcohol, chew tobacco, and smoke marijuana than were students who did not participate in extracurricular athletic activities. These findings, while encouraging, ought to be verified through confidential self-

60   reports of high school students themselves. Nonetheless, these findings offer support for the notion that participation in sports promotes health and wellness.

Conversely, Wadler and Hainline (1989) have suggested that athletes may be more likely to experiment

65   with recreational and ergogenic aids than individuals

141

not participating in athletics. Physically, athletes might use recreational drugs to cope with the pain of injury rehabilitation. Mentally, stress (arising from the competitive demands of sports) and low self-confidence are issues that might lead athletes to recreational drug use. Furthermore, the "culture" of the particular sport might socialize athletes into drug use (e.g., baseball and smokeless tobacco) (Anshel, 1998). However, there is little evidence to suggest that recreational drug use is higher for athletes than nonathletes.

Ergogenic Aids

Unlike recreational substances, use of ergogenic aids is more likely in competitive athletic settings (Dyment, 1987). Wadler and Hainline (1989) have pointed out five instances that might lead athletes to utilize performance-enhancing pharmacological aids: (1) athletes who are at risk for not making a team or achieving the level of performance they desire; (2) athletes who are approaching the end of their career and are striving to continue to compete in their sport; (3) athletes who have weight problems and are seeking a means to increase or decrease weight; (4) athletes who are battling injuries and are trying to find ways to heal quicker; and (5) athletes who feel external pressure, such as from teammates, coaches, and parents, to use performance-enhancing drugs. Little research has contradicted the notion that those participating in sports are more disposed to use ergogenic aids. However, the findings of Anderson and colleagues (1991) did not support the notion that there is an anabolic steroid epidemic in collegiate athletics. Although their study did not examine whether athletes more frequently use anabolic steroids than do nonathletes, Anderson et al. concluded that steroid use by intercollegiate athletes did not increase over a four-year span. However, the prevalence of ergogenic aids a decade later has multiplied, with the advent of over-the-counter supplements (Hendrickson & Burton, 2000).

Educational Interventions

While the relationship between drug use and participation in organized athletics is still unclear, few disagree that early identification of, and education about, drug use is necessary. Andrews and Duncan (1998) have noted that cigarette smoking that begins during adolescence proceeds to more frequent use in the two years following high school. Furthermore, onset of drug use has been found to be a major determinant of adolescent morbidity and failure to perform age-related social roles (Grant & Dawson, 1998). In light of these facts, identification of substance use patterns during the high school years is important for preventing and curbing at-risk behaviors that might arise later in an individual's life.

Sports organizations have made it their mission to deter substance use by athletes. In 1986, the National Collegiate Athletic Association implemented a national drug education and drug-testing program for its member institutions (Anderson et al., 1991). Other organizations at various levels of sports have also adopted programs to monitor and police drug use behaviors in athletes (Shields, 1995). The Massachusetts Interscholastic Athletic Association (MIAA) has initiated one such program for high school athletic programs in the state (Massachusetts Interscholastic Athletic Association, 1999). The cornerstone of this intervention is the MIAA Chemical Health Eligibility Rule.

During the season of practice or play, a student shall not, regardless of the quantity, use or consume, possess, buy/sell or give away any beverage containing alcohol; any tobacco product; marijuana; steroids; or any controlled substance.... The penalty for the first violation is that a student shall lose eligibility for the next two (2) consecutive interscholastic events or two (2) weeks of a season in which the student is a participant, whichever is greater. If a second or subsequent violation occurs, the student shall lose eligibility for the next twelve (12) consecutive interscholastic events or twelve (12) consecutive weeks, whichever is greater, in which the student is a participant.

It is the desire of the MIAA that this rule will not only be effective during the athletic season, but lead to an overall healthier lifestyle. High school coaches and athletic directors are responsible for implementing this rule and levying punishments as infractions occur. Adams (1992) found that students favored the eligibility rule and would like to see it strictly enforced. Furthermore, student athletes supported the notion of mandatory/random drug testing in high school athletics. Although drug intervention programs have been supported by both administrators and athletes, their efficacy must still be determined.

Purpose of the Present Study

The purpose of this study was to examine the incidence of drug use by interscholastic high school athletes, and to see if participation in interscholastic athletics is related to a healthier lifestyle, and specifically decreased use of recreational drugs and ergogenic aids year-round. Exploring possible differences in drug use patterns between athletes and nonathletes was a central element. This study sought to replicate previous high school drug use and abuse surveys conducted in the state of Massachusetts (Adams, 1992; Gardner & Zaichkowsky, 1995).

Besides the desire to update the findings on substance use habits since 1991, two other issues motivated this research. First, drug use by athletes has received a great deal of media attention. For example, the supplement androstenedione came to wide public attention during the baseball season in which Mark McGwire broke the home run record. Second, the governing bodies of state high school athletics have instituted wellness programs, drug education, and specific rules to prevent drug use. This study examined descriptive data relating to the effectiveness of these rules and programs.

Method

Participants

One thousand five hundred fifteen students, representing 15 high schools within the state of Massachusetts, were surveyed. Male students represented 51% of the sample ($n = 773$), while female students accounted for 49% ($n = 742$). Thirty-five percent were freshmen, 24.6% were sophomores, 23.4% were juniors, and 17% were in their senior year of high school. Seventy-four percent reported they had participated in one or more formally sanctioned interscholastic sports within the past 12 months.

The 150-item questionnaire used in this study was based on previous studies that have examined drug use patterns among high school students and student athletes (Adams, 1992; Anderson & McKeag, 1985; Johnston, O'Malley, & Bachman, 1999; Gardner & Zaichkowsky, 1995; Zaichkowsky, 1987). It included questions about students' drug use within the past 12 months, and made "nonuse" as stringent a classification as possible. Consistent with previous studies, both recreational and ergogenic substance use was self-reported. Recreational substances included alcohol, cigarettes, smokeless tobacco, marijuana, cocaine, and psychedelic drugs. Ergogenic aids included major pain medications, anabolic steroids, barbiturates, amphetamines, androstenedione, and creatine. A final section of the questionnaire asked students to address the effectiveness of the Massachusetts Interscholastic Athletic Association's substance use rules and educational interventions.

Table 1
Drug Use Patterns Among High School Athletes and Nonathletes

	Athletes (%)	Nonathletes (%)	Total (%)
Alcohol	68.8	68.4	68.7
Cigarettes**	36.1	44.0	38.4
Smokeless tobacco	8.0	7.7	7.9
Marijuana	37.5	42.9	39.1
Cocaine**	3.1	7.2	4.3
Psychedelics***	9.8	18.1	12.3
Creatine**	10.4	4.4	8.6
Androstenedione	2.3	2.1	2.2
Anabolic steroids	2.5	3.4	2.8
Pain medication	29.3	31.9	30.1
Barbiturates	3.7	6.1	4.4
Amphetamines	6.8	9.6	7.6

**Significant difference between athletes and nonathletes at the .01 level.
***Significant difference between athletes and nonathletes at the .001 level.

Procedure

Permission to conduct the study was obtained from the principals of 15 randomly selected public high schools in Massachusetts. Each principal agreed to allow between 100 and 180 students to participate in the study, and assigned a school athletic director or wellness coordinator to be the primary contact person for the researchers.

Each contact person was asked to select students who were representative of the school's gender, ethnic, and athletic demographics to participate in the study. Students were categorized as athletes if they participated on any state-sanctioned interscholastic athletic team. Upon creating the sample, the principal investigator and each school's contact person selected a class period and date in which to administer the questionnaire.

The principal investigator and two research assistants visited the 15 schools over a period of a month and a half. Students were administered the questionnaire in the school auditorium or cafeteria. They were assured that they would remain anonymous, that their responses would be viewed only by researchers, and that all information would be kept confidential. The questionnaire took approximately 30 minutes to complete.

Data Analysis

The frequencies of all variables were calculated. Descriptive statistics and chi square analyses were conducted using the Statistical Package for the Social Sciences (SPSS).

Results

Athlete/Nonathlete Differences

Chi square analyses indicated statistically significant differences between athletes and nonathletes in reported use of 4 of the 12 substances (see Table 1). In terms of recreational drugs, significantly more nonathletes than interscholastic athletes have smoked cigarettes, $\chi^2(1, N = 520) = 7.455, p < .01$. Nonathletes also reported using cocaine, $\chi^2(1, N = 59) = 11.491, p < .01$, and psychedelics, $\chi^2(1, N = 171) = 18.382, p < .001$, with greater frequency. One ergogenic aid, creatine, was used significantly more by athletes than nonathletes, $\chi^2(1, N = 115) = 7.455, p < .01$. Athletes were less likely to use marijuana, amphetamines, and barbiturates than were nonathletes, although the differences fell just short of being statistically significant.

Interscholastic Drug Intervention Feedback

The Massachusetts Interscholastic Athletic Association's Chemical Health Eligibility Rule seeks to discourage the use of recreational and ergogenic substances by high school athletes. Sixty-eight percent of the student athletes were aware of this rule (see Table 2). Thirty-eight percent reported having violated the rule; only 12% of these student athletes reported having been punished by school officials. Thirteen percent of those caught breaking the rule said they had not been punished. Seventy-one percent believed that some of their teammates had violated the Chemical Health Eligibility Rule.

Not only does the MIAA set drug use rules for student athletes, but it also seeks to implement intervention programs. Fifty-seven percent of the athletes stated that their coaches further this mission by discussing the issue of drug use and abuse. Thirty-one percent of the athletes expressed interest in drug education programs provided by the athletic department, while 48% stated that they would submit to random drug testing.

Table 2
Interscholastic Athletes' Perceptions of Drug Intervention Effectiveness

Topic	Yes	No
Do you know the Chemical Health Eligibility Rule?	68%	32%
Have you violated this rule during the season?	38%	62%
Have you received a penalty if you violated this rule?	12%	88%
Have you been caught and not been penalized?	13%	87%
Have any of your teammates violated this rule?	71%	29%
Does your coach discuss the issue of drugs?	57%	43%
Would you submit to voluntary random drug testing?	48%	52%
Are you interested in drug prevention programs from the athletic department?	31%	69%

Discussion

270   The results of this study appear to reflect current trends in substance use by high school students when compared with national averages (see Johnston et al., 1999). One encouraging finding was that cigarette smoking in Massachusetts was lower than national
275   averages. Roughly 38% of the students surveyed here reported smoking at least one cigarette as compared with the lowest estimate of 51% of the adolescents surveyed by the National Institute on Drug Abuse (Johnston et al., 1999). Massachusetts has engaged in
280   an aggressive antitobacco campaign over the last decade, which might account for this finding.

Previous research suggests three possible reasons for adolescent drug use: experimentation, social learning, and body image concerns (Anshel, 1998; Collins,
285   2000). Experimentation with drugs has been associated with boredom and is often supported by adolescents' belief that they are impervious to the harmful side effects of dangerous substances. Social learning theory states that individuals will take their drug use cues
290   from others in the environment. Modeling of parents' and friends' behavior is a prime example of social learning. Last, individuals have been found to use certain drugs to improve their appearance.

Recreational Substances

It has been suggested that recreational drug use
295   does not differ for athletes and nonathletes (Adams, 1992; Anshel, 1998; Dyment, 1987; Wadler & Hainline, 1989). The results of the present study were mixed in regard to student athlete and nonathlete substance use differences. There were no significant dif-

300   ferences for three of the six recreational drugs: alcohol, marijuana, and smokeless tobacco.

It is clear that alcohol use is socially accepted (Bailey & Rachal, 1993; Bush & Iannotti, 1992; Reifman et al., 1998), which might explain the high percentage of
305   students who consumed alcohol and the lack of difference in alcohol use between athletes and nonathletes. Further, the media provide opportunities for high school students to model the drinking behaviors of their professional and collegiate counterparts (Collins,
310   2000). Although the peer group influences the use of most substances, the culture of sports has also promoted alcohol use.

Slightly over 37% of the athletes reported smoking marijuana in the last year as opposed to about 43% of
315   the nonathletes. This is similar to the pattern for cigarette smoking, although the difference between athletes and nonathletes for marijuana was not significant ($p <$ .052). Even though marijuana and cigarettes are two different types of drugs, it seems that the athletes were
320   more aware of the negative impact smoking any kind of substance has on athletic performance.

Conversely, the lack of conclusive difference in marijuana use may reflect the availability of marijuana, the rising social acceptability of the drug, and the de-
325   sire to experiment (Johnston et al., 1999). In addition, athletes might not perceive marijuana as being as harmful as cocaine or psychedelics, and therefore may be more inclined to try the perceived lesser of two evils.

330   Marijuana has often been labeled a "gateway" drug to more addictive substances (Bush & Iannotti, 1992), yet the present study does not support this contention. Perhaps participation in athletics acts as a barrier to the use of more addictive substances. The significantly
335   lower use of cocaine and psychedelics by athletes can possibly be explained by the commitment necessary to participate in high school athletics. Seasons are year-round for some athletes, and others may be multisports athletes. After-school practices and weekend competi-
340   tions leave student athletes with less time for drug use/experimentation and less time to recover. Thus, organized athletics might reduce the desire of youth to indulge in more addictive and socially unacceptable drugs.

Ergogenic Aids

345   There was no significant difference between athletes and nonathletes for most ergogenic aids (anabolic steroids, androstenedione, pain medication, barbiturates, and amphetamines), which is a positive finding. This suggests that the culture of high school athletics in
350   Massachusetts does not encourage widespread use of these illicit substances. However, it should be noted that the lack of differences might reflect body image issues, specifically in regard to nonathletes who take steroids. Steroids increase an individual's muscle mass,
355   thus increasing self-confidence (Anshel, 1998). Addi-

tionally, muscle-building substances provide the opportunity for individuals to live up to societal standards for physical appearance. Similarly, amphetamines may be used to lose weight and help an individual achieve the "ideal" figure. These substances may not necessarily be utilized to improve athletic performance, but rather to help students improve their body image (Anshel, 1998).

The lack of differences for most of the ergogenic aids might further be explained by the skill level of the typical high school athlete. Wadler and Hainline (1989) have pointed out that few adolescents compete at "elite" levels. In light of this fact, there is little need for illicit performance-enhancing substances in the average high school athlete's competitive endeavors. As the competitive demands get greater and the opposition tougher, one might expect the usage levels of ergogenic aids to increase (Wadler & Hainline, 1989).

The sole difference in the use of ergogenic aids by athletes and nonathletes was for creatine, a nutritional supplement. High school athletes were more than twice as likely to use creatine than were nonathletes. The legality and availability of creatine are perhaps the greatest reasons for the higher level of use among athletes, who are likely trying to gain a competitive edge (Dyment, 1987).

Intervention

Can the differences in illicit drug use behaviors between student athletes and nonathletes be explained by interscholastic chemical health programs? While it would appear that the eligibility rule has helped in policing the substance use of interscholastic athletes, many are still unaware of this rule or ignore it. Seventy-one percent of the athletes reported that teammates have violated the Chemical Health Eligibility Rule. Furthermore, almost 40% of the athletes admitted to having broken this rule, with 13% having not been penalized after being caught. These figures bring the effectiveness of the rule and its enforcement into question. Only 57% reported that their coaches addressed the issue of substance use and abuse, which indicates that this is an educational opportunity that needs to be strengthened.

Educating this population is not an easy feat. A majority of the students were not interested in any further drug interventions. Over half said they would not submit to voluntary random drug testing, and 69% were not interested in drug prevention programs provided by their athletic departments. These findings indicate a change in student attitudes over the last decade. Adams (1992) found that a majority of student athletes were receptive to the idea of random drug testing and additional substance abuse programming through their athletic departments. One reason for the change might be that students have been saturated with drug education. Alternatively, the fact that athletes generally used fewer illicit substances than nonathletes might suggest

that athletes felt they had already acquired healthful behaviors. Furthermore, recent studies have suggested that drug education programming needs to begin early (Faigenbaum, Zaichkowsky, Gardner, & Micheli, 1998), and interventions aimed at high school athletes might be too late for high success rates.

Conclusion

Despite this study's large sample size, one must be cautious regarding generalization of the findings. The high school and sports cultures examined here might only be representative of Massachusetts or the northeastern United States. Because the social circumstances of adolescents and their athletic participation greatly influence their substance use behaviors, more must be done to understand the social climate of high school athletics.

Nevertheless, the present study suggests that participation in athletics is related to a healthier lifestyle. It also reveals that marijuana and alcohol are the two primary substances where more education and intervention are necessary. Furthermore, this study suggests that coaches and administrators must assess the efficacy of their drug prevention programs and their efforts to enforce rules and regulations.

Athletic activities provide many opportunities to promote healthful behaviors. Therefore, sports organizations ought to assess the needs of their athletes and provide effective interventions in a timely manner.

References

Adams, C. L. (1992). *Substance use of Massachusetts high school student athletes.* Unpublished doctoral dissertation, Boston University.

Anderson, W. A., Albrecht, R. R., McKeag, D. B., Hough, D. O., & McGrew, C. A. (1991). A national survey of alcohol and drug use by college athletes. *The Physician and Sportsmedicine, 19,* 91–104.

Anderson, W. A., & McKeag, D. B. (1985). *The substance use and abuse habits of college student athletes* (Report No. 2). Mission, KS: The National Collegiate Athletic Association.

Andrews, J. A., & Duncan, S. C. (1998). The effect of attitude on the development of adolescent cigarette use. *Journal of Substance Abuse, 10,* 1–7.

Anshel, M. H. (1998). Drug abuse in sports: Causes and cures. In J. M. Williams (Ed.), *Applied sport psychology: Personal growth to peak performance* (pp. 372–387). Mountain View, CA: Mayfield Publishing Company.

Bailey, S. L., & Rachal, J. V. (1993). Dimensions of adolescent problem drinking. *Journal of Studies on Alcohol, 54,* 555–565.

Bush, P. J., & Iannotti, R. J. (1992). Elementary schoolchildren's use of alcohol, cigarettes, and marijuana and classmates' attribution of socialization. *Drug and Alcohol Dependence, 30,* 275–287.

Collins, G. B. (2000). Substance abuse and athletes. In D. Begel & R. W. Burton: (Eds.), *Sport psychiatry.* New York: W. W. Norton & Company.

Dyment, P. G. (1987). The adolescent athlete and ergogenic aids. *Journal of Adolescent Health Care, 8,* 68–73.

Faigenbaum, A. D., Zaichkowsky, L. D., Gardner, D. E., & Micheli, L. J. (1998). Anabolic steroid use by male and female middle school students. *Pediatrics, 101,* p. e6.

Gardner, D. E., & Zaichkowsky, L. (1995). *Substance use patterns in Massachusetts high school athletes and nonathletes.* Unpublished manuscript.

Grant, B. F., & Dawson, D. A. (1998). Age of onset of drug use and its association with DSM-IV drug abuse and dependence: Results from the National Longitudinal Alcohol Epidemiologic Survey. *Journal of Substance Abuse, 10,* 163–173.

Hendrickson, T. P., & Burton, R. W. (2000). Athletes' use of performance-enhancing drugs. In D. Begel & R. W. Burton (Eds.), *Sport psychiatry.* New York: W. W. Norton & Company.

Johnston, L. D., O'Malley, P. M., & Bachman, J. G. (1999). *National survey results on drug use from the Monitoring the Future study, 1975–1998: Volume 1. Secondary school students* (NIH Publication No. 99–4660). Rockville, MD: National Institute on Drug Abuse.

Massachusetts Interscholastic Athletic Association. (1999). *Massachusetts Interscholastic Athletic Association wellness manual.* Milford, Massachusetts.

Mayer, R. R., Forster, J. L., Murray, D. M., & Wagenaar, A. C. (1998). Social settings and situations of underage drinking. *Journal of Studies on Alcohol, 59,* 207–215.

Nurco, D. N. (1985). A discussion of validity. In B. A. Rouse, N. J. Kozel, & L. G. Richards (Eds.), *Self-report methods of estimating drug use: Meeting current challenges to validity* (NIDA Research Monograph No. 57, DHHS Publication No. ADM 85-1402). Washington, DC: U.S. Government Printing Office.

Reifman, A., Barnes, G. M., Dintscheff, B. A., Farrell, M. P., & Uhteg, L. (1998). Parental and peer influences on the onset of heavier drinking among adolescents. *Journal of Studies on Alcohol, 59,* 311–317.

Shephard, R. J. (2000). Importance of sport and exercise to quality of life and longevity. In L. Zaichkowsky & D. Mostofsky (Eds.), *Medical and psychological aspects of sport and exercise.* Morgantown, WV: FIT.

Shields, E. W., Jr. (1995). Sociodemographic analysis of drug use among adolescent athletes: Observations–perceptions of athletic directors–coaches. *Adolescence, 30,* 849–861.

Wadler, G. I., & Hainline, B. (1989). *Drugs and the athlete.* Philadelphia: F. A. Davis Company.

Zaichkowsky, L. (1987). *Drug use patterns in Massachusetts high school athletes and nonathletes.* Unpublished manuscript.

Acknowledgments: The researchers would like to thank the Massachusetts Governor's Committee on Physical Fitness and Sports for the grant that supported this study, and Bill Gaine and the Massachusetts Interscholastic Athletic Association for their assistance and support.

Address correspondence to: Adam H. Naylor, School of Education, Boston University, 605 Commonwealth Avenue, Boston, Massachusetts 02215. E-mail: adamnaylor@juno.com

Exercise for Article 22

Factual Questions

1. Barbiturates are classified as
   A. a recreational drug.   B. an ergogenic drug.

2. According to a study reported in the literature review, do student athletes support the notion of mandatory/random drug testing in high school athletics?

3. Male students represented what percentage of the sample?

4. Permission to conduct the study was obtained from whom?

5. What percentage of the athletes reported using cocaine? What percentage of nonathletes reported using cocaine?

6. Was the difference between the two percentages in your answer to question 5 statistically significant? If yes, at what probability level?

7. What percentage of the student athletes reported that their coaches discussed the issue of drugs?

8. Which drug often has been labeled a "gateway" drug?

Questions for Discussion

9. In this study, a relatively large number of schools (15) was represented. To what extent does this increase your confidence in the results? Explain. (See lines 178–180.)

10. The students were asked to report on their drug use during the past 12 months. Do you think that this is an appropriate time interval? Explain. (See lines 193–195.)

11. The contact person at each school was asked to select students who were representative of the school's gender, ethnic, and athletic demographics to participate in the study. In your opinion, was this a good way to select the sample? (See lines 214–216.)

12. The students were assured that they would remain anonymous, that their responses would be viewed only by researchers, and that all information would be kept confidential. In your opinion, how important were these assurances? Do you think that some students might still deny their illicit drug use even though they were given these assurances? Explain. (See lines 226–229.)

13. The researchers mention the northeastern United States as an area to which these results "might only be representative." Do you agree? Explain. (See lines 419–422.)

14. The researchers state that "the present study suggests that participation in athletics is related to a healthier lifestyle." Do you agree? Do you also think that this study provides evidence that participation in athletics *causes* a reduction in students' substance use? Explain. (See lines 427–428.)

Quality Ratings

Directions: Indicate your level of agreement with each of the following statements by circling a number from 5 for strongly agree (SA) to 1 for strongly disagree (SD). If you believe an item is not applicable to this research article, leave it blank. Be prepared to explain your ratings.

A. The introduction establishes the importance of the study.

   SA   5   4   3   2   1   SD

B. The literature review establishes the context for the study.

   SA   5   4   3   2   1   SD

C. The research purpose, question, or hypothesis is clearly stated.

SA   5   4   3   2   1   SD

D. The method of sampling is sound.

SA   5   4   3   2   1   SD

E. Relevant demographics (for example, age, gender, and ethnicity) are described.

SA   5   4   3   2   1   SD

F. Measurement procedures are adequate.

SA   5   4   3   2   1   SD

G. All procedures have been described in sufficient detail to permit a replication of the study.

SA   5   4   3   2   1   SD

H. The participants have been adequately protected from potential harm.

SA   5   4   3   2   1   SD

I. The results are clearly described.

SA   5   4   3   2   1   SD

J. The discussion/conclusion is appropriate.

SA   5   4   3   2   1   SD

K. Despite any flaws, the report is worthy of publication.

SA   5   4   3   2   1   SD

Article 23

A Comparison of American and Taiwanese Students: Their Math Perception

YEA-LING TSAO
Taipei Municipal Teachers College

ABSTRACT. The major purpose of this study was to attempt to understand some of the reasons for mathematics perception of Taiwanese children compared to American children. The study was conducted with elementary schools in the Denver metropolitan area and Taipei, Taiwan in which fifth graders in each city (21 and 37, respectively) were selected as target subjects in the study. To determine if attitudes and beliefs have a profound effect on American students' performance in mathematics, researchers believe that it may be helpful to compare American students to Chinese students. By providing comparative data, the researcher found marked differences in the beliefs of American and Taiwanese students in three areas under investigation: how to do well in mathematics, what math solutions should be, and motivation. The present study makes a potentially important contribution to our understanding of child development and education in two cultures.

From *Journal of Instructional Psychology*, *31*, 206–213. Copyright © 2004 by Project Innovation, Inc. Reprinted with permission.

Poor performance by American students on tests of mathematics and science has reached the level of a national crisis. Why is this? Study after study has reported on one or another facet of the low standing of Americans in international competition. For example, in a recent cross-national study of mathematics achievement, American students in the eighth and twelfth grades were below the international average in problem solving, geometry, algebra, calculus, and other areas of mathematics. In contrast, Japanese eighth graders received the highest average scores of children from 20 countries, and, at the twelfth-grade level, Japanese students were second only to Chinese students in Hong Kong (Garden, 1987). We must ask why this is the case. Why are Chinese students consistently among the top scorers in cross-national studies of achievement and American students consistently below the international average?

The primary purpose of this research project was to attempt to provide some answers to this question. The researcher was interested in exploring cross-cultural differences in mathematics perception and attitudes of younger children. The major concern was to describe the context in which different levels of achievement occur in these two cultures. The researcher sought to identify not only contexts that appear to be important in explaining differences observed in the early years but also those that might be related to the cross-cultural differences in achievement that have been found among older children and youth. What effect does it have on our children's performance in mathematics? The researcher hopes these questions can be answered in further research.

Literature Review

Logically, children's academic achievement is related to three major factors: their intelligence, their experiences at school, and their experiences at home. With regard to the first factor, it seems unlikely that cross-national differences in academic achievement among Chinese, Japanese, and American children can be accounted for by differences in general intelligence. There is no evidence that Chinese and Japanese children are more intelligent than American children.

According to Schoenfeld (1989), the way people engage in mathematical activities is shaped by their conception of mathematics. There have been many studies that confirm that affective factors shape how students behave. For instance, perceived personal control (Lefcourt, 1982), and perceived usefulness of mathematics (Fennema & Sherman, 1978) are all positively correlated with achievement in mathematics (Schoenfeld, 1989). However, it is unclear if there is a cause-and-effect relationship between affective factors and achievement in mathematics. It is interesting to note that Schoenfeld (1989) found that the strongest correlation was between mathematical performance and perceived mathematical ability.

Children's academic achievement is given a more central role in some cultures than in others. In developing countries such as Taiwan, personal advancement is closely linked to academic achievement, and there is great emphasis on education. In Japan, where natural resources are limited, progress in technology and science is essential for the nation's economic health, and such progress is highly dependent on having a well-educated work force. Other cultures have different goals. Some value experiences that stimulate children to think and build up a broad fund of knowledge, regardless of whether such experiences result in higher school grades; others stress the importance of children developing a sense of self-worth. The goal of education in these societies is not only the acquisition of specific types of knowledge but also the development of children who feel good about themselves and their capabilities; self-confidence is believed to facilitate later learning. In other words, while some cultures value activities that help a child master prescribed skills, others, such as that in the United States, value experiences that will make a child more creative and confident (Stevenson, Lee, Chen, Stigler, Lee, Hsu, & Kitamura, 1990).

Chinese students must go through a series of rigorous entrance exams in order to get into a top university. Forty percent of Chinese students will make it to one of these universities. It is clear that these exams provide intense motivation for students in China to perform well. It would appear that the teachers in China put a great emphasis on teaching in preparation for these national exams. They do in fact do this, but they emphasize conceptual understanding and applications of math to the real world instead of just computations.

Reynolds and Walberg (1992) found that motivation and home environment have a strong indirect effect on achievement. They also found that motivation appeared to be a stronger indicator of mathematics attitude than home environment. This would suggest that the students are responsible for changing their attitude toward mathematics and that their home environment is less influential. However, this could be very difficult for students in the United States if they are consistently hearing that it is okay to not be good in mathematics.

American teachers spent twice as much time on educating students in language arts than they did on mathematics (Stevenson, Lee, & Stigler, 1986). Chinese teachers spent equal amounts of time on language arts and mathematics. Furthermore, teachers in the U.S. are allowed to organize their classrooms according to their own desires, not to a national standard (Stevenson, Lee, & Stigler, 1986). Also, Stevenson, Lee, and Stigler (1986, 1987) found that American teachers only spent about 22% of their time in the classroom imparting information, whereas Chinese teachers spent about 60% of classroom time imparting information. Chinese students spent 240 days a year in school, whereas American students only spent 178 days in school (Stevenson, Lee, & Stigler, 1986; 1987). Upon closer analysis of schools in China and the U.S., it has been found that students in Taiwan spend five-and-a-half days in school a week compared to only five days a week for American students. Further, children in Taiwan spend more time in the day studying mathematics than their American counterparts (Stigler, Lee, Lucker, & Stevenson, 1982; Stigler, Lee, & Stevenson, 1987).

There appear to be issues such as how teachers', parents', and society's attitudes and beliefs affect our children. Research completed by Haladyna, Shaughnessy, and Shaughnessy (1983) found that there is a strong association between teacher quality measures and attitude toward mathematics. It is interesting to note that when teachers were asked what factors may influence students' performance in mathematics, 41% of American teachers believed that innate intelligence was more important than studying hard, which was just the opposite of Chinese teachers (Stigler, Chen, & Lee, 1993). It was also found that American mothers felt that success in school was attributed to ability and Chinese mothers felt that success was to due to effort. Stigler, Chen and Lee (1993) found that even though Americans seem to be aware of the trouble that the American educational system is in, they still feel that the schools are doing a "good" or "excellent" job in educating their children. Parents have a high regard for their children's academic performance even though they continue to be outperformed by their Chinese counterparts.

In Taiwan, the Ministry of Education specifies the curriculum for all schools in great detail. The ministry publishes all textbooks; furthermore, every school in Taiwan uses the same textbooks (Stigler, Lee, & Stevenson, 1986). However, in the United States there is a great deal of variation among textbook series (Stigler, Lee, Lucker, & Stevenson, 1982). This is due to the fact that there is not a national curriculum in the United States. All the textbooks in both countries use a common international system of mathematical notation and Arabic numerals (Stigler, Lee, Lucker, & Stevenson, 1982). Stigler, Lee, Lucker, and Stevenson (1982) also found that the Taiwanese curriculum lagged behind the United States' curriculum when concepts and skills were introduced. Therefore, it does not appear as if only the curriculum in the United States should be blamed for American students' low scores in comparison to Chinese students.

In studies of parental evaluations of children's capabilities, the closer the match between parental evaluations and the child's ability, the better the developmental outcome (e.g., Miller, 1988). Parents whose views are realistic are more likely to adapt interactions with their child to a level appropriate to the child's abilities than are parents who overestimate or underestimate what their child is capable of doing. The same effect would be expected at the societal level: Members of some societies may generally be realistic in evaluating themselves and their children, and others may be biased and give excessively favorable or unfavorable ratings. Realistic evaluation should create a more positive environment for academic achievement (Stevenson, Lee, Chen, Stigler, Lee, Hsu, & Kitamura, 1990). Parents' perceptions of their child's capabilities are an important factor in their expectations for that child. For instance, the U.S. culture has a tendency to place a higher value on achievement in sports than in mathematics (Geary, 1996). The Asian culture, on the other

hand, prioritizes mathematical learning. In fact, the elders of the culture believe that high achievement in
185 mathematics is an important goal for the younger members of the culture (Geary, 1996). It is clear that education is highly valued in China. In fact, ongoing education is the norm.

Stevenson, Lee, Chen, Stigler, Lee, Hsu, and Kita-
190 mura (1990) stated that the degree to which parents, family, and other members of society become involved in children's development and education is likely to differ, depending on the society's conception of the individual in relation to these entities. Chinese and
195 American children do have very different experiences at school. These differences in the cultural valuation of mathematics translate into differences in the invest-ment of children, parents, and teachers in learning mathematics, and are likely to be the primary source of
200 differences in mathematical ability between East Asian and U.S. children (Geary, 1996; Stevenson & Stigler, 1992). According to research by Hackett and Betz (1989), mathematics performance was significantly and positively correlated with attitudes toward mathemat-
205 ics. Stigler, Chen, and Lee concluded that the achieve-ment gap is "unlikely to diminish until there are marked changes in the attitudes and beliefs of Ameri-can parents and students about education" (Stigler, Chen, & Lee, 1993, p. 57).

Methodology

Participants

210 The study was conducted with fifth-grade children from Taipei, Taiwan, and Denver, Colorado. Taipei is a large modern city that is relatively comparable to Den-ver. The researcher selected one public elementary school from each city and surveyed one classroom
215 from each school. The Taipei classroom had 37 stu-dents and the Denver classroom consisted of only 21 students as target subjects in the study.

The researcher chose elementary schoolchildren as the subjects for two reasons. First, the researcher
220 wanted to know if cross-cultural differences in achievement emerged during these early years of schooling. If this proved to be the case, it would be difficult to account for cross-cultural differences in achievement primarily in terms of the educational prac-
225 tices of the schools. A second reason for focusing on elementary schoolchildren was to gain some under-standing of the early antecedents of the large differ-ences that appear later in middle and senior high school.

Instrument

230 A questionnaire containing 39 closed questions was developed by Alan Schoenfeld (1989) and was used with his permission in this study. All items were pre-sent in the form of a seven-point rating scale, ranging from 1 = "strongly agree" to 7 = "strongly disagree."
235 The questionnaire contained questions related to stu-dents' perception of what mathematics is and how to

do well in it, what mathematics solutions should be, how math problems can be solved, how mathematics is learned, and student motivation. The students rated
240 each of the first 33 questions on a seven-point scale with one being strongly agree, four being neutral, and seven being strongly disagree. The last six questions were concerned with gender, grades, and perception of their parents' attitudes toward mathematics. The ques-
245 tionnaire was determined to be highly reliable with an alpha of 0.8468.

Procedure

In this study, the fifth-grade students were asked to answer the questionnaire. Due to the fact that the re-searcher was unable to go to Taipei to conduct the
250 study, the teacher who is a friend of the researcher dis-tributed the questionnaire at her convenience. How-ever, the researcher was able to distribute the surveys in the Denver school. Typically, the questionnaire took only 10–15 minutes to complete.

Data Analysis

255 The form of the data collected contained the atti-tude measure from a Likert-type scale and personal information. The researcher compared the means of each question in the questionnaire and used a two-tailed t test to analyze the data. Then the researcher
260 categorized some of the related questions to determine if there was a correlation between categories.

Result

Specific prior hypotheses were not developed be-cause information from previous work was insufficient to allow confidence to be developed about the char-
265 acteristic of each culture. Although it was not the re-searcher's purpose to evaluate the usefulness of the constructs that have emerged from this work explaining differences in achievement in the two cultures at issue, the researcher did use them to help organize some con-
270 siderations. The researcher used a two-tailed t test to compare the mathematical perceptions between Chi-nese and American students. The means of each ques-tion in the questionnaire was also compared. Among the 33 items, 23 items were significantly different be-
275 tween American and Chinese students' answers: items 1, 3, 4, 5, 6, 7, 8, 12, 14, 15, 16, 18, 19, 20, 21, 22, 24, 25, 26, 28, 29, 31, and 33.

The following items were grouped into six catego-ries, with the thought that some questions asked might
280 have the same concept. Table 1 displays the six catego-ries and the mean score of the items that were signifi-cantly different for the two cultures.

Discussion of Results

The researcher found marked differences in the be-liefs of American and Taiwanese students in many of
285 the areas under investigation. The data show significant differences in the means for the category of what mathematics is. It is interesting to note that the ques-tions in this category suggest that mathematics are

Table 1
Six Categories: The Mean Score of the Items Shows Significant Differences in the Two Cultures

Number of category	Concept	Contained items
1	What mathematics is	1,* 2, 3,* 31*
2	How to do well in it	14,* 28*
3	What mathematics solutions should be	4,* 5,* 6,* 15*
4	How math problems can be solved	7,* 8,* 11, 12,* 13
5	How mathematics is learned	10, 27
6	Student motivation–negative	19,* 22*
	Student motivation–positive	20,* 23, 24*

*$p < .01$

mostly numbers. The Taiwanese students tended to
disagree or feel neutral about these statements. However, the American children tended to agree with this
perception of mathematics.

The second category of how to do well in mathematics also showed significant differences in the mean
scores. The American students strongly agreed that
memorization was the key to doing well in mathematics. If they could memorize all the formulas and how to
do them, then they would do fine in the class, even if
they did not understand what they were doing. It is
hardly the most creative or logical of acts, but it also is
a creative discipline in math where one can discover
and learn to be logical. Their Taiwanese counterparts,
on the other hand, were again more apt to disagree with
this belief.

The category of what math solutions should be encompassed where there could be more than one right
solution to a problem. Again a significant difference in
the mean score was determined. American students
believed the solution to be right answers. Taiwanese
students' responses were more flexible. Taiwanese
students strongly disagreed with the idea that in
mathematics they are either right or wrong. However,
the American students tended to strongly agree with
this idea.

The category of how math problems can be solved
and how mathematics is learned did not show significant differences in the two cultures. For the last category, the researcher broke up the category of motivation into two parts: negative motivation and positive
motivation. There were significant differences between
the two sub-categories for the two cultures. The negative motivation subcategory encompassed the idea of
learning math because it was required or because of
fear of punishment. The Taiwanese answers showed
that they are affected by this negative motivation. They
tended to agree with these statements. However, the
American students strongly disagreed with these statements. Instead, the American students were more influenced by positive motivation such as wanting to do
well in class or impress the teacher.

There were a few individual questions that were of
interest to the researcher. Table 2 shows the mean
score for each culture. There was a significant difference in the mean scores. American students believed
that solving mathematics problems depended on knowing the rules. Mathematics was presumed to be more
rule-bound. Taiwanese students tended to agree that
good teaching practice in mathematics consisted of
making sure students knew how to use the rules. On the
other hand, students also thought that good teaching
practice consisted of showing students lots of different
ways to look at the same question. The researcher also
found the reason Taiwanese students believed school
math was useful in real life was that they might have
been more preoccupied with learning itself rather than
being concerned with self-perceptions.

What is interesting to note is that even though the
Taiwanese students' perceptions of mathematics was
overall more positive than their American counterparts,
they seemed to be learning mathematics mainly because of the fear of punishment. This area should
probably receive more attention in future research studies. Even though the Taiwanese students hinted that
they learned mathematics for negative reasons, they did
have a more positive perception of mathematics than
their American counterparts. This is most likely due to
the fact that their culture places such a high value on
mathematics achievement and it in turn trickles down
into the schools. The two cultures' perceptions of
mathematics was clearly different, but the students did
share some of the same beliefs regarding mathematics
that take place inside class and mathematics that take
place outside.

From past international studies of achievement, we
know that Taiwan continues to outperform the United
States in mathematics achievement. The researcher also
found (Tsao, 2000) that there are marked differences in
the attitudes and beliefs of the two cultures toward
mathematics and in the students' attitudes and beliefs
toward mathematics. This difference in mathematics
achievement could be the effect of the Taiwanese's
more positive perception of mathematics. Further, it
appears that the negative attitude of the American cul-

Table 2

Question	Mean score USA	Mean score Taiwan	p value
Math is mostly facts and procedures that have to be memorized	2.3000	4.2432	0.000*
Math is just a way of thinking about space, numbers, and problems	2.2000	5.2222	0.000*
In mathematics something is either right or wrong	1.6500	5.5833	0.000*
The best way to do well in math is to memorize all of the formulas	1.8500	4.2162	0.000*
I'll get in trouble if I don't try to learn math	4.2000	2.4324	0.003*
Different math courses cover unrelated topics	2.6500	4.8649	0.000*
Some people are good at math and some aren't	1.3500	2.9189	0.000*
When you get the wrong answer to a math problem, it is absolutely wrong–there's no room for argument	3.2105	5.1351	0.000*

*$p < .01$

ture could be one factor causing the low international achievement scores in mathematics.

These differences in the cultural valuation of mathematics translate into differences in the investment of children, parents, and teachers in learning mathematics, and are likely to be the primary source of the mathematical ability differences comparing East Asian and U.S. children (Geary, 1996). According to research by Hackett and Betz (1989), mathematics performance was significantly and positively correlated with attitudes toward mathematics. Stigler, Chen, and Lee (1993) concluded that the achievement gap is "unlikely to diminish until there are marked changes in the attitudes and beliefs of American parents and students about education" (p. 57).

There is still a great need for further investigation into the differences between the two cultures' perceptions of mathematics. In further studies, researchers should do a series of questionnaires and interviews of students from elementary school through college in order to pinpoint an age level or grade level at which students' attitudes and beliefs toward mathematics begin to change. Other studies should study the students' parents and teachers in order to get a better understanding of what their attitudes and beliefs are.

Limitations

The major limitation of this study is that they are convenience samples and small samples from each country. A larger number of samples would not only have resulted in more reliable and generalized conclusions about the effects of math perception between American and Taiwan students, but would also allow a more systematic study of the relationship between math perception and performance outcome in mathematics.

Educational Implications

The goal of education in these societies is not only the acquisition of specific types of knowledge, but also the development of children who feel good about themselves and their capabilities. Self-confidence is believed to facilitate later learning. In other words, while some cultures value activities that help a child master prescribed skills, others, such as those in the United States, value experiences that will make a child more creative and confident. The degree to which parents, family, and other members of society become involved in children's development and education is likely to differ, depending on the society's conception of the individual in relation to these entities. The firmness of boundaries separating individuals, families, and groups has important implications for children's development. In some cultures, such as that in the United States, the individual is deemed to be responsible for his or her accomplishments and difficulties; in others, such as the Chinese cultures, members of the family, teachers, or a larger group—such as pupils in the same classroom—are expected to assume some of the responsibility. As the interdependence among individuals increases, their mutual obligations to each other also increase. Individuals in such situations work hard not only to satisfy their own goals but also to meet the goals set by their families, and the success of the group is valued as highly as the success of particular individuals within the group.

The greater the cultural emphasis on effort, the more likely it is that parents and teachers will believe that they can be instrumental in aiding children in their academic achievement. This belief is transmitted to children, and they, too, come to believe that diligence will lead to success. If, however, adults believe that innate ability imposes critical limitations on children's progress in school, it seems unlikely that they would be motivated to make such strong efforts at assistance. Taiwan, like other countries influenced by the Confucian belief in human malleability, is among the cultures that place great weight on the possibility of advancement through effort.

It would be helpful if more studies that focus on af-

fective issues would have stronger links to research on
450 other topics related to the improvement of practice in
mathematics education. Although little has been done
to connect research on affective issues to these kinds of
studies of cultural influences on mathematics learning,
455 such connections should be able to link differences in
achievement to beliefs that are connected to cultural
influences.

References

Fennema, E., & Sherman, J. (1978). Sex-related differences in mathematics achievement, spatial visualization, and affective factors. *American Educational Research Journal, 14.* 51–71.

Garden, R. A. (1987). The second IEA mathematics study. *Comparative Education Review, 31,* 47–68.

Geary, D. C., Salthouse, T. A., Chen, G., & Fan, L. (1996). Are East Asian versus American differences in arithmetical ability a recent phenomenon? *Developmental Psychology, 32,* 254–262.

Geary, D. C. (1996). Biology, culture, and cross-national differences in mathematical ability. In R.J. Stemberg & T. Ben-Zeev (Eds.), *The Nature of Mathematical Thinking* (pp. 145–171). Mahwah, New Jersey: Lawrence Erlbaum, Publishers.

Hackett, G., & Betz, N. E. (1989). An exploration of the mathematics self-efficacy/mathematics performance correspondence. *Journal for Research in Mathematics Education, 20,* 261–273.

Haladyna, T., Shaughnessy, J., & Shaughnessy, J. M. (1983). A causal analysis of attitude toward mathematics. *Journal for Research in Mathematics Education, 14,* 19–2.9.

Lefcourt, H. M. (1982). Locus of control. Hillsdale, NJ: Erlbaum.

Miller, S. A. (1988). Parents' Beliefs about Children's Cognitive Development. *Child Development, 59,* 259–85.

Reynolds, A. J., & Walberg, H. J. (1992). A process model of mathematics achievement and attitude. *Journal for Research in Mathematics Education, 23,* 306–328.

Schoenfeld, A.H. (1989). Explorations of students' mathematical beliefs and behavior. *Journal for Research in Mathematics Education, 20,* 338–355.

Stevenson, H. W., Chen, C., & Lee, S. (1993). Mathematics achievement of Chinese, Japanese, and American children: Ten years later. *Science, 259,* 53–58.

Stevenson, H. W., Lee, S. Y., Chen, C., Stigler, J. W., Lee, S., Hsu, C. C., & Kitamura, S. (1990). Contexts of achievement: A study of American, Chinese, and Japanese children. *Monographs of the society for research in Children Development, 55.* (Serial No. 221).

Stevenson, H. W., Lee, S., & Stigler, J. W. (1986). Mathematics achievement of Chinese, Japanese, and American children. *Science, 231,* 693–699.

Stigler, J. W., Lee, S., Lucker, G. W., & Stevenson, H. W. (1982). Curriculum and achievement in mathematics: A study of elementary school children in Japan, Taiwan, and the United States. *Journal of Educational Psychology, 74,* 315–322.

Stigler, J. W., Lee, S., & Stevenson, H. W. (1987). Mathematics classrooms in Japan, Taiwan, and the United States. *Child Development, 56,* 1272–1285.

Tsao, Y. L. (2000). Do the attitudes and beliefs of a culture have an effect on students' performance in mathematics? Unpublished manuscript. University of Northern Colorado.

Address correspondence to: Dr. Yea-Ling Tsao, Math Computer Science Education Department, Taipei Municipal Teachers College, No. 1, Ai-Guo West Road, Taipei, 100, Taiwan. E-mail: tsaoyealing@hotmail.com

Exercise for Article 23

Factual Questions

1. According to the literature review, American teachers spend about 22% of their time imparting information. What is the corresponding percentage for Chinese teachers?

2. How many children from Denver participated in this study?

3. On the seven-point rating scale used in this study, what does a "7" stand for?

4. Did the USA sample *or* the Taiwan sample have a higher mean score on "Math is mostly facts and procedures that have to be memorized"?

5. What was the mean score of the Taiwan sample on "The best way to do well in math is to memorize all of the formulas"?

6. Are all the differences between means in Table 2 statistically significant at the $p < .01$ level?

Questions for Discussion

7. How desirable would it be in a future study of this type to use students from more than two cities? Explain.

8. Do you think that this study identifies *causes* of the differences in mathematics achievement between American and Chinese students? Explain.

9. The researcher discusses a major limitation of this study in lines 399–406. Do you agree? In your opinion, is the limitation serious enough to affect the validity of the results of this study? Explain.

10. If you were conducting a study on the same topic, what changes, if any, would you make in the research methodology?

Quality Ratings

Directions: Indicate your level of agreement with each of the following statements by circling a number from 5 for strongly agree (SA) to 1 for strongly disagree (SD). If you believe an item is not applicable to this research article, leave it blank. Be prepared to explain your ratings.

A. The introduction establishes the importance of the study.

SA   5   4   3   2   1   SD

B. The literature review establishes the context for the study.

SA   5   4   3   2   1   SD

C. The research purpose, question, or hypothesis is clearly stated.

SA   5   4   3   2   1   SD

D. The method of sampling is sound.

SA   5   4   3   2   1   SD

E. Relevant demographics (for example, age, gender, and ethnicity) are described.

    SA   5   4   3   2   1   SD

F. Measurement procedures are adequate.

    SA   5   4   3   2   1   SD

G. All procedures have been described in sufficient detail to permit a replication of the study.

    SA   5   4   3   2   1   SD

H. The participants have been adequately protected from potential harm.

    SA   5   4   3   2   1   SD

I. The results are clearly described.

    SA   5   4   3   2   1   SD

J. The discussion/conclusion is appropriate.

    SA   5   4   3   2   1   SD

K. Despite any flaws, the report is worthy of publication.

    SA   5   4   3   2   1   SD

Article 24

Learning to Love Reading:
Interviews with Older Children and Teens

LINDA TERAN STROMMEN
Educational Consultant

BARBARA FOWLES MATES
Long Island University

ABSTRACT. Students in sixth and ninth grades were surveyed to determine attitudes toward reading and identify factors associated with the development of a love of reading.

From *Journal of Adolescent & Adult Literacy*, *48*, 188–200. Copyright © 2004 by International Reading Association. Reprinted with permission.

Certainly, learning to read is valued by many cultures, and the ability to read is regarded as the most fundamental goal of education. However, though most children in the United States do learn to read, many
5 leave school unable to read beyond the most basic functional level. The degree to which schools are effective purveyors of reading education and the methods used to teach reading has become the subject of controversy. However, factors that foster a child's love of
10 reading have, for the most part, been left out of the debate.

Many studies of the early stages of reading acquisition have shown that the home environment and support from a parent or other adult may be essential to
15 encouraging literacy development (Adoni, 1995; Bissex, 1980; Bloom, 1970, 1973; Cambourne, 1995; Clark, 1984; Durkin, 1966; Fader, 1983; Forester, 1986; Hall & Moats, 2000; Harste, Burke, & Woodward, 1982; Morrow, 1983; Neuman, 1980, 1986; Tay-
20 lor, 1983; Teale, 1984; Yaden, 1986). Although such studies largely focused on the acquisition of reading skills, more recently McKenna, Kear, and Ellsworth (1995) surveyed children's attitudes toward reading and concluded that children's views of recreational and
25 academic reading are tied to reading ability as well as to community norms and beliefs. Their work documented a change in children's attitudes toward reading that typically evolves from enthusiasm to comparative indifference by the end of the elementary school years.
30 A meta-analysis of research on reading (National Institute of Child Health and Human Development, 2000) listed no recent studies that address the love of reading or its relation to reading achievement.

The preponderance of research findings suggest
35 that few children, skilled readers or not, choose to de-vote their leisure time to reading. Surveys of school-children's reading practices (Anderson, Hiebert, Scott, & Wilkinson, 1985; Anderson, Wilson, & Fielding, 1988; Himmelweit & Swift, 1976; Lyness, 1952;
40 Moffitt & Wartella, 1992; Neuman, 1980, 1986, 1995) have shown that young people across all age groups devote very little time to recreational reading, and this has been true since the 1940s. While studies that survey the reading practices, leisure time use, and aca-
45 demic achievement of older children and teens (Anderson et al., 1988; Greaney & Hegarty, 1987; Greaney & Neuman, 1983; Lewis & Teale, 1980; Long & Henderson, 1973; Neuman, 1981, 1986, 1995) revealed patterns of behavior and suggested that children's percep-
50 tions about reading influenced this behavior (Neuman, 1995), they did not explain the genesis of attitudes about reading. Teens spend even less time reading than younger children (Moje, Young, Readence, & Moore, 2000), despite the fact that they also spend less time
55 watching television. Kubey and Csikzentmihalyi (1990) reported that "the average American teenager watches more than 21 hours of TV each week but devotes only 5.6 hours a week to homework and a mere 1.8 hours to pleasure reading" (p. 24). Nevertheless,
60 several investigators (Greaney, 1980; Neuman, 1986, 1995; Searls, Mead, & Ward, 1985) have failed to find a significant relationship between time spent reading and time spent watching television for any age group.

Nell's research into the psychology of reading for
65 pleasure (1988) documented factors that contribute to a book's readability and made a significant contribution to our understanding of how reading can be emotionally satisfying. Additionally, Moore, Bean, Birdyshaw, and Rycik (1999) posited that "vicariously stepping
70 into text worlds can nourish teens' emotions and psyches as well as their intellects" (p. 102). However, little in the research literature on reading addresses the factors that lead some young people to embrace the satisfactions afforded by recreational reading. This is true
75 despite the fact that a recent position paper on teen literacy (Moore et al., 1999) noted that a desire to read is an important cornerstone of adolescents' literacy achievement.

Smith (1988) has argued that we learn to read, and become literate in the process, simply by reading. In *The Power of Reading* (1993), Krashen explored research findings that supported Smith's idea and the role reading for pleasure plays in a child's literacy development. Krashen stated that

the relationship between reported free voluntary reading and literacy development is not always large, but it is remarkably consistent. Nearly every study that has examined this relationship has found a correlation, and it is present even when different tests, different methods of probing reading habits, and different definitions of free reading are used. (p. 7)

Krashen concluded that children who frequently read for pleasure

will become adequate readers, acquire a large vocabulary, develop the ability to understand and use complex grammatical constructions, develop a good writing style, and become good (but not necessarily perfect) spellers. Although free voluntary reading alone will not ensure attainment of the highest levels of literacy, it will at least ensure an acceptable level. (p. 84)

Those who do not develop the habit of reading for pleasure may have "a very difficult time reading and writing at a level high enough to deal with the demands of today's world" (p. x). With this view in mind, we sought to determine factors that contribute to and support a child's learning to love to read.

Procedure

We wished to identify older children and teens for whom reading extended texts is a significant, pleasurable, recreational activity and consistent part of daily life, hereafter identified as *Readers*, as well as a comparable group who seldom or never choose to read for pleasure, hereafter called *Not-readers*. (We chose this term rather than *Nonreaders* in order to avoid the inaccurate implication that children and teens in this group lack reading skills.) To make these identifications, we designed, pilot-tested, and distributed questionnaires to a cross-section of sixth-grade students attending a suburban middle school outside a large northeastern U.S. city and to ninth-grade students in the same school district. The questionnaire was administered by classroom teachers who followed a specific set of instructions we provided.

The students who completed the questionnaire represented the available spectrum of academic achievement, including remedial and honors students. The participants were heterogeneously grouped sixth-grade students in four core (English/social studies) classes (*n* = 65), and ninth-grade students in five homogeneously grouped English classes (*n* = 86), including one remedial and one honors group. A total of 151 students responded to the written questionnaire. A numerical identification system was used to protect the anonymity of all students. The language spoken at home, reading ability, and level of academic achievement were not controlled.

The questionnaire—presented as a survey of leisure time use by students—included, in addition to basic demographic information, a broad range of questions in the following categories:

1. Activities engaged in outside of school (students were asked to estimate time per day spent at activities such as sports, music lessons, leisure activities, media use, reading for pleasure, homework, and chores).
2. Self-perceptions and attitudes (likes and dislikes, self-description).
3. Reading practices and materials (novels, informational books, magazines; reading compared with other leisure activities; reading practices of family members and friends; availability of reading materials in the home).

We included this broad range of items to mask our specific objective and to help us place reading activities in the context of students' lives.

Embedded within the 10-page questionnaire was a seven-item Literacy Index, which was designed to identify both Readers and Not-readers. On the basis of interviews conducted as part of a pilot study, we had concluded that time spent reading books was a more reliable indicator of a love of reading than time spent reading shorter print texts. The content and scoring for these items is indicated in Table 1.

The questionnaire yielded only a small number of Readers whose answers to the index questions clearly distinguished them from the rest of the respondents. Four sixth-grade students and 8 ninth-grade students (12 students in all out of a total of 151, or approximately 8% of the students) met all of the criteria as listed in Table 1 and were identified as Readers. It should be emphasized that we sought to identify those young people who read extended texts as a form of enjoyable recreation, not those characterized by excellent reading skills alone.

Of the sixth-grade Readers, three were female and one was male. One sixth-grade Reader participated in a special remedial reading program. Of the ninth-grade Readers, two were male and six were female. One ninth-grade Reader was designated as having a learning disability and two ninth-grade Readers were honors students.

The greatest number of students surveyed at both grade levels fell into our Not-reader category. Not-readers were also distributed across remedial, general, and honors classes. A small number of students gave one or two answers on the index that fell into the Reader category, but because they otherwise most resembled Not-readers they were grouped with the latter. Our primary intention was to identify a group of young people who clearly loved to read.

Table 1
Literacy Index Items

	Reader response	Not-reader response
1. I enjoy reading a good book.	Selected this item	Did not select this item
2. Favorite leisure activity?	Named reading	Named other activities
3. Books read in past three years.	20 or more	0–5
4. Novels read in past year.	Several (not school assigned)	None
5. I prefer to read.	Selected this item	Did not select item
6. Time spent reading for pleasure on a typical weekday.	30 minutes or more	No time spent
7. Describe a "perfect" day.	Included a period of reading	No reading

190 It is interesting to note that reading skill and academic achievement (as characterized by students in subsequent interviews) were not definitive factors in distinguishing Readers from Not-readers. Several Not-readers were honors students, while a few Readers 195 claimed to struggle with reading and writing assignments.

In response to items on the questionnaire, all of the students in both groups indicated that literacy materials, such as newspapers and reference books, were 200 available in their homes. Many students had computers at home, and all had access to computers in school. There were no notable differences in students' reported television viewing habits, with Readers and Not-readers alike reporting three to four hours of television 205 viewing per day (though most said the TV was often "just on" while they pursued other activities, such as completing homework, looking at magazines, or chatting online with friends). In addition, there was no noteworthy difference in the nature and number of ex-210 tracurricular activities, such as music lessons, sports, clubs, or time spent with friends. Readers did not prove to be less social or less occupied with activities than Not-readers, though general studies ninth-grade Not-readers did report being less involved in organized ac-215 tivities than their classmates.

The questionnaire proved to have validity as a tool for identifying Readers and Not-readers. In all cases, students who were later interviewed confirmed their preliminary classification as Reader or Not-reader. 220 Each readily agreed with our characterization of them as either a person who enjoys reading and does so often or as one who does not enjoy reading and never reads books for recreation.

All students identified as Readers and an equal 225 number of Not-readers were invited by letter to meet with one of the principal investigators for a one-on-one interview that focused on their leisure-time reading practices. Interviews were approved by parents and arranged by a school staff member. These took place at 230 the schools during the student's free period.

Because of scheduling difficulties, only five of the eight ninth-grade students identified as Readers could be interviewed. All four of the sixth-grade Readers were interviewed. Four sixth-grade Not-readers and

235 five ninth-grade Not-readers were selected who, insofar as possible, matched the Readers in terms of gender and academic tracking. We had anticipated some reluctance on the part of Not-readers to be characterized as such, but this did not occur.

240 Interviews were informal, following a protocol of guided, open-ended questions. The interview questions were derived from the following research questions:

1. Are there consistent attributes of the social environment of Readers that appear to maintain read-245 ing activity?
2. Are there consistent early childhood and ongoing experiences that promote interest in reading?
3. Do students who identify themselves as Readers display similar ideas and attitudes about the ap-250 peal of reading?
4. Are these ideas and attitudes different from those of Not-readers?

All interviews were audiotaped, with the permission of the student, and transcribed in full by the interviewer. 255 A sample of interview questions is listed in Table 2.

Findings

The methods we used to examine the interview data were determined by the size of the sample and the intensive nature of this research. The two investigators independently studied each recorded interview to 260 search for important features that recurred in interviews with Readers and were largely absent from those of Not-readers. The identified features were extensively discussed and clarified. The resulting list of features was then used to reexamine each interview protocol to 265 ensure that it was broadly characteristic of Readers alone. At this time, we chose examples that typified each feature among Readers as well as examples from Not-readers to help illustrate our findings.

The clear differences between Readers and Not-270 readers that were indicated in the survey data were confirmed under the closer scrutiny of one-on-one interviews. When we analyzed the interviews in light of our research questions, several significant themes emerged. Profiles of individuals who were classified as Readers 275 or Not-readers revealed unique features of each student's experiences, but also a number of clear common threads within each of the two groups. We found the

Table 2
Sample Interview Questions

Questions for Readers	Questions for Not-readers
Your responses to the questionnaire show that you enjoy reading. Do you agree? Why do you like to read?	Your responses to the questionnaire show that you dislike reading. Do you agree? Why don't you enjoy reading?
How do you decide what to read?	Do you ever feel like reading a book or magazine article? Internet info or chat? Why?
Where do you get the things you read?	What things to read are in your home?
Do you ever talk about things you read with family or friends?	Do other family members talk about things they read?
If your friends told you about a great story that was available on film and book, would you see the movie or read the book? Why?	Same as for Readers. Also: If your friends told you about a great book, would you give it a try?
What is it about reading that makes you want to spend time reading?	What is it about reading that makes you not want to read?
Is there anything that your parents did that contributed to your enjoyment of reading? What?	Is there any experience that you remember that may have contributed to your dislike of reading? What?
Do you remember any of the first books read to you? Which were your favorites?	Same as for Readers.
Do you think your parents like to read? What makes you think they do or don't?	Same as for Readers.
Do you think it's important to be a reader? Why?	Same as for Readers.
Do your friends (or a best friend) enjoy reading? Why do you think they do or do not?	Same as for Readers.
Do you think people need to be able to read well? Why?	Same as for Readers.

following commonalities to hold across the age groups. All student names are pseudonyms.

280 *Readers regularly interact around books with other members of their social circle who love to read.* All the Readers interviewed reported discussing what they read with other interested readers. These conversations, which regularly took place between the Reader and a 285 family member or close friend, were characterized by Readers as simply "what we do." Discussions about books allow young people to draw upon the reading experiences of other members of their social circle and to see reading as part of their social life.

290 Mark, a ninth-grader, was typical of the Readers interviewed. Mark recalled that when he was quite young, his mother would readily drop everything to read to him at his request. Now that he is a teen, this interaction has evolved. He and his mother and 295 younger sister, who is also an avid reader, recommend books to one another and discuss them later. Mark commented that his mother "put me on to Agatha Christie. She also reads the books I'm reading. It gets annoying sometimes. I'll put a bookmark in and come 300 back 10 minutes later and my mom'll be reading it."

All three share a love of Agatha Christie mysteries, which they swap and discuss. Mark laughingly remarked that he and his sister "use books as a threat, like 'if you don't take your plate off the table, I'll tell 305 you who did it!'—because they're usually murder mysteries—so both of us have to put our dishes in the dishwasher."

Recounting stories or talking about character and plot with another enthusiastic reader was an important 310 element of Readers' experiences. Anne, a ninth-grade Reader, described how stories from books enhanced her interest in reading and also provided her with material to share with friends and family:

> We tell each other stories [from books]. I read books and 315 then tell her [her mother], and she reads my books. She tells me stories of her books and I read hers. So we go back and forth. Sometimes, I share stories with my friends. If it has to do with a topic we're talking about, I'll bring up the book that I read and tell them the situa- 320 tion.

Though Readers extended this interaction to their peers, the pattern was always established within the family. Ken, a sixth-grade Reader, said he is most likely to talk about books with his dad, who recom- 325 mends action and mystery books, and with his two best friends. Ken told the interviewer,

> I mean, we don't set aside time to book chat like on Oprah. But we'll talk about books, and we'll see if there's anything that none of us have read before and if 330 it's just the same old. And we'll talk about mysteries where the person you least expect, like the old granny, is the one who did it.

Nicole, a ninth-grade Reader, explained how her cousins conveyed their love of reading to her and thus 335 played a role in building her own interest:

My older cousins told me about books. They'd tell me these great stories and say, "try reading this and you'll find the more detailed story." In elementary school my cousins would tell me about other novels they had read when they were my age. Also, I have some cousins who are my age and they're big readers.... They would tell me about this book and I would try to find it and read it.

Readers learned from family or other members of their social circle that reading can be an entertaining, diverting, enjoyable, sociable, and therefore worthwhile activity. Anne, a ninth-grade Reader, said that her mother's love of reading

encouraged me because also it seemed fun. She liked the books that she read, she would tell me about them, and it seemed interesting. I was just like, "Why is reading a book so much fun?" So I decide to try it, and it is fun.

Peer-group approval was not a big issue with Readers, even in adolescence. Most Readers had many friends who did not choose to read for pleasure. None were judgmental about this, but most believed that by choosing not to read their friends were missing out on a good thing.

In contrast to Readers, Not-readers' family reading experiences were more variable, did not continue beyond early childhood, and did not evolve to include discussions about the characters or events in books. The older sibling of one Not-reader had suggested books for her to read but had not done so regularly. Several Not-readers mentioned that their parents said they should read more because reading would make them smarter. Jessica, a ninth-grade Not-reader, said that talking about books was "not really a big part" of family discussions, which tended to be "about current events but not about books."

This lack of family discussions about books may account for our finding that over half of our Not-reader subjects claimed to have enjoyed reading until between 9 and 11 years of age. At this point, they told us they lost interest in childhood favorites and found no alternative reading material that appealed to them. Mary, a sixth-grade Not-reader, told the interviewer, "I read Goosebumps every night. Maybe I gave up reading because I phased out of the Goosebumps books." Jake, a ninth-grade Not-reader, commented, "I had a time—like when I was 8 or 9—when I liked Ramona Quimby and the Beverly Cleary books that I could read. And that stopped when I was about 10." Apparently, these students did not have the support of a family member who enjoyed reading to suggest and share appropriate books.

Readers see being an active member of a community of readers as an important part of their identity. An important attribute of each Reader's environment is that it includes others who read for pleasure. Mark, a ninth-grade Reader, said, "I was surrounded with it. There were always books lying around the house. They [his parents] were always reading." Both parents of Ken (a sixth-grade Reader) are also avid readers who, according to Ken, read the newspaper "cover to cover, each day" and, by his estimate, several books a week. Ken, who sees himself as a Reader in a family of avid readers, gave this description:

It's part of my life, because that's what I do. Like, I'll go out in my tree house and I'll stay and read books like jungle and mystery and secret agent books. There's a rule in the house that I have to read a book a week, but I usually read three books a week. In the summer I have a lot of things going on, but I'll usually read a book a day.

Brian, a ninth-grade Reader who was designated as having a learning disability by his school, said he did not begin reading until he was 8 or 9. Nevertheless, Brian thinks of himself as a reading member of a reading family:

They're teachers. They just love to read. They read everything. Everyone in my house reads. Not just one person reads. Everyone. When I was smaller there was one time when everyone had to read. It was like "Reading Time!" Now I do it even at school in my free time.

Not-readers, in contrast, did not see recreational reading as an important part of their families' lives. They described parents and siblings as occasional readers who might read magazines, newspapers, and work-related material, or as people who do not enjoy reading at all. They said their parents were "too busy" to read or were involved in other activities. They did not see being a reader as an important aspect of their own identity or the identity of family members.

Parents or other family members of Readers explicitly prioritize reading as a recreational activity. Readers see reading as an activity that plays a significant and enjoyable role in the life of one or more family members or friends. Nicole, a ninth-grade Reader, recalled,

My mother likes to read these big books in Korean. When they [her parents] have free time they read, usually a few times a week. Sometimes at night I'll see the light on and they're usually reading. My mother and grandmother read books to me when I was little and taught me to read by reading to me and with me. They consider it very important. When I was young they would always say to read more. "Don't watch TV, read!" They do that with my sisters now.

Not-readers had different experiences. Several of them mentioned that a parent occasionally told them that they should read more in order to do well in school or become smarter. But Not-readers believed their parents did not see reading as a priority for themselves or for the family.

Jessica, a ninth-grade Not-reader, offered an account that differed somewhat from other Not-readers. She mentioned that her parents

read current events, and also my mother went back to school about five years ago and is starting her own practice so she's reading a lot of psychotherapy books. And

159

my father reads a lot of fiction and nonfiction books. I guess they read mostly every day.

But, when asked if her parents encouraged her to spend time reading, Jessica said, "When I was younger they tried to get me to read; my uncle would bring me books. It's just not something I have motivation to do. My parents never really thought it was that important, basically."

Readers have access to plentiful, varied reading materials. As our survey indicated, and the interviews confirmed, basic reading materials were available at home to all of the young people with whom we met. For Readers, however, interest in reading was sustained by an involved parent or other family member who continued to provide access to a variety of books as the child matured and to guide the child's choices. For Not-readers, this type of support was far less evident, especially once the child entered school.

Stephanie, a sixth-grade Reader, told the interviewer,

> I own a lot of books. Actually, my mother and sister and my sister's friends [and I] are starting a mother–daughter book club. I thought I would announce at the first meeting that I would start a sort of library because I have so many books—at least a hundred. I have four boxes in the attic, and a whole shelf in our playroom.

Not-readers had vague memories of engaging with books during playtime or at bedtime. Only four Not-readers interviewed recalled owning books as a child. Asked if she had her own books, Jessica, a ninth-grade Not-reader, stated, "I have books in my room that have been given to me and have not been read."

Readers recalled frequent visits to a public library or bookseller, and most told us this activity continued to the present. Corinne, a ninth-grade Reader, described her experience:

> Yes, we went to the library very often. I still go often. Once every two weeks or so. I walked to the library as soon as I was old enough to go by myself. I was in a reading club on the weekend. There was story time, then a book club. You would tell about your book, then we had pizza.

Those Not-readers who recalled being taken to the library said that this practice ended, along with being read to by a parent, once they entered school, or that trips to the library were made infrequently and only for the purpose of obtaining a book for a school assignment. Samantha, a ninth-grade Not-reader, spoke of occasionally visiting a local bookseller: "I'll go with a friend and sit there and read. But I don't buy the books because I'll never get a chance to read them."

Readers love reading. Readers had vivid and fond memories of their early encounters with books and talked with great enthusiasm about specific books read to them when they were very young. Brian, a ninth-grade Reader, told the interviewer,

> There was one, I don't remember what it was called, about some boy, and he was afraid of his basement. He thought that these goblin guys were in his basement and he beat them with a broom and they got smaller and smaller at the end. I read that constantly. I still have all of my books.

Corinne, a ninth-grade Reader, recalled,

> *The Giving Tree.* I remember it's about how much a little boy uses the tree and as he gets older he uses it more and more and they have kind of a relationship. It was so sad for the tree, so upsetting. The boy is so selfish. He gives nothing back to the tree. But the tree is happy.

Readers told of having established a reading ritual (usually the bedtime story) that had never really ended. In fact, they could not imagine a day when they would not read, if only for a short while, before turning out the lights at night. Mark, a ninth-grade Reader, commented, "I like reading so much. I can't picture myself without it."

The Readers we interviewed said they love to read because reading stimulates their imagination; takes them to new places; and introduces them to new ideas, events, and elements of human emotion. Several also said that books give them a wealth of detail not available through television and film and told how they imagine a setting or the intensity of emotion in their mind's eye, something they cannot do when watching television or a movie. Brian, a ninth-grade Reader, commented,

> It's always fun to read. You're just sitting there and there's this whole other world waiting. You're reading something and the whole world stops when you close the book. And when you open it up again—okay—let's turn it back on again. It's weird when you think about it.

Anne, a sixth-grade Reader, said, "You can read and no one tells you how the picture should be. It's just your mind that's going with the words and it can be any picture you want it to be...you're making your own little story." Ken, a sixth-grade Reader, reflected,

> It takes me to places that I always wanted to be. Like, I read detective books and I feel like I'm the person trying to solve the case. Or, say I want to go to some undiscovered planet but I'm stuck in my house, I'll just read the book. I like the fact that you can be a totally different person and that you can have different abilities. It's almost like a game. In books you have the ability to see the future, or fly. On TV you don't use your imagination. It's like the TV is your imagination. In books you can determine the setting and the atmosphere of the story. Say it's a dark street. In your imagination you can have a street with dumpsters, say people on the side, dogs and garbage, and you can really get into it more and that makes the story more exciting.

Readers prefer reading to other sources of information or entertainment because they feel reading provides greater depth of understanding, more details, more insights on character, and an understanding of interpersonal relationships, as well as a basis for empa-

565 thy. Nicole, a ninth-grade Reader, commented, "Sometimes it relates to my life too, because you read about someone who has similar problems, and other times you just realize about other people's problems."

Readers also like the portability and companion-570 ability of books and enjoy choosing what, when, and where to read. Most carried a book when traveling. With a book at hand they knew they would never be bored. As Mark, a ninth-grade Reader, noted, "A book is good company." Ken, a sixth-grade Reader, de-575 scribed the pleasure of choosing a book to read, as well as the place to read it, in keeping with the mood created by the weather.

> Today it's nice out. I'd probably want to read a Hardy Boys or this book called *The Prodigal Spy*. And well, on
580 rainy days, or just an ordinary day, I'll sit and read my textbook or books about early explorers and ancient civilizations.

Stephanie, a sixth-grade Reader, smiled as she said, "You can sink into a book…or on a rainy day you can 585 always sit and read. You can have dreams about it. I dream I'm the character. You can put aside your problems. It's another world."

Not-readers had no comparable feelings to relate. Most recalled other activities more vividly and talked 590 about playing outside, involvement with sports and time spent "hanging out" with friends. However, Not-readers, particularly those who are high-achieving, spoke of the value of reading, an activity they see as virtuous and admirable. In contrast, only one of the 595 Readers mentioned this self-improvement aspect of reading: Corinne, a ninth-grade Reader, told the interviewer, "It's easier for me to understand things when they're written down because I've read so many books. And it's easier to write because I know how authors 600 place their words." Brian, a ninth-grade Reader, appeared at first to share this utilitarian view, but then his thoughts took quite a different direction.

> You learn a lot from reading. Like, there's some reading you should do. Some people are better off without read-605 ing. They don't understand where the writer is coming from. If I've got a book to read, I want to know about the author. People just see things for what they are. A lot of people don't care for the emotional stuff and don't like reading and say it's a waste of time. It's a waste of time 610 because they don't understand. It's like the arts—you have to be into it to understand it. You have to be into the themes.

School is not the critical factor, though a teacher's enthusiasm might be. Even though our interviews took 615 place in a school setting, the subject of school played a minor role in all of our conversations. All of the Readers interviewed clearly connected a love of reading with experiences provided outside of school.

None of the students interviewed mentioned read-620 ing instruction or reading skill as something that supported their enjoyment of reading, though one Not-reader told us that poor reading ability contributed to

his dislike of reading. Another Not-reader recalled en-joying some of the books assigned in school when he 625 was younger (through fourth grade) but could not remember even being interested enough to complete a single assigned book since that time. In fact, only two Readers said they truly enjoyed reading the novels assigned for classes or their textbooks. Readers tended to 630 see assigned reading as something to be accomplished quickly in order to make time for books of their own choice.

Samantha, a ninth-grade Not-reader, offered some insight into an aspect of the school reading experience 635 that may diminish the pleasure of reading:

> I just don't enjoy reading books and textbooks. I mean they're easier to read than primary documents and it's better than learning from the activities we do, but I don't enjoy reading them. It's become a chore. It's just not 640 pleasurable. It's so fact filled and you have to know everything—knowing that I have to know everything for a test….

Readers and Not-readers in all classes told us they scan assigned material to locate answers to questions 645 posed by teachers rather than read assignments in full.

When asked what teachers had done to contribute to their enjoyment of reading, several Readers recalled early grade-school teachers who invited students to borrow books from classroom libraries or suggested 650 particular books. Brian, a ninth-grade Reader, told of a teacher who spoke about books with real passion:

> There's a teacher who's getting a lot of people to read. Not me. I'm already into books, but a lot of people in our grade. It's like her one goal in life is to make everyone 655 enjoy and love reading. She gets so into it. She loves it.

Though our survey did not support Brian's impression that his teacher's passion for reading had per-suaded "a lot of people to read," this particular teacher and a few others were praised by Readers because they 660 demonstrated an enthusiasm for books, had "lots of books" in their classrooms, let students borrow books, and read aloud in class frequently.

Readers read (no matter what). Readers said that they read books for pleasure every day, or nearly every 665 day, no matter how busy they are. Several of the Not-readers we interviewed expressed open admiration for their friends who are voracious readers, claiming to be baffled by how these students find the time to read books of their choice given the pressure of school as-670 signments and after-school activities. Over half the Not-readers said they were "too busy" to read for pleasure. However, all of the Readers saw distractions from schoolwork and other activities as a nonissue. Though some said they did not have as much time to 675 read as they would like, all Readers made time for reading because it was enjoyable to them. Because our original survey questions did not reveal any significant differences in reported involvement in other activities between Readers and Not-readers, it does not appear

680 that the demands of school assignments and activities dictate the choices young people make about reading. Rather, attitudes about reading determine these choices.

Readers told of reading a great variety of written 685 material as well as almost any available print, including advertising on cereal boxes, even labels and the like. Ken, a sixth-grade Reader, commented,

> Usually, I'm late for school 'cause I'll be reading. Like, when my dad's reading the newspaper I'll usually take a
690 > section from him and start reading that. And I'll read pamphlets that my mom has, and I'll read tags on my shirt and stuff.

In contrast, Not-readers told us reading was too "tedious," "slow," or "boring" to engage their interest. 695 All but one of the Not-readers told us they do not enjoy reading novels because written material is too detailed and takes too long to get to the point, or because they do not understand what the author is trying to convey. Not-readers described reading in terms of purpose 700 rather than pleasure. They saw reading as a means to improve vocabulary or to access information (if not available from another source), and to manage one's affairs (for example, to fill out a job application). But, given the choice, all Not-readers would see the movie 705 rather than read the book. In fact, Not-readers, even those whose reading skills were excellent, avoid reading whenever possible.

All but two of the Not-readers interviewed told us they valued reading and cited not having sufficient 710 time as the principal reason for not engaging in reading as a recreational activity. Samantha, a ninth-grade Not-reader, told the interviewer, "I never feel I have enough time to read…if I had more time I would just read. Definitely." When asked what occupied her time, 715 Samantha replied that drawing takes up her time, and "flipping through magazines because I'm interested in fashion design." Clearly, Samantha and other Not-readers choose to fill leisure time with activities other than reading.

720 Like many Not-readers, Samantha told us she believed that peers who include recreational reading in their daily schedules read at a fast rate and therefore require less time for reading. This notion was commonly held by Not-readers although Nell's (1988) 725 work (which shows that reading for pleasure most often proceeds at an unhurried pace) did not support this assumption. Readers, however, saw reading as intrinsically worthwhile and something they "always" find time for.

What It Takes to Become a Reader

730 Although this research involves close study of a relatively small group of older children and teens, the profiles of Readers in our survey clearly indicate that becoming a Reader is not a simple matter of attaining fluency. The Readers we interviewed believed that 735 reading was a worthwhile way to spend leisure time because it was pleasurable. Not-readers were of the opinion that reading was boring, tedious, and a waste of their time.

Our study suggests that when parents establish a 740 routine of reading to their young children, they foster an early interest in books that can be maintained if a variety of books is made available as children mature and their interests change. Easy access to the books that a particular Reader finds enjoyable enables reading 745 to continue as an attractive alternative to other activities for young people. All but one of the Readers in our study acknowledged that family or friends shared books or bought books for them or that visits to the library were a frequent family activity that continued to 750 be supported as they grew older. In addition, parents (or other close family members) who read for recreation provide a model for the children to emulate. Parents who schedule a time for family reading activities clearly demonstrate reading is a priority.

755 The ongoing dialogue about books that takes place between parents and children seems to have a particularly important role in the development of a child's love of reading. Discussions about books among family members demonstrate the pleasure that books inspire, 760 spark a Reader's interest, help Readers to make reading selections, and make it possible for Readers to become participants in an activity that their immediate social circle, and the wider culture, values and esteems. Adults who encourage such activity send a powerful 765 message about the pleasures of reading. This may be key to developing the perception of oneself as a Reader. In addition, because these informal conversations about books are congenial, they bring a social, refreshing, and renewing component to the reading 770 experience. Readers learn, through social interaction with other Readers, that reading is entertaining and stimulating.

Implications

If it is true, as previous research seems to indicate, that by reading for pleasure young people can attain 775 literacy competence, then encouraging a child's love of reading is a desirable goal. In addition, Readers' experiences with books, and their obvious pleasure in sharing them with us, made it clear that reading can be a wonderful, satisfying, and enriching activity for those 780 who are fortunate enough to become engaged by it.

Those who would hope to foster a young person's love of reading must acknowledge that, while students surely benefit when teachers recognize the need to motivate them to read, young people must see themselves 785 as participant readers in a community that pursues reading as a significant and enjoyable recreational activity if reading is to become a lifelong endeavor. To this end, the child's immediate culture, the family, must invest itself in the process to demonstrate the 790 pleasure reading affords by regularly reading aloud to young children, making age- and interest-appropriate

795 books easily available as the child matures, providing a model for children to emulate, scheduling time for family reading, and demonstrating the social nature of reading and encouraging interest through conversations about the books family members read.

References

Adoni, H. (1995). Literacy and reading in a multimedia environment. *Journal of Communication, 45*, 152–174.

Anderson, R., Hiebert, E., Scott, J., & Wilkinson, I. (1985). *Becoming a nation of readers: The report of the Commission on Reading*. Washington, DC: National Institute of Education.

Anderson, R., Wilson, P., & Fielding, L. (1988). Growth in reading and how children spend their time outside of school. *Reading Research Quarterly, 23*, 285–303. doi:10.1598/RRQ.23.3.2

Bissex, G. (1980). *GNYS at work*. Cambridge, MA: Harvard University Press.

Bloom, L. (1970). *Language development: Form and function in emerging grammar*. Cambridge, MA: Harvard University Press.

Bloom, L. (1973). *One word at a time*. Paris: Mouton.

Cambourne, B. (1995). Towards an educationally relevant theory of literacy learning: Twenty years of inquiry. *The Reading Teacher, 49*, 182–190.

Clark, M. (1984). Literacy at home and at school: Insights from the study of young fluent readers. In H. Goelman, A. Oberg, & F. Smith (Eds.), *Awakening to literacy* (pp. 122–130). Portsmouth, NH: Heinemann.

Durkin, D. (1966). *Children who read early*. New York: Teachers College Press.

Fader, D. (1983). Literacy and family. In R. Bailey & R. Fosheim (Eds.), *Literacy for life: The demand for reading and writing* (pp. 236–247). New York: Modern Language Association.

Forester, A. (1986). Apprenticeship in the art of literacy. In D. Tovey & J. Kerber (Eds.), *Roles in literacy learning: A new perspective* (pp. 66–72). Newark, DE: International Reading Association.

Greaney, V. (1980). Factors related to amount and type of leisure reading. *Reading Research Quarterly, 15*, 337–357.

Greaney, V., & Hegarty, M. (1987). Correlates of leisure-time reading. *Journal of Research in Reading, 10*, 3–32.

Greaney, V., & Neuman, S. (1983). Young people's view of reading: A cross-cultural perspective. *The Reading Teacher, 37*, 158–163.

Hall, S., & Moats, L. (2000, Spring). Why reading to children is important. *American Educator*, pp. 26–33.

Harste, J., Burke, C., & Woodward, V. (1982). Children's language and world: Initial encounters with print. In J. Langer & M. Smith-Burke (Eds.), *Reader meets author: Bridging the gap* (pp. 105–131). Newark, DE: International Reading Association.

Himmelweit, H., & Swift, B. (1976). Continuities and discontinuities in media usage and taste: A longitudinal study. *Journal of Social Issues, 32*, 133–156.

Krashen, S. (1993). *The power of reading: Insights from the research*. Englewood, CO: Libraries Unlimited.

Kubey, R., & Csikzentmihalyi, M. (1990). *Television and the quality of life: How viewing shapes everyday experience*. Hillsdale, NJ: Erlbaum.

Lewis, R., & Teale, W. (1980). Another look at secondary students' attitudes toward reading. *Journal of Reading Behavior, 12*, 187–201.

Long, B., & Henderson, F. (1973). Children's use of time: Some personal and social correlates. *Elementary School Journal, 73*, 193–199.

Lyness, P. (1952). The place of mass media in the lives of boys and girls. *Journalism Quarterly, 29*, 43–54.

McKenna, M., Kear, D., & Ellsworth, A. (1995) Children's attitudes toward reading: A national survey. *Reading Research Quarterly, 30*, 934–956.

Moffitt, M., & Wartella, E. (1992). Youth and reading: A survey of leisure reading pursuits of female and male adolescents. *Reading Research and Instruction, 31*, 1–17.

Moje, E., Young, J., Readence, J., & Moore, D. (2000). Reinventing adolescent literacy for new times: Perennial and millennial issues. *Journal of Adolescent & Adult Literacy, 43*, 400–407.

Moore, D., Bean, T., Birdyshaw, D., & Rycik, J. (1999). *Adolescent literacy: A position statement for the Commission on Adolescent Literacy of the International Reading Association*. Newark, DE: International Reading Association.

Morrow, L. (1983). Home and school correlates of early interest in literature. *Journal of Educational Research, 76*, 221–223.

National Institute of Child Health and Human Development. (2000). *Report of the National Reading Panel: Teaching children to read: An evidence-based assessment of the scientific research literature in reading and its implications for reading instruction* (NIH Publication No. 00-4769). Washington, DC: U.S. Government Printing Office.

Nell, V. (1988). *Lost in a book: The psychology of reading for pleasure*. New Haven, CT: Yale University Press.

Neuman, S. (1980). Why children read: A functional approach. *Journal of Reading Behavior, 12*, 333–336.

Neuman, S. (1981). *Effects of television on reading behavior*. Willimantic: Eastern Connecticut State College. (ERIC Document Reproduction Service No. ED205941)

Neuman, S. (1986). Television, reading and the home environment. *Reading Research and Instruction, 25*, 173–183.

Neuman, S. (1995). *Literacy in the television age: The myth of the TV effect* (2nd ed.). Norwood, NJ: Ablex.

Searls, D., Mead, N., & Ward, B. (1985). The relationship of students' reading skills to TV watching, leisure time reading and homework. *Journal of Reading, 29*, 158–162.

Smith, F. (1988). *Understanding reading*. Hillsdale, NJ: Erlbaum.

Taylor, D. (1983). *Family literacy*. Exeter, NH: Heinemann.

Teale, W. (1984). Home background and young children's literacy development. In H. Goelman, A. Oberg, & F. Smith (Eds.), *Awakening to literacy* (pp. 173–206). Portsmouth, NH: Heinemann.

Yaden, D. (1986). Issues related to home influence on young children's print-related development. In D. Yaden & S. Templeton (Eds.), *Metalinguistic awareness and beginning literacy* (pp. 145–148). Portsmouth, NH: Heinemann.

Address correspondence to: Linda Teran Strommen, 30 Smith Street, Glen Head, NY 11545. E-mail: ltstrommen@aol.com

Exercise for Article 24

Factual Questions

1. Why did the researchers choose the term *Not-readers* instead of the term *nonreaders*?

2. How was the anonymity of the students protected?

3. Did the researchers "mask" their specific research objective?

4. Approximately what percentage of the 151 students were identified as *Readers*?

5. How many of the *Readers* were interviewed?

6. Were the interviews audiotaped?

Questions for Discussion

7. What is your opinion of the validity of the Literacy Index Items in Table 1? Do you think that some of the items are more important than others for identifying *Readers*? (See lines 155–162.)

8. In your opinion, how important is the information in the paragraph starting with line 216 (in which the validity of the questionnaire is discussed)? Explain.

9. If you had conducted this study, would you have used open-ended questions such as those in Table 2 *or* would you have used forced-choice items (i.e., items with choices)? Explain.

10. For the interviews, the researchers attempted to match the *Readers* and *Not-readers* in terms of gender and academic tracking. Is this important? Explain.

11. In the Findings section of this research article, there are many more direct quotations of participants' responses than in most other articles in this book. Do you think that the inclusion of numerous direct quotations is a strength of this article? To what extent did the quotations help you understand the findings? Explain.

12. To what extent do you think this research has helped to identify the causes of learning to love reading? Explain. Consider the entire article when answering this question, with special attention to lines 730–772.

Quality Ratings

Directions: Indicate your level of agreement with each of the following statements by circling a number from 5 for strongly agree (SA) to 1 for strongly disagree (SD). If you believe an item is not applicable to this research article, leave it blank. Be prepared to explain your ratings.

A. The introduction establishes the importance of the study.

SA   5   4   3   2   1   SD

B. The literature review establishes the context for the study.

SA   5   4   3   2   1   SD

C. The research purpose, question, or hypothesis is clearly stated.

SA   5   4   3   2   1   SD

D. The method of sampling is sound.

SA   5   4   3   2   1   SD

E. Relevant demographics (for example, age, gender, and ethnicity) are described.

SA   5   4   3   2   1   SD

F. Measurement procedures are adequate.

SA   5   4   3   2   1   SD

G. All procedures have been described in sufficient detail to permit a replication of the study.

SA   5   4   3   2   1   SD

H. The participants have been adequately protected from potential harm.

SA   5   4   3   2   1   SD

I. The results are clearly described.

SA   5   4   3   2   1   SD

J. The discussion/conclusion is appropriate.

SA   5   4   3   2   1   SD

K. Despite any flaws, the report is worthy of publication.

SA   5   4   3   2   1   SD

Article 25

A Study of Parents of Violent Children

ELLIOTT H. SCHREIBER
Rowan University

KAREN N. SCHREIBER
New Jersey Division of Vocational Rehabilitation

SUMMARY. This study, based on in-depth interviews of 25 parents of violent children and a control group of 25 parents of nonviolent children, concerned the parents' personalities. Parents were between 22 and 48 years of age and were from middle and lower middle socioeconomic backgrounds. Differences in classification by the non-blinded interviewers of parents into the two groups on six behavior characteristics were significant on χ^2 tests. Some recommendations are made for further research.

From *Psychological Reports*, *90*, 101–104. Copyright © 2002 by Psychological Reports. Reprinted with permission.

The present study investigated the personality characteristics of parents of a group of violent children as violence has increasingly involved numerous youth in Western society (Bandura, Ross, & Ross, 1961; Hicks,
5 1965; Patterson, 1986; Schreiber, 1988, 1990; Lewinsohn, Hopps, Roberts, Seeley, & Andrews, 1993; Edelbrock, Rende, Plomin, & Thompson, 1995; Schreiber & Schreiber, 1998).

More work on and knowledge about violence is
10 needed and also on the parents of violent children according to Lane (1997), Widom (1989), and Rutter, MacDonald, LeCouteur, Harrington, Bolton, and Bailey (1990). This was recently supported by continued violence in public schools. The research of Johnson
15 (1972), Loeber (1990), Mussen, Conger, and Kagan (1995), Feshback (1970), Lahey, Loeber, Hart, Frick, Applegate, Zhang, Green, and Russo (1995), and Zimmerman (1994) on violence motivated this study to assess the relation of behavioral characteristics of par-
20 ents of violent children with their children's behavior. The above references suggested the importance of six personality characteristics of parents of violent children who were referred from public schools and compared with those of parents of nonviolent children.

Method

Sample

25 In the sample were 50 parents from middle and lower-middle socioeconomic classes. All the parents were between 22 and 48 years of age ($M = 34$ yr.). The parents gave written consent and were referred from the public schools. There were 25 parents of violent
30 children and 25 parents of nonaggressive (well-functioning) children as controls. The children who

were defined as violent had made assaultive acts on people, set fires, and killed animals. Their parents were 13 Euro-American, 8 African American, and 4 Latin
35 American families. The control group of parents included 15 Euro-American, 7 African American, and 3 Latin American families. For three families of the former and two families of the latter, there was one maternal parent as a result of divorce. One family from
40 each group was excluded because they moved from the area ($N = 25$). The children's ages ranged from 6 to 15 years, with a mean age of 9.5 yr.

Procedure

The parents of the violent children came from five local communities in which the children attended spe-
45 cial education classes in New Jersey. These children with violent behavior were diagnosed by the school psychiatrist as having the diagnostic classifications of oppositional defiant disorder ($n = 10$) and conduct disorder ($n = 15$). One notes that eight had a secondary
50 diagnosis of attention deficit disorder. The control group of parents was selected at random from four communities in the same geographical area.

All parents were interviewed for two hours in their homes by the authors on separate visits, separated by 2
55 mo. Each parent was evaluated on six behavioral characteristics from the literature on violent children and adolescents (Redl & Wineman, 1951; Despert, 1970; Loeber & Schmaling, 1985; Schreiber, 1988). Those personality characteristics most commonly linked to
60 violent behavior in children were abusive behavior (verbal or physical), impulsivity, immaturity, insecurity, emotionally cold, and inconsistent behavior (English & English, 1961). Differential analysis of the responses of these 50 parents was made. None of the
65 parents was aware of the purpose of the study. The decision to classify each parent's responses as yes or no, that is, as indicating each personality characteristic, was made independently by each interviewer. Their decisions were made largely on the basis of predomi-
70 nantly positive or negative responses to single and direct questions about the behavior of the parent as reflecting each personality characteristic (abusive, impulsive, immature, insecure, emotionally cold, and inconsistent behavior). Questions were repeated and ex-
75 plained in a consistent manner to all the parents. Exam-

Table 1
Classification of Interview Responses by Parents of Two Groups on Six Personality Characteristics

Interviewer	Personality characteristic	Parents of violent group		Parents of control group		χ^2
		Yes	No	Yes	No	
1	Abusive	18	7	4	21	17.60
	Impulsive	20	5	8	17	11.68
	Immature	19	6	7	18	11.60
	Insecure	20	5	6	19	17.10
	Emotionally cold	19	6	5	20	17.10
	Inconsistent behavior	20	5	4	21	22.26
2	Abusive	17	8	3	22	18.10
	Impulsive	22	3	4	21	28.98
	Immature	21	4	5	20	22.96
	Insecure	23	2	4	21	32.48
	Emotionally cold	18	7	5	20	12.90
	Inconsistent behavior	22	3	2	23	35.78

$*p < .001$.

iners were knowledgeable about these participants and so were not blinded.

Results and Discussion

80 The classifications by the interviewers of the behavioral responses of all parents were tabulated and analyzed by chi square. Since frequencies of several cells were below 5, the Yates correction for continuity was applied. The results by interviewers were not made known until the end of the research.

85 Table 1 contains classifications of the interview responses, Interviewers 1 and 2, and separates parents by group. The parents' responses were assigned a "Yes" or "No" categorization on six behavioral characteristics. Chi square showed a significant difference in distribution of parents by group on all six personality 90 characteristics ($p < .001$). More parents of the violent group were identified as showing characteristics of personality disturbance than parents of the control group on a two-tailed test.

Analysis by interviewers showed consistency re-95 garding greater presence of disturbed behavioral characteristics in the responses of parents of violent children. The findings encourage further research with larger samples, different age groups, and varying types of population as well as involving interviewers blind to 100 history and related matters. Research on parental discipline, attitudes, and development of violent behavior would be helpful.

References

Bandura, A., Ross, D., & Ross, S. (1961). Transmission of aggression through imitation of aggressive models. *Journal of Abnormal and Social Psychology, 63*, 575–582.

Despert, J. L. (1970). *The emotionally disturbed child.* New York: Doubleday.

Edelbrock, C., Rende, R., Plomin, R., & Thompson, L. A. (1995). A twin study of competence and problem behavior in childhood and adolescence. *Journal of Child Psychology and Psychiatry and Allied Disciplines, 36*, 775–785.

English, H. B., & English, A. C. (1961). *A comprehensive dictionary of psychological and psychoanalytical terms.* New York: Longman & Green.

Feshbach, S. (1970). Aggression. In P. H. Mussen (Ed.), *Carmichael's manual of child psychology.* Vol. 2. New York: Wiley, pp. 281–291.

Hicks, D. J. (1965). Imitation and retention of film-mediated aggressive peer and adult models. *Journal of Personality and Social Psychology, 2*, 97–100.

Johnson, R. N. (1972). *Aggression in men and animals.* Philadelphia, PA: Saunders.

Lahey, B. B., Loeber, R., Hart, E. L., Frick, P. J., Applegate, B., Zhang, Q., Green, S. M., Russo, M. R. (1995). Four-year longitudinal study of conduct disorders in boys: Patterns and predictors of persistence. *Journal of Abnormal Psychology, 104*, 89–93.

Lane, R. (1997). *Murder in America.* Columbus, OH: Ohio State Univer. Press.

Lewinsohn, P. M., Hopps, H., Roberts, R. E., Seeley, J. R., & Andrews, J. A. (1993). Adolescent psychopathology: I. Prevalence and incidence of depression and other DSM-III–R disorders in high school students. *Journal of Abnormal Psychology, 102*, 133–144.

Loeber, R. (1990). Development and risk factors of juvenile antisocial behavior and delinquency. *Clinical Psychology Review, 10*, 1–41.

Loeber, R., & Schmaling, K. B. (1985). Empirical evidence of overt and covert patterns of antisocial conduct problems: A meta-analysis. *Journal of Abnormal Child Psychology, 13*, 337–352.

Mussen, P. H., Conger, J. J., & Kagan, J. (1995). Child development and personality. New York: Harper & Row.

Patterson, G. R. (1986). Performance models for antisocial boys. *American Psychologist, 41*, 432–444.

Redl, F., & Wineman, D. (1951). *Children who hate.* New York: Free Press.

Rutter, M., MacDonald, H., LeCouteur, A., Harrington, R., Bolton, P., & Bailey, A. (1990). Genetic factors in child psychiatric disorders: II. Empirical findings. *Journal of Child Psychology and Psychiatry, 31*, 39–83.

Schreiber, E. H. (1988). *Aggression and violence in human behavior.* Lexington, MA: Ginn.

Schreiber, E. H. (1990). *Abnormal behavior.* Lexington, MA: Ginn.

Schreiber, E. H., & Schreiber, D. E. (1998). Use of hypnosis with a case of acquaintance rape. *Australian Journal of Clinical and Experimental Hypnosis, 26*, 72–75.

Widom, C. S. (1989). The cycle of violence. *Science, 244*, 160–166.

Zimmerman, M. (1994). Diagnosing personality disorders: Review of issues and research methods. *Archives of General Psychiatry, 51*, 225–245.

Address correspondence to: Elliott H. Schreiber, Ed.D., 708 Camden Avenue, Moorestown, NJ 08057.

Appendix

Interview Form

1. What types of discipline do you use with your children? Please explain.

2. Do you have a great deal of patience or little patience with your children? For example, do you have a long or short fuse with the children? Elaborate.

3. Describe your personal and social relationships with the family members. Also, discuss your responsibilities in the family.

4. How secure do you feel about your role with the children? Describe your feelings about yourself and your role.

5. Describe how you handle affection with your children. Elaborate on some personal experiences.

6. Do you use the same discipline techniques on a daily basis? Describe your feelings on discipline and behavior.

Exercise for Article 25

Factual Questions

1. What suggested the importance of the six personality characteristics that were examined in this study?

2. What was the mean age of the parents?

3. Who interviewed the parents?

4. Were the parents made aware of the purpose of the study?

5. How many of the parents of violent children were classified as abusive by Interviewer 2?

6. There were significant differences between the two groups of parents on how many of the personality characteristics?

Questions for Discussion

7. In lines 25–27, the researchers describe characteristics that suggest the two groups of families were similar demographically. Is it important to know this? Are there other demographics that might have been considered? Explain.

8. The violent children attended special education classes. How important would it be to know whether the control group children also attended special education classes? (See lines 43–52.)

9. The interviewers knew which parents had violent children and which did not (i.e., they were not blinded). Could this affect the validity of the findings? Explain.

10. In your opinion, does this study indicate that the six personality characteristics of parents influence the behavior of their children? Explain.

11. If you were to conduct a study on the same topic, what changes in the research methodology, if any, would you make?

Quality Ratings

Directions: Indicate your level of agreement with each of the following statements by circling a number from 5 for strongly agree (SA) to 1 for strongly disagree (SD). If you believe an item is not applicable to this research article, leave it blank. Be prepared to explain your ratings.

A. The introduction establishes the importance of the study.

SA   5   4   3   2   1   SD

B. The literature review establishes the context for the study.

SA   5   4   3   2   1   SD

C. The research purpose, question, or hypothesis is clearly stated.

SA   5   4   3   2   1   SD

D. The method of sampling is sound.

SA   5   4   3   2   1   SD

E. Relevant demographics (for example, age, gender, and ethnicity) are described.

SA   5   4   3   2   1   SD

F. Measurement procedures are adequate.

SA   5   4   3   2   1   SD

G. All procedures have been described in sufficient detail to permit a replication of the study.

SA   5   4   3   2   1   SD

H. The participants have been adequately protected from potential harm.

SA   5   4   3   2   1   SD

I. The results are clearly described.

SA   5   4   3   2   1   SD

J. The discussion/conclusion is appropriate.

SA   5   4   3   2   1   SD

K. Despite any flaws, the report is worthy of publication.

SA   5   4   3   2   1   SD

Article 26

Smoking Cessation for High School Students: Impact Evaluation of a Novel Program

MEGHAN L. O'CONNELL
Yale-Griffin Prevention Research Center

MATTHEW FREEMAN
Yale University School of Medicine

GEORGIA JENNINGS
Yale-Griffin Prevention Research Center

WENDY CHAN
Yale-Griffin Prevention Research Center

LAURA S. GRECI
Yale-Griffin Prevention Research Center

IRINA D. MANTA
Yale University School of Medicine

DAVID L. KATZ
Yale-Griffin Prevention Research Center

ABSTRACT. This pilot study was designed to evaluate the feasibility and the impact of a smoking-cessation program that would meet the specific needs of high school students. Feedback from focus groups conducted with adolescent smokers at a Connecticut high school was used to develop a tailored intervention. Intervention components included commonly used behavioral strategies, with additional options to assist students to quit smoking, including use of bupropion, concomitant support for parent smoking cessation, stress management, and physician counseling. On completion, 20 of the 22 enrolled students remained committed to quitting. Twenty-seven percent of students quit smoking, and 69% of those who continued to smoke reduced the number of cigarettes smoked per day by an average of 13. Providing additional options to students and additional support for concomitant parental cessation may enhance the appeal of adolescent smoking-cessation programs. Further investigation into efficacy of bupropion use for adolescent cessation is warranted.

From *Behavior Modification*, *28*, 133–146. Copyright © 2004 by Sage Publications, Inc. Reprinted with permission.

Tobacco use is the leading cause of premature (preventable) death in the United States (Centers for Disease Control and Prevention [CDC], 1994) and will result in death or disability for half of all regular users
5 (CDC, 1999). Tobacco use among teenagers is in particular an enormous public-health concern. Tobacco use onset, regular use, and dependence often begin during adolescence (CDC, 1994; Elders, Perry, Eriksen, & Giovino, 1994). Behavior patterns are set during
10 this time and often continue into adulthood (Caplan, 1995). The 1998–1999 National Youth Tobacco Survey (CDC, 2000) indicates that 63.5% of U.S. high school students have smoked cigarettes during their lifetime, with 34.8% having smoked during the past 30
15 days and 20.1% smoking on a daily basis. It is estimated that in the United States alone, 3,000 young people become regular smokers every day, and the proportion of youth addicted to cigarettes is growing

(Lamkin, Davis, & Kamen, 1998). There is a great
20 need for innovative tobacco-cessation programs targeting adolescents (Schubiner, Herrold, & Hunt, 1998; Sussman, Lichtman, Ritt, & Pallonen, 1999), as intervention during this life stage has the potential to reach smokers before the habit becomes well established
25 (Elders et al., 1994).

Despite frequent studies on the prevalence of cigarette smoking among adolescents and the proliferation of programs to prevent initiation of cigarette use, few studies of smoking-cessation interventions for youth
30 have been reported. Although some adolescent smoking-cessation programs have been implemented in schools, few have been evaluated (Lamkin et al., 1998). Existing cessation programs for adolescents (Dino et al., 2001; Sussman, Dent, & Lichtman, 2001)
35 aim to enhance participant problem-solving skills for managing personal barriers to quitting, help in coping with physical and psychological withdrawal symptoms, and encourage identification of situations that trigger the urge to smoke. Bupropion, a monocyclic antide-
40 pressant that may help relieve some of the anxiety associated with smoking cessation (Nichols, 1999), has been efficacious in adult programs (Hurt et al., 1997), although evidence to support its use for smoking cessation in adolescents is lacking.
45 This article reports the results of a tailored smoking-cessation program developed for students at one Connecticut high school.

Method

Focus Groups

Using methods described by Krueger (Krueger, 1994), the research team conducted focus groups with
50 11th- and 12th-grade students. Students evaluated and suggested modifications of existing smoking-cessation programs used in Connecticut, including the American Lung Association's Nicotine Challenge (American Lung Association, n.d.) and an adapted version of the
55 adult Smoke Stoppers program (Smoke Stoppers,

1998), and identified barriers to smoking cessation that had not been addressed.

Students were recruited for focus groups in April and May of 2000 by the high school nurse, the school outreach worker, and through public-address system announcements. A prescreening questionnaire identified 45 eligible students (23 males, 22 females) who were invited to participate in one of eight single-gender focus groups. Students were eligible if they were current and regular smokers (defined as smoking more than one cigarette per day) (Farkas et al., 1996). The average number of participants in each group was five.

Structured, open-ended questions were used to guide discussions, along with videotape segments and materials from the established cessation programs. Key questions related to personal experiences with smoking (e.g., addiction, interest in quitting, and friends' and parents' smoking status), likes and dislikes of former program components, and opinions of elements proposed for inclusion in the pilot program. Researchers also inquired about logistical considerations for recruiting students and about implementing the program in the school. Each focus group lasted 90 minutes and was audiotaped. The students were provided with $25, pizza, and soda for their participation.

The pilot smoking-cessation program was developed and revised based on clear consensus among focus-group participants about the inclusion or the exclusion of specific intervention components. Clear consensus was defined by researchers as total agreement or agreement among a large majority of participants, with no dissent.

Program Components

Unique program components, including pharmacotherapy, concurrent parental intervention, stress management, and physician involvement were incorporated into a tailored intervention. These components were considered complementary to the features of currently used programs. Bupropion was viewed as a possible strategy to assist students in their quitting efforts; however, focus groups did not support use of nicotine replacement. A parental-intervention component was planned to educate parents about effects of household smoke on their child's ability to quit and to increase awareness of ways they could support their teenager's efforts to quit. Cessation support for parents was also available upon request as an adjunct to the adolescent program.

In addition to the above intervention components, weekly group meetings were planned based on effective strategies used in prior cessation programs that were deemed acceptable to focus groups. Strategies employed were based principally on the transtheoretical model of change (Prochaska & DiClemente, 1983) and a recent adaptation emphasizing the importance of an individualized approach to raising motivation, and/or lowering barriers to change (Katz, 2001). This behavioral component included exercises for students to further choose personalized strategies for preparing to quit and remaining smoke free by learning skills to overcome barriers. Various techniques to deal with personal cravings, stress, and peer pressures were incorporated to encourage participants to try many strategies. Specific tips were given to help students consider and to help open dialogue about the various ways to avoid personal triggers to smoke. Discussion also served to help students identify alternate ways to relieve stress, how to seek support from family and friends, and what to say to friends who offer cigarettes. Motivational videos and contracts with students were also used.

Recruitment

Faculty, counselors, and administrators referred interested students for a 20-minute to 30-minute assessment with the school nurse; other students were self-referred. The transtheoretical model (Prochaska & DiClemente, 1983) of behavior change was used to identify appropriate candidates for the program. Students determined to be of contemplator status or greater in the stages of change were encouraged to take part. The school nurse engaged in short discussions with students in the precontemplator stage in an attempt to move them closer to the contemplator stage. These students received information about the program to encourage future participation.

Based on student opinion that lack of parental support was an important impediment to cessation, parents were addressed during school orientation in September 2000. Messages about health risks associated with adolescent smoking and the influence parents have on their child's smoking behavior were delivered. The new program was presented as an opportunity for parents to help students quit. All parents received a letter in the mail with answers to frequently asked questions and tips on how to support their children's attempts to quit smoking.

Program Implementation

Enrollment commenced following protocol approval by the pertinent Institutional Review Board (Griffin Hospital, Derby, CT). Twenty-two 11th- and 12th-grade students who had been smoking for at least 2 years and were motivated to quit enrolled in the pilot adolescent smoking-cessation intervention program. Intake assessments were completed prior to the intervention, including baseline measures of smoking habits, information on perceived impediments to smoking cessation, and students' desire to try strategies to overcome these barriers.

Participants were screened for seizure and eating disorders, as well as use of other medications before being given the option of the addition of 300 mg of bupropion per day for up to 3 months (with parental permission). Verbal and written, student and parental

Table 1
Student Ratings of the Helpfulness of Intervention Components

Program component	Extremely helpful or quite helpful			Somewhat helpful			Not helpful		
	%	Male	Female	%	Male	Female	%	Male	Female
Weekly meetings	57	7	1	29	2	2	14	2	0
Developing strategies to cut down	43	6	0	43	5	1	14	0	2
Physician involvement	29	3	1	50	5	2	21	2	1
Discussion of ways to stay smoke-free	36	5	0	50	5	2	14	1	1
Video	29	3	1	57	6	2	14	2	0
Tip sheet	21	3	0	29	3	1	50	5	2
Parent discussion with physician	14	2	0	21	2	1	64	7	2
Relaxation tape	7	1	0	21	3	0	71	7	3
Zyban* (9 out of 14 respondents used Zyban)	11	1	0	44	3	1	44	3	1
Relaxation session	0	0	0	43	5	1	57	6	2
Contract	0	0	0	21	2	1	79	9	2

Note. Ratings did not differ significantly between male and female respondents. $N = 14$ (11 males, 3 females).
*Zyban is a brand name for bupropion.

consent was obtained prior to drug dispensation by the school nurse.

Referrals to outside agencies were made for students with other chemical dependencies (determination of dependency was made by the school nurse and the outreach worker).

The program spanned November and December of 2000 and was coordinated and run by the school nurse and the school outreach worker, with support from the research team. Smoking-cessation group sessions were held during rotating class periods. On completion of the intervention, student quit data were collected and process-evaluation questionnaires were completed.

There were no adult smoking-cessation programs available in the community. Interested parents of enrolled students were provided contact information for the study personnel and offered guidance in their quit effort. As appropriate, parents were offered bupropion and physician counseling.

Analysis

Students were asked to complete surveys to report their smoking status and to rate how helpful each program component was toward their efforts to quit or reduce smoking. Chi-square statistics and Fisher's exact tests (for analyses where expected cell-frequency counts were less than five) were used to assess associations between gender and quit or reduction rates as well as intervention component ratings. Analyses were performed to compare numbers of male and female students who quit smoking and who quit or reduced smoking. Comparisons were also made to assess frequency with which male and female students rated a program component as being helpful in their efforts to quit or reduce smoking.

Results

At the end of the program (following Week 8), 20 out of 22 students (91%) were surveyed about their experiences as members of the program, and 14 of 22 students provided feedback on the usefulness of specific program components. For analysis purposes, the two students who were lost to follow-up were considered to be smoking.

Six out of 22 students (27%) reported being smoke free. The average number of cigarettes smoked per day among students who were not able to quit decreased from 22 per day prior to the program to 9; 11 of the 16 who remained smokers (69%) had cut down on the number of cigarettes smoked per day. Overall, 17 of 22 respondents either completely quit or significantly cut down (77%) throughout the course of the program. Numbers of male and female students who quit smoking were comparable (males: 4 out of 15 [27%]; females: 2 out of 7 [29%]; $p = 0.38$). There was also no difference in the number of students who quit or reduced smoking by gender (males: 5 out of 7 [71.4%]; females: 11 out of 15 [73.3%]; $p = 0.38$). The majority (79%) of students who continued to smoke stated that they would participate in such a program again.

Eleven students (50%) whose parents provided written consent were started with a two-week supply of bupropion. More than 40% of students taking bupropion reported that it was somewhat useful as an aid for quitting. However, 7 of the 11 students using the medication reported sleep disturbance. One person each reported headache and stomach upset. Although 8 of 11 students taking bupropion reported taking the medication regularly, as directed, facilitators believed this to be untrue, as some students returned unused packets of medication.

Components of the intervention that received the highest ratings regarding their helpfulness were meeting weekly as a group, the development of personal strategies to cut down and refrain from smoking, the use of a motivational video, and talking with the physician. The majority (86%) of students rated each of these as somewhat helpful, quite helpful, or extremely helpful. Components of the program that were considered helpful by smaller percents of students included bupropion, relaxation techniques, and the physician's conversation with parents. Comparison by chi-square testing revealed no significant differences in male and female students' ratings of each component (see Table 1).

Sixty percent (12 out of 20) of participants reported having at least one smoking parent or other family member. Among these participants, 75% viewed the smoking habits of a family member as an impediment to their own quitting. Some students reported that more parental involvement would be beneficial; however, 55% did not believe that their parents would be interested in learning about ways to support students' efforts.

Discussion

Student recruitment into the smoking-cessation program following the focus groups was greater by a factor of three than that experienced during previous years at the same school. Whether this resulted from school presentation and focus-group participation or the lessons learned from them is unclear; however, modifications made to the prior promotion and the enrollment process clearly enhanced student interest in the program. Methods for maintaining interest and maintaining contact with the students were effective, as indicated by the 13% dropout rate. The specific components of this program, preprogram focus groups, or both may have value for all schools sponsoring smoking-cessation interventions.

The 27% quit rate among participants in this pilot program is relatively high compared to prior programs with adolescents, the previously highest recorded quit rate being approximately 22% (Dino et al., 2001). Quit rates did not differ significantly between males and females. Differences in the degree of difficulty experienced by males and females while attempting to quit were not determined; however, a recent study suggests that male and female adolescents may require gender-specific intervention (Dino et al., 2001). Therefore, preferences among this student population for gender-specific programs will be ascertained at a 12-month follow-up and considered for future study.

Inclusion of pharmacotherapy was considered acceptable by more than half of the participants. Willingness to try pharmacological therapies as an aid to smoking-cessation efforts may have important implications for future treatment of nicotine addiction among adolescents. Efficacy of this approach for adolescent smokers is as yet uncertain; the strong student support for making bupropion available demonstrated in this study may be important to consider in the design of future programs. Use of bupropion for smoking cessation has been found to increase the probability of successful quitting among adult smokers (Holm & Spencer, 2000; Hurt et al., 1997) and may produce similar results in adolescents if taken correctly. Parental supervision may be necessary to ensure bupropion is taken regularly and at recommended intervals to maximize helpful effects and avoid side effects such as sleeplessness.

Acceptance of the use of bupropion by 11 of the 13 parents contacted suggests that they are willing to consider this approach to smoking cessation in their children. Further, the process of obtaining informed parental consent for use of bupropion may have engaged parents in a complementary quit effort of their own—an ancillary benefit.

Successful adolescent smoking cessation may require efforts to increase parental awareness of the benefits of expressing concerns about smoking and ways to support family members who are trying to quit. Provision of communication-skills training for parents and their teenagers may also be beneficial. A study examining parental influences on adolescents' transitions from nonsmoker to experimenter and from experimenter to established-smoker status demonstrated that lack of perceived parental concern about smoking distinguished experimenters who progressed to regular smoking from those who did not; problem-solving communication with parents was found to be protective (Distefan, Gilpin, Choi, & Pierce, 1998). Concurrent smoking-cessation programs for parents of teenagers attempting to quit are also likely to be of profound importance. This study attempted to encourage parents who smoke to consider quitting. However, no programs were available in the community to meet the needs of adults who desired assistance. More work is required to determine effective ways to engage parents in efforts to support their teenager's quit attempts, regardless of whether they are willing to make personal quit attempts. Without parental support, it seems unlikely that adolescents will be successful in their attempts to quit smoking.

There is evidence to suggest that the average smoker requires multiple quit attempts before quitting for good (Hymowitz, Sexton, Ockene, & Grandits, 1991; Zhu, Sun, Billings, Choi, & Malarcher, 1999). Many participants in this study who have not quit smoking have reduced the number of cigarettes smoked per day. Cutting down on number of cigarettes smoked not only reduces health risks associated with smoking but also may lessen the difficulty experienced in attempting to quit in the future. Results of this experience support available evidence suggesting that adolescents are aware of the dangers associated with cigarette smoking and are often motivated to quit (Engels,

Knibbe, de Vries, & Drop, 1998; Houston, Kolbe, & Eriksen, 1998) but find quitting prohibitively difficult (CDC, 1994; Lamkin et al., 1998).

350   Research indicates that tailoring health messages and interventions to individual needs may enhance smoking-cessation outcomes (Juszczak & Sadler, 1999; Strecher et al., 1994). It is well recognized that disease-prevention efforts targeting adolescents must be con-

355   sidered in the context of adolescent development. Therefore, timing and tailoring of interventions to suit adolescent target groups is recommended (Juszczak & Sadler, 1999), particularly to support behaviors throughout each stage of change (Damrosch, 1991).

360   Students emphasized the desire for a program that is not rigid but offers various options for different needs. Thus, making options such as pharmacotherapy, physician contact, and parental involvement available may enhance the appeal of smoking-cessation programs

365   even for students who may not be interested in these particular intervention components.

Limitations of the study should be noted. The 27% quit rate is promising; however, long-term evaluation data are not yet available. Conclusions as to efficacy of

370   the program in terms of sustained-quit and smoking-reduction rates are premature. Students participating in this study are part of a fairly homogeneous group made up of predominantly white teenagers with moderate to high socioeconomic status, and the study sample is

375   quite small. Therefore, population-based generalizations cannot be made, and further research is needed to determine if the proposed program components are relevant for other adolescent groups. It is unclear to what extent participation in focus-group interviews by

380   some program members influenced interest in the program. Therefore, replication of the program may require alternate methods to establish similar rates of participation. Sophisticated methods to verify self-reported quit and smoking-reduction rates were not

385   available due to financial constraints.

Conclusions

Student demand for and commitment to this smoking-cessation program as well as the promising quit rate warrant further investigation into school-based methods of assisting adolescents to quit smoking. Pre-

390   intervention focus groups may add independent value by conferring a sense of local ownership and thereby attract program participants. Pharmacological intervention as part of a comprehensive program represents a possible additional means of overcoming certain resis-

395   tances to change; however, further study is required, and a controlled means of monitoring compliance may be necessary. Parental involvement and support is recommended and further research into appropriate and effective ways of engaging parents in efforts to assist

400   their teenagers to quit smoking (and to consider quitting themselves) is encouraged. Finally, refinements in the process of identifying individual impediments to

smoking cessation and to offering strategies tailored to an individual's impediment profile offer the promise of

405   greater success and warrant increased attention.

References

American Lung Association. Connecticut Chapter (n.d.). Nicoteen Challenge. Retrieved from www.lungusa.com

Caplan, D. (1995). Smoking: issues and interventions for occupational health nurses. *AAOHN Journal*, 43, 633–644.

Centers for Disease Control and Prevention. (1994). Guidelines for school health programs to prevent tobacco use and addiction. *Mortality and Morbidity Weekly Report*, 43, 1–18.

Centers for Disease Control and Prevention. (1999). *Best practices for comprehensive tobacco control programs—August 1999*. Atlanta, GA: U.S. Department of Health and Human Services, Centers for Disease Control and Prevention, National Center for Chronic Disease Prevention and Health Promotion, Office on Smoking and Health.

Centers for Disease Control and Prevention. (2000). Youth tobacco surveillance—United States, 1998–1999. *Mortality and Morbidity Weekly Report*, 49, vi–94.

Damrosch, S. (1991). General strategies for motivating people to change their behavior. *The Nursing Clinics of North America*, 26, 833–843.

Dino, G., Horn, K., Goldcamp, J., Maniar, S., Fernandez, A., & Massey, C. (2001). Statewide demonstration of not on tobacco: A gender-sensitive teen smoking cessation program. *Journal of School Nursing*, 17, 90–97.

Distefan, J. M., Gilpin, E. A., Choi, W. S., & Pierce, J. P. (1998). Parental influences predict adolescent smoking in the United States, 1989–1993. *Journal of Adolescent Health*, 22, 466–474.

Elders, M. J., Perry, C. L., Eriksen, M. P., & Giovino, G. A. (1994). The report of the surgeon general: Preventing tobacco use among young people. *American Journal of Public Health*, 84, 543–547.

Engels, R. C., Knibbe, R. A., de Vries, H., & Drop, M. J. (1998). Antecedents of smoking cessation among adolescents: Who is motivated to change? *Preventive Medicine*, 27, 348–357.

Farkas, A., Pierce, J., Zhu, S., Rosbrook, B., Gilbin, E., Berry, C., et al. (1996). Addiction versus stages of change models in predicting smoking cessation. *Addiction*, 91, 1271–1280.

Holm, K., & Spencer, C. (2000). Bupropion: A review of its use in the management of smoking cessation. *Drugs*, 59, 1007–1024.

Houston, T., Kolbe, L. J., & Eriksen, M. P. (1998). Tobacco-use cessation in the '90s—Not "adults only" anymore. *Preventive Medicine*, 27(5 Pt 3), A1–A2.

Hurt, R. D., Sachs, D. P., Glover, E. D., Offord, K. P., Johnston, J. A., Dale, L. C., et al. (1997). A comparison of sustained-release bupropion and placebo for smoking cessation. *New England Journal of Medicine*, 337, 1195–1202.

Hymowitz, N., Sexton, M., Ockene, J., & Grandits, G. (1991). Baseline factors associated with smoking cessation and relapse: MRFIT Research Group. *Preventive Medicine*, 20, 590–601.

Juszczak, L., & Sadler, L. (1999). Adolescent development: Setting the stage for influencing health behaviors. *Adolescent Medicine*, 10, 1–11.

Katz, D. (2001). Behavior modification in primary care: The pressure system model. *Preventive Medicine*, 32, 66–72.

Krueger, R. (1994). *Focus groups: A practical guide for applied research* (2nd ed.). London: Sage.

Lamkin, L., Davis, B., & Kamen, A. (1998). Rationale for tobacco cessation interventions for youth. *Preventive Medicine*, 27(5 Pt 3), A3–A8.

Nichols, M. (1999). The use of bupropion hydrochloride for smoking cessation therapy. *Clinical Excellence for Nurse Practitioners*, 3, 317–322.

Prochaska, J. O., & DiClemente, C. C. (1983). Stages and processes of self-change of smoking: Toward an integrative model of change. *Journal of Consulting and Clinical Psychology*, 51, 390–395.

Schubiner, H., Herrold, A., & Hunt, R. (1998). Tobacco cessation and youth: The feasibility of brief office interventions for adolescents. *Preventive Medicine*, 27(5 Pt. 3), A47–A54.

Smoke Stoppers. (1998). Smoke stoppers participant kit—Adult group program. West Chester, PA.

Strecher, V. J., Kreuter, M., Den Boer, D. J., Kobrin, S., Hospers, H. J., & Skinner, C. S. (1994). The effects of computer-tailored smoking cessation messages in family practice settings. *Journal of Family Practice*, 39, 262–270.

Sussman, S., Dent, C. W., & Lichtman, K. L. (2001). Project EX: Outcomes of a teen smoking cessation program. *Addictive Behaviors*, 26, 425–438.

Sussman, S., Lichtman, K., Ritt, A., & Pallonen, U. (1999). Effects of thirty-four adolescent tobacco use cessation and prevention trials on regular users of tobacco products. *Substance Use & Misuse*, 34, 1469–1503.

Zhu, S. H., Sun, J., Billings, S. C., Choi, W. S., & Malarcher, A. (1999). Predictors of smoking cessation in U.S. adolescents. *American Journal of Preventive Medicine*, 16, 202–207.

Acknowledgments: This study was supported financially by a tobacco mini grant from the Connecticut Southwest Area Health Education Council and the Connecticut Orange Drug and Alcohol Action Council. We gratefully acknowledge the participation of Amity High School's students and staff, the support of the Connecticut American Lung Association and of St. Vincent's Hospital, Bridgeport, CT, and the technical assistance of Michelle LaRovera.

About the authors: Meghan L. O'Connell, M.P.H., is currently a project coordinator at the Yale-Griffin Prevention Research Center. Her research focuses on adult- and adolescent-tobacco-use prevention, as well as the prevention and control of obesity. She has a particular interest in adolescent health. She earned her M.P.H. from Curtin University in Perth, Australia. Matthew Freeman earned his M.P.H. in chronic-disease epidemiology from the Yale University School of Medicine. He is currently in the nurse-practitioner program at The Ohio State University. His field of interest is adolescent and college health. Georgia Jennings, M.P.H., is the deputy director of the Yale-Griffin Prevention Research Center, where her primary interest is modifying health-risk behaviors through community-based participatory research. She is currently engaged in a yearlong project in Spain related to her interest in developing international collaborations to address the growing list of common public health challenges, especially those related to cardiovascular disease. She received her M.P.H. from the Yale University School of Medicine. Wendy Chan, M.P.H., is a biostatistician in the Community and Preventive Medicine Department of the Mount Sinai School of Medicine. She is currently performing statistical analysis for association studies to understand the role of genetic polymorphisms on chronic disease, disease progression, nutrient processing, metabolism of environmental contaminants, and pubertal development. She received her M.P.H. from Emory University. Laura S. Greci, M.D., M.P.H., completed her residency in internal medicine/preventive medicine at Griffin Hospital/Yale University in June 2002 and has recently finished her M.P.H. degree requirements from the Yale University School of Public Health. She is participating in research projects involving adult vaccination usage in the inpatient setting, the application of laboratory tests for disease diagnosis (e.g., diabetes), and race and ethnic differences in motor-vehicle fatality rates. After her residency, she plans to continue to research interests in clinical preventive medicine and health promotion in New Mexico, where she attended medical school at the University of New Mexico. Irina D. Manta is a research assistant at the Yale-Griffin Prevention Research Center. David L. Katz, M.D., M.P.H, F.A.C.P.M., is an associate clinical professor of epidemiology and public health and medicine and the director of medical studies in public health at the Yale University, School of Medicine. A board-certified specialist in both internal medicine and preventive medicine and public health, Katz earned his B.A. from Dartmouth College, his M.D. from the Albert Einstein School of Medicine, and his M.P.H. from the Yale University School of Medicine. Recipient of the American College of Preventive Medicine's Rising Star award in 2001, Katz is a former preventive-medicine residency director, founder and director of an Integrative Medicine Center in Derby, CT; and director of the Centers-for-Disease-Control-funded Yale-Griffin Prevention Research Center, where he oversees a research staff of more than 20. In his role as director, Katz serves as principal investigator for numerous studies related to obesity prevention and control, nutrition effects on health, behavior change, and chronic-disease prevention.

Address correspondence to: Meghan L. O'Connell, Yale Griffin PRC, 30 Division Street, Derby, CT 06418.

Exercise for Article 26

Factual Questions

1. The pilot smoking-cessation program for this research was developed and revised on what basis?

2. How were the participants recruited?

3. How many students enrolled in the program?

4. Who coordinated and ran the program?

5. Why did the facilitators believe that some students did not take bupropion as directed?

6. The quit rate in this program was 27%. According to the researchers, what is the previously highest reported quit rate in the literature?

Questions for Discussion

7. What is your opinion on the use of focus groups to plan this program? Do you think that it would be better to rely on expert opinion instead of students' opinions? Explain. (See lines 48–87.)

8. In your opinion, are the program components described in sufficient detail? Explain. (See lines 88–125.)

9. Does the fact that Table 1 includes only three females affect your interpretation of the data in it? Explain.

10. The data on the effectiveness of the program are based on self-reports by students. Are there advantages and disadvantages to using self-reports for such data? Explain.

11. The researchers describe limitations in lines 367–385. In your opinion, are all the limitations important? Are some more important than others?

12. Based on the information in this report, would you be in favor of using public funds to support additional evaluations of this program? Explain.

Quality Ratings

Directions: Indicate your level of agreement with each of the following statements by circling a number from 5 for strongly agree (SA) to 1 for strongly disagree (SD). If you believe an item is not applicable to this research article, leave it blank. Be prepared to explain your ratings.

A. The introduction establishes the importance of the study.

SA   5   4   3   2   1   SD

B. The literature review establishes the context for the study.

SA   5   4   3   2   1   SD

C. The research purpose, question, or hypothesis is clearly stated.

       SA   5   4   3   2   1   SD

D. The method of sampling is sound.

       SA   5   4   3   2   1   SD

E. Relevant demographics (for example, age, gender, and ethnicity) are described.

       SA   5   4   3   2   1   SD

F. Measurement procedures are adequate.

       SA   5   4   3   2   1   SD

G. All procedures have been described in sufficient detail to permit a replication of the study.

       SA   5   4   3   2   1   SD

H. The participants have been adequately protected from potential harm.

       SA   5   4   3   2   1   SD

I. The results are clearly described.

       SA   5   4   3   2   1   SD

J. The discussion/conclusion is appropriate.

       SA   5   4   3   2   1   SD

K. Despite any flaws, the report is worthy of publication.

       SA   5   4   3   2   1   SD

Article 27

Evaluation of a Standards-Based Supplemental Program in Reading

DUANE INMAN
Berry College

LESLIE MARLOW
Berry College

BENNIE BARRON
Northwestern State University

ABSTRACT. This pilot descriptive study examined expressed perceptions of a diverse group of teachers who, in the 2002–2003 school year, piloted implementation of a new standards-based supplemental program in reading/language arts, EduSTRANDS. Over 600 teachers in 153 schools using a supplemental, standards-based reading/language arts program were surveyed on their impressions of the features and effectiveness of the program. Standard assessment scores from the schools were compared for the year immediately preceding the use of the materials and for the first year of use of the materials. Overall, teacher evaluations of the program were positive. Scores increased at all tested levels except in sixth grade.

From *Reading Improvement, 41,* 179–187. Copyright © 2004 by Project Innovation, Inc. Reprinted with permission.

Political, sociological, and educational changes hallmarked the school atmosphere in the United States at the opening of the 21st century. The enactment of the No Child Left Behind Act of 2001, signed on January 8, 2002, provided the impetus for educators to take a closer look at classroom practices and subsequent student outcomes. The ultimate goal is to instruct in a manner which results in the highest possible student performance on standardized achievement measures, thus addressing the demand for stronger accountability for results (www.ed.gov/nclb). Within the next decade "…2013–2014, all students will reach high standards, at a minimum attaining proficiency or better in reading/language arts." Where student performance is found to be at less-than-desirable levels, measures must be taken to implement sound, research-based methodology. Students must be provided with advantageous education programs which address mandated standards and which have been found to be correlated with increased student performance on measures of their standards-based outcomes (NCLBA, 2002). The high standards on which student performance is to be based will come from the professional educational organizations. Specifically, national guidelines established by the International Reading Association (IRA) and by the National Council of Teachers of English (NCTE) for reading and language arts will play a primary role in student evaluation.

In response to the demand for students to achieve at high levels and to meet specified standards, all states have mandated a statewide testing program for all of their students. For example, yearly in Louisiana, students at specific grade levels are tested using the Louisiana Statewide Norm-Referenced Testing Program in order to ascertain their levels of achievement in comparison with national results (Louisiana State Education Progress Report, 2001–2002). The results of this test provide a standard measure for student achievement and can provide an indication of school progress on a year-to-year basis.

This pilot descriptive study examined expressed perceptions of a diverse group of teachers who, in the 2002–2003 school year, piloted implementation of a new standards-based supplemental program in reading/language arts, EduSTRANDS. The EduSTRANDS materials address each of the standards set forth by IRA/NCTE and include multiple activities and strategies to introduce, reinforce, and evaluate student performance. Content examples and practice are provided for each identified skill. Lessons are arranged vertically between grades as well as horizontally within grades for grades 1–8. Well-designed instructional approaches support effective reading instruction. According to the American Federation of Teachers (2003), the following components are needed to effectively teach reading: comprehension strategies, vocabulary instruction, systematic and explicit instruction regarding written English, decoding skills, and phonemic/phonics instruction. The EduSTRANDS materials which address these components were developed in response to numerous teacher requests for a coherent way to ensure all reading/language arts standards could be adequately and thoroughly addressed. Extant basal texts and available curricula often were limited in their consideration of the entire set of standards at particular grade levels.

Over 20 years ago reading research specialists investigated and identified primary instructional areas which were critical to students' success in reading (Share, Jorm, Maclean, & Matthews, 1984; Miller & Ellsworth, 1985). This research continued into the mid-1990s when studies began to emphasize the need for teachers to adapt and supplement lessons in order to meet the unique needs of individual students (Turner, 1995; Snow, Burns, & Griffin, 1998; Pressley, 1998; Pressley, Rankin, & Yokoi, 1996). More recently, the findings of the National Reading Panel (2000), a re-examination of the findings of the National Reading Panel (Camilli, Vargas, & Yurecko, 2003) and research by Farstrup and Samuels (2002) re-emphasized the importance of a comprehensive reading program that allows for specific skill instruction in a variety of areas.

There are a number of programs which have been developed which claim to meet the criteria set forth by these research programs. However, limited independent research is available on the effectiveness of these programs.

Support for the approach taken in this evaluative project was supplied by the IRA 2002 Position Statement on Standards Based Reading Instruction which identifies specific questions to be addressed when reviewing instructional materials:

- Does this program or instructional approach provide systematic and explicit instruction in the particular strategies that have been proven to relate to high rates of achievement in reading for the children I teach?
- Does the program or instructional approach provide flexibility for use within the range of learners in the various classrooms where it will be used? Are there assessment tools that assist teachers in identifying individual learning needs? Are there a variety of strategies and activities that are consistent with diverse learning needs?
- Does the program or instructional approach provide a collection of high-quality literary materials that are diverse in levels of difficulty, genre, topic, and cultural representation to meet the individual needs and interests of the children with whom it will be used?

As an outgrowth from the IRA (2002) Position Statement, the following research questions were addressed by this study:

1. What is the nature of the population of teachers currently using the EduSTRANDS materials?
2. What are the expressed teacher opinions of the materials?
3. What is the nature and direction of change in student scores on the Louisiana Statewide Norm-Referenced Testing Program instrument in the schools using the EduSTRANDS program?

Population

Nineteen school systems within Louisiana participated in this pilot study. Six hundred twelve teachers from 153 schools cooperated in the implementation and assessment of the EduSTRANDS program. The schools ranged from fewer than 200 to over 500 total enrollment, grades K thru 12, and were located in diverse settings including rural, suburban, and urban with

a wide diversity of ethnicities and economic levels represented by the 77,000 students using the program. Although some of the schools served grades K–12, only teachers actively engaged in teaching grades K–8 or using the EduSTRANDS materials for remediation in higher grades were surveyed.

Instrument

The EduSTRANDS Teacher Opinion Survey is composed of two major sections: Section One, containing seven items related to demographic information of the teachers and their classrooms, and Section Two containing 14 items. The 14 items assessed expressed teacher perceptions regarding EduSTRANDS materials organization, practical aspects for using the materials, alignment with standards, and preparation for standard evaluation instruments. The instrument was developed by a panel of university professors specializing in reading, research, and education. The materials were peer reviewed and piloted for clarity by classroom teachers, and revised multiple times prior to being disseminated to the target population.

Information concerning student performance within the schools was obtained from the Louisiana school report cards, available as public domain information.

Limitations

Survey research, when conducted through the mail, typically results in respondent participation of less than 20% (Losh, 2003; Zhu, 2001). Generally, these respondents have strong feelings regarding the topic, either positive or negative, which influences their decision to participate (Gall, Gall, & Borg, 2003).

This descriptive study does not attempt to demonstrate a causal effect for the program as indicated by student performance, although information regarding student performance for the year immediately prior to using EduSTRANDS and for the first year of the use of EduSTRANDS is included for comparison purposes. To reach definite conclusions within the first year of implementation would be premature as both students and teachers needed some time to become familiar with the materials, not only with how to use them but how to most effectively integrate them into each instructional/curricular program.

Data Analysis and Procedures

All data were tabulated and analyzed using the SPSS-x program running the Windows XP environment.

In early spring of 2003, survey packets were sent to each of the participants. Each packet contained a letter of explanation, a survey form, and a self-addressed, stamped envelope for return. The return was anonymous with no identifiers for teacher, school, or school system included on either the envelope or the response form. There was no follow-up on the initial mailing. Approximately 30% of the completed surveys were returned, a rate which is well in excess of the 20% ex-

Table 1
Demographic Information

Teaching assignment	K–4	5–8	8–12	Other	
	54%	22%	9%	12%	
Years' experience	1–3	4–10	11–20	> 20	
	9%	32%	25%	31%	
Education level	Bachelor's	Master's	Master's +	Some college	
	57%	15%	21%	3%	
School enrollment	< 200	200–300	300–400	400–500	> 500
	25%	8%	23%	19%	24%
Class size	< 15	15–20	21–25	26–30	30+
	12%	48%	30%	9%	0%

pected response rate for one-wave mail surveys (Losh, 2003; Zhu, 2001).

Results

Demographics

Respondent demographics are summarized in Table 1. The majority of the teachers (76%) taught in grades 1–8 with only 9% at higher grades. Twelve percent expressed that their assignment was "other," which probably indicates that their teaching assignments were multiple levels or special classes not specified on the questionnaire. This was an experienced group of teachers with only 9% having fewer than four years of teaching experience. They taught in a wide variety of school sizes and 79% had a class size of 15–25 students. Fifty-seven percent of the respondents had a bachelor's degree, with an additional 36% having at least a master's degree. The remaining 3% indicated "some" college.

Program Opinions

In looking at the individual components of the satisfaction section of the survey, there is strong support from the teachers regarding the usefulness of the materials in the three categories—practical aspects of use (Table 2), alignment with standards (Table 3), and materials organization (Table 4). Noteworthy are the items in which there was over 85% agreement or strong agreement. These items were: well-organized materials, ease of use, alignment with content standards, alignment with state benchmarks, usefulness for enrichment, and usefulness for extended practice. In looking for items of agreement between the 80% and 85% levels, teachers expressed agreement that the materials were ready for immediate use, complemented the reading and language arts programs, provided a variety of formats, and accommodated student needs. There were two remaining items with which at least 75% of the respondents agreed: The materials complement the basal in use, and the materials provide ease of lesson modification.

Table 2
Practical Aspects of Use

	Strongly agree/agree	Strongly disagree/ disagree	Neither
Ready for immediate use	80.8%	5.5%	9.3%
Ease of use of all materials	88.5%	2.8%	8.2%
Ease of lesson modifications	76.4%	2.8%	19.9%
Accommodates for student needs	82.3%	1.7%	10.4%
Use as enrichment	85.2%	2.8%	11.0%
Use for extended practice	89.6%	.6%	8.8%

Table 3
Alignment with Standards

	Strongly agree/agree	Strongly disagree/ disagree	Neither
Aligned with content standards	88.5%	1.1%	9.9%
Aligned with state benchmarks	85.2%	1.1%	13.2%
IOWA test	66.5%	3.9%	29.1%
LEAP test	67.6%	3.3%	28.6%

Table 4
Materials Organization

	Strongly agree/agree	Strongly disagree/ disagree	Neither
Well-organized materials	85.7%	2.2%	8.8%
Complements basal	74.7%	2.2%	20.3%
Complements reading/language arts curriculum	82.4%	2.8%	14.3%
Variety of lesson formats	81.3%	4.8%	13.7%

Thus, there was agreement by more than 3/4 of the teachers with the usefulness of all the features of the program. When looking at the portion of the population which disagreed with the 14 items, there were no items with which there was disagreement at greater than 5.5%.

Outcomes

An examination of the progress of test scores within the schools using EduSTRANDS reveals that there were higher scores at all levels (Table 5) on the Louisiana Statewide Norm-Referenced Testing Program between spring 2002 and spring 2003 results except at grade 6. All differences were significant at the $p > .05$ level. While this does not necessarily indicate a causal relationship between the use of the program and test scores, it does indicate that significant progress is being made in almost every grade where the program is in effect.

Table 5
Comparison of Mean Scores, 2002–2003

Grade level	Mean scores	
	2002	2003
3	48.31	52.22
5	46.13	51.75
6	48.50	41.98
7	46.17	47.14

Discussion

It is necessary to provide appropriate reading instruction to all students beginning in the early grades of elementary school and extending throughout middle and high school. To become good readers, students must develop an awareness of the skills needed for decoding as well as the ability to read text accurately and fluently and the ability to apply comprehension strategies as they read. Research included in the report from The National Reading Panel (2002) emphasized that teachers needed to adjust the instruction in these areas in order to meet the specific needs of their students. The program examined through this survey has materials that incorporate this component so that students receive instruction and support that integrates with the current classroom materials to supplement learning endeavors in reading. The results of the teacher satisfaction survey indicate that teachers are highly in agreement that the features of the program meet the requirements for an effective, research-based set of materials. According to the respondents, the versatility of the EduSTRANDS program provides teachers with the tools that are critical to the teaching of reading.

Additionally, an examination of the test scores indicates gains at almost all levels. Based on test score results and teacher evaluations, there appears to be no discernable distinction between the effectiveness of this program in grades K–8 and its use in specific remedial instruction at the high school level. It is strongly recommended that additional research be done with respect to student progress for the populations using the program, and comparisons be made with non-participant peers to discover if the change in scores is indeed causal.

References

American Federation of Teachers (2003). www.aft.org/edissues/reading/

Camilli, G., Vargas, S. & Yurecko, M. (2003). Teaching children to read: The fragile link between science and federal education policy. *Education Policy Analysis Archives, 11*(15). Retrieved [Dec. 2003] from http://epaa.asu.edu/epaa/v11n15

Farstrup, A. and Samuels, S., Eds. (2002). *What research has to say about reading instruction.* Newark, Delaware.

Gall, M., Gall, J. & Borg, W. (2003). *Introductory Statistics.* Boston, Allyn and Bacon.

International Reading Association (2002). *What is evidence-based reading instruction?* Newark, Delaware.

Losh, S. C. (2003). http://edf5481-01.fa02.fsu.edu/Guide5.html.

Louisiana Department of Education (2003). *2001–2002 Louisiana State Education Progress.* Baton Rouge, Louisiana.

Miller, J. & Ellsworth, R. (1985). The evaluation of a two-year program to improve teacher effectiveness in reading instruction. *Elementary School Journal, 85.*

National Reading Panel (2000). *Teaching children to read: An evidenced-based assessment of the scientific research literature on reading and its implications for reading instruction.* Washington, DC.

Pressley, M. (1998). *Reading instruction that works: The case for balanced teaching.* New York: Guilford Press.

Pressley, M., Rankin, J., & Yokoi, L. (1996). A survey of instructional practices of primary teachers nominated as effective in promoting literacy. *Elementary School Journal, 96,* 363–384.

Share, D., Jorm, A., Maclean, R. & Matthews, R. (1984). Sources for individual differences in reading acquisition. *Journal of Educational Psychology, 76,* 1309–1324.

Snow, C., Burns, M. & Griffin, P. (Eds.). (1998). *Preventing reading difficulties in young children.* Washington, DC.: National Academy Press.

Turner, J. (1995). The influence of classroom contexts on young children's motivation for literacy. *Reading Research Quarterly, 30,* 410–441.

U. S. Department of Education (2002). Executive summary. The No Child Left Behind Act of 2001 http://www .ed.gov.offices/OESE/esea/execsumm.html.

Zhu, Y. (2001). http://biostat.coph

About the authors: Drs. Duane Inman and Leslie Marlow, Charter School of Education/Human Sciences, Berry College, Mount Berry, GA. Dr. Bennie Barron, Teacher Education Center, Northwestern State University, Natchitoches, LA.

Address correspondence to: Dr. Duane Inman, Charter School of Education/Human Sciences, 2277 Martha Berry Hwy. NW, Mount Berry, GA 30149.

Exercise for Article 27

Factual Questions

1. Who developed the instrument used in this program evaluation?

2. Was the instrument pilot tested?

3. Do the researchers claim that this evaluation shows a causal effect (i.e., the effect of the program on student performance)?

4. The researchers cite a study suggesting that when survey research is conducted through the mail, the typical respondent participation is less than what percentage?

5. What percentage of the responding teachers taught in grades higher than 8th grade?

6. Were all the differences in mean student performance from 2002 to 2003 statistically significant? If yes, at what probability level?

Questions for Discussion

7. The researchers state that this is a pilot study. Do you agree? If yes, what could be done to make it a more definitive study? (See line 41.)

8. Does the description of the EduSTRANDS program give you an adequate overview of it? Explain. (See lines 41–65.)

9. The response rate was approximately 30%. In your opinion, is this a serious limitation of this program evaluation? (See lines 179–182.)

10. In your opinion, how important would it be to include a control group in a future study of student outcomes resulting from the EduSTRANDS program? Explain. (See lines 223–233.)

11. This evaluation focuses on teachers' perceptions of a program. Do you think that this is equally important to student outcomes when evaluating an educational program? Explain.

Quality Ratings

Directions: Indicate your level of agreement with each of the following statements by circling a number from 5 for strongly agree (SA) to 1 for strongly disagree (SD). If you believe an item is not applicable to this research article, leave it blank. Be prepared to explain your ratings.

A. The introduction establishes the importance of the study.

SA 5 4 3 2 1 SD

B. The literature review establishes the context for the study.

SA 5 4 3 2 1 SD

C. The research purpose, question, or hypothesis is clearly stated.

SA 5 4 3 2 1 SD

D. The method of sampling is sound.

SA 5 4 3 2 1 SD

E. Relevant demographics (for example, age, gender, and ethnicity) are described.

SA 5 4 3 2 1 SD

F. Measurement procedures are adequate.

SA 5 4 3 2 1 SD

G. All procedures have been described in sufficient detail to permit a replication of the study.

SA 5 4 3 2 1 SD

H. The participants have been adequately protected from potential harm.

SA 5 4 3 2 1 SD

I. The results are clearly described.

SA 5 4 3 2 1 SD

J. The discussion/conclusion is appropriate.

SA 5 4 3 2 1 SD

K. Despite any flaws, the report is worthy of publication.

SA 5 4 3 2 1 SD

Article 28

Program to Reduce Behavioral Infractions and Referrals to Special Education

JAY GOTTLIEB
New York University

SUSAN POLIRSTOK
Lehman College of the City University of New York

From *Children & Schools: A Journal of the National Association of Social Workers*, 27, 53–57. Copyright © 2005 by National Association of Social Workers. Reprinted with permission.

This article reports the results of a professional development program using positive behavioral interventions designed to reduce the number of behavioral infraction reports and referrals to special education and
5 to improve academic achievement. Clinical personnel participated in all of the training sessions and were encouraged to explore how their interactions with teachers could support the "positive intervention" program. Not only can clinical personnel offer caring and
10 support for teachers who are committed to examining their management practices and making changes, they also can serve as resources when discussing students who present with severe physical, behavioral, or social-emotional challenges. From a clinical perspective,
15 helping teachers meet the individual and more specialized intervention needs of students with special challenges can begin only when classroom climate, organization, and structure have been addressed. The importance of these broad issues has been noted by Pollo-
20 way, Patton, and Serna (2001), who maintained that classroom organization and management are essential "precursors to teaching."

Intervention Sites

Three elementary schools from an inner-city school district, schools A, B, and C, were chosen for interven-
25 tion on the basis of requests to the district superintendent for assistance with classroom management and concerns about the rate of referral to special education. All three schools had similar student populations—primarily low-income racial and ethnic minority stu-
30 dents. On average, 40.3 percent of the schools' student populations were African American, 55.7 percent were Latino, 3.2 percent were Asian, and .8 percent were white. The proportion of students receiving free lunch across the three schools ranged from 91 percent to 99
35 percent. All three schools had characteristics commonly found in inner-city elementary schools: high teacher turnover, poor staff morale, low academic

achievement, and substantial poverty and social fragmentation in the community.
40 In the first school selected for training, school A (a K–8 school with about 550 students, of whom approximately 300 were in grades K–5), teachers forwarded to the principal 625 anecdotal reports of behavioral infractions by students in grades K–5. This was
45 42 percent more than the 360 reports forwarded to the principal during the preceding school year for the elementary-level students. School A also had an extremely high rate of special education referrals, which was of great concern to the school district administra-
50 tion; 11.2 percent of the school's K–5 population was referred, compared with an average of 4.7 percent for the whole school district. The referral rate of 11.2 percent placed this school in the upper 5 percent of all 811 primary and middle schools in the city for which data
55 were available. In schools B and C, trained during the following school year, student referrals to special education represented 8 percent of the enrollment in each school, almost double the average district special education referral rate.

Schoolwide Training Program

60 At the request of the district superintendent and the principals of schools A, B, and C, a training program for all administrators, clinical personnel, teachers, and paraprofessionals in these three schools was initiated. The training focused on behavior management proce-
65 dures using positive behavioral interventions to increase the level of teacher praise and reinforcement of students and reduce the use of punishment and negative teacher comments. This is in keeping with trends in behavioral intervention, which stress positive interven-
70 tions over negative and punitive strategies (Smith, Polloway, Patton, & Dowdy, 2004).
Careful crafting of classroom rules, contingent teaching, use of teacher praise, development of hierarchies of no-cost or low-cost tangible reinforcers, and
75 selective ignoring were among the techniques taught. These techniques have been widely documented in the literature as effective in promoting student learning (Lloyd, Forness, & Kavale, 1998). The program sought to empower teachers to create high-approval class-
80 rooms that children would find emotionally safe to take

Table 1
Professional Development Program Results Compared with the Preceding Year

Target outcomes	Preceding year comparison data *n*	After professional development program *n*	Percent improvement %
Behavioral infractions reports for school A	625	246	−61
Special education referrals for school A	30	11	−63
Special education referrals for schools B and C	32	22	−31
Students reading at grade level in school A (%)	27	35.3	8.3†
Students reading at grade level in schools A, B, and C (%)	28.8	32.2	3.5‡

Notes. †Overall school district performance showed a 3.5 percent increase across all 15 elementary schools in the district compared with the 8.3 percent increase in school A. ‡Overall school district performance showed a 1.5 percent decline across all 15 elementary schools in the district compared with the 3.5 percent increase for schools A, B, and C.

the necessary risks to tackle difficult academic tasks and change inappropriate behaviors.

An overriding intent when developing the training program was to minimize demands on teachers. Steps were taken to ensure that teachers did not have to do things that were overly demanding of their time. The rationale was that if teachers were asked to do things that were too taxing or foreign to their normal routines, they would not attempt the required activities, an outcome often evident when new programs are initiated.

In school A, training began immediately before school opened for the academic year and the last session occurred in mid-January. The seven half-days that were available between September and January for training were the entire allotment of contractually mandated professional development days through mid-year. In late March, a 45-minute follow-up session was provided to review key points that were covered during the seven sessions; this refresher session took place during the monthly faculty meeting. Schools B and C were trained jointly during the following year; only five half-day sessions were available for the professional development program between September and January. Similarly, a follow-up refresher session in March was held for both schools at their regular monthly faculty meetings.

The 150-minute professional development sessions typically began with a question and answer period, during which teachers raised questions about problems they encountered in their classes. The trainer encouraged group discussions to address these problems. Another portion of each session focused on a specific behavior management technique and how that technique could be used in classrooms.

The techniques taught in the professional development program were the following:

1. How to develop classroom rules that are behaviorally specific (that is, few in number and stated positively)
2. How to teach classroom rules to foster student ownership of academic and behavioral performance (that is, increase locus of control through self-monitoring)
3. How to increase teacher consciousness about language used with students to praise or reprimand and whether teacher comments were appropriate given classroom rules (that is, how to be a contingent teacher in the use of approval and disapproval)
4. How to increase the number of positive statements made by teachers to individual students and to the whole class compared with the number of negative statements (that is, how to be a high-approval teacher and change the approval-disapproval ratio in the classroom)
5. How to develop reinforcement systems that were "user-friendly" in terms of time and record keeping (that is, limit the complexity of the system)
6. How to use selective ignoring while trying to "catch students being good" (that is, change the focus from "catching students being bad")
7. How to work with high-frequency disruptive behaviors by reducing them gradually over time (that is, set realistic behavior change goals that recognize that change is often a slow process).

Time was allotted during each training session for participants to meet in small groups, usually by grade level taught, to discuss how the techniques presented could be applied in their classrooms in a developmentally appropriate way. Clinical personnel were integrated into these small-group discussions and provided a developmental perspective about what strategies might work with particular grades. Group members' collective sharing during training sessions led to other discussions outside the program. Participants were learning how to collaborate and support each other with respect to general classroom management issues, as well as issues related to the special needs of individual children.

Outcomes

The evaluation of outcomes varied slightly according to the data available in individual schools (see Table 1). Standardized achievement tests and referrals for special education were available in all three schools. Other data, such as the number of behavioral infraction

181

reports forwarded to the principal, were available only for school A.

Information on behavioral infractions in school A was provided by the principal. The number of behavioral infraction reports that the principal received from the teachers was recorded monthly. The number of referrals to special education and reasons for the referrals were obtained from the clinical team responsible for processing special education referrals for each of the schools. Members of the clinical team assigned to each school received the referrals and accompanying documentation, conducted the multidisciplinary assessments, and determined eligibility and placement recommendations. Information on referrals from each clinical team was gathered in mid-June.

Behavioral Infraction Reports

In the year preceding the training, 625 behavioral infraction reports were sent to the principal in school A, a significant increase over the 360 reports submitted the year before. During the school year in which the professional development program was offered, 246 behavioral infraction reports were forwarded, a reduction of 61 percent over the preceding year and 32 percent over the year before that.

Referrals to Special Education

Special education referrals to the clinical team for behavioral problems were collected in schools A, B, and C. In school A, data on referrals to special education declined from 30 the preceding year to 11 during the training year, a 63 percent reduction. Referral rates for special education in schools B and C dropped 31 percent during the training year compared with the preceding year.

Academic Achievement

School achievement data on standardized reading tests administered to all schools in the city were used as measures of academic achievement. During the school year preceding the professional development program, 27 percent of the students in school A scored at or above grade level on the California Test of Basic Skills, which was administered annually to all students in city school systems beginning in the third grade. In the year immediately following the training, 35.3 percent of the students in school A scored at or above grade level. The increase of 8.3 percent of children reading at or above grade level was substantially higher than the 3.5 percent average increase for that inner-city school district as a whole across its 15 elementary schools. It was also the first time in six years that reading scores in school A had improved.

Reading scores for schools A, B, and C at the end of the second training year were compared with the other 12 elementary schools in the district. The percentage of children reading at or above grade level in the three schools that received the professional development program increased from 28.8 percent to 32.3 percent. During the same period, scores for the other 12 schools declined from 39.2 percent reading at or above grade level to 37.7 percent. Although the district had allocated the same level of resources for literacy development in all 15 elementary schools, the three schools that received the professional development program improved five percentage points beyond the other schools. Only two of the 12 schools in the comparison group improved their performance during the same time period.

School Climate

As a consequence of the professional development program, tangible changes in school climate were noted in schools A, B, and C. Observational data supplied by the principals characterized the nature of these changes:

- Teachers treated children with greater respect.
- There was less "backbiting" among teachers than in previous years.
- The faculty seemed less stressed.
- Teacher-paraprofessional teams functioned more consistently and more effectively with regard to classroom management. Itinerant teachers saw positive changes in the school environment.
- Clinical staff interacted with teachers in a broader context as resource personnel.

Changes in school climate occurred even though not every teacher had adopted the program. Principals reported that about one-third of the teachers attempted the program and dropped it within a day or two, claiming that it was not effective. Another third attempted to implement the behavioral program, stopped, and then resumed it, sometimes for several iterations. The final third of the teachers implemented the program and stuck with it for the duration of the school year. Asked why some teachers believed that the program was unsuccessful, the principals responded that teachers who saw the program as a failure were seeking total and immediate elimination of the inappropriate behaviors they were trying to improve. When the behaviors were not eliminated immediately, the teachers concluded that the program was not viable. Teachers who kept coming back to the program were more willing to accept a gradual reduction in inappropriate behavior as a criterion for success. Changing classroom behavior of whole classes or individual students requires that teachers courageously examine their use of reinforcement and punishment and the provision of incentives to foster engagement of students in the change process. For teachers who had the patience to work with the program, results were evident.

Implications

This professional development program confirmed what researchers and teachers typically say about classrooms—that successful behavior management is a critical prerequisite for successful academic instruction. Less time spent on managing behavior translates into more time available for instruction. This finding is supported in the literature: "Effective classroom management is required if students are to benefit from any form of instruction, especially in inclusive classrooms where students display a wide range of diversity (Jones & Jones, 2001)" (Smith et al., 2004, p. 42).

As a result of this professional development program, behavioral infraction reports and conduct-related special education referrals declined substantially. When teachers were provided with the skills to manage disruptive behavior, they referred fewer students for special education. In reviewing the referrals to special education over the intervention period, we noted that the nature of these referrals shifted from primarily conduct-related referrals to more academic referrals that were skill specific. Overall, all three schools improved on the variables targeted for intervention. However, school A showed greater improvement than schools B and C. This may be due in part to the fact that school A was trained by itself over seven half-day sessions, whereas schools B and C were trained together over five half-day sessions. The differences in the number of half-day training sessions that were available each year were a function of mandated professional development time from which the district could not deviate. Moreover, training two schools together could have affected the teachers' comfort level when sharing concerns regarding their teaching and management. Finally, the role and reputation of the principal as a leader and respected colleague could have affected the performance of each of these schools. School A's principal was highly regarded by the staff and attended all training sessions and actively participated throughout the program, whereas the principals of schools B and C supported the program and encouraged the staff but did not actively participate in the sessions. This suggests that the active participation of the principal in this type of schoolwide intervention may be a critical variable.

This schoolwide approach to improving behavior significantly affected school climate and highlighted the roles clinical personnel can play in supporting school change. Clinical personnel met more often with groups of teachers to discuss reinforcement programs for whole classes as well as individual students with special needs. The gap between "in-classroom personnel" (teachers and paraprofessionals) and "out-of-classroom personnel" (clinical psychologists and social workers) was bridged by this positive intervention program.

The professional development program highlighted in this article recognizes the importance of creating school communities rich with approval and opportunities for success. Interactions between teachers and students that are characterized by high approval can contribute to a successful instructional program and a positive school climate, which can yield the types of academic and behavioral gains described in this work.

References

Lloyd, J. W., Forness, S. R., & Kavale, K. A. (1998). Some methods are more effective than others. *Intervention in School and Clinic, 33*, 195–200.

Polloway, E. A., Patton, J. R., & Serna, L. (2001). *Strategies for teaching learners with special needs* (7th ed.). Columbus, OH: Merrill.

Smith, T. E., Polloway, E. A., Patton, J. R., & Dowdy, C. A. (2004). *Teaching students with special needs in inclusive settings* (4th ed.). Boston: Pearson.

Acknowledgment: This work was supported by a grant from the New York Community Trust to New York University.

About the authors: Jay Gottlieb, Ph.D., is professor of special education, Department of Teaching and Learning, New York University, New York, NY. Susan Polirstok, Ed.D., is associate dean, Department of Specialized Services in Education, and professor of special education, Lehman College of the City University of New York.

Address correspondence to: Dr. Susan Polirstok, Lehman College of the City University of New York, 250 Bedford Park Boulevard West, Bronx, NY 10468. E-mail: susan.polirstok@lehman.cuny.edu

Exercise for Article 28

Factual Questions

1. The three schools were selected for this program based on requests to the district superintendent for assistance with what?

2. How did the professional development sessions typically begin?

3. Were the clinical personnel (trainers) integrated into the small-group discussion sessions?

4. What was the percent improvement in behavioral infraction reports for school A?

5. What percentage of the students in school A was reading at grade level after the professional development program?

6. Who supplied the observational data on school climate?

Questions for Discussion

7. The professional development session lasted 150 minutes. In your opinion, is this long enough for the implementation of a program such as this one? (See line 107.)

8. Keeping in mind that this is a research report and not a professional development guide, is the implementation of the program described in sufficient detail to provide you with a clear understanding of it? (See lines 107–160.)

9. In your opinion, is the observational process used by the principals to collect data on school climate described in sufficient detail? Explain. (See lines 229–268.)

10. Does it surprise you that one-third of the teachers attempted the program and dropped it within a day or two, claiming that it was not effective? Explain. (See lines 244–248.)

11. Does the data in this report convince you that this program deserves to be explored in further research? Explain.

Quality Ratings

Directions: Indicate your level of agreement with each of the following statements by circling a number from 5 for strongly agree (SA) to 1 for strongly disagree (SD). If you believe an item is not applicable to this research article, leave it blank. Be prepared to explain your ratings.

A. The introduction establishes the importance of the study.

SA   5   4   3   2   1   SD

B. The literature review establishes the context for the study.

SA   5   4   3   2   1   SD

C. The research purpose, question, or hypothesis is clearly stated.

SA   5   4   3   2   1   SD

D. The method of sampling is sound.

SA   5   4   3   2   1   SD

E. Relevant demographics (for example, age, gender, and ethnicity) are described.

SA   5   4   3   2   1   SD

F. Measurement procedures are adequate.

SA   5   4   3   2   1   SD

G. All procedures have been described in sufficient detail to permit a replication of the study.

SA   5   4   3   2   1   SD

H. The participants have been adequately protected from potential harm.

SA   5   4   3   2   1   SD

I. The results are clearly described.

SA   5   4   3   2   1   SD

J. The discussion/conclusion is appropriate.

SA   5   4   3   2   1   SD

K. Despite any flaws, the report is worthy of publication.

SA   5   4   3   2   1   SD

Article 29

The "Stay Alive From Education" (SAFE) Program: Description and Preliminary Pilot Testing*

TAMARA TUCKER WILKINS
Minnesota State University

ABSTRACT. Traffic accidents are the leading cause of death among young people in the United States. Nearly half of these accidents involve the consumption of alcohol and/or drugs, and seat belts are not worn in over 85% of all motor vehicle accidents. SAFE is a one-hour behavior modification program that informs students of the dangers associated with driving under the influence of drugs and/or alcohol and not wearing seat belts. Pretests and posttests were offered to 60 students to determine preliminary efficacy of the program. Quantitative data and open-ended comments seem to suggest that students may change their driving behaviors due to the influence of this presentation.

From *Journal of Alcohol and Drug Education*, *45*, 1–11. Copyright © 2002 by American Alcohol and Drug Information Foundation. Reprinted with permission.

Introduction

According to the National Highway Traffic Safety Administration (1996), traffic accidents are the leading cause of death among young people in the United States. Approximately 15 youths between the ages of 16 and 20 die every day from injuries incurred during a traffic crash. This rate is twice that of the general population. A vehicular accident claims the life of one teenager every 90 minutes. Nearly half these wrecks involve the consumption of alcohol and/or drugs. Seat belts are not worn in 85% to 90% of all motor vehicle accidents (National Highway Traffic Safety Administration, 1996).

Figures for Florida, the location of the current study, are even more disturbing. Florida ranks third in the nation in terms of traffic fatalities. One out of every 15 teenage drivers has a traffic accident every year, and teenage drivers are more likely to die in wrecks than any other age group. Almost two-thirds of the 2,806 traffic fatalities in 1996 involved occupants not wearing seat belts. Alcohol is a factor in one out of every three traffic fatalities (Florida Department of Highway Safety and Motor Vehicles, 1997). While teenage drivers between the ages of 15 and 17 constitute 2.2% of the state's motor vehicle operators, they appear in 5% of all vehicle crashes and represent 4% of the driver fatalities.

The budgetary outlays associated with the medical care of trauma victims are staggering. The average cost for dispatching paramedics and their equipment to an accident scene exceeds the $1,700 mark. The typical traffic fatality commands a price tag that hovers around $425,000 (U.S. Department of Transportation, 1996). Because these numbers are likely to continue their upward spiral, policy makers have a keen interest in promoting intervention programs aimed at reducing this highway carnage.

The "Stay Alive From Education" (SAFE) program was initiated by two paramedics from the Metro Dade (Miami) Fire Rescue in 1990 and was first presented in South Florida area high schools. Response was favorable, and some observers mentioned they would like to see the program take place throughout the state. As a result, various chapters of SAFE were formed throughout Florida. A "chapter" is simply a location where local emergency medical service personnel have been trained and certified to present SAFE. The Tallahassee Chapter is the first unit to include the local police department. Traffic homicide investigators and certified paramedics present a one-hour program to high school students about the dangers of driving under the influence of alcohol or drugs, not wearing seat belts, and the trauma associated with these dangers. The purpose of this manuscript is to describe the SAFE program, its goals, and report preliminary results from a pilot testing of high school students.

The SAFE program presentation consists of three phases. Introductions start the first phase. Presenters quickly move into a casual, informal discussion of the goals of the program, definitions of traumatic injury and death, and what constitutes a medical versus trauma call. Graphic photographs of traffic victims who are roughly the same age as those in the audience are passed around while various props are being set up for later use. Descriptive accounts of "what happened"

---

* For more information on the SAFE program, contact Vince Easevoili (305-852-2651) or Ralph Jimenez (305-375-9543).

65 in various photos are offered. Students learn that seat belts were not worn, that alcohol and/or other drugs were involved in all the accidents depicted, and that all of the victims they just saw in the photos died as a result of their injuries.

70   The second phase is essentially a demonstration of physics. By placing an egg in a jar and shaking it, the laws of physics are obvious when the shaking is abruptly stopped. The egg is broken, and students appear to realize that the same thing often happens to a
75 person's brain during a traffic crash. The presenter asks for a show of hands of those who do not use their seat belt all the time, no matter where they sit in the vehicle, and the reasons why. Some common responses are, "I don't think about it," "I'm too lazy," "I'm going
80 somewhere close by—right around the corner," "Seat belts are uncomfortable," "It wrinkles my clothes," "I have air bags and an automatic seat belt," or "I'm in the backseat!" The SAFE presenter, upon hearing the excuse of being in the backseat, says, "See this picture?
85 See these two guys in the backseat? They weren't wearing their seat belts. The two in the front were. The two in the back became the objects in motion, like the egg in the jar, until the movement was stopped by the heads of the two people in the front seat. When the
90 rescue team arrived at the scene, all four were dead from massive head injuries. They found the teeth of the guys in the backseat embedded in the back of the heads of the guys in the front seat."

    The third phase involves the recruitment of a stu-
95 dent volunteer who will play the part of an injured "crash victim." Paramedics demonstrate and decipher the medical consequences associated with driving while under the influence of alcohol and/or drugs. They inform students that all intoxicated persons are likely
100 not to receive pain relievers due to the high risks associated with combining drugs and/or alcohol with pain relievers and anesthesia. Likewise, they graphically depict what happens when a car accident victim does not wear a seat belt. This role playing is done in a real-
105 istic fashion by strapping a student volunteer to a backboard. Students see their fellow classmate role-play a crash victim who is strapped down and perforated with various tubes for blood and medication disbursement. The hope, of course, is that students will empatheti-
110 cally relate the experience of trauma to their own lives. Because hands-on techniques are employed rather than lectures, students gain insight of what paramedics and traffic homicide officers encounter when they respond to a traumatic traffic accident. Paramedics show stu-
115 dents how trauma victims are treated in the field on a step-by-step basis, and traffic homicide officers share their experiences of telling family members about the death of their loved ones.

    The primary goal of SAFE is to change, modify, or
120 "recondition" the behavior of students who participate in irresponsible driving behaviors so they become more responsible drivers and riders. Behavior modification

involves at least four stages. The four stages include identifying the target behavior(s), gathering baseline
125 data, developing techniques of punishment and reinforcement, and execution and evaluation (Weiten, 1994; Watson & Tharp, 1989).

    The target behaviors entail wearing a seat belt and driving "drug/alcohol" free. Paramedics and traffic
130 homicide officers offer statistics and graphic details from their personal experiences to paint a picture of real-life tragedies that stem from irresponsible driving. The "egg in the jar" demonstrates the consequences or punishments of irresponsible driving behaviors. Fur-
135 thermore, the discomfort experienced by the student volunteer who is strapped to a wooden backboard for approximately 15 minutes amplifies the message. While paramedics assure the volunteer and the audience that these feelings are minor, had a real accident
140 occurred, the pain would be intense and last significantly longer. The final stage involves encouraging observers to adopt safe driving habits. The targeted goals are to convince students to wear seat belts, require those who ride with them to wear seat belts, and
145 refuse to drive or ride with someone who is under the influence of alcohol and/or drugs.

    The tactics employed by SAFE place it within the genre of a "shock" program. It is similar to "Scared Straight," where juveniles are shocked into the realities
150 associated with incarceration. At the conclusion of the "Scared Straight" program, teens who took part in this Juvenile Awareness Project recall their experiences of the program, the time with prisoners, and the prison location or scene. Deemed successful by audiences,
155 "Scared Straight" was made into an Oscar-winning TV documentary and filmed at Rahway State Prison in New Jersey. Reasons for the program's success were perceived to be the growing crime problem (i.e., at the time), a reduction in support for rehabilitation, and a
160 "dramatic promise of a new, synthetic solution for delinquency" (Heeren & Shichor, 1984).

    While there is little conclusive evidence that shock incarceration programs have a positive effect on offender behavior over time, analyses of these programs
165 suggest that intense supervision efforts via "shock" programs play a critical role in limiting some irresponsible behaviors (MacKenzie & Brame, 1995). Several community-based intervention programs are similar in the implementation of strong "shock" techniques. An-
170 tipregnancy programs attempt to show the realities of being a full-time parent, and some AIDS prevention programs use similar "shock" format approaches. In an evaluative study of AIDS prevention programs, Ostrow (1989) offers four determinants of behavioral change as
175 crucial elements of effective education. He claims "effective education" to be the behavior-changing mechanism of choice. Determinants of behavioral change include: (1) general factual knowledge of the problem, (2) perceived susceptibility or risk, (3) perceived sever-
180 ity, and (4) perceived benefits and costs. These pro-

Table 1
Self-Report Participant Scores Prior to and One Month After Exposure to the SAFE Presentation

n = 60 Statement		Always	Most of the time	Sometimes	Never	Mean	*sd*	*t*
How often do you…								
wear your seat belt while rid-	Pretest	32	21	6	1	1.60	0.74	5.56**
ing in the front seat?	Posttest	52	8	–	–	1.13	0.34	
wear your seat belt while rid-	Pretest	7	24	16	13	2.58	0.96	3.77**
ing in the backseat?	Posttest	28	21	10	1	1.87	1.52	
ride in a car where the driver	Pretest	23	27	9	1	1.80	0.75	2.66**
wears a seat belt?	Posttest	31	25	4	–	1.55	0.62	
ride in a car where all passen-	Pretest	5	19	29	7	2.63	0.80	3.36*
gers wear seat belts?	Posttest	10	29	19	2	2.22	0.76	
ride in a car where driver has	Pretest	1	1	28	30	3.45	0.62	– 4.46**
used alcohol or drugs?	Posttest	–	1	8	51	3.83	0.42	
see other students driving in	Pretest	11	10	38	1	2.48	0.81	5.71**
an unsafe manner?	Posttest	18	27	15	–	1.95	0.75	

* Denotes significance at .01 level of analysis, two-tailed.
** Denotes significance at .001 level of analysis, two-tailed.

grams share a similar feature with the SAFE project. Each presentation is very dramatic, and presenters seek to jolt kids (and others) into a picture of reality where enormous adverse consequences derive from irrespon-
185 sible behavior.

Other preventive literature centers around the need to get entire communities involved in traffic safety education programs. Designated driver programs are one such effort. These community-based programs are
190 intended to offer intoxicated persons an alternative to getting behind the wheel and driving. A designated driver is one person in a group of two or more drinkers who agrees not to drink alcoholic beverages and to transport the members of the group home safely. Many
195 communities who participate in this type of program offer safe travel in the form of a free or subsidized taxicab ride if a designated driver is not available (National Highway Traffic Safety Administration, 1994). Other educational program efforts include Maryland's
200 "Kids in Safety Seats" Program, which targets child passenger safety; California's Contra Costa County Prevention Program, which advocates helmet usage by motorcyclists and bicyclists, and Rhode Island's Community Traffic Safety Program, which focuses on is-
205 sues related to pedestrian safety (National Highway Traffic Safety Administration, 1993).

The founders of SAFE have good intentions of rousing community support and participation. In some cities, presentations of SAFE have been offered to the
210 general public. While some individuals and groups take advantage of this opportunity, SAFE presenters are mainly concerned with the program's effectiveness on young, more risk-taking attendees. The program has not yet received any independent empirical attention to
215 determine whether it is effective. The evaluation model employed in this research project is often referred to as an "outcome model" (Adams, 1975). An outcome model seeks to ascertain how effective or efficient an agency or program is in attaining goals. Determining

220 the impact of SAFE on *stated* attitudinal and participant *reported* behavioral changes is the primary goal of this descriptive and evaluative research project.

Procedure

Several local high school classes participated in the SAFE program during the spring of 1998. Quantitative
225 data and open-ended questionnaires were obtained using self-administered surveys. The data set for this study is made up of two participating classes, for a total of 60 students. Regular attendees of two high school classes were selected based upon convenience to the
230 SAFE presenters. It was not necessary to gain parental consent in order to distribute questionnaires to students. The information was collected both before the program presentation and 30 days later. This pretest/posttest design is a common tool in evaluating in-
235 tervention strategies.

Upon arrival for the program, students completed a pretest or pre-program survey. Demographics were asked in an attempt to ascertain identifiable characteristics. That is, participants' date of birth, sex, and
240 race/ethnicity were asked in order to match the anonymous questionnaires. One month after the SAFE program was presented, the same participants were offered a post-program survey. The follow-up questionnaire was designed exactly like the pre-program question-
245 naire with one exception: Students were asked whether they thought the SAFE program should be repeated for new students and the reasons behind their feelings. Sixty pre-program surveys were matched by demographic information with post-program surveys and
250 serve as the study group.

Results

The study group participants were 52% male (*n* = 31) and 48% female (*n* = 29). Concerning race and/or ethnicity, 60% stated they were white, 37% marked black, and 3% chose Hispanic. As of April 1, 1998, all
255 participants were of legal driving age in Florida. One

person was 18 years of age, 18 students were 17 years old, and 41 were 16 years old.

Table 1 presents the results of a paired-samples *t* test, which compares the means for responses offered in the pretest and the posttest. Average scores concerning how often students claim to wear a seat belt while riding in the front seat dropped from the original mean score of 1.60 to 1.13 during the posttest period. Because wearing a seat belt while riding in the front seat is required by state law, many students probably already engage in such behavior on a regular basis. For those who profess to use a seat belt less often, it appears that statistically significant changes were indicated. In other words, a month later, SAFE participants reported a higher level of seat-belt usage while riding in the front seat. Students specify they are more likely to use a seat belt while in the backseat as well (*t* = 3.77, *p* = .01). Thus, it would appear that the SAFE program satisfied its desired goal of altering stated seat belt use.

While students have little or no control over what another driver does concerning the use of safety belts, there is a significant difference between the first and second timeframes under evaluation (*t* = 2.66, *p* = .01). It may be that the SAFE presentation made students more adept at noticing when a driver was or was not wearing a seat belt. Two students even offered comments to the fact that they will now say something or put pressure on their friends and family members to "always" fasten their seat belts.

The fourth question under evaluation deals with the frequency of riding in a motor vehicle when all passengers are wearing seat belts. The difference from Phase I to Phase II was also statistically significant. This finding may also reflect the assumption that persons of this age group have little or no control over what others do, but at least they may ask others to buckle up.

Perhaps the most risky of driving behaviors involves the driver's use of alcohol and/or drugs. Both before and after the SAFE presentation, students know driving under the influence of alcohol and/or drugs is dangerous. Statistically significant differences were found from Time 1 to Time 2. Prior to the SAFE presentation, 30 students said that they would sometimes (or more frequently) ride with a driver they knew was intoxicated, and 30 students said they would "never" ride with an intoxicated driver. After the presentation, 51 of the 60 students under evaluation declared they would "never" ride with a driver who had been drinking alcohol and/or using drugs. Subjects were also asked how often they see other students driving in an unsafe manner. Statistically significant differences are detected, with more students seeing unsafe driving occurring more frequently (*t* = 5.71, *p* = .01). While not entirely conclusive, it is quite possible that the differences may be due to an increased level of awareness by participants as dramatically stressed by the SAFE program presenters.

Students were asked if the SAFE program should be repeated next year for new students and why. Of the 60 responses, all but one student said the program should be made available. Once again, the written comments about the SAFE presentation were overwhelmingly positive:

"Yes, definitely! It gives us a huge reality check of what could happen when [driving and] using drugs/alcohol and not wearing a seat belt."

"The SAFE program reviewed a lot of things I already knew, but it taught me a lot of new things too."

"It opened my eyes to what can really happen when you get into a wreck."

"The students who come here next year need to learn this stuff the same as us. It helps."

"Those pictures scared us. They made us think. Others need to learn to think too."

"It changed my views about driving in an unsafe manner."

"If I wouldn't have seen those pictures, a seat belt would never cross my mind."

"It put that lasting thought about not wearing seat belts in my mind."

Finally, it is important to mention that neither sex nor racial background played a role in how the program was perceived, as indicated by an analysis of variance (i.e., ANOVA) or test comparison of Phase I to Phase II. In other words, no systematic differences or effects were found to be statistically relevant based on the demographic characteristics of participants. This may be evidence the program generates a fairly uniform picture for all students regardless of social category.

Limitations of the Study

There are, at minimum, four major limitations to the present study. First, this study only describes the SAFE program and reports on stated behavioral changes. Any actual changes in driving behavior cannot be calculated. This preliminary study was undertaken to simply describe the program and to ask students if they thought the program was effective. It was not in the scope of this project to physically observe any behavioral changes.

Second, there was no control group involved. Students who participated in the SAFE presentation were not compared to students who were absent, dropped out of high school, or who did not attend a SAFE demonstration. This makes the significance of any outcome measure dubious and uncertain.

Third, only short-term self-reported effects are included in the evaluation. Whether or not any long-term effects or lasting impacts result in behavioral changes simply cannot be determined. In order to conclude any long-term or ultimate effects, the same sample of students would have to complete another questionnaire at some point in the future. Because high school drivers serve as the primary SAFE presentation population, it is unlikely that a follow-up, long-term study will be tackled. Locating the same participating subjects after an extended period of time (e.g., after graduation) would require both time and money.

Fourth, the sample was selected out of convenience to those collecting the data and is relatively small in number ($n = 60$). Thus, any conclusions drawn from this study may be exaggerated and empirically limited. In a future study, a systematic sampling frame should be developed and sample size increased. These two steps would help increase inference or the ability to generalize results to an overall population.

Discussion

The purpose of this study was to describe and evaluate the "Scared Straight" driving behavior-modification program known as SAFE. The evidence shows that this program does change or modify responses regarding irresponsible driving in the short-term. However, it is not known whether it generates any behavior or long-term educational effects. Knowing that the program has short-term benefits, school and police administrators may want to manipulate student behavior by presenting SAFE just prior to those "special occasions" that are marked by high traffic fatality rates. For example, some thought might go into conducting a SAFE campaign one week prior to homecoming, the senior prom, graduation, or another event that has the potential to be marred by traffic accidents and their aftermath. Additionally, a "booster" presentation may be helpful as one might anticipate the program would experience a decaying effect with the passage of time. Until a longitudinal design is implemented, it is difficult to say just what degree of decay exists.

High school students are the primary targets of the current SAFE project. However, college students, and even the public at large, may be appropriate participants in the SAFE program should funding for such be available. If the changes are as dramatic as the high school student participants openly state, the current figures may indicate a potentially downward trend in the rate of traffic fatalities. If increased awareness occurs and responsible driving behaviors replace irresponsible ones, for whatever length of time, the result may be health instead of harm and/or life rather than death.

Last, the demand for evaluative research has surged in recent years. Because of budgetary constraints and limitations, studying the process and effectiveness of particular programs is necessary (Williamson, Karp, Dalphin, & Gray, 1992). Economic costs are involved in programs like this one, but these costs are incomparable to that of the human suffering and loss of life, which all too often accompany irresponsible driving behaviors. While limited by the time period under evaluation, this research project indicates the SAFE program is well received by participants and is a potentially relevant and beneficial behavior modification program.

References

Adams, S. (1975). *Evaluative research in corrections: A practical guide.* Washington, D.C.: U.S. Department of Justice.

Florida Department of Highway Safety and Motor Vehicles. (1997). *Publication of annual statistics.* Tallahassee, FL: State of Florida.

Heeren, J., & Shichor, D. (1984). Mass media and delinquency prevention: The case of Scared Straight. *Deviant Behavior, 5*(1–4), 375–386.

MacKenzie, D., & Brame, R. (1995). Shock incarceration and positive adjustment during community supervision. *Journal of Quantitative Criminology, 11*(2), 111–142.

National Highway Traffic Safety Administration. (1996). *Annual publication.* Washington, D.C.: Government Printing Office.

National Highway Traffic Safety Administration. (1994). *A guide to developing a community-based designated driver program.* Washington, D.C.: Government Printing Office.

National Highway Traffic Safety Administration. (1993). *Commitment, communication, cooperation: Traffic safety and public health working together to prevent traffic injury.* Washington, D.C.: Government Printing Office.

Ostrow, D. G. (1989). AIDS prevention through effective education (Living with AIDS: Part II). *Daedalus, 118*(3): 229.

United States Department of Transportation. (1996). *Annual report.* Washington, D.C.: Government Printing Office.

Watson, D., & Tharp, R. (1989). *Self-directed behavior: Self-modification for personal adjustment.* Pacific Grove, CA: Brooks and Cole Publishing Co.

Weiten, W. (1994). *Psychology: Themes and variations* (2nd ed.). Pacific Grove, CA.

Williamson, J., Karp, D., Dalphin, J., & Gray, P. (1992). *The research craft: An introduction to social research methods.* Glenview, IL: Scott, Foresman and Company.

Address correspondence to: Tamara Tucker Wilkins, 109 Morris Hall—Dept. of Law Enforcement, Minnesota State University, Mankato, MN 56001-8400. Phone: (507) 389-1118 or 389-2721. E-mail: tamara.wilkins@mankato.msus.edu

Exercise for Article 29

Factual Questions

1. In Florida, teenage drivers between the ages of 15 and 17 constitute 2.2% of the state's motor vehicle operators. They appear in what percentage of all vehicle crashes?

2. In "Scared Straight," juveniles are shocked into the realities associated with what?

3. On the pretest, how many students reported always wearing seat belts while riding in the backseat? How many students reported always doing this on the posttest?

4. Was the difference between the two means for riding in a car where the driver has used alcohol or drugs statistically significant? If yes, at what probability level was it significant?

5. In response to the question regarding whether the SAFE program should be repeated next year for new students, how many answered in the affirmative?

6. The researcher discusses four limitations of this evaluation. What is the third limitation?

Questions for Discussion

7. In your opinion, are the three phases of the program described in sufficient detail? Explain. (See lines 56–118.)

8. To calculate the means in Table 1, a score of 1 was assigned to "Always," a score of 2 to "Most of the time," a score of 3 to "Sometimes," and a score of 4 to "Never." Hence, for wearing your seat belt while riding in the front seat, the *decrease* in the mean from 1.60 to 1.13 indicates a change of behavior in the desired direction (i.e., more students wearing seat belts). Would you have scored the questions in this way? If not, would you have given a score of 4 to "Always," a score of 3 to "Most of the time," and so on? Explain.

9. The Results section includes both quantitative and qualitative information. (See lines 319–335 for qualitative results.) In your opinion, are both types of information equally important? If not, which do you think is more important? Explain.

10. The researcher notes that this evaluation is limited because it reports on only "stated behavioral changes." In other words, it depends on self-reports. In your opinion, is this an important limitation? Explain. (See lines 345–379.)

11. The researcher notes that there was no control group. In your opinion, is this an important limitation? Explain. (See lines 354–359.)

12. If you were a member of a school board, would you be inclined to vote to fund the SAFE program based on the information in this study? Would you request that the program be evaluated again (if it were funded in your school district)? Explain. (See lines 414–421.)

Quality Ratings

Directions: Indicate your level of agreement with each of the following statements by circling a number from 5 for strongly agree (SA) to 1 for strongly disagree (SD). If you believe an item is not applicable to this research article, leave it blank. Be prepared to explain your ratings.

A. The introduction establishes the importance of the study.

SA   5   4   3   2   1   SD

B. The literature review establishes the context for the study.

SA   5   4   3   2   1   SD

C. The research purpose, question, or hypothesis is clearly stated.

SA   5   4   3   2   1   SD

D. The method of sampling is sound.

SA   5   4   3   2   1   SD

E. Relevant demographics (for example, age, gender, and ethnicity) are described.

SA   5   4   3   2   1   SD

F. Measurement procedures are adequate.

SA   5   4   3   2   1   SD

G. All procedures have been described in sufficient detail to permit a replication of the study.

SA   5   4   3   2   1   SD

H. The participants have been adequately protected from potential harm.

SA   5   4   3   2   1   SD

I. The results are clearly described.

SA   5   4   3   2   1   SD

J. The discussion/conclusion is appropriate.

SA   5   4   3   2   1   SD

K. Despite any flaws, the report is worthy of publication.

SA   5   4   3   2   1   SD

Article 30

Looking for a Struggle: Exploring the Emotions of a Middle School Reader

CHERI FOSTER TRIPLETT
Virginia Polytechnic Institute and State University

ABSTRACT. Struggling readers often feel alienated from teachers and frustrated by social comparisons. However, it is possible to create contexts in which struggling readers experience success and begin to redefine themselves.

From *Journal of Adolescent & Adult Literacy, 48,* 214–222. Copyright © 2004 by International Reading Association. Reprinted with permission.

The purpose of this case study was to explore a middle school student's emotions in the tutoring context in order to better understand the "struggles" facing a struggling reader. The study revolved around a sixth
5　grader, Mitchell; his mother, Joan (both names are pseudonyms); and me—his reading tutor. When we first talked about the possibility of tutoring for Mitchell, Joan's eyes welled up with tears. She reported that Mitchell had struggled with reading since
10　the early grades but had learned some compensatory strategies that had helped him. Now in the sixth grade, Mitchell was reading at a third-grade level, and according to Joan, reading had become increasingly frustrating for him.

15　The terms *struggling*, *frustrated*, and *tears* immediately brought to mind an array of negative emotions. As a tutor, I was interested in exploring the emotions of this struggling reader. Could Mitchell's emotions offer clues about how to help him? After reading literature in
20　cognitive psychology explaining that emotions are a result of our individual interpretations of particular situations or contexts, I was convinced that studying a student's emotions could provide clues about how that student is interpreting the tutoring context. I was also
25　convinced that understanding the emotions of a struggling reader could benefit other tutors and teachers as well.

A Cognitive Explanation of Emotions

According to research in cognitive psychology, emotions emerge from a conceptual appraisal process
30　in which an individual infers and interprets to make sense of a situation. Initial or primary appraisals are made concerning the personal relevance of the situation, followed by secondary appraisals concerning perceived control over the situation (Lazarus, 1991; Smith,

35　1991). Emotions such as happiness or pride are linked to primary appraisals that a situation is beneficial to the individual. Emotions such as anger or fear are linked to primary appraisals that a situation is harmful to the individual. Differentiations between challenge and
40　frustration, pride and gratitude are distinguished by secondary appraisals. For instance, pride and gratitude have identical primary appraisals of personal benefit, but they are distinguished by the secondary appraisal of accountability. Pride is a result of perceived self-
45　accountability. Gratitude is a result of perceived "other-accountability" (Parkinson, 1994; Smith, 1991).

This appraisal process may help to explain some of the emotions encountered in previous literacy research. For example, Oldfather (1994) discovered a range of
50　feelings associated with students' experiences when not motivated for literacy learning. Students openly expressed anger and helplessness. Some students' statements were direct appraisals that learning situations were out of their control and that they were not
55　accountable for their frustrations. For instance, one angry student explained, "Teachers kind of get on your back and everything. I really get mad" (p. 13). If we use the appraisal process to interpret this student's anger, we know he perceives the learning context as
60　somehow harmful or not beneficial (primary appraisal), and that he perceives another as accountable for the situation (secondary appraisal). Also, in Allen, Michalove, and Shockley (1993), one student's pride was evidenced in his comments: "I'm learning to
65　read!... Want me to show you?... Want me to read it to you?...Ooh, this is my favorite part!" (p. 71). Another student was grateful to those around her for their assistance: "I read big words. Ms. Willis and Ms. Shockley read books and I read and they tell it when I don't
70　know a word. I learn if I read. Ms. Shockley, Ms. Willis, and my sister, my eleven-year-old sister, will help" (p. 105). In their quotes, these students revealed that the ability to read is personally relevant and beneficial (primary appraisals), but they differed in their
75　secondary appraisals of accountability. The first student saw himself as accountable; he expressed the confidence and excitement that often accompany feelings of pride. The second student consistently mentioned

those who helped her; she expressed gratitude toward her teachers and her sister.

A Social Explanation of Emotions

These cognitive explanations of emotion did help me to understand our tutoring interactions; however, they only seemed to scratch the surface of the emotional issues surrounding Mitchell's struggle to be a successful reader. Thus, after analyzing data for only a short period, I realized that there were themes that were better explained by social theories. In essence, I realized that Mitchell's struggle was not just a result of his individual interpretation of one particular context— Mitchell's struggle was being socially constructed in a variety of contexts and in numerous relationships.

Social constructionism emphasizes that knowledge is formulated between participants in a social relationship (Hruby, 2001). This theory is somewhat different from the social *constructivism* attributed to Vygotsky, in that constructivism can be considered a cognitive description of knowledge and *constructionism* can be considered a social description of knowledge. Emotions have likewise been described from a social constructionist perspective. Scheff (1997) explained that emotions are created within our social relationships. He described feelings of enjoyment and pride as associated with relationships of solidarity. He described feelings of shame, fear, anger, and indifference and associated them with alienating relationships. By situating thoughts and feelings within social contexts, social constructionism provides a framework for understanding how interactions in a classroom can influence a student's emotional responses and how a student's struggle can be socially constructed.

Literacy research framed by social constructionism (Hinchman, Bourcy, Thomas, & Olcott, 2002; McCarthey, 2001; Moje, 2000) has detailed how particular contexts and particular relationships help to construct students' literacy identities, including notions of struggle. McCarthey (2001) concluded that students who identify well with school and with teachers tend to be more successful in school literacy practices and those who find their identities defined by other aspects of their lives may not be as successful in school literacy practices.

Procedures and Methods

This qualitative study took place in the context of tutoring during four months of biweekly, one-hour sessions. All data collection took place in and around the tutoring context or in the small university snack shop, where parents often waited to pick up their children. Written retrospective narratives and interviews informed me of what took place in Mitchell's reading history before I began to tutor. Other data sources included field notes (i.e., theoretical, methodological, tutorial, and personal), artifacts, and ongoing tape-recorded interviews. Triangulation of perspectives was an important aspect of this case study. The emic per-

spectives of parent and student, or what may be termed *lay theories*, provided a richer, more intersubjective explanation of the emotions in this context (Mathison, 1993).

Constant comparative methods (Glaser & Strauss, 1967; Strauss & Corbin, 1990) were used for data analysis. Although constant comparative analysis originated in the context of grounded theory (Glaser & Strauss), it has been used in a variety of educational studies as an analytic induction method—even in studies not intending to develop grounded theory (Merriam, 1998). In this study, constant comparative methods were not used for the purpose of developing theory but for their systematic approach. This approach involves closely attending to data sources and noticing what patterns emerge (open coding), noting categories or themes, and then beginning to describe the properties that exemplify each category by comparing and contrasting subsequent data.

Constant comparative analysis provides an opportunity to recognize and use the recursiveness of the research process. As categories are identified, a type of theoretical sampling takes place in which emerging concepts influence subsequent data collection. At the same time, data are revisited in order to clarify the categories and subcategories. The findings are then discussed in relation to theories from the original literature review and in relation to new theories to explain unfamiliar categories (Strauss & Corbin, 1990). For example, one category or theme that emerged during data collection was Mitchell's socioemotional relationship with teachers. I sought other explanations because this category was not best explained by the literature in cognitive psychology. Visiting the social constructionist literature provided a richer, more colorful and thus more credible interpretation of the data (Lather, 1991).

Other measures were also taken to provide credibility. Triangulation of perspectives, triangulation of data sources, and member checks (LeCompte & Preissle, 1993; Merriam, 1998) validated emerging categories. Member checks consisted of open-ended interviews in which I asked for feedback or clarification regarding emerging concepts, as well as informal conversations throughout to share my own thoughts about what I was interpreting.

Findings and Discussion

Cognitive Explanations: Looking for a Struggle

As I began to notice particular patterns of emotion in the tutoring context, I was perplexed when I did not see or hear any evidence of a struggle. I assumed I would hear negative emotions expressed, such as frustration, anger, or disappointment because of Mitchell's reading history. Joan explained that Mitchell had always struggled with reading and that he had worked with many tutors. She said, "He is always falling apart when he works on his reading, writing, and spelling.... He often cries." Even during our first meeting together,

190 when some students seem apprehensive about working with a new person, Mitchell seemed relaxed and somewhat relieved that our initial meeting was focused on conversation instead of testing. Likewise, throughout our semester together, Mitchell expressed positive emotions about tutoring:

195   Mitchell: [interview] I like funny books like this, and like *Matilda* [Dahl, 1998, Puffin], they make me laugh!

      Cheri: [field notes] Mitchell and I laugh a lot! We both love this book!

200   Joan: [interview] I've noticed that I hear you both laughing when I pass by your office…. I thought, well, they sound like they are having a good time!

Fun, laughter, and enjoyment were expressed in the 205 context of tutoring. For example, one afternoon as Joan and I were discussing Mitchell's progress over a cup of coffee, I told her how much I enjoyed getting to know Mitchell and that "he is fun, interesting, and thoughtful." She said that "he always really enjoyed tutoring" 210 and that "he looked forward to it!" These contextual responses of fun, laughter, and enjoyment indicate primary appraisals of personal benefit.

All three case study participants also consistently commented on Mitchell's obvious pride and success in 215 reading tasks. During one session, I recorded my thoughts as Mitchell reacted to his obvious success on a spelling assessment:

[Mitchell is pleased. I can tell as we go along by his expression…he is obviously excited!]

220   Cheri: What do you think about that? You spelled 17 out of 20 words correctly and distinguished between the short vowel *a* and short vowel *e*!

    Mitchell: [with a coy grin on his face] I'm good!

      Cheri: Yes, indeed!

225 Mitchell also began to experience some pride in his successes at school. He came to my office a little early one day and excitedly reported, "When I have reading or spelling at school, I've noticed that I am reading the big words a lot better! I have also noticed when I am 230 spelling…that I am not getting mixed up." According to the emotion appraisal process, pride and success can be linked to secondary appraisals of self-accountability.

Emotions and Motivation in Literacy Contexts

What aspects of tutoring may have influenced Mitchell's appraisal of personal benefit, resulting in 235 feelings of fun, laughter, and enjoyment? What aspects of tutoring may have influenced Mitchell's appraisal of self-accountability, resulting in feelings of pride and success? Several aspects of tutoring contributed to Mitchell's positive feelings, such as having opportuni-240 ties to make choices, participating in activities that were personally relevant, working within his instructional level, and having opportunities to experience

success. These aspects were apparent in my notes from our first meeting:

245 We spent the first 20 minutes talking about Mitchell's upcoming soccer trip…. We talked about the kinds of books Mitchell likes to read. He mentioned *Matilda*, so we discussed Roald Dahl and compared the movie *Matilda* with the book…. The last 30 minutes, Mitchell read aloud three 250 different passages from the Qualitative Reading Inventory—second-, third-, and fourth-grade passages. He seemed relieved that I asked him to read "easy stuff" before we moved on to the passages that were more difficult.

I continued to focus on choice and personal rele-255 vance throughout the semester. Each book that we read together was a book that Mitchell chose to read, based on his own interests. We spent a lot of time laughing over books like *There's a Boy in the Girls' Bathroom* (Sachar, 1988, Yearling), *The Mouse and the Motorcy-260 cle* (Cleary, 1990, HarperTrophy), and *Matilda* because Mitchell liked funny books. We also spent time reading soccer magazines and newspaper articles about World Cup Soccer. Writing opportunities came from these readings, such as writing predictions about what would 265 happen in the next chapter or writing about a favorite soccer player. Writing opportunities also arose from personal narratives such as a fishing trip in which Mitchell caught a huge shark. Personal letter writing and letter reading were a natural part of Mitchell's de-270 sire to keep in touch with his friends and family—these were a vital part of our concentration on reading, writing, and spelling. For example, Mitchell wrote a letter to his mother. We looked for spelling errors in his first draft, circling a few obvious mistakes. We then used 275 those particular spelling patterns to create a word sort together by writing words in columns, cutting them apart, and sorting them again into appropriate columns.

Oldfather and Wigfield (1996) explained that students feel motivated for literacy learning when they

280 experience learning environments as places to pursue personal interests, as places in which they can achieve at least some degree of self-determination and participation in shaping aspects of their own learning agenda, as places 285 in which their ideas and their literate actions are taken seriously. (p. 101)

Unfortunately, Mitchell perceived most of his experiences of reading, writing, and spelling at school as "not very interesting." He reported a literacy history of boredom, anxiety over testing, competition for points 290 and grades, rarely getting to choose what he read, and always reading "hard stuff."

Reading, writing, and spelling within Mitchell's instructional level certainly benefited his feelings of success. Through ongoing assessment, such as running 295 records, spelling inventories, and writing samples, I was able to be attentive to his growth so that tasks were challenging but not frustrating. Morris (1996) identified "diligent, unrelenting attention to instructional level" as essential to success in tutoring. I also realized 300 early on that Mitchell had difficulty recognizing and celebrating his own successes. Each week I asked him to focus on what he did well, such as reading with expression, breaking down big words by looking at syllables, or sorting numerous words into the correct word-pattern column. Asking Mitchell to be attentive to his successes no doubt contributed to his feelings of pride—for once, he had an opportunity to think of himself as a successful reader.

Social Explanations: Contexts and Relationships of Struggle

Social relationships were very important to Mitchell, and his mother and I both noticed that he had unique socioemotional strengths. Joan commented, "Mitchell will make it in this world…. He always has good friends, he's often the leader of his social group, [and] he's very popular with the other kids." Comments like these from his mother and my ongoing notes about Mitchell's emphasis on social relationships caused me to query, "Mitchell talks about his friends a lot: playing with friends, wanting to finish his work so he can talk with friends, how he hopes to have good friends when he moves to Alabama. Do most kids talk about their friends this much?" When we were able to use this strength through writing letters to friends and family, writing personal stories, and reading books that highlighted relationships (e.g., *There's a Boy in the Girls' Bathroom*), Mitchell flourished.

Social comparisons at school. Mitchell's socioemotional strengths were often portrayed in his ability to empathize with his peers. Throughout our four months together, Mitchell expressed concerns about the social comparisons made in his literacy experiences. He expressed concern for himself but also for his peers. For example, Mitchell reported "feeling bad" in years past when he "never got the prizes" offered by Accelerated Reader. However, he also reported that he "felt bad for his friends" from other classes who were not good readers because they never got their points and they "hated Accelerated Reader." Mitchell relayed a history of concerns over Accelerated Reader. He was happy to finally have a teacher who treated students "fair" when it came to Accelerated Reader points. In an informal, audiotaped interview he explained that he was really happy that his teacher set goals that everyone could reach:

Mitchell: Other classes have to do more. I think they have to read a bunch of books for points to get…like cameras and other big prizes like that…and some kids can't read that many and they don't get prizes.

Cheri: Does everybody get the points they need in your class?

Mitchell: Yeah, last time we all got the points we need…we all got [an ice cream] bar!

Mitchell also reported some embarrassment about the color codes that were used on Accelerated Reader books to mark their level. He said his friends always knew when he got a third-grade book, and that sometimes he checked out "books that are really too hard" because his friends were reading them. Unfortunately, other social comparisons plagued Mitchell's reading history as well. When I asked him to tell me more about reading third-grade books, Mitchell immediately reported frustration over always being in the "low reading group." He seemed to be angry about this issue when he talked about it. When I asked Mitchell to explain how these reading groups made him feel, he replied, "I just…I really don't know what to say…it just made me feel dumb."

Although there have been studies reporting positive effects (McGinn & Parrish, 2002; Topping & Paul, 1999), Accelerated Reader has also been criticized for its competitive reward system (Biggers, 2001; Stevenson & Camarata, 2000). Extrinsic rewards and incentive programs like those offered by Accelerated Reader have also been criticized for decreasing students' intrinsic motivation to read (Carter, 1996; Gambrell, 1996; Pavonetti, Brimmer, & Cipielewski, 2003). Likewise, ability grouping has received a wide range of criticisms, from lack of effectiveness to negative emotional effects on students (Allington, 1983; Slavin, 1986). Although teachers and researchers in the early 1990s (Allington, 1992; Berghoff & Egawa, 1991; Flood, Lapp, Flood, & Nagel, 1992) suggested an alternative to ability grouping with the use of flexible groupings, teachers and researchers continue to debate the issue (Pallas, Entwisle, Alexander, & Stluka, 1994; Wilkinson & Townsend, 2000; Worthy & Hoffman, 1996).

Socioemotional relationships. One-on-one tutoring gave Mitchell and me the time to develop a positive and supportive socioemotional relationship. This was essential to Mitchell's success in tutoring. We began each tutoring session by catching up on our daily lives and recording our personal thoughts in our notebooks. He shared stories about fishing trips and soccer matches. I shared stories about hiking trips and books I was reading.

Mitchell had positive and supportive socioemotional relationships with his friends, his family, his coach, and his tutor. Mitchell described talking with these people in a relational and personal way. For instance, Mitchell said his coach was "like a friend 'cause he's nice and jokes around with me and my friends…and talks with me and my friends." He likewise described his mother as his friend. Joan and Mitchell continuously expressed pride in each other's accomplishments. It is interesting that enjoyment, fun, laughter, and pride were expressed about these relationships. Scheff (1997), explaining the importance of our socioemotional relationships from a social constructionist perspective, relayed that feelings of enjoyment and pride in relationships evidence solidarity and interdependence.

Scheff (1997) described a type of "We-ness" associated with relationships of interdependence. Unfortunately, the relationships that could not be defined by this "We-ness" were Mitchell's relationships with most teachers. The talk that Mitchell associated with many teachers was directive in nature but not relational. When I asked Mitchell to explain the difference between his coach and his teachers, he poignantly replied, "The teachers that like you as a person...they also think you are smart. They talk and laugh and talk to you in the hallways and stuff. Then there are ones who don't really talk to you at all. You don't know what they think of you," Mitchell's interpretation of his interactions with most teachers involved anger, fear, and indifference. Mitchell shared with me that he was often afraid to ask his teachers for help because "they'll get mad like you didn't listen or something." Joan concurred that relationships with teachers had been "a constant battle."

As I tried to make sense of Mitchell's thoughts about certain relationships with adults, I began an open-ended interview to make sure I was getting the message straight. Even after four months of developing camaraderie, I was jarred by his candor.

Cheri: Mitchell, I wanted to ask you some questions today because I want to see if I'm getting the message straight here, OK? [Mitchell nods.] You've told me a lot about your coach and your teachers. How is your coach like your teachers? Or how is he different from your teachers?

Mitchell: [He pauses and seems to be thinking about it.] I have seven teachers, right? Only one, my third-period teacher, he's the only one that I can remember ever joking around with me and my friends and stuff. That teacher is like my coach—then all the other teachers, they just don't like teaching so they don't kid around and stuff...that's different from my coach.

Cheri: So, are you saying that your coach likes coaching soccer, but most of your teachers don't like teaching?

Mitchell: Well, they are always in a bad mood...getting mad...and yelling at kids...like they don't like being around you.

Cheri: So, your third-period teacher is like your coach? [Mitchell nods.] How else are they alike?

Mitchell: They joke around and talk...and they try to make it fun.

Cheri: Are they trying to be friends with you?

Mitchell: Yeah and like, the sixth-period teacher, she definitely doesn't want to be friends. She doesn't care if all the kids hate her!

Cheri: Well, does your coach like what he is coaching? I mean, does he like soccer? [Mitchell nods.] But what about your teachers...do they—

Mitchell: [Mitchell interrupts with an answer before I finish the question.] They don't like what they teach and they don't like teaching.

Social constructionism and literacy identity. Mitchell's anger and fear evidenced his alienation from school literacy contexts. Similar to McCarthey's (2001) findings, Mitchell did not identify with school or with teachers and had not experienced success in school literacy contexts or in relationships with teachers. Although Mitchell did not see himself as a successful reader or writer, he saw himself as a successful soccer player. McCarthey (2001) concluded "teachers need to provide students with opportunities to connect their literate selves with other aspects of their identity" (p. 145). When Mitchell's interests (i.e., soccer, socioemotional relationships, humor) were incorporated into our reading and writing activities, Mitchell began to redefine himself as a reader and writer.

McCarthey and Moje (2002) further highlighted how contexts can influence our identities, including the way we are positioned by people and practices. The social comparisons made in school literacy contexts made Mitchell feel dumb. He expressed anger, embarrassment, and frustration associated with reading groups and Accelerated Reader. Because there were no social comparisons in our one-on-one tutoring context, Mitchell was able to focus on his own successes and recognize his own improvements. Likewise, a one-on-one context gave us the opportunity to develop a positive and supportive socioemotional relationship.

Because Mitchell made meaning through relationships, he perceived the amount of and nature of verbal interaction between himself and teachers to be a key factor in his understanding of who he was as a learner. It is possible that teachers differentiated their feedback to Mitchell because he has had difficulty in school. There is research supporting the fact that teachers respond differently to those who are struggling, including more directives and less relational feedback (Allington, 1983). Phelps and Weaver's (1999) research, exploring the public and personal voices of adolescents in literacy classrooms, revealed that relationships with teachers have a major influence on students' willingness to participate in classroom dialogue. These researchers discovered that students did not speak up when they feared ridicule from the teacher. Qualitative accounts of successful literacy instruction include descriptions of teachers who take time to build personal relationships with individual students (Dillon, 1989; Ladson-Billings, 1994; Oldfather, 1994).

Create a Context for Success

This study offers insight into the context-specific and relationship-specific emotions of a literacy learner. A student's feelings of enjoyment tell us that he interprets his experience as personally beneficial. Feelings of pride tell us that he sees himself as accountable for his successes. Feelings of anger and frustration signal that he sees that someone else is responsible for his lack of success. If a reader is feeling a struggle, then he or she interprets the situation as not beneficial, and the reader interprets that someone else is accountable for the experience. Likewise, this study identifies the specific aspects of tutoring that contributed to Mitchell's feelings of enjoyment and pride, such as having opportunities to make choices, participating in activities that were personally relevant, working within his instructional level, and focusing on his successes. As a tutor, I was able to create a context in which Mitchell did not experience feelings of struggle.

Also, this look at one middle school reader's emotions helps us to understand how feelings related to struggle, such as anger, frustration, and fear, can be socially constructed in particular contexts and in particular relationships. It is unfortunate that Mitchell experienced a literacy struggle at school and with teachers. The social comparisons made through reading groups and Accelerated Reader made Mitchell feel dumb. Lack of personal relevance in reading and writing activities made Mitchell feel unmotivated. Relationships with teachers made Mitchell feel fearful, angry, and alienated.

This study questions the notion of struggle and our practice of labeling students as struggling readers. If we consider that Mitchell was a successful literacy learner in one context and a struggling reader in another context, then we are challenged to create contexts in which a student experiences success. According to McCarthey and Moje (2002), "When we consider identities to be social constructions, and thus always open for change and conflict depending on the social interaction we find ourselves in, we open possibilities for rethinking the labels we so easily use to identify students" (p. 230).

References

Allen, J., Michalove, B., & Shockley, B. (1993). *Engaging children: Community and chaos in the lives of young literacy learners.* Portsmouth. NH: Heinemann.

Allington, R. (1983). The reading instruction provided readers of differing reading abilities. *Elementary School Journal, 83,* 548–559.

Allington, R. (1992). Reconsidering instructional groupings. *Reading Horizons, 32,* 349–355.

Berghoff, B., & Egawa, K. (1991). No more "rocks": Grouping to give students control of their learning. *The Reading Teacher, 44,* 536–541.

Biggers, D. (2001). The argument against Accelerated Reader. *Journal of Adolescent & Adult Literacy, 45,* 72–75.

Carter, B. (1996). Hold the applause!: Do Accelerated Reader and Electronic Bookshelf send the right message? *School Library Journal, 42,* 22–25.

Dillon, D. (1989). Showing them that I want them to learn and that I care about who they are: A microethnography. *American Educational Research Journal, 26,* 227–259.

Flood, J., Lapp, D., Flood, S., & Nagel, G. (1992). Am I allowed to group? Using flexible patterns for effective instruction. *The Reading Teacher, 45,* 608–616.

Gambrell, L. (1996). Creating classroom cultures that foster reading motivation. *The Reading Teacher, 50,* 14–25.

Glaser, B. G., & Strauss, A. L. (1967). *The discovery of grounded theory: Strategies for qualitative research.* Chicago: Aldine.

Hinchman, K., Bourcy, L., Thomas, H., & Olcott, K. (2002). Representing adolescents' literacies: Case studies of three white males. *Reading Research and Instruction, 3,* 229–246.

Hruby, G. (2001). Sociological, postmodern, and new realism perspectives in social constructionism: Implications for literacy research. *Reading Research Quarterly, 36,* 48–62. doi: 10.1598/RRQ.36.1.3

Ladson-Billings, G. (1994). *The dreamkeepers: Successful teachers of African American children.* San Francisco: Jossey-Bass.

Lather, P. (1991). *Getting smart: Feminist research and pedagogy within the postmodern.* New York: Routledge.

Lazarus, R. S. (1991). *Emotion and adaptation.* Oxford, UK: Oxford University Press.

LeCompte, M., & Preissle, J. (1993). *Ethnography and qualitative design in educational research.* New York: Academic Press.

Mathison, S. (1993). From practice to theory to practice. In D. Flinders & G. Mills (Eds.), *Theory and concepts in qualitative research: Perspectives from the field* (pp. 55–67). New York: Teachers College Press.

McCarthey, S. (2001). Identity construction in elementary readers and writers. *Reading Research Quarterly, 36,* 122–151. doi: 10.1598/RRQ.36.2.2

McCarthey, S., & Moje, E. (2002). Conversations: Identity matters. *Reading Research Quarterly, 37,* 228–238. doi: 10.1598/RRQ.37.2.6

McGinn, J., & Parrish, A. (2002). Accelerating ESL students' reading progress with Accelerated Reader. *Reading Horizons, 42,* 175–189.

Merriam, S. (1998). *Qualitative research and case study applications in education.* San Francisco: Jossey-Bass.

Moje, E. (2000). "To be part of the story": The literacy practices of gangsta adolescents. *Teachers College Record, 102,* 651–690.

Morris, D. (1996). A case study of middle school reading disability. *The Reading Teacher, 49,* 368–377.

Oldfather, P. (1994). *When students do not feel motivated for literacy learning: How a responsive classroom culture helps.* Athens, GA: National Reading Research Center.

Oldfather, P., & Wigfield, A. (1996). Children's motivations for literacy learning. In L. Baker, P. Afflerbach, & D. Reinking (Eds.), *Developing engaged readers in school and home communities* (pp. 89–113). Mahwah, NJ: Erlbaum.

Pallas, A., Entwisle, D., Alexander, K., & Stluka, M. F. (1994). Ability group effects: Instructional, social or institutional? *Sociology of Education, 67,* 27–46.

Parkinson, B. (1994). Emotion. In B. Parkinson & A. M. Colman (Eds.), *Emotion and motivation* (pp. 1–21). New York: Longman.

Pavonetti, L., Brimmer, K., & Cipielewski, J. (2003). Accelerated Reader: What are the lasting effects on the reading habits of middle school students exposed to Accelerated Reader in the early grades? *Journal of Adolescent & Adult Literacy, 46,* 300–311.

Phelps, S., & Weaver, D. (1999). Public and personal voices in adolescents' classroom talk. *Journal of Literacy Research, 31,* 321–354.

Scheff, T. (1997). *Emotions, the social bond, and human reality.* Cambridge, MA: Cambridge University Press.

Slavin, R. (1986). *Ability grouping and student achievement in the elementary schools* (Synthesis Report No. 1). Baltimore: Center for Research on Elementary and Middle Schools.

Smith, C.A. (1991). The self, appraisal and coping. In C. R. Snyder & D. R. Forsythe (Eds.), *Handbook of social and clinical psychology: The health perspective* (pp. 116–137). Elmsford, NY: Pergamon.

Stevenson, J., & Camarata, J. (2000). Imposters in whole language clothing: Undressing the Accelerated Reader program. *Talking Points, 11,* 8–11.

Strauss, A., & Corbin, J. (1990). *Basics of qualitative research: Grounded theory procedures and techniques.* Newbury Park, CA: Sage.

Topping, K., & Paul, T. (1999). Computer-assisted assessment of practice at reading: A large scale survey using Accelerated Reader data. *Reading and Writing Quarterly, 15,* 213–231.

Wilkinson, I. A. G., & Townsend, M. A. R. (2000). From Rata to Rimu: Grouping for instruction in best practice New Zealand classrooms. *The Reading Teacher, 53,* 460–471.

Worthy, J., & Hoffman, J. (1996). Critical Questions: Is ability grouping in first grade a negative? *The Reading Teacher, 49,* 65–67.

Address correspondence to: Cheri Foster Triplett, College of Human Resources and Education, 318 War Memorial Hall, Virginia Tech, Blacksburg, VA 24061-0313. E-mail: ctriplet@vt.edu

Exercise for Article 30

Factual Questions

1. What is the explicitly stated purpose of this study?

2. This study took place in the context of tutoring that lasted how long?

3. How was the researcher "informed" of Mitchell's reading history before the researcher began to tutor?

4. In addition to the "tutoring context," where else were the data collected?

5. What did "member checks" consist of?

6. Did the student express positive emotions about tutoring?

Questions for Discussion

7. This is a case study of a single student. Before reading this article, to what extent did you believe that case studies are useful sources of information? Has reading it changed your belief? Explain.

8. In your opinion, how important is the discussion of social theories in lines 81–121 for establishing a framework for this study? Explain.

9. In line 122, the researcher refers to this as a "qualitative study." Do you agree with this classification? If yes, what features of this research study distinguish it from a quantitative study?

10. To what extent is the use of multiple data sources a strength of this study? (See lines 127–132.)

11. Before reading this article, how familiar were you with "constant comparative methods"? To what extent does the material in lines 138–169 better inform you of these methods?

12. In your opinion, is the dialogue in lines 437–472 an important part of the Results section of this research article? Explain.

13. Do you think that this study has important implications for tutors who work with struggling readers? Explain.

Quality Ratings

Directions: Indicate your level of agreement with each of the following statements by circling a number from 5 for strongly agree (SA) to 1 for strongly disagree (SD). If you believe an item is not applicable to this research article, leave it blank. Be prepared to explain your ratings.

A. The introduction establishes the importance of the study.

SA   5   4   3   2   1   SD

B. The literature review establishes the context for the study.

SA   5   4   3   2   1   SD

C. The research purpose, question, or hypothesis is clearly stated.

SA   5   4   3   2   1   SD

D. The method of sampling is sound.

SA   5   4   3   2   1   SD

E. Relevant demographics (for example, age, gender, and ethnicity) are described.

SA   5   4   3   2   1   SD

F. Measurement procedures are adequate.

SA   5   4   3   2   1   SD

G. All procedures have been described in sufficient detail to permit a replication of the study.

SA   5   4   3   2   1   SD

H. The participants have been adequately protected from potential harm.

SA   5   4   3   2   1   SD

I. The results are clearly described.

SA   5   4   3   2   1   SD

J. The discussion/conclusion is appropriate.

SA   5   4   3   2   1   SD

K. Despite any flaws, the report is worthy of publication.

SA   5   4   3   2   1   SD

Article 31

Walk and Talk: An Intervention for Behaviorally Challenged Youths

PATRICIA A. DOUCETTE
Alberta, Canada

ABSTRACT. This qualitative research explored the question: Do preadolescent and adolescent youths with behavioral challenges benefit from a multimodal intervention of walking outdoors while engaging in counseling? The objective of the Walk and Talk intervention is to help the youth feel better, explore alternative behavioral choices, and learn new coping strategies and life skills by engaging in a counseling process that includes the benefits of mild aerobic exercise, and that nurtures a connection to the outdoors. The intervention utilizes a strong therapeutic alliance based on the Rogerian technique of unconditional positive regard, which is grounded and guided by the principles of attachment theory. For eight weeks, eight students (aged 9 to 13 years) from a middle school in Alberta, Canada, participated weekly in the Walk and Talk Intervention. Students' self-reports indicated that they benefited from the intervention. Research triangulation with involved adults supported findings that indicated the students were making prosocial choices in behavior, and were experiencing more feelings of self-efficacy and well-being. Limitations, new research directions, and subsequent longitudinal research possibilities are discussed.

From *Adolescence*, *39*, 373–388. Copyright © 2004 by Libra Publishers, Inc. Reprinted with permission.

Western societies have seen an increase in violence and antisocial behavior in schools and communities (Pollack, 1998). Juvenile crime rates have increased fourfold since the early 1970s (Cook & Laub, 1997). After the shock of the Columbine school massacre in the United States and other violent incidents, communities are demanding interventions to help prevent similar occurrences.

Traditional approaches for various youth behavior challenges have assumed the behavior needs to be controlled and contained by using behavioral and social learning approaches (Moore, Moretti, & Holland, 1998). Many current interventions rely on adaptations of behavior modification strategies to provide structure and control. The tenets of some programs for troubled youth are based on a hierarchy of control, authority, and power. The framework of behavior and behavioral boundaries is directed by coercive control with token economies and earned privileges that are enforced by systems involving revoking social and recreational activities (Moore, Moretti, & Holland, 1998). I question and challenge this type of philosophy. Intrinsic motivation for making positive behavioral choices and taking responsibility and ownership for behavior is unlikely to become the behavioral response when behavior is controlled by others. Research (Deci & Ryan, 1985) suggests intrinsic motivation involves self-determination, self-awareness of one's needs, and setting goals to meet those needs. I believe that many behaviorally challenged youths have experienced interactions with key adults that have been punitive, rejecting, and untrustworthy (Moore, Moretti, & Holland, 1998; Staub, 1996). Therefore, many current interventions based on behavioral strategies and coercive control have limited effectiveness (Moore, Moretti, & Holland, 1998; Staub, 1996).

New treatment methods that adopt a therapeutic approach that is grounded and guided by the principles of attachment theory may engage a therapeutic process with the results of youths' prosocial behavioral choices (Centers for Disease Control, 1991; Ferguson, 1999; Holland, Moretti, Verlaan, & Peterson, 1993; Keat, 1990; Moffitt, 1993; Moore, Moretti, & Holland, 1998). By participating in a casual walk outdoors, there can be the physiological advantage of mild aerobic exercise (Franken, 1994; Hays, 1999; Fox, 1997; Baum & Posluszny, 1999; Kolb & Whishaw, 1996, 1998). I believe, as do others (Anderson, 2000; Glaser, 2000; Tkachuk & Martin, 1999; Real Age Newsletter, 2001a), that human beings have a natural bond with the outdoors and other living organisms. By nurturing this bond with a walk outdoors, positive well-being and health can result (Tkachuk & Martin, 1999; Hays, 1999; Orlick, 1993; Real Age Newsletter, 2001b).

Walk and Talk Intervention

The Walk and Talk intervention has its fundamental philosophy in Bronfenbrenner's (1979) social ecological theory of behavior, which views the child, family, school, work, peers, neighborhood, and community as interconnected systems. Youths' problem behavior can be attributed to dysfunction between any one or more combinations of these systems (Borduin, 1999). By understanding these dynamics, the Walk and Talk Intervention attempts to provide a support network that encourages youths to reconnect with self and the environment through an attachment process, a counseling process, and a physiological response resulting in feelings of self-efficacy.

The Walk and Talk intervention utilizes three components to engage youths. The counseling component of the Walk and Talk intervention borrows seven principles from the Orinoco program used at the Maples Adolescent Centre near Vancouver, British Columbia (Moore, Moretti, & Holland, 1998, pp. 10–18). These principles are driven by an underlying understanding of attachment theory. These principles are as follows:

1. All behavior has meaning. The meaning of the behavior is revealed by understanding the internal working model of the person generating the behavior.

2. Early and repeated experiences with people who care for us set a foundation for our internal working models of relationship with self and others. Our earliest experiences have a profound effect on how we approach relationships, school, work, and play.

3. Biological legacies such as cognitive, emotional, and physical capabilities are an interactive part of our experience and contribute to our working model of relationships with self and others.

4. Internal working models are constantly changing in the context of relationships and expertise. These models are constantly revised based on experience. Experience can be added to but not subtracted.

5. Interpersonal relationships are a process of continuous reciprocal interplay of each person's internal working model with others. It is not possible to hold oneself apart from this interplay.

6. We understand ourselves in relation to others. A sense of self includes our sense of how others view and respond to us.

7. Enduring change in an individual's behavior occurs only when there is change in the internal working model supported by change in the system one lives in and if there is sufficient time, opportunity, and support to integrate the new experience.

The counseling component of the Walk and Talk intervention is interlaced with new strategies for positive life skills and attempts to incorporate solution-focused brief therapy (Riley, 1999). Through counseling, youths discover solutions by way of simple interventions while experiencing positive regard in Rogerian fashion (Rogers, 1980). Focus is kept on youths' strengths while collaborating for change (Riley, 1999; Orlick, 1993). Identifying highlights is an important element of each walk. Highlights are used to teach youths to think positively so they can reframe their experiences in a way that enhances well-being (Orlick, 1993). By being able to illuminate the good in things that happen in daily life, youths can find inner strength and resilience when experiencing negative events or reactions from others (Orlick, 1993). Youths who have an inner source of reworking setbacks in daily life will be more likely to cope with stress effectively.

The ecopsychology component of the Walk and Talk intervention is tied to the psychological processes that bring people closer to the natural world. Some research suggests that humans have a natural bond with other living organisms, and nurturing that connection may provide a health benefit (Roszak, Gomes, & Kanner, 1995; Real Age Newsletter, 2001a). By walking outdoors, the outdoor connection is nurtured, facilitating youths' awareness of their environment.

The physiological component engages the youths in aerobic exercise. Considerable research supports the use of exercise to alleviate many types of mental illness and enhance feelings of well-being (Tkachuk & Martin, 1999). Some research suggests that as little as ten minutes of daily exercise is enough to generate mood-elevating neurochemicals (Real Age Newsletter, 2001b). Recognizing the importance of exercise to well-being is a critical aspect of the Walk and Talk intervention.

The intervention for behaviorally challenged youths combines the benefits of a strong therapeutic alliance based on the Rogerian technique of unconditional positive regard (Rogers, 1980), integrated with mild aerobic exercise that occurs outdoors in a place of natural beauty. The research goal is to discover if this combination has a beneficial effect on selected youths and their problem behaviors.

The impetus for this research is to understand the epidemiology and etiology of the problem behaviors while attempting to implement an effective preventative intervention. One objective is to provide fertile ground for the youths to explore and understand alternative behavioral choices. This phenomenological qualitative research approach assumes that the participants are existential individuals and as such, actions, verbalizations, everyday patterns, and ways of interacting can reveal an understanding of human behavior (Addison, 1992). A basic principle of existentialism suggests that each and every expression—even the most insignificant and superficial behavior—reveals and communicates who that individual is (Sartre, 1957). It is hoped that the participants will acquire a stronger self-understanding via a therapeutic alliance, aerobic exercise, experiencing a connection to the outdoors, and be able to choose to make a behavior change.

By understanding and utilizing attachment theory (Ainsworth & Bowlby, 1991; Bowlby, 1969; Centers for Disease Control, 1991; Ferguson, 1999; Holland, Moretti, Verlaan, & Peterson, 1993; Keat, 1990; Moffitt, 1993; Moore, Moretti, & Holland, 1998) and Rogerian (1980) methods to guide the counseling with a walk outdoors, it is hoped that youths' self-esteem will increase as they become connected to another person (myself) and the outdoors.

Why do some young people sabotage themselves with nonproductive behaviors? I believe if an intervention can be introduced and then utilized by youths who have a history of these behaviors, they can be redirected to satisfying, productive lives regardless of their prior personal history. The intervention will help behaviorally troubled youths to feel better and do better by being internally motivated to choose prosocial behavior.

The plasticity, resilience, and remarkable adaptability of youths to their unique selves and situations has been a catalyst for my research. The importance of attachment (as defined by Ainsworth, 2000) and understanding attachment theory (Ainsworth, 2000; Bowlby, 1969) cannot be understated. The Walk and Talk intervention provides a safe place for youths to discover new positive coping strategies that can benefit them throughout life.

Method

The middle school principal assigned the student outreach support worker to select appropriate individuals for the Walk and Talk intervention. The assistant superintendent, a licensed psychologist, was selected as a resource and liaison in case crises should arise. A consent form was signed by a school district representative. Further, consent forms were sent to the parents of participants.

The eight intervention respondents chosen were coded by school assessors as behaviorally challenged and in need of special education. I first met with each of the eight youths for a preintervention interview that allows us to become acquainted and for me to familiarize myself with their understanding of their behavioral challenges. Specifically, the youths' problem behaviors as indicated by school representatives, parents and/or guardians were identified as conduct disorder as described in the *Diagnostic and Statistical Manual of Mental Disorders* (American Psychiatric Association, 1994). Conduct disorders include violating rules, aggressiveness that threatens or causes physical harm to others, bullying, extortion, lack of respect for self and others, suicide attempts, truancy, initiating frequent fights, and various charges by the police, such as breaking and entering (DSM-IV, 1994). The problem behaviors were repetitive, resulting in unsuccessful functioning within the school, community, and often family setting.

By utilizing a collaborative, qualitative approach, I disclosed the intentions of the Walk and Talk intervention. I believe this approach facilitated development of alliance, empowerment of the participant, and engagement as the expert (Creswell, 1998; Flick, 1998). My role as researcher was that of an active, interested learner (Creswell, 1998; Flick, 1998). This collaborative, qualitative approach bridges the gap between participant and researcher. A collaborative approach has been preferred for youths since it engages and honors them as their own expert (Axline, 1947/1969; Oaklander, 1978); youths are usually not in control of many decisions that affect them.

Interviews were conducted before and after the six-week Walk and Talk intervention. The first interview included an introduction by me and the youths. They were asked to draw a picture of themselves performing any activity of their choice. Sheets of 8" × 11" white paper and ten assorted gel pens were provided. These pens were chosen because of their popularity with children of all ages. Upon completion of the drawings, the youths were asked to make a list of at least five of their strengths. Next they were asked to list at least five weaknesses. The final activity was to write a short autobiographical incident about something that had made an impression, whether positive or negative. After each activity, discussion was encouraged. A goal of the interview was to start the youths thinking about self, and for me, to learn what they think and feel. At the close of the interview, I prepared them for the week of walking and talking, emphasizing that it would be their opportunity to talk about whatever came to mind and the talks would be confidential—except in extreme situations, for instance, statements about harming themselves or others.

By conducting the first interview in this manner, it was hoped the youths would start to self-disclose in some or all of the modalities. Also, it provides baseline insight as to how the youths feel at that time. The self-portraits of each youth were examined by a licensed art therapist, Maxine Junge, and myself. Maxine Junge (personal communication, February 18, 2002) provides the caution that what she offered were guesses, hypotheses, and impressions. The autobiographical pieces gave insight into issues considered important by these youths.

The interview was fairly ambitious, but the researcher did not press the youths with the agenda. It was hoped that an alliance would be established wherein trust and respect would be shared. This started the counseling process. It is important to discover what this process is for the youths and report it. It is important to discover the meaning the youths give to events and resulting actions (Maxwell, 1996). It was the youths' reality that this qualitative approach attempts to understand (Maxwell, 1996). The youths were the focus and their phenomenological experience was explored while psychoeducational interventions were suggested and discussed when appropriate.

It was the counselor's role to help the youths clarify and reframe belief constructs while helping to identify and translate the subconscious into the conscious (Hays, 1999). How youths behave and speak reflects subconscious thoughts and feelings (Hunter, 1987). It was the counselor's role to help the youths identify the connectedness to place and others, identify and verbalize one or more successful survival skills while introducing new conscious approaches that encourage the cognitive strategy of stop, think, do. Introducing young people to the hope of a future that is rewarding and positive and one they can manage and control is a paramount goal. When appropriate, they will be introduced to various life skills that can improve the quality of their life (Orlick, 1993). By learning about positive thinking, positive self-talk, stress management, relaxation skills, imagery, anger physiology, anger management, communication with "I-statements," focusing and refocusing, new behavioral choices can be made (Orlick, 1993). Learning one, two, or more key life skills can enhance the youths' lives.

I met with each respondent for six consecutive weeks, once a week, for approximately 30–45 minutes per session. Each session entailed a walk on the school grounds. This did not include the pre- and post-interviews. The eight participants began their first walk and talk between December 12, 2001, and January 28, 2002. This wide range of start times was due to the waiting period for parental consents and then arranging appropriate times with the teachers. Also, at the end of December and early January, there was a two-week school break, which caused a delay in beginning some first sessions. The total walk and talk time allotted was 45 minutes but because of time needed to dress appropriately, actual walk and talk time was about 30 minutes. At the start of each walk I asked the youths what they wanted to discuss. If there was not anything in particular they wanted to say, I asked them for highlights in their lives since I last saw them a week ago. Highlights are positive events, positive experiences, comments, personal accomplishments or anything that has lifted the quality of the moment for that child (Orlick, 1993, 1998). Next, I asked them about their low lights. Understanding and verbalizing that life is filled with highs and lows begins the journey of self-discovery and also allows the youth to discuss alternative strategies for dealing with problems.

Throughout the six-week Walk and Talk intervention, I introduced strategies for dealing with stress, identifying what was stressful for the youth, discussing the importance of positive self talk, mental imagery, visualization techniques, and focusing and refocusing techniques (Orlick, 1993, 1998). Most of the youths chosen for this intervention had anger-management challenges. When appropriate, anger management techniques, combined with the cognitive strategy of stop, think, do were introduced. Understanding anger cycles and the physiology of anger was discussed. One of the life skills introduced was learning the rules of using assertiveness rather than aggressiveness and utilizing I-statements to convey feelings to others. When appropriate these types of life skills were introduced and practiced in mock situations. Positive life skill techniques were woven into the counseling session during most sessions.

The intervention was completed with a post interview. When gathering data from the youths, respondents were informed that the research was intended to help them in the future; therefore, answering honestly is important. Respondents were told there were no right or wrong responses. They were to feel free to talk openly. Similar to the pre-intervention interview, youths were asked to draw a picture of themselves in an activity. Next they were asked to write their strengths and weaknesses. At that time, I showed each youth the drawing from their pre-intervention interview, and we compared the strengths and weaknesses from before and after the intervention. Together we noted the differences. I asked each youth: What has changed since we started? What did you like about walk and talk? What didn't you like about it? What was helpful? What wasn't helpful? What are your concluding comments and remarks? Do you think it would be good for other youths to participate? I asked them what they thought about the art they produced and about the strengths and weaknesses they identified. I assessed self-esteem via the self-portrait they had drawn, comparing pre- and post-intervention responses. Several methods of communicating with the youths (i.e., art, structured exercise, open-ended questions, and discussion of their experience) made my report of their phenomenological experience more complete.

Results and Discussion

I chose a phenomenological approach because I wanted to capture the essence of the youths' experience as told by them. Did they feel better and do better? The youths' experience was reported as I observed it. I assessed their experience of the Walk and Talk intervention as told to me by them along with collateral observation and/or information given to me by parents, teachers, and other involved school personnel. The ecopsychology aspect of this intervention can be replicated in any safe outdoor environment.

The only given variables in this research are the common denominators of age, youths from 9 to 13 years old, and the individual, problematic behaviors, although variations in etiology and epidemiology exist. The factors relating to the causes of the behaviors are individual. The systemic distribution of impacting incidents and contributing components to each youth's behavior vary. By offering a multimodal approach it was hoped that the youths' experiences would be positive and result in prosocial behavior.

As the qualitative researcher, it was my mandate to utilize rigorous data collection procedures (Creswell, 1998). As a researcher, it was also my intent to maintain my distance in order to promote objectivity but still engage them as a counselor. To achieve this result requires walking a fine line. To preserve scientific clarity, conscious effort was required. However, a positive interpersonal relationship was necessary for the success of the research intervention and of the qualitative approach. The characteristics and assumptions of the phenomenological qualitative approach to research necessitates that the participant's view be the entire reality of the study (Creswell, 1998). As such, the reality was purely and subjectively portrayed as an experiential component of the study. To analyze the data, multiple approaches and multiple traditions were included. This was done to provide a fuller, holistic view and richer understanding of the process which occurred during time in the field.

Combining the three components of counseling, ecopsychology, and physiological enhancement creates a new intervention for behaviorally challenged youths. The youths who completed the intervention stated that it helped them clarify feelings. Overall, I believe the Walk and Talk intervention benefited each youth who completed the intervention. The following discussion provides specifics about the individual participants.

Youth A

Youth A's participation helped him to become more self-aware of his struggles with his sister and father. Although strategies were discussed, I do not believe that Youth A assimilated many new life skills. He needed much more individual time and attention to help him cope with the number of problems he faces outside of school. However, his art therapy work showed a definite improvement. The first drawing was very small, not grounded, and "floating," which the art therapist suggested indicated a feeling of smallness, powerlessness, and lack of self-esteem. The final drawing depicted a well-defined boy and girl—Youth A and little sister—in his bedroom with all his prized possessions. Both children were smiling and he looked like a protective big brother. His teacher's comments about Youth A indicated that the Walk and Talk intervention had benefited Youth A, at least for the days of each Walk and Talk. The teacher believed Youth A needed more continuous intensive help. Youth A made positive comments about his experience in intervention: He liked talking about his feelings and learning focusing and refocusing skills. His before-and-after strengths ratio was 12/15, indicating that he believed he had more strengths on the completion day of Walk and Talk than on the starting day. His weaknesses ratio was 9/3, indicating that at the start of Walk and Talk he believed he had many more weaknesses than when he finished.

Youth B

I believe there was a significant improvement with Youth B. Each week he self-disclosed more and more. He was eager to talk about his problems and challenges as time went on. Toward the end of the intervention, he was walking with his head held high rather than downcast. He was very pleased to report his new, fun relationship with his big brother. His teacher told me throughout the intervention of his improved coping and social skills in the classroom. She gave me detailed accounts of how Youth B avoided confrontations by using newly acquired social skill strategies. In the last discussion with the teacher (on the last day of the intervention) she revealed a violent outburst in his classroom. It was on that day physical abuse charges were reported to social services regarding his mother. Although the teacher could not understand Youth B's incongruent behavior, I knew it all fit.

His before-and-after strengths ratio was 5/8, indicating that he believed he had more strengths on the completion day of Walk and Talk than on the starting day. In addition, three of the strengths mentioned were social skills. His weaknesses ratio was 4/0, indicating that at the start of Walk and Talk he believed he had four weaknesses and when he finished, he had none. Youth B indicated Walk and Talk was a helpful intervention for him.

The art therapist's comments regarding his drawings indicate that he was a boy possibly filled with fear and anger. The drawings denoted a developmental problem in that they depicted a small and insignificant figure.

Youth C

I think there was a huge improvement with Youth C. He seemed to self-disclose more and more each week. He utilized the life-skill techniques we discussed, practiced them throughout the week, and eagerly reported back to me. His self-esteem soared with each new success he experienced. He would retell with enthusiasm his weekly attempts at new life skills and his successes along with some failures. His teacher echoed my sentiments noticing a remarkable change of attitude in the classroom, his cooperation with peers, and positive choices in behavior. His brother commented on their newly improved relationship.

His before-and-after strengths ratio was 5/5. On completion day of Walk and Talk, three of his five strengths were social skills, whereas on starting day none were social skills. His weaknesses ratio was 5/2, indicating that at the start of Walk and Talk, he had many more weaknesses than when he finished. At the start he indicated that two of his five weaknesses were social skills and at completion, one of his two weaknesses was his temper. I viewed these changes as exemplifying a raised level of self-awareness. Youth C very enthusiastically claimed Walk and Talk was a positive event for him.

The art therapist noted that his first drawing depicted a small, faceless, insignificant boy, and his final drawing was very similar. Sadly, after completion of the intervention, charges of parental child abuse were reported to social services.

Youth D

Youth D was reintegrated into the regular classroom toward the end of the Walk and Talk intervention. I think his participation in the intervention was one of many support efforts that helped him improve his overall success and well-being. During Walk and Talk he talked about his daily challenges. He seemed to develop a self-awareness over time. His teacher reported positive changes: he had started to react appropriately and to accept "no" without bursting into tears. He utilized self-chosen time outs and self-talk to help him control his emotions. His teacher indicated that he was more polite and considerate with others. Youth D reported that Walk and Talk had been a great experience for him.

His before-and-after strengths ratio was 7/8. On completion day of Walk and Talk, one of his eight strengths was a social skill. His weaknesses ratio was 5/5. The art therapy assessment for his first drawing suggested an ineffectual, fearful, and avoidant child. His final drawing was grounded, but still revealed a faceless self. Youth D's before-and-after drawings lack depth and involvement.

Youth E

I believe Youth E benefited from his participation in the Walk and Talk intervention but needed intensive ongoing help. He seemed to have a very low self-image that was controlled by external events. His troubled home life, parents' divorce, and taking a daily drug cocktail for various problems contributed to his need for external support. His teacher agreed. The teacher also said that Youth E had benefited greatly from participating in Walk and Talk. In the classroom he was much calmer and cooperative, thereby experiencing more personal success—something he clearly needed. Youth E said Walk and Talk was good for him because he could get his feelings out.

The art therapist's assessment of his artwork was of a boy with high intelligence, with a good self-image. This was contradictory to the boy I knew. Both of his pictures were grounded but showed an avoidant boy who did not know how to handle his impulses.

His before-and-after strengths ratio was 5/8. On completion day of Walk and Talk, seven of his eight strengths were social skills. This was impressive. His weaknesses ratio was 5/1. In his first meeting he identified two social skills weaknesses as being related to being bullied. In our final meeting he admitted that arguing was his weakness. I believe he had acquired more self-awareness over the intervention time and learned new coping strategies.

Youth F

It was difficult for me to assess whether Youth F, the only female participant, benefited from the intervention. I often wondered what she was learning and what bothered her. However, I found her participation in the ecopsychology aspect remarkable. She became transformed from a girl who threw rocks at birds to one who tried to gently approach them and stroke them. She became increasingly aware of the surrounding trees, an occasional wandering dog, and the variety of birds. She seemed to enjoy the physical aspects of the intervention. I believe she was extremely athletic and often mentioned this to her. Her teacher queried me after the second Walk and Talk to learn what life skills we were concentrating on. The teacher collaborated with me to help the girl control her impulsivity by reminding her when it was appropriate to focus, refocus, stop, think, do, rub her lucky penny, and apply any other life skill strategies I had mentioned. Also, Youth F's mother phoned me to offer collaboration in helping her daughter use life skills at home. Youth F experienced behavioral improvement during the intervention time as reported by all triangulation sources. Youth F told me that Walk and Talk was great.

The art therapist's assessment of her artwork suggested possible organic problems. I agreed. Her before-and-after strengths ratio was 15/7. Her weaknesses ratio was 5/0. I believe Youth F could use ongoing outside support.

Youth G

Youth G was a total pleasure to have as a participant of Walk and Talk. Although he was mildly developmentally delayed, he was eager to learn new positive life skills. He readily became attached to the outdoor environment, becoming keenly aware of the birds, trees, and sounds. He often made observations that I found remarkable, although his kind, gentle spirit was often squelched in his daily struggles with academics and interpersonal relationships, but because of his resilience and willingness to discuss his problems, he could find solutions readily. His teachers believed Youth G's success was ongoing after he participated in a behavioral program. Youth G's teachers concurred that the Walk and Talk intervention had probably helped to illuminate his positive choices.

Youth G's art assessment denoted his developmental lag. The drawings before-and-after showed him wearing a sport shirt with the number twelve (his lucky number) and playing volleyball. Neither drawing reflected a grounded individual. His before-and-after strengths ratio was 5/5. In his first meeting he identified two social skills as being strengths. In the last meeting he identified three social skills as such. His weaknesses ratio was 1/3. I believe this indicated a keener self-awareness. I believe Youth G benefited enormously from his participation in the Walk and Talk intervention.

Youth H

Youth H identified seven strengths and two weaknesses. He liked to talk about playing and watching hockey. His art was not grounded and very simple. The art therapist noted that his drawing was very protected and defensive, indicating possible anger and aggression.

Youth H was removed from the intervention after one meeting. At the time of our first meeting, the

teacher's aid strongly argued against his being a participant in the Walk and Talk intervention. Youth H had been selected by the student outreach worker, and his parents had consented to his participation. The new
630 school guidance counselor contacted me with concerns and recommended that he be pulled from the intervention. Due to these objections, Youth H was withdrawn. My advice to future Walk and Talk interventionists is to enlist the support of all people who are in favor of a
635 youth's participation in the program. Otherwise, what happened to Youth H could happen to others.

Overall, the research results were positive. From the teachers' perspective, my perspective, and the youths' comments, the intervention seemed to benefit
640 them on many fronts. Introducing alternative life-skill strategies was a key counseling component of the intervention. All youths found the focusing and refocusing exercise beneficial, and many adopted the technique to everyday life. Focusing and refocusing can
645 facilitate learning to experience life fully. By practicing focusing and refocusing exercises, youths can learn to closely observe what is seen, listen intently to what is heard, feel fully and connect completely when interacting with others (Orlick, 1993). The focusing and refo-
650 cusing technique utilized aspects of the intervention's ecopsychological component by weaving a life-skill technique into a closer awareness of self and facets of the outdoors that otherwise would go unnoticed. After applying the technique outdoors it was readily transfer-
655 able to indoor situations.

It is my belief that to varying degrees, the youths benefited from the experience of counseling outdoors enhanced by the physiological "boost" provided by aerobic exercise. Walking allowed for physical release,
660 something very important for these active youths. Feelings, problems, and sometimes solutions to problems materialized. All respondents found talking about such problems to be beneficial. These respondents were chosen because of their difficulty in managing social
665 situations.

Assuming my findings are correct and the intervention can be deemed successful, will the intervention have long-term effects? I can only speculate. Follow-up longitudinal studies are recommended. Suggestions
670 for future research include using control groups with various problem behaviors as well as groups with no problem behaviors, groups with and without the ecopsychological component, groups with and without the walking component. I also advise utilizing quantita-
675 tive methods to measure success. Possibly my strongest recommendation is to do the Walk and Talk intervention in warm weather.

Conclusions

A possible limitation of this research could be its subjective nature. Further, my subjectivity presupposes
680 that most people with attachment difficulties respond favorably to Carl Rogers' (1980) therapeutic approach of positive personal regard.

Inclement weather could deter respondents from wholehearted participation. Unfortunately, the session
685 times, once established, were not flexible since they were incorporated into the school day.

This research approached behavioral challenges from an individual vantage point rather than a systemic or societal perspective. Some researchers (e.g.,
690 Grossman, 1999) view youths' turmoil and violence as resulting from the ills of society (i.e., television, movies, and videogame violence). The present research does not address these types of cultural concerns of society on a macro level.
695 In sum, I would like to see the Walk and Talk intervention used in middle schools and high schools and utilized by mental health practitioners. Once youths have completed the intervention, I recommend periodical refreshers on a monthly basis. Walk and Talk re-
700 freshers will give the youths a time to reconnect with the outdoors, self, and reinstate positive behaviors and life skills.

References

Addison, R. (1992). Grounded hermeneutic research. In B. F. Crabtree & W. L. Miller (Eds.), *Doing qualitative research* (pp. 110–124). Newbury Park, CA: Sage Publications.

Ainsworth, M. (2000). Maternal sensitivity scales (original work published in 1969). Available at http://www.psy.sunysb.edu/ewaters/senscoop.htm

Ainsworth, M., & Bowlby, J. (1991). An ethological approach to personality development. *American Psychologist, 46,* 333–341.

American Psychiatric Association. (1994). *Diagnostic and statistical manual of mental disorders* (4th ed.). Washington, DC: Author.

Anderson, N. (2000). *Testimony of the Office of the Director of National Institutes of Health, Department of Health and Human Services regarding mind/body interactions and health before the United States Senate, September 22, 1998.* Available at http://www.apa.org/ppo/scitest923.html

Axline, V. (1947/1969). *Play therapy.* New York: Ballantine Books.

Baum, A. & Posluszny, D. (1999). Health psychology: Mapping biobehavioral contributions to health and illness. *Annual Review of Psychology, 50,* 137–163.

Borduin, C. (1999). Multisystemic treatment of criminality and violence in adolescents. *Journal of the American Academy of Child and Adolescent Psychiatry, 38,* 242–249.

Bowlby, J. (1969). *Attachment: Attachment and loss* (Vol. 1). New York: Basic Books.

Bronfenbrenner, U. (1979). *The ecology of human development: Experiments by nature and design.* Cambridge, MA: Harvard University Press.

Centers for Disease Control. (1991). Forum on youth violence in minority communities: Setting the agenda for prevention. *Public Health Reports, 106,* 225–253.

Cook, P. J., & Laub, J. H. (1997). The unprecedented epidemic in youth violence. In M. Tonry & M. H. Molore (Eds.), *Crime and justice* (pp. 101–138). Chicago, IL: University of Chicago Press.

Creswell, J. W. (1998). *Qualitative inquiry and research design: Choosing among five traditions.* Thousand Oaks, CA: Sage Publications.

Deci, E., & Ryan, R. (1985). *Intrinsic motivation and self determination in human behavior.* New York: Plenum Press.

Ferguson, G. (1999). *Shouting at the sky: Troubled teens and the promise of the wild.* New York: Thomas Dunne Books.

Flick, U. (1998). *An introduction to qualitative research.* Thousand Oaks, CA: Sage Publications.

Fox, K. (1997). Let's get physical. In K. R. Fox (Ed.), *The physical self: From motivation to well being* (pp. vii–xiii). Champaign, IL; Human Kinetics.

Franken, R. (1994). *Human motivation.* Pacific Grove, CA: Brooks-Cole Publishers.

Glaser, R. (2000). *Mind-body interactions, immunity, and health.* Available at http://www.apa.org/ppo/mind.html

Grossman, D. (1999). *Stop teaching our kids to kill: A call to action against TV, movie, and video game violence.* New York: Crown Books.

Hays, K. (1999). *Working it out.* Washington, DC: American Psychological Association.

Holland, R., Moretti, M., Verlaan, V., & Peterson, S. (1993). Attachment and conduct disorder: The response program. *Canadian Journal of Psychiatry*, *38*, 420–431.

Hunter, M. (1996). *Psych yourself in!* Vancouver, BC: SeaWalk Press.

Keat, D. (1990). *Child multimodal therapy*. Norwood, NJ: Ablex Publishing.

Kolb, B., & Whishaw, I. (1996). *Human neuropsychology*. New York: W. H. Freeman.

Kolb, B., & Whishaw, I. (1998). Brain plasticity and behavior. *Annual Review of Psychology*, *49*, 43–64.

Maxwell, J. (1996). *Qualitative research design: An interactive approach*. Thousand Oaks, CA: Sage Publications.

Moffitt, T. (1993). Adolescence-limited and life-course persistent antisocial behavior: A developmental taxonomy. *Psychological Review*, *100*, 674–701.

Moore, K., Moretti, M., & Holland, R. (1998). A new perspective on youth care programs: Using attachment theory to guide interventions for troubled youth. *Residential Treatment for Children and Youth*, *15*, 1–24.

Oaklander, V. (1978). *Windows to our children: A gestalt therapy approach to children and adolescents*. Moab, UT: Real People Press.

Orlick, T. (1993). *Free to feel great: Teaching children to excel at living*. Carp, Ontario, Canada: Creative bound.

Orlick, T. (1998). *Feeling great*. Carp, Ontario, Canada: Creative Bound.

Pollack, W. (1998). *Real boys*. New York: Henry Holt & Co.

Real Age Newsletter. (2001a, May 18). *The call of the wild, tip of the day*. Available at http://www.realage.com/

Real Age Newsletter (2001b, October 9). *Quick mood fix, tip of the day*. Available at http://www.realage.com/

Riley, S. (1999). Brief therapy: An adolescent intervention. *Art Therapy: Journal of the American Art Therapy Association*, *16*, 83–86.

Rogers, C. (1980). *A way of being*. Boston: Houghton Mifflin.

Roszak, T., Gomes, M., & Kanner, A. (1995). *Ecopsychology: Restoring the earth, healing the mind*. San Francisco, CA: Sierra Club Books.

Sartre, J. P. (1957). *Existentialism and human emotions*. New York: The Wisdom Library.

Staub, E. (1996). Altruism and aggression in children and youth. In R. Feldman (Ed.), *The psychology of adversity* (pp. 115–144). Amherst, MA: University of Massachusetts Press.

Tkachuk, G. A., & Martin, G. L. (1999). Exercise therapy for patients with psychiatric disorders: Research and clinical implications. *Professional Psychology: Research and Practice*, *30*, 275–282.

Acknowledgments: The author wishes to thank the youths who participated in this research. Their energy, spirit, and resilience are an inspiration. The author also thanks Michele Clark and Maxine Junge, Goddard College, Plainfield, Vermont, for their input and insight regarding this research.

Address correspondence to: Patricia A. Doucette, 240 Grizzly Crescent, Canmore, Alberta, T1W 1B5 Canada. E-mail: pdoucett@ telusplanet.net

Exercise for Article 31

Factual Questions

1. Did the researcher use a consent form?

2. At the pre-intervention interview, what did the researcher ask the participants to do after completing their self-drawing?

3. Does the researcher state that she attempted to use rigorous data collection procedures and to remain objective?

4. Youth A reported 12 strengths at the pre-interview. How many did he report at the post-interview?

5. The researcher reported a "huge improvement" for which youth?

6. Which youth was removed from the intervention after one meeting?

Questions for Discussion

7. What is your opinion on the use of drawings of the self to collect data on self-concept? (For example, see lines 243–248, 266–273, 370–374, and 432–440.)

8. In your opinion, are the specific strategies used in the Walk and Talk intervention described in sufficient detail? Explain. (See lines 334–351.)

9. The researcher suggests the use of control groups in future research. In your opinion, is this an important suggestion? Explain. (See lines 669–674.)

10. Do you agree with the researcher on the need for quantitative methods to measure success? Explain. (See lines 674–675.)

11. Do you agree with the researcher that a possible limitation of this research is its subjective nature? Explain. (See lines 678–682.)

12. Overall, has this researcher convinced you that the Walk and Talk intervention is a promising method to use with other students? Why? Why not?

Quality Ratings

Directions: Indicate your level of agreement with each of the following statements by circling a number from 5 for strongly agree (SA) to 1 for strongly disagree (SD). If you believe an item is not applicable to this research article, leave it blank. Be prepared to explain your ratings.

A. The introduction establishes the importance of the study.

SA   5   4   3   2   1   SD

B. The literature review establishes the context for the study.

SA   5   4   3   2   1   SD

C. The research purpose, question, or hypothesis is clearly stated.

SA   5   4   3   2   1   SD

D. The method of sampling is sound.

SA   5   4   3   2   1   SD

E. Relevant demographics (for example, age, gender, and ethnicity) are described.

SA   5   4   3   2   1   SD

F. Measurement procedures are adequate.

    SA   5   4   3   2   1   SD

G. All procedures have been described in sufficient detail to permit a replication of the study.

    SA   5   4   3   2   1   SD

H. The participants have been adequately protected from potential harm.

    SA   5   4   3   2   1   SD

I. The results are clearly described.

    SA   5   4   3   2   1   SD

J. The discussion/conclusion is appropriate.

    SA   5   4   3   2   1   SD

K. Despite any flaws, the report is worthy of publication.

    SA   5   4   3   2   1   SD

Article 32

A Qualitative Examination of
Graduate Advising Relationships:
The Advisee Perspective

LEWIS Z. SCHLOSSER
University of Maryland

SARAH KNOX
Marquette University

ALISSA R. MOSKOVITZ
Marquette University

CLARA E. HILL
University of Maryland

ABSTRACT. Sixteen 3rd-year counseling psychology doctoral students were interviewed about their relationships with their graduate advisors. Of those students, 10 were satisfied and 6 were unsatisfied with their advising relationships. Satisfied and unsatisfied students differed on several aspects of the advising relationship, including (a) the ability to choose their advisors, (b) the frequency of meetings with their advisors, (c) the benefits and costs associated with their advising relationships, and (d) how conflict was dealt with in the advising relationship. Furthermore, all of the satisfied students reported that their advising relationships became more positive over time, whereas many of the unsatisfied students reported that their advising relationships got worse (e.g., became more distant) over time.

From *Journal of Counseling Psychology*, *50*, 178–188. Copyright © 2003 by the American Psychological Association. Reprinted with permission.

We believe, as do many others (e.g., Gelso, 1979, 1993, 1997; Gelso & Lent, 2000; Magoon & Holland, 1984; Schlosser, 2002; Schlosser & Gelso, 2001), that the graduate advising relationship can profoundly af-
5 fect a psychology graduate student's professional development within and even beyond her or his training program. This is because advisors typically facilitate their advisees' progress through the program, work with students on research requirements (i.e., theses and
10 dissertations), and serve in other capacities for their students (e.g., providing clinical supervision, facilitating professional development). Despite the importance of the advising relationship, however, an extensive literature review revealed only one published empirical
15 study focused specifically on advisor-advisee relationships (i.e., Schlosser & Gelso, 2001).

Schlosser and Gelso (2001) constructed and validated the Advisory Working Alliance Inventory (AWAI), a paper-and-pencil, self-report measure to
20 assess the working alliance between the advisor and advisee from the advisee's perspective. The advisory working alliance was defined as "that portion of the relationship that reflects the connection between advisor and advisee that is made during work toward com-
25 mon goals" (p. 158). That study provided initial evidence of the importance of the working alliance in the graduate advising relationship. For example, student ratings of the advisory working alliance were related positively to student self-ratings of research self-
30 efficacy and attitudes toward research. In addition, students' perceptions of the advisory alliance were positively correlated with students' perceptions of the advisor's expertness, attractiveness, and trustworthiness. These findings underscore the advisor's role in terms
35 of facilitating relevant outcomes in advisees, as well as the importance of the advisor's personal and professional qualities in forming and maintaining working alliances with advisees.

Schlosser and Gelso's (2001) study was limited,
40 however, in that they only examined perceptions of the advisory working alliance. The working alliance, although important, does not fully capture all of the components of the graduate advising relationship (Gelso & Schlosser, 2001; Hill, 1997; Schlosser &
45 Gelso, 2001). For example, personal (e.g., non-school-related) relationships might form between advisor and advisee that are not a part of the advisory working alliance yet are still important components of the overall advising relationship. In addition, as the advising rela-
50 tionship naturally progresses over time and the student matures professionally from student to colleague, the faculty-student relationship is also likely to undergo changes. The AWAI was not designed to examine the evolution of the advising relationship throughout
55 graduate school. Therefore, we believe that there is a need for research that examines the advising relationship more broadly than the AWAI currently allows.

Before proceeding, however, we believe it is important to distinguish between *mentoring* and *advising*.
60 This distinction is important to make because the construct of mentoring has received a fair amount of atten-

tion in the literature (e.g., Hollingsworth & Fassinger, 2002; Russell & Adams, 1997), and mentoring has been suggested as an important aspect of protégé professional development (Gelso & Lent, 2000). We do not, however, see advising and mentoring as synonymous. *Mentoring* refers to a positive relationship in which protégés learn professional skills (Cronan-Hillix, Gensheimer, Cronan-Hillix, & Davidson, 1986; Russell & Adams, 1997), whereas *advising* refers to a positive or negative relationship in which guidance may or may not be provided with regard to professional skill development (Schlosser & Gelso, 2001). For the present study, *advising* is a more appropriate term than *mentoring*. First, graduate advising relationships can be positive or negative. Because the term *mentor* has an inherently positive connotation (Schlosser & Gelso, 2001), students are not likely to report having poor relationships with mentors. Second, although a few students report being assigned or finding a mentor, more often they report being assigned or finding an advisor. For example, Schlosser and Gelso (2001) found that 100% of the 281 graduate student respondents indicated that they had an advisor, whereas Cronan-Hillix et al. (1986) found that only half the students in their sample reported having a mentor. Finally, definitions of *mentor* have been inconsistent in the research, and no proposed definition of *mentor* describes a graduate advisor adequately (i.e., definitions have either been overly simplified or too complex). For these reasons, we decided that the term *advisor* was more appropriate for the current study. This decision allowed us to define the construct of *advisor* clearly, and removed the positive bias inherent in *mentor* so that participants could talk about nonpositive experiences they might have had with their advisors.

We defined *advisor* as the faculty member who has the greatest responsibility for helping guide the advisee through the graduate program. In addition, the advisor may influence the advisees' professional development (e.g., research, practice, career choice). It is important to note that counseling psychology doctoral programs use several different words to identify the person who performs the roles and functions of what we have termed an *advisor* (e.g., *advisor, major professor, committee chair, dissertation chair*) (Schlosser & Gelso, 2001).

Given the lack of empirical research on advising relationships, we thought that a qualitative methodology would be a good way to probe advisees' experiences deeply without constraining responses. We also believed that qualitative research would allow for a different, and potentially richer, description of advising relationships by using words rather than numbers for data. In addition, we wanted to know about specific aspects of the advising relationship because we felt that they would paint a more complete picture of the advising relationship, which would in turn illuminate participants' other responses.

Hence, we used the consensual qualitative research (CQR) methodology developed by Hill, Thompson, and Williams (1997). In CQR, a small number of cases is examined extensively to gain an in-depth understanding of the phenomenon, data analysis is conducted using a consensual group process, and conclusions emerge inductively from the data. In addition, an auditor checks the consensus judgments yielded by the analyses to ensure that the conclusions are as unbiased as possible and are based on data. We selected the CQR methodology (over other qualitative approaches) because CQR possesses some notable strengths. First, CQR uses multiple judges, as well as an auditor, thereby lessening the likelihood that any one person's perspective will unduly influence the data analysis process. Second, CQR provides a consistent yet flexible approach to the data gathering process. The interview is semistructured, which provides consistency across cases, yet allows for flexibility wherein interviewers may deviate from the protocol as needed on the basis of an individual participant's responses.

Our purpose in this study was to investigate students' perceptions of their relationships with their graduate advisors. To accomplish this task, we queried participants about several major areas of their advising relationships, including descriptions of the relationship itself (e.g., its foci), expectations about the relationship, and interpersonal interactions between themselves and their advisors. We were also interested in understanding the gains and costs students associated with their advising relationships, as well as any changes in the relationship over time. We chose to focus on counseling psychology (as opposed to other applied areas of psychology) in order to examine the advising relationship intensely in one area of psychology.

Method

Participants

Advisees. Sixteen 3rd-year counseling psychology doctoral students (14 women, 2 men; 14 Caucasian, 2 biracial) from nine universities participated in this study. Advisees ranged in age from 24 to 50 years ($M = 33.63$, $SD = 8.47$) and had been with their current advisor from 5 to 36 months ($M = 28.56$, $SD = 8.93$). Three had changed advisors at some point in their graduate program, and 13 indicated no such change. Ten advisees identified their current advisors as female, 6 as male; advisees estimated that their advisors were African American (3), Asian American (1), Caucasian (10), and multiracial (2). Students estimated the age of their current advisor to be between 31 and 70 years ($M = 44.53$, $SD = 9.96$).

Interviewers and judges. Three researchers conducted the audiotaped interviews and served as the primary research team: a 28-year-old Caucasian male, a 39-year-old Caucasian female, and a 24-year-old Caucasian female. At the beginning of the study, one researcher was a 4th-year graduate student in a coun-

175 seling psychology doctoral program, another was an assistant professor in a department of counseling and educational psychology, and another was a 2nd-year student in a counseling master's program. A 52-year-old Caucasian female professor in a department of psy-

180 chology served as the auditor. (All are authors of this article.)

Prior to conducting the interviews, the primary team discussed their own experiences as advisees, as well as their biases about the advising relationship.

185 During data analysis, similar discussions occurred periodically to enable the team to be mindful of their biases and try to set them aside. We briefly report these expectations to provide context for the analysis. Two of the researchers had extremely positive advising rela-

190 tionships focused mainly on research, career guidance, and program requirements. One researcher had never been a doctoral student and did not have clear expectations about the doctoral advising relationship. The auditor, who had advised students for 27 years, felt that

195 advising was one of her favorite job tasks; she thought that the major focus of the relationship was research, and that the relationship varied across advisees.

Measures

Demographic form. The demographic form requested that participants provide basic information

200 about age, gender, race, year in doctoral program, duration of current advising relationship, and whether or not they had ever changed advisors during doctoral training. Participants also answered questions about their advisors' gender, race, and estimated age.

205 *Interview protocol.* The first, semistructured interview opened with questions designed to gather general information about the advising relationship, such as a description of the advisor and the advising relationship, how the advisee and advisor had been matched, and the

210 focus of the advising relationship. In the next section of the interview, we sought specific information about the advising relationship to provide context for the advisees' experience. Thus, we inquired about the frequency and modality (i.e., individual or group) of advi-

215 sor-advisee meetings, behaviors related to professional development, and students' comfort level regarding sharing personal and professional issues with their advisors. The interview then moved to questions about the benefits and costs of the advising relationship, as

220 well as about conflict management between advisee and advisor. In closing the interview, we asked advisees to describe the strongest memories of their advising relationships and to rate their advising relationships on a 5-point Likert-type scale (1 = *very negative*, 3 =

225 *mixed*, 5 = *very positive*). Each question was asked of every participant, but the interviewers probed for additional information as was deemed necessary to develop a more complete understanding of that particular advising relationship.

230 A follow-up interview provided an opportunity for the researchers to ask any questions that may have arisen after the initial interview and for the participant to provide clarifications and/or alter previous comments. It also provided a chance for both researcher

235 and participant to explore any further thoughts and reactions that might have been stimulated by the first interview.

Procedures

Recruiting advisees. Twelve programs were randomly selected from the list of counseling psychology doctoral programs accredited by the American Psycho-

240 logical Association (APA; American Psychological Association, 1999). The training directors of these programs were sent a letter asking if we could contact their 3rd-year students to invite them to participate in a

245 study of graduate advising relationships. The letter explained that interested program directors need only provide the names and addresses of their current 3rd-year doctoral students. We believed that 3rd-year doctoral students would be able to talk about their advising

250 relationships with some substance because they would have greater perspective on their experiences in graduate school with their advisors than their counterparts in the first 2 years of their training. Furthermore, we thought that these students would be engaged in sig-

255 nificant ongoing work with their advisors during the interview period. We specifically did not select more advanced students because we believed that they would report very different experiences from students in the midst of their program. As the more advanced student

260 prepares for internships and jobs, the advising relationship is likely to change from that of advisor-advisee to that of peer or colleague. Finally, empirical research (Schlosser & Gelso, 2001) has identified the length of the advising relationship as an important factor to con-

265 sider. For all these reasons, we selected 3rd-year doctoral students.

Training directors were told that participants would complete two confidential, taped phone interviews in which they would respond to questions concerning

270 their advising relationship. Directors were assured that confidentiality would be maintained by the use of code numbers, and that no researcher would ask about the identity of the student's advisor or program. Two weeks after the first contact with program directors,

275 those who had not yet provided names and addresses of 3rd-year counseling psychology doctoral students were recontacted by phone and again invited to participate. For those who declined or still did not respond, this ended their involvement. For those who provided the

280 requested information about students, this also ended their involvement, as any further contact was made with the students directly.

Upon receiving lists of 3rd-year doctoral students from program training directors, a member of the pri-

285 mary team contacted students by letter and invited

them to participate in a study of graduate advising relationships, informing them of where we had obtained their contact information. The letter explained that those who agreed to participate would be asked questions about their advising relationship in two taped phone interviews, the first lasting about an hour, the second about 10 min. They were assured that their responses would be confidential via the assignment of code numbers, and that no researcher would make any attempt to identify participants' advisors or programs. Those who agreed to participate were asked to complete and return the consent and demographic forms included with the letter. Participants were also asked to give their names and phone numbers to enable the interviewer to arrange for the first interview. The first interview protocol was also included in this mailing, with the hope that it would help potential participants decide whether or not they wished to participate, and that it would stimulate the responses of those who chose to participate. Upon receipt of the consent and demographic forms, one of the primary researchers called the participant to set up the first interview.

We contacted 12 graduate programs dispersed nationally using the procedures described above. Nine out of these 12 programs provided us with a list of 3rd-year doctoral students or the e-mail address of their program's electronic mailing list. Of the 52 packets mailed and the two e-mail messages sent to program electronic mailing lists, 16 students agreed to participate.

Interviewing. Each of the primary team members completed both the initial and follow-up interviews with 5 to 6 participants. At the end of each interview, the researcher made notes on the interview, indicating how long the interview took and the interviewer's ability to build rapport with the participant. At the conclusion of the first interview, the follow-up interview was scheduled (typically 2 weeks after the initial interview). At the end of the follow-up interview, the interviewer debriefed the participant, then asked if she or he wanted to comment on a draft of the final results.

Transcripts. The interviews were audiotaped and transcribed verbatim (except for minimal encouragers). All identifying information for participant, advisor, and program was removed, and each participant was assigned a code number to maintain confidentiality.

Draft of final results. Those participants who requested one ($n = 8$) were sent a draft of the final results of the study for their comments. Participants were asked to comment on the degree to which their individual experiences were captured by the group results. They were also asked to confirm that their confidentiality had been maintained. Only 1 participant returned comments; she indicated that she was glad the study had been conducted and felt that we had captured her experiences as an advisee. She also offered some suggestions for future research.

Procedures for Analyzing Data

Consensual Qualitative Research (CQR) methods (Hill et al., 1997) were used to analyze the data. The essence of CQR is reaching consensus about the meaning and categorization of the data. Consensus is achieved through the primary team discussing their individual perceptions and then agreeing on a final conceptualization. At least some disagreement is the norm but is worked through until eventual agreement is reached. Two of the three members of the primary team knew each other well, whereas the third was initially less known. In addition, the second author (i.e., the assistant professor) was more familiar with the methodology than the other two members of the primary team (i.e., the graduate students).

The key features of CQR are a reliance on words rather than numbers to describe phenomena, as well as the intensive study of a small number of cases. Additionally, the context of the whole case is used to understand specific parts of the experience, and the analysis process is inductive, with understanding built from observations of the data rather than imposing a structure on the data ahead of time. Finally, the process involves dividing responses to open-ended questions from interviews into domains (i.e., topic areas), constructing core ideas (i.e., abstracts or brief summaries) for all material within each domain for each individual case, and then developing categories to describe the themes in the core ideas within domains across cases (cross-analysis). Consensus is achieved to ensure that the "best" construction is developed considering all of the data, and an auditor checks the consensus judgments to ensure that the primary team does not overlook important data. Finally, the primary team continually returns to the raw data to make sure that their conclusions are sound and are based on the data.

Coding of domains. A "start list" (Miles & Huberman, 1994) of domains was developed by the primary team by grouping the questions (on the basis of content) from the interview protocol. The domains were altered after reviewing the first few transcripts and then further refined by going through additional transcripts. Additional changes were made throughout the process to reflect the emerging data. Once the domains were set, the cases that had been initially coded were reexamined, and their coding was modified to be consistent with the domain list. Using the transcripts, the three judges independently assigned each meaning unit (a complete thought, ranging from one phrase to several sentences) from each transcript into one or more domains. The judges discussed the assignment of meaning units into domains until consensus was reached.

Coding of core ideas. Each judge independently read all data within each domain for a specific case and wrote what she or he considered to be the core ideas (i.e., concise descriptions of the general concepts of the data). Judges discussed each core idea until they reached consensus about content and wording. A con-

Table 1
Domains and Categories of Satisfied and Unsatisfied Cases

Domain	Category	Frequency of:	
		Satisfied cases	Unsatisfied cases
Description of advising relationship (AR)	Positive	Typical	—
	Negative or shallow/null/businesslike	—	General
Advisor–advisee pairing	Chose	Typical	—
	Assigned	Variant	General
Meetings with advisor	Individual meetings	General	General
	Group meetings	Typical	Variant
	Frequent meetings	Typical	—
	Infrequent meetings	Variant	General
Focus on AR	Research a part of AR	General	Typical
	Research not a part of AR	—	Variant
	Program requirements part of AR	General	Typical
	Career guidance part of AR	Typical	—
	Career guidance not part of AR	—	Typical
Professional interactions with advisor	Advisor encouraged student to participate in conferences and/or introduced them to important people	Typical	Variant
	Advisor did not encourage student to participate in conferences and/or introduce them to important people	Variant	Typical
Comfort disclosing information with advisor			
Professional	Very comfortable	Typical	Variant
	Cautious	Variant	Typical
Personal	Cautious	Typical	General
	Very comfortable	Variant	—
Expectations about AR			
Initial	Collegial/supportive AR	Typical	General
	Program guidance/help with dissertation	Variant	Typical
Changes	Want more guidance	Typical	—
	No changes	Variant	—
	Expectations unmet and were lowered	—	General
Benefits of the AR	Nonspecific gains	General	General
	Positive growth as a researcher	Typical	—
	Accessibility of advisor	Typical	—
	Positive growth as a therapist	Variant	—
Costs of the AR	Needs not met by advisor so student goes elsewhere	Typical	General
	Lack of mentoring	—	General
	Inaccessibility of advisor	—	Typical
	Political disadvantages	—	Typical
Conflict management between advisor and advisee	Dealt with openly; working through conflict strengthens AR	Typical	—
	No conflict in AR	Variant	—
	Conflict/disconnection is avoided/not discussed in AR	—	Typical
Changes in AR over time	Became more positive	General	—
	Became more distant/got worse	—	Typical
	Stayed the same	—	Variant
Strongest memory of AR	Positive memory	General	Typical
	Negative memory	—	Variant

Note. For the satisfied group (*n* = 10), general = all 10 cases represented; typical = 5–9 cases represented, variant = 2–4 cases represented. For the unsatisfied group (*n* = 6), general = all 6 cases represented; typical = 3–5 cases represented, variant = 2 cases represented. Dashes indicate no category for the indicated domain.

sensus version was then developed for each case, which included the core ideas and the corresponding interview data for each of the domains. The auditor examined the consensus version of each case and checked the accuracy of both the domain coding and the wording of the core ideas, making comments and suggestions for changes. The judges then discussed the auditor's remarks and again reached consensus.

Cross-analysis. The purpose of the cross-analysis is to cluster the core ideas within domains across cases.

The initial cross analyses were done on 14 of the 16 cases, with 2 cases left out as a stability check (Hill et al., 1997). Each member of the primary team examined the core ideas from all cases for each domain and independently created categories that best captured these core ideas. The team then came to consensus on the conceptual labels of the categories and the specific core ideas that belonged in each category.

After this initial set of categories was established, the judges returned to the final consensus versions of each case to determine whether the cases contained data not previously coded for any of the categories. If such data were discerned (as determined by a consensus judgment of the primary team), the consensus version of the case was altered accordingly to reflect this category, and the core idea was then added to the appropriate category in the cross-analysis. Categories and domains were thus continually revised until everyone felt assured that the data were well represented. The auditor then reviewed the cross-analysis; the auditor's suggestions were considered by the primary team and incorporated if consensus was reached.

Stability check. After the initial cross-analysis was complete, the remaining 2 cases (temporarily omitted in the initial cross-analysis) were added back in to see if the designations of general, typical, and variant changed, and also to see if the team felt that new categories needed to be added to accommodate the new cases. The remaining cases did not alter the results substantially, and hence the findings were considered stable.

Results

During data analysis, it became apparent that our participants were describing two very different kinds of advising relationships. For this reason, we divided the sample on the basis of whether the student was satisfied or unsatisfied with her/his relationship with her/his advisor. To determine how to categorize each of the 16 cases (i.e., satisfied or unsatisfied), we looked at the participants' responses to their description of the advising relationship (e.g., positive, neutral, or negative). In cases where the decision was not clear, we incorporated a more complete review of the data (i.e., looking at the majority of the transcript) to assess whether or not a particular participant was satisfied. Cases were not deemed "satisfied" or "unsatisfied" until consensus among the primary team members was reached. After consensus was reached, we used the students' Likert-type ratings of their advising relationships to "triangulate" our findings (i.e., to collect data from different methods; Hill et al., 1997). Students whom we deemed (via the process just described) satisfied with their advising relationships consistently rated these relationships as 4 or greater on a 5-point Likert scale (5 = *very positive*; $M = 4.65$, $SD = 0.75$). Conversely, students whom we deemed unsatisfied with their advising relationships consistently rated these relationships as 3 or lower ($M = 2.75$, $SD = 0.42$).

We structured the results on a domain by domain basis. Within each domain, we first present findings that emerged from the 10 students who were satisfied with their advising relationships. Then, we present results from the 6 students who were not satisfied with their advising relationships. Table 1 displays results for both the satisfied and unsatisfied cases. For the satisfied cases, categories were considered general if all 10 cases were represented, typical if there were 5 to 9 cases, and variant if there were 2 to 4 cases. For the unsatisfied cases, categories were considered general if all 6 cases were represented, typical for 3 to 5 cases, and variant if there were only 2 cases.

Description of Advising Relationship

Typically, satisfied students described their advising relationships as positive. For example, one student stated, "I feel very comfortable with her and I don't mean warm and fuzzy all the time; I feel comfortable expressing disagreements to her, and I know when disagreements come up, we are able to bring it to the table and talk about it." Similarly, students also reported that their advisors were supportive, friendly, collegial, and respectful; 2 students indicated that their advisors worked to level the playing field so they did not feel a power differential.

Unsatisfied students generally described their advising relationships as negative or neutral. One student, for example, felt that it was hard to establish rapport with her advisor because he was cold and distant. Other students saw their advising relationships as shallow or businesslike. For instance, 1 student felt that her advisor was superficial, and another student experienced her advisor as focusing solely on classes and as disinterested in her as a person.

Advisor–Advisee Pairing

Satisfied students typically reported that they were able to choose their advisor and only variantly reported being assigned to their advisor. In contrast, all 6 unsatisfied students reported that they had been assigned to work with their advisor upon entry to the doctoral program.

Meetings with Advisor

Students satisfied with their advising relationships generally indicated having individual meetings with their advisors, whether regularly scheduled or spontaneous. In addition, students typically reported being a part of group meetings (e.g., research teams) with their advisors. With regard to frequency, satisfied students typically reported frequent meetings (e.g., weekly) with their advisors, and only variantly reported infrequent meetings (e.g., once per semester).

Unsatisfied students generally had infrequent individual meetings with their advisors (e.g., once or twice a semester). These students also variantly were part of group meetings with their advisors. One student, for example, was a member of her advisor's research team.

Focus of the Advising Relationship

Satisfied students described several foci of the advising relationship. First, they generally reported that research was a part of the advising relationship, whether related to theses, dissertations, or other projects. For example, 1 student reported that he was working with his advisor on multiple aspects of his dissertation (i.e., getting participants, analyzing data, and writing up the results). Second, students generally reported that discussing program requirements was a part of their advising relationship. Some examples of these requirements include coursework, dissertation, internship, comprehensive examinations, and annual student reviews. Third, satisfied students typically reported that they focused on career guidance with their advisors as a part of their advising relationship. For example, 1 student reported discussing career aspirations with her advisor and receiving guidance from her advisor about what the student needed to do to achieve those aspirations.

Unsatisfied students also described several foci of the advising relationship. First, they typically reported that research was a part of the advising relationship, whether related to theses or dissertations, or to other projects. These students also variantly reported that research was not part of the advising relationship. One student, for instance, indicated that her advisor was not interested in her dissertation. Second, unsatisfied students typically indicated that program requirements were a part of the advising relationship. Some students, for example, felt that dealing with the tasks of graduate school was the only reason that they had relationships with their advisors. Third, career guidance was typically not a part of advising relationships for unsatisfied students. One student, for example, felt that her advisor was inaccessible for discussing career concerns.

Professional Interactions with Advisor

Typically, satisfied students indicated that their advisors encouraged them to participate in professional conferences and/or introduced them to important people. For example, 1 student indicated that his advisor encouraged conference attendance because they were positive, enjoyable professional experiences. Variantly, however, these students indicated that their advisors did not encourage conference participation and/or make important introductions.

In contrast to the satisfied students, unsatisfied students typically indicated that their advisors did not encourage them to participate in professional conferences nor introduce them to important people. Only variantly did students indicate that such activities occurred. For example, 1 student indicated that her advisor encouraged her to present her research at a conference.

Comfort Disclosing Professional Information with Advisor

Satisfied students typically reported feeling very comfortable disclosing aspects of their professional lives to their advisors. One student shared her insecurities about her abilities, and another student talked about his doubts concerning his career choice. Variantly, students reported feeling cautious talking about their professional lives with their advisors. Here, 1 student, who was concerned about how much to disclose, indicated that she talked in a very general, nondefensive manner because she did not want to sound like she has "a *DSM-IV* diagnosis."

Unsatisfied students, however, typically reported feeling cautious talking about their professional lives with their advisors. One student indicated that she was never comfortable talking to her advisor because he was unpredictable (i.e., sometimes supportive, other times not). Another student felt that sharing any negative feelings would be politically unsafe.

Comfort Disclosing Personal Information with Advisor

Typically, satisfied students indicated caution about sharing personal information with their advisors. One student stated that she would only share personal information as it affected her professional life, whereas other students indicated that it was simply not their style to share too much of themselves in a professional context. Variantly, some students did express a high degree of comfort sharing personal information with their advisors. In fact, 1 student indicated that he would have been less satisfied with his advising relationship if he could not have talked about personal information with his advisor.

All 6 unsatisfied students indicated being cautious sharing personal information with their advisors. One student felt that her advisor was not interested in her personally and that she could not talk to her advisor because he was "like a stranger" to her. Another student said that he was not comfortable sharing anything about his personal life with his advisor.

Initial Expectations from the Advising Relationship

Satisfied students typically indicated that they had expected a collegial or supportive relationship with their advisor. One student, for example, expected her advisor to be a "mentor" and professional role model; another student wanted someone who was interested in the person's whole experience of graduate school (i.e., professional and personal matters). Students variantly expected program guidance and help with their dissertations. For example, one student wanted her advisor's assistance to complete her coursework and dissertation in a timely fashion.

Interestingly, unsatisfied students generally indicated that they, too, expected a collegial and/or supportive relationship with their advisors. For example, 1 student expected to be interpersonally close with the faculty and with her advisor; however, this student reported that her expectations were unmet. Students also typically expected program guidance and help with their dissertations. One student, for example, expected her advisor to discuss her progress in the program.

Change in Students' Expectations Since Entering Graduate School

Typically, satisfied students indicated wanting even more guidance now from their advisors than they had initially expected. One student, for instance, felt that she needed to learn as much as possible during her remaining time in the program and hoped that her advisor would "give me what I need before I leave." Students variantly reported no changes in expectations.

Generally, students who were unsatisfied with their advising relationships indicated that their expectations of their advisors were unmet or lowered over time. As an illustration, 1 student now asked little of her advisor and felt that her advisor gave little to her. Another student stated, "I expected more personal interest in me and more help adjusting.... I expected my advisor to give a shit about me."

Benefits of the Advising Relationship

Students satisfied with their advising relationships generally reported various, nonspecific gains. For example, one student felt that she received fairly large gains from her advisor with regard to teaching, whereas another student felt that her advisor was an excellent role model. Other students acknowledged receiving help with how to navigate a doctoral program successfully, how to apply for and obtain clinical internships, and how to network. In the first of two typical categories, students reported positive growth in their work as researchers. For instance, students reported learning how to design and complete research projects, run statistical analyses, and write manuscripts. In the second typical category, students indicated that their advisors were accessible. For example, several students commented that their advisors' doors were always open and that students felt comfortable dropping in without an appointment. Finally, students variantly reported positive growth in their work as therapists. Students here reported positive changes in their clinical skills and increased counseling self-efficacy (note that the advisor had also served as the clinical supervisor at some point for these students).

In the second group of students, despite being unsatisfied, they nevertheless generally reported nonspecific gains from their advising relationships. For example, 1 advisee felt that her advisor gave her a political advantage because the advisor could "pull more weight" in the department, whereas another student felt that research opportunities were available to her because of her advisor.

Costs of the Advising Relationship

Satisfied students typically reported that they went to other sources (e.g., other faculty, supervisors, or students) if their advisor was not meeting some of their needs. For example, 1 student said that he sought out a neuropsychologist for content advice on his dissertation, and another student reported relying on her classmates for support. Students also typically reported some political disadvantages because of their advising relationships (e.g., negative assumptions made about students by others based on their advisors' interests or interpersonal style). One student, for example, was seen as being disinterested in research and disorganized because her advisor was known to have these qualities. Another student felt concerned that her advisor, as an

assistant professor, lacked the power to speak her mind openly to her colleagues and to support the student if the student wanted to do something different from the norm.

Whereas only some of the satisfied students reported going to other sources if their advisor was not meeting their needs, all 6 of the unsatisfied students reported having to go elsewhere to get their advising needs met. For example, 1 student said that she sought out everything she needed from other people because she did not get anything from her advisor. Students also generally reported a lack of mentoring by their advisors. For example, 1 student felt like she had to figure everything out for herself and was mad and resentful toward her advisor because of this lack of guidance. Another student described her advising relationship as not fostering her development as a professional. Finally, students typically reported that their advisors were inaccessible. As an illustration, 1 student reported talking with her advisor only once all year in an informal, unplanned meeting in the hallway.

Conflict Management Between Advisor and Advisee

Satisfied students typically reported that conflict was dealt with openly and that working through any conflict strengthened the advising relationship. Several students, for instance, felt that their advisors were very open, so they felt comfortable addressing difficult subjects. Furthermore, 1 student reported that processing conflict improved the depth of her advising relationship. Students variantly reported a lack of conflict in the advising relationship.

Unsatisfied students typically reported that conflict was avoided or not discussed in their advising relationship. As examples, one student felt like she would avoid her advisor or "kiss her ass" if there was any conflict; another student thought her advisor was unaware of any conflict, and a 3rd student indicated that her advisor's personality style "would not allow for conflict."

Changes in Advising Relationship Over Time

Students who were satisfied with their advising relationships generally reported that their advising relationships became more positive over time. Most of these students indicated that they had grown closer to their advisors and felt that their comfort with their advisors had increased as a result of getting to know their advisors better.

Typically, unsatisfied students reported that they became more distant from their advisors or that their advising relationships worsened over time. For example, some of these students began to critically examine their advising relationships, mostly because they felt mistreated, which led them to feel disappointed with their advisors. Other students felt that their advisors became less accessible during the course of their graduate program, contributing to students' dissatisfaction with the advising relationship. Unsatisfied students variantly reported that their advising relationships stayed the same or became more positive. One student, for example, though still globally dissatisfied with her advising relationship, gained some respect for her advisor after initially seeing her advisor in a fairly negative light.

Strongest Memory of Advising Relationship

Satisfied students generally recalled positive events as the strongest memory of their advising relationship, whether about professional or personal issues. For example, 1 student felt like a professional and a peer when her advisor approached her about publishing her thesis, whereas another student felt personally special when her advisor left a conversation with other faculty members to come check on the student soon after the death of the student's father.

Unsatisfied students reported that the strongest memories of their advising relationships were typically positive, in which they felt supported about professional issues. For example, 1 student remembered her advisor inviting several students to her home for a potluck dinner and giving a workshop on how to submit proposals for professional conferences. Variantly, students recalled negative events in which they felt rejected by their advisors. For example, when 1 student approached her advisor because she needed to talk about an important issue, the advisor's response was, "How long will this take?" The student felt like her advisor "blew" her "off"; as a result of this interaction, the student did not want any further interactions with her advisor.

Discussion

Overall, several differences were noted between satisfied and unsatisfied advising relationships. Thematically, most of these discrepancies can be clustered into interpersonal (e.g., satisfaction, comfort disclosing, conflict management) and instructional (e.g., research, career guidance, and professional development) components. Interpersonal components focus on the relational concerns between advisors and advisees, whereas instructional components focus on the didactic or task-focused nature of advisor-advisee interactions related to training (Kahn & Gelso, 1997). The recognition of interpersonal and instructional components of professional psychology training is consistent with previous empirical research on research training (Gelso, 1997; Kahn & Gelso, 1997) and graduate advising (Schlosser & Gelso, 2001). In addition, some other issues emerged (i.e., how advisor and advisee were paired to work together, expectations about the advising relationship) that did not fit cleanly into either cluster yet appear to be important features of the advising relationship. Each is amplified below.

Interpersonal Components

Students who were satisfied with their advising relationships described the relationship as positive, re-

ported having rapport with their advisors, and felt that these relationships improved over time. This finding is consistent with Schlosser and Gelso (2001), who found that advisor-advisee rapport was an important component of a good advisory working alliance. Conversely, students who were unsatisfied with their advising relationships described these relationships as shallow, businesslike, or negative. It may be that unsatisfied students did not get what they were seeking from their advising relationships or perceived more costs than benefits and thus were not satisfied. Alternatively (or perhaps additively), these students may have been exposed to negative advising, which can be potentially damaging to the student (Gelso & Lent, 2000).

Our results also indicated that comfort disclosing professional information with the advisor happens more frequently in satisfied (vs. unsatisfied) advising relationships. Satisfied students typically felt very comfortable disclosing professional information to the advisor, whereas unsatisfied students were cautious doing so. Students who felt comfortable disclosing professional information may have received implicit and/or explicit messages from their advisors that this material was appropriate for advisory meetings, and/or these students felt validated by their advisors when these issues were discussed. For unsatisfied students, a lack of trust between student and advisor may explain the caution in disclosing. This mistrust may also reflect an absence of the interpersonal connection between advisor and advisee that Schlosser and Gelso (2001) found to be an important aspect of a positive advisory working alliance.

Interestingly, students were almost uniformly cautious when it came to sharing personal information with their advisors, regardless of satisfaction with their advising relationships. This may point to the role that students think the advising relationship should play (i.e., it is for professional purposes, not personal ones). Several students (both satisfied and unsatisfied) said that they did not want to share personal information unless it affected their professional work. However, a few students (notably the satisfied students) in our sample reported enjoying the personal (i.e., non-work-related) relationship with their advisors, and felt that they would be less satisfied with their advising relationships without those personal interactions complementing the professional activities. Therefore, individual advisee personality differences may have dictated the degree to which personal interactions were sought out and/or expected from the advisor. Finally, the advisor's preferences also certainly played a role in the degree to which student and advisor discussed personal and professional information. Advisors may have encouraged or discouraged advisees from sharing personal and/or professional information depending on what they perceived to be their role as advisor.

When it came to conflict management, large differences were noted between satisfied and unsatisfied students. Satisfied students reported that open processing of conflict strengthened the advising relationship; the healthy resolution of interpersonal conflict may have even enhanced satisfaction with the advising relationship. In contrast, unsatisfied students reported that conflict was avoided or not discussed. For the unsatisfied students, this conflict avoidance was usually seen as a function of the advisor's personality (e.g., not allowing for or addressing conflict) or the student's interpersonal style (e.g., showing deference to authority).

Instructional Components

All students had individual meetings with their advisors, and several reported being part of a group (e.g., research team) in which they had regular contact with their advisor. The key difference between satisfied and unsatisfied students was in the frequency of these meetings. In satisfied relationships, contact was quite frequent (e.g., once a week), whereas unsatisfied students saw their advisors as little as once a semester or even once a year. Thinking about the myriad potential functions of the advisor, it is hard to imagine accomplishing very much with annual or semesterly meetings; it is also difficult to imagine having a meaningful relationship with such minimal contact. Conversely, frequent contact was likely to have allowed satisfied students to feel supported and guided by their advisors, as well as having a place to get their needs met. Although frequent meetings do not guarantee a positive advising relationship, regular student-advisor contact was the norm for satisfied students in our sample.

Research appears to have been an essential component of the advising relationship in counseling psychology Ph.D. programs. This finding makes intuitive sense, as completion of the dissertation is a graduation requirement; faculty may also encourage students to be on other research teams. Although advising varies by program, many satisfied students in our sample reported that their advisors served as a guide through both the research process and other aspects of the training program (e.g., coursework, comprehensive examinations). These findings are consistent with the extant literature on graduate advising (Gelso & Schlosser, 2001; Schlosser, 2002). Research was still seen as an important part of unsatisfied advising relationships; however, these students often felt that their advisors did not guide them enough or were not interested in the students' research.

Another significant difference between satisfied and unsatisfied students was the focus on career guidance in the advising relationship. Satisfied students typically received such guidance, whereas unsatisfied students typically did not. Because the purpose of graduate training is the preparation for a professional career, the absence of career guidance was likely an important loss for these students. As evidenced by some of our participants' remarks, the lack of career

guidance appears to have contributed to students' dissatisfaction with the advising relationship.

Professional development proved to be another important area in this cluster of instructional components. Encouragement to participate in professional conferences and introductions to people at conferences typically occurred in the context of a satisfied advising relationship and not in unsatisfied ones. These advisor behaviors are likely to communicate the advisor's interest and investment in the student's career. For unsatisfied students whose advisors tended not to encourage conference participation or make professional introductions, the message may have been perceived as, "I don't care about your career," regardless of the advisor's intent. Students may also have ignored an advisor's encouragement if they perceived the advising relationship as less than positive.

Perhaps one of the more obvious differences between satisfied and unsatisfied students was the perceived benefits and costs associated with the advising relationship. By definition, satisfied students reported more gains and fewer costs than did their unsatisfied counterparts. Of more interest here is the information about the aspects that are likely to be benefits of a good advising relationship (e.g., student growth as a scientist-practitioner, accessibility of advisor). However, these undoubtedly do not represent all of the benefits necessary for a student to be satisfied with her or his advising relationship. In fact, we believe that other gains (e.g., social support from the advisor) might be facilitative to the advising relationship. Responses from our unsatisfied students point to specific factors (i.e., unmet needs forcing the student to seek help elsewhere, lack of mentoring, inaccessibility of the advisor, political disadvantages) that were absent in their advising relationships. Looking across the data, it appears that professional mentoring and advisor accessibility may be crucial aspects of the advising relationship.

Other Issues

One emergent issue from our results was how students and advisors were paired to work together. Specifically, satisfied students were allowed to choose their advisors, whereas unsatisfied students were assigned to an advisor. Thus, the simple procedure of allowing students to choose an advisor may facilitate the development of a positive and successful advising relationship. Because students often have little control or power in their graduate programs, the ability to choose one's advisor may be tremendously empowering. Conversely, being assigned to an advisor may frustrate the student and could contribute to dissatisfaction with the advising relationship. If the student is assigned to work with an advisor, however, the freedom to change to a different advisor may enhance the student's satisfaction with the advising relationship.

With regard to changes in students' expectations about the advising relationship, satisfied students either

965 wanted continued guidance from their advisors or reported no changes in their expectations (often because
those expectations were met). In contrast, unsatisfied
students consistently indicated that their initial expectations were unmet and often were even lowered. For
970 these students, having their expectations go unmet appears to have tainted their advising relationships, as
several unsatisfied students reported now wanting
nothing from their advisors. The findings suggest that it
is important for students and advisors to talk about
975 expectations about their relationships; not having such
a discussion may set up students and advisors for later
disappointment.

Summary and Conclusions

In sum, the positive advising relationship could be
described as one in which the members have a good
980 rapport, process conflict openly, and work together to
facilitate the advisee's progress through the graduate
program and development as an emerging professional.
This description shares some common elements with
descriptions of mentoring relationships (e.g.,
985 Hollingsworth & Fassinger, 2002; Russell & Adams,
1997). Although a mentoring type of advising relationship may be highly desirable, results from the current
study suggest that not all students enjoy that kind of
relationship with their advisors. Thus, to build positive
990 advising relationships, both student and advisor must
be thoughtful and purposeful about the formation and
maintenance of their relationship, paying attention to
each person's expectations and goals.

Conversely, students who are unsatisfied with their
995 advising relationships (and have relationships that are
neutral or negative) are unlikely to refer to their advisors as mentors because the term mentor connotes a
positive valence. Rather, they might report negative
mentoring behaviors, as demonstrated by 1 of our par-
1000 ticipants who wanted only that his advisor "give a shit"
about him. Recently, some research (i.e., Johnson &
Huwe, 2002) has identified dysfunctional aspects of
mentoring (e.g., mentor neglect, boundary violations,
relational conflict). Such aspects parallel the current
1005 results from the unsatisfied students, who likewise discussed advisor unavailability and interpersonal conflict. If advisor and advisee were able to identify dysfunctional aspects of their relationship, perhaps they
could work together toward improving the quality of
1010 that relationship.

Satisfaction with the advising relationship may
mean that the relationship is good, or perhaps "good
enough" (Gelso, 2001). In a satisfied relationship, students may not perceive missing aspects of the relation-
1015 ship as harmful (i.e., the positive nature of the relationship outweighs what is perceived as lacking). For example, a satisfied student might not care as much about
having a more "personal" relationship with the advisor
if the student's needs are met in other areas by the ad-
1020 visor (e.g., dissertation, career guidance). Conversely,

an unsatisfied student may be more sensitive to "missing" aspects of the advising relationship and may experience them as damaging and/or painful because the
overall relationship is not good enough to compensate
1025 for such absent elements.

Results from the current study support the notion
that advising and mentoring, although not synonymous,
do share some common characteristics. Because of the
potential overlap between these two areas, an examina-
1030 tion of the similarities and differences between the advising and mentoring literatures might be fruitful as a
guide for future researchers. However, because of the
diversity within the mentoring literature (i.e., mentoring has been studied in many arenas, including busi-
1035 ness and industry, academia, and community mental
health, among others), some parameters are necessary.
First, data from Green and Bauer (1995) suggest that
mentoring is contextually bound (i.e., mentoring is
defined by the arena), and as such, differs across set-
1040 tings (e.g., business and industry, academia). Hence,
only research investigating how mentoring in academia
is consistent with or divergent from graduate advising
will be considered. Second, because the current study
focused on the advisee's perceptions of the graduate
1045 advising relationship, this discussion will be likewise
limited in its scope, focusing on research about the
protégé's perceptions of the mentoring relationship.
Under these parameters, the mentoring literature is
limited to two main areas (i.e., providing descriptive
1050 data about mentoring and examining research-related
student outcomes); these are the two areas that are discussed below as they pertain to advising relationships.

Descriptive studies have revealed what characteristics protégés deem important in a mentor. For example,
1055 several studies (Cronan-Hillix et al., 1986; Knox &
McGovern, 1988; Wilde & Schau; 1991) found that
good mentors were typically interested in and supportive of their students, possessed knowledge and demonstrated competence, and evidenced excellent inter-
1060 personal skills. These mentors were able to use such
qualities to form and maintain relationships with their
protégés, as well as to collaboratively work with them.
Conversely, bad mentors were described as having
extremely poor interpersonal skills, lacking interest in
1065 and support for their students, demonstrating incompetence, lacking knowledge, and being inaccessible and
unavailable to the student-protégé.

When comparing the above research with the results of the current study, it appears that mentoring and
1070 advising do share some common characteristics. In
both advising and mentoring, there is a strong emphasis
on the interpersonal connection between members of
the dyad, a connection that may be the most powerful
aspect in the advising relationship. When rapport be-
1075 tween advisor and advisee exists, the advisee gets support, knowledge, safety, time, and attention from the
advisor. In addition, both advising and mentoring focus
partially on the collaborative work (e.g., research) be-

217

tween student and faculty. Thus, advising and mentoring both possess psychosocial and career-related functions. There are also aspects of advisors and mentors that are seen as consistently negative. One example is the availability and accessibility of the advisor or mentor, which appears to consistently differentiate positive advising relationships from negative ones (i.e., in positive advising relationships, advisors are more available or accessible than they are in negative advising relationships).

In reviewing outcome studies of mentoring in academia, we found that these pieces of research have focused largely on research-related outcomes for students, such as research productivity and research self-efficacy; however, this research has yielded inconsistent findings. For example, two studies found that students' perceptions of the mentoring relationship was not important in predicting their scholarly activity (Green & Bauer, 1995; Kahn, 2001), whereas other research (e.g., Cronan-Hillix et al., 1986; Hollingsworth & Fassinger, 2002) suggested that mentoring can promote student research self-efficacy and productivity (measured by research publications and presentations). Empirical research has consistently found positive correlations between the graduate advising relationship and research outcomes (Schlosser, 2002; Schlosser & Gelso, 2001). The findings from the current study are consistent with the previous research on advising relationships and suggest that advising relationships can have positive effects where research related outcomes are concerned.

Finally, it is important to note that *negative mentoring* is not likely describing a negative relationship but rather a positive relationship with the presence of some negative behaviors (Eby, McManus, Simon, & Russell, 2000). In comparison, *negative advising* is likely describing a negative relationship with severity ranging from relatively minor (e.g., ambivalent feelings about advising relationship) to harmful and psychonoxious. This distinction, which should be incorporated into future research, is likely because of the positive valence attached to the term *mentor*, whereas the term *advisor* is more neutral.

Limitations

Our intent was to investigate the advising relationship in graduate school from the perspective of the student-advisee. We recognize that the results are limited to this sample of 16 3rd-year counseling psychology doctoral students who responded to requests for participation. Because of the potential for self-selection bias, these results may not be representative of those students who chose not to participate. In addition, our sample was mostly Caucasian women; although they make up the majority of psychology graduate students, it could be problematic to generalize our findings to other student groups (e.g., males, advisees of color). Furthermore, until empirical research has examined advising relationships in the other applied areas of psychology (i.e., clinical, school), we do not know if our findings are limited to APA-accredited counseling psychology programs or whether they also reflect advising relationships in these other areas. As noted by Schlosser and Gelso (2001), the developmental stage of the graduate student may play a significant role in the advising relationship. Thus, students at different stages of training may describe their advising relationships in different terms.

We also realize that only the advisees' perspectives were assessed in this study, and as such, we lack the advisors' views about the graduate advising relationship; further inquiry is underway to examine the advisor's perceptions. Additionally, some students may not have wanted to discuss their advisors in a negative light, either because of respect for their advisors or because they feared that their identity (or the identity of their advisor) could be revealed. Finally, it also may have been hard for participants to articulate certain aspects of their relationships because they may not have been aware of their feelings.

Implications for Research and Practice

Our study suggests that students perceive the advising relationship to be an important aspect of their graduate training; this is consistent with previous research (Gelso, 1997). There are a few issues to consider regarding the graduate advising relationship. First, the decision of whether to assign advisees to advisors or to allow them to choose seems important. This decision, which may affect the advising relationship, also communicates the program's position with regard to the students having a voice. Second, frequent contact with one's advisor and the sense of advisor accessibility appears to be a simple yet powerful factor in contributing to satisfaction with the advising relationship. Obviously, the actual frequency of meetings will vary depending on the needs of the student. However, the student may perceive the advisor as inaccessible if the advisor is overloaded with advisees or has no time to meet with the advisee. This speaks to the issue of advisor load (i.e., limiting the number of advisees) so that advisors can devote adequate attention to each advisee. Another issue pertains to the degree of satisfaction with the advising relationship; this may be related to the kind of match between student and advisor. For example, similar interests (e.g., research, career goals, or interpersonal style) may contribute to the perception of match between advisee and advisor; the converse is also likely to be true (i.e., dissimilar interests could detract from perceptions of fit).

Future inquiry could also examine specific types of advisor-advisee interactions (e.g., cross-cultural advising relationships), as well as the effects of the advising relationship on relevant outcomes for students (e.g., completion of the doctoral degree, satisfaction with graduate school, career choice and satisfaction) and faculty members (e.g., feelings of generativity, job satisfaction). In addition, the training environment may affect the advising relationship, so examining the overall training environment along with the advisor-advisee relationship would be worthwhile. Finally, the role of the advising relationship seems to change over time. Thus, research examining the advising relationship at different points in time (e.g., beginning of graduate training, during internship) may yield fruitful results.

1195

References

American Psychological Association (1999). *Accredited programs in counseling psychology.* Retrieved July 17, 1999, from http://www.apa.org/ed/counspsy.html

Cronan-Hillix, T., Gensheimer, L. K., Cronan-Hillix, W. A., & Davidson, W. S. (1986). Students' views of mentors in psychology graduate training. *Teaching of Psychology, 13,* 123–127.

Eby, L. T., McManus, S. E., Simon, S. A., & Russell, J. E. A. (2000). The protégé's perspective regarding negative mentoring experiences: The development of a taxonomy. *Journal of Vocational Behavior, 57,* 1–21.

Gelso, C. J. (1979). Research in counseling: Methodological and professional issues. *Counseling Psychologist, 8,* 7–35.

Gelso, C. J. (1993). On the making of a scientist-practitioner: A theory of research training in professional psychology. *Professional Psychology: Research and Practice, 24,* 468–476.

Gelso, C. J. (1997). The making of a scientist in applied psychology: An attribute by treatment conception. *Counseling Psychologist, 25,* 307–320.

Gelso, C. J. (2001, August). Toward a theory of the advising relationship in graduate education: Or the "good enough" relationship. In S. Knox (Chair), *Exploring graduate advising relationships in counseling psychology.* Symposium conducted at the Annual Convention of the American Psychological Association, San Francisco, CA.

Gelso, C. J., & Lent, R. W. (2000). Scientific training and scholarly productivity: The person, the training environment, and their interaction. In S. D. Brown & R. W. Lent (Eds.), *Handbook of counseling psychology* (3rd ed., pp. 109–139), New York: Wiley.

Gelso, C. J., & Schlosser, L. Z. (2001). Studying the graduate advising relationship: New concepts and findings. *Psychotherapy Bulletin, 36,* 6–8.

Green, S. G., & Bauer, T. N. (1995). Supervisory mentoring by advisers: Relationships with doctoral student potential, productivity, and commitment. *Personnel Psychology, 48,* 537–561.

Hill, C. E. (1997). The effects of my research training environment: Where are my students now? *Counseling Psychologist, 25,* 74–81.

Hill, C. E., Thompson, B. J., & Williams, E. N. (1997). A guide to conducting consensual qualitative research. *Counseling Psychologist, 25,* 517–572.

Hollingsworth, M. A., & Fassinger, R. E. (2002). The role of faculty mentors in the research training of counseling psychology doctoral students. *Journal of Counseling Psychology, 49,* 324–330.

Johnson, W. B., & Huwe, J. M. (2002). Toward a typology of mentorship dysfunction in graduate school. *Psychotherapy: Theory/Research/Practice/Teaching, 39,* 44–55.

Kahn, J. H. (2001). Predicting the scholarly activity of counseling psychology students: A refinement and extension. *Journal of Counseling Psychology, 48,* 344–354.

Kahn, J. H., & Gelso, C. J. (1997). Factor Structure of the Research Training Environment Scale Revised: Implications for research training in applied psychology. *The Counseling Psychologist, 25,* 22–37.

Knox, P. L., & McGovern, T. V. (1988). Mentoring women in academia. *Teaching of Psychology, 15,* 39–41.

Magoon, T. M., & Holland, J. L. (1984). Research training and supervision. In S. D. Brown & R. W. Lent (Eds.), *Handbook of counseling psychology* (pp. 682–715). New York: Wiley.

Miles, M. B., & Huberman, A. M. (1994). *Qualitative data analysis: An expanded sourcebook* (2nd ed.). Thousand Oaks, CA: Sage.

Russell, J. E. A., & Adams, D. M. (Eds.) (1997). Mentoring [Special Issue]. *Journal of Vocational Behavior, 51.*

Schlosser, L. Z. (2002). *The Advisory Working Alliance Inventory: Further scale development and validation.* Unpublished doctoral dissertation, University of Maryland, College Park.

Schlosser, L. Z., & Gelso, C. J. (2001). Measuring the working alliance in advisor-advisee relationships in graduate school. *Journal of Counseling Psychology, 48,* 157–167.

Wilde, J. B., & Schau, C. G. (1991). Mentoring in graduate schools of education: Mentees' perceptions. *Journal of Experimental Education, 59,* 165–179.

Acknowledgments: We express our gratitude to our team of research assistants at the University of Maryland and Marquette University for their help with transcription. We are also grateful to Charles J. Gelso for his helpful comments on a draft of this article. This study was presented as part of a symposium at the 109th Annual Convention of the American Psychological Association, San Francisco, California, August 2001.

About the authors: Lewis Z. Schlosser is now at the Department of Psychiatry, New York Presbyterian Hospital, Weill Medical College of Cornell University. Sarah Knox and Alissa R. Moskovitz are with the Department of Counseling and Educational Psychology, School of Education, Marquette University. Clara E. Hill is in the Department of Psychology, University of Maryland.

Address correspondence to: Sarah Knox, Department of Counseling and Educational Psychology, School of Education, Marquette University, Milwaukee, Wisconsin 53201. E-mail: sarah.knox @marquette.edu

Exercise for Article 32

Factual Questions

1. What was the mean age of the participants?

2. How were the twelve programs selected? From what list were they selected?

3. Was there a follow-up with program directors who did not initially provide names and addresses of students?

4. According to the researchers, what is the "essence" of CQR?

5. The researchers state that there are two "key features" of CQR. The first is reliance on words rather than numbers to describe phenomena. What is the second one?

6. In the results, a "typical" response is defined as a response given by how many of the ten participants?

Questions for Discussion

7. Many educational studies are conducted in just one school setting. This study was conducted in nine universities. In your opinion, is the use of nine instead of one an important strength of this study? Explain.

8. Is the researchers' description of their backgrounds and personal experiences with graduate advising especially relevant? Would the study be weaker without it? (See lines 155–197.)

9. In your opinion, is asking participants for their reactions to the draft of the results an important strength of this study? (See lines 331–341.)

10. In your opinion, is the description of the procedures for analyzing the data in lines 342–439 sufficient to give you a clear idea of how the data were analyzed? Explain.

11. Do you find any of the Results in lines 440–772 especially interesting? Especially surprising? Explain.

12. The Results section of this report is longer than the Results section of most other research articles in this book. Do you think that the Results section in this article could be shortened without losing important information? Explain. (See lines 440–772.)

13. The researchers describe the limitations of their study in lines 1122–1156. Do you think that some of the limitations are more important than others? Explain.

Quality Ratings

Directions: Indicate your level of agreement with each of the following statements by circling a number from 5 for strongly agree (SA) to 1 for strongly disagree (SD). If you believe an item is not applicable to this research article, leave it blank. Be prepared to explain your ratings.

A. The introduction establishes the importance of the study.

SA   5   4   3   2   1   SD

B. The literature review establishes the context for the study.

SA   5   4   3   2   1   SD

C. The research purpose, question, or hypothesis is clearly stated.

SA   5   4   3   2   1   SD

D. The method of sampling is sound.

SA   5   4   3   2   1   SD

E. Relevant demographics (for example, age, gender, and ethnicity) are described.

SA   5   4   3   2   1   SD

F. Measurement procedures are adequate.

SA   5   4   3   2   1   SD

G. All procedures have been described in sufficient detail to permit a replication of the study.

SA   5   4   3   2   1   SD

H. The participants have been adequately protected from potential harm.

SA   5   4   3   2   1   SD

I. The results are clearly described.

SA   5   4   3   2   1   SD

J. The discussion/conclusion is appropriate.

SA   5   4   3   2   1   SD

K. Despite any flaws, the report is worthy of publication.

SA   5   4   3   2   1   SD

Article 33

The Developmental Progression of Children's Oral Story Inventions

EUGENE GEIST
Ohio University

JERRY ALDRIDGE
University of Alabama, Birmingham

ABSTRACT. This study investigated stories that children created after being told the Grimm version of selected tales. These stories were told as an instruction to the children on story structure and to familiarize children with ideas of plot, character, and conflict in stories. This cross-sectional study considered what differences are evident in the oral fairy tales that children tell at different ages. Stories from children in kindergarten, first grade, second grade, and third grade were collected and analyzed.

For the purpose of this study, the following research questions were asked. These questions guided the research and eventually became the major coding categories.

1. Is there a developmental difference in the type of story (i.e., personal narrative, fantasy, realistic fiction) children tell when they are asked to invent a fairy tale?
2. Are there developmental differences in the content of children's stories among age groups?
3. Are there developmental differences in how children organize the content of their invented fairy tales?

A qualitative research methodology was used for this study. Children's orally invented stories were tape-recorded and transcribed. The data were analyzed using content analysis of the transcripts.

This study indicates that children's orally told invented fairy tales can be used (a) to promote cognitive development, (b) to assess cognitive development, and (c) to identify emotional conflicts that children are experiencing. This study also indicates that second grade is a good time to promote creativity and imaginations as this was the age in which children were most confident in their imaginative abilities.

Few studies have been conducted on children's oral story inventions (Aldridge, Eddowes, Ewing, & Kuby, 1994). Studies on children's interest in folk and fairy tales have not touched on children's invented "fairy tales" and how they can reflect developmental issues.
5 There have been many examinations of written retellings of fairy tales (Boydston, 1994; Gambrell, Pfeiffer, & Wilson, 1985; Morrow, 1986). However, few works have examined oral stories invented by children. In-
10 vented oral stories can give a valuable insight into a

child's cognitive, affective, and creative development (Allan & Bertoia, 1992; Markham, 1983; Sutton-Smith, 1985).

This study investigated stories that children created
15 after being told the Grimm version of selected tales. These stories were told as an instruction to the children on story structure and to familiarize children with ideas of plot, character, and conflict in stories. The Grimm (1993) versions were chosen because the literature
20 suggests that they are the closest to the oral tradition (Zipes, 1988). This cross-sectional study considered what differences are evident in the oral fairy tales that children tell at different ages. Stories from children in kindergarten, first grade, second grade, and third grade
25 were collected and analyzed (Geist & Aldridge, 1999).

For the purpose of this study, the following research questions were asked. These questions guided the research and eventually became the major coding categories.

30 1. Is there a developmental difference in the type of story (i.e., personal narrative, fantasy, realistic fiction) children tell when they are asked to invent a fairy tale?
2. Are there developmental differences in the content
35 of children's stories among age groups?
3. Are there developmental differences in how children organize the content of their invented fairy tales?

Method

A qualitative research methodology was used for
40 this study. Children's orally invented stories were tape-recorded and transcribed. The data were analyzed using content analysis of the transcripts. According to Carney (1972), "content analysis is any technique for making inferences by objectively and systematically identify-
45 ing specified characteristics of messages" (p. 25).

A semistructured interview format was used to collect data. The children were asked to make up a fairy tale and tell it to the researcher. The researcher prompted the subject if there was a long pause. The
50 researcher also had the child start over if the child was engaging in a retelling of a story that the researcher

recognized. The data were then analyzed using a content analysis.

Participants

Convenience sampling was the method used to select study participants. The classrooms chosen were believed to facilitate the expansion of a developing theory because the sample was homogeneous. All subjects were African American and from low socioeconomic families. The subjects for this study were students in four classrooms at an elementary school in a low socioeconomic area of an urban city in the southeastern United States. The racial makeup of the sample was 100% African American.

Data Collection

Each classroom participated in a 45-minute lesson on fairy tales and story structure each day for 4 days. The lesson consisted of reading and discussing the plots and characters of fairy tales. After the 4 days, the children were asked, individually, to make up a fairy tale and tell it orally. The stories were tape-recorded and transcribed. A content analysis of the transcripts was performed as described by Carney (1992).

One kindergarten, one first-grade, one second-grade, and one third-grade classroom, each with approximately 15 students, participated in this study. Each classroom was given an identical session on fairy tales and story structure. This session consisted of reading fairy tales to the students and discussing the aspects of the story. The specific description of the 5 days of storytelling and discussion are found in Geist and Aldridge (1999). These procedures were modified from Allan and Bertoia (1992) by Boydston (1994). Allan and Bertoia developed a procedure to initiate the discussion of fairy tales. This outline was used for seventh graders; however, because this study was interested in students in kindergarten, first, second, and third grades, a procedure modified by Boydston (1994) was used for this study. Boydston's outline was developed for second graders but is appropriate for the ages targeted in this study.

Data Analysis

Analysis of the data was generated from the transcripts of the audiotapes. The research questions served as a guide for conducting the analysis. Each question became a major coding category broken down by age. The results of each age were then compared to each other to build a model of children's invented fairy tales. Bogdan and Biklen (1992) stated that preassigned coding systems are developed when researchers explore particular topics or aspects of the study.

Inter-rater reliability was conducted on this study by having an educational professional with extensive knowledge of fairy tales and their form, function, and uses independently categorize the data. Another rater was trained in content analysis and was experienced in the content analysis method. This researcher had performed qualitative studies on fairy tales and children's storytelling in the past. The two raters participated in two practice sessions of reading and analyzing children's oral invented stories.

The recordings were transcribed and copied. The independent rater and the researcher received identical copies of the transcripts. Because the three foreshadowed questions that were used as a framework for the categories, the independent rater was given a copy of the foreshadowed questions. Each rater read the transcripts as many times as needed and noted themes related to genre, content, and organization. Each rater then independently compared the common themes from each grade and constructed a model for genre, content, and organization.

Both raters discussed the method for analysis before beginning. When a theme or thread was identified, it was highlighted by a colored marker that identified it with other items that belonged with that thread. The rater wrote notes in the margin next to this highlighted text. Then all of the text passages with the same color highlight were collected by grade. The rater then reread the passages and came up with a phrase or word that best described the common characteristics of those passages. The descriptive phrases were then compared to the phrases for the other grades to determine if a model could be constructed. Often, there was more than one model that was evident in each of the categories.

These themes and models were then compared. The themes and models that were consistent between the two raters were retained and clarified. The themes and models that were not consistent between the two raters were not included. Each story was then categorized independently by each rater into the rough model that had been developed.

Results

Findings from this study suggest a developmental shift in the genre, content, and organization of children's oral invented stories. The genre of the children's stories moved from the fantastical to stories based on personal experiences. Kindergarten children told mostly fantasy stories, first and second graders told mostly realistic fiction, and third graders told mostly personal narratives.

The content of the children's stories showed development in two areas. First, there was development in the basis of their stories. Kindergarten children based their stories on previously heard material, first graders based theirs on familiar surroundings, second graders based their inventions on their imagination, and third graders tended to base their stories on personal experiences.

Second, there was development in how parents were depicted in the stories. Kindergartners, first, and second graders depicted parents as heroes and comforters. Third graders depicted parents as authority figures.

The content of the stories of all the grades contained reflections of the children's fears and concerns from everyday life. Fears about being kidnapped or other stresses, such as performance anxiety and social pressures, were reflected in their stories.

The organization of the stories moved from disjointed sentences to a coherent whole story. States that could be delineated were (a) disjointed, (b) phrase disjointed, (c) short-utilitarian, (d) sidetracked, and (e) coherent whole.

Genre

The development of genre moved from the fantastical notions of kindergartners to the realistic personal narratives of third graders. Kindergartners told fantastical stories of talking umbrellas, flying to Mars, magic, and evil witches that turned children into food. First and second graders told realistic fiction stories about hunters, kings, queens, and an occasional witch; however, almost all of the actions of the characters were in the realm of possibility. Third graders tended to tell personal narratives that related directly to their life experiences; they were simply retelling events that happened to them or to someone they knew.

The study suggests the genre was influenced by three things. First, it was influenced by the classroom context. In the kindergarten classroom, the researcher observed a lot of fantasy literature. Children heard stories daily about talking animals and fantastical actions in the books the teachers read to them. However, as the grades progressed, the researcher observed that the teachers provided more realistic literature and less fantasy. This, in turn, affected the genre of the stories that the children told. Second was the children's developing understanding of the difference between fantasy and reality. As children begin to understand the concept of causality and move into concrete operations, the concept of what is possible and logical versus what is illogical, magical, and impossible becomes more delineated. The second- and third-grade stories reflect this move toward reality-based stories. Third was the base material that children chose. As we have already mentioned, children tended to choose more personal material as they got older until at third grade they tell personal, true to life personal narratives. Obviously, this shift is going to affect the genre of the story that they tell. This will be discussed further in the examination of the content of the children's stories.

Content

There were three developmental themes that could be delineated in the content of the children's stories. The first was the basis that the children used to construct their stories. The second was the role of parents in the children's stories. Third, the content of all the grades contained reflections of children's fears and concerns.

Children in kindergarten based their stories on previously heard material. They did not appear confident in their ability to be successful in making up a story on their own, so they used stories that they had heard or read recently to build their story around. First graders were a little more sure of themselves so they did not need specific stories on which to base their inventions. However, they still needed to base the settings and characteristics on things that were familiar to them. This gave them the framework for their stories. By second grade, the children did not need outside structure on which to build their stories. They could rely on their imagination completely as the basis for their stories. In third grade, the surge of imagination noted in second grade appeared to be gone. Either by discouragement or development, children had given up on imagination as the basis of their stories. These children told personal narratives that used personal experiences as the basis for their inventions. These types of stories required little or no imagination.

A second developmental theme evident in the content of the children's orally invented stories was that at around third grade children began to consider peers, rather than parents, as their primary social contacts. This transition was reflected in their stories. In kindergarten and first grade, children were still primarily dependent on their parents for social and emotional interaction. However, around second grade they began to bond with peers, and the peer group became their primary social group with many third graders.

Before third grade, parents in children's stories were heroes and comforters. It was they who rescued the child from the grasp of the monster. A major shift had occurred in the third graders' stories, when parents were depicted as strict authority figures who were present to judge and punish. Third grade children's stories showed a common theme of fear of parental reprisals in this sample.

The stories also show a reflection of children's fears and anxieties. Children are surrounded with stress that is often not released. Stories offer children this release. The stories of all the grades contained personal reflections of fears and stresses. Especially prevalent were fears of kidnap and murder. The children in this particular school had experience with a classmate being kidnapped and murdered, so it is not surprising that this fear appeared in their stories.

Organization

Three developmental aspects of children's organization of invented stories were determined in this study. These included:

1. There was a clear developmental sequence to the way children organized their stories.
2. Egocentrism decreased through interactions in the social environment.
3. The distinction of the difference between fantasy and reality developed with age.

270 Even after the children were involved in the 4-day workshop on fairy tales, a developmental pattern still emerged. This suggests that there are aspects to children's understanding of story structure that are developmental and cannot be totally directly taught. The

275 workshop focused on the characters, settings, plot, and organization of fairy tales. The children were instructed that fairy tales have a clear beginning, middle, and end; the beginning contains an introduction of the characters, setting, and problems; the middle of the story dis-

280 cusses how the characters go about solving the problems; and the end of the story contains the resolution. Thus, the children were familiar with the parts of the stories, and still a majority of the children were unable to use the information given in the workshops to con-

285 struct a coherent whole story. This suggests that the progression through stages of organization is developmental and not based on training.

There was a cognitive developmental sequence in the organization of children's oral invented stories. So

290 distinct were the differences, a developmental model can be proposed based on the data. The first stage can be characterized by the children being unable to form a coherent, ordered whole story. They told disjointed stories in which individual thoughts were juxtaposed.

295 This is consistent with the findings of Piaget (1958) that children could not order a story into a coherent whole until about the age of 8.

In the second stage, the children could string a series of thoughts together into coherent phrases; how-

300 ever, the phrases of about two or three sentences were juxtaposed against other phrases to which they had little relationship. In the third stage, children told short, utilitarian stories that just included the basics of a story with no elaboration. The children were attempting to

305 keep their stories ordered and coherent and, if there was too much information, they got confused.

The fourth stage showed the result of this confusion. Children got sidetracked because they included more elaboration and lost track of the original story-

310 line. Eventually, they got back on track and ended the story on the same theme with which they started. The final stage was characterized by children telling a coherent, elaborate story from beginning to end without getting sidetracked.

Conclusions and Implications

315 This study showed that literacy is not totally in the domain of social knowledge. The learning of words, letters, and rules of language must be passed down through the culture; these aspects of literacy cannot be invented by children without help. However, there are

320 aspects of literacy that involve what Piaget deemed logico-mathematical knowledge. This study suggests that story structure is, at least partially, logico-mathematical knowledge. The part–whole relationship (Piaget, 1970) plays a part in the structure of children's

325 stories. The children in this study all received direct

instruction on story structure, but still a developmental sequence was evident. Children's understanding of story structure is dependent on more than direct instruction.

330 Story structure is learned through interaction with text and words rather than through direct instruction. Children will invent story structure by telling and writing stories. The reactions from the audience and from their rereading or listening to other students' stories

335 cause disequilibrium, which, according to Piaget (1970), leads to development.

This study indicates that children's orally told invented fairy tales can be used (a) to promote cognitive development, (b) to assess cognitive development, and

340 (c) to identify emotional conflicts that children are experiencing. This study also indicates that second grade is a good time to promote creativity and imagination, as this was the age in which children were most confident in their imaginative abilities.

345 Orally invented stories can be used to promote cognitive development. Each time children tell a story, they must attempt first to order it mentally. This mental activity promotes the construction of knowledge. A developmental sequence to the organization of orally

350 told stories appears evident from the stories children told in this study. To promote the movement through these developmental stages, children must be provided with the opportunity to tell stories to an audience and receive social interaction. Each time the child tells a

355 story, the reaction from the audience causes disequilibrium. If the audience does not understand the story, the child must examine why the audience did not understand it. This type of construction through social interaction was also described by Kamii (2000) in math

360 development. This works just as well for storytelling. The feedback from peers helps the child to overcome the limitations of egocentrism and egocentric thought.

Orally told invented fairy tales can also be used for assessment of children's cognitive abilities. This can

365 give a teacher an idea of the areas in which a child might need work. This study was consistent with Piaget (1952) with regard to developmental sequences through which children must progress. This sequence can be used to assist in screening students who might

370 need assistance.

These stories can be used to identify emotional differences or possible traumas in children's lives. As this study and others have shown (Allan, 1988; Allan & Bertoia, 1992), children include stressful events and

375 emotional problems they are dealing with in their stories. These orally told stories could help screen for physical and sexual abuse, fears and concerns, and emotional problems.

While this study showed promise for identifying

380 developmental changes in children's oral storytelling inventions from kindergarten through third grade, much more research needs to be done. Researchers should also seek to "identify individual and cultural

385 variations in the discourse and oral inventions of young children" (Geist & Aldridge, 1999, p. 822).

References

Aldridge, J., Eddowes, A., Ewing, J., & Kuby, P. (1994). Analytical psychology, constructivism, and education. *Journal of Instructional Psychology, 21,* 359–367.

Allan, J. (1988). *Inscapes of the child's world.* Dallas, TX: Spring Publications.

Allan, J., & Bertoia, J. (1992). *Written paths to healing.* Dallas, TX: Spring Publications.

Bogdan, R., & Biklen, S. (1992). *Qualitative research for educators* (2nd ed.). Boston: Knopp.

Boydston, R. (1994). *Written retellings of fairy tales.* Unpublished doctoral dissertation, University of Alabama at Birmingham, Birmingham, Alabama.

Carney, T. F. (1972). *Content analysis: A technique for systematic inference from communication.* Winnipeg, Manitoba: University of Manitoba Press.

Gambrell, L. B., Pfeiffer, W. R., & Wilson, R. M. (1985). The effects of telling upon reading comprehension and recall of text information. *Journal of Educational Research, 78,* 216–220.

Geist, E. A., & Aldridge, J. (1999). Genre, content, and organization of kindergarten children's oral story inventions. *Psychological Reports, 85,* 817–822.

Grimm Brothers. (1993). *The complete Brothers Grimm fairy tales.* New York: Pantheon Books.

Kamii, C. (2000). *Young children reinvent arithmetic* (2nd ed.). New York: Teachers College Press.

Markham, R. H. (1983). The fairy tale: An introduction to literature and the creative process. *College English, 45,* 31–45.

Morrow, L. M. (1986). The effect of structural guidance in story retellings of children's dictation of original stories. *Journal of Reading Behavior, 18,* 135–151.

Piaget, J. (1952). *The thought and language of the child.* London: Humanities Press.

Piaget. J. (1958). *The growth of logical thinking from childhood to adolescence.* New York: Basic Books.

Piaget, J. (1970). *Structuralism.* New York: Basic Books.

Sutton-Smith, B. (1985). The development of fictional narrative performances. *Topics in Language Disorders, 7,* 1–10.

Zipes, J. (1988). *The Brothers Grimm.* New York: Routledge.

Address correspondence to: Dr. Eugene Geist, Ohio University, W324 Grover Center, Athens, OH 45701.

Exercise for Article 33

Factual Questions

1. According to Carney (1972), what is "content analysis"?

2. How many first-grade classrooms participated in this study?

3. The themes and models that were included had to be consistent among how many raters?

4. Children at what grade level told mostly fantasy stories?

5. At what grade level(s) did the children's stories reflect children's fears and concerns of everyday life?

6. At what grade level did children begin to consider peers, rather than parents, as their primary social contacts?

Questions for Discussion

7. The researchers state that they used a "convenience sample." What do you think this term means?

8. The researchers state that all four classrooms were given an identical session on fairy tales and story structure. Is it important to know that they were "identical"? Explain.

9. In your opinion, is the description of the lessons adequate? If no, what else would you like to know about them? (See lines 66–89.)

10. The authors discuss "inter-rater reliability." In your opinion, how important is this information for evaluating the reliability of the results of this study? Explain. (See lines 99–140.)

11. Do you agree with the researchers that orally told stories could help screen for physical and sexual abuse, fears and concerns, and emotional problems? (See lines 376–378.)

12. This study is qualitative and does not report any statistical analyses. In your opinion, is the study "scientific"? Explain.

13. If you were conducting a study on the same topic, what changes, if any, would you make in the research methodology? Explain.

Quality Ratings

Directions: Indicate your level of agreement with each of the following statements by circling a number from 5 for strongly agree (SA) to 1 for strongly disagree (SD). If you believe an item is not applicable to this research article, leave it blank. Be prepared to explain your ratings.

A. The introduction establishes the importance of the study.

SA   5   4   3   2   1   SD

B. The literature review establishes the context for the study.

SA   5   4   3   2   1   SD

C. The research purpose, question, or hypothesis is clearly stated.

SA   5   4   3   2   1   SD

D. The method of sampling is sound.

SA   5   4   3   2   1   SD

E. Relevant demographics (for example, age, gender, and ethnicity) are described.

    SA   5   4   3   2   1   SD

F. Measurement procedures are adequate.

    SA   5   4   3   2   1   SD

G. All procedures have been described in sufficient detail to permit a replication of the study.

    SA   5   4   3   2   1   SD

H. The participants have been adequately protected from potential harm.

    SA   5   4   3   2   1   SD

I. The results are clearly described.

    SA   5   4   3   2   1   SD

J. The discussion/conclusion is appropriate.

    SA   5   4   3   2   1   SD

K. Despite any flaws, the report is worthy of publication.

    SA   5   4   3   2   1   SD

Article 34

Teacher Beliefs About Instructional Choice: A Phenomenological Study

TERRI FLOWERDAY
University of Nebraska, Lincoln

GREGORY SCHRAW
University of Nebraska, Lincoln

ABSTRACT. We interviewed 36 practicing teachers using phenomenological methods to examine what, when, where, and to whom teachers offer choice. Teachers participated in pilot, interview, and member-check phases. Our final results focused on the following main points: (a) teachers believe that choice promotes learning and motivation; (b) choice is used in a number of ways; (c) teachers have a variety of reasons for giving choices; (d) teachers imposed limits on classroom choice based on (e) student age, ability, and prior knowledge and (f) teacher experience, efficacy, and management style.

From *Journal of Educational Psychology*, 92, 634–645. Copyright © 2000 by the American Psychological Association. Reprinted with permission.

This study examines teachers' beliefs about instructional choice in the classroom. We undertook this study because we are frequently asked by preservice teachers to comment on the role of choice in the classroom.
5 Unfortunately, we have had very little to say on this topic because there is virtually no research base on either the effects of choice on learning or on how teachers implement choice in the classroom. Our goal in this study is to describe in teachers' own words what
10 types of choices they offer students, how they decide when and to whom choices should be given, and why they offer these choices.

The present research uses semistructured interviews to examine teachers' beliefs about the use of choice in
15 their classrooms. We draw on phenomenological methodology in which a select group of participants describe a phenomenon in their own words. The purpose of this methodology is to generate rather than test theory. Below, we summarize previous research on choice
20 and highlight some of the limitations of these studies. We then describe our methodology in more detail and summarize our main findings. Theoretical consequences of our findings, as well as their relationship to existing psychological theories, are reserved for the
25 Discussion section of this article.

Empirical Research on Choice and Learning

There is little research on choice. However, there is extensive literature that examines the role controlling environments (e.g., teachers and structured classroom settings) play in autonomy and learning (Flink, Bog-
30 giano, & Barrett, 1990; Grolnick & Ryan, 1987; Miserandino, 1996; Ryan, Connell, & Grolnick, 1992). These studies suggest that controlling environments reduce a sense of personal autonomy and intrinsic motivation and result in decreased learning and poorer
35 attitudes about school (Enzle & Anderson, 1993; Weinert & Helmke, 1995). A number of other studies have examined the role that perceived control (i.e., self-judgments of personal competence or autonomy) plays in intrinsic motivation (Boggiano, Main, & Katz,
40 1988; Skinner, Wellborn, & Connell, 1990; Williams & Deci, 1996). These studies indicate that greater perceived autonomy results in higher levels of intrinsic motivation and enjoyment, especially when the desire for control is high (Law, Logan, & Baron, 1994).
45 A small but important set of choice-related studies has appeared in the computerized testing literature. These studies typically compare computer-adapted tests (CAT; i.e., those in which a computer selects test items for an examinee) with self-adapted tests (SAT;
50 i.e., those in which examinees select test items from one of several preassigned difficulty levels). Rocklin and O'Donnell (1987) and Rocklin, O'Donnell, and Holst (1995) found that college students performed better on a self-adapted test compared with a computer-
55 adapted version. Wise, Plake, Johnson, and Roos (1992) showed that individuals taking the self-adapted version reported significantly lower posttest anxiety. Wise, Roos, Plake, and Nebelsick-Gullet (1994) found that the type of test one completes has no effect on
60 posttest anxiety provided one is allowed to choose the test's format (i.e., CAT vs. SAT). In a follow-up study, Wise, Roos, Leland, Oats, and McCrann (1996) reported that individuals with a high desire for control were significantly more likely to select a self-adapted
65 rather than a computer-adapted test. Thus, the ability to choose how one is tested appears to reduce anxiety, regardless of the type of test one takes, and especially if one has a high desire for control. It can be concluded that choice, under these conditions, leads to a decrease
70 in negative affect (anxiety) or improved affect.

We also identified four studies that examined the effect of choice on learning outcomes. Zuckerman,

Porac, Lathin, Smith, and Deci (1978) asked 80 college students to select puzzles they would like to work on during an experimental session. Forty yoked pairs were created such that each individual in the choice condition selected three of six puzzles to work on, then indicated how much time he or she would allot to each puzzle. Individuals in the yoked group were assigned the puzzles and the same time allotments selected by individuals in the choice group. Individuals who were allowed to choose reported a greater feeling of control, indicated that they would be more willing to return for another session of puzzle solving, and spent significantly more time solving similar puzzles in a free-choice period at the end of the experiment.

Cordova and Lepper (1996) examined the role of choice when elementary school children used computer-aided learning environments to improve arithmetical and problem-solving skills. Allowing children to make choices positively affected several measures of affective engagement, including perceived competence, a preference for greater task difficulty, overall liking, and a greater willingness to stay after class compared with students in a control group. In contrast, there were few significant effects for choice with respect to cognitive engagement variables. Specifically, choice had no impact on use of hints, use of complex problem-solving operations, or the amount of strategic play, although those students given choice performed significantly better on a follow-up math test. A related study by Parker and Lepper (1992) also failed to report differences in cognitive engagement as a function of choice.

Schraw, Flowerday, and Reisetter (1998) conducted two experiments that examined the effect of choice on reading engagement among adults. Experiment 1 compared three groups: those who chose from among three equivalent texts (i.e., free choice), those who were assigned a text under the assumption that other readers declined to read it (i.e., forced choice), and those who were assigned a text without additional information (i.e., control group). None of the groups differed with respect to multiple choice test performance, essays written about the text, or holistic understanding of the text's meaning. Groups did not differ either with respect to interest and personal reactions but differed on several self-report indices of postexperimental satisfaction. Experiment 2 divided a large group into two subgroups, half receiving the option to choose what to read, the other half being assigned a text. The two groups did not differ on any of the cognitive measures or on affective reactions to the text. The free choice group, however, reported more interest in the text and more satisfaction with their research participation experience.

Research results show that choice has mixed effects on engagement and learning. Most studies report an increase in positive affect when individuals are given choices, even when choice has no simultaneous effect on learning. In contrast, few studies report consistently positive effects of choice on learning. Typically, choice had no effect at all on learning, although it appears, on the basis of research from the computerized adaptive testing literature, that choice may have a positive effect if the test taker has a strong desire for control. The main conclusion to emerge from this research is that choice positively affects affect but has little impact on performance.

The research described above has three general limitations. One is that all of these studies examined the consequences of choices rather than reasons for giving choices in the first place. Second, none of these studies examined the role of teachers in the choice-implementation process. Third, there is no explicit theory of choice stated in any of these studies, either in terms of how to administer choices or what to expect once one does so. Thus, after conducting this review, we still were no closer to answering the basic question posed by so many of our teachers: "Should I give my students choices, and if so, what kind?"

The Present Study

We conducted the present research to understand better the role of teachers in the choice-implementation process. We were interested especially in teachers' beliefs about why they give their students choices, although we also asked teachers to describe the use and consequences of those choices. Our main goal was to codify teachers' beliefs about choice. A secondary goal was to discuss the implications of the present research for an emergent theory of choice.

We focused on three aspects of teacher choice, including what choices teachers offer to their students, when and to whom teachers offer choice, and how teachers perceive the effectiveness of the choices they offer students. We used the qualitative tradition of phenomenology to construct a data-driven account of teachers' beliefs about choice (Creswell, 1998; Moustakas, 1994). The purpose of phenomenological research is to describe a phenomenon using the participants' own words.

The present study included three main stages. Semistructured (i.e., open-ended) interviews were conducted in a pilot study ($N = 8$), and a second interview protocol was developed on the basis of teacher feedback obtained in the pilot study. The revised interview questions were used in Stage 2 of the study, which consisted of preliminary written responses by 36 teachers to seven questions, followed by in-depth, one-on-one interviews of teachers using the same seven questions. These items were designed to address the three main research questions described above. Consistent with phenomenological methods (Creswell, 1998; Moustakas, 1994), we present our findings at three levels of specificity, including descriptive analysis, thematic analysis, and interpretive analysis of underlying models (Wolcott, 1994). The purpose of descriptive analysis is to summarize the range of responses and emergent points of agreement to each of the seven questions in the structured interviews. The purpose of thematic analysis is to interpret emergent themes across the full set of interviews. The purpose of interpretive analysis is to propose a preliminary model of teacher choice. The third stage consisted of member checks in which three teachers reviewed and critiqued our final results.

Method

Methodological Framework

We used the qualitative method of phenomenology in this study because there is no existing theory of choice. Phenomenological design is appropriate when one's goal is to explore a phenomenon about which little has been written. The researcher collects information from knowledgeable participants who are asked to describe the phenomenon, and the researcher then analyzes themes and interprets the data. The results can be used to build a theory that can later be tested. According to Creswell (1998, p. 15), "qualitative research is multi-method in focus, involving an interpretive, naturalistic approach in which the researcher attempts to make sense of or interpret phenomena in terms of the meanings people bring to them." The data are, by nature, descriptive and composed of words or pictures rather than numbers, as is the case in quantitative research. The researcher's purpose is to describe and interpret the perspective of the participant (Bogdan & Biklen, 1992). Toward this end, the researcher begins to collect in-depth experiential information from a select group of participant informants.

Participants

The purpose of phenomenological research is to explore and describe a phenomenon, such as instructional choice in the classroom, from the perspective of a target group made up of individuals who have insight into the specific phenomenon being examined. A semistructured interview format is utilized. The use of criterion sampling (Creswell, 1998) gives the researcher access to in-depth information on the target topic recorded from the perspective of a specific group of participants. This necessitates the use of informants who have considerable experience with the phenomenon. Participants are selected on the basis of their ability to speak directly to the topic under investigation.

Participants for the pilot study ($N = 8$) and participants for the main study ($N = 36$) were classroom teachers attending summer classes at a large Midwestern university. Criteria for participation included enrollment in graduate courses in educational psychology, learning theory, or research methods, in addition to at least 1 year of K–12 classroom teaching experience. All participants had bachelor's degrees, and approximately one-third also held master's degrees. A variety of content areas were represented, including science, math, social studies, special education, elementary education, technology, art, music, and foreign language. Both rural and urban school districts were

represented, as were small and large schools. Years of experience in the classroom ranged from 1 year to 29 years. Approximately 60% of the participants were female, and 40% were male. Complete demographic information is provided in the Appendix.

Data Collection

The primary source of data is verbal responses from a series of in-depth interviews with participants. Terri Flowerday entered into dialogue with each informant, gathering information, reviewing the information for clarity and intent, and finally, checking for accuracy of interpretation through participant feedback. In the initial series of interviews, responses were tape-recorded, then transcribed into narrative text, and data were analyzed using phenomenological methods outlined in Moustakas (1994). Responses were coded and themes established, which resulted in an interview protocol consisting of seven questions. Additionally, it was decided that future participants would be given these questions prior to the taped portion of the interview. In this way, the teachers would be able to preview the questions, formulate answers, and write brief responses to serve as cues for the taped portion of the interview.

The second series of interviews consisted of 1-hr interviews with each of the 36 teacher–participants. Each participant was given a three-page handout that included six personal profile items (subjects taught, years' teaching experience, grade levels taught, number of students per class, degrees held, size and setting of school), and the following seven interview questions:

1a. What types of instructional choices do you give your students? Examples might include choices of reading materials, topics of study, forms of assessment, etc.

1b. Are these choices unlimited or limited? Please describe.

2. Why do you give students choices? What is your rationale for doing so?

3. Is giving choices a good strategy for accomplishing your goals for student learning? Is it successful? Please explain.

4. How do students respond to being given choices?

5. To whom do you give choices? Are there individual differences that you consider such as (a) developmental level or age of students, (b) ability or achievement level of students, (c) course content, and (d) level of motivation, etc.?

6. Do you think more or less choice is being given in classrooms today as opposed to when you were in K–12? Why do you say this?

7. When is choice a good idea? Is choice ever a bad idea? Please explain.

Participants were asked to spend 20 min previewing the questions and completing the demographic information. The researcher encouraged participants to write brief responses for each question to serve as cues. After 20 min, the researcher returned and the interview began. The discussion focused on the seven protocol questions. Participants were instructed to respond as

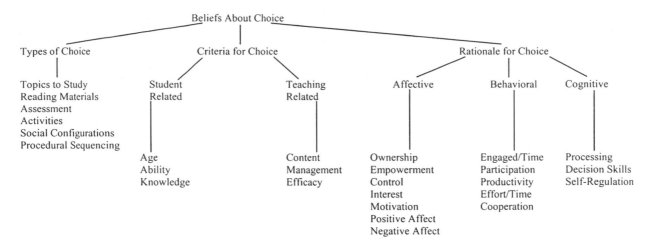

Figure 1. Teacher beliefs about choice.

openly and honestly as possible and were encouraged to add any information they believed to be relevant. Interviewing took place in two conference rooms in a building on campus, and each session lasted approximately 1 hr.

After finishing the teacher interviews, the tape recordings were transcribed. The researcher carefully read the transcripts and listened to the tapes, looking for significant statements reflecting participant experiences and beliefs about choice. The statements were coded and categories established. This process of horizontalization of the data culminated in a list of nonrepetitive themes. A structural description of the phenomenon was developed, and Terri Flowerday interpreted the results such that a composite description was arrived at. Gregory Schraw reviewed a random sample of transcripts and listened to the tapes. The researchers met to discuss interpretation and revise categories and themes. The discussion continued until complete agreement was reached.

Triangulation

A number of steps were taken to triangulate the data. First, data from the initial eight teacher interviews were compared with data obtained from the later 36 interviews. Consistent patterns emerged. Second, both written and verbal responses were obtained from the participants. Verbal responses were later transcribed into written form. The researcher compiled written fieldnotes during and immediately following each interview with regard to contextual observations. There were consistent themes cutting across the verbal and written data. Third, researcher interpretations were checked for accuracy by asking participants to confirm researcher interpretations and to provide clarification when necessary. The fourth step was to have Gregory Schraw review the written responses and fieldnotes, listen to a random sample of taped interviews, and make a separate determination of themes and interpretations (i.e., conduct an audit). The researchers then

met to discuss the data, thematic analysis, and interpretive conclusions. Dialogue continued until consensus was reached.

A fifth step was to conduct individual member checks with three additional classroom teachers. Participants were recruited from a different section of the same class taught during the spring semester. Criteria for participation were the same as for the main study. The purpose of the member check was to verify that our final results were consistent with teachers' beliefs and classroom experiences. Teachers were debriefed about the purpose of the member check process and about our final results. Debriefing focused on five aspects of our results: (a) teachers believe that choice promotes learning and motivation; (b) choice was used in a number of ways; (c) teachers had a variety of reasons for giving choices and implemented choice on the basis of this rationale; (d) student age, ability, and prior knowledge were factors to be considered; and (e) teacher experience, efficacy, and management style influenced beliefs about choice.

Teachers participating in the member-check phase of the study represented elementary, middle level, and senior high schools. Both female and male teachers were interviewed. The member-check phase consisted of individual 1-hr interviews that were tape-recorded and transcribed. Teachers were informed about the purpose and procedures of the two initial interview phases, and teacher responses were described. Participants were shown a thematic representation of teacher responses (see Figure 1), and the researcher explained the key points and rationale for the model. Participants were encouraged to ask questions and provide feedback. Next, teachers were given approximately 15 min to reflect on the model and write comments. The final 30 min were devoted to participant–researcher dialogue during which teacher input was solicited and clarification provided. Determining the degree to which participants endorsed or wanted revisions in the model was our goal. Participant notes and verbal responses were analyzed using qualitative methods consistent with phenomenological design. We met to discuss the results and concluded that participants in the member check overwhelmingly endorsed the themes represented in Figure 1 and the interpretations we made.

Results

Thematic Analysis

Thirty-six teachers responded individually to each of the seven questions described above. Responses were categorized around three broad thematic topics, shown in Figure 1. The *types-of-choice* category refers to six areas of choice that teachers commonly offer to students. The *criteria-for-choice* category refers to characteristics of students and teachers that affect choice. The *rationale-for-choice* category refers to affective, behavioral, and cognitive reasons for giving choices to students.

Types of Choices

All participants were asked to describe the types of instructional choices they gave to their students. Choices varied as a function of content areas (e.g., science, literature, elementary education, music, social studies) and educational levels (e.g., kindergarten, fourth grade, middle school, senior high school), although all teachers agreed on six main types of choice, including: (a) topics of study; (b) reading materials; (c) methods of assessment; (d) activities; (e) social arrangements; and (f) procedural choices. These themes are consistent with the recommendations for student choice made by educational researchers. For example, Shevin and Klein (1984) suggested giving choice among various objects and activities, choice of whether or not to engage in an activity, choice of when to terminate an activity, choice of partners for activities, and choice of sequence of activities as appropriate for novice decision makers in educational settings.

Choices of topics for study and of reading materials were mentioned most frequently. Topics were chosen for research papers, in-class projects, and presentations. Choice of reading materials included type of genre (e.g., fiction or biography) and choice of authors. For example, one teacher stated, "I generally lay out an overall plan of topics and let students make decisions about material within the topics." Assessment choices included the type and frequency of assessments and criteria for evaluation, such as rubric development. A typical teacher response was to let students select "from among different forms of assessment such as essay test questions, exams, or book reports versus final projects." Choice of activities varied substantially depending on the age of students. Younger students were given choices about what to do, whereas older students were given more choices about how to do it. These choices centered around how to allocate one's learning time in the classroom. One physical education teacher indicated how she allowed students to "choose what type of equipment they want to use, like basket-

ball or yellow ball or activities such as dribbling or shooting." Choice of social arrangement was important to students and included decisions about working in pairs or small groups, seating arrangements, and choosing group members when collaborative projects were assigned. Students were allowed to make a number of procedural choices as well, including when to take tests, what order to study prescribed topics, and when assignments were due.

Criteria for Choices

Teachers described a number of factors that affected the use of choice in the classroom. Student-related themes focused on characteristics of students, such as age, ability level, and amount of prior knowledge, that influence teacher decisions about the use of choice. Teaching-related themes focused on characteristics of the teaching environment, such as course content, teacher management style, and teaching efficacy, that affect the use of choice.

Student-related themes. Most teachers stated that older students need more choices than younger students. Seventy-six percent of the teachers who discussed student age as a determining factor in their use of choice said that older students were better candidates for instructional choice due to maturity and better decision-making skills. Older students also have well-established interests and should be allowed to pursue those interests. Teachers were concerned that younger students could be overwhelmed by too many choices. Typical responses included the following:

> "I give more choices to older students; younger children need more structure and can't deal as well with decisions."

> "I give [fewer] choices to younger students since their responses tend to be predictable and less mature."

> "Choice is a bad idea when students are developmentally not ready to decide what to learn."

> "Choice is negative when maturity of students is too low."

In contrast to the majority position, some teachers argued that choice should be increased in elementary classrooms. Four of the 36 teachers stated that choice is more important for younger children than for older children. These teachers suggested that it is never too early to start teaching decision-making and self-regulation skills that spontaneously emerge from choice making, and that even 5-year-olds benefit from frequent presentation of choice. They argued that younger students need choice at least as much, if not more, than older students because they have little experience with decision making. One teacher claimed that "students need to be able to think for themselves, so we need to start providing choices when they are younger." Another stated succinctly that "little kids need to explore; they are interested in everything; they need choices."

485   Student ability was an important variable as well. The majority of teachers (11 of 13) who discussed ability level indicated that higher achieving or higher ability students benefit more from choice than do their lower ability peers because they are better able to util-

490   ize the choices they are given. A high school math and computer teacher offered a common response when he stated,

> My more capable students will take that choice and use it creatively. I think with my less capable students, espe-
> 495   cially in math, there are so many fundamentals you have to cover. You know choice is going to make them more interested but they have to have a minimal level of information first.

Additional comments included the following state-
500   ments:

> "More and different types of choices can be given to high achievers."

> "More capable students get more choices."

> "The higher the achiever, the more choice. Low achievers
> 505   need more structure."

> "High ability means more choice in my class."

> "I think the gifted kids need to be challenged; they need lots of options."

Teachers suggested prior knowledge has a signifi-
510   cant impact on the degree to which students benefit from choice. Most teachers indicated that students use choice most effectively when they possess a certain degree of background knowledge in a subject area or have attained a basic level of procedural skill. A vari-
515   ety of teacher comments indicated that choices have less utility when students are relative novices:

> "Giving choices depends on the student's level of learn-ing, the material, and on how far into the course the student has gone."

> 520   "I give them choices once I feel they have a good grasp of the foundations."

> "Choice is a good idea when students have a good foun-dation of principles and they need to learn to apply them."

> 525   "Students benefit from choice when they have familiarity with content, with me and my expectations, and have a certain amount of background information."

> "Choice is a good idea when they (the students) have some background knowledge to go off of and not a good
> 530   idea when they have no knowledge to make a good choice with."

Teaching-related themes. Course content affects the use of choice in the classroom. Topics that require se-quencing, such as mathematics, were deemed less
535   amenable to choice. One high school math teacher said, "Certain material needs to be covered and in a system-atic, orderly way," adding, "There is little room for choice." Another teacher agreed: "In my math classes, I give choices of which problems to work but that's
540   about all."

Other subject areas, such as history and literature, were believed to be better suited to instructional choice. Choices were given on what topic to study, such as the Civil Rights Movement or the Cold War,
545   and how to assess learning using a variety of measures, such as written tests, class presentations, and projects. One high school psychology teacher told us, "Because everything is interesting in psychology, students need to choose what to research" and because it is an elec-
550   tive course, "Students are more invested and need more choices." A high school creative writing teacher said, "Students need to choose topics they are interested in so they will be motivated to write about them." Busi-ness teachers also discussed the importance of instruc-
555   tional choice as a way of making projects relevant. "Students need to select companies or products to study that are meaningful to them." They can "choose the newspaper articles they want to bring in for discus-sion," and "they choose the software they want to use."
560   Art, music, and drama teachers indicated that choice is essential for the development of creativity:

> "Choices are given in music selection, in what uniforms to wear, and in what types of groups we will form."

> "Students have choices of which play to do, and what
> 565   parts to try out for."

> "My art students are given choices of subject matter and imagery; choice benefits those who have skill and crea-tivity in the visual arts."

The physical education teachers who were inter-
570   viewed offered choices of "activities to focus on," "equipment to use," and "partners or groups to practice drills with."

Teachers' classroom management styles affected the use of choice. Teachers who valued student auton-
575   omy were most likely to support the use of choice. Nevertheless, all teachers believed that choice could be used effectively even in tightly controlled classrooms. Most teachers also believed it was important to yield some control of the classroom to students and that
580   choice was an important way to do so. For example, one teacher stated that "choice allows students to be accountable for their actions; they made the choice so they follow through." Making choices also helps stu-dents learn about consequences. As one teacher said,
585   "Basically, students always have a choice of doing or not doing, of studying or not studying, but they also have to face the consequences." Teachers also reported using choice to reinforce positive behavior, as the fol-lowing quotes indicate:

> 590   "I give my kids choices after they have done a good job on an assignment."

> "I let my students choose as a positive consequence based on earlier behavior."

> "Giving my students choice helps build rapport between
> 595   them and me; they show more respect."

Students who are allowed to make choices "invest more energy in learning" and "feel a certain responsibility to participate." Students respond to choice by "becoming very trustworthy," by "making good decisions," and by "working cooperatively together."

The use of choice was linked to teachers' efficacy. Most teachers reported using more choice as they became more experienced over the years and as they became more comfortable throughout the course of each academic year. Several teachers mentioned that choice-giving in their classrooms had not truly been incorporated until after they had multiple years of teaching experience. As the following comments indicate, more choices were offered to students as teachers became more efficacious:

"At first, I didn't give many choices but gradually I started adding options and alternatives."

"I think it's more work to give choices and new teachers have enough to deal with already."

"I give more choices than I used to because I've learned how to handle their reactions."

"I am more comfortable giving choices now and have more of them built into my lessons."

Rationale for Choice

Teachers' responses fell into one of three subcategories that reflected affective, behavioral, and cognitive rationales for choice. "Affective" rationales focused on changing attitudes and increasing affective engagement. "Behavioral" rationales emphasized the role of choice in increasing student effort and participation. "Cognitive" rationales highlighted the effect of choice on levels of processing and cognitive engagement. Additionally, teachers cited increased self-regulation and improved decision-making skills.

Affective rationales for choice. Teachers give students choices because choices have a positive effect on attitude and affective engagement. Words and phrases that were used to describe student response to choice included *empowered, sense of control, responsibility, ownership, motivated, enthusiastic, satisfaction, excited, appreciative,* and *sense of purpose.* The majority of teachers said that choice produces positive effects on students most of the time. However, teachers also conceded that some students react negatively to choice, preferring to be "just told what to do." Terms such as *overwhelmed, confused,* and *nervous* were used to describe negative affective response.

Roughly 70% of teachers mentioned student *ownership* as the most important affective consequence of choice. One teacher said of her students, "It gives them more ownership of learning, promotes collaboration (sometimes) and more buy in." Another teacher said the reason for giving students choice was that they developed "ownership, (became) more motivated and committed to learning. Ownership is a factor; children are more likely to follow through on a choice they feel they made." The belief that ownership is positive and leads to an increase in learning provides the basis for their rationale of choice giving. One teacher said,

I believe that students feel a sense of ownership to a project if they have chosen it. In turn, I believe, the ownership factor leads to more enthusiasm, better quality work, and the student will be more likely to remember something they value.

Another teacher reported, "On projects where they (the students) had a choice, they had more ownership in them and put forth more effort."

Empowerment was a second term used frequently to explain why choice is important for students. Various teachers reported, "Because students feel empowered, they respond in a responsible way"; "Students who are given choices feel empowered and when they feel empowered, they are more apt to take control of or responsibility for their own learning"; and "I think young children might have a more difficult time (making choices); however, this might still make them feel empowered."

Many participants also used choice to give students control of the learning process. One teacher said choice is important because "most times, it promotes success; control of learning," and another teacher simply stated, "It gives the students more control of their learning. I like them to feel they have an element of control in what they're doing; they'll do a better job." One high school teacher commented, "I give choices because it works. Especially in high school, students need to take some control of their learning [and] the environment. Students need to have some control; a sense of their own directedness."

Teachers claimed that choice enhances motivation by increasing interest and that this can occur in two ways. First, choice increases interest by providing the opportunity for students to select what they are already interested in. Second, choice may generate interest where previously it did not exist. A large number of teachers discussed the motivational properties of choice and the potential for interest generation. These teachers believe that choice has a positive motivational effect on students because it increases interest and engagement. One high school teacher stated that choice "promotes involvement, matches student interests; there is less groaning." Choice also "taps creativity, interest, and adds variety." Choice gives students the "satisfaction of solving a problem that they are interested in." Teachers also reported that "choice is a good idea when a student is able to tailor assignments to their own interests" and "students are given choices so they will be interested in the subject, motivated." A computer teacher said, "If they (students) are allowed to pick a topic, they have more interest in what they're doing; they're not going to choose a topic they aren't interested in." She added, "Any time a student is interested in what they're learning, they seem to be more motivated."

One participant stated that "choice is good for motivation. A nonmotivated student will get choices in hopes of motivating him." Another teacher reported,

"Student self-efficacy and motivation are positively affected by giving students a feeling they are invested in the course." Yet another teacher indicated that he gives his students choice because of "the motivation factor," which "causes students to stick with it and they seem to learn more." A secondary school teacher, when asked why she gives students choices, responded "motivation; taking time to choose helps them focus, it seems to give them a feeling of responsibility, a vested interest; it's *my* topic. It motivates them to get started and I can usually see a sense of pride as they work."

Many teachers also linked the opportunity for choice to positive affect or the alleviation of negative affect. One participant stated that students are "usually more excited and willing to start their research when they have chosen their own topic." In computer class, "they are thrilled when they get to choose their activity." Additionally, "many seem relieved; it eases pressure." One teacher reported, "Most students say that learning is more fun, meaningful, and they feel proud of their work." Another participant stated that it "gives students more confidence if they get to make the choices instead of always being told what to do." An industrial technology instructor mentioned that "students don't feel threatened when you give them choices; it works really well that way."

Although teachers agreed that giving students choice is usually a good strategy for improving attitude and learning, several also pointed out that occasionally there is a student who reacts negatively to choice. When asked how students react to choice, one middle school teacher responded, "Some of them, when you say you're giving them a choice, say, 'We'd rather just be given a normal assignment.' They really don't know what they're going to do." She continued, "I don't let them off the hook right away but I try to give them suggestions and if I know the student, I know what they might be interested in." Another participant reported, "Sometimes, they (students) respond with skepticism, like 'what's the catch?'" One teacher explained, "Some of my students don't like having to make a choice; they feel that I should facilitate entirely."

Behavioral rationales for choice. Most teachers claimed that choice is related positively to student behaviors such as time on task, participation in classroom activities, demonstration of effort, cooperation, and respect. "The class comes together tremendously; when students choose, they generally participate more fully," said one teacher. Choice "helps them to be more actively engaged," and students "usually work harder, give better effort" when they have chosen the activity. Other teachers said, "Choice makes students responsible for their behavior" and "in math, some students can meet more objectives if they don't have to repeat learned activities but can work at their own pace." One middle school teacher explained that as a result of choice, "reports and presentations are always extremely well done but sometimes important topics aren't cho-

sen." A high school teacher said, "We know from business research that if you give everyone the opportunity to make decisions, their productivity will increase; that's what I see."

In most but not all cases, the behavioral responses to choice were perceived positively. Some teachers, however, pointed out that there can also be behavioral pitfalls associated with choice. For example, when given choices, "Some students fall back on easy, comfortable topics and don't push themselves; they get lazy." Choice can "allow the student to stagnate on a favorite topic or activity; not explore new territory." Giving students a choice of topics for a research paper can provide an opportunity "to avoid the assignment" by turning in a previously written piece of work.

Cognitive rationales for choice. When teachers were asked specifically about the effects of choice on student learning, nearly everyone indicated they believed their students learn more when choices are offered, even though this conclusion is not supported by empirical findings (Schraw et al., 1998). Teachers emphasized two cognitive subthemes: (1) greater level of cognitive engagement with deeper processing, and (2) greater self-regulation and the development of decision-making skills. First, choice is believed to be responsible for increasing student engagement with learning materials and classroom activities. Choice is believed to be beneficial because it provides students with the opportunity to explore topics for which they have intrinsic interest, leads to greater engagement, deeper processing, and better recall. A special education teacher whose students she described as "at-risk teens" said that giving students appropriate choices encouraged them to interact with the material. She indicated that they spend more time studying "if they are interested, if they want to know more about the issue." A middle school science teacher said he believes that when students are given choices "they definitely make the commitment to learning, use higher level thinking." He went on to say, "They (the students) think more about the way the whole thing fits together, especially when you give choices for assessment." Another teacher said of the relationship between choice and learning, "Choice makes education more meaningful. There is more permanence, more learning."

Teachers also suggested that choice encourages self-regulation and is necessary for the development of decision-making skills. The perception of learning as self-determined causes the student to invest more time, energy, and effort in the process because it is "uncool to fail at something you have chosen." This feeling of responsibility for producing a desirable outcome may be the mechanism by which engagement, strategy use, and learning are increased. One teacher reported, "I believe choice leads to self-regulation of learning." A foreign language teacher commented, "I think it is more likely to lead to the use of metacognitive skills as students make decisions about the direction of their learning." Participants said that choice is associated with "increased self-monitoring" and "thinking and decision-making skills." Choice, participants said, allows students to learn to "evaluate options and develop decision-making skills." Students "learn from their choices; even if they make a bad choice, they can learn from it." Simply put, "Choice builds learning skills."

Summary

The themes summarized above make it clear that teachers possess a variety of beliefs about use of choice in the classroom. Most teachers have spent a great deal of time thinking about the implementation and consequences of choice. Typically, several student-related factors are considered. These factors or themes shown in Figure 1 are consistent with educational research as well. For example, Shevin and Klein (1984) concluded that students' ages and ability levels affect the use of choice in the classroom. Shapiro and Cole (1994, p. 136) reported that "not all choices are appropriate for all students." Shapiro and Cole (1994, p. 137) went on to say, "As students increase in age and ability level, they may benefit from expanded choice." Zimmerman and Martinez-Pons (1990) concluded that high-ability students were better able to use self-regulation strategies when allowed to do so. Sweet, Guthrie, and Ng (1998) concluded that low-achieving students benefit less from choice than their high-achieving counterparts. Aguilar and Petrakis (1989) found that prior experience and skill level were influential factors in students' choice of sports and in their level of participation in sports-related activities.

Support for teacher-related variables (e.g., course content, management style, experience, and efficacy) can be found in the research literature as well. Choice has been used successfully in many content areas, including art (Amabile & Gitomer, 1984), reading (Guthrie & McCann, 1997; Pressley, Yokoi, Rankin, Wharton-McDonald, & Mistretta-Hampston, 1997; Turner, 1995), and foreign language (Bruning, Flowerday, & Trayer, 1999). Teachers' management styles, experiences, and efficacies play a role in implementation of choice. Woolfolk and Hoy (1990) reported that teachers' beliefs about their personal teaching efficacies (their personal abilities to influence student learning outcomes) affects their philosophies of classroom management and instructional style. Teachers with greater personal efficacy tend to operate from a humanistic orientation in which "self-discipline is substituted for strict control" (Woolfolk & Hoy, 1990, p. 84). Bandura (1993) concurred that "teachers' beliefs in their personal efficacy to motivate and promote learning affect the types of learning environments they create and the level of progress their students achieve" (p. 117). Bandura (1997) and Lent, Brown, and Hackett (1994) also suggested that self-efficacy is instrumental in the appraisal and implementation of occupational and academic choices.

Final Results

The thematic results reported above provide a descriptive account of teachers' beliefs in their own words. This section organizes those themes into an integrated structural description of teacher beliefs about choice (Moustakas, 1994). The purpose of the structural description is to provide an analysis of themes reported by teachers.

Teachers discussed at length their beliefs about choice, distinguishing between positive and negative effects of choice on affective (e.g., engagement and motivation) and cognitive (e.g., learning) engagement. Teachers strongly agreed that choice improves affective response by increasing students' ownership, interest, creativity, and personal autonomy. This claim has been made by a number of choice proponents (Deci, 1992; Kamii, 1991; Kohn, 1993). Many teachers stated that choice increases student creativity and flow as well, a claim consistent with recent qualitative analyses of the creative process (Amabile, 1996; Csikszentmihalyi, 1996). There also was a consensus among teachers that judicious use of choice in the classroom improves student–teacher relationships by demonstrating that teachers have confidence in students' ability to self-regulate their learning. Teachers agreed that choice improves cognitive processes such as student engagement, strategy use, and decision making because students are more motivated to perform well when they set their own goals and decide how to reach them. These claims have not been supported with any degree of consistency, although there have been a few empirical studies that specifically address these issues (Hannifin & Sullivan, 1996; Schraw et al., 1998).

All of the teachers we interviewed held positive beliefs about the use of choice in the classroom. However, most of the same teachers expressed some concerns about the overuse of choice. One concern was that too much choice becomes counterproductive. Teachers believed that too many choices can overwhelm students, especially younger students who are less skilled at making their own educational decisions. There was consensus as well that choice may allow unmotivated students to take the path of least resistance. These claims are consistent with findings in business (Williams, 1998) and psychology (Tafarodi, Milne, & Smith, 1999) that indicate that choice is most effective when it includes two equally valued alternatives. Choices between two unequal alternatives or alternatives that are not valued may result in negative outcomes because of what Kohn (1993) refers to as "pseudo-choice."

Teachers offered students choices in six areas. Choices were offered most frequently with respect to topics for term papers and research projects and what to read during recreational reading periods throughout the day. Teachers consistently reported that choice promotes engagement and learning because students select topics they are knowledgeable about and are interested in. Classroom assessment was another area where teachers offered a variety of choices. Most choices concerned the type, frequency, and criteria for assessment. Teachers felt it was motivating for students to help select the criteria used to evaluate their work even though teachers did not do so frequently. Teachers also offered a variety of choices regarding classroom social arrangements. These choices typically concerned seating arrangements, choosing group members, and whether students would work alone or in pairs. Although teachers felt that choice in social arrangements was important, choice was limited to ensure that students had a variety of social experiences and interacted in an academic work setting with other students they would not interact with if they were not required to do so. Previous research has suggested that a variety of social experiences are advantageous for students compared with a more limited array of experiences that would result if students consistently selected in-class partners (Cooper, 1999; Zimmerman, 2000). Teachers offered students a variety of choices regarding classroom procedures such as when to complete assignments, in what order the class would cover main topics, and when to be tested. Procedural choice facilitated learning because it gave students an opportunity to better accommodate individual academic interests and extracurricular activities such as athletics, music, and performing arts.

Teachers gave students choices for two main reasons, one of which they discussed at length (i.e., enhancement of classroom experience), and one of which they rarely discussed explicitly (i.e., reward of effort and good behavior). Teachers indicated that choice resulted in increased student engagement, sense of control, and motivation. This claim is supported by a number of empirical studies based on self-determination theory (Deci, Vallerand, Pelletier, & Ryan, 1991; Ryan & Deci, 2000). Choice is used as well to promote deeper cognitive processing and creativity (Kamii, 1991; Kohn, 1993). Teachers also use choice to improve students' decision-making skills. Teachers frequently commented that many of their students were rather unskilled in this regard, presumably because they are rarely given meaningful choices in academic settings. There are no empirical studies that have examined this relationship.

Teachers also used choice as a reward for effort or good behavior. Few of the teachers we interviewed discussed this aspect of choice explicitly, although it became apparent, based on their comments about when and where they used choice, that it was used frequently as a reward. Teachers were most likely to give choices to older, competent, self-regulated students who had previously demonstrated the ability to use choice wisely. In addition, some teachers gave students choices as a reward for extra effort, improved achievement, or attempts to comply with rules or circumstances they did not enjoy.

Although teachers said they offered choices to every student, and did so regularly, they also stated that options should be limited to increase chances of a positive outcome. Most teachers provided a limited-choice menu to students in which they were required to choose from an array of teacher-selected options.

Teachers repeatedly indicated that several student-related and teacher-related variables affect the use of choice. Age, prior knowledge, and student achievement were mentioned by participants as factors to be considered when making decisions about choice. Older students are given more choices than are younger students because they possess more knowledge and decision-making skills. Teachers also suggested that older students have a stronger need for autonomy and control of their academic progress. This claim is supported by a variety of studies indicating that older students respond more favorably in less controlling environments compared with younger students (Flink et al., 1990; Grolnick & Ryan, 1987). Level of prior knowledge should be considered. High-knowledge students are entrusted with more important choices such as selecting a topic for a major research or creative project than are low-knowledge students. Achievement level affects the number and scope of classroom choice. Self-regulated students are given more choices than are less-regulated students. Choices did not appear to differ as a function of gender or social competence.

The amount of choice given to students is influenced by a number of teacher-related variables. Perhaps the most important of these is teacher self-efficacy. Many teachers indicated that they increased the use of choice throughout their careers, in part due to the extra time and effort needed to administer choices and in part because they felt a greater need for control in their early years. Teachers continue to give more choices to their students in academic settings where they themselves feel intellectually and psychologically autonomous. A second closely related factor is experience. The more experience a teacher has in a particular topic area, the more likely she or he is to offer choice. Course content is another important variable. Teachers in the physical or biological sciences and in mathematics offered fewer choices overall than teachers in the arts and social sciences. This phenomenon was due to two factors: the crucial role of foundational knowledge in the sciences and the naturally occurring instructional sequence implicit in math and science courses. Last, teachers' management styles affected the use of choice. Some teachers believed that classrooms were more efficient when teachers assumed control for student learning. These teachers offered less choice, although even the most teacher-centered individuals believed that regular choices were of benefit to motivation and learning. In contrast, some teachers believed in student-centered classrooms that offered more choices. Although teachers differed in their management styles and usage of choice, there did not appear to be noticeable differences in their attitudes about the effectiveness of choice. Thus, whether teachers use choice a little or a lot, when they do use it, most feel that it promotes motivation and learning.

Feedback from Final Member Checks

Teachers interviewed in the final member-check phase of the study enthusiastically supported the thematic representation of teacher practices and beliefs as presented in Figure 1. All three participants indicated that results were consistent with their understanding and perceptions of instructional choice in the classroom. A fifth-grade teacher stated, "I think it is very thorough; I think it covers everything in depth." He indicated that he uses many of the choices represented with his own students. The rationale-for-choice section was particularly well received. Participants commented that the categories were useful for thinking about rationale and that they had used similar reasoning when deciding about choices for their students. One middle school language arts teacher was especially interested in the types of choices being offered and indicated agreement with all the categories and themes. A high school social studies and Spanish teacher was interested in the teaching-related themes, suggesting that management style and teacher efficacy were very important determinants of decision making about provision of choice. She stated, "Some teachers are very teacher-centered, controlling, and don't provide these opportunities; it might overwhelm some." Also, the secondary teacher reinforced the belief that there was potential for choice to backfire, leading to negative affective, behavioral, and cognitive effects. Member-check participants overwhelmingly endorsed the teacher-belief themes and made no recommendations for substantial additions or deletions from the model.

Discussion

We focus on three main points in this discussion: (1) summarization of our initial research questions, (2) a summarization of guidelines for the use of choice in the classroom on the basis of our findings, and (3) implications for future research.

Summary of Findings

This study examined three questions related to teachers' beliefs about instructional choice. These questions focused on what kind of choices teachers give to students, when and to whom they give them, and why they give them. We explored these questions for two reasons. The first reason is that we are frequently asked questions by preservice and practicing teachers about how to use choice in the classroom. Thus far, we have relied solely on our own personal experiences to answer these questions because there are no systematic research findings to draw from. We believe the present findings, based on the classroom practices of 36 teachers, offer a number of explicit guidelines. A second reason is that there is no existing theory of teacher choice. We undertook the present study in part to begin to generate a preliminary model of teacher choice that can be refined and tested by subsequent research.

Our first question focused on what kinds of choices teachers offer their students. Most choices fall into one of six categories, including topic of study, reading materials, methods of assessment, order of activities, social arrangements, and procedural choices. Most choices center on topic of study or reading materials. Fewer choices were given with regard to classroom assessment, in part because teachers were required to conduct certain kinds of assessment and in part because students often lacked a clear idea of what needed to be assessed or how to do so. Nevertheless, teachers felt that some choice of assessment greatly enhanced a students' sense of autonomy and personal control. Choice of learning activities was also common. Teachers offered students a variety of choices with respect to homework, in-class free time, as well as alternative ways to demonstrate their knowledge. A number of social relationship choices were given, although these choices were given cautiously. In general, teachers did not give students social options until a certain degree of competence had been demonstrated. We discuss this phenomenon in more detail below.

Three factors emerged as important constraints on who is given choice: age, ability, and prior knowledge. This pattern closely matched previous research (Shapiro & Cole, 1994). Teachers give older students more choices even though many teachers emphasized the need for authentic choices for younger students. Students of higher ability or those who demonstrate higher performance are given more choices as well. The rationale is that self-regulated students can be trusted to make wise choices and use the opportunities provided by choice more efficiently. This assumption is supported by recent empirical findings (Zimmerman, 2000). Prior knowledge was also considered in making decisions about who is given choice. Teachers had strong beliefs that knowledgeable students are best able to make wise choices and work autonomously once given a choice. Teachers were aware of the potential interactions among age, ability, and prior knowledge. A number of participants indicated that knowledge compensates in part for age and ability; thus, it was possible to give high-knowledge younger students more choices than low-knowledge older students. Nevertheless, teachers also emphasized the role of "choice equity" in the classroom, indicating choice can be appropriately structured in such a way as to benefit all students regardless of age, ability, or level of prior knowledge.

Teachers' comments about when they give choices were especially interesting. Participants agreed that all students should be given choices on a regular basis even when they are young. However, a closer analysis of teachers' comments indicated they made an implicit distinction between generative and maintenance functions of choice, often opting for the latter. By generative function, we mean the assumption that choice causes (i.e., generates) self-determination because it gives students a greater sense of control, interest, and better decision-making skills. Agreeing with this assumption suggests that teachers should use choice in a proactive manner to motivate their students. In contrast, many teachers used choice as a reward to "maintain" existing behaviors; that is, choice was used in the classroom as a consequence rather than as a causal antecedent of self-determined behaviors. For example, students who were performing well could choose their partner for an upcoming class project, or students who performed well on one assignment were given more choices on the next assignment. This pattern seemed somewhat contradictory to us given the explicit theoretical emphasis on the generative function of choice in research literature. From our perspective, it appears that teachers implicitly believe that choice causes self-determination but paradoxically act as if self-determination should be rewarded by choice. Future research will look more closely at this inconsistency between theory and practice. It may be that choice serves as a cognitive–behavioral reinforcer as well as a source of intrinsic motivation.

Teachers gave students choices for three main reasons. The first was to increase student self-determination. All teachers felt the self-determined students were more motivated and more likely to be deeply engaged in classroom learning. This assumption is closely aligned with the main assumptions of self-determination theory (Deci & Ryan, 1987; Deci et al., 1991). The second reason for giving choice was to increase personal interest, which was seen as a major catalyst for improving learning. Teachers felt that interest was necessary for total engagement (Deci, 1992). A third reason was to provide an opportunity for students to practice their decision-making skills. Teachers stressed that students would not become facile at making wise choices unless they were given the opportunity to do so and gained feedback about their progress (Reeve, Bolt, & Cai, 1999).

Guidelines for Classroom Practice

The present findings have a number of implications for teaching. The most obvious of these is that teachers believe that choice matters to students. All teachers in the study offer their students choices, and most do so regularly. On a day-to-day basis, teachers offer more choices to older, higher ability, and more knowledgeable students than others, although all teachers felt it is important to maintain some degree of choice equity. A second implication concerns what kinds of choices to give students. All of the teachers we interviewed gave students choices about what to study, especially in their free time or when they were working in small groups. The rationale is that students will select tasks and materials that are of interest to them and therefore experience greater motivation to learn. None of the teachers expressed any misgivings about this strategy. A third implication concerns how to sequence choices. Participants agreed that simple choices were most appropriate for younger or less capable students and that all students should be eased into the year with simple choices.

Our interviews yielded a considerable amount of data in which a wide variety of suggestions were made for using choice in the classroom. We offer a number of general conclusions that most or all teachers agreed with.

When to use choice: (a) in all grades, but older students need more choices as student competence and self-regulation increase; and (b) when students know a lot about the task or topic.

Where to use choice: (a) in a variety of settings (e.g., math, history); (b) on different tasks (e.g., homework, assessment); and (c) for academic and social activities.

How to use choice: (a) offer simple choices at first; (b) help students practice making good choices; (c) provide feedback about the choice; (d) use team choices for younger students; (e) provide information that clarifies the choice; and (f) offer choices within a task (e.g., ordering, sequence, topic).

Implications for Future Research

The present findings raise several broad issues for future research. One concerns the extent to which teachers' beliefs about choice can be validated empirically. Current research supports many of the claims that teachers make regarding positive affective engagement, satisfaction, and empowerment. However, there is less support for the claim that choice significantly improves deeper learning. A second issue is whether the use of choice in a generative or maintenance manner affects intrinsic motivation, engagement, or learning. One possibility is that choice used as a reward could undermine intrinsic motivation (Kohn, 1993). Studies are needed to determine whether performance contingencies attached to choice undermine its potentially positive effects. A third issue pertains to how teachers' usage of choice is related to their own teaching self-efficacies. None of the teachers in this study explicitly addressed this issue, although many mentioned that they offered more choices as their careers advanced and students became more self-regulated. We suspect that high-efficacy teachers offer more choices to their students than do low-efficacy teachers (Calderhead, 1996; Pajares, 1992). Fourth, a much better understanding is needed of the relationship between choice and interest. All of the teachers we interviewed stated that choice increased interest because it allowed students to select what they liked and already knew about. However, it is unclear presently

1280 whether choice exerts a causal influence on interest, or if interest contributes to learning separate from choice.

Appendix

Demographic Information from Current Study (N = 36)

Item	Total
Male	14 (39%)
Female	22 (61%)
Grade levels taught	
Elementary (K–5)	8 (22%)
Secondary (6–12)	28 (78%)
Degrees held	
Bachelor's only	24 (67%)
Bachelor's and master's	12 (33%)
Description of schools	
Small	15 (41%)
Medium–large	21 (59%)
Rural	18 (50%)
Urban	18 (50%)
Subjects represented	
Elementary curriculum	7
Business	5
Computer technology	10
Language arts–English	12
Math	6
Music–art	2
Physical education	6
Science	11
Social sciences	8
Special education	4
Industrial technology	1
World languages	5

Item	N	Minimum	Maximum	M	SD
Number of students per class	36	1.00	35.00	20.77	7.54
Years of teaching experience	36	1.00	29.00	8.06	7.58

References

Aguilar, T. E., & Petrakis, E. (1989). Development and initial validation of perceived competence and satisfaction measures for racquet sports. *Journal of Leisure Research, 21*, 133–149.

Amabile, T. M. (1996). *Creativity in context.* Boulder, CO: Westview.

Amabile, T. M., & Gitomer, J. (1984). Children's artistic creativity: Effects of choice in task materials. *Personality and Social Psychology Bulletin, 10*, 209–215.

Bandura, A. (1993). Perceived self-efficacy in cognitive development and functioning. *Educational Psychologist, 28*, 117–148.

Bandura, A. (1997). *Self-efficacy: The exercise of control.* New York: Freeman.

Bogdan, R. C., & Biklen, S. K. (1992). *Qualitative research for education: An introduction to theory and methods.* Boston: Allyn & Bacon.

Boggiano, A. K., Main, D. S., & Katz, P. A. (1988). Children's preference for challenge: The role of perceived competence and control. *Journal of Personality and Social Psychology, 54*, 134–141.

Bruning, R., Flowerday, T., & Trayer, M. (1999). Developing foreign language frameworks: An evaluation study. *Foreign Language Annals, 32*, 159–176.

Calderhead, J. (1996). Teachers: Beliefs and knowledge. In D. C. Berliner & R. C. Calfee (Eds.), *Handbook of educational psychology* (pp. 709–725). New York: Simon & Schuster Macmillan.

Cooper, M. A. (1999). Classroom choices from a cognitive perspective on peer learning. In A. M. O'Donnell & A. King (Eds.), *Cognitive perspectives on peer learning* (pp. 215–234). Mahwah, NJ: Erlbaum.

Cordova, D. I., & Lepper, M. R. (1996). Intrinsic motivation and the process of learning: Beneficial effects of contextualization, personalization, and choice. *Journal of Educational Psychology, 88*, 715–730.

Creswell, J. W. (1998). *Qualitative inquiry and research design: Choosing among five traditions.* Thousand Oaks, CA: Sage.

Csikszentmihalyi, M. (1996). *Creativity: Flow and the psychology of discovery and invention.* New York: Harper-Collins.

Deci, E. L. (1992). The relation of interest to the motivation of behavior: A self-determination theory perspective. In A. Renninger, S. Hidi, & A. Krapp (Eds.), *The role of interest in learning and development* (pp. 43–70). Hillsdale, NJ: Erlbaum.

Deci, E. L., & Ryan, R. M. (1987). The support of autonomy and control of behavior. *Journal of Personality and Social Psychology, 53*, 1024–1037.

Deci, E. L., Vallerand, R. J., Pelletier, L. G., & Ryan, R. M. (1991). Motivation and education: The self-determination perspective. *Educational Psychologist, 26*, 325–346.

Enzle, M. E., & Anderson, S. C. (1993). Surveillant intentions and intrinsic motivation. *Journal of Personality and Social Psychology, 64*, 257–266.

Flink, C., Boggiano, A. K., & Barrett, M. (1990). Controlling teaching strategies: Undermining children's self-determination and performance. *Journal of Personality and Social Psychology, 59*, 916–924.

Grolnick, W. S., & Ryan, R. M. (1987). Autonomy in children's learning: An experimental and individual difference investigation. *Journal of Personality and Social Psychology, 52*, 890–898.

Guthrie, J. T., & McCann, A. D. (1997). Characteristics of classrooms that promote motivations and strategies for learning. In J. T. Guthrie & A. Wigfield (Eds.), *Reading engagement: Motivating readers through integrated instruction* (pp. 128–148). Newark, DE: International Reading Association.

Hannafin, R. D., & Sullivan, H. J. (1996). Preferences and learner control over amount of instruction. *Journal of Educational Psychology, 88*, 162–173.

Kamii, C. (1991). Toward autonomy: The importance of critical thinking and choice making. *School Psychology Review, 20*, 382–388.

Kohn, A. (1993, September). Choices for children: Why and how to let students decide. *Phi Delta Kappan*, 8–20.

Law, A., Logan, H., & Baron, R. S. (1994). Desire for control, felt control, and stress inoculation training during dental treatment. *Journal of Personality and Social Psychology, 67*, 926–936.

Lent, R. W., Brown, S. D., & Hackett, G. (1994). Toward a unifying social cognitive theory of career and academic interest, choice, and performance. *Journal of Vocational Behavior, 45*, 79–122.

Miserandino, M. (1996). Children who do well in school: Individual differences in perceived competence and autonomy in above-average children. *Journal of Educational Psychology, 88*, 203–214.

Moustakas, C. (1994). *Phenomenological research methods.* Thousand Oaks, CA: Sage.

Pajares, M. F. (1992). Teachers' beliefs and educational research: Cleaning up a messy construct. *Review of Educational Research, 62*, 307–322.

Parker, L. E., & Lepper, M. R. (1992). The effects of fantasy contexts on children's learning and motivation: Making learning more fun. *Journal of Personality and Social Psychology, 62*, 625–633.

Pressley, M., Yokoi, L., Rankin, J., Wharton-McDonald, R., & Mistretta-Hampston, J. (1997). *A survey of the instructional practices of Grade-5 teachers nominated as effective in promoting literacy* (Reading Research Report No. 85). Athens, GA: University of Georgia and University of Maryland, with the National Reading Research Center.

Reeve, J., Bolt, E., & Cai, Y. (1999). Autonomy-supportive teachers: How they teach and motivate students. *Journal of Educational Psychology, 91*, 537–548.

Rocklin, T., & O'Donnell, A. M. (1987). Self-adapted testing: A performance-improving variant of computerized adaptive testing. *Journal of Educational Psychology, 79*, 315–319.

Rocklin, T. R., O'Donnell, A. M., & Holst, P. M. (1995). Effects and underlying mechanisms of self-adapted testing. *Journal of Educational Psychology, 87*, 103–116.

Ryan, R., Connell, J., & Grolnick, W. (1992). When achievement is not intrinsically motivated: A theory of internalization and self-regulation in school. In K. Boggiano & T. Pittman (Eds.), *Achievement and motivation: A social developmental perspective* (pp. 167–188). Cambridge, UK: Cambridge University Press.

Ryan, R. M., & Deci, E. L. (2000). Self-determination theory and the facilitation of intrinsic motivation, social development, and well-being. *American Psychologist, 55*, 68–78.

Schraw, G., Flowerday, T., & Reisetter, M. (1998). The role of choice in reader engagement. *Journal of Educational Psychology, 90*, 705–714.

Shapiro, E. S., & Cole, C. L. (1994). *Behavior change in the classroom: Self-management intervention.* New York: Guilford Press.

Shevin, M., & Klein, N. K. (1984). The importance of choice-making skills for students with severe disabilities. *Journal of the Association for Persons with Severe Handicaps, 9*, 159–166.

Skinner, E. A., Wellborn, J. G., & Connell, J. P. (1990). What it takes to do well in school and whether I've got it: A process model of perceived control and children's engagement and achievement in school. *Journal of Educational Psychology, 82*, 22–32.

Sweet, A. P., Guthrie, J. T., & Ng, M. M. (1997). Teacher perceptions and student reading motivation. *Journal of Educational Psychology, 90*, 210–223.

Tafarodi, R. W., Milne, A. B., & Smith, A. J. (1999). The confidence of choice: Evidence for an augmentation effect on self-perceived performance. *Personality and Social Psychology Bulletin, 25, 11*, 1405.

Turner, J. C. (1995). The influence of classroom contexts on young children's motivation for literacy. *Reading Research Quarterly, 30*, 410–441.

Weinert, F. E., & Helmke, A. (1995). Learning from wise mother nature or big brother instructor: The wrong choice as seen from an educational perspective. *Educational Psychologist, 30,* 135–142.

Williams, G. C., & Deci, E. L. (1996). Internalization of biopsychosocial values by medical students: A test of self-determination theory. *Journal of Personality and Social Psychology, 70,* 767–779.

Williams, S. (1998). An organizational model of choice: A theoretical analysis differentiating choice, personal control, and self-determination. *Genetic, Social, and General Psychology Monographs, 124,* 465–491.

Wise, S. L., Plake, B. S., Johnson, P. L., & Roos, L. L. (1992). A comparison of self-adapted and computerized adaptive tests. *Journal of Educational Measurement, 29,* 329–339.

Wise, S. L., Roos, L. L., Leland, V. L., Oats, R. G., & McCrann, T. O. (1996). The development and validation of a scale measuring desire for control on examinations. *Educational and Psychological Measurement, 56,* 710–718.

Wise, S. L., Roos, L. L., Plake, B. S., & Nebelsick-Gullet, L. J. (1994). The relationship between examinee anxiety and preference for self-adapted testing. *Applied Measurement in Education, 7,* 81–91.

Wolcott, H. F. (1994). *Transforming qualitative data: Description, analysis, and interpretation.* Thousand Oaks, CA: Sage.

Woolfolk, A. E., & Hoy, W. K. (1990). Prospective teachers' sense of efficacy and beliefs about control. *Journal of Educational Psychology, 82,* 81–91.

Zimmerman, B. J. (2000). Attaining self-regulation: A social–cognitive perspective. In M. Boekarts, P. Pintrich, & M. Zeidner (Eds.), *Handbook of self-regulation* (pp. 13–39). San Diego: Academic Press.

Zimmerman, B. J., & Martinez-Pons, M. (1990). Student differences in self-regulated learning: Relating grade, sex, and giftedness to self-efficacy and strategy use. *Journal of Educational Psychology, 82,* 51–59.

Zuckerman, M., Porac, J., Lathin, D., Smith, R., & Deci, E. L. (1978). On the importance of self-determination for intrinsically-motivated behavior. *Personality and Social Psychology Bulletin, 4,* 443–446.

Acknowledgments: Special thanks go to Douglas Kauffman for his helpful assistance on an earlier version of this article.

Address correspondence to: Terri Flowerday, University of Nebraska—Lincoln, 309 Bancroft Hall, Lincoln, NE 68588-0384. E-mail may be sent to Gregory Schraw at gschraw@unl.edu

Exercise for Article 34

Factual Questions

1. According to the researchers, the purpose of phenomenological methodology is to
   A. test theory.   B. generate theory.

2. In their review of empirical research on choice and learning, the researchers state that the research they describe has three general limitations. What is the first one they mention?

3. According to the researchers, the purpose of phenomenological research is to describe a phenomenon using what?
   A. The researchers' own words.
   B. The participants' own words.
   C. The words of previous researchers.

4. What were the participants for the pilot study and the main study attending?

5. What did the participants do immediately before being interviewed?

6. "Triangulation of data" refers to collecting and/or interpreting data using more than one method. What was the third method used to triangulate the data in this study?

7. Most teachers (i.e., participants) stated that which group of students were given more choices?
   A. Younger students.   B. Older students.

8. What was the mean (*M*) number of years of teaching experience?

Questions for Discussion

9. In the first stage of their research, the researchers conducted a pilot study using eight participants. In your opinion, how important is this aspect of the research? Does it give you more confidence in the results of the study? Explain.

10. Have the researchers described their "methodological framework" in lines 194–214 adequately? Have they adequately justified the use of qualitative methodology instead of quantitative methodology? Explain.

11. To what extent does the use of "member checks" by the researchers increase your confidence in the validity of the results of this study? (See lines 339–380.)

12. What aspects of the results, if any, surprised you? Were any of the results especially interesting to you? Explain.

13. According to the Appendix just above the references for this article, 78% of the participants were secondary school teachers. Does this fact influence your interpretation of the results? Explain.

14. If you were to conduct a follow-up study on the same topic, would you build on this study by conducting an additional qualitative study *or* would you conduct a quantitative study? Explain.

Quality Ratings

Directions: Indicate your level of agreement with each of the following statements by circling a number from 5 for strongly agree (SA) to 1 for strongly disagree (SD). If you believe an item is not applicable to this research article, leave it blank. Be prepared to explain your ratings.

A. The introduction establishes the importance of the study.

SA   5   4   3   2   1   SD

B. The literature review establishes the context for the study.

SA   5   4   3   2   1   SD

C. The research purpose, question, or hypothesis is clearly stated.

SA   5   4   3   2   1   SD

D. The method of sampling is sound.

SA   5   4   3   2   1   SD

E. Relevant demographics (for example, age, gender, and ethnicity) are described.

SA   5   4   3   2   1   SD

F. Measurement procedures are adequate.

SA   5   4   3   2   1   SD

G. All procedures have been described in sufficient detail to permit a replication of the study.

SA   5   4   3   2   1   SD

H. The participants have been adequately protected from potential harm.

SA   5   4   3   2   1   SD

I. The results are clearly described.

SA   5   4   3   2   1   SD

J. The discussion/conclusion is appropriate.

SA   5   4   3   2   1   SD

K. Despite any flaws, the report is worthy of publication.

SA   5   4   3   2   1   SD

Article 35

Student Perceptions of the Transition from Elementary to Middle School

University of North Carolina

From *Professional School Counseling*, 5, 339–345. Copyright © 2002 by American School Counselor Association. Reprinted with permission.

Transitions are often a difficult time of life. The stress and challenge inherent in adjustment can create developmental crises for even the heartiest individuals. Helping students in transition is similarly challenging. To facilitate successful transitions, helping professionals such as school counselors should consider the developmental tasks of various stages, the coping abilities and flexibility of individuals, and the potent systemic and contextual factors of influence.

School personnel recognize the difficult transition students undertake when moving from one level of schooling to another. The transition from elementary to middle school may be especially challenging because it often involves significant school and personal change. One consideration is that most middle school environments differ significantly from the elementary environment (Perkins & Gelfer, 1995). Contextual transitions commonly include additional and unfamiliar students and school staff, and multiple sets of behavioral and classroom rules and expectations.

This contextual change during the transition to middle school is heightened by personal change. Physical, emotional, and social changes that occur in puberty have been associated with heightened emotionality, conflict, and defiance of adults (Berk, 1993). Although pubertal changes have been viewed more as an opportunity than a crisis (Papalia, Olds, & Feldman, 2001), the varied timing of preadolescent development is difficult for students (Berk, 1993). Pubertal changes occur at different times and at different rates for students in the same grade. Therefore, as students transition to middle school, they confront both external contextual changes and internal pubertal changes.

Research has highlighted the developmental and academic difficulties often associated with the transition from elementary to middle school. Both boys and girls show a significant increase in psychological distress across the transition to middle school (Chung, Elias, & Schneider, 1998; Crockett et al., 1989). Even though declines in achievement and increased distress are not gender exclusive, boys tend to show a significant drop in academic achievement, while girls seem to experience a greater level of psychological distress after the transition (Chung et al., 1998). Also, during the transition, girls find peer relationships most stressful, whereas boys find peer relationships, conflict with authority, and academic pressures as equal stressors (Elias, Ubriaco, Reese, Gara, Rothbaum, & Haviland, 1992).

Along with psychological and academic outcomes, studies have shown that student motivation and attitudes toward school tend to decline during the transition to middle school (Anderman, 1996; Harter, 1981; Simmons & Blyth, 1987). Eccles et al. (1993) used "stage-environment fit" to describe the poor fit between the developmental needs of preadolescents and the environment of middle school or junior high school (e.g., academic tracking, increasing competition, and awareness of personal peer group status). Declining student motivation and attitude were highlighted by Simmons and Blyth, who found more negative consequences for students in the transition from elementary to middle school as compared to students making the same grade transition in K–8 schools.

While most of the research describes the negative outcomes associated with the transition to middle school, several authors also suggested interventions to reduce negative outcomes. Schumacher (1998) identified social, organizational, and motivational factors as important aspects of successful interventions. Eccles et al. (1993) suggested strategies designed to create a school context appropriate to developmental levels of preadolescents. These included building smaller communities within the school, using teaming and cooperative learning, eliminating tracking, empowering teachers, and improving student/teacher relationships. Similarly, Felner et al. (1993) found teaching teams and advisory programs as important preventative interventions for students in transition.

Although much of the research has either noted the detrimental effects of the school transition or suggested interventions, few investigations have sought student perceptions during the transition to middle school.

Arowosafe and Irvin (1992) interviewed students about the transition at the end of the sixth-grade year. They asked students about stressors, school safety, perceptions of school, and what people told them about middle school. Students reported heightened levels of stress related to safety concerns in the school. They also noted that students report friends and the information they received from others as critical factors that affect the transition experience.

The purpose of the current investigation was to learn more about student perceptions during the transition from elementary to middle school. The research questions were:

- What questions do students have about middle school?
- What specific concerns do students have about middle school?
- What aspects of middle school do students see as positive?
- What do students think middle school will be like?
- Whom do students turn to for help during the transition into middle school?
- What is important for students to know about coming to middle school?

Method

Participants

The research was conducted in four phases. For phases I and II, participants included all 331 fifth-grade students in a large, rural, Southeastern public school district. Participants included students from three different elementary schools that were scheduled to enter one large middle school (sixth to eighth grade). The mean age was 11.8 years, with a range of 10 to 13 years old. Racial composition of the participants included 59% white students ($n = 195$), 37% black students ($n = 122$), and 4% other ($n = 14$). There were 175 females (53%) and 156 males (47%). Approximately 45% ($n = 149$) were on free or reduced lunch during the fifth-grade year.

At the start of the sixth-grade year (phase III), 103 students (four home-base classrooms) were randomly selected from the 331 fifth-grade students. Demographic information mirrored that of the first sample. Phase IV included a purposeful sample of participants ($n = 97$), again from the 331 fifth-grade students, who experienced success at the middle school. The sample was selected in December of the sixth-grade year. Success was defined by average or better grades (no grade lower than a C), appropriate behavior (no more than one behavior referral), and regular attendance (no more than two unexcused absences) during the first academic marking period (9 weeks) of sixth grade. The researcher felt that perceptions and insight from students with generally positive records, rather than a random or complete sample, would be valuable for understanding student perceptions of the transition. The phase IV sample included students with similar demographics as compared to the participants for the earlier phases.

Setting

Due to the contextual influence on this research (i.e., the significance of elementary school and middle school context), it is important to provide data about the setting. In the participating elementary schools, students attend neighborhood schools that use self-contained classrooms. This middle school is centrally located in the large rural county. The middle school uses teaching teams, four teachers per team that cover primary subjects, and each student has one of those teachers for a home base. As with most middle schools, students move between four to six teachers and are introduced to lockers, showering in gym class, and more responsibility than in elementary school. Students from this district can also travel for up to one and one-half hours each way on a bus to and from their middle school. Although middle school students commute to school on a bus with students from similar geographic areas, students also ride with all students in grades 6 to 12 in the school district.

Procedure

A longitudinal analysis of student perceptions occurred in four phases, starting in January of fifth grade and concluded in December of sixth grade. In phase I (January of the fifth-grade year), the participants submitted questions about middle school. In phase II (May of the fifth-grade year), the participants completed a questionnaire designed to discover more information about student perspectives. In phase III (in August—the start of the sixth-grade year in middle school), students completed a questionnaire similar to the one used in phase II. The phase III questionnaire was administered in home base at the conclusion of the first two weeks of school. In the last phase, phase IV (December of the sixth-grade year), a purposeful sample of selected successful students completed a questionnaire that repeated questions from phases II and III. The phase IV questionnaire was administered at a meeting of selected students led by the school counselor to assist in planning for the upcoming year.

Data Collection

One writing assignment and three questionnaires were used to elicit student perspectives during the transition. In phase I, participants were asked to write any questions they had about middle school. In phase II, the participants completed a five-item questionnaire. One item of the questionnaire asked students to select concerns from a list of 13 themes. A second item, consisting of the same 13 themes, asked students to select positive aspects. The checklist items were generated from themes written by students in phase I, and each checklist included an open-ended response. The checklists were identical and included items such as changing classes, using your locker, getting good grades, older students, and making friends. The questionnaire also assessed general feelings about coming to middle school. One question asked students to indicate how they feel about coming to middle school (worried, a little worried, a little excited, or excited). Additionally, an open-ended question was included to assess perceptions of what middle school would be like. Finally, one question asked students to select the person or persons they felt were most helpful to them during the transition to middle school (teachers, counselors, parents, friends, or someone else).

During phase III, students completed a second questionnaire in home base. This seven-item questionnaire inquired about academic strategies and goals for sixth grade. Included in the questionnaire were items replicated from previous phases. Students were asked what, if any, questions they had about middle school and what concerns they had about middle school.

The third questionnaire again replicated previous questions. This six-item questionnaire included open-ended questions about concerns and best aspects of middle school. The questionnaire also replicated the question about the person or persons who helped students during the transition to middle school. These questions were worded as reflections over the past transition year (e.g., "What were the best aspects about coming to middle school?"). The questionnaire also included an open-ended question to seek students' recommendations for helping fifth-grade students in the transition to middle school for the next academic year. Finally, the questionnaire concluded with one question about class schedule and one about team membership.

Data Analysis

The open-ended writing assignment and series of questionnaire responses were analyzed for content and qualitative themes concerning the transition. Data were subjected to content analysis to identify emergent themes in the responses. Because categories in a content analysis should be completely exhaustive and mutually exclusive, a step classification system (Holsti, 1969) was used. First, each participant's response was categorized into a meaning unit. Meaning units are described as perceived shifts in attitude or a shift in the emotional quality of a response (Giorgo, 1985). These units are not meant to be independent, but rather expressions of aspects of the whole response. For the writing assignment, each question listed by students was coded as a meaning unit. In questionnaires, individual question responses were also coded as meaning units. Open-ended questions on the questionnaires were analyzed for meaning shifts and coded accordingly. For example, a response such as "both scary and fun" would be coded as two separate meaning units. The data, divided into meaning units, describe meaningful aspects of the response, with minimal inferences from the researcher (Seidman, 1991).

After meaning units were coded and tabulated for all data, the researcher examined the coding for their thematic meaning and collapsed coded content into larger themes. Larger themes were identified from the most frequent responses emerging from the initial coding. For example, one student wrote eight separate questions. Although all eight questions were distinct meaning units, the first five focused on rules and procedures, while the last three listed concerns about bullies and older students. Additionally, several responses did not collapse into larger categories and were judged atypical. These responses represented less than 3% of the total responses.

Researcher and Researcher Bias

The researcher is a white male who at the time of the study was a practicing school counselor at the middle school. Although student perceptions formed the base of all conclusions, the researcher also had assumptions that may have influenced the results. As a school counselor, research bias included an increased focus on personal/social adjustment during the transition. The researcher also assumed a level of anxiety concerning the transition to middle school.

Results

Phase I—January of Fifth-Grade Year

What questions do students have about going to middle school? Three hundred thirty-one participants submitted a total of 555 questions. Most students submitted 3 to 5 questions, with a range from 1 to 15. Twenty-eight percent ($n = 156$) of the questions focused on rules and procedures (e.g., "What's the consequence for being late?"), 16% ($n = 90$) on class schedules in sixth grade (e.g., "Do sixth graders get to do chorus?"), 11% ($n = 60$) on PE or gym class (e.g., "Do you get to play basketball in gym class?"), 9% ($n = 52$) on expectations for sixth graders (e.g., "Do you have a lot of work to do?"), and 9% ($n = 52$) on lunch (e.g., "If you have last lunch, do you always have pizza?"). The remaining questions (27%) addressed topics (each one comprised less than 5% of the total) that included lockers, extracurricular programs, recess, teachers, and sports. Of particular note and consistent with current events in schools today, a few of the questions concerned school violence or safety. For example, two questions included "What happens if you threaten to hurt a teacher?" and "Do people kill people in middle school?"

Phase II—May of Fifth-Grade Year

What specific concerns do students have about coming to middle school? A total of 735 concerns were selected by the 331 participants. The frequency of selected concerns was spread somewhat evenly over the 13 choices provided in the questionnaire. In fact, no one response comprised more than 15% of the total selections. The most frequent responses included older students, 14% ($n = 102$); homework, 13% ($n = 98$);

using one's locker, 12% (n = 88); and getting good grades, 12% (n = 85). Only lunchroom, bathrooms, and the open-ended choice received little attention (comprised less than 1%).

Which aspects of middle school do students see as positive? A total of 808 items were selected by the 331 participants. Parallel to the worries of fifth-grade students, students selected a variety of potential positive aspects of middle school. The most mentioned aspects included making friends, 16% (n = 130); gym/PE class, 15% (n = 124); using your locker, 11% (n = 90); and both changing classes and getting good grades, 10% (n = 82 for each). Only the open choice received less than 1% (n = 10).

What do students think middle school will be like? A total of 329 meaning units were coded from the responses by the 331 participants. Forty-five percent of the responses listed that middle school will be "fun" (n = 148), 14% of the responses mentioned that middle school will be "exciting" (n = 46), 11% of responses suggested it will be "cool" (n = 36), while 9% of the responses listed "hard" or "scary" (n = 31). A variety of other responses (each category represented less than 5% of the total) included "weird," "tight," "good," "awesome," and "like a maze."

Whom do students turn to for help during the transition to middle school? A total of 480 choices were selected by the 331 participants. Thirty-five percent of the responses specified friends (n = 166), 22% parents (n = 105), 21% teachers (n = 103), 14% school counselor (n = 68), while 8% mentioned other sources including "cousins," "siblings," and "other family" (n = 38).

Phase III—August of the Sixth-Grade Year

What questions do students have about middle school? A total of 91 responses were reported by 103 randomly selected participants from phases I and II. Thirty-four percent of the responses indicated no questions about middle school (n = 31), 16% of responses centered on rules and procedures (n = 15; e.g., "Can I have one more minute extra to change classes?"), 15% of the responses focused on homework (n = 14; e.g., "How much homework do we get?"), and 7% of the responses focused on classes (n = 6; e.g., "Do I have to take an elective?"). The remaining responses (n = 31) were varied, and each category accounted for less than 5% of the total.

What specific concerns do students have about middle school? A total of 115 responses were tabulated from the 103 randomly selected participants from phases I and II. Twenty-four percent of the responses focused on bullies or older students (n = 28; e.g., "Being picked on on the bus with the older kids"), 19% about getting lost in the building (n = 22; e.g., "Getting lost"), and 19% about doing well in classes (n = 22; e.g., "I am worried that I might not do as well as I have in the past years"). Fourteen percent of the responses

suggested there were no concerns (n = 16) and 7% of the responses centered on being tardy to class (n = 8; e.g., "What happens if I am a minute late to class?"). The remaining responses (n = 27) were varied, and each category accounted for less than 5% of the total responses.

Phase IV—December of Sixth-Grade Year

What were the most difficult aspects of middle school? A total of 152 responses were listed by the 97 participants from a purposeful sample of successful students in phases I and II. Twenty-six percent of the responses focused on getting lost (n = 40; e.g., "Fear of getting lost"), 13% on making friends (n = 19; e.g., "Getting to know people"), 11% on learning the class schedule (n = 17; e.g., "Knowing how to change classes"), 10% on lockers (n = 16; e.g., "Opening your locker"), 8% on getting to class on time (n = 12; e.g., "Tardies, all of them you can get"), and 5% of responses indicated there were no difficulties. The remaining responses (n = 50) were varied, and no category accounted for more than 5% of the total.

What were the best aspects of being in middle school? A total of 118 responses were reported from 97 participants of a purposeful sample of successful students from phases I and II. Forty-three percent centered on freedom/choices (n = 51; e.g., "You get more freedom, like not having to walk in lines"), 18% focused on friends (n = 21; e.g., "Get more time to talk to friends"), 16% on classes (n =19; e.g., "Different and better classes"), and 13% on lockers (n = 15; e.g., "You get your own space and can put stuff in your locker"). The remaining responses (n = 12) were varied, and each category accounted for less than 5% of the total.

Who helped students the most with the transition to middle school? A total of 131 choices represented the people most helpful to the 97 participants. Forty percent of the responses selected friends (n = 52), 23% chose teachers (n = 30), 19% selected parents (n = 25), 11% selected other family (n = 14; e.g., "brothers," "cousins"), while 8% selected the school counselor (n = 10).

What is important to tell fifth-grade students about coming to middle school? Of the 158 responses from the 97 participants, 23% felt it was most important to tell fifth-grade students about rules (n = 36; e.g., "You can't chew gum"), 18% reported expectations/responsibilities (n = 29; e.g., "You have to do your homework to go to incentive day"), 10% where classes and other items are located (n = 16; e.g., "Art is on the eighth-grade hall"), 9% that it is fun (n = 14; e.g., "It is more fun than elementary school"), 8% there are nice teachers (n =12; e.g., "Teachers are pretty nice"), and 6% that it is not hard (n = 9; e.g., "Most of the classes are easy, except social studies"). The remaining responses (n = 69) accounted for categories represented by less than 5% of the total.

Discussion

Students' questions about middle school were dominated by rules and procedures throughout the transition from fifth to sixth grade. Although school rules may be a typical part of orientation programs, being explicit and thorough about rules and procedures seems crucial. The data suggest that students are keenly aware of the contextual change in the transition. Although sixth-grade students at times may exhibit adolescent characteristics, it seems important to remember that these students need an "elementary" orientation concerning rules and procedures. Rules such as walking in the halls or keeping one's hands to oneself, or procedures such as reporting to class before the tardy bell seem simplistic, but these rules and procedures are what students asked about the most. In fact, students 9 weeks into the sixth grade still reflected that expectations and responsibilities were most important to tell fifth-grade students. Although class scheduling is often the start and focus of the orientation process for students in fifth grade, these data suggest that rules/procedures and expectations are most important to students.

Student worries about middle school include a wide variety of topics. Although orientation programming attempts to minimize these concerns, these data indicate that it is important to address a variety of worries involved in the transition. In fact, the spread and frequency of reported worries suggest that there is a generalized or overall persistent level of worry for most students in transition. This conclusion is similar to research suggesting the difficulty of school transitions (Chung et al., 1998; Crockett et al., 1989).

It is also noteworthy both in the fifth grade and at the start of the sixth-grade year that older students or bullies were a particular concern. This echoes findings from Arowosafe and Irvin's (1992) study in which students reported safety as a concern because of rumors about older students. Orientation programming could address this persistent concern by including older students as tour guides or peer mentors in the school to ease the transition. Alternatively, schoolwide bullying programs may help alleviate student concerns about school safety. It is also important to note that homework and doing well in classes seem to be of particular concern to students in both fifth grade and the start of sixth grade. Students' academic concerns may suggest that it is important to build students' confidence in the classroom by teaching homework and study skills. In light of research (Anderman, 1996; Harter, 1981; Simmons & Blyth, 1987) that suggests academic and motivational declines in the transition, addressing these concerns seems especially important. Additionally, getting lost in middle school is a main concern of students upon reflection in December of the sixth-grade year. This fear could be addressed by providing school tours or comprehensive class schedule-based orientations.

Although intervention or orientation programming can be useful to address questions and worries, designing orientation programs that facilitate and build upon student enthusiasm and confidence might provide encouragement to overcome worries and build motivation during the transition. Students recorded more entries for positive aspects than concerns and indicated excitement about a variety of aspects of middle school. In fact, 70% of the student responses were positive to the open-ended question, "What will middle school be like?" During the transition, orientation leaders should highlight aspects of middle school that students seem to enjoy, including increased freedom and choices, the opportunity to change classes, and having their own lockers. Also, it is important to note that students mentioned friends as the top source of help during the transition. This finding supports the need to include peers in transition interventions and orientation programming. Upon reflecting about the transition, sixth-grade students suggest it is important to tell fifth graders that middle school is fun and there are nice teachers.

Although a few studies have found students that thrive in the transition (Crockett et al., 1989; Hirsch & Rapkin, 1987), these data contradict most of the previous research reporting the transition as a rather negative event for students (Anderman, 1996; Chung et al., 1998; Crockett et al., 1989; Elias, Gara, & Ubriaco, 1985; Harter, 1981; Simmons & Blyth, 1987). This study suggests that there are equal, if not more positive, aspects related to the transition to middle school from the student perspective.

This study revealed the importance of including a variety of people in the transition or orientation program. Although school counselors are often responsible for transition planning, students reported that friends, parents, and teachers are all sources of help in the transition. Again, friends and peers are reported as the most frequent resource for students in transition. However, some peers may not provide accurate or helpful information. In this way, it may be useful to identify role-model students who exhibit a desire and skill set that would make them good candidates to help students in transition. An ambassador or peer-helping program may be extremely helpful in the transition (Arowosafe & Irvin, 1992). In fact, Mittman and Packer (1982) found that students attribute a good start frequently to the presence of old friends and the making of new friends. This type of peer support has a strong relationship with adolescent mental health (Hirsch & DeBois, 1992).

Similarly, including teachers and parents in programming is important. Although teachers often provide an orientation to their individual classrooms, integrating teachers in a systemic way may be useful. For example, teachers may have unique classroom rules or procedures, but perhaps a combined orientation can be presented by teachers about general topics such as hall passes or discipline referrals. Arowosafe and Irvin

525 (1992) suggested that teachers can be integrated in advisor/advisee activities. Similarly, although parents are included in open house and class scheduling in most cases, it seems important that parents are informed about rules/procedures and expectations in the middle school.

530 Arowosafe and Irvin (1992) also suggested it is important to provide parent consultation on the transition to middle school, as they found most parents tended to provide warnings rather than positive information about middle school. In this way, parent orientation can

535 strengthen and support student orientation to the middle school. Students look for help from parents during the fifth-grade year, while teachers replace parents to become more important during the sixth-grade year. This shift in adult influence fits developmentally as

540 preadolescents struggle to form an identity independent of family. Interestingly, students still continue to desire adult assistance throughout the transition.

Limitations

With only one primary researcher, qualitative data coding is limited. No researcher can enter into a study

545 without bias (Rowan, 1981). With only one researcher involved with data analysis and only one school district, this study requires replication. Interviews, rather than questionnaires, with students may also elicit richer information about difficulties and positive aspects of

550 the transition. All of the data are self-report, which has inherent limitations.

Implications for School Counselors

Data from this research and the research to date (e.g., Arowosafe & Irvin, 1992; Crockett et al., 1989; Eccles & Midgley, 1989) on school transition suggest

555 that preventive or proactive programming is needed to assist students with the elementary to middle school transition. The transition provides both a challenge and opportunity for school counselors. This research suggests the following guidelines for school counselors

560 coordinating transition programs: (a) rules, expectations, and responsibilities are the primary concern of students and should be presented early in fifth grade and infused throughout the transition year (this is also an excellent opportunity to include administrators and

565 teachers in transition programming), (b) school counselors have an opportunity both to address concerns and stressors and to promote positive aspects of the transition to middle school, (c) transition programs should include peers, family, and teachers as students

570 look to significant others for help, and (d) transition programs should evolve throughout the transition year as student perceptions and needs change.

References

Anderman, E. (1996). The middle school experience: Effects on the math and science achievement of adolescents with LD. *Journal of Learning Disabilities, 31,* 128–138.

Arowosafe, D., & Irvin, J. (1992). Transition to a middle level school: What kids say. *Middle School Journal, 24*(2), 15–19.

Berk, L. (1993). *Infants, children, and adolescents.* Needham Heights, MA: Allyn & Bacon.

Chung, H., Elias, M., & Schneider, K. (1998). Patterns of individual adjustment changes during the middle school transition. *Journal of School Psychology, 36,* 83–101.

Crockett, L., Peterson, A., Graber, J., Schulenburg, J., & Ebata, A. (1989). School transitions and adjustment during early adolescence. *Journal of Early Adolescence, 9,* 181–210.

Eccles, J., & Midgley, C. (1989). Stage/environment fit: Developmentally appropriate classrooms for early adolescents. In R. Ames & C. Ames (Eds.), *Research on motivation in education* (Vol. 3, pp. 139–186). New York: Academic.

Eccles, J., Wigfield, A., Midgley, C., Reuman, D., Mac Iver, D., & Feldlaufer, H. (1993). Negative effects of traditional middle schools on students' motivation. *The Elementary School Journal, 93,* 553–574.

Elias, M., Gara, M., & Ubriaco, M. (1985). Sources of stress and support in children's transition to middle school: An empirical analysis. *Journal of Clinical Child Psychology, 14,* 112–118.

Elias, M., Ubriaco, M., Reese, A., Gara, M., Rothbaum, P., & Haviland, M. (1992). A measure of adaptation to problematic academic and interpersonal tasks of middle school. *Journal of School Psychology, 30,* 41–57.

Felner, R., Brand, S., Adan, A., Mulhall, P., Flowers, N., Sartain, B., & Du-Bois, D. (1993). Restructuring the ecology of the school as an approach to prevention during school transitions: Longitudinal follow-ups and extensions of the School Transition Environment Project (STEP). *Prevention in Human Services, 10*(2), 103–136.

Giorgo, A. (1985). *Phenomenology and psychological research.* Pittsburgh, PA: Duquesne University.

Harter, S. (1981). A new self-report scale of intrinsic versus extrinsic orientation in the classroom: Motivational and informational components. *Developmental Psychology, 17,* 300–312.

Hirsch, B., & DeBois, D. (1992). The relation of peer support and psychological symptomatology during the transition to junior high school: A two-year longitudinal analysis. *American Journal of Community Psychology, 20,* 333–347.

Hirsch, B., & Rapkin, B. (1987). The transition to junior high school: A longitudinal study of self-esteem, psychological symptomatology, school life, and social support. *Child Development, 58,* 1235–1243.

Holsti, O. (1969). *Content analysis for the social sciences and humanities.* Reading, MA: Addison-Wesley.

Mittman, A., & Packer, M. (1982). Concerns of seventh graders about their transition to junior high school. *Journal of Early Adolescence, 2,* 319–338.

Papalia, D., Olds, S., & Feldman, R. (2001). *Human development* (8th ed.). New York: McGraw-Hill.

Perkins, P., & Gelfer, J. (1995). Elementary to middle school: Planning for transition. *The Clearing House, 68,* 171–173.

Rowan, J. (1981). A dialectical paradigm for research. In P. Reason & J. Rowan (Eds.), *Human inquiry* (pp. 93–112). New York: John Wiley.

Schumacher, D. (1998). *The transition to middle school* (Report No. EDO-PS-98-6). Washington, DC: Clearinghouse on Elementary and Early Childhood Education. (ERIC Document Reproduction Service No. ED 422 119)

Seidman, I. (1991). *Interviewing as qualitative research: A guide for researchers in education and the social sciences.* New York: Columbia Teachers Press.

Simmons, R., & Blyth, D. (1987). *Moving into adolescence: The impact of pubertal change and school context.* Hawthorne, NY: Aldine de Gruyter.

Acknowledgment: This research was sponsored by the American School Counselor Association Practitioner Grant.

Exercise for Article 35

Factual Questions

1. According to the literature review, after the transition, girls seem to experience a greater level of what (in comparison with boys)?

2. The students were in which grade when phase I of the study was conducted?

3. How were the 103 students for phase III selected from the 331 fifth-grade students?

4. "Meaning units" are described as perceived shifts in what?

5. For phase I, what is the total number of questions submitted by participants?

6. In phase III, what percentage of the respondents indicated no questions about middle school?

7. In his discussion of the results, the researcher indicates that the participants' questions about middle school were dominated by what?

Questions for Discussion

8. Phase IV of the study was limited to students who had experienced success at the middle school. What is your opinion on the researcher's decision to limit this phase to just those who were successful? (See lines 125–127.)

9. What is your opinion on the researcher's definition of "success," which is stated in lines 128–133?

10. Some of the data collection was open-ended (e.g., asking students to write their questions about middle school). In addition, there were closed-ended questions in which students selected from choices. What is your opinion on these two approaches to data collection? Are they both needed in a study of this type? Explain.

11. The researcher describes the qualitative data analysis in lines 225–258. In your opinion, is it described in adequate detail? Explain.

12. In your opinion, how important is the material on "Researcher and Researcher Bias"? (See lines 259–267.)

13. The researcher describes the limitations of the research in lines 543–551. Do you think that the results of this research are valuable despite the limitations? Explain.

14. If you were to conduct research on the same topic, what changes in the research methodology, if any, would you make?

Quality Ratings

Directions: Indicate your level of agreement with each of the following statements by circling a number from 5 for strongly agree (SA) to 1 for strongly disagree (SD). If you believe an item is not applicable to this research article, leave it blank. Be prepared to explain your ratings.

A. The introduction establishes the importance of the study.

SA   5   4   3   2   1   SD

B. The literature review establishes the context for the study.

SA   5   4   3   2   1   SD

C. The research purpose, question, or hypothesis is clearly stated.

SA   5   4   3   2   1   SD

D. The method of sampling is sound.

SA   5   4   3   2   1   SD

E. Relevant demographics (for example, age, gender, and ethnicity) are described.

SA   5   4   3   2   1   SD

F. Measurement procedures are adequate.

SA   5   4   3   2   1   SD

G. All procedures have been described in sufficient detail to permit a replication of the study.

SA   5   4   3   2   1   SD

H. The participants have been adequately protected from potential harm.

SA   5   4   3   2   1   SD

I. The results are clearly described.

SA   5   4   3   2   1   SD

J. The discussion/conclusion is appropriate.

SA   5   4   3   2   1   SD

K. Despite any flaws, the report is worthy of publication.

SA   5   4   3   2   1   SD

Article 36

Project D.A.R.E. Outcome
Effectiveness Revisited

STEVEN L. WEST
Virginia Commonwealth University

KERI K. O'NEAL
University of North Carolina, Chapel Hill

OBJECTIVES. We provide an updated meta-analysis on the effectiveness of Project D.A.R.E. in preventing alcohol, tobacco, and illicit drug use among school-aged youths.

METHODS. We used meta-analytic techniques to create an overall effect size for D.A.R.E. outcome evaluations reported in scientific journals.

RESULTS. The overall weighted effect size for the included D.A.R.E. studies was extremely small (correlation coefficient = 0.011; Cohen's d = 0.023; 95% confidence interval = –0.04, 0.08) and nonsignificant (z = 0.73, NS).

CONCLUSIONS. Our study supports previous findings indicating that D.A.R.E. is ineffective.

From *American Journal of Public Health*, *94*, 1027–1029. Copyright © 2004 by American Journal of Public Health. Reprinted with permission.

In the United States, Project D.A.R.E. (Drug Abuse Resistance Education) is one of the most widely used substance abuse prevention programs targeted at school-aged youths. In recent years, D.A.R.E. has been
5 the country's largest single school-based prevention program in terms of federal expenditures, with an average of three-quarters of a billion dollars spent on its provision annually.[1] Although its effectiveness in preventing substance use has been called into question, its
10 application in our nation's schools remains very extensive.[2–6]

Given the recent increases in alcohol and other drug use among high school and college students,[7] the continued use of D.A.R.E. and similar programs seems
15 likely. In a meta-analysis examining the effectiveness of D.A.R.E., Ennett et al.[3] noted negligible yet positive effect sizes (ranging from 0.00 to 0.11) when outcomes occurring immediately after program completion were considered. However, this analysis involved 2 major
20 limitations. First, Ennett et al. included research from nonpeer-reviewed sources, including annual reports produced for agencies associated with the provision of D.A.R.E. services. While such an inclusion does not necessarily represent a serious methodological flaw,
25 use of such sources has been called into question.[8]

Second, Ennett and colleagues included only studies in which postintervention assessment was con-

ducted immediately at program termination. As noted by Lynam et al.,[6] the developmental trajectories of drug
30 experimentation and use vary over time. Thus, if individuals are assessed during periods in which rates of experimentation and use are naturally high, any positive effects that could be found at times of lower experimentation will be deflated. Likewise, assessments
35 made during periods in which experimentation and use are slight will exaggerate the overall effect of the intervention.

Ideally, problems such as those just described could be solved by the use of large-scale longitudinal studies
40 involving extensive follow-up over a period of years. There have been several longer-term follow-ups, but the cost of such efforts may limit the number of longitudinal studies that can be conducted. In the present analysis, we attempted to overcome this difficulty by
45 including a wider range of follow-up reports, from immediate posttests to 10-year postintervention assessments, in an updated meta-analysis of all currently available research articles reporting an outcome evaluation of Project D.A.R.E.

Methods

50 We conducted computer searches of the *ERIC*, *MEDLINE*, and *PsycINFO* databases in late fall 2002 to obtain articles for the present study. In addition, we reviewed the reference lists of the acquired articles for other potential sources. We initially reviewed roughly
55 40 articles from these efforts; 11 studies appearing in the literature from 1991 to 2002 met our 3 inclusion criteria, which were as follows:

1. The research was reported in a peer-reviewed journal; reports from dissertations/theses, books, and unpublished manuscripts were not included. We
60 selected this criterion in an attempt to ensure inclusion of only those studies with rigorous methodologies. As noted, a previous meta-analysis of Project D.A.R.E. included research from nonreviewed sources, a fact that critics have suggested
65 may have added error to the reported findings.[8]

2. The research included a control or comparison group (i.e., the research must have involved an experimental or quasi-experimental design).

Table 1
Primary Articles Included in the Meta-Analysis

Study (year)	Sample	r	d	95% confidence interval
Ringwalt et al. (1991)[18]	5th and 6th graders (n = 1270; 52% female/48% male; 50% African American/40% Anglo/10% other), posttested immediately	0.025	0.056	−0.06, 0.16
Becker et al. (1992)[19]	5th graders (n = 2878), posttested immediately	−0.058	−0.117	−0.19, −0.04
Harmon (1993)[20]	5th graders (n = 708), posttested immediately	0.015	0.030	−0.12, 0.18
Ennett et al. (1994)[21]	7th and 8th graders (n = 1334; 54% Anglo/22% African American/9% Hispanic/15% other), 2 years post-D.A.R.E.	0.000	0.000[a]	−0.11, 0.11
Rosenbaum et al. (1994)[22]	6th and 7th graders (n = 1584; 49.7% female/50.3% male; 49.9% Anglo/24.7% African American/8.9% Hispanic/16.5% other), 1 year post-D.A.R.E.	0.000	0.000[a]	−0.10, 0.10
Wysong et al. (1994)[23]	12th graders (n = 619), 5 years post-D.A.R.E.	0.000	0.000[a]	−0.16, 0.16
Dukes et al. (1996)[24]	9th graders (n = 849), 3 years post-D.A.R.E.	0.035	0.072	−0.06, 0.21
Zagumny & Thompson (1997)[25]	6th graders (n = 395; 48% female/52% male), 4–5 years post-D.A.R.E.	0.184	0.376	0.07, 0.68
Lynam et al. (1999)[6]	6th graders (n = 1002; 57% female/43% male; 75.1% Anglo/20.4% African American/0.5% other), 10 years post-D.A.R.E.	0.000	0.000[a]	−0.15, 0.15
Thombs (2000)[26]	5th through 10th graders (n = 630; 90.4% Anglo/5.5% African American/4.1% other), posttested at least 1 to 6 years post-D.A.R.E.	0.025	0.038	−0.15, 0.23
Ahmed et al. (2002)[14]	5th and 6th graders (n = 236; 50% female/50% male/69% Anglo/24% African American/7% other), posttested immediately	0.198	0.405	0.01, 0.80

Note. r = correlation coefficient; d = difference in the means of the treatment and control conditions divided by the pooled standard deviation. Negative signs for r and d indicate greater effectiveness of control/comparison group.
[a]Assumed effect size.

3. The research included both preintervention and postintervention assessments of at least 1 of 3 key variables: alcohol use, illicit drug use, and tobacco use. We chose to include only those effect sizes that concerned actual substance use behaviors, since the true test of a substance use prevention effort is its impact on actual rates of use.

Using these criteria, we refined the original list of studies to 11 studies (Table 1). We calculated effect sizes using the procedures outlined by Rosenthal.[9] Meta-analysis results are commonly presented in the form of either a correlation coefficient (r) or the difference in the means of the treatment and control conditions divided by the pooled standard deviation (Cohen's d).[10] Since both are ratings of effect size, they can readily be converted to one another, and, if not provided in the original analyses, they can be calculated via F, t, and χ^2 statistics as well as means and standard deviations.[9] We calculated both estimations for the individual included studies and for the overall analysis. As discussed by Amato and Keith,[11] tests of significance used in meta-analyses require that effect sizes be independent; therefore, if 2 or more effect sizes were generated within the same outcome category, we used the mean effect size. We also used the procedure for weighting effect sizes suggested by Shadish and Haddock[12] to ensure that all effect sizes were in the form of a com-mon metric. In addition, we calculated 95% confidence intervals (CIs) for each study and for the overall analysis.

Results

The average weighted effect size (r) for all studies was 0.011 (d = 0.023; 95% CI = −0.04, 0.08), indicating marginally better outcomes for individuals participating in D.A.R.E. relative to participants in control conditions. The fact that the associated CI included a negative value indicates that the average effect size was not significantly greater than zero at $p < .05$. According to the guidelines developed by Cohen,[13] both of the effect sizes obtained were below the level normally considered small. Four of the included studies noted no effect of D.A.R.E. relative to control conditions, and 1 study noted that D.A.R.E. was less effective than the control condition.

Furthermore, the 6 reports indicating that D.A.R.E. had more positive effects were for the most part small (Figure 1). The largest effect size was found in a report in which the only outcome examined was smoking. Finally, we conducted a test of cumulative significance to determine whether differences existed between D.A.R.E. participants and non-D.A.R.E. participants. This test produced nonsignificant results (z = 0.73, NS).

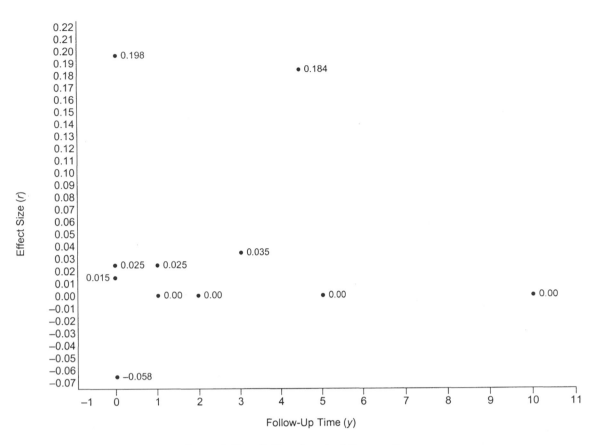

Figure 1. Plot of effect sizes, by follow-up time.

Discussion

Our results confirm the findings of a previous meta-analysis[3] indicating that Project D.A.R.E. is ineffective.
125 This is not surprising, given the substantial information developed over the past decade to that effect. Critics of the present analysis might argue that, despite the magnitude of our findings, the direction of the effect of D.A.R.E. was generally positive. While this is the case,
130 it should be emphasized that the effects we found did not differ significantly from the variation one would expect by chance. According to Cohen's guidelines,[13] the effect size we obtained would have needed to be 20 times larger to be considered even small. Given the
135 tremendous expenditures in time and money involved with D.A.R.E., it would appear that continued efforts should focus on other techniques and programs that might produce more substantial effects.

Our findings also indicate that D.A.R.E. was mini-
140 mally effective during the follow-up periods that would place its participants in the very age groups targeted. Indeed, no noticeable effects could be discerned in nearly half of the reports, including the study involving the longest follow-up period. This is an important con-
145 sideration for those involved in program planning and development.

As noted earlier, progression in regard to experimentation and use varies over time. Use of alcohol and other drugs reaches a peak during adolescence or

150 young adulthood and decreases steadily thereafter.[7,15] Such a developmental path would be expected of all individuals, regardless of their exposure to a prevention effort. Ideally, individuals enrolled in a program such as D.A.R.E. would report limited or no use during their
155 adolescent and young adult years. The fact that half of the included studies reported no beneficial effect of D.A.R.E. beyond what would be expected by chance casts serious doubt on its utility.

One shortcoming of our analysis should be noted.
160 In many of the studies we included, individual students were the unit of analysis in calculating effects. As noted by Rosenbaum and Hanson,[16] this practice tends to lead to overestimates of program effectiveness, since the true unit of analysis is the schools in which the stu-
165 dents are "nested." Because our meta-analysis was limited to the types of data and related information available from the original articles, the potential for such inflation of program effectiveness exists. However, the overall effect sizes calculated here were small and non-
170 significant, and thus it is unlikely that inclusion of studies making this error had a significant impact on the current findings.

An additional caveat is that all of the studies included in this analysis represent evaluations of what is
175 commonly referred to as the "old D.A.R.E.": programs generally based on the original formulations of the D.A.R.E. model. In response to the many critiques of

the program, the D.A.R.E. prevention model was substantially revamped in 2001, thanks in part to a \$13.6
180 million grant provided by the Robert Wood Johnson
Foundation.[17] The revisions to the model have since
given rise to programs working under the "new
D.A.R.E." paradigm. However, at the time of the writing of this article we were unable to find any major
185 evaluation of the new D.A.R.E. model in the research
literature, and the effectiveness of such efforts has yet
to be determined.

References

1. McNeal RB, Hanson WB. An examination of strategies for gaining con-
vergent validity in natural experiments: D.A.R.E. as an illustrative case
study. *Eval Rev.* 1995;19:141–158.
2. Donnermeyer J, Wurschmidt T. Educators' perceptions of the D.A.R.E.
program. *J Drug Educ.* 1997;27:259–276.
3. Ennett ST, Tobler NS, Ringwalt CL, Flewelling RL. How effective is
Drug Abuse Resistance Education? A meta-analysis of Project D.A.R.E.
outcome evaluations. *Am J Public Health.* 1994;84:1394–1401.
4. Hanson WB. Pilot test results comparing the All Stars Program with
seventh-grade D.A.R.E.: Program integrity and mediating variable
analysis. *Subst Use Misuse.* 1996;31:1359–1377.
5. Hanson WB, McNeal RB. How D.A.R.E. works: An examination of
program effects on mediating variables. *Health Educ Behav.*
1997;24:165–176.
6. Lynam DR, Milich R, Zimmerman R, et al. Project D.A.R.E: No effects
at 10-year follow-up. *J Consult Clin Psychol.* 1999;67:590–593.
7. Johnston LD, O'Malley PM, Bachman JG. *National Survey Results on
Drug Use From the Monitoring the Future Study, 1975–1998. Volume 1:
Secondary School Students.* Rockville, Md: National Institute on Drug
Abuse; 1999. NIH publication 99–4660.
8. Gorman DM. The effectiveness of D.A.R.E. and other drug use prevention programs. *Am J Public Health.* 1995;85:873.
9. Rosenthal R. *Meta-Analytic Procedures for Social Research.* 2nd ed.
Thousand Oaks, Calif: Sage Publications; 1991.
10. DasEiden R, Reifman A. Effects of Brazelton demonstrations on later
parenting: A meta-analysis. *J Pediatr Psychol.* 1996;21:857–868.
11. Amato PH, Keith B. Parental divorce and well-being of children: A
meta-analysis. *Psychol Bull.* 1991;110:26–46.
12. Shadish WR, Haddock CK. Combining estimates of effect size. In: Cooper H, Hedges LV, eds. *The Handbook of Research Synthesis.* New
York. NY: Russell Sage Foundation; 1994:261–281.
13. Cohen J. *Statistical Power Analysis for the Behavioral Sciences.* 2nd ed.
Hillsdale, NJ: Lawrence Erlbaum Associates; 1998.
14. Ahmed NU, Ahmed NS, Bennett CR, Hinds JE. Impact of a drug abuse
resistance education (D.A.R.E.) program in preventing the initiation of
cigarette smoking in fifth- and sixth-grade students. *J Natl Med Assoc.*
2002;94:249–256.
15. Shedler J, Block J. Adolescent drug use and psychological health: A
longitudinal inquiry. *Am Psychol.* 1990;45:612–630.
16. Rosenbaum DP, Hanson GS. Assessing the effects of a school-based
drug education: A six-year multilevel analysis of Project D.A.R.E. *J Res
Crime Delinquency.* 1998;35:381–412.
17. Improving and evaluating the D.A.R.E. school-based substance abuse
prevention curriculum. Available at: http://www.rwjf.org/programs/
grantDetail.jsp?id=040371. Accessed January 8, 2003.
18. Ringwalt C, Ennett ST, Holt KD. An outcome evaluation of Project
D.A.R.E. (Drug Abuse Resistance Education). *Health Educ Res.*
1991;6:327–337.
19. Becker HK, Agopian MW, Yeh S. Impact evaluation of drug abuse resistance education (D.A.R.E.). *J Drug Educ.* 1992;22:283–291.
20. Harmon MA. Reducing the risk of drug involvement among early adolescents: An evaluation of drug abuse resistance education (D.A.R.E.).
Eval Rev. 1993;17:221–239.
21. Ennett ST, Rosenbaum DP, Flewelling RL, Bieler GS, Ringwalt CL,
Bailey SL. Long-term evaluation of drug abuse resistance education.
Addict Behav. 1994;19:113–125.
22. Rosenbaum DP, Flewelling RL, Bailey SL, Ringwalt CL, Wilkinson DL.
Cops in the classroom: A longitudinal evaluation of drug abuse resistance education (D.A.R.E.). *J Res Crime Delinquency.* 1994;31:3–31.
23. Wysong E, Aniskiewicz R, Wright D. Truth and D.A.R.E.: Tracking
drug education to graduation and as symbolic politics. *Soc Probl.*
1994;41:448–472.
24. Dukes RL, Ulllman JB, Stein JA. Three-year follow-up of drug abuse
resistance education (D.A.R.E.). *Eval Rev.* 1996;20:49–66.
25. Zagumny MJ, Thompson MK. Does D.A.R.E. work? An evaluation in
rural Tennessee. *J Alcohol Drug Educ.* 1997;42:32–41.
26. Thombs DL. A retrospective study of D.A.R.E.: Substantive effects not
detected in undergraduates. *J Alcohol Drug Educ.* 2000;46:27–40.

Acknowledgments: Portions of this research were presented at the
Eighth Annual Meeting of the Society for Prevention Research,
Montreal, Quebec, Canada, June 2000.

About the authors: Steven L. West is with the Department of Rehabilitation Counseling, Virginia Commonwealth University, Richmond. Keri K. O'Neal is with the Center for Developmental Science,
University of North Carolina, Chapel Hill. Drs. West and O'Neal
contributed equally to all aspects of study design, data analysis, and
the writing of this article. No protocol approval was needed for this
study.

Address correspondence to: Steven L. West, Ph.D., Virginia Commonwealth University, Department of Rehabilitation Counseling,
1112 East Clay St., Box 980330, Richmond, VA 23298-0330. E-
mail: slwest2@vcu.edu

Exercise for Article 36

Factual Questions

1. To identify the articles for this meta-analysis, the
researchers conducted computer searches of which
three databases?

2. Which study had the largest effect size (r)? (Identify it by the name of the author and year of publication.) What was the value of r in this study?

3. What was the average weighted effect size (r) for
all studies included in this meta-analysis?

4. The study with the largest effect size examined
only one outcome. What was the outcome?

5. According to Figure 1, the study with the longest
follow-up time had what effect size?

6. Were the researchers able to find any major
evaluations of the *new* D.A.R.E. paradigm?

Questions for Discussion

7. The researchers do not describe the D.A.R.E. program components. In your opinion, would it have
been desirable for them to do so? Explain.

8. What is your opinion of the researchers' decision
to include only research reported in peer-reviewed
journals? (See lines 58–66.)

9. What is your opinion of the researchers' decision
to include only evaluations that included a control
or comparison group? (See lines 67–69.)

10. Does it surprise you that the study by Becker et al.
in Table 1 has negative effect sizes? Explain.

11. In Table 1, 95% confidence intervals are reported. What is your understanding of the meaning of these intervals?

12. What is your opinion on the researchers' suggestion in lines 134–138? Is your opinion based on the data in this meta-analysis? Explain.

Quality Ratings

Directions: Indicate your level of agreement with each of the following statements by circling a number from 5 for strongly agree (SA) to 1 for strongly disagree (SD). If you believe an item is not applicable to this research article, leave it blank. Be prepared to explain your ratings.

A. The introduction establishes the importance of the study.

SA   5   4   3   2   1   SD

B. The literature review establishes the context for the study.

SA   5   4   3   2   1   SD

C. The research purpose, question, or hypothesis is clearly stated.

SA   5   4   3   2   1   SD

D. The method of sampling is sound.

SA   5   4   3   2   1   SD

E. Relevant demographics (for example, age, gender, and ethnicity) are described.

SA   5   4   3   2   1   SD

F. Measurement procedures are adequate.

SA   5   4   3   2   1   SD

G. All procedures have been described in sufficient detail to permit a replication of the study.

SA   5   4   3   2   1   SD

H. The participants have been adequately protected from potential harm.

SA   5   4   3   2   1   SD

I. The results are clearly described.

SA   5   4   3   2   1   SD

J. The discussion/conclusion is appropriate.

SA   5   4   3   2   1   SD

K. Despite any flaws, the report is worthy of publication.

SA   5   4   3   2   1   SD

Article 37

Relational Aggression in Middle School: Educational Implications of Developmental Research

JINA S. YOON
Wayne State University

ELIZABETH BARTON
Wayne State University

JENNIFER TAIARIOL
Wayne State University

ABSTRACT. With increasing attention to school violence and aggression, it is argued that more covert, natured, subtle conflicts among students should be carefully examined and addressed to prevent negative outcomes. This article provides an overview of current knowledge on relational aggression including its definition, its link to a number of adjustment difficulties, and contexts contributing to the maintenance of relational aggression. Based on the review of empirical findings, educational implications for teachers and school administrators are discussed with an emphasis on an urgent need to promote a greater understanding of relational aggression and to develop effective, innovative approaches in schools. The discussion also includes specific recommendations for prevention and intervention of relational aggression in middle school.

From *Journal of Early Adolescence*, 24, 303–318. Copyright © 2004 by Sage Publications. Reprinted with permission.

With increasing media and public interest in conflict and violence in school, there have been many demands for creating positive, safe school environments that facilitate students' learning activities. Given that
5 students' perceptions of physical and psychological safety precede their academic engagement and adjustment (Baker, 1998), these initiatives are a welcome sign. However, much of the current discussion in these efforts is limited to more noticeable forms of conflict
10 such as school violence and physical bullying. For example, Elliott, Hamburg, and Williams (1998) offered a narrow definition of school violence: "Violence refers to the threat or use of physical force with the intention of causing physical injury, damage, or intimidation
15 of another person" (p. 13). Although conflicts that involve threats and the use of physical force may warrant immediate attention because of possible serious physical harm, they are relatively rare in occurrence (Mulvey & Cauffman, 2001). Research further indicates that
20 interpersonal conflicts in the form of physical violence are only part of school experiences and that there are various sources of subtle interpersonal conflicts that are beyond physical harm thereby inflicting psychological and emotional harm on victims (Batsche, 1997). It is

25 clear that our efforts to create positive school experiences should target a wide range of conflicts that penetrate students' social experiences.

In fact, researchers in developmental psychology have identified a set of interpersonal behaviors and
30 attitudes among students that inflict serious emotional harm but go unnoticed by teachers and parents. Crick and colleagues (1999) defined relational aggression as "behaviors that harm others through damage (or the threat of damage) to relationships or feelings of accep-
35 tance, friendship or group inclusion" (p. 77). In contrast to physical aggression (i.e., hitting, kicking) that involves bodily injuries, relational aggression involves interpersonally manipulative behaviors (Crick & Grotpeter, 1995). These behaviors include direct control
40 (e.g., "You can't be my friend unless…"), social alienation (e.g., giving peers the silent treatment), rejection (e.g., telling rumors or lies about a peer so that others in the group will reject him or her), and social exclusion (e.g., excluding a peer from play or a social group)
45 (Crick, Casas, & Nelson, 2002). Relational aggression has been found in children as young as 3 years old (Crick, Casas, & Ku, 1999), whereas more sophisticated and covert forms of relational aggression have been found in middle childhood (Crick, Bigbee, &
50 Howes, 1996) and adolescence (Bjorkqvist, Osterman, & Lagerspetz, 1994). In addition, forms of relational aggression have been found in romantic relationships (Crick et al., 1999).

Although many relationally aggressive behaviors
55 are frequently reported and present significant concerns in middle schools, limited discussion exists regarding prevention and intervention issues that educators face. Also lacking in the literature is comprehensive understanding of relational aggression in developmental and
60 environmental contexts such as peer, family, and school environments. The purposes of this article are to review current developmental research in relational aggression and to discuss its educational implications for teachers and school administrators.
65 Relational aggression was originally conceptualized as a form of aggression that may be more prevalent

among females. Although the aggression literature primarily focused on overt aggression (i.e., physical), which is displayed more in boys than girls, the gender difference disappears when both relational and overt (i.e., physical or verbal) aggression are considered (Crick & Grotpeter, 1995; Rys & Bear, 1997). The hypothesis that girls, compared to boys, are more likely to engage in relational aggression received initial support (Bosworth, Espelage, & Simon, 1999; Crick & Grotpeter, 1996). However, more recent studies also reported that male and female students engage in the same level of relational aggression (Crick, Casas, & Mosher, 1997; Roecker-Phelps, 2001). A more consistent finding is that social and emotional effects of relational victimization are greater for girls than boys (Crick et al., 1996; Paquette & Underwood, 1999). That is, although boys and girls receive the same levels of relational aggression, girls perceive it as more hurtful than boys do.

Less explored is how relational aggression should be addressed. Of particular challenge to teachers, parents, and administrators is that they may not directly witness the act because of the covert nature of relational aggression. Students report that teachers are unwilling to get involved, although students do agree that teachers should intervene in relational aggression situations (Casey-Cannon, Hayward, & Gowen, 2001). Teachers' low levels of involvement may reflect a widely accepted belief that some relationally aggressive behaviors are normative for adolescents (e.g., "middle school kids are just mean") and are transient (e.g., "they usually grow out of it").

Although most research has been conducted at the elementary level and aggression, youth violence, and victimization in general decrease with age (Olweus, 1993), relational aggression in middle childhood and adolescence may be more salient because of developmental milestones in this period. Significant growth in cognitive and social areas takes place in middle school, and these developmental changes affect interpersonal relationships in quality and structure. We argue that these developmental issues should be taken into consideration in understanding the covert, manipulative nature of relational aggression. Adolescents seek independence from parents and have increasing interest in peers. As their social network extends to include both same-sex and opposite-sex peer groups, social status and acceptance in peer groups become more critical than ever. An important developmental task at this age is to effectively navigate through peer relationships and successfully resolve interpersonal conflicts through which they increase levels of social competence. In particular, peer relationships that involve emotional closeness and intimacy become an important part of their social life (Savin-Williams & Berndt, 1990). In this developmental context, a possible attempt to hurt an intimate friendship or social reputation would be perceived as an enormous threat and is most likely to

have significant implications in peer relationships. It has been also speculated that with increased needs for peer acceptance, relational aggression may be used as a way to fit in (Espelage & Holt, 2001).

In addition, advances in social cognition appear to be involved in relational aggression. For example, adolescents in general enhance their social understanding (Hill & Palmquist, 1978), which leads to more sophisticated goal setting and complex social problem solving (Kreitler & Kreitler, 1987; Moshman, 1993). In addition, they become increasingly skilled at understanding the complicated process of subtle, nonverbal behaviors and their impact on interpersonal relationships (Selman, 1980). Developmentally, adolescents increasingly use negotiation and bargaining in resolving interpersonal conflicts and decrease their reliance on power assertion and detachment (Laursen, 1993). Increased social understanding and conflict resolution abilities are critical skills in developing and maintaining close peer relationships. Conversely, cognitively sophisticated adolescents might be best suited to engage in relational aggression, as they are most able to perceive manipulative and harmful methods for interacting. For instance, Sutton and Smith (1999) indicated that bullying behaviors involving relational aggression are most frequently committed by adolescents with highly sophisticated social cognition skills. It is also possible that relationally aggressive teens resort to power assertion and detachment methods in peer conflicts with better understanding of forms of aggression most hurtful to the victim (Hennington, Hughes, Cavell, & Thompson, 1998). These cognitive changes may explain the shift to more sophisticated forms of relational aggression in middle school (Crick et al., 1999).

It is possible that relational aggression decreases as teens' peer relationships become more mature and less conflictual (Seidman, Aber, Allen, & French, 1996). However, relational aggression has been reported beyond early adolescence in high school (Roecker-Phelps, 2001) and college (Werner & Crick, 1999). More important, relational aggression has been linked to a wide range of difficulties for both victims and perpetrators, thus indicating that effective prevention and intervention are warranted for the pattern of behaviors that one may consider developmentally normal.

Adjustment Difficulties Associated with Relational Aggression

The social and psychological maladjustment associated with relational aggression is as far-reaching and stable as those of physical aggression (Galen & Underwood, 1997). Recent studies have found that victims of relational aggression tend to be more depressed, anxious, and have lower self-esteem (Casey-Cannon et al., 2001; Crick & Grotpeter, 1996; Ladd & Ladd, 2001). In addition, children who are frequent targets of relational aggression are more rejected and less accepted by their peer groups (Crick et al., 2001; Ju-

180 vonen, Nishina, & Graham, 2001). Furthermore, victims of chronic relational aggression are more likely to view that they are the cause of mistreatment by others (Ladd & Ladd, 2001). That view may, in turn, render them to repeated victimization, thus perpetuating their low self-esteem and overall adjustment difficulties. The pattern of social and emotional maladjustment from victimization appears to be more pervasive for girls (Paquette & Underwood, 1999). Given that, compared to boys, girls are more relationship oriented and place a higher value on intimacy (Tannen, 1990), experiences of relational aggression pose greater threats to girls, thus resulting in more negative outcomes in their functioning.

Those who are relationally aggressive also experience poor outcomes. Relationally aggressive girls are more likely to experience externalizing symptoms associated with oppositional defiant and conduct disorders (Prinstein, Boergers, & Vernberg, 2001). Relationally aggressive children are more likely to be disliked and lack prosocial behavior compared to nonaggressive children (Crick & Grotpeter, 1995).

There is a moderate relation between relational and overt aggression ($r = .60$ to $.75$; Crick et al., 2001), and a number of students exhibit both forms of aggression. The research suggests the poorest outcomes for this group compared to the nonaggressive and aggressive groups with one form of aggression. In a diverse adolescent sample, students who experienced both overt and relational victimization were most severely maladjusted and reported the highest level of depression, loneliness, and externalizing problems (Prinstein et al., 2001). Despite the moderate relation between the two forms of aggression, it is important to note that relational aggression makes a unique contribution to adjustment beyond overt aggression (see Crick et al., 2001).

Taken together, research findings indicate that relationally aggressive behaviors are linked to a number of concurrent and future adjustment problems for both victims and perpetrators and that the association is robust (Crick et al., 1999). Special attention is needed to address and prevent negative outcomes associated with perpetrators and victims of relational aggression. Furthermore, emerging evidence suggests that relational aggression involves more than victims and perpetrators and may be shaped and maintained in various contexts.

Context of Relational Aggression

Research on the etiology of relational aggression is limited to date. One promising area of recent investigation is parental influence in the family context. So far, parental conflict, coercion, and psychological control have been examined as possible links to the development of relational aggression. Parents may invalidate a child's feelings, threaten to withdraw love or affection, or use sarcasm and power-assertive discipline (Maccoby & Martin, 1983). For example, Nelson and Crick

(2001) found that maternal coercive control and maternal corporal punishment were significantly associated with relational aggression for boys. For girls, paternal psychological control was positively associated with relational aggression.

Another possible family context of relational aggression is sibling relationships. It is well established that physical aggression in sibling relationships has a strong influence on the acquisition of aggressive behaviors (Dunn & Munn, 1986; Patterson, 1986). Recent studies report that relational aggression is more frequently reported among sibling dyads than physical aggression (O'Brien, 1999) and that relational aggression in sibling relationships is linked to conflicts, depressive symptoms, and low self-worth (Updegraff, Denning, & Thayer, 2003). The direct link between relational aggression in sibling and peer relationships has not been documented yet. However, it is likely that levels of relational aggression in sibling relationships are most likely to play a role in levels of relational aggression exhibited in peer relationships given that sibling interactions serve as a model and training ground for learning social behaviors (Azmitia & Hesser, 1993; Patterson, 1982).

Peer group is another important context to consider because victimization experiences occur in a group context (Pellegrini, Bartini, & Brooks, 1999; Salmivalli, Lagerspetz, Bjorkqvist, Osterman, & Kaukiainen, 1996). Victims in middle school are often teased and threatened by groups of students who assume different roles (e.g., leaders, bystanders, etc.), "not necessarily by one school yard bully" (Salmivalli et al., 1996, p. 3). Particularly, the peer context of relational aggression is unique because the aggressive behaviors focus on manipulating and damaging interpersonal relationships in peer groups. For example, according to Grotpeter and Crick (1996), friends who are highly intimate and exclusive often behave more aggressively within the friendship than they do toward peers who are not their close friends. In addition, relationally aggressive students have perceived support from their peer group and report the same number of friends as those who are not relationally aggressive and report the same levels of intimacy and closeness with friends. These findings indicate that relational aggression may be endorsed and collaborated by other students in a peer group.

Meanwhile, the victims of relationally aggressive children report high levels of conflict and betrayal (Grotpeter & Crick, 1996). Consistent with this pattern, studies found that victims of relational aggression are repeatedly exposed to the same type of aggression over time. Along with other factors, victims may present themselves as more vulnerable in their relationships with perpetrators, thus increasing chances of victimization because of a number of reasons, such as the limited number of alternative friends and higher needs for intimacy (Crick et al., 1999).

Further research should examine the complex processes of peer influence including how individual group members participate in victimization of relational aggression as perpetrators, bystanders, and collaborators and how certain small peer groups deter or encourage relational aggression. For example, during early adolescence, cliques (small peer groups with an average of five to six individuals of the same sex and age) emerge based on shared activities and friendships, and dominate social experiences. Given the intimate and exclusive nature of cliques, it will be interesting to explore the group dynamics of cliques in relation to relational aggression.

Similarly, classroom and school environments are other important contexts to consider. Growing literature on bullying and school violence points to classroom and school environments playing critical roles in the maintenance of students' aggressive behaviors (Barth, Dane, Dunlap, Lochman, & Wells, 2001; Song & Swearer, 2002) and overall adjustment (Yoon, 2003). A general attitude among teachers and school administrators has been that interpersonal aggression, or meanness, is a normative developmental feature of middle school students (Jeffrey, Miller, & Linn, 2001). This sentiment may explain teachers' indifferent perceptions and attitudes toward relational aggression. Specifically, teachers perceive relationally aggressive behaviors as less serious than verbal or physical aggression and are less likely to intervene (Craig, Henderson, & Murphy, 2000). When asked to respond to hypothetical situations that involve relational aggression, teachers are more likely to ignore or get less involved and are less sympathetic to the victims compared to overt aggression (Yoon & Kerber, 2003). Teachers' passive approaches to dealing with relational aggression are disconcerting. Of particular concern that stems from the absence of a consistent effort to address relational aggression is its impact on the victims and perpetrators. When victims of bullying perceive their plight as going unnoticed, they are less likely to feel safe in their school environment, thus possibly affecting their school experience (Casey-Cannon et al., 2001; Yoon & Kerber, 2003). Specifically, teachers' ignoring is likely to set an expectation for students by sending an inappropriate message that the behaviors are tolerated and even permitted.

Implications for Teachers and School Administrators

A review of the developmental literature suggests that (a) relational aggression is associated with a number of short- and long-term adjustment difficulties, (b) it should be understood in the larger picture of adolescent development, and (c) it is a manifestation of a complex interplay between individual characteristics of victims and perpetrators and the contexts of family, peer, and school. Few intervention programs that specifically address relational aggression exist. Classroom curriculums for anti-bullying efforts have become popular, yet empirical support for these programs is limited. In addition, many programs focus on physical aggression and verbal threats and do not include relational aggression (i.e., McDonald, Billingham, Conrad, Morgan, & Payton, 1997; Walker et al., 1998). Furthermore, the programs are geared more toward elementary levels (see Mytton, DiGuiseppi, Gough, Taylor, & Logan, 2002, for a comprehensive review for elementary-level programs). *Bully Proofing Your School: A Comprehensive Approach for Elementary Schools* (Garrity, Jens, Porter, Sager, & Short-Camilli, 2000) and *Steps to Respect: A Bullying Prevention Program* (Committee for Children, 1998) are two examples of school-based, skill-building programs for youth designed to teach children ways to build more respectful and caring peer relationships.

Although empirically proven treatment programs specifically targeting relational aggression are lacking at this point, current literature on anti-bullying and school violence intervention programs provides a broader discussion as to how socially aggressive, intimidating behaviors should be addressed in school (see Olweus, 1991; Swearer & Doll, 2001). Furthermore, this literature review on relational aggression clearly provides a number of critical implications for teachers and school administrators. First of all, there is an urgent need to promote a greater understanding of relational aggression and to develop effective, innovative approaches in schools. More important, drawing from an ecological perspective (Swearer & Doll, 2001), we argue that any systematic effort should include assessments of both participants' individual characteristics (i.e., victims and perpetrators) and the contextual variables that are at work in the development and maintenance of relational aggression (Olweus, 1993; Underwood, Galen, & Paquette, 2001). The following discussion will focus on specific implications for prevention and intervention of relational aggression in middle school.

Teacher prevention/intervention strategies. A first step toward reducing relational aggression in the classroom involves educating teachers and school administrators on identifying signs of relational aggression and the potential deleterious effects of these behaviors. Teachers should investigate relational victimization as a possible source of social difficulties and school maladjustments among students, and they should learn how to identify relational aggressors in their classrooms. Students (both relational aggressors and victims) may benefit from support services (i.e., social support groups, skills groups, consultations) in school where they can learn to cope with victimization, learn constructive means of conflict resolution, and assist in setting up proactive plans that reduce risks for destructive interpersonal interactions. In fact, research suggests that high levels of social support, such as close friendships, buffer children from negative outcomes of victimization (Prinstein et al., 2001). Then, promoting positive peer relationships is an important area of intervention.

410 Teachers with developed knowledge of relational aggression and victimization are more likely to identify, manage, and intervene during these destructive episodes. Craig et al. (2000) found that witnessing and recognizing relational aggression and possessing levels
415 of empathy were predictors of intolerant attitudes toward relational aggressive behaviors. These researchers also found that prospective teachers were less likely to identify social isolation as bullying behaviors, and they tended to feel that physical bullying behavior was the
420 most severe and warranted intervention as compared to relational bullying. According to interview data (Simmons, 2002), students reported that teachers are either unaware of what is going on or uninvolved in helping students have better social experiences. Unfortunately,
425 teachers' mishandling and lack of involvement in relational aggression behaviors can be interpreted as condoning the behaviors, thereby creating a hidden curriculum that reinforces bullying behaviors (Yoon & Kerber, 2003).

430 Indeed, teacher education and training programs on relational aggression should be included in antibullying efforts currently underway in many schools. To best reduce the negative impact of relational aggression in middle school, teacher education and train-
435 ing programs should (a) enhance the knowledge of relational bullying behaviors, (b) improve skills for identifying and assessing behaviors associated with relational aggression in their classrooms, and (c) produce attitudinal changes toward intervention and pre-
440 vention of relational aggression. Formal sociometric assessment may be burdensome or unnecessary, but classroom-wide anonymous surveys of students and/or observation can be used to better understand students' peer relationships and perceptions about school. Once
445 the concerns are identified, problem-solving processes can be facilitated by teachers through class discussions. Doll, Siemers, Nickolite, and Song (2003) demonstrated how teachers and a consultant examined a classroom environment using the ClassMap procedure and
450 facilitated discussions among middle school students. Although it does not directly address relational aggression, teachers can use similar approaches in addressing a wide range of negative peer relationships including physical and relational aggression.

455 In addition, educational efforts on building constructive teacher–student relationships and establishing respectful classroom environments are also recommended for curbing relational aggression in middle school. For example, Positive Behavioral Interventions
460 and Support, an empirically proven program, promotes improvements in teachers' instructional styles, classroom routines, and settings to develop more harmonious and effective learning environments (Taylor-Greene et al., 1997). The teacher component may be

465 particularly important given recent student reports that some teachers and other school staff model hostile behaviors (Song & Swearer, 2002).

School-wide prevention/intervention strategies. Peer relationships characterized by relational aggres-
470 sion must be viewed from the perspective of the bully and the victim and therefore interventions must be developed and implemented to address both parties in the interaction. Too often, prevention and intervention strategies focus only on changing the behavior of the
475 bully, yet it is the bully–victim and occasional witness relationship that must also change. Developing and implementing a cookie-cutter approach to reducing relational aggressive behaviors will not result in positive interactions among the participants in the future. It
480 is not effective to target intentional aggression by bullies without focusing on victim behavior, as well. Therefore, developing and implementing the prevention and intervention plan requires a conscious effort to target the context of the relationship and situations in
485 which relational aggression occurs. More important, the entire school climate or culture that condones relational aggression must be clearly identified and changed. It is well documented that the perceived school climate affects students' psychosocial and aca-
490 demic functioning (Baker, 1998; Shouse, 1996; Solomon, Watson, Battistich, Schaps, & Delucchi, 1996).

For these reasons, school-wide prevention/intervention strategies may be more appropriate. Schoolwide strategies, if implemented in a comprehensive
495 manner, are designed to affect all aspects of the school community including the teaching staff, administration, support staff, parents/guardians, and student body. School-wide initiatives should include changes in school policies and procedures, staff development, bul-
500 lying assessments, curriculum support, and programming initiatives. For example, conflict resolution programs are implemented in many schools, such as the Second Step Program for prekindergarten and 9th-grade students (Flannery, Huff, & Manos, 1996) and
505 the PeaceBuilders for grades 1 through 5 (Grossman et al., 1997) with some success in improving school climate. These programs should include discussions of specific examples that involve relational aggression through which students not only learn to successfully
510 resolve conflicts but also build a climate of disapproving it. Raising awareness within schools and educating students about the detrimental effects of rumors, peer isolation, and other interpersonal manipulation may be an important part of a systematic approach. This would
515 further promote peer mediation, not necessarily teacher-directed intervention that may not be highly desired by some students. Consistent with the systematic approach in creating a positive school climate, class and school rules should reflect strong disapproval
520 of relationally aggressive behaviors and should be clearly communicated to students and parents.

Others recommend that schools should address relationally aggressive behaviors by promoting the respect of individual differences among students (Espelage & Asidao, 2001). Early adolescents' social worlds center around small, intimate peer groups (i.e., cliques) that are often formed on the basis of shared interests and activities (Ennett & Bauman, 1996). In this process, they are more likely to seek similarities and affiliation. However, as these groups become more distinctive, their memberships become more exclusive by nature, thereby highlighting differences and an us-versus-them mentality. Given this developmental context, promoting the genuine respect of individual differences may be a challenging but very critical one to be persistently pursued.

Barton (2003) suggested that the hallmarks of American schools contribute to the isolation and segregation of students thereby allowing relational aggression to flourish. Kipnis (1999) further argued that schools condone bullying, teasing, and cliques by dividing and labeling students according to their academic and/or athletic gifts. Students are likely to continue these lines of separation and maintain their position within the school hierarchy (Barton, 2000). Barton (2000) recommended that school-based programs target "belief systems and teach tolerance, acceptance, and respect through effective communication and constructive resolution" (p. 108). Unnecessary divisions and hostile relationships (e.g., teacher–administrator relationships) would create an organizational climate that perpetuates disrespect and intolerance among students.

Schools should also include parents/guardians in programming efforts to reduce the expression of relational behaviors. It is critical to provide parents/guardians with opportunities to improve their knowledge, skills, and attitudes on relational aggression and its deleterious impact on child development, as these destructive behaviors may be modeled by family members. Teacher conferences and whole-school assemblies are wonderful methods for highlighting the seriousness of relational aggression and outlining the school plan for reducing these destructive relationships. Again, these methods are intended to promote a positive school environment through parent–school collaboration and have been effective in reducing more direct bullying (Orpinas, Horne, & Staniszewski, 2003). Educational training in constructive conflict resolution methods may also be offered by the school for interested parents/guardians as a component of the whole-school intervention program. For example, the Positive Behavioral Intervention and Support Program requires a collaborative approach between families and professionals to alter problem behaviors and create support systems for the student (Todd, Horner, & Sugai, 1999).

Creating a school environment that guarantees physical safety and psychological security of students is an important task to promote academic, social, and emotional competences. We argued in this article that relational aggression is a complex phenomenon that undermines many important aspects of student adjustment. The covert nature of interpersonal conflicts should not be ignored in our examination of school violence. The research findings support that relational aggression is maintained and further perpetuated in many different contexts (i.e., family, peer, and school). A thorough assessment of each context and multilevel prevention and intervention programs are recommended for relational aggression as well as violent behaviors among students. The timing of these intervention efforts seems critical in middle school. Espelage and Holt (2001) found that after the transition to middle school, the 6th graders reported more use of teasing and other bullying behaviors than 7th and 8th graders. As they establish new social structures and strive for their own social standing, any systematic intervention effort may be more needed and cost-effective for the purpose of prevention.

References

Azmitia, M., & Hesser, J. (1993). Why siblings are important agents of cognitive development: A comparison of siblings and peers. *Child Development, 64*, 430–444.

Baker, J. A. (1998). The social context of school satisfaction among urban, low-income, African American students. *School Psychology Quarterly, 13*, 25–44.

Barth, J. M., Dane, H. E., Dunlap, S. T., Lochman, J. E., & Wells, K. C. (2001, April). *Classroom and school environment influences on aggression, peer acceptance, and academic focus.* Paper presented at the biennial meeting of the Society for Research on Child Development, Minneapolis, MN.

Barton, E. A. (2000). *Leadership strategies for safe schools.* Arlington Heights, IL: Skylight Professional Development.

Barton, E. A. (2003). *Bully prevention: Tips and strategies for school leaders and classroom teachers.* Arlington Heights, IL: Pearson Professional Development.

Batsche, G. M. (1997). Bullying. In G. C. Bear, K. M. Minke, & A. Thomas (Eds.), *Children's needs II: Development, problems and alternatives* (pp. 171–179). Bethesda, MD: National Association of School Psychologists.

Bjorkqvist, K., Osterman, L., & Lagerspetz, K. M. J. (1994, June). *Patterns of aggression among adolescents of three age groups: A cross cultural comparison.* Paper presented at the 13th biennial meeting of the International Society for the Study of Behavioral Development, Amsterdam, Netherlands.

Bosworth, K., Espelage, D., & Simon, T. (1999). Factors associated with bullying behavior among early adolescents. *Journal of Early Adolescence, 19*, 341–362.

Casey-Cannon, S., Hayward, C., & Gowen, K. (2001). Middle-school girls' reports of peer victimization: Concerns, consequences, and implications. *Professional School Counseling, 5*, 138–147.

Committee for Children. (1998). *Steps to respect: A bullying prevention program.* Seattle, WA: Author.

Craig, W. M., Henderson, K., & Murphy, J. G. (2000). Prospective teachers' attitudes toward bullying and victimization. *School Psychology International, 21*, 5–21.

Crick, N. R., Bigbee, M. A., & Howes, C. (1996). Gender differences in children's normative beliefs about aggression: How do I hurt thee? Let me count the ways. *Child Development, 67*, 1003–1014.

Crick, N. R., Casas, J. F., & Ku, H. (1999). Physical and relational peer victimization in preschool. *Developmental Psychology, 35*, 376–385.

Crick, N. R., Casas, J. F., & Mosher, M. (1997). Relational and overt aggression in preschool. *Developmental Psychology, 33*, 579–588.

Crick, N. R., Casas, J. F., & Nelson, D. A. (2002). Toward a more comprehensive understanding of peer maltreatment: Studies of relational victimization. *Current Directions in Psychological Science, 11*, 98–101.

Crick, N. R., & Grotpeter, J. K. (1995). Relational aggression, gender, and social–psychological adjustment. *Child Development, 66*, 710–722.

Crick, N. R., & Grotpeter, J. K. (1996). Children's treatment by peers: Victims of relational and overt aggression. *Development and Psychopathology, 8*, 367–380.

Crick, N. R., Nelson, D. A., Morales, J. R., Cullerton-Sen, C., Casas, J. F., & Hickman, S. E. (2001). Relational victimization in childhood and adolescence: I hurt you through the grapevine. In J. Juvonen & S. Graham (Eds.), *Peer harassment in school: The plight of the vulnerable and victimized* (pp. 196–214). New York: Guildford.

Crick, N. R., Werner, N. E., Casas, J. F., O'Brien, K. M., Nelson, D. A., Grotpeter, J. K., et al. (1999). Childhood aggression and gender: A new look at an old problem. In D. Bernstein (Ed.), *Nebraska symposium on motivation* (Vol. 45). Lincoln: University of Nebraska Press.

Doll, B., Siemers, E., Nickolite, M., & Song, S. (2003, April). *Using Class-Maps Consultation to make classrooms healthy places to learn.* Paper presented at the annual meeting of National Association of School Psychologists, Toronto, Canada.

Dunn, J., & Munn, P. (1986). Sibling quarrels and maternal intervention: Individual differences in understanding and aggression. *Journal of Child Psychology and Psychiatry, 27*, 583–595.

Elliott, D. S., Hamburg, B. A., & Williams, K. R. (1998). *Violence in American schools.* New York: Cambridge University Press.

Ennett, S., & Bauman, K. (1996). Adolescent social networks: School, demographic and longitudinal considerations. *Journal of Adolescent Research, 11*, 194–245.

Espelage, D. L., & Asidao, C. (2001). Interviews with middle school students: Bullying, victimization, and contextual variables. *Journal of Emotional Abuse, 2*, 49–62.

Espelage, D. L., & Holt, M. K. (2001). Bullying and victimization during early adolescence: Peer influences and psychosocial correlates. *Journal of Emotional Abuse, 2*, 123–142.

Flannery, D. L., Huff, C., & Manos, M. (1996). Youth gangs: A developmental perspective. In T. Gullotta, G. Adams, & R. Montemayor (Eds.), *Advances in adolescent development: Delinquency, juvenile justice, and adolescence* (Vol. 10). Thousand Oaks, CA: Sage.

Galen, B., & Underwood, J. K. (1997). A developmental investigation of social aggression among children. *Developmental Psychology, 33*, 589–600.

Garrity, C., Jens, K., Porter, W., Sager, N., & Short-Camilli, C. (2000). *Bully proofing your school: A comprehensive approach for elementary schools.* Longmont, CO: Sopris West.

Grossman, P. W., Neckerman, H. J., Koepsell, T., Liu, P. Y., Asher, K. N., Beland, K., et al. (1997). Effectiveness of a violence prevention curriculum among children in elementary school: A randomized controlled trial. *Journal of the American Medical Association, 277*, 1605–1611.

Grotpeter, J. K., & Crick, N. R. (1996). Relational aggression, overt aggression, and friendship. *Child Development, 67*, 2328–2338.

Hennington, C., Hughes, J. N., Cavell, T. A., & Thompson, B. (1998). The role of relational aggression in identifying aggressive boys and girls. *Journal of School Psychology, 36*, 457–477.

Hill, J., & Palmquist, W. (1978). Social cognition and social relations in early adolescence. *International Journal of Behavior Development, 1*, 1–36.

Jeffrey, L. R., Miller, D., & Linn, M. (2001). Middle school bullying as a context for the development of passive observers to the victimization of others. *Journal of Emotional Abuse, 2*, 143–156.

Juvonen, J., Nishina, A., & Graham, S. (2001). Self-views versus peer perceptions of victim status among early adolescents. In J. Juvonen & S. Graham (Eds), *Peer harassment in school: The plight of the vulnerable and victimized* (pp. 25–48). New York: Guildford.

Kipnis, A. (1999). *Angry young men: How parents, teachers, and counselors can help "bad boys" become good men.* San Francisco: Jossey-Bass.

Kreitler, S., & Kreitler, H. (1987). Conceptions and processes of planning: The developmental perspective. In S. L. Frieman, E. K. Scholnick, & R. R. Cocking (Eds.), *Blueprints for thinking* (pp. 205–272). Cambridge, UK: Cambridge University Press.

Ladd, B. K., & Ladd, G. W. (2001). Variations in peer victimization: Relations to children's maladjustment. In J. Juvonen & S. Graham (Eds.), *Peer harassment in school: The plight of the vulnerable and victimized* (pp. 25–48). New York: Guildford.

Laursen, B. (Ed.). (1993). Conflict management among close peers. In *Close friendships in adolescence: New directions for child development* (pp. 39–54). San Francisco: Jossey-Bass.

Maccoby, E. E., & Martin, J. A. (1983). Socialization in the context of the family. In A. J. Sameroff, M. Lewis, & S. M. Miller (Eds.), *Handbook of developmental psychopathology* (pp. 75–91). New York: Plenum.

McDonald, L., Billingham, S., Conrad, T., Morgan, A. O., & Payton, E. (1997). Families and schools together (FAST): Integrating community development with clinical strategies. *Families in Society—The Journal of Contemporary Human Services, 78*, 140–155.

Moshman, D. (1993). Adolescent reasoning and adolescent rights. *Human Development, 36*, 27–40.

Mulvey, E. P., & Cauffman, E. (2001). The inherent limits of predicting school violence. *American Psychologist, 56*, 797–802.

Mytton, J., DiGuiseppi, C., Gough, D., Taylor, R., & Logan, S. (2002). School based violence prevention programming: Systematic review of secondary prevention trials. *Archives of Pediatrics and Adolescent Medicine, 156*, 752–762.

Nelson, D. A., & Crick, N. R. (2001). Parental psychological control: Implications for childhood physical and relational aggression. In B. K. Barber (Ed.),

Intrusive parenting: How psychological control affects children and adolescents (pp. 161–189). Washington, DC: American Psychological Association.

O'Brien, K. M. (1999). Relational and physical aggression in aggressive and nonaggressive children's sibling relationships: Do gender, gender composition and birth position influence aggressive behavior towards siblings? *Dissertation Abstracts International, 60*(5B), 2388.

Olweus, D. (1991). Bully/victim problems among school children: Basic facts and effects of a school based intervention program. In D. Pepler & K. Rubin (Eds.), *The development and treatment of childhood aggression* (pp. 411–438). Hillsdale, NJ: Erlbaum.

Olweus, D. (1993). Bullying at school: What we know and what we can do. Oxford, UK: Blackwell.

Orpinas, P., Horne, A. M., & Staniszewski, D. (2003). School bullying: Changing the problem by changing the school. *School Psychology Review, 32*, 431–444.

Paquette, J. A., & Underwood, M. K. (1999). Young adolescents' experiences of peer victimization: Gender differences in accounts of social and physical aggression. *Merrill-Palmer Quarterly, 45*, 233–258.

Patterson, G. R. (1982). *Coercive family process.* Eugene, OR: Castalia.

Patterson, G. R. (1986). The contribution of siblings to training for fighting: A microsocial analysis. In D. Olweus, J. Block, & M. Radke-Yarrow (Eds.), *Development of antisocial and prosocial behavior: Research, theories, and issues* (pp. 235–261). New York: Academic Press.

Pellegrini, A. D., Bartini, M., & Brooks, F. (1999). School bullies, victims, and aggressive victims: Factors relating top group affiliation and victimization in early adolescence. *Journal of Educational Psychology, 91*, 216–224.

Prinstein, M. J., Boergers, J., & Vernberg, E. M. (2001). Overt and relational aggression in adolescents: Social–psychological adjustment of aggressors and victims. *Journal of Clinical Child Psychology, 30*, 479–491.

Roecker-Phelps, C. E. (2001). Children's responses to overt and relational aggression. *Journal of Clinical and Child Psychology, 30*, 240–252.

Rys, G. S., & Bear, G. G. (1997). Relational aggression and peer rejection: Gender and developmental issues. *Merrill-Palmer Quarterly, 43*, 87–106.

Salmivalli, C., Lagerspetz, K., Bjorkqvist, K., Osterman, K., & Kaukiainen, A. (1996). Bullying as a group process: Participant roles and their relations to social status within the group. *Aggressive Behavior, 22*, 1–15.

Savin-Williams, R. C., & Berndt, T. J. (1990). Friendship and peer relationships. In S. S. Feldman & G. R. Elliott (Eds.), *At the threshold: The developing adolescent* (pp. 277–307). Cambridge, MA: Harvard University Press.

Seidman, E., Aber, J. L., Allen, L., & French, S. E. (1996). The impact of the transition to high school on the self-system and perceived social context of poor urban youth. *American Journal of Community Psychology, 24*, 489–515.

Selman, R. (1980). *The growth of interpersonal understanding.* New York: Academic Press.

Shouse, R. C. (1996). Academic press and sense of community: Conflict, congruence, and implications for student achievement. *Social Psychology of Education, 1*, 47–68.

Simmons, R. (2002). *Odd girls out: The hidden culture of aggression in girls.* New York: Harcourt.

Solomon, D., Watson, M., Battistich, V., Schaps, E., & Delucchi, K. (1996). Creating classrooms that students experience as communities. *American Journal of Community Psychology, 24*, 719–748.

Song, S. Y., & Swearer, S. M. (2002, February). *An ecological analysis of bullying in middle school: Understanding school climate across the bully-victim continuum.* Paper presented at the Annual Convention of the National Association of School Psychologists, Chicago.

Sutton, J., & Smith, P. (1999). Bullying as a group process: An adaptation of the participant role approach. *Aggressive Behavior, 25*, 97–111.

Swearer, S. M., & Doll, B. (2001). Bullying in schools: An ecological framework. *Journal of Emotional Abuse, 2*, 7–23.

Tannen, D. (1990). *You just don't understand!* New York: Ballantine.

Taylor-Greene, S., Brown, D., Nelson, L., Longton, J., Gassman, T., Cohen, J., et al. (1997). School-wide behavioral support: Starting the year off right. *Journal of Behavioral Education, 7*, 99–112.

Todd, A., Horner, R., & Sugai, G. (1999). Self-monitoring and self-recruited praise: Effects on problem behavior, academics engagement, and work completion in a typical classroom. *Journal of Positive Behavior Interventions, 1*, 66–76.

Underwood, M. K., Galen, B. R., & Paquette, J. A. (2001). Top ten challenges for understanding gender aggression in children: Why can't we all just get along? *Social Development, 10*, 248–266.

Updegraff, K. A., Denning, D. J., & Thayer, S. M. (2003, April). *Sibling relational aggression: Links to sibling relationship quality and adolescent adjustment.* Paper presented at the biennial meeting of the Society for Research in Child Development, Tampa, FL.

Walker, H. M., Kavanagh, K., Stiller, B., Golly, A., Seveverson, H. H., & Feil, E. G. (1998). First step to success: An early intervention approach for preventing school antisocial behavior. *Journal of Emotional and Behavioral Disorders, 6*, 66–80.

Werner, N. E., & Crick, N. R. (1999). Relational aggression and social psychological adjustment in a college sample. *Journal of Abnormal Psychology, 108*, 615–623.

Yoon, J. (2003, April). *Victimization experiences, classroom climate and school adjustment.* Poster presented at the biennial meeting of the Society of Research in Child Development, Tampa, FL.

Yoon, J., & Kerber, K. (2003). Bullying: Elementary teachers' attitudes and intervention strategies. *Research in Education, 69,* 27–35.

Address correspondence to: Jina S. Yoon, Educational Psychology, 347 College of Education, Wayne State University, Detroit, MI 48202. E-mail: jyoon@wayne.edu

Exercise for Article 37

Editor's note: This article is a literature review, not a report of original research. Hence, the exercise for this article is different from the others.

Directions: Indicate your level of agreement with each of the following statements by circling a number from 5 for strongly agree (SA) to 1 for strongly disagree (SD). If you believe an item is not applicable to this literature review, leave it blank. Be prepared to explain your ratings.

A. The introduction establishes the importance of the topic.

   SA   5   4   3   2   1   SD

B. The literature review is well organized.

   SA   5   4   3   2   1   SD

C. The literature review is free of ambiguous statements.

   SA   5   4   3   2   1   SD

D. Relevant demographics (for example, age, gender, and ethnicity) are discussed in the review.

   SA   5   4   3   2   1   SD

E. The conclusions are appropriate.

   SA   5   4   3   2   1   SD

F. The literature review has important implications.

   SA   5   4   3   2   1   SD

G. Despite any flaws, the literature review is worthy of publication.

   SA   5   4   3   2   1   SD

Appendix A

Criteria for the Evaluation of Educational Research

Suggested Scale:

5—Excellent (A model of good practice.)
4—Good (A few minor defects.)
3—Mediocre (Not good, not bad.)
2—Poor (Some serious defects.)
1—Completely incompetent (A horrible example.)

Title

1. Title is well related to content of article.

Problem

2. Problem is clearly stated.

3. Hypotheses are clearly stated.

4. Problem is significant.

5. Assumptions are clearly stated.

6. Limitations of the study are stated.

7. Important terms are defined.

Review of Literature

8. Coverage of the literature is adequate.

9. Review of literature is well organized.

10. Studies are examined critically.

11. Source of important findings is noted.

12. Relationship of the problem to previous research is made clear.

Procedures

13. Research design is described fully.

14. Research design is appropriate to solution of the problem.

15. Research design is free of specific weaknesses.

16. Population and sample are described.

17. Method of sampling is appropriate.

18. Data-gathering methods or procedures are described.

19. Data-gathering methods or procedures are appropriate to the solution of the problem.

20. Data-gathering methods or procedures are used correctly.

21. Validity and reliability of data-gathering procedures are established.

Data Analysis

22. Appropriate methods are selected to analyze data.

23. Methods used in analyzing the data are applied correctly.

24. Results of the analysis are presented clearly.

25. Tables and figures are effectively used.

Summary and Conclusions

26. Conclusions are clearly stated.

27. Conclusions are substantiated by the evidence presented.

28. Conclusions are relevant to the problem.

29. Conclusions are significant.

30. Generalizations are confined to the population from which the sample was drawn.

Form and Style

31. Report is clearly written.

32. Report is logically organized.

33. Tone of the report displays an unbiased, impartial, scientific attitude.

Appendix B

Quality Control in Qualitative Research*

This topic describes some of the specific techniques that qualitative researchers use to establish the dependability and trustworthiness of their data.[1]

One technique is to use multiple sources for obtaining data on the research topic. The technical name for this is **data triangulation**. For instance, for a qualitative study of discrimination in an employment setting, a researcher might interview employees, their supervisors, and the responsible personnel officers. To the extent that the various sources provide similar information, the data can be said to be corroborated.

The methods used to collect data can also be triangulated. For instance, a researcher might conduct individual interviews with parents regarding their child-rearing practices and then have the same participants provide data via focus groups. This would be an example of **methods triangulation**.

Note that in *data triangulation*, typically two or more types of participants (such as employees and supervisors) are used to collect data on a research topic. In contrast, in *methods triangulation*, only one type of participant (such as parents) is used to provide data but two or more methods are used to collect the data.

An important technique to assure the quality of qualitative research is to form a *research team*, with each member of the team participating in the collection and analysis of data. This can be thought of as **researcher triangulation**, which reduces the possibility that the results of qualitative research represent only the idiosyncratic views of one individual researcher.

Sometimes, it is helpful to form a **team of researchers with diverse backgrounds**. For instance, for a study on the success of minority students in medical school, a team of researchers that consists of both medical school instructors and medical school students might strengthen the study by providing more than one perspective when collecting and analyzing the data.

The issue of having diversity in a research team is addressed in Example 1, which is from a qualitative research report on gender issues. The researchers point out that gender diversity in their research team helps to provide a "comprehensive view."

EXAMPLE 1
Diversity in a research team: Gender and sexuality issues were analyzed by all three researchers. That our research team included one man and two women probably helped us have a comprehensive view of the different meanings of gender issues.[2]

Oral interviews and focus groups are typically audiotaped and then transcribed. Sometimes, transcription is difficult because certain participants might not speak distinctly. In addition, transcribers sometimes make errors. Therefore, checking the accuracy of a transcription helps to ensure the quality of the data. In Example 2, a sample of segments was checked.

EXAMPLE 2
Checking the accuracy of transcriptions: Each audiotaped session was transcribed verbatim. Segments of the transcriptions were checked randomly against the audiotapes for accuracy.[3]

In the analysis of data, each member of a research team should initially work independently (without consulting each other) and then compare the results of their analyses. To the extent that they agree, the results are more dependable. This technique examines what is called **interobserver agreement**.[4] When there are disagreements, often they can be resolved by having the researchers discuss their differences until they reach a consensus.

The use of an outside expert can also help to ensure the quality of the research. A researcher's peer (such as another experienced qualitative researcher) can examine the process used to collect data, the resulting data

---

*From Patten, M. L. (2005). *Understanding research methods: An overview of the essentials* (5th ed.). Los Angeles: Pyrczak Publishing. Reprinted with permission.

[1] The terms "dependability" and "trustworthiness" in qualitative research loosely correspond to the terms "reliability" and "validity" in quantitative research.

[2] Rasera, E. F., Vieira, E. M., & Japur, M. (2004). Influence of gender and sexuality on the construction of being HIV positive as experienced in a support group in Brazil. *Families, Systems, & Health, 22*, 340–351.

[3] Lukens, E. P., Thorning, H., & Lohrer, S. (2004). Sibling perspectives on severe mental illness: Reflections on self and family. *American Journal of Orthopsychiatry, 74*, 489–501.

[4] In qualitative research, this is sometimes called *intercoder agreement*. In quantitative research, this concept is called *interobserver reliability*.

and the conclusions, and then provide feedback to the researcher. This process is called **peer review**. Under certain circumstances, the peer who provides the review is called an **auditor**.

The dependability of the results can also be enhanced by a process called **member checking**. This term is based on the idea that the participants are "members" of the research team. By having the participants/members review the results of the analysis, researchers can determine whether their results "ring true" to the participants. If not, adjustments can be made in the description of the results.